Seeing Ourselves

Seeing Ourselves

Classic, Contemporary, and Cross-Cultural Readings in Sociology

Fifth Edition

Edited by

John J. Macionis
Kenyon College

Nijole V. Benokraitis
University of Baltimore

Upper Saddle River, New Jersey 07458

Library of Congress Cataloging-in-Publication Data

Seeing ourselves : classic, contemporary, and cross-cultural readings in sociology / edited by John J. Macionis, Nijole V. Benokraitis.—5th ed.
p. cm.
Includes bibliographical references and index.
ISBN 0-13-081358-3 (alk. paper)
1. Sociology. I. Macionis, John J. II. Benokraitis, Nijole V. (Nijole Vaicaitis)
HM586.S44 2000
301—dc21 00-038561

VP, Editorial director: Laura Pearson
Publisher: Nancy Roberts
Acquisitions editor: Christopher DeJohn
Managing editor: Sharon Chambliss
Editorial/production supervision and
interior design: Barbara Reilly
Editorial assistant: Christina Scalia
Prepress and manufacturing buyer: Mary Ann Gloriande
Director of marketing: Gina Sluss
Cover art director: Jayne Conte
Cover design: Bruce Kenselaar
Cover art: Maurice Brazil Prendergast, American (1859–1924), *Ramparts, St. Malo*, oil on canvas. David David Gallery, Philadelphia/SuperStock.

This book was set in 10/12 Times New Roman by DM Cradle Associates and was printed and bound by Hamilton Printing Company.
The cover was printed by Phoenix Color Corp.

A Division of Pearson Education
Upper Saddle River, New Jersey 07458

Printed in the United States of America
10 9 8 7 6 5 4 3

ISBN: 0-13-081358-3

Prentice-Hall International (UK) Limited, *London*
Prentice-Hall of Australia Pty. Limited, *Sydney*
Prentice-Hall Canada Inc., *Toronto*
Prentice-Hall Hispanoamericana, S.A., *Mexico*
Prentice-Hall of India Private Limited, *New Delhi*
Prentice-Hall of Japan, Inc., *Tokyo*
Pearson Education Asia Pte. Ltd., *Singapore*
Editora Prentice-Hall do Brasil, Ltda., *Rio de Janeiro*

Contents

Socialization

Social Interaction in Everyday Life

Groups and Organizations

Aging and the Elderly

The Economy and Work

Politics, Government, and the Military

Family

Collective Behavior and Social Movements

Social Change and Modernity

Preface

"Change is one thing," Bertrand Russell pointed out, "progress is another." This new edition of *Seeing Ourselves* brings Russell's words to life. To be sure, the readings in this anthology highlight the many ways our world is changing. But pointing to change is just part of the history. In addition, classroom readings must help students ask questions about the shape of our society: Are social changes—involving technology, the economy, international relations, and social movements at home—improving quality of life? For whom? What should our goals for the future be? Our purpose in revising *Seeing Ourselves* is to present to students the many social changes that are shaping their lives as well as to help them think critically about the kind of world they will build in the twenty-first century.

Seeing Ourselves presents the very best of sociological thought, from the work of the discipline's pioneers to the men and women who are doing today's cutting-edge research. The selections explore both U.S. society and global trends. This reader provides excellent material for a wide range of courses, including introductory sociology, social problems, cultural anthropology, social theory, social stratification, American studies, women's studies, and marriage and the family.

THE THREE C'S: CLASSIC, CONTEMPORARY, AND CROSS-CULTURAL

Since its introduction a decade ago, *Seeing Ourselves* has been the most popular reader in the discipline. The new, fifth edition offers seventy-seven selections that represent the breadth and depth of sociology. *Seeing Ourselves* is not only the most extensive anthology available, it is the only one that systematically weaves together three kinds of selections. For each general topic typically covered in a sociology course, three types of articles are included: *classic, contemporary*, and *cross-cultural.*

Classic articles—thirty in all—are sociological statements of recognized importance and lasting significance. Included here are the ideas of sociology's founders and shakers—including Emile Durkheim, Karl Marx, Max Weber, Georg Simmel, Ferdinand Tönnies, as well as Margaret Mead,

W. E. B. Du Bois, Louis Wirth, George Herbert Mead, Thomas Robert Malthus, and Charles Horton Cooley. Also found here are more recent contributions by Alfred Kinsey, Jessie Bernard, Robert Merton, Erving Goffman, Peter Berger, Kingsley Davis and Wilbert Moore, C. Wright Mills, Talcott Parsons, Leslie White, and Jo Freeman.

We recognize that not everyone will agree about precisely which selections warrant the term "classic." We hope, however, that instructors will be pleased to see the work of so many outstanding men and women—carefully edited with undergraduate students in mind—available in a single, affordable source.

Twenty-four *contemporary* selections focus on current sociological issues, controversies, and applications. These articles show sociologists at work and demonstrate the importance of ongoing research. They make for stimulating reading and offer thought-provoking insights about ourselves and the surrounding world. Among the contemporary selections in *Seeing Ourselves* are Earl Babbie on the importance of sociological research, George Ritzer on McDonaldization and jobs, James Davison Hunter on today's "culture wars," Jay Coakley offering a sociological analysis of sport, Dianne Herman pointing out the cultural roots of sexual violence, Deborah Tannen explaining why the two sexes often talk past each other, Robert Michael et al. reporting how many sexual partners U.S. adults really have, George Gerbner on television and violence, Andrew Hacker on the state of black and white America, Patricia Hill Collins analyzing the plight of women of color, Nijole Benokraitis on patterns of subtle discrimination, John Macionis sketching the shape of the coming "cyber-society," William Julius Wilson describing the rising desperation of some inner-city residents, William O'Hare profiling affluent Latinos, Roseann Giarrusso et al. on the increasing importance of grandparenting, Catharine MacKinnon's view of pornography as a form of domination, David Popenoe's contention that fatherhood is in serious decline, Jonathan Kozol's charges of "savage inequalities" in our schools, Ruth Zambrana et al. on the health of Latino families, James Jasper and Dorothy Nelkin's account of the animal rights movement, Lester Brown's survey of the state of the world's environment, and Joe Feagin and Robert Parker's assessment of the role of big business in the life of today's cities.

The twenty-three *cross-cultural* selections offer sociological insights about the striking cultural diversity of the United States and the larger world. Included are well-known works such as "Body Ritual among the Nacirema" by Horace Miner, "India's Sacred Cow" by Marvin Harris, "The Amish: A Small Society" by John Hostetler, J.M. Carrier's "Homosexual Behavior in Cross-Cultural Perspective," and Elijah Anderson's "The Code of the Streets." Other articles explore issues and problems including the state of American Indians, how familiar gestures can offend people in other societies, how Japanese and U.S. business people behave according to different sets of rules, the staggering burden of African poverty, women's social standing around the world, the rising number of elderly people worldwide, cross-cultural patterns of mate selection, Islam's view of women, academic achievement among Southeast Asian immigrants, and the rising global population. Cross-cultural selections stimulate critical thinking about social diversity in North America as well as broaden students' understanding of other cultures.

ORGANIZATION OF THE READER

This reader parallels the chapter sequence common to textbooks used in introductory sociology. Instructors can easily and effectively use these articles in a host of other courses, just as teachers can assign articles in whatever order they wish. For each of the twenty-three general topics, a cluster of three or four articles is presented, each cluster including at least one classic, one contemporary, and one cross-cultural selection. The expansive coverage of these seventy-seven articles ensures that instructors can choose readings well suited to their own classes.

The first grouping of articles describes the distinctive sociological perspective, brings to life the promise and pitfalls of sociological research, and demonstrates the discipline's applications to a variety of issues. The selections that follow focus on key concepts: culture, society, socialization, social interaction, groups and organizations, deviance, and human sexuality. The focus then turns to various dimensions of social inequality, with attention to class, gender, race and ethnicity, and aging. The major social institutions are covered next, including the economy and work; politics, government, and the military; family; religion; education; and health and medicine. The final sets of articles explore dimensions of global transformation—including population growth, urbanization, the natural environment, social movements, and social change.

A NOTE ON LANGUAGE

All readings are presented in their original form; the editors have not altered any author's language. Readers should be aware that some of the older selections—especially the classics—use male pronouns rather than more contemporary gender-neutral terminology, and one article employs the term "Negro." We have not changed the language in any article, wishing not to violate the historical authenticity of any document. That said, we urge faculty and students, with the original articles in hand, to consider the significance of changing language in their analysis of the author's ideas.

TEACHING FEATURES

This reader has two features that enhance the learning of students. First, a brief introduction, preceding each selection, presents the essential argument and highlights important issues to keep in mind while completing the reading. Second, each article is followed by three or four "Critical-Thinking Questions" that develop the significance of the reading, help students evaluate their own learning, and stimulate class discussion.

INTERNET SITES

Readers are also invited to visit our sociology Web sites. At **http://www.prenhall.com/macionis** students will find online study guides for the Macionis introductory texts *(Sociology* and *Society: The Basics),* including discussion topics, test questions, and Internet links. Another site, **http://www.thesociologypage.com** (or **http://www.macionis.com**), provides information about the field of sociology, biographies of key sociologists, recent news of interest to sociologists, and more than fifty links to worthwhile Internet sites.

Also, **http://www.prenhall.com/benokraitis** offers more than 400 "hot links" to topics such as theory, sociological research, culture, socialization, interaction and communication, sexuality, race and ethnicity, gender roles, aging, work, marriage, health, family violence, and social change.

INSTRUCTOR'S TEST ITEM FILE

Prentice Hall also supports *Seeing Ourselves* with a Test Item File, prepared by Leda A. Thompson. For each of the seventy-seven selections in this reader, the Test Item File provides instructors with six multiple-choice questions (with answers) and several essay questions for easy test creation. The multiple-choice questions are also available on computer disk for users of IBM and Macintosh personal computers.

CHANGES TO THE FIFTH EDITION

We are grateful to our colleagues at hundreds of colleges and universities who have made *Seeing Ourselves* a part of their courses. Energized by this unparalleled reception, the editors have now produced an even stronger edition. Here are the key changes:

*1. **Sixteen new articles,*** of a total of seventy-seven, appear in the fifth edition. As one might expect, changes to classic selections are limited: in this case, to a new selection from Alfred Kinsey's groundbreaking study of human sexuality. There are eight new contemporary selections, including Jay Coakley, "How Would a Sociologist Look at Sport?"; Earl Babbie, "The Importance of Social Research"; George Ritzer, "McJobs: McDonaldization and the Workplace"; Robert Michael et al., "Sex in America: How Many Partners Do We Have?"; Andrew Hacker, "Who Has How Much and Why?"; Roseann Giarrusso et al., "How the Grandparent Role Is Changing"; Jonathan Kozol, "Savage Inequalities: Children in U.S. Schools"; and James Jasper and Dorothy Nelkin, "The Animal Rights Movement as a Moral Crusade."

In addition, this fifth edition offers seven new cross-cultural selections, enriching the anthology's multicultural and global content. The new selections in this category are Elijah Anderson, "The Code of the Streets"; C. Matthew Snipp, "A Comeback for American Indians"; Naomi Neft and Ann D. Levine, "Women in Today's World"; Frank Hobbs and Bonnie Damon, "Our Aging World"; Adrian Karatnycky, "Freedom in the World: A Global Survey"; J. Kenneth Smail, "Let's *Reduce* Global Population!"; and Janet Hadley, "Abortion Movements in Poland, Great Britain, and the United States."

2. A new cluster of articles on human sexuality. Many sociology courses now include discussion of human sexuality. In this revision, therefore, the editors have added three selections on this topic: Alfred Kinsey's classic study of sexual orientation; Robert Michael, John Gagnon, Edward Laumann, and Gina Kolata's "Sex in America: How Many Partners Do We Have?"; and J. M. Carrier's "Homosexual Behavior in Cross-Cultural Perspective."

3. A continued emphasis on diversity. In *Seeing Ourselves*, "diversity" involves three important objectives. First is *global* content. The editors have worked hard to include in this collection the work of sociologists from around the world. Twenty-one of the selections in this edition deal primarily with social patterns beyond the borders of the United States. Second, "diversity" refers to *multicultural* issues. The selections in this edition of *Seeing Ourselves* highlights the lives of African Americans, Asian Americans, Latinos, and American Indians and other native peoples, as well as women and men from all social class backgrounds. This anthology, in short, brings to the center the lives of people often pushed to the margins of society. Third, "diversity" means presenting to students arguments from *different points of view.* Using this reader, students will grapple with important issues and debates reflecting various positions on the political spectrum.

4. A small change in topic ordering. In this edition, we have reversed the order of the cluster dealing with gender and the cluster dealing with race and ethnicity. This small change, reflecting the suggestion of several classroom instructors, gives students more experience discussing social inequality before they focus on race, a topic that some students find difficult to discuss in class.

As in the past, we invite faculty and students to share their thoughts and reactions to this reader. Write to John Macionis at the Department of Anthropology-Sociology, Olof Palme House, Kenyon College, Gambier, Ohio 43022-9623 or to Nijole Benokraitis at the Department of Sociology, University of Baltimore, 1420 North Charles Street, Baltimore, Maryland 21201-5779. E-mail addresses are macionis@kenyon.edu and nbenokraitis@ubmail.ubalt.edu

ACKNOWLEDGMENTS

The editors are grateful to a number of colleagues for their help in preparing this reader. First, the

relationship between writers and publishers is a distinctive mix of friendship, creative tension, and a shared commitment to do the best job possible. For her unwavering support from the outset, we wish to express our gratitude to Nancy Roberts, publisher, at Prentice Hall. Sharon Chambliss, managing editor for sociology, coordinated myriad tasks and shepherded this edition's production with her usual calm and good cheer. Special thanks go to Barbara Reilly, production editor, for her commitment to excellence and her meticulous attention to detail.

Nijole Benokraitis is grateful to Linda Fair, secretary of the Division of Criminology, Criminal Justice, and Social Policy, at the University of Baltimore and to Taneisha Sanders, graduate research assistant, for their invaluable assistance in preparing many of the articles for publication. Both editors are indebted to Amy Marsh Macionis for her skillful editorial review of the entire manuscript.

A number of other colleagues offered critical comments, which have improved the final book: Afrola Anwary, Concordia College; Kathleen A. Asburg, Community College of Philadelphia; Frank Barter, Community College of Philadelphia; Scott H. Beck, East Tennessee State University; Marshall A. Botkin, Frederick Community College; Joseph E. Boyle, Virginia Polytechnic Institute and State University; Julie V. Brown, University of North Carolina, Greensboro; Meredith A. Myers, University of Georgia; Ron Pagnucco, Mt. St. Mary's College; Barry Perlman, Community College of Philadelphia; Salvador Rivera, State University of New York—Cobleskill; Ron L. Shamufell, Community College of Philadelphia; and Randall J. Thomson, North Carolina State University.

Finally, recognizing the fact that the academic profession too often undervalues the core role of teaching, John Macionis and Nijole Benokraitis dedicate *Seeing Ourselves* to the men and women who have committed their lives to educating today's undergraduates, helping them to develop the skills and the insights that will play a part in reshaping tomorrow's world.

Seeing Ourselves

1

The Promise of Sociology

C. Wright Mills

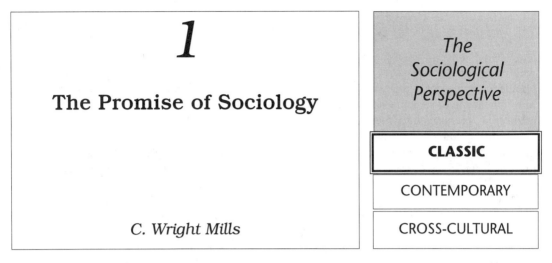

The Sociological Perspective

CLASSIC

CONTEMPORARY

CROSS-CULTURAL

To C. Wright Mills, the sociological imagination *is a special way to engage the world. To think sociologically is to realize that what we experience as* personal problems *are often widely shared by others like ourselves. Thus, many personal problems are actually* social issues. *For Mills, one of sociology's most outspoken activists, the sociological imagination encouraged collective action to change the world in some way.*

Nowadays men often feel that their private lives are a series of traps. They sense that within their everyday worlds, they cannot overcome their troubles, and in this feeling, they are often quite correct: What ordinary men are directly aware of and what they try to do are bounded by the private orbits in which they live; their visions and their powers are limited to the close-up scenes of job, family, neighborhood; in other milieux, they move vicariously and remain spectators. And the more aware they become, however vaguely, of ambitions and of threats which transcend their immediate locales, the more trapped they seem to feel.

Underlying this sense of being trapped are seemingly impersonal changes in the very structure of continent-wide societies. The facts of contemporary history are also facts about the success and the failure of individual men and women. When a society is industrialized, a peasant becomes a worker; a feudal lord is liquidated or becomes a businessman. When classes rise or fall, a man is employed or unemployed; when the rate of investment goes up or down, a man takes new heart or goes broke. When wars happen, an insurance salesman becomes a rocket launcher; a store clerk, a radar man; a wife lives alone; a child grows up without a father. Neither the life of an individual nor the history of a society can be understood without understanding both.

Yet men do not usually define the troubles they endure in terms of histor-

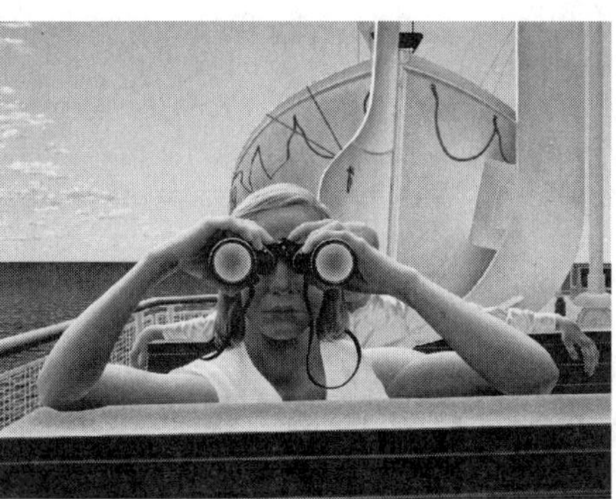

Alex Colville (1920–), *To Prince Edward Island*, 1965, acrylic emulsion on masonite, 61.9 x 92.5 cm. National Gallery of Canada, Ottawa. © NGC/MBAC.

Source: From *The Sociological Imagination* by C. Wright Mills. Copyright © 1959 by Oxford University Press, Inc. Renewed 1987 by Yaraslava Mills. Used by permission of Oxford University Press, Inc.

ical change and institutional contradiction. The well-being they enjoy, they do not usually impute to the big ups and downs of the societies in which they live. Seldom aware of the intricate connection between the patterns of their own lives and the course of world history, ordinary men do not usually know what this connection means for the kinds of men they are becoming and for the kinds of history-making in which they might take part. They do not possess the quality of mind essential to grasp the interplay of man and society, of biography and history, of self and world. They cannot cope with their personal troubles in such ways as to control the structural transformations that usually lie behind them.

Surely it is no wonder. In what period have so many men been so totally exposed at so fast a pace to such earthquakes of change? That Americans have not known such catastrophic changes as have the men and women of other societies is due to historical facts that are now quickly becoming "merely history." The history that now affects every man is world history. Within this scene and this period, in the course of a single generation, one-sixth of mankind is transformed from all that is feudal and backward into all that is modern, advanced, and fearful. Political colonies are freed; new and less visible forms of imperialism installed. Revolutions occur; men feel the intimate grip of new kinds of authority. Totalitarian societies rise, and are smashed to bits—or succeed fabulously. After two centuries of ascendancy, capitalism is shown up as only one way to make society into an industrial apparatus. After two centuries of hope, even formal democracy is restricted to a quite small portion of mankind. Everywhere in the underdeveloped world, ancient ways of life are broken up and vague expectations become urgent demands. Everywhere in the overdeveloped world, the means of authority and of violence become total in scope and bureaucratic in form. Humanity itself now lies before us, the super-nation at either pole concentrating its most coordinated and massive efforts upon the preparation of World War III.

The very shaping of history now outpaces the ability of men to orient themselves in accordance with cherished values. And which values? Even when they do not panic, men often sense that older ways of feeling and thinking have collapsed and that newer beginnings are ambiguous to the point of moral stasis. Is it any wonder that ordinary men feel they cannot cope with the larger worlds with which they are so suddenly confronted? That they cannot understand the meaning of their epoch for their own lives? That—in defense of selfhood—they become morally insensible, trying to remain altogether private men? Is it any wonder that they come to be possessed by a sense of the trap?

It is not only information that they need—in this Age of Fact, information often dominates their attention and overwhelms their capacities to assimilate it. It is not only the skills of reason that they need—although their struggles to acquire these often exhaust their limited moral energy.

What they need, and what they feel they need, is a quality of mind that will help them to use information and to develop reason in order to achieve lucid summations of what is going on in the world and of what may be happening within themselves. It is this quality, I am going to contend, that journalists and scholars, artists and publics, scientists and editors are coming to expect of what may be called the sociological imagination.

The sociological imagination enables its possessor to understand the larger historical scene in terms of its meaning for the inner life and the external career of a variety of individuals. It enables him to take into account how individuals, in the welter of their daily experience, often become falsely conscious of their social positions. Within that welter, the framework of modern society is sought, and within that framework the psychologies of a variety of men and women are formulated. By such means the personal uneasiness of individuals is focused upon explicit troubles and the indifference of publics is transformed into involvement with public issues.

The first fruit of this imagination—and the first lesson of the social science that embodies it—is the idea that the individual can understand his own experience and gauge his own fate only by locating himself within his period, that he can know his own chances in life by becoming aware of those of all individuals in his circumstances. In many ways it is a terrible lesson; in many ways a magnificent one. We do not know the limits of man's capacities for supreme effort or willing degradation, for agony or glee, for pleasurable brutality or the sweetness of reason. But in our time we have come to know that the limits of "human nature" are frighteningly broad. We have come to know that every individual lives, from one generation to the next, in some society; that he lives out a biography, and that he lives it out within some historical sequence. By the fact of his living he contributes, however minutely, to the shaping of this society and to the course of its history, even as he is made by society and by its historical push and shove.

The sociological imagination enables us to grasp history and biography and the relations between the two within society. That is its task and its promise. To recognize this task and this promise is the mark of the classic social analyst. It is characteristic of Herbert Spencer—turgid, polysyllabic, comprehensive; of E. A. Ross—graceful, muckraking, upright; of Auguste Comte and Emile Durkheim; of the intricate and subtle Karl Mannheim. It is the quality of all that is intellectually excellent in Karl Marx; it is the clue to Thorstein Veblen's brilliant and ironic insight, to Joseph Schumpeter's many-sided constructions of reality; it is the basis of the psychological sweep of W. E. H. Lecky no less than of the profundity and clarity of Max Weber. And it is the signal of what is best in contemporary studies of man and society.

No social study that does not come back to the problems of biography, of history, and of their intersections within a society has completed its intellectual journey. Whatever the specific problems of the classic social analysts, however limited or however broad the features of social reality they have examined, those who have been imaginatively aware of the promise of their work have consistently asked three sorts of questions:

1. What is the structure of this particular society as a whole? What are its essential components, and how are they related to one another? How does it differ from other varieties of social order? Within it, what is the meaning of any particular feature for its continuance and for its change?
2. Where does this society stand in human history? What are the mechanics by which it is changing? What is its place within and its meaning for the development of humanity as a whole? How does any particular feature we are examining affect, and how is it affected by, the historical period in which it moves? And this period—what are its essential features? How does it differ from other periods? What are its characteristic ways of history-making?
3. What varieties of men and women now prevail in this society and in this period? And what varieties are coming to prevail? In what ways are they selected and formed, liberated and repressed, made sensitive and blunted? What kinds of "human nature" are revealed in the conduct and character we observe in this society in this period? And what is the meaning for "human nature" of each and every feature of the society we are examining?

Whether the point of interest is a great power state or a minor literary mood, a family, a prison, a creed—these are the kinds of questions the best social analysts have asked. They are the intellectual pivots of classic studies of man in society—and they are the questions inevitably raised by any mind possessing the sociological imagination. For that imagination is the capacity to shift from one perspective to another—from the political to the psychological; from examination of a single family to comparative assessment of the national budgets of the world; from the theological school to the military establishment; from considerations of an oil industry to studies of contemporary poetry. It is the capacity to range from the most impersonal and remote transformations to the most intimate features of the human self—and to see the relations between the two. Back of its use there is always the urge to know the social and historical meaning of the individual in the society and in the period in which he has his quality and his being.

That, in brief, is why it is by means of the sociological imagination that men now hope to grasp what is going on in the world, and to understand what is happening in themselves as minute points of the intersections of biography and history within society. In large part, contemporary man's self-conscious view of himself as at least an outsider, if not a permanent stranger, rests upon an absorbed realization of social relativity and of the transformative power of history. The sociological imagination is the most fruitful form of this self-consciousness. By its use men whose mentalities have swept only a series of limited orbits often come to feel as if suddenly awakened in a house with which they had only supposed themselves to be familiar. Correctly or incorrectly, they often come to feel that they can now provide themselves with adequate summations, cohesive assessments, comprehensive orientations. Older decisions that once appeared sound now seem to them products of a mind unaccountably dense. Their capacity for astonishment is made lively again. They acquire a new way of thinking, they experience a transvaluation of values: In a word, by their reflection and by their sensibility, they realize the cultural meaning of the social sciences.

Perhaps the most fruitful distinction with which the sociological imagination works is between "the personal troubles of milieu" and "the public issues of social structure." This distinction is an essential tool of the sociological imagination and a feature of all classic work in social science.

Troubles occur within the character of the individual and within the range of his immediate relations with others; they have to do with his self and with those limited areas of social life of which he is directly and personally aware. Accordingly, the statement and the resolution of troubles properly lie within the individual as a biographical entity and within the scope of his immediate milieu—the social setting that is directly open to his personal experience and to some extent his willful activity. A trouble is a private matter: Values cherished by an individual are felt by him to be threatened.

Issues have to do with matters that transcend these local environments of the individual and the range of his inner life. They have to do with the organization of many such milieux into the institutions of an historical society as a whole, with the ways in which various milieux overlap and interpenetrate to form the larger structure of social and historical life. An issue is a public matter: Some value cherished by publics is felt to be threatened. Often there is a debate about what that value really is and about what it is that really threatens it. This debate is often without focus if only because it is the very nature of an issue, unlike even widespread trouble, that it cannot very well be defined in terms of the immediate and everyday environments of ordinary men. An issue, in fact, often involves a crisis in institutional arrangements, and often too it involves what Marxists call "contradictions" or "antagonisms."

In these terms, consider unemployment. When, in a city of 100,000, only one man is unemployed, that is his personal trouble, and for its relief we properly look to the character of the man, his skills, and his immediate opportunities. But when in a nation of 50 million employees, 15 million men are unemployed, that is an issue, and we may not hope to find its solution within the range of opportunities open to any one individual. The very structure of opportunities has collapsed. Both the correct statement of the problem and the range of possible solutions require us to consider the economic and political institutions of the society, and not merely the personal situation and character of a scatter of individuals.

Consider war. The personal problem of war, when it occurs, may be how to survive it or how to die in it with honor; how to make money out of it; how to climb into the higher safety of the military apparatus; or how to contribute to the war's termination. In short, according to one's values, to find a set of milieux and within it to survive the war or make one's death in it meaningful. But the structural issues of war have to do with its causes; with what types of men it throws up into command; with its effects upon economic and political, family and religious institutions, with the unorganized irresponsibility of a world of nation-states.

Consider marriage. Inside a marriage a man and a woman may experience personal troubles, but when the divorce rate during the first four years of marriage is 250 out of every 1,000 attempts, this is an indication of a structural issue having to do with the institutions of marriage and the family and other institutions that bear upon them.

Or consider the metropolis—the horrible, beautiful, ugly, magnificent sprawl of the great city. For many upper-class people, the personal solution to "the problem of the city" is to have an apartment with private garage under it in the heart of the city and, forty miles out, a house by Henry Hill, garden by Garrett Eckbo, on a hundred acres of private land. In these two controlled environments—with a small staff at each end and a private helicopter connection—most people could solve many of the problems of personal milieux caused by the facts of the city. But all this, however splendid, does not solve the public issues that the structural fact of the city poses. What should be done with this wonderful monstrosity? Break it up into scattered units, combining residence and work? Refurbish it as it stands? Or, after evacuation, dynamite it and build new cities according to new plans in new places? What should those plans be? And who is to decide and to accomplish whatever choice is made? These are structural issues; to confront them and to solve them requires us to consider political and economic issues that affect innumerable milieux.

Insofar as an economy is so arranged that slumps occur, the problem of unemployment becomes incapable of personal solution. Insofar as war is inherent in the nation-state system and in the uneven industrialization of the world, the ordinary individual in his restricted milieu will be powerless—with or without psychiatric aid—to solve the troubles this system or lack of system imposes upon him. Insofar as the family as an institution turns women into darling little slaves and men into their chief providers and unweaned dependents, the problem of a satisfactory marriage remains incapable of purely private solution. Insofar as the overdeveloped megalopolis and the overdeveloped automobile are built-in features of the overdeveloped society, the issues of urban living will not be solved by personal ingenuity and private wealth.

What we experience in various and specific milieux, I have noted, is often caused by structural changes. Accordingly, to understand the changes of many personal milieux we are required to look beyond them. And the number and variety of such structural changes increase as the institutions within which we live become more embracing and more intricately connected with one another. To be aware of the idea of social structure and to use it with sensibility is to be capable of tracing such linkages among a great variety of milieux. To be able to do that is to possess the sociological imagination. . . .

CRITICAL-THINKING QUESTIONS

1. Why do people in the United States tend to think of the operation of society in personal terms?

2. What are the practical benefits of the sociological perspective? Are there liabilities?

3. What does Mills have in mind in suggesting that by developing the sociological imagination we learn to assemble *facts* into *social analysis?*

The Sociological Perspective

CLASSIC

CONTEMPORARY

CROSS-CULTURAL

2

Invitation to Sociology

Peter L. Berger

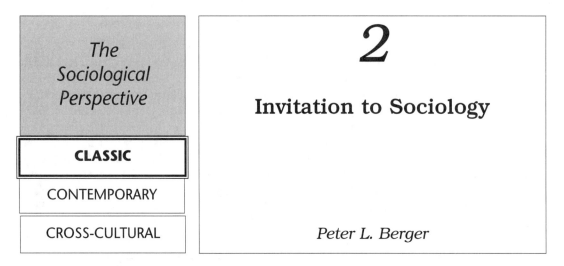

Using the sociological perspective changes how we perceive the surrounding world, and even ourselves. Peter Berger compares thinking sociologically to entering a new and unfamiliar society—one in which "things are no longer what they seem." This article should lead you to rethink your social world, so that you become aware of issues that you may never before have considered.

. . . It can be said that the first wisdom of sociology is this—things are not what they seem. This too is a deceptively simple statement. It ceases to be simple after a while. Social reality turns out to have many layers of meaning. The discovery of each new layer changes the perception of the whole.

Anthropologists use the term "culture shock" to describe the impact of a totally new culture upon a newcomer. In an extreme instance such shock will be experienced by the Western explorer who is told, halfway through dinner, that he is eating the nice old lady he had been chatting with the previous day—a shock with predictable physiological if not moral consequences. Most explorers no longer encounter cannibalism in their travels today. However, the first encounters with polygamy or with puberty rites or even with the way some nations drive their automobiles can be quite a shock to an American visitor. With the shock may go not only disapproval or disgust but a sense of excitement that things can *really* be that different from what they are at home. To some extent, at least, this is the excitement of any first travel abroad. The experience of sociological discovery could be described as "culture shock" minus geographical displacement. In other words, the sociologist travels at home—with shocking results. He is unlikely to find that he is eating a nice old lady for dinner. But the discovery, for instance, that his own church has considerable money invested in the missile industry or that a few blocks from his home there are people who engage in cultic orgies may not be drastically different in emotional impact. Yet we would not want to imply that sociological discoveries are always or even usually outrageous to moral sentiment. Not at all. What they have in common with exploration in distant lands, however, is the sudden illumination of new and unsuspected facets of human existence in

---

society. This is the excitement and, as we shall try to show later, the humanistic justification of sociology.

People who like to avoid shocking discoveries, who prefer to believe that society is just what they were taught in Sunday school, who like the safety of the rules and the maxims of what Alfred Schuetz has called the "world-taken-for-granted," should stay away from sociology. People who feel no temptation before closed doors, who have no curiosity about human beings, who are content to admire scenery without wondering about the people who live in those houses on the other side of that river, should probably also stay away from sociology. They will find it unpleasant or, at any rate, unrewarding. People who are interested in human beings only if they can change, convert, or reform them should also be warned, for they will find sociology much less useful than they hoped. And people whose interest is mainly in their own conceptual constructions will do just as well to turn to the study of little white mice. Sociology will be satisfying, in the long run, only to those who can think of nothing more entrancing than to watch men and to understand things human. . . .

To ask sociological questions, then, presupposes that one is interested in looking some distance beyond the commonly accepted or officially defined goals of human actions. It presupposes a certain awareness that human events have different levels of meaning, some of which are hidden from the consciousness of everyday life. It may even presuppose a measure of suspicion about the way in which human events are officially interpreted by the authorities, be they political, juridical, or religious in character. If one is willing to go as far as that, it would seem evident that not all historical circumstances are equally favorable for the development of sociological perspective.

It would appear plausible, in consequence, that sociological thought would have the best chance to develop in historical circumstances marked by severe jolts to the self-conception, especially the official and authoritative and generally accepted self-conception of a culture. It is only in such circumstances that perceptive men are likely to be motivated to think beyond the assertions of this self-conception and, as a result, question the authorities. . . .

Sociological perspective can then be understood in terms of such phrases as "seeing through," "looking behind," very much as such phrases would be employed in common speech—"seeing through his game," "looking behind the scenes"—in other words, "being up on all the tricks."

. . . We could think of this in terms of a common experience of people living in large cities. One of the fascinations of a large city is the immense variety of human activities taking place behind the seemingly anonymous and endlessly undifferentiated rows of houses. A person who lives in such a city will time and again experience surprise or even shock as he discovers the strange pursuits that some men engage in quite unobtrusively in houses that, from the outside, look like all the others on a certain street. Having had this experience once or twice, one will repeatedly find oneself walking down a street, perhaps late in the evening, and wondering what may be going on under the bright lights showing through a line of drawn curtains. An ordinary family engaged in pleasant talk with guests? A scene of desperation amid illness or death? Or a scene of debauched pleasures? Perhaps a strange cult or a dangerous conspiracy? The facades of the houses cannot tell us, proclaiming nothing but an architectural conformity to the tastes of some group or class that may not even inhabit the street any longer. The social mysteries lie behind the facades. The wish to penetrate these mysteries is an analogon to sociological curiosity. In some cities that are suddenly struck by calamity this wish may be abruptly realized. Those who have experienced wartime bombings know of the sudden encounters with unsuspected (and sometimes unimaginable) fellow tenants in the air-raid shelter of one's apartment building. Or they can recollect the startling morning sight of a house hit by a bomb during the night, neatly sliced in half, the facade torn away and the previously hidden interior mercilessly revealed in the daylight. But in most cities that one may normally live in, the facades must be penetrated by one's own inquisitive intrusions. Similarly, there are historical situations in which the facades of society are violently torn apart and all but the most incurious are forced to see that there was a reality behind the facades all along. Usually this does not happen, and the facades continue to confront us with seemingly rocklike permanence. The perception of the reality behind the facades then demands a considerable intellectual effort.

A few examples of the way in which sociology "looks behind" the facades of social structures might serve to make our argument clearer. Take, for instance, the political organization of a community. If one wants to find out how a modern American city is governed, it is very easy to get the official information about this subject. The city will have a charter, operating under the laws of the state. With some advice from informed individuals, one may look up various statutes that define the constitution of the city. Thus one may find out that this particular community has a city-manager form of administration, or that party affiliations do not appear on the ballot in municipal elections, or that the city government participates in a regional water district. In similar fashion, with the help of some newspaper reading, one may find out the officially recognized political problems of the community. One may read that the city plans to annex a certain suburban area, or that there has been a change in the zoning ordinances to facilitate industrial development in another area, or even that one of the members of the city council has been accused of using his office for personal gain. All such matters still occur on the, as it were, visible, official, or public level of political life. However, it would be an exceedingly naive person who would believe that this kind of information gives him a rounded picture of the political reality of that community. The sociologist will want to know above all the constituency of the "informal power structure" (as it has been called by Floyd Hunter, an American sociologist interested in such studies), which is a configuration of men and their power that cannot be found in any statutes, and probably cannot be read about in the newspapers. The political scientist or the legal expert might find it very interesting to compare the city charter with the constitutions of other similar communities. The sociologist will be far more concerned with discovering the way in which powerful vested interests influence or even control the actions of officials elected under the charter. These vested interests will not be found in city hall, but rather in the executive suites of corporations that may not even be located in that community, in the private mansions of a handful of powerful men, perhaps in the offices of certain labor unions, or even, in some instances, in the headquarters of criminal organizations. When the sociologist concerns himself with power, he will "look behind" the official mechanisms that are supposed to regulate power in the community. This does not necessarily mean that he will regard the official mechanisms as totally ineffective or their legal definition as totally illusionary. But at the very least he will insist that there is another level of reality to be investigated in the particular system of power. In some cases he might conclude that to look for real power in the publicly recognized places is quite delusional. . . .

Let us take one further example. In Western countries, and especially in America, it is assumed that men and women marry because they are in love. There is a broadly based popular mythology about the character of love as a violent, irresistible emotion that strikes where it will, a mystery that is the goal of most young people and often of the not-so-young as well. As soon as one investigates, however, which people actually marry each other, one finds that the lightning-shaft of Cupid seems to be guided rather strongly within very definite channels of class, income, education, [and] racial and religious background. If one then investigates a little further into the behavior that is engaged in prior to marriage under the rather misleading euphemism of "courtship," one finds channels of interaction that are often rigid to the point of ritual. The suspicion begins to dawn on one that, most of the time, it is not so much the emotion of love that creates a certain kind of relationship, but that carefully predefined and often planned relationships eventually generate the desired emotion. In other words, when certain conditions are met or have been constructed, one allows oneself "to fall in love." The sociologist investigating our patterns of "courtship" and marriage soon discovers a complex web of motives related in many ways to the entire institutional structure within which an individual lives his life—class, career, economic ambition, aspirations of power and prestige. The miracle of love now begins to look somewhat synthetic. Again, this need not mean in any given instance that the sociologist will declare the romantic interpretation to be an illusion. But, once more, he will look beyond the immediately given and publicly approved interpretations. . . .

We would contend, then, that there is a debunking motif inherent in sociological consciousness. The sociologist will be driven time and again, by the very logic of his discipline, to debunk the social systems he is studying. This unmasking tendency need not necessarily be due to the sociologist's temperament or inclinations. Indeed, it may happen that the sociologist, who as an individual may be of a conciliatory disposition and quite disinclined to disturb the comfortable assumptions on which he rests his own social existence, is nevertheless compelled by what he is doing to fly in the face of what those around him take for granted. In other words, we would contend that the roots of the debunking motif in sociology are not psychological but methodological. The sociological frame of reference, with its built-in procedure of looking for levels of reality other than those given in the official interpretations of society, carries with it a logical imperative to unmask the pretensions and the propaganda by which men cloak their actions with each other. This unmasking imperative is one of the characteristics of sociology particularly at home in the temper of the modern era. . . .

CRITICAL-THINKING QUESTIONS

1. How can we explain the fact that people within any society tend to take their own way of life for granted?
2. What does Berger think is the justification for studying sociology?
3. What is involved in sociological "debunking"? How are others likely to respond to sociological insights?

The Sociological Perspective

CLASSIC

CONTEMPORARY

CROSS-CULTURAL

3

How Would a Sociologist Look at Sport?

Jay J. Coakley

Sociologists apply the sociological perspective to just about any aspect of life. Here, Jay Coakley describes the sociology of sport, highlighting how the focus of a sociologist differs from that of a psychologist. Notice how this point of view links sport to most other areas of our lives, including culture, the economy, education, family life, and religion.

WHAT IS THE SOCIOLOGY OF SPORT?

. . . Most people in the field would agree that the sociology of sport is a subdiscipline of sociology that focuses on the relationship between sport and society. Its major goals are to understand the following:

1. The relationships between sport and other spheres of social life, such as family, education, politics, the economy, the media, and religion
2. The social organization, group behavior, and social interaction patterns that exist within sport settings
3. The cultural, structural, and situational factors affecting sport and sport experiences
4. The social processes that occur in conjunction with sport, processes such as socialization, competition, cooperation, conflict, social stratification, and social change.

Source: *Sport in Society: Issues and Controversies*, 4th ed., by Jay J. Coakley (St. Louis: Times Mirror/Mosby, © 1990), pp. 2–6. Reprinted with permission of W. B. Saunders Company.

Unlike the psychology of sport, the sociology of sport is not directly concerned with issues related to motivation, perception, cognition, personality, and individual performance in sport. Instead, it is concerned with how the behavior of individuals and groups within sport is influenced by social relationships, past social experiences, and the social settings in which sport activities occur. On a more general level it is concerned with the organization of sport itself and how that organization is created, maintained, and changed by people who have differing interests, opportunities, and resources.

A psychological approach focuses on factors within individuals, whereas a sociological approach focuses on the social settings in which people respond to and influence one another. Sociologists are concerned with how social settings are created by people, how those settings are organized, how they influence behavior, and how people change them through their own actions and relationships.

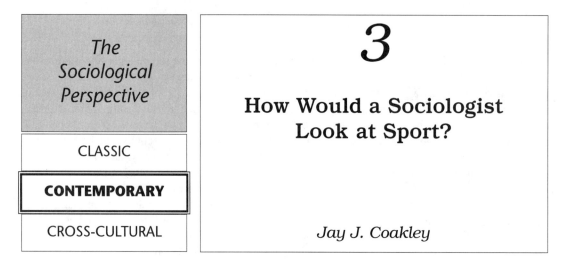

When a topic like violence in sport is studied, sociologists want to know why rates of violence among athletes and spectators change over time and why they vary from one country to another and from group to group within countries. They also want to know why violence is associated with some sports and not others and why some events become scenes for violence while others are peaceful. The search for answers to these questions focuses on historical circumstances, social conditions, political and economic factors, and the relationships of the people involved. Sociological research attempts to discover consistent patterns of violence across a variety of social settings and to find the connections among these patterns and the characteristics of the settings themselves. When connections are found, sociologists make suggestions about how social relationships and social conditions may be changed to control rates of violent behavior.

A psychologist, on the other hand, studies violence in sport by looking at the attitudes, emotions, perceptions, and response patterns of athletes and spectators as individuals. Questions are asked about how individuals perceive the actions of others and how those actions serve as stimuli for violent responses. There are also questions about how violent attitudes and behavioral tendencies are developed, how they become a part of a person's personality structure, and how they may be changed through conditioning or therapy.

Research in the sociology of sport sometimes creates controversy. This is because sociologists often call attention to the need for changes in the organization of sport and society. This often threatens some people, especially those in positions of power and control in sport and in society at large. These people are the ones with the most to lose if changes are made in social relationships and social organization. After all, their power and control have been achieved within existing social structures, and changes in those structures could jeopardize their positions. This leads them to favor approaches to sport that explain problems in terms of the characteristics of individuals rather than in terms of social conditions. If problems are blamed on individuals, solutions will emphasize better ways of controlling people and teaching them how to adjust to the world as it is rather than emphasizing changes in the way that world is organized.

The potential for controversy in the sociology of sport can be illustrated by looking at some of the research findings on participation in sport by women in many countries around the world. Research shows that married women with children have lower rates of participation than other categories of people. The reason for this is that these women don't have the resources or the opportunities to become involved in sports. They are short of free time; they don't have money for child care; they often lack transportation; there are few sport programs related to their interests and needs; and their husbands often expect them to be responsible for the needs of everyone in the family. It is easy to see the potential for controversy in the position that changes should be made to increase participation rates among these women. Recommendations for change would *not* focus on giving motivational talks to the women themselves. Instead, the recommendations would focus on the need for child care, for affordable opportunities to participate, for equal access to opportunities, for changes in the ways husbands and wives define their relationships with each other, and for legal changes enabling the daughters of these women to have the same opportunities as their sons.

As you can see, these recommendations are controversial. They call for community resources to be reallocated on the basis of new priorities, for men to share the resources they use for their sport programs, for husbands to share in child care and homemaking, for the development of job opportunities for women so they will have the resources needed to make choices, and for political representatives to pass laws that redefine the rights of women. Such changes threaten those who benefit from the way things are organized now. This is why the sociology of sport is sometimes seen as too critical and negative. Studying the relationship between sport and society certainly can help us understand more about the world in which we live, but it also forces us to take a critical look at the social conditions that affect our lives on and off playing fields. . . .

WHY STUDY THE SOCIOLOGY OF SPORT?

The most obvious answer to this question is that sport cannot be ignored because it is such a pervasive part of life in contemporary society. It does not take a sociologist to call our attention to the fact that during the twentieth century the popularity and visibility of sport have grown dramatically in many countries around the world. A survey of the mass media shows that newspapers in most cities devote entire sections of their daily editions to the coverage of sport. This is especially true in North America, where newsprint about sport frequently surpasses the space given to the economy, politics, or any other single topic of interest. Radio and television stations bring numerous hours of live and taped sporting events to people all around the world. Sport personalities serve as objects of attention—as heroes and antiheroes. Young people in many countries are apt to be more familiar with the names of top-level athletes than with the names of their national religious, economic, and political leaders. For a large segment of people of all ages in industrialized countries, sport is likely to be included in their everyday lives through their involvement as participants or spectators, through their reading, or through their conversations with friends and acquaintances. . . .

In most industrial countries, sport is related to each of the major spheres of social life, such as the family, education, politics, economics, and religion. For example, in North America millions of children are involved in a variety of organized sport activities throughout the year. It is primarily their parents who organize leagues, coach teams, and attend games. *Family* schedules are altered to accommodate practices and games. These schedules are also affected by the patterns of sport involvement among adult family members. Watching televised sport events sometimes disrupts family life and at other times provides a collective focus for family attention. In some cases relationships between family members are nurtured and played out during sport activities or in conversations about these activities.

At all levels of *education*, sport has become an integral part of the experiences of North American students. Most schools in the United States and Canada sponsor interscholastic sport teams, and it is not uncommon for these teams to attract more attention than academic programs do among students and community residents. At the university level, some schools even use their teams to promote the quality of their academic programs, making or losing large amounts of money in the process. In the United States some large universities have public relations profiles built on (or seriously damaged by) the reputations of their sport programs.

In the *political* arena, sport is often linked to feelings of national pride. Despite frequent complaints about mixing sport and politics, most North Americans have no second thoughts about displaying national flags and playing national anthems at sporting events. Political leaders at various levels of government have been known to promote themselves by associating with sport as both participants and spectators. In fact, it has become a tradition for U.S. presidents to make congratulatory post game phone calls to the locker rooms of national championship teams. On the international level, sport has become a hotbed of political controversy in recent years. And both the United States and Canada, as well as most other countries around the world, have used sport as a means to enhance their reputations in international political relationships.

The *economics* of most Western industrial countries have been affected by the billions of dollars spent every year for tickets to games, sports equipment, participation fees, athletic club membership dues, and bets placed on favorite teams and athletes. The economies of many local communities have been affected by the existence of major sport teams. In some countries tax dollars have occasionally been used to partially support those teams. In the United States there are universities that gross millions of dollars per week at their football games and pay their athletes the equivalent of minimum wages. The major television networks in the United States are now paying the National Football League (NFL) $500 million per year for the rights to televise games, and athletes in the major professional team sports have average salaries as high as $625,000 (in the National Basketball Association). Advertisers have paid over $1 million for a single minute of commercial television time during the Super Bowl, and they have paid well over a million dollars to have their corporate names associated with national teams and major events such as the Olympics.

There is even a relationship between sport and *religion*. For example, local churches and church groups in both the United States and Canada are some of the most active sponsors of athletic teams and leagues. Parishes and congregations have been known to revise their Sunday service schedules to accommodate their members who would not miss an opening kickoff in an NFL game for anything—not even their religious beliefs. Religious rituals are increasingly used in conjunction with sport participation, and there are a few large nondenominational religious organizations that have been created for the sole purpose of attracting and converting athletes to Christian beliefs. Other religious organizations have used athletes as spokespersons for their belief systems in the hope of converting people who strongly identify with sports.

In addition to being linked to the major spheres of social life in contemporary society, sport and sport participation in most countries have been given ideological support through the formation of belief systems that outline the positive consequences of sport for individuals and society. For example, it is popularly believed that sport builds character, provides outlets for aggressive energy, and serves as the basis for group unity and solidarity. In capitalist countries it is believed that sport involvement leads to the development of competitive traits; in socialist countries it is believed that it leads to cooperation and commitment to the group. Regardless of differences in political or economic systems, people in most countries tend to believe that sport is positively linked to their ways of life. This is especially true in industrialized societies, although many developing nations have promoted sport and sport involvement as means to develop individual character and enhance their reputations in the international political arena.

Now let's get back to our original question: Why study the sociology of sport? It could be said that studying the sociology of sport is important because it will help us learn more about human behavior and the settings in which that behavior occurs. Furthermore, sport offers a unique context for the study of social processes and relationships. Sport teams provide ideal settings for studying group interaction and the inner workings of large organizations (Ball, 1975). The public nature of sport activities and events allows easy access to information on a variety of questions related to the sociological understanding of behavior. These are all good reasons for sociologists to be interested in studying sport. After all, the science of sociology is concerned with understanding everyday life, learning how behavior is influenced by the settings in which it occurs, and learning how people can change those settings through their own actions. . . .

CRITICAL-THINKING QUESTIONS

1. From a sociological point of view, how is sport much more than just a form of recreation and physical conditioning?
2. Why do you think sport is such a major part of our way of life in the United States?
3. According to the reading, what is the value of looking at sport—or other elements of our lives—from a sociological point of view?

REFERENCE

BALL, D. W. 1975. A note on method in the sociology of sport. In *Sport and social order*, eds. D. W. Ball and J. W. Loy. Reading, Mass.: Addison-Wesley.

The Sociological Perspective

CLASSIC

CONTEMPORARY

CROSS-CULTURAL

4

Body Ritual among the Nacirema

Horace Miner

Most people take their life for granted; when they think about society at all, it is usually viewed as both natural and good. To help us step back from our society, anthropologist Horace Miner describes the Nacirema, a peculiar people living in North America (whose lives should strike you as familiar). Miner's intellectual sleight-of-hand illustrates how the sociological perspective involves detachment, so that everyday life becomes something new and unusual.

The anthropologist has become so familiar with the diversity of ways in which different peoples behave in similar situations that he is not apt to be surprised by even the most exotic customs. In fact, if all of the logically possible combinations of behavior have not been found somewhere in the world, he is apt to suspect that they must be present in some yet undescribed tribe. This point has, in fact, been expressed with respect to clan organization by Murdock (1949:71). In this light, the magical beliefs and practices of the Nacirema present such unusual aspects that it seems desirable to describe them as an example of the extremes to which human behavior can go.

Professor Linton first brought the ritual of the Nacirema to the attention of anthropologists twenty years ago (1936:326), but the culture of this people is still very poorly understood. They are a North American group living in the territory between the Canadian Cree, the Yaqui and Tarahumare of Mexico, and the Carib and Arawak of the Antilles. Little is known of their origin, although tradition states that they came from the east. According to Nacirema mythology, their nation was originated by a culture hero, Notgnihsaw, who is otherwise known for two great feats of strength—the throwing of a piece of wampum across the river Pa-To-Mac and the chopping down of a cherry tree in which the Spirit of Truth resided.

Nacirema culture is characterized by a highly developed market economy which has evolved in a rich natural habitat. While much of the people's time is devoted to economic pursuits, a large part of the fruits of these labors and a considerable portion of the day are spent in ritual activity. The focus of this activity is the human body, the appearance and health of which loom as a dominant concern in the ethos of the people. While such concern is certainly not unusual, its ceremonial aspects and associated philosophy are unique.

Source: "Body Ritual among the Nacirema" by Horace Miner. Reproduced by permission of the American Anthropological Association from *American Anthropologist,* vol. 58, no. 3, June, 1956. Not for further reproduction.

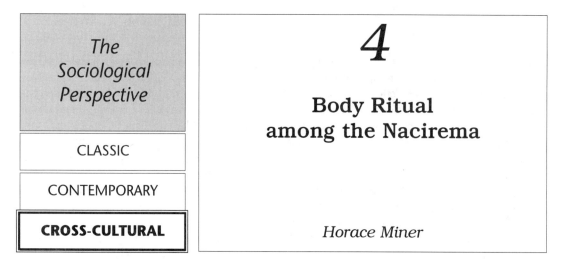

The fundamental belief underlying the whole system appears to be that the human body is ugly and that its natural tendency is to debility and disease. Incarcerated in such a body, man's only hope is to avert these characteristics through the use of the powerful influences of ritual and ceremony. Every household has one or more shrines devoted to this purpose. The more powerful individuals in this society have several shrines in their houses, and, in fact, the opulence of a house is often referred to in terms of the number of such ritual centers it possesses. Most houses are of wattle and daub construction, but the shrine rooms of the more wealthy are walled with stone. Poorer families imitate the rich by applying pottery plaques to their shrine walls.

While each family has at least one such shrine, the rituals associated with it are not family ceremonies but are private and secret. The rites are normally only discussed with children, and then only during the period when they are being initiated into these mysteries. I was able, however, to establish sufficient rapport with the natives to examine these shrines and to have the rituals described to me.

The focal point of the shrine is a box or chest which is built into the wall. In this chest are kept the many charms and magical potions without which no native believes he could live. These preparations are secured from a variety of specialized practitioners. The most powerful of these are the medicine men, whose assistance must be rewarded with substantial gifts. However, the medicine men do not provide the curative potions for their clients, but decide what the ingredients should be and then write them down in an ancient and secret language. This writing is understood only by the medicine men and by the herbalists who, for another gift, provide the required charm.

The charm is not disposed of after it has served its purpose, but is placed in the charm-box of the household shrine. As these magical materials are specific for certain ills, and the real or imagined maladies of the people are many, the charm-box is usually full to overflowing. The magical packets are so numerous that people forget what their purposes were and fear to use them again. While the natives are very vague on this point, we can only assume that the idea in retaining all the old magical materials is that their presence in the charm-box, before which the body rituals are conducted, will in some way protect the worshipper.

Beneath the charm-box is a small font. Each day every member of the family, in succession, enters the shrine room, bows his head before the charm-box, mingles different sorts of holy water in the font, and proceeds with a brief rite of ablution. The holy waters are secured from the Water Temple of the community, where the priests conduct elaborate ceremonies to make the liquid ritually pure.

In the hierarchy of magical practitioners, and below the medicine men in prestige, are specialists whose designation is best translated "holy-mouth-men." The Nacirema have an almost pathological horror of and fascination with the mouth, the condition of which is believed to have a supernatural influence on all social relationships. Were it not for the rituals of the mouth, they believe that their teeth would fall out, their gums bleed, their jaws shrink, their friends desert them, and their lovers reject them. They also believe that a strong relationship exists between oral and moral characteristics. For example, there is a ritual ablution of the mouth for children which is supposed to improve their moral fiber.

The daily body ritual performed by everyone includes a mouth-rite. Despite the fact that these people are so punctilious about care of the mouth, this rite involves a practice which strikes the uninitiated stranger as revolting. It was reported to me that the ritual consists of inserting a small bundle of hog hairs into the mouth, along with certain magical powders, and then moving the bundle in a highly formalized series of gestures.

In addition to the private mouth-rite, the people seek out a holy-mouth-man once or twice a year. These practitioners have an impressive set of paraphernalia, consisting of a variety of augers, awls, probes, and prods. The use of these objects in the exorcism of the evils of the mouth involves almost unbelievable ritual torture of the client. The holy-mouth-man opens the client's mouth and, using the above-mentioned tools, enlarges any holes which decay may have created in the teeth. Magical materials are put into these holes. If there are no naturally occurring holes in the teeth, large sections of one or more teeth are gouged out so that the supernatural substance can be applied. In the client's view, the purpose of these ministrations is to arrest decay and to draw friends. The extremely sacred and traditional character of the rite is evident in the fact that the natives return to the holy-mouth-man year after year, despite the fact that their teeth continue to decay.

It is to be hoped that, when a thorough study of the Nacirema is made, there will be careful inquiry into the personality structure of these people. One has but to watch the gleam in the eye of a holy-mouth-man, as he jabs an awl into an exposed nerve, to suspect that a certain amount of sadism is involved. If this can be established, a very interesting pattern emerges, for most of the population shows definite masochistic tendencies. It was to these that Professor Linton referred in discussing a distinctive part of the daily body ritual which is performed only by men. This part of the rite involves scraping and lacerating the surface of the face with a sharp instrument. Special women's rites are performed only four times during each lunar month, but what they lack in frequency is made up in barbarity. As part of this ceremony, women bake their heads in small ovens for about an hour. The theoretically interesting point is that what seems to be a preponderantly masochistic people have developed sadistic specialists.

The medicine men have an imposing temple, or *latipso,* in every community of any size. The more elaborate ceremonies required to treat very sick patients can only be performed at this temple. These ceremonies involve not only the thaumaturge but a permanent group of vestal maidens who move sedately about the temple chambers in distinctive costume and headdress.

The *latipso* ceremonies are so harsh that it is phenomenal that a fair proportion of the really sick natives who enter the temple ever recover. Small children whose indoctrination is still incomplete have been known to resist attempts to take them to the temple because "that is where you go to die." Despite this fact, sick adults are not only willing but eager to undergo the protracted ritual purification, if they can afford to do so. No matter how ill the supplicant or how grave the emergency, the guardians of many temples will not admit a client if he cannot give a rich gift to the custodian. Even after one has gained admission and survived the ceremonies, the guardians will not permit the neophyte to leave until he makes still another gift.

The supplicant entering the temple is first stripped of all his or her clothes. In everyday life the Nacirema avoids exposure of his body and its natural functions. Bathing and excretory acts are performed only in the secrecy of the household shrine, where they are ritualized as part of the body-rites. Psychological shock results from the fact that body secrecy is suddenly lost upon entry into the *latipso.* A man, whose own wife has never seen him in an excretory act, suddenly finds himself naked and assisted by a vestal maiden while he performs his natural functions into a sacred vessel. This sort of ceremonial treatment is necessitated by the fact that the excreta are used by a diviner to ascertain the course and nature of the client's sickness. Female clients, on the other hand, find their naked bodies are subjected to the scrutiny, manipulation, and prodding of the medicine men.

Few supplicants in the temple are well enough to do anything but lie on their hard beds. The daily ceremonies, like the rites of the holy-mouth-men, involve discomfort and torture. With ritual precision, the vestals awaken their miserable charges each dawn and roll them about on their beds of pain while performing ablutions, in the formal movements of which the maidens are highly trained. At other times they insert magic wands in the supplicant's mouth or force him to eat substances which are supposed to be healing. From time to time the medicine men come to their clients and jab magically treated needles into their flesh. The fact that these temple ceremonies may not cure, and may even kill, the neophyte, in no way decreases the people's faith in the medicine men.

There remains one other kind of practitioner, known as a "listener." This witch-doctor has the power to exorcise the devils that lodge in the heads of people who have been bewitched. The Nacirema believe that parents bewitch their own children. Mothers are particularly suspected of putting a curse on children while teaching them the secret body rituals. The counter-magic of the witch-doctor is unusual in its lack of ritual. The patient simply tells the "listener" all his troubles and fears, beginning with the earliest difficulties he can remember. The memory displayed by the Nacirema in these exorcism sessions is truly remarkable. It is not uncommon for the patient to bemoan the rejection he felt upon being weaned as a babe, and a few individuals even see their troubles going back to the traumatic effects of their own birth.

In conclusion, mention must be made of certain practices which have their base in native esthetics but which depend upon the pervasive aversion to the natural body and its functions. There are ritual fasts to make fat people thin and ceremonial feasts to make thin people fat. Still other rites are used to make women's breasts larger if they are small, and smaller if they are large. General dissatisfaction with breast shape is symbolized in the fact that the ideal form is virtually outside the range of human variation. A few women afflicted with almost inhuman hypermammary development are so idolized that they make a handsome living by simply going from village to village and permitting the natives to stare at them for a fee.

Reference has already been made to the fact that excretory functions are ritualized, routinized, and relegated to secrecy. Natural reproductive functions are similarly distorted. Intercourse is taboo as a topic and scheduled as an act. Efforts are made to avoid pregnancy by the use of magical materials or by limiting intercourse to certain phases of the moon. Conception is actually very infrequent. When pregnant, women dress so as to hide their condition. Parturition takes place in secret, without friends or relatives to assist, and the majority of women do not nurse their infants.

Our review of the ritual life of the Nacirema has certainly shown them to be a magic-ridden people. It is hard to understand how they have managed to exist so long under the burdens which they have imposed upon themselves. But even such exotic customs as these take on real meaning when they are viewed with the insight provided by Malinowski when he wrote (1948: 70):

> Looking from far and above, from our high places of safety in the developed civilization, it is easy to see all the crudity and irrelevance of magic. But without its power and guidance early man could not have mastered his practical difficulties as he has done, nor could man have advanced to the higher stages of civilization.

CRITICAL-THINKING QUESTIONS

1. Did you understand that Miner is describing the "American"—"Nacirema" spelled backwards? Why do we not recognize this right away?
2. Using Miner's approach, describe a baseball game, an auction, shoppers in a supermarket, or a college classroom.
3. What do we gain from being able to "step back" from our way of life as Miner has done here?

REFERENCES

Linton, R. 1936. *The study of man.* New York: Appleton-Century.

Malinowski, B. 1948. *Magic, science and religion.* Glencoe, Ill.: Free Press.

Murdock, G. P. 1949. *Social structure.* New York: Macmillan.

Sociological Research

CLASSIC

CONTEMPORARY

CROSS-CULTURAL

5

The Case for Value-Free Sociology

Max Weber

The following is part of a lecture given in 1918 at Germany's Munich University by Max Weber, one of sociology's pioneers. Weber lived in politically turbulent times, in which the government and other organizations were demanding that university faculty teach the "right" ideas. Weber responded to these pressures by encouraging everyone to be politically involved as citizens; yet, he maintained that the teachers and scholars should prize dispassionate analysis rather than political advocacy. This selection stimulates critical thinking about the mix of fact and value that is found in all sociological research.

Let us consider the disciplines close to me: sociology, history, economics, political science, and those types of cultural philosophy that make it their task to interpret the sciences. It is said, and I agree, that politics is out of place in the lecture-room. It does not belong there on the part of the students. . . . Neither does [it] belong in the lecture-room on the part of the [instructors], and when the [instructor] is scientifically concerned with politics, it belongs there least of all.

To take a practical stand is one thing, and to analyze political structures and party positions is another. When speaking in a political meeting about democracy, one does not hide one's personal standpoint; indeed, to come out clearly and take a stand is one's damned duty. The words one uses in such a meeting are not means of scientific analysis but means of canvassing votes and winning over others. They are not plowshares to loosen the soil of contemplative thought; they are swords against the enemies: Such words are weapons. It would be an outrage, however, to use words in this fashion in a lecture or in the lecture-room. If, for instance, "democracy" is under discussion, one considers its various forms, analyzes them in the way they function, determines what results for the conditions of life the one form has as compared with the other. Then one confronts the forms of democracy with nondemocratic forms of political order and endeavors to come to a position

Source: Excerpts from *From Max Weber: Essays in Sociology* by Max Weber, edited by H. H. Gerth and C. Wright Mills. Translation copyright © 1946, 1958 by H. H. Gerth and C. Wright Mills. Used by permission of Oxford University Press, Inc.

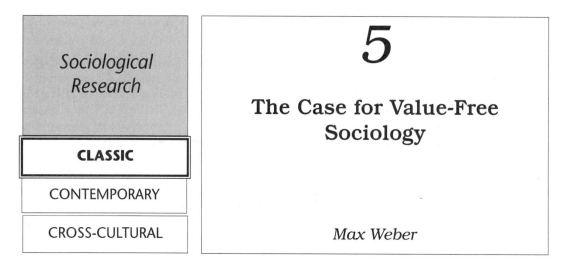

where the student may find the point from which, in terms of his ultimate ideals, he can take a stand. But the true teacher will beware of imposing from the platform any political position upon the student, whether it is expressed or suggested. "To let the facts speak for themselves" is the most unfair way of putting over a political position to the student.

Why should we abstain from doing this? I state in advance that some highly esteemed colleagues are of the opinion that it is not possible to carry through this self-restraint and that, even if it were possible, it would be a whim to avoid declaring oneself. Now one cannot demonstrate scientifically what the duty of an academic teacher is. One can only demand of the teacher that he have the intellectual integrity to see that it is one thing to state facts, to determine mathematical or logical relations or the internal structure of cultural values, while it is another thing to answer questions of the *value* of culture and its individual contents and the question of how one should act in the cultural community and in political associations. These are quite heterogeneous problems. If he asks further why he should not deal with both types of problems in the lecture-room, the answer is: because the prophet and the demagogue do not belong on the academic platform.

To the prophet and the demagogue, it is said: "Go your ways out into the streets and speak openly to the world," that is, speak where criticism is possible. In the lecture-room we stand opposite our audience, and it has to remain silent. I deem it irresponsible to exploit the circumstance that for the sake of their career the students have to attend a teacher's course while there is nobody present to oppose him with criticism. The task of the teacher is to serve the students with his knowledge and scientific experience and not to imprint upon them his personal political views. It is certainly possible that the individual teacher will not entirely succeed in eliminating his personal sympathies. He is then exposed to the sharpest criticism in the forum of his own conscience. And this deficiency does not prove anything; other errors are also possible, for instance, erroneous statements of fact, and yet they prove nothing against the duty of searching for the truth. I also reject this in the very interest of science. I am ready to prove from the works of our historians that whenever the man of science introduces his personal value judgment, a full understanding of the facts *ceases*. . . .

The primary task of a useful teacher is to teach his students to recognize "inconvenient" facts—I mean facts that are inconvenient for their party opinions. And for every party opinion there are facts that are extremely inconvenient, for my own opinion no less than for others. I believe the teacher accomplishes more than a mere intellectual task if he compels his audience to accustom itself to the existence of such facts. I would be so immodest as even to apply the expression "moral achievement," though perhaps this may sound too grandiose for something that should go without saying.

CRITICAL-THINKING QUESTIONS

1. Why does Weber seek to set the campus apart from society as an "ivory tower"?
2. How is the classroom a distinctive setting in terms of political neutrality? If instructors cannot be entirely free from value positions, why should they strive to point out "inconvenient facts" to their students?
3. Do you see arguments *for* instructors presenting passionate advocacy of issues that are of great political and moral significance?

Sociological Research

CLASSIC

CONTEMPORARY

CROSS-CULTURAL

6

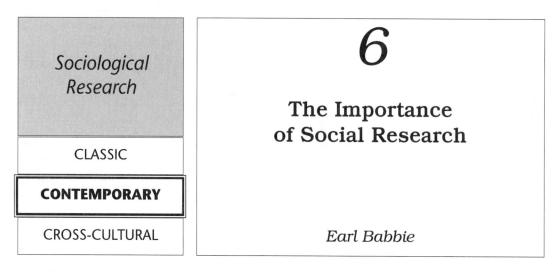

The Importance of Social Research

Earl Babbie

How *do we know what we know? Tradition, religion, laws, the media, personal experiences, and people in authority shape our everyday beliefs and behaviors. In this selection, Earl Babbie argues that social problems such as poverty could be diminished if policymakers and the general public based their responses on rigorous social science research results rather than emotions and stereotypes.*

. . . We can't solve our social problems until we understand how they come about, persist. Social science research offers a way to examine and understand the operation of human social affairs. It provides points of view and technical procedures that uncover things that would otherwise escape our awareness. Often, as the cliché goes, things are not what they seem; social science research can make that clear. One example illustrates this fact.

Poverty is a persistent problem in the United States, and none of its intended solutions is more controversial than *welfare*. Although the program is intended to give the poor a helping hand while they reestablish their financial viability, many complain that it has the opposite effect.

Part of the public image of welfare in action was crystallized by Susan Sheehan (1976) in her book, *A Welfare Mother*, which describes the situation of a three-generation welfare family, suggesting that the welfare system trapped the poor rather than liberat[ed] them. Martin Anderson (1978:56) agreed with Sheehan's assessment and charged that the welfare system had established a caste system in America, "perhaps as much as one-tenth of this nation—a caste of people almost totally dependent on the state, with little hope or prospect of breaking free. Perhaps we should call them the Dependent Americans."

George Gilder (1990) has spoken for many who believe the poor are poor mainly because they refuse to work, saying the welfare system saps their incentive to take care of themselves. Ralph Segalman and David Marsland (1989:6–7) support the view that welfare has become an intergenerational way of life for the poor in welfare systems around the world. Children raised in welfare families, they assert, will likely live their adult lives on welfare:

> This conflict between the intent of welfare as a temporary aid (as so understood by most of the public) and welfare as a permanent right (as understood by the

---

Source: From *Practice of Social Research* (with InfoTrac), 8th edition, by E.R. Babbie, copyright © 1998. Reprinted with permission of Wadsworth Publishing, a division of Thomson Learning.

welfare bureaucracy and welfare state planners) has serious implications. The welfare state nations, by and large, have given up on the concept of client rehabilitation for self-sufficiency, an intent originally supported by most welfare state proponents. What was to have been a temporary condition has become a permanent cost on the welfare state. As a result, welfare discourages productivity and self-sufficiency and establishes a new mode of approved behaviour in the society—one of acceptance of dependency as the norm.

These negative views of the effects of the welfare system are widely shared by the general public, even among those basically sympathetic to the aims of the program. Greg Duncan (1984: 2–3) at the University of Michigan's Survey Research Center points out that census data would seem to confirm the impression that a hard core of the poor have become trapped in their poverty. Speaking of the percentage of the population living in poverty at any given time, he says,

> Year-to-year changes in these fractions are typically less than 1 percent, and the Census survey's other measures show little change in the characteristic of the poor from one year to the next. They have shown repeatedly that the individuals who are poor are more likely to be in families headed by a woman, by someone with low education, and by blacks.
>
> Evidence that one-eighth of the population was poor in two consecutive years, and that those poor shared similar characteristics, is consistent with an inference of absolutely no turnover in the poverty population. Moreover, the evidence seems to fit the stereotype that those families that are poor are likely to remain poor, and that there is a hard-core population of poor families for whom there is little hope of self-improvement.

Duncan continues, however, to warn that such snapshots of the population can conceal changes taking place. Specifically, an unchanging percentage of the population living in poverty does not necessarily mean the *same* families are poor from year to year. Theoretically, it could be a totally different set of families each year.

To determine the real nature of poverty and welfare, the University of Michigan undertook a "Panel Study of Income Dynamics" in which they followed the economic fate of 5,000 families from 1969 to 1978, or ten years, the period supposedly typified by Sheehan's "welfare mother." At the beginning, the researchers found that in 1978, 8.1 percent of these families were receiving some welfare benefits and 3.5 percent depended on welfare for more than half their income. Moreover, these percentages did not differ drastically over the ten-year period (Duncan 1984: 75).

Looking beyond these surface data, however, the researchers found something you might not have expected. During the ten-year period, about one-fourth of the 5,000 families received welfare benefits at least once. However, only 8.7 percent of the families were ever dependent on welfare for more than half their income. *"Only a little over one-half of the individuals living in poverty in one year are found to be poor in the next, and considerably less than one-half of those who experience poverty remain persistently poor over many years"* (Duncan 1984:3; emphasis original).

Only 2 percent of the families received welfare each of the ten years, and less than 1 percent were continuously dependent on welfare for the ten years. Table 1 summarizes these findings.

These data paint a much different picture of poverty than people commonly assume. In a summary of his findings, Duncan (1984:4–5) says:

> While nearly one-quarter of the population received income from welfare sources at least once in the decade, only about 2 percent of all the population could be characterized as dependent upon this income for extended periods of time. Many families receiving welfare benefits at any given time were in the early stages of recovering from an economic crisis caused by the death, departure, or disability of a husband, a recovery that often lifted them out of welfare when they found full-time employment, or remarried, or both. Furthermore, most of the children raised in welfare families did not themselves receive welfare benefits after they left home and formed their own households.

Many of the things social scientists study—including [the issue of welfare] you've just read about—generate deep emotions and firm convictions in most people. This makes effective inquiry into the facts difficult at best; all too often,

TABLE 1 Incidence of Short- and Long-Run Welfare Receipt and Dependence, 1969–1978

	Percent of U.S. Population:	
	Receiving Any Welfare Income	*Dependent on Welfare for More than 50% of Family Income*
Welfare in 1978	8.1%	3.5%
Welfare in 1 or more years, 1969–78	25.2	8.7
Welfare in 5 or more years, 1969–78	8.3	3.5
Welfare in all 10 years, 1969–78	2.0	0.7
"Persistent welfare" (welfare in 8 or more years), 1969–78	4.4	2.0

Source: Greg J. Duncan, *Years of Poverty, Years of Plenty: The Changing Fortunes of American Workers and Families* (Ann Arbor: University of Michigan, 1984), 75.

researchers manage only to confirm their initial prejudices. The special value of social science research methods is that they offer a way to address such issues with logical and observational rigor. They let us all pierce through our personal viewpoints and take a look at the world that lies beyond our own perspectives. And it is that "world beyond" that holds the solutions to the social problems we face today.

At a time of increased depression and disillusionment, we are continually tempted to turn away from confronting social problems and retreat into the concerns of our own self-interest. Social science research offers an opportunity to take on those problems and discover the experience of making a difference after all. The choice is yours; I invite you to take on the challenge. . . .

CRITICAL-THINKING QUESTIONS

1. What does Babbie mean when he says that "things are not what they seem" when we read about controversial issues such as welfare?

2. Many people believe that welfare has become an intergenerational way of life. What data does Babbie present that challenge such beliefs?

3. In the classical selection ("The Case for Value-Free Sociology"), Max Weber asserts that "The primary task of a useful teacher is to teach [her/his] students to recognize 'inconvenient' facts—I mean facts that are inconvenient for their party opinions." Do you think some instructors (and students) feel pressure to conform to approved points of view, whether religious or political? Should faculty and students ignore research findings that contradict such perspectives?

REFERENCES

ANDERSON, MARTIN. 1978. *Welfare: The political economy of welfare reform in the United States*. Stanford, Calif.: Hoover Institution Press.

DUNCAN, GREG J., with RICHARD D. COE, et al. 1984. *Years of poverty, years of plenty: The changing fortunes of American workers and families*. Ann Arbor: Survey Research Center Institute.

GILDER, GEORGE. 1990. The nature of poverty. In *The American polity reader*, eds. A. Serow, W. Shannon, and E. Ladd, 658–63. New York: Norton.

SEGALMAN, RALPH, and DAVID MARSLAND. 1989. *Cradle to grave: Comparative perspectives on the state of welfare*. New York: St. Martin's Press.

SHEEHAN, SUSAN. 1976. *A welfare mother*. New York: Mentor.

7

Sensitivity in Field Research: A Study of Policing in Northern Ireland

John D. Brewer

Sociological Research

CLASSIC

CONTEMPORARY

CROSS-CULTURAL

Max Weber (see Reading 5) encouraged social scientists to be value-free in their research. Even when researchers attempt to be value-free, however, their data-gathering strategies are often shaped by social, religious, and ideological constraints. As John Brewer observes, conducting research on controversial topics or in sensitive locations—such as Northern Ireland—may be politically, psychologically, and physically threatening to both researchers and respondents. Brewer posits that fieldwork often requires making a number of pragmatic compromises that "depart from the textbook portrayal of ideal research practice."

Textbooks on research methods rarely mention the problems that arise when undertaking research on controversial topics or conducting it in sensitive locations. When the question of sensitivity is considered, it is usually approached from the perspective of ethics (e.g., Rainwater & Pittman, 1966). Comments range from the naive to the prosaic, so there is little textbook advice on which to draw. Therefore the issues raised by it can only be addressed in the context of specific studies where this was a problem. For example, Punch (1989) has recently reflected on his study of police corruption in Amsterdam and noted how the sensitivity of the topic caused several personal and professional difficulties. The catalyst here is the author's ethnographic study of routine police work by the Royal Ulster Constabulary (RUC) in East Belfast, Northern Ireland (see Brewer, 1991).[1]

The interest that the RUC has as a police force derives entirely from the political and social context in which it operates. The RUC has been forced to adopt a high political profile in its attempts to contain Northern Ireland's social and political divisions, resulting in controversy but also professional expertise in security policing (on the RUC, see Brewer, Guelke, Hume, Moxon-Browne, & Wilford, 1988; Weitzer, 1985). But this context is both a spur and a hindrance to the researcher. Policing in Northern Ireland is an emotive topic in a sensitive environment, and this sensitivity has implications for the research, especially its design and location, and the validity and reliability of the results. In documenting these effects, this [reading] will provide more than the usual anecdotal confessions of a researcher. If reflexivity on the part of authors is a vital quality in helping others understand how social scientific knowledge is produced, as Woolgar has recently claimed (1988), these

Source: "Sensitivity as a Problem in Field Research: A Study of Routine Policing in Northern Ireland," by John D. Brewer, in *Researching Sensitive Topics*, ed. Claire M. Renzetti and Raymond M. Lee, pp. 125–28, 130–37, 140–41, 144.

reflections are important to demonstrate some of the social processes lying behind and operating upon this study. . . .

SENSITIVITY AS A PROBLEM

Five types of problems were encountered in studying the RUC—problems of *technique, methodology, ethics, social context,* and *personal security*. These terms will become clearer upon discussion of the specific problems that arose in each type. Briefly, however, *technical* problems are problems of technique and practice; *methodological* problems describe the broader theoretical and epistemological issues raised by one's technique and practice; while *ethical* problems describe the moral dilemmas raised by the research. These three types are common to all research to whatever kind, topic, or location. The last two are more closely associated with research in sensitive settings or on controversial topics. *Contextual* problems are those that arise from the social, political and economic environment within which the research takes place; while problems of *personal security* are self-explanatory and refer to the researcher's physical safety.

Clearly, these problems are not restricted to sensitive research. No research takes place in a vacuum and this context can have a bearing upon it, whether in terms of the nonavailability of funds, the ease of access, or public reception of the findings. The point is merely that these contextual problems are more severe when dealing with sensitive topics or working in sensitive locations. They become a prominent feature of the research design and fieldwork, having to be continually borne in mind by the researcher at all stages of the research rather than just contemplated as a vague possibility or a theoretical truism once fieldwork is completed. Similarly, it is possible to have one's physical safety threatened during any research. But mostly the danger arises from the everyday life activities required in the research and is quite incidental to the topic and geographic location of the research itself. It is also so unlikely to occur that it is not a major element of the researcher's thoughts. By the very sensitivity of their topic or location, however, some pieces of research make the danger less incidental and more real.

In the research discussed here, problems of context and security are integrally linked. Indeed, in studying the RUC in Northern Ireland, problems of personal security are a direct consequence of the context within which the research occurs. But the reason they have been distinguished is because these two types of problems do not necessarily go together. Problems of personal security can be quite real and paramount without there being any serious contextual problems, and vice versa. For example, an ethnographic study of a sensitive topic, such as organized crime in the United States, might cause one or two problems of personal security for the researcher, but the social and political context of the research adds few special problems. . . .

STUDYING THE RUC

Anyone planning research on the RUC has first to confront the major contextual problem that the research will end up on the public and not just the academic domain. This causes problems of personal security because researchers may become seen as endorsing the force or be intimidated into passing on information that would threaten the personal security of respondents. These were intractable problems and had to be lived with if the sensitivity of the topic was not to lead to the abandonment of the research at the very beginning. Once adapted to, a technical issue was then faced. The chief constable's permission for the research was necessary if the researchers were not to be morally responsible for getting those policemen and women who talked to us privately sacked because they had done so without the chief constable's permission. Members of the force over whom this threat does not hang or by whom it is treated lightly, such as ex-policemen and women or disgruntled members of the force, are too unrepresentative to give a balanced view of policing. Therefore it was necessary to undertake an overt study and to obtain permission for the research from the chief constable.

Many different kinds of research require the permission of a gatekeeper, including all overt police research, which is the reason Holdaway chose to undertake his research covertly (see Holdaway, 1982). If the research is overt, the reliability of the data depends upon what control the gatekeeper demands, something Douglas calls retrenchment from the front (Douglas, 1972), and the integrity of the researcher in withstanding such pressure. Research of policing in divided societies is especially likely to provoke suspicion about its reliability for these reasons. Hence it is worth explaining that, once permission was granted, no limits were laid down by senior officers and no censorship role was retained by the RUC. The fieldworker, or research assistant, was able to spend as much time in the field as the principal investigator thought necessary. No restrictions were placed on her going out on patrol, traveling in vehicles, or going to incidents of routine police duty. The particular section[2] upon whom we came to focus attention was decided by us, not the police management. Visits were allowed to other stations, including, on three occasions, those in areas of high tension in West and North Belfast. We also visited the Women's Police Unit, which deals entirely with sex crimes.

Given that the permission of the gatekeeper was necessary, there was a further technical problem of how to design the research so that the suspicion of outsiders could be overcome. Suspicion is a trait of all police officers but was a particular contextual problem in Northern Ireland because of the extra security risks the RUC face in opening up their leviathan to strangers. A technical problem such as this raises interesting methodological questions because it forces researchers to ask which style of research is better suited to overcoming respondents' resistance. It was thought that a questionnaire that asked police officers about controversial issues, especially when put by a total stranger, would be unreliable because of the reluctance of respondents to give truthful answers. Research on the police that has used mailed questionnaires has suffered from a low response rate (e.g., Policy Studies Institute, 1983). Ethnographic research has special qualities suited to dealing with controversial topics in sensitive locations. It entails a gradual and progressive contact with respondents, which is sustained over a long period, allowing rapport to be established slowly with respondents over time. It also allows researchers to participate in the full range of experiences involved in the topic. This is why a great deal of the best police research is based on the ethnographic method and why members of several other unusual, offbeat, difficult, or demanding occupations have been studied in this way, such as truck drivers (Hollowell, 1968), traffic wardens (Richman, 1983), cocktail waitresses (Spradley & Mann, 1975), and prison wardens (Jacobs & Retsky, 1975).

To be successful, however, ethnographic research demands a considerable time commitment. This is true especially with sensitive topics where the researcher's penetration into the field takes longer and, once successful, continually needs to be reinforced by intensive contact. This time factor created a technical problem that was overcome by employing a research assistant to be responsible for data collection. There are methodological limitations to team ethnography of this sort, however, that constitute another implication of sensitivity for methodology and technique. It was the research assistant who participated in the field while the principal investigator remained distant from it, and it is impossible to know how much of the research assistant's experiences in the field were lost when writing up the notes secondhand for the principal investigator. Team ethnography is more feasible, however, if principal investigators can overcome a further technical problem and design the research in such a way as to compensate for their distance from the field. This can be done by giving the research assistant a special role not restricted to data collection, especially in writing up the research. The reliance on a research assistant was not an easy solution to the time problem, for it created an insurmountable ethical problem, in that the research assistant also faced problems of personal security.

At the stage of obtaining access, new problems arose and old ones reappeared. A major technical problem was for the research to be presented to the gatekeeper in such a way that permission would be given, something that the chief constable had never before done. On the assumption that the chief constable considered certain topics to be too sensitive, the researchers needed to be careful in how they designed and presented the research. The key to this no doubt lay in the attraction to the RUC of the idea of research on how routine policing is affected by Northern Ireland's security situation and the appeal of giving ordinary policemen and women an opportunity to express their views about policing. The experience of other police forces who had granted researchers permission illustrated that no great difficulties were created as a result, and permitting the research is in accord with the professionalism that is the core value of senior officers in the RUC. It is worth noting here that this topic has less attraction for ordinary policemen and women. Although they might take pleasure in thinking someone is interested in what their views are, it is they who run the risks associated with answering someone's questions and from being observed while doing their job. This is what Fox and Lundman (1974:53) mean when they say that there are two gates within police organizations that affect access—winning the support of both senior managers and the ordinary members of the force who are the subjects of the research. This point will be returned to later, for the caution of suspicion of ordinary policemen and women created numerous technical problems at the stage of data collection. . . .

Because of the nature of the Northern Ireland context, religion is a major means by which people assess identity and political attitudes. The research assistant was Catholic, presenting the problem of whether or not to reveal this fact to the largely Protestant respondents—something that would not have been a problem in most other contexts. It was initially decided to conceal her religion because we thought it would be a sensitive matter for respondents and might make penetration into the field harder. People in Northern Ireland are very skilled in telling identity (Burton, 1979), however, and it was quite easily uncovered. It is difficult to estimate precisely how sensitive this proved to be for respondents, although, as we shall argue shortly, there are grounds for our claim that it was not a source of systematic bias. The fieldworker's religion was, however, useful in automatically placing on the agenda the issue of police attitudes towards Catholics, as was her sex in relation to sexism within the force.

It is well known that the personal characteristics of a participant observer affect his or her research practice (see Hunt, 1984; Warren, 1988; Warren & Rasmussen, 1977; Wax, 1979) and that being female brings its own problems in the field. In this regard, the fieldworker's experiences with the RUC are similar to those of other young female researchers, in being subject to sexual hustling, fraternity, and paternalistic attitudes from male respondents (see Easterday, Papademas, Shorr, & Valentine, 1977). There also are, however, advantages to being female. Young female researchers may be treated as "acceptable incompetents" (Lofland, 1971:100) and perceived as nonthreatening (Easterday et al., 1977:344; Warren & Rasmussen, 1977:360–61). As Jennifer Hunt (1984) showed in respect to her work on the police, these qualities can increase a female researcher's penetration in the field and facilitate the development of rapport. . . .

It is worth outlining the ways we attempted to resolve these problems to allow readers to assess whether or not they were overcome. To help engender trust and familiarity, the fieldworker's contact in the station was restricted at the beginning to a few hours a shift once a week, gradually being built up to a full shift, including nights, twice a week. Fieldwork took place over a twelve-month period between 1987 and 1988 and was sufficiently prolonged to avoid the criticism that brief "smash and grab" ethnographies often deserve. Initially, the fieldworker's relations with respondents in the field were especially and unusually effusive, which runs counter to the norm in ethnographic research. She was seen as a light relief from the boredom or demands of the shift, and, as a female, she was treated as a "pretty face" in a working environment that is heavily masculine (for similar experiences, see Easterday et al., 1977; Hunt, 1984; Warren & Rasmussen, 1977). As contact in the field increased, and the presence of the fieldworker became routine, her treatment by respondents likewise became routine. It was only at that point that we felt confident that the fieldworker was being talked to by respondents as a person rather than as some novel sex object, and the veracity of what they said could be treated by us with more confidence. We therefore dispute Van Maanen's (1981:480) view that researchers on the police have to be male to be able to participate fully in the occupational culture of the police (for the difficulties in establishing rapport experience by a male researcher on the police, see Warren & Rasmussen, 1977:358).

What is more important than gender is the personality and skill of the fieldworker in overcoming the feelings of suspicion the police have of all outsiders, especially in the more enclosed and threatened world of the RUC. In our case, the fieldworker's sex seemed no bar to her obtaining access to the masculine canteen culture of policemen or to participating in conversations on the topics that are popular in that culture. Given the men's conventional views of gender roles, being female actually facilitated the introduction of topics of a more emotional kind in which women are commonsensically thought to be more interested. Respondents therefore talked freely about stress, death, the paramilitary threat and its effect on the family. These are particularly pertinent in Northern Ireland's police force (for a discussion of respondents' feelings about being in danger, see Brewer, 1990). Moreover, it also allowed entry into the policewomen's world, which using Van Maanen's logic, would have been denied a male fieldworker.

While no researcher, irrespective of his or her sex, can ever be totally sure that respondents are being truthful, our research design compensated for this. It is difficult to sustain untruths and false masks over twelve months of contact in the field, particularly when this contact involves sharing very private moments with respondents, such as those provided when in the canteen, during the quiet hours of the night shift, when riding in the back of a vehicle, or accompanying them in the guard post on sentry duty. After several months of working full eight-hour shifts, the constables frequently forgot that an outsider was present, or no longer cared, and the fieldworker experienced moments when it would have been difficult to maintain a front. While a few policemen tried to the bitter end to avoid conversations with the fieldworker, sufficient rapport was established over time for the majority to talk quite openly to her about what are highly sensitive and controversial topics in a Northern Ireland context. It is for this reason that data mostly comprise accounts and verbatim records of spontaneous conversations in natural situations.[3]

As one further measure of the rapport that was established, most respondents eventually became assured enough in her presence to express their feelings about being the subject of research. Over a twelve-month period, a fieldworker's persistent inquisitiveness is bound to become something of an irritant, and Van Maanen notes how fieldworkers cannot expect to be liked by all respondents (1982:111). But, leaving aside instances of momentary irritation, of which there were many, most respondents became confident enough in the fieldworker's presence to express what were no doubt widely held fears about the research. Sometimes these concerns were expressed through humor and ribaldry. The fieldworker became known among some policemen as "old nosebag," and there were long-running jokes about spelling people's names correctly in Sinn Fein's *Republican News*, the party newspaper of the Irish Republican Army (IRA). On one occasion, the concerns were expressed through anger. Toward the end of a long and tiring night shift, when news was coming through of the murder of another member of the RUC, one policeman in particular decided to put the fieldworker through a test of trust:

POLICE CONSTABLE 1: Look, just hold on a wee minute. What gives you the right to come here and start asking us these personal questions about our families and that. . . . You're not going to learn anything about the police while you're here. They're not going to tell you anything. . . . And you know why? Because you're always walking about with that bloody notebook writing everything down, and you're not getting anywhere near the truth. . . . Like what use is this research you're doing anyway? Is it going to do me or my mates any good? What you doing it for? 'Cos let me tell you, the only people who are going to be interested in your bloody research are the authorities.

WOMAN POLICE CONSTABLE: Can't you see that? They're just using you. . . .

POLICE CONSTABLE 1: See this research, as far as I'm concerned you'll learn nothing. It's a waste of time. To be honest, I couldn't give a monkey's fart about your research. If you really want to learn something you should have started at the top. It's them you need to be looking at. They don't care about the family man getting shot, they don't care about the families. The guy shot tonight will be forgotten about in another few weeks. It's them you should be talking to. The so-called big men at the top don't care about us.

WOMAN POLICE CONSTABLE: But it's us who are getting shot and blown up.

POLICE CONSTABLE 2: I'll tell you this. See when I come in here on a night, it's not the IRA I'm worried about, it's them upstairs.

POLICE CONSTABLE 1: I don't care what you're writing down, just as long as I don't see it in *Republican News*. Maybe the police has made me this way, but do you not see that if you're going to come in here asking me questions about my family, if you're going to want to know all these things, I've got to be able to trust you. Like after this tonight, I'd let you come out in a vehicle with me. (Field notes [FN], 30/8/87:33–45)

This extract is useful to illustrate how the fieldworker, in the one policeman's own admission, both needed to be tested and was successful in passing. There were many different sorts of trials set for the fieldworker,[4] and the apologies other members of the section afterward gave her because of this policeman's conduct is proof that they too were successfully passed. But this particular extract is useful for another reason in that it shows, through the subplots that appear within it, the range of issues provoked by the research about which respondents were sensitive. Some of these are worth highlighting in greater detail as a means of contextualizing the data and illustrating the contingencies operating upon them. . . .

Another technical problem of great significance at the stage of data collection is that of recording data (see Van Maanen, 1982). The ethnographer's conventional notepad can be obtrusive, yet, when the time in the field extends to a full eight-hour shift, it is impossible to do without this aid. One way of allaying fears is by taking notes in as unobtrusive a manner as possible. This is done by reducing the visibility of the pad and the physical activity of note taking; occasionally foregoing it when the situation seemed appropriate, as in the canteen or recreation and television rooms; and emphasizing that the notebooks were not secret. We reiterated this from time to time by showing them pages from the field notes and extracts from the data. Methodologically, however, it is impossible to know the reactive effects of this obtrusive form of recording data. But, in the context of Northern

Ireland, where police officers are so sensitive about security, it would have been even more suspicious and disruptive if the research assistant had taken frequent and lengthy absences to surreptitiously record data.

Inasmuch as most of the data collection was done by the research assistant, the principal investigator had to face the moral problem that the bulk of the physical danger at this juncture was borne by someone else. In Northern Ireland, people become inured to such risks, but, even so, the fieldwork was based in East Belfast, where the specific risks associated with fieldwork were negligible. Yet the fact still remained it was not the principal investigator who ran them.

Before moving to the final research stage of dissemination of results, it is worth noting a significant difference between our experience in data collection and usual police research: namely, the reversal in the process of retrenchment. Many studies describe a retrenchment from the front (Douglas, 1972) that occurred as police management sought to control or influence the research design and practice. What retrenchment we experienced was from below and occurred during data collection, which illustrates that working daily with the fieldworker was a source of greater sensitivity to ordinary policemen and women than was the idea of research to senior officers (for similar experiences, see Punch, 1989). The techniques by which a minority of respondents sought to impose limits from below included direct refusals to answer questions "for security reasons," occasional resorts to lying, and frequent use of coded conversations in which the meaning was concealed by maintaining a protective hold on the background knowledge to the conversation and the meaning of phrases. Sometimes they would drive off in their vehicle without the fieldworker. On one occasion, they locked her in the car when they went to a call, and sometimes they wound up the window to prevent her overhearing. Once, upon getting out of the car, they deliberately maneuvered the vehicle so as to trap the fieldworker to prevent her accompanying them. Dodges like this immediately make one suspicious about what they had to hide, and they tended to occur when they were wishing to do some personal business while on duty or simply avoid work. Such techniques were therefore popular among the lazy. These were the sorts of respondents who nicknamed the fieldworker "tell her nothin' " and "nosebag" and tried to assert informal checks on colleagues who were conversing with the fieldworker by reminding them of the notepad and that she writes everything down.

At the final stage of research, there was the technical problem of withdrawing from the field and publishing in such a way that the chief constable would not deny future researchers the opportunity to obtain permission. It was easy to anticipate that, in the Northern Ireland context, the results would have, temporarily at least, a high public profile, and, as researchers, we needed to be sensitive to the fact that the results might have been given a political slant, leading to further problems of personal security. Rainwater and Pittman's (1966) reflection on their study of a controversial housing development project identifies publication of the results as an acute problem. People's bigotry can be inflamed by what they read, and the results can be interpreted by members of the public in whatever way they want. Careful use of prose was therefore important. Agonizing over prose was also necessary to avoid revealing information that might be used to threaten the physical safety of respondents. There is a more intractable ethical issue behind these difficulties, for researchers have no control over the ideological use to which the data might be put. . . .

CRITICAL-THINKING QUESTIONS

1. What does Brewer mean by "contextual problems" in conducting field research? What does he mean by "sensitive" research?

2. Brewer describes a number of problems that he and his research assistant encountered in studying the RUC. What were the obstacles? How

did Brewer and his colleague try to overcome these problems?

3. Consider controversial and sensitive topics such as abortion, homosexuality, and assisted suicide. Can researchers study these issues without succumbing to ethical or political biases?

NOTES

1. The research reported here was funded by the ESRC on grant number E00232246. I also wish to acknowledge the assistance of Kathleen Magee in data collection.

2. A "section" is an administrative unit comprising the group of policemen and women on duty for the shift. In other forces, it is usually referred to as a "relief." A section numbers about twenty constables plus a small number of officials. Each section has at least one policewoman.

3. Van Maanen has argued that most ethnographic data are talk based (1982:140).

4. Other researchers have noted the trials and tests to which they have been put by subjects in the field (see Douglas, 1972; Van Maanen, 1982).

REFERENCES

BREWER, J. D. 1990. Talking about danger: The RUC and the paramilitary threat. *Sociology,* 24: 657–74.

BREWER, J. D. 1991. *Inside the RUC: Routine policing in a divided society*. Oxford: Oxford University Press.

BREWER, J. D., A. GUELKE, I. HUME, E. MOXON-BROWNE, and R. WILFORD. 1988. *Police, public order, and the state.* London: Macmillan.

BURTON, F. 1979. *Politics of legitimacy*. London: Routledge & Kegan Paul.

DOUGLAS, J. D. 1972. Managing fronts in observing deviance. In *Observing deviance*, ed. J. D. Douglas. New York: Random House.

EASTERDAY, L., D. PAPADEMAS, L. SCHORR, and C. VALENTINE. 1977. The making of a female researcher. *Urban Life*, 6: 333–48.

FOX, J. C., and R. LUNDMAN. 1974. Problems and strategies in gaining access in police organizations. *Criminology*, 12: 52–69.

HOLDAWAY, S. 1982. An insider job: A case study of covert research. In *Social research ethics*, ed. M. Bulmer. London: Macmillan.

HOLLOWELL, P. 1968. *The lorry driver*. London: Routledge & Kegan Paul.

HUNT, J. 1984. The development of rapport through the negotiation of gender in fieldwork among the police. *Human Organization*, 43: 283–96.

JACOBS, J., and H. RETSKY. 1975. Prison guards. *Urban Life and Culture,* 4: 5–29.

LOFLAND, J. 1971. *Analyzing social settings*. Belmont, Calif.: Wadsworth.

Policy Studies Institute. 1983. *Police and people in London: A survey of police officers.* London: Policy Studies Institute.

PUNCH, M. 1989. Researching police deviance. *British Journal of Sociology*, 40: 177–204.

RAINWATER, L., and D. PITTMAN. 1966. Ethical problems in studying a politically sensitive and deviant community. *Social Problems*, 14: 357–66.

RICHMAN, J. 1983. *Traffic wardens*. Manchester: Manchester University Press.

SPRADLEY, J., and B. MANN. 1975. *The cocktail waitress*. New York: John Wiley.

VAN MAANEN, J. 1981. The informant game: Selected aspects of ethnographic research in police organizations. *Urban Life*, 9: 469–94.

VAN MAANEN, J. 1982. Fieldwork on the beat. In *Varieties of qualitative research*, ed. J. Van Maanen. Beverly Hills, Calif.: Sage.

WARREN, C. A. B. 1988. *Gender issues in field research*. Newbury Park, Calif.: Sage.

WARREN, C. A. B., and P. RASMUSSEN. 1977. Sex and gender in field research. *Urban Life,* 6: 349–69.

WAX, R. H. 1979. Gender and age in fieldwork and fieldwork education. *Social Problems*, 26: 509–22.

WEITZER, R. 1985. Policing a divided society. *Social Problems*, 33: 41–55.

WOOLGAR, S. 1988. *Knowledge and reflexivity*. London: Sage.

8

Symbol: The Basic Element of Culture

Leslie A. White

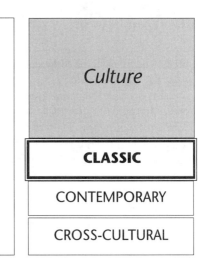

Leslie A. White, a noted anthropologist, argues in this selection that the key to human existence is the ability to use symbols. While all animals are capable of complex behavior, only humanity depends on symbolic activity. This is the special power that underlies our autonomy as the only creatures who live according to meanings we set for ourselves. Thus symbols convert our animal species into humanity, in the process transforming social behavior into true civilization.

. . . All human behavior originates in the use of symbols. It was the symbol which transformed our anthropoid ancestors into men and made them human. All civilizations have been generated, and are perpetuated, only by the use of symbols. It is the symbol which transforms an infant of *Homo sapiens* into a human being; deaf mutes who grow up without the use of symbols are not human beings. All human behavior consists of, or is dependent upon, the use of symbols. Human behavior is symbolic behavior; symbolic behavior is human behavior. The symbol is the universe of humanity. . . .

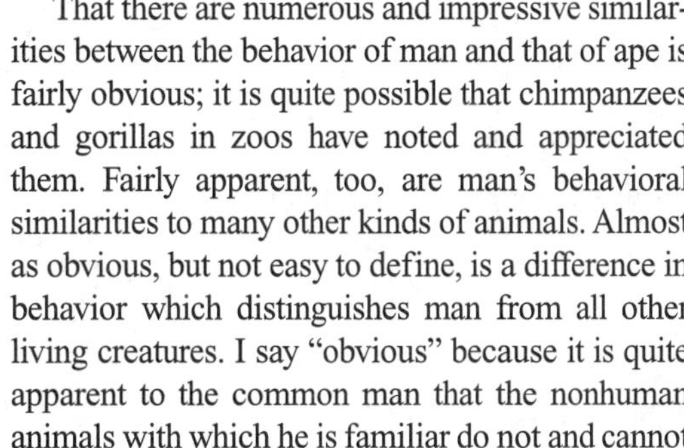

That there are numerous and impressive similarities between the behavior of man and that of ape is fairly obvious; it is quite possible that chimpanzees and gorillas in zoos have noted and appreciated them. Fairly apparent, too, are man's behavioral similarities to many other kinds of animals. Almost as obvious, but not easy to define, is a difference in behavior which distinguishes man from all other living creatures. I say "obvious" because it is quite apparent to the common man that the nonhuman animals with which he is familiar do not and cannot enter, and participate in, the world in which he, as a human being, lives. It is impossible for a dog, horse, bird, or even an ape, to have *any* understanding of the meaning of the sign of the cross to a Christian, or of the fact that black (white among the Chinese) is the color of mourning. No chimpanzee or laboratory

rat can appreciate the difference between Holy water and distilled water, or grasp the meaning of *Tuesday, 3,* or *sin.* No animal save man can distinguish a cousin from an uncle, or a cross cousin from a parallel cousin. Only man can commit the crime of incest or adultery; only he can remember the Sabbath and keep it Holy. It is not, as we well know, that the lower animals can do these things but to a lesser degree than ourselves; they cannot perform these acts of appreciation and distinction *at all.* It is, as Descartes said long ago, "not only that the brutes have less Reason than man, but that they have none at all.". . .

A symbol may be defined as a thing the value or meaning of which is bestowed upon it by those who use it. I say "thing" because a symbol may have any kind of physical form; it may have the form of a material object, a color, a sound, an odor, a motion of an object, a taste.

The meaning, or value, of a symbol is in no instance derived from or determined by properties intrinsic in its physical form: The color appropriate to mourning may be yellow, green, or any other color; purple need not be the color of royalty; among the Manchu rulers of China it was yellow. . . . The meaning of symbols is derived from and determined by the organisms who use them; meaning is bestowed by human organisms upon physical things or events which thereupon become symbols. Symbols "have their signification," to use John Locke's phrase, "from the arbitrary imposition of men."

All symbols must have a physical form otherwise they could not enter our experience. . . . But the meaning of a symbol cannot be discovered by mere sensory examination of its physical form. One cannot tell by looking at an *x* in an algebraic equation what it stands for; one cannot ascertain with the ears alone the symbolic value of the phonetic compound *si;* one cannot tell merely by weighing a pig how much gold he will exchange for; one cannot tell from the wave length of a color whether it stands for courage or cowardice, "stop" or "go"; nor can one discover the spirit in a fetish by any amount of physical or chemical examination. The meaning of a symbol can be grasped only by nonsensory, symbolic means. . . .

Thus Darwin says: "That which distinguishes man from the lower animals is not the understanding of articulate sounds, for as everyone knows, dogs understand many words and sentences."[1]. . .

The man differs from the dog—and all other creatures—in that *he can and does play an active role in determining what value the vocal stimulus is to have, and the dog cannot.* The dog does not and cannot play an active part in determining the value of the vocal stimulus. Whether he is to roll over or go fetch at a given stimulus, or whether the stimulus for roll over be one combination of sounds or another is a matter in which the dog has nothing whatever to "say." He plays a purely passive role and can do nothing else. He learns the meaning of a vocal command just as his salivary glands may learn to respond to the sound of a bell. But man plays an active role and thus becomes a creator: Let *x* equal three pounds of coal and it does equal three pounds of coal; let removal of the hat in a house of worship indicate respect and it becomes so. This creative faculty, that of freely, actively, and arbitrarily bestowing value upon things, is one of the most commonplace as well as *the* most important characteristic of man. Children employ it freely in their play: "Let's pretend that this rock is a wolf.". . .

All culture (civilization) depends upon the symbol. It was the exercise of the symbolic faculty that brought culture into existence, and it is the use of symbols that makes the perpetuation of culture possible. Without the symbol there would be no culture, and man would be merely an animal, not a human being.

Articulate speech is the most important form of symbolic expression. Remove speech from culture and what would remain? Let us see.

Without articulate speech we would have no *human* social organization. Families we might have, but this form of organization is not peculiar to man; it is not *per se,* human. But we would have no prohibitions of incest, no rules prescribing exogamy and endogamy, polygamy, monogamy. How could marriage with a cross cousin be prescribed, marriage with a parallel cousin proscribed, without articulate speech? How could rules which prohibit plural mates possessed simultaneously but permit them if possessed one at a time, exist without speech?

Without speech we would have no political, economic, ecclesiastic, or military organization; no codes of etiquette or ethics; no laws; no science, theology, or literature; no games or music, except on an ape level. Rituals and ceremonial paraphernalia would be meaningless without articulate speech. Indeed, without articulate speech we would be all but toolless: We would have only the occasional and insignificant use of the tool such as we find today among the higher apes, for it was articulate speech that transformed the nonprogressive tool-using of the ape into the progressive, cumulative tool-using of man, the human being.

In short, without symbolic communication in some form, we would have no culture. "In the Word was the beginning" of culture—and its perpetuation also.

To be sure, with all his culture man is still an animal and strives for the same ends that all other living creatures strive for: the preservation of the individual and the perpetuation of the [species]. In concrete terms these ends are food, shelter from the elements, defense from enemies, health, and offspring. The fact that man strives for these ends just as all other animals do has, no doubt, led many to declare that there is "no fundamental difference between the behavior of man and of other creatures." But man does differ, not in *ends* but in *means*. Man's means are cultural means: Culture is simply the human animal's way of living. And, since these means, culture, are dependent upon a faculty possessed by man alone, the ability to use symbols, the difference between the behavior of man and of all other creatures is not merely great, but basic and fundamental.

The behavior of man is of two distinct kinds: symbolic and nonsymbolic. Man yawns, stretches, coughs, scratches himself, cries out in pain, shrinks with fear, "bristles" with anger, and so on. Nonsymbolic behavior of this sort is not peculiar to man; he shares it not only with the other primates but with many other animal species as well. But man communicates with his fellows with articulate speech, uses amulets, confesses sins, makes laws, observes codes of etiquette, explains his dreams, classifies his relatives in designated categories, and so on. This kind of behavior is unique; only man is capable of it; it is peculiar to man because it consists of, or is dependent upon, the use of symbols. The nonsymbolic behavior of *Homo sapiens* is the behavior of man the animal; the symbolic behavior is that of man the human being. It is the symbol which has transformed man from a mere animal to a human animal. . . .

The infant of the species *Homo sapiens* becomes human only when and as he exercises his symbol faculty. Only through articulate speech—not necessarily vocal—can he enter the world of human beings and take part in their affairs. The questions asked earlier may be repeated now. How could a growing child know and appreciate such things as social organization, ethics, etiquette, ritual, science, religion, art, and games without symbolic communication? The answer is of course that he could know nothing of these things and have no appreciation of them at all. . . .

Children who have been cut off from human intercourse for years by blindness and deafness but who have eventually effected communication with their fellows on a symbolic level are exceedingly illuminating. The case of Helen Keller is exceptionally instructive. . . .

Helen Keller was rendered blind and deaf at an early age by illness. She grew up as a child without symbolic contact with anyone. Descriptions of her at the age of seven, the time at which her teacher, Miss Sullivan, came to her home, disclosed no *human* attributes of Helen's behavior at all. She was a headstrong, undisciplined, and unruly little animal.

Within a day or so after her arrival at the Keller home, Miss Sullivan taught Helen her first word, spelling it into her hand. But this word was merely a sign, not a symbol. A week later Helen knew several words but, as Miss Sullivan reports, she had "no idea how to use them or that everything has a name." Within three weeks Helen knew eighteen nouns and three verbs. But she was still on the level of signs; she still had no notion "that everything has a name."

Helen confused the word signs for "mug" and "water" because, apparently, both were associated with drinking. Miss Sullivan made a few attempts to clear up this confusion but without success. One morning, however, about a month after Miss Sullivan's arrival, the two went out to the pump in the garden. What happened then is best told in their own words:

> I made Helen hold her mug under the spout while I pumped. As the cold water gushed forth, filling the mug, I spelled "w-a-t-e-r" into Helen's free hand. The word coming so close upon the sensation of cold water rushing over her hand seemed to startle her. She dropped the mug and stood as one transfixed. A new light came into her face. She spelled "water" several times. Then she dropped on the ground and asked for its name and pointed to the pump and the trellis, and suddenly turning round she asked for my name. . . . *In a few hours she had added thirty new words to her vocabulary.*

But these words were now more than mere signs as they are to a dog and as they had been to Helen up to then. They were *symbols.* Helen had at last grasped and turned the key that admitted her for the first time to a new universe: the world of human beings. Helen describes this marvelous experience herself:

> We walked down the path to the well-house, attracted by the fragrance of the honeysuckle with which it was covered. Someone was drawing water and my teacher placed my hand under the spout. As the cool stream gushed over one hand she spelled into the other the word *water,* first slowly, then rapidly. I stood still, my whole attention fixed upon the motion of her fingers. Suddenly I felt a misty consciousness as of something forgotten—a thrill of returning thought; and somehow *the mystery of language was revealed to me.* I knew then that "w-a-t-e-r" meant the wonderful cool something that was flowing over my hand. That living word awakened my soul, gave it light, hope, joy, set it free!

Helen was transformed on the instant by this experience. Miss Sullivan had managed to touch Helen's symbol mechanism and set it in motion. Helen, on her part, grasped the external world with this mechanism that had lain dormant and inert all these years, sealed in dark and silent isolation by eyes that could not see and ears that heard not. But now she had crossed the boundary and entered a new land. Henceforth the progress would be rapid.

"I left the well-house," Helen reports, "eager to learn. Everything had a name, and each name gave birth to a new thought. As we returned to the house every object which I touched seemed to quiver with life. That was because I saw everything with the strange new sight that had come to me."

Helen became humanized rapidly. "I see an improvement in Helen from day to day," Miss Sullivan wrote in her diary, "*almost from hour to hour.* Everything must have a name now. . . . She drops the signs and pantomime she used before as soon as she has words to supply their place. . . . We notice her face grows more expressive each day. . . ."

A more eloquent and convincing account of the significance of symbols and of the great gulf between the human mind and that of minds without symbols could hardly be imagined.

The natural processes of biologic evolution brought into existence in man, and man alone, a new and distinctive ability; the ability to use symbols. The most important form of symbolic expression is articulate speech. Articulate speech means communication of ideas; communication means preservation—tradition—and preservation means accumulation and progress. The emergence of the faculty of symboling has resulted in the genesis of a new order of phenomena: an extra-somatic, cultural order. All civilizations are born of, and are perpetuated by, the use of symbols. A culture, or civilization, is but a particular kind of form which the biologic, life-perpetuating activities of a particular animal, man, assume.

Human behavior is symbolic behavior; if it is not symbolic, it is not human. The infant of the genus *Homo* becomes a human being only as he is introduced into and participates in that order of phenomena which is culture. And the key to this world and the means of participation in it is—the symbol.

CRITICAL-THINKING QUESTIONS

1. Why does White argue that a deaf mute unable to communicate symbolically is not fully human? What opposing argument might be made? What position would White take in the pro-choice versus pro-life abortion controversy?

2. Because the reality we experience is based on a particular system of symbols, how do we tend to view members of other cultures? What special efforts are needed to overcome the tendency to treat people of different cultures as less worthy than we are?

3. How did gaining the capacity to use symbols transform Helen Keller? How did this ability alter her capacity for further learning?

NOTE

1. Charles Darwin, *The Descent of Man,* chap. 3.

Culture

CLASSIC

CONTEMPORARY

CROSS-CULTURAL

9

Manifest and Latent Functions

Robert K. Merton

Robert Merton made a major contribution to structural-functional theory by pointing out that social patterns have both manifest and latent functions. Manifest functions are those consequences that are familiar, planned, and generally recognized. Latent functions, on the other hand, are unfamiliar, unplanned, and widely overlooked. For this reason, Merton argued, comprehending latent functions is a special responsibility of sociologists. Merton illustrates this process by offering observations about the pattern of conspicuous consumption.

. . . Armed with the concept of latent function, the sociologist extends his inquiry in those very directions which promise most for the theoretic development of the discipline. He examines the familiar (or planned) social practice to ascertain the latent, and hence generally unrecognized, functions (as well, of course, as the manifest functions). He considers, for example, the consequences of the new wage plan for, say, the trade union in which the workers are organized or the consequences of a propaganda program, not only for increasing its avowed purpose of stirring up patriotic fervor, but also for making large numbers of people reluctant to speak their minds when they differ with official policies, etc. In short, it is suggested that the *distinctive* intellectual contributions of the sociologist are found primarily in the study of unintended consequences (among which are latent functions) of social practices, as well as in the study of anticipated consequences (among which are manifest functions).

[Illustration]: The Pattern of Conspicuous Consumption. The manifest purpose of buying consumption goods is, of course, the satisfaction of the needs for which these goods are explicitly designed. Thus, automobiles are obviously intended to provide a certain kind of transportation; candles, to provide light; choice articles of food to provide sustenance; rare art products to provide aesthetic pleasure. Since these products *do* have these uses, it was largely assumed that these encompass the range of socially significant functions. Veblen indeed suggests that this was ordinarily the prevailing view (in the pre-Veblenian era, of course): "The end of acquisition and accumulation is conventionally held to be the consumption of the goods accumulated. . . . This is at least felt to be the economically legitimate end of acquisition, *which alone it is incumbent on the theory to take account of.*"[1]

Source: Reprinted with the permission of The Free Press, a Division of Simon & Schuster, from *Social Theory and Social Structure*, revised and enlarged edition by Robert K. Merton.

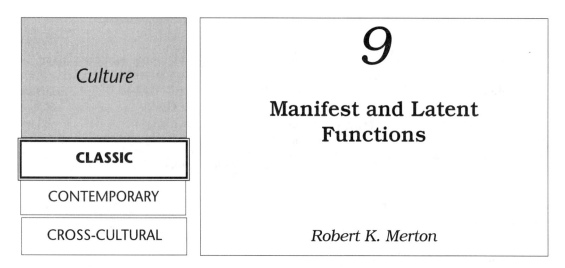

However, says Veblen in effect, as sociologists we must go on to consider the latent functions of acquisition, accumulation, and consumption, and these latent functions are remote indeed from the manifest functions. "But, it is only when taken in a sense of far removed from its naive meaning [i.e., manifest function] that the consumption of goods can be said to afford the incentive from which accumulation invariably proceeds." And among these latent functions, which help explain the persistence and the social location of the pattern of conspicuous consumption, is [the fact that] . . . it results in a *heightening or reaffirmation of social status.*

The Veblenian paradox is that people buy expensive goods not so much because they are superior but because they are expensive. For it is the latent equation ("costliness = mark of higher social status") which he singles out in his functional analysis, rather than the manifest equation ("costliness = excellence of the goods"). Not that he denies manifest functions *any* place in buttressing the pattern of conspicuous consumption. These, too, are operative. . . . *It is only that these direct, manifest functions do not fully account for the prevailing patterns of consumption. Otherwise put, if the latent functions of status-enhancement or status-reaffirmation were removed from the patterns of conspicuous consumption, these patterns would undergo severe changes of a sort which the "conventional" economist could not foresee.*

CRITICAL-THINKING QUESTIONS

1. Why, according to Merton, is the study of latent functions one of the important tasks of sociologists?
2. Distinguish between the manifest and latent functions of owning designer clothing, a fine car, or a large home.
3. According to Thorstein Veblen, whom Merton cites in his analysis, does the higher cost of various goods typically attest to their higher quality? Why or why not?
4. Identify some of the manifest and latent functions of (a) a primary school spelling bee, (b) sports, and (c) attending college.

NOTE

1. Thorstein Veblen, *Theory of the Leisure Class* (1899) (New York: Vanguard Press, 1928), p. 25.

Culture

CLASSIC

CONTEMPORARY

CROSS-CULTURAL

10

The Rape Culture

Dianne F. Herman

Culture is vital in the human species, but some cultural patterns are destructive. Dianne Herman argues that, by linking sexuality and violence, the United States is a "rape culture" that undermines healthy relationships. Although "date rape" has always existed, it has only recently been seen, by social scientists and practitioners, as a form of violence. However, many young adults—including college students—still view date rape as a "normal" part of dating.

When Susan Griffin wrote, "I have never been free of the fear of rape," she touched a responsive chord in most women.[1] Every woman knows the fear of being alone at home late at night or the terror that strikes her when she receives an obscene telephone call. She knows also of the "minirapes"—the pinch in the crowded bus, the wolf whistle from a passing car, the stare of a man looking at her bust during a conversation. Griffin has argued, "Rape is a kind of terrorism which severely limits the freedom of women and makes women dependent on men."[2]

Women live their lives according to a rape schedule. . . .

Because of the aggressive–passive, dominant–submissive, me-Tarzan–you-Jane nature of the relationship between the sexes in our culture, there is a close association between violence and sexuality. Words that are slang sexual terms, for example, frequently accompany assaultive behavior or gestures. "Fuck you" is meant as a brutal attack in verbal terms. In the popular culture, "James Bond alternately whips out his revolver and his cock, and though there is no known connection between the skills of a gunfighter and love-making, pacifism seems suspiciously effeminate."[3] The imagery of sexual relations between males and females in books, songs, advertising, and films is frequently that of a sadomasochistic relationship thinly veiled by a romantic facade. Thus, it is very difficult in our society to differentiate rape from "normal" heterosexual relations. Indeed our culture can be characterized as a rape culture because the image of heterosexual intercourse is based on a rape model of sexuality.

LEGAL DEFINITIONS OF RAPE

If healthy heterosexuality were characterized by loving, warm, and reciprocally satisfying actions,

---

Source: "The Rape Culture," by Dianne F. Herman, in *Women: A Feminist Perspective,* 3d ed., ed. Jo Freeman (Mountain View, Calif.: Mayfield, 1984).

then rape could be defined as sex without consent, therefore involving either domination or violence. Instead, rape is legally defined as sexual intercourse by a male with a female, *other than his wife,* without the consent of the woman and effected by force, duress, intimidation, or deception as to the nature of the act. The spousal exemption in the law, which still remains in effect in most states, means that a husband cannot be guilty of raping his wife, even if he forces intercourse against her will. The implication of this loophole is that *violent, unwanted* sex does not necessarily define rape. Instead, rape is *illegal* sex—that is, sexual assault by a man who has no legal rights over the woman. In other words, in the law's eyes, violence in legal sexual intercourse is permissible, but sexual relations with a woman who is not one's property is not.

From their inception, rape laws have been established not to protect women, but to protect women's property value for men.

Society's view of rape was purely a matter of economics—of assets and liabilities. When a married woman was raped, her husband was wronged, not her. If she was unmarried, her father suffered since his investment depreciated. It was the monetary value of a woman which determined the gravity of the crime. Because she had no personal rights under the law, her own emotions simply didn't matter.[4] Because rape meant that precious merchandise was irreparably damaged, the severity of the punishment was dependent on whether the victim was a virgin. In some virgin rapes, biblical law ordered that the rapist marry the victim, since she was now devalued property.[5] The social status of the victim was also important, as a woman of higher social status was more valuable. . . .

Due to pressure from feminist groups, the legal definition of rape has been broadened in many states over the last decade.[6] Evidentiary rules requiring corroboration, cautionary instructions, psychiatric examinations, and prior sexual history have been eliminated or revised in most states. A survey of 151 criminal-justice professionals in Florida, Michigan, and Georgia found that these types of reforms in rape-law legislation have received widespread acceptance and approval. "Further, the findings suggest that law reform need not generate the confusion, uncertainty, or antagonism predicted by some early analysts."[7]

Some jurisdictions have established categories of sexual offenses that allow for sex-neutral assaults, taking into account that men and children, as well as women, can be victims. Others have allowed prosecution when sexual assaults include acts other than penetration of the vagina by the penis, such as sodomy or oral copulation. The latest struggle has been to remove the spousal exemption in the laws, so that husbands are not immune to prosecution for rape by their wives. Each of these changes reflects an evolving understanding that rape laws should not be in existence to regulate control of virginal female bodies for sole ownership by one man; rather, rape should be defined as a sexual assault and crime of violence by one person against another.[8]

HOW COMMON IS RAPE?

There was a steady increase in the rape rate between the mid-sixties and 1980, when it leveled off. In 1964, 11.2 rapes and attempted rapes were reported nationally per 100,000 inhabitants. That figure climbed to 26.1 reports per 100,000 by 1974, and, in the 1980s, has fluctuated between 33.5 and 37.9.[9] Since male victims rarely report rape, this means that, in 1987, 73 of every 100,000 females in the United States reported that they were victims of rape or attempted rape.[10]

These statistics are based on *reported* rapes. Victimization surveys indicate that for every reported rape, an additional one to three rapes have occurred but have not been reported.[11] Diana E. H. Russell's 1978 study of 930 San Francisco women found that 44 percent reported at least one completed or attempted rape.[12] Only 8 percent, or less than one in twelve, of the total number of incidents were ever reported to the police. Using Russell's findings, the actual incidence of rape is twenty-four times higher than FBI statistics indicate.

In addition, a woman is probably less safe from rape in this country than she is in any other developed nation. The United States has one of the highest rape rates in the world.[13] In 1984, the United States had 35.7 rapes per 100,000 people. The Bureau of Justice Statistics found European nations had an average of 5.4 rapes per 100,000 inhabitants in that same year.[14]

VICTIMS OF RAPE

Many myths surround the crime of rape, but perhaps most common are those that imply that the victim was responsible for her own victimization. Projecting the blame on the woman is accomplished by portraying her as a seductress. The conventional scenario is one of a man who is sexually aroused by an attractive, flirtatious woman. But the image of the rape victim as seductive and enticing is at odds with reality. Rapes have been committed on females as young as six months and as old as ninety-three years. Most victims tend to be very young. In one study in Philadelphia of reported rapes in 1958 and 1960, 20 percent of the victims were between ten and fourteen years of age; another 25 percent were between fifteen and nineteen.[15] According to data compiled in 1974 by Women Organized Against Rape, 41 percent of rape victims seen in hospital emergency rooms in Philadelphia were sixteen or younger. The category with the highest frequency of victims was the range between thirteen and sixteen years of age.[16] A comprehensive review of the literature on rape victimization published in 1979 noted that the high-risk ages are adolescents (aged thirteen to seventeen) and young adults (aged eighteen to twenty-four).[17] In 1985, The National Crime Survey, based on findings from a continuous survey of a representative sample of housing units across the United States, reported that the rape rate is highest for those white women between ages sixteen and nineteen, and for those black women between ages twenty-five and thirty-four.[18]

. . . Rape is a crime commonly committed by an assailant who is known to the victim. Even in cases where women do report to the police, victim and offender are frequently acquainted. In a study of 146 persons admitted to the emergency room of Boston City Hospital during a one-year period from 1972 to 1973 with a complaint of rape, 102 of these rapes were reported to police. Forty of these victims who reported the assault knew their assailant.[19] Burgess and Holmstrom believe that victims who know their rapists are less apt to report the crime. Their study found that victims who reported rapes by assailants known to them had more difficulty establishing their credibility than did victims raped by strangers, and these cases had a higher likelihood of dropping out of the criminal-justice system.[20]. . .

In 1982, *Ms.* magazine reported a series of studies on college campuses confirming that, even given new and more liberal attitudes about premarital sex and women's liberation, date rape and other forms of acquaintance rape may be reaching epidemic proportions in higher education. In some cases, women have even been assaulted by men ostensibly acting as protective escorts to prevent rape.[21] A 1985 study of over 600 college students found that three-quarters of the women and more than one-half of the men disclosed an experience of sexual aggression on a date. Nearly 15 percent of the women and 7 percent of the men said that intercourse had taken place against the woman's will.[22] The victim and offender had most likely known each other almost one year before the sexual assault. Date rape occurred most frequently when the man initiated the date, when he drove to and from and paid for the date, when drinking took place, and when the couple found themselves alone either in a car or indoors. In these instances, it appears that college men may feel they have license to rape.

In explaining date rape, one set of authors has stated,

> . . . women are often seen as legitimate objects of sexual aggression. Rape can be viewed as the logical extension of a cultural perspective that defines men as possessors of women. The American dating system, in particular, places females in the position of sexual objects purchased by men. Women are groomed to compete for men who will shower them with attention and favors, men are socialized to expect sexual reward (or at least to try for that reward) for their attention to women. This perspective presents the woman as a legitimate object of victimization: If a man is unable to seduce a woman, and yet has provided her with certain attention and gifts, then he has a right to expect sexual payment. Only the situation of rape by a total stranger escapes the influence of this reasoning. In any other case, if a woman knows her attacker even slightly, she is likely to be perceived as a legitimate victim of a justified aggressor.[23]

The tendency to dismiss rape allegations when victim and offender know each other has contributed to the silence that surrounds marital rape. Finkelhor and Yllo in their study of marital rape found that only one textbook on marriage and the family of the thirty-one they surveyed mentioned rape or anything related to sexual assault in marriage.[24] These authors cite studies that indicate that at least 10 percent of all married women questioned on this topic report that their husbands have used physical force or threats to have sex with them.[25] Marital rape may be the most common form of sexual assault: More than two times as many of the women interviewed had been raped by husbands as had been raped by strangers.[26]. . . Husbands' desires to frighten, humiliate, punish, degrade, dominate, and control their spouses were found to be the most common motivations for the sexual assaults. In their 1980–81 study of Boston area mothers, Finkelhor and Yllo found that about half of the marital rape victims were also battered.[27] Many cases were uncovered in which wives were tortured through sadistic sexual assaults involving objects. Many more were humiliated by being forced to engage in distasteful or unusual sexual practices. One-quarter of the victims in their survey were sexually attacked in the presence of others—usually their children.[28] Many times, the rape was the final violent act in a series of physical and emotional abuses or the payback when a woman filed for separation or divorce. Sadly, many women suffer years of abuse thinking that the assaults are caused by their failure to be good wives or feeling that they have no way out and that this is the lot of the married woman. Too often, their husbands justify their attacks on their wives by blaming the wives for causing their loss of control, or by saying that they are entitled to treat their spouses any way they choose.

Because rape so frequently involves people who know each other, most rapists and their victims are of the same race and age group. In 1985, approximately 80 percent of all rapes and attempted rapes were intraracial.[29] One reason that the myth that rapes are interracial dies hard is that cases of this type frequently receive the most publicity. In a study of rape in Philadelphia, researchers discovered that the two major newspapers, when they reported on rape cases, mentioned mainly interracial offenses. Intraracial rapes were only occasionally mentioned.[30] Gary LaFree examined the effect of race in the handling of 881 sexual assaults in a large midwestern city. He found that black males who assaulted white women received more serious charges, longer sentences, and more severe punishment in terms of executed sentences and incarceration in the state penitentiary.[31] Although black women are three times more likely to be raped than are white women, rape is least prosecuted if the victim is black.[32] The rape of poor, black women is not an offense against men of power.

WHY MEN RAPE

. . . One of the most surprising findings of studies on rape is that the rapist is normal in personality, appearance, intelligence, behavior, and sexual drive.[33] Empirical research has repeatedly failed to find a consistent pattern of personality type or character disorder that reliably discriminates the rapist from the nonrapist. According to Amir, the only significant psychological difference between the rapist and the normal, well-adjusted male appears to be the greater tendency of the former to express rage and violence. But this finding probably tends to overemphasize the aggressive personality characteristics of rapists, since generally only imprisoned rapists have been studied. Those few rapists who are sentenced to prison tend to be the more obviously violent offenders. In fact, studies by some researchers have found one type of rapist who is fairly meek and mild-mannered.[34] What is clear is that the rapist is not an exotic freak. Rather, rape evolves out of a situation in which "normal" males feel a need to prove themselves to be "men" by displaying dominance over females.

In our society, men demonstrate their competence as people by being "masculine." Part of this definition of masculinity involves a contempt for anything feminine or for females in general. Reported rapes, in fact, are frequently associated with some form of ridicule and sexual humiliation, such as urination on the victim, anal intercourse, fellatio, and ejaculation in the victim's face and hair. Insertion into the woman's vagina of broomsticks, bottles, and other phallic objects is not an uncommon coup de grace.[35] The overvaluing of toughness expresses itself in a disregard for anything associated with fragility. In the rapist's view, his assertion of maleness is automatically tied to a violent repudiation of anything feminine.

Most rapes are not spontaneous acts in which the rapist had no prior intent to commit rape but was overcome by the sexual provocations of his victim. Statistics compiled from reported rapes show that the overwhelming majority are planned. In one study, 71 percent of all reported rapes were prearranged, and another 11 percent were partially planned. Only 18 percent were impulsive acts.[36] Planning is most common in cases of group rape. Even when the rapist is acting alone, a majority of the rapes involves some manipulations on the part of the offender to place his victim in a vulnerable situation that he can exploit. . . .

Most convicted rapists tend to project the blame on others, particularly the victim. Schultz found that the sex offender is twice as likely to insist on his innocence as is the general offender.[37] "In two-thirds of the cases one hears, 'I'm here on a phoney beef,' or 'I might have been a little rough with her but she was asking for it,' or 'I might have done it but I was too drunk to remember.'"[38] They also rationalize the act by labeling their victims "bad" women. Some rapists excuse and deny their crime by portraying the victim as a woman of questionable sexual reputation or as a person who has placed herself in a compromising position, thus "getting what she deserved."[39]. . .

American culture produces rapists when it encourages the socialization of men to subscribe to values of control and dominance, callousness and competitiveness, and anger and aggression, and when it discourages the expression by men of vulnerability, sharing, and cooperation. In the end, it is not only the women who become the victims of these men, but also the offenders themselves, who suffer. These men lose the ability to satisfy needs for nurturance, love, and belonging, and their anger and frustration from this loss expresses itself in acts of violence and abuse against others. The tragedy for our society is that we produce so many of these hardened men.

SOCIETY'S RESPONSE TO RAPE

. . . The police have considerable discretion in determining whether a crime has been committed. In 1976, according to a study by the FBI, 19 percent of all forcible rapes reported to the police were unfounded.[40] *Unfounding* simply means that the police decide there is no basis for prosecution. . . .

According to many studies, one of the most frequent causes of unfounding rape is a prior relationship between the participants. In the Philadelphia study, 43 percent of all date rapes were unfounded. The police, according to the researcher, seemed to be more concerned that the victim had "assumed the risk" than they were with the fact that she had not given consent to intercourse.[41]

Another common reason police unfound cases is the apparent lack of force in the rape situation. The extent of injuries seems to be even more important in the decision to unfound than is whether the offender had a weapon.[42] There is no requirement that a male businessperson must either forcibly resist when mugged or forfeit protection under the law. But proof of rape, both to the police and in court, is often required to take the form of proof of resistance, substantiated by the extent of injuries suffered by the victim. Yet local police departments frequently advise women not to resist if faced with the possibility of rape.

> In a confusion partially of their own making, local police precincts point out contradictory messages: They "unfound" a rape case because, by the rule of their own male logic, the woman did not show normal resistance; they report on an especially brutal rape case and announce to the press that the multiple stab wounds were the work of an assailant who was enraged because the woman resisted.[43]

The victim is told that if she was raped it was because she did not resist enough. But if she fights back and is raped and otherwise assaulted, police blame her again for bringing about her own injuries because of her resistance. . . .

One reason physicians are reluctant to diagnose injuries as caused by a sexual assault is due to their reluctance to have to give up their valuable time to testify on behalf of the prosecution. In the early seventies, the District of Columbia newspapers reported that doctors of D.C. General Hospital were intentionally giving negative medical reports of rape victims so they would not be called to court. In one case that reached the appeals court, the doctor had reported absolutely no injuries even though police photographs showed bruises and scratches on the victim's face. As a result, the trial court dismissed the rape charges and the defendants were only found guilty of assault with intent to commit rape.[44]

For many women, the experience of having their account of the events scrutinized, mocked, or discounted continues in the courtroom. Women have often said that they felt as though they, not the defendants, were the persons on trial. According to Burgess and Holmstrom, "Going to court, for the victim, is as much of a crises as the actual rape itself."[45] They quote one victim shortly after she appeared in district court: "I felt like crying. I felt abused. I didn't like the questions the defense was asking. I felt accused—guilty 'til proven innocent. I thought the defense lawyer made it a big joke."[46] They relate how one twelve-year-old girl had a psychotic breakdown during the preliminary court process.[47]

The victim, by taking the case to court, incurs extensive costs, both psychological and financial. Expecting to testify just once, she is likely to have to repeat her story at the hearing for probable cause, to the grand jury, and in superior-court sessions. To convey the discomfort of such a process, feminists have recommended that individuals imagine having to tell an audience all the details of their last sexual experience. In addition to exposing themselves to public scrutiny, rape victims may be subject to harassment from the friends or family of the perpetrator.

Financially, the time away from work nearly always stretches beyond expectations. According to Burgess and Holmstrom, the victims they accompanied to court were often forced to sit three to four hours in the courthouse, only to be told that the case had been continued. After they and their witnesses had taken time off from work and, in some cases, traveled great distances, they were less than enthusiastic about the idea of seeing justice done.[48] Wood has said, "Due to the traumatic experience which a victim must go through in order to attempt to secure the attacker's successful prosecution, it is amazing any rape cases come to trial."[49]

Even if the victim is resilient enough to pursue her case, she may encounter prejudicial attitudes from judges and juries. . . . Shirley Feldman-Summers and Karen Lindner investigated the perceptions of victims by juries and found that, as the respectability of the victim decreased, the jury's belief that the victim was responsible for the rape increased.[50] In a sense, juries have created an extralegal defense. If the complainant somehow "assumed the risk" of rape, juries will commonly find the defendant guilty of some lesser crime or will acquit him altogether.[51] "A seventeen-year-old girl was raped during a beer-drinking party. The jury probably acquitted, according to the judge, because they thought the girl asked for what she got."[52] In one case, according to Medea and Thompson, "a woman who responded with 'fuck off' when approached lost her case because 'fuck' is a sexually exciting word."[53] If the victim knew the offender previously, especially as an intimate, juries will be reluctant to convict:

> In one case of "savage rape," the victim's jaw was fractured in two places. The jury nevertheless acquitted because it found that there may have been sexual relations on previous occasions, and the parties had been drinking on the night of the incident.[54]

. . . Despite attempts to educate the public about the dynamics of rape, myths still persist. Martha Burt, in a study of almost 600 Minnesota residents, found that most believed that "Any healthy woman can resist a rapist." "In the majority of rapes, the victim was promiscuous or had a bad reputation." "If a girl engages in necking or petting and she lets things get out of hand, it is her fault if her partner forces sex on her." "One reason that women falsely report a rape is that they frequently have a need to call attention to themselves." Burt found that rapists also subscribed to these myths in attempts to excuse and rationalize their behavior.[55] The implication of her study is that the general population's attitudes toward women who are raped is very similar to the rapist's view of his victim.

During the 1986–87 school year, a survey was taken of over 1500 sixth to ninth graders who attended the Rhode Island Rape Crisis Center's assault-awareness program in schools across the state. The results of the survey strongly indicated that even the next generation of Americans tends to blame the victim of sexual assault. For example, 50 percent of the students said a woman who walks alone at night and dresses seductively is asking to be raped. In addition, most of the students surveyed accepted sexually assaultive behavior as normal. Fifty-one percent of the boys and 41 percent of the girls stated that a man has a right to force a woman to kiss him if he has spent "a lot of money" on her. Sixty-five percent of the boys and 57 percent of the girls in junior high schools said it is acceptable for a man to force a woman to have sex if they have been dating for more than six months. Eighty-seven percent of the boys and 79 percent of the girls approved of rape if the couple were married. Interestingly, 20 percent of the girls and 6 percent of the boys taking the survey disclosed that they had been sexually abused.[56]

In cases of rape, judges, juries, police, prosecutors, and the general public frequently attribute blame and responsibility to the victim for her own victimization. Unfortunately, these negative responses are often compounded by reactions from family and friends. Encounters with parents, relatives, friends, and spouses many times involve either anger at the victim for being foolish enough to get raped or expressions of embarrassment and shame that family members will suffer as a result of the attack. . . .

THE RAPE CULTURE

. . . As long as sex in our society is construed as a dirty, low, and violent act involving domination of a male over a female, rape will remain a common occurrence. The erotization of male dominance means that whenever women are in a subordinate position to men, the likelihood for sexual assault is great. We are beginning to see that rape is not the only way in which women are sexually victimized, and that other forms of sexual exploitation of women are rampant in our society.[57] Feminists have raised our consciousness about rape by developing rape crisis centers and other programs to assist victims and their families, by reforming laws and challenging politicians, by training professionals in medicine and in the criminal-justice system, and by educating women and the general public on the subject. They are also enlightening us about pornography; sexual harassment on the job and in higher education; sexual exploitation in doctor, dentist, and therapist relations with patients; and sexual assault in the family, such as incest and rape in marriage.

Rape is the logical outcome if men act according to the "masculine mystique" and women act according to the "feminine mystique." But rape does not have to occur. Its presence is an indication of how widely held are traditional views of appropriate male and female behavior, and of how strongly enforced these views are. Our society is a rape culture because it fosters and encourages rape by teaching males and females that it is natural and normal for sexual relations to involve aggressive behavior on the part of males. To end rape, people must be able to envision a relationship between the sexes that involves sharing, warmth, and equality, and to bring about a social system in which those values are fostered.

CRITICAL-THINKING QUESTIONS

1. According to Herman, what is the link between sexuality and violence in U.S. culture? Why is it sometimes difficult to differentiate rape from normal heterosexual relations in our culture?
2. Why does date rape occur? What about marital rape?
3. How do rapists rationalize their behavior? How does our society respond to rape?

NOTES

1. Susan Griffin, "Rape: The All-American Crime," *Ramparts,* 10 (Sept., 1971), 26.
2. Ibid., 35.
3. Ibid., 27.
4. Carol V. Horos, *Rape* (New Canaan, Conn.: Tobey, 1974), p. 4.
5. Ibid., p. 5.
6. Rosemarie Tong, *Women, Sex and the Law* (Totowa, N.J.: Rowman & Allanheld, 1984), pp. 90–123.
7. Barbara E. Smith and Jane Roberts Chapman, "Rape Law Reform Legislation: Practitioner's Perceptions of the Effectiveness of Specific Provisions," *Response,* 10 (1987), 8.
8. Tong, op. cit., pp. 90–123.
9. *Forcible Rape: An Analysis of Legal Issues,* 2. Table I reports the rape rate for each year from 1960 to 1975. Figures for subsequent years can be found in *Uniform Crime Reports: Crime in the United States* (Federal Bureau of Investigation, U.S. Department of Justice, Washington, D.C.) for each year.
10. *Uniform Crime Reports for the United States* (Washington, D.C.: U.S. Department of Justice, 1987), 14.
11. Duncan Chappell, "Forcible Rape and the Criminal Justice System: Surveying Present Practices and Reporting Future Trends," in *Sexual Assault,* eds. Marcia J. Walker and Stanley L. Brodsky (Lexington, Mass.: Lexington Books, 1976), p. 22. Annual surveys by the federal government report that from 1973 to 1986, between 41 and 61 percent of all rapes and attempted rapes were reported to the police. Bureau of Criminal Justice Statistics Bulletin, *Criminal Victimization—1986,* Table 5, p. 4. However, the National Institute of Law Enforcement and Criminal Justice reported in *Forcible Rape: Final Project Report,* March 1987, that "the *actual* number of rapes in the United States is approximately four times the reported number" (p. 15).
12. Diana E. H. Russell, *Sexual Exploitation* (Beverly Hills, Calif.: Sage, 1984), pp. 35–36.
13. Diana Scully and Joseph Marolla, " 'Riding the Bull at Gilley's': Convicted Rapists Described the Rewards of Rape," *Social Problems,* 32 (Feb., 1985), 252.
14. *International Crime Rates*, NCJ-110776 (Special Report by the Bureau of Justice Statistics), May, 1988, Table 1, p. 2.
15. Menachem Amir, *Patterns in Forcible Rape* (Chicago: University of Chicago Press, 1971), p. 341.
16. Women Organized Against Rape, *W.O.A.R. Data* (Philadelphia: mimeo., 1975), p. 1.
17. Russell, op. cit., p. 79.
18. U.S. Department of Justice, Bureau of Justice Statistics, *Criminal Victimization in the United States, 1985,* NCJ-104273, May, 1987, Table 9, p. 18.
19. Lynda Lytle Holmstrom and Ann Wolbert Burgess, *The Victim of Rape* (New Brunswick, N.J.: Transaction, 1983), p. xxi.
20. Ibid.

21. Karen Barrett, "Date Rape, a Campus Epidemic?" *Ms.,* 11 (Sept., 1982), 130.

22. "Date Rape: Familiar Strangers," *Psychology Today* (July, 1987), p. 10.

23. Susan H. Klemmack and David L. Klemmack, "The Social Definition of Rape," in *Sexual Assault,* eds. Marcia J. Walker and Stanley L. Brodsky (Lexington, Mass.: Lexington Books, 1976), p. 136.

24. David Finkelhor and Kersti Yllo, *License to Rape; Sexual Abuse of Wives* (New York: Holt, Rinehart and Winston, 1985), p. 6.

25. Ibid., pp. 6–7.

26. Ibid., p. 8.

27. Ibid., pp. 22, 113.

28. Ibid., p. 133.

29. *Criminal Victimization—1985,* Table 37, p. 39.

30. Comment, "Police Discretion and the Judgment that a Crime Has Been Committed—Rape in Philadelphia," *University of Pennsylvania Law Review,* 117 (1968), 318.

31. Gary D. LaFree, "The Effect of Sexual Stratification by Race on Official Reactions to Rape," *American Sociological Review,* 45 (1980), 842.

32. *Criminal Victimization—1985,* Table 7, p. 17.

33. Menachem Amir, op. cit., 314. See also Benjamin Karpman, *The Sexual Offender and His Offenses* (New York: Julian Press, 1954), pp. 38–39.

34. See, for example, Camille E. LeGrand, "Rape and Rape Laws: Sexism in Society and Law," *California Law Review,* 61 (1973), 922; and Marray L. Cohen, Ralph Garofalo, Richard Boucher, and Theoharis Seghorn, "The Psychology of Rapists," *Seminars in Psychiatry,* 3 (Aug. 1971), 317.

35. Brownmiller, op. cit., p. 195.

36. Amir, op. cit., p. 334.

37. Leroy Schultz, "Interviewing the Sex Offender's Victim," *Journal of Criminal Law, Criminology and Police Science,* 50 (Jan./Feb., 1960), 451.

38. R. J. McCaldon, "Rape," *Canadian Journal of Corrections,* 9 (Jan., 1967), 47.

39. Scully and Marolla, op. cit., 542.

40. *1976 Uniform Crime Reports,* 16.

41. Comment, "Police Discretion," 304.

42. See, for example, Duncan Chappell et al., "Forcible Rape: A Comparative Study of Offenses Known to the Police in Boston and Los Angeles," in *Studies in the Sociology of Sex,* ed. James M. Henslin (New York: Appleton-Century-Crofts, 1971), p. 180.

43. Ibid., p. 291.

44. Janet Bode, *Fighting Back* (New York: Macmillan, 1987), pp. 130–31; *United States* v. *Benn* 476 F.2d. 1127, 1133 (1973).

45. Ann Wolbert Burgess and Lynda Lytle Holmstrom, *Rape: Victims of Crisis* (Bowie, Md.: Robert Brady, 1974), p. 197.

46. Ibid.

47. Ibid., p. 211.

48. Ibid., p. 200.

49. Pamela Lakes Wood, "The Victim in a Forcible Rape Case: A Feminist View," *American Criminal Law Review,* 7 (1973), 335.

50. Shirley Feldman-Summers and Karen Lindner, "Perceptions of Victims and Defendants in Criminal Assault Cases," *Criminal Justice and Behavior,* 3 (1976), 327.

51. Note, "The Rape Corroboration Requirement: Repeal Not Reform," *Yale Law Journal,* 81 (1972), 1379.

52. Wood, op. cit., 341–42.

53. Andrea Medea and Kathleen Thompson, *Against Rape* (New York: Farrar, Straus and Giroux, 1974), p. 121.

54. Wood, op. cit., 344–45.

55. Martha R. Burt, "Cultural Myths and Supports for Rape," *Journal of Personality and Social Psychology,* 38 (1980), 855.

56. Jacqueline J. Kikuchi, "What Do Adolescents Know and Think about Sexual Abuse?" (paper presented at the National Symposium on Child Victimization, Anaheim, Calif., April 27–30, 1988).

57. See, for example, Lin Farley, *Sexual Shakedown* (New York: Warner, 1978); Kathleen Barry, *Female Sexual Slavery* (New York: Avon, 1979); Andrea Dworkin, *Pornography: Men Possessing Women* (New York: Putnam, 1981).

11

India's Sacred Cow

Culture

CLASSIC

CONTEMPORARY

CROSS-CULTURAL

Marvin Harris

Anthropologist Marvin Harris uses the approach of cultural ecology to investigate how exotic and seemingly inexplicable cultural patterns may turn out to be everyday strategies for human survival in a particular natural environment. In this article, he offers his own favorite example: Why do people in India—many of whom are hungry—refuse to eat beef from the "sacred cows" that are found most everywhere?

Whenever I get into discussions about the influence of practical and mundane factors on lifestyles, someone is sure to say, "But what about all those cows the hungry peasants in India refuse to eat?" The picture of a ragged farmer starving to death alongside a big fat cow conveys a reassuring sense of mystery to Western observers. In countless learned and popular allusions, it confirms our deepest conviction about how people with inscrutable Oriental minds ought to act. It is comforting to know—somewhat like "there will always be an England"—that in India spiritual values are more precious than life itself. And at the same time it makes us feel sad. How can we ever hope to understand people so different from ourselves? Westerners find the idea that there might be a practical explanation for Hindu love of the cow more upsetting than Hindus do. The sacred cow—how else can I say it?—is one of our favorite sacred cows.

Hindus venerate cows because cows are the symbol of everything that is alive. As Mary is to Christians the mother of God, the cow to Hindus is the mother of life. So there is no greater sacrilege for a Hindu than killing a cow. Even the taking of human life lacks the symbolic meaning, the unutterable defilement, that is evoked by cow slaughter.

According to many experts, cow worship is the number one cause of India's hunger and poverty. Some Western-trained agronomists say that the taboo against cow slaughter is keeping one hundred million "useless" animals alive. They claim that cow worship lowers the efficiency of agriculture because the useless animals contribute neither milk nor meat while competing for croplands and foodstuff with useful animals and hungry human beings. . . .

It does seem that there are enormous numbers of surplus, useless, and uneconomic animals, and that this situation is a direct result of irrational

---

Source: From *Cows, Pigs, Wars, and Witches: The Riddles of Culture* by Marvin Harris.

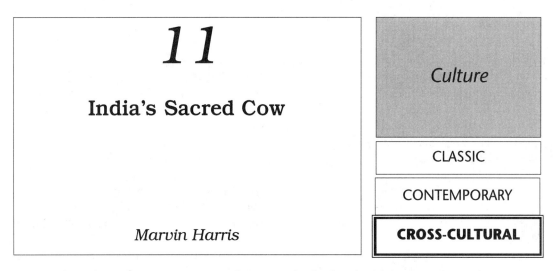

Hindu doctrines. Tourists on their way through Delhi, Calcutta, Madras, Bombay, and other Indian cities are astonished at the liberties enjoyed by stray cattle. The animals wander through the streets, browse off the stalls in the market place, break into private gardens, defecate all over the sidewalks, and snarl traffic by pausing to chew their cuds in the middle of busy intersections. In the countryside, the cattle congregate on the shoulders of every highway and spend much of their time taking leisurely walks down the railroad tracks.

To Western observers familiar with modern industrial techniques of agriculture and stock raising, cow love seems senseless, even suicidal. The efficiency expert yearns to get his hands on all those useless animals and ship them off to a proper fate. And yet one finds certain inconsistencies in the condemnation of cow love. When I began to wonder if there might be a practical explanation for the sacred cow, I came across an intriguing government report. It said that India had too many cows but too few oxen. With so many cows around, how could there be a shortage of oxen? Oxen and male water buffalo are the principal source of traction for plowing India's fields. For each farm of ten acres or less, one pair of oxen or water buffalo is considered adequate. A little arithmetic shows that as far as plowing is concerned, there is indeed a shortage rather than a surplus of animals. India has 60 million farms, but only 80 million traction animals. If each farm had its quota of two oxen or two water buffalo, there ought to be 120 million traction animals—that is, 40 million more than are actually available.

The shortage may not be quite so bad since some farmers rent or borrow oxen from their neighbors. But the sharing of plow animals often proves impractical. Plowing must be coordinated with the monsoon rains, and by the time one farm has been plowed, the optimum moment for plowing another may already have passed. Also, after plowing is over, a farmer still needs his own pair of oxen to pull his oxcart, the mainstay of the bulk transport throughout rural India. Quite possibly private ownership of farms, livestock, plows, and oxcarts lowers the efficiency of Indian agriculture, but this, I soon realized, was not caused by cow love.

The shortage of draft animals is a terrible threat that hangs over most of India's peasant families. When an ox falls sick a poor farmer is in danger of losing his farm. If he has no replacement for it, he will have to borrow money at usurious rates. Millions of rural households have in fact lost all or part of their holdings and have gone into sharecropping or day labor as a result of such debts. Each year hundreds of thousands of destitute farmers end up migrating to the cities, which already teem with unemployed and homeless persons.

The Indian farmer who can't replace his sick or deceased ox is in much the same situation as an American farmer who can neither replace nor repair his broken tractor. But there is an important difference: Tractors are made by factories, but oxen are made by cows. A farmer who owns a cow owns a factory for making oxen. With or without cow love, this is a good reason for him not to be too anxious to sell his cow to the slaughterhouse. One also begins to see why Indian farmers might be willing to tolerate cows that give only 500 pounds of milk per year. If the main economic function of the zebu cow is to breed male traction animals, then there's no point in comparing her with specialized American dairy animals, whose main function is to produce milk. Still, the milk produced by zebu cows plays an important role in meeting the nutritional needs of many poor families. Even small amounts of milk products can improve the health of people who are forced to subsist on the edge of starvation.

Agriculture is part of a vast system of human and natural relationships. To judge isolated portions of this "ecosystem" in terms that are relevant to the conduct of American agribusiness leads to some very strange impressions. Cattle figure in the Indian ecosystem in ways that are easily overlooked or demeaned by observers from industrialized, high-energy societies. In the United States, chemicals have almost completely replaced animal manure as the principal source of farm fertilizer. American farmers stopped using manure when they began to plow with tractors rather than mules or horses. Since tractors excrete poisons rather than fertilizers, a commitment to large-scale machine farming is almost of necessity a commitment to the use of chemical fertilizers. And around the world today there has in fact grown up a vast integrated petrochemical-tractor-truck industrial complex that produces farm machinery, motorized transport, oil and gasoline, and chemical fertilizers and pesticides upon which new high-yield production techniques depend.

For better or worse, most of India's farmers cannot participate in this complex, not because they worship their cows, but because they can't afford to buy tractors. Like other underdeveloped nations, India can't build factories that are competitive with the facilities of the industrialized nations nor pay for large quantities of imported industrial products. To convert from animals and manure to tractors and petrochemicals would require the investment of incredible amounts of capital. Moreover, the inevitable effect of substituting costly machines for cheap animals is to reduce the number of people who can earn their living from agriculture and to force a corresponding increase in the size of the average farm. We know that the development of large-scale agribusiness in the United States has meant the virtual destruction of the small family farm. Less than 5 percent of U.S. families now live on farms, as compared with 60 percent about a hundred years ago. If agribusiness were to develop along similar lines in India, jobs and housing would soon have to be found for a quarter of a billion displaced peasants.

Since the suffering caused by unemployment and homelessness in India's cities is already intolerable, an additional massive build-up of the urban population can only lead to unprecedented upheavals and catastrophes.

With this alternative in view, it becomes easier to understand low-energy, small-scale, animal-based systems. As I have already pointed out, cows and oxen provide low-energy substitutes for tractors and tractor factories. They also should be credited with carrying out the functions of a petrochemical industry. India's cattle annually excrete about 700 million tons of recoverable manure. Approximately half of this total is used as fertilizer, while most of the remainder is burned to provide heat for cooking. The annual quantity of heat liberated by this dung, the Indian housewife's main cooking fuel, is the thermal equivalent of 27 million tons of kerosene, 35 million tons of coal, or 68 million tons of wood. Since India has only small reserves of oil and coal and is already the victim of extensive deforestation, none of these fuels can be considered practical substitutes for cow dung. The thought of dung in the kitchen may not appeal to the average American, but Indian women regard it as a superior cooking fuel because it is finely adjusted to their domestic routines. Most Indian dishes are prepared with clarified butter known as *ghee,* for which cow dung is the preferred source of heat since it burns with a clean, slow, long-lasting flame that doesn't scorch the food. This enables the Indian housewife to start cooking her meals and to leave them unattended for several hours while she takes care of the children, helps out in the fields, or performs other chores. American housewives achieve a similar effect through a complex set of electronic controls that come as expensive options on late-model stoves.

Cow dung has at least one other major function. Mixed with water and made into a paste, it is used as a household flooring material. Smeared over a dirt floor and left to harden into a smooth surface, it keeps the dust down and can be swept clean with a broom.

Because cattle droppings have so many useful properties, every bit of dung is carefully collected. Village small fry are given the task of following the family cow around and of bringing home its daily petrochemical output. In the cities, sweeper castes enjoy a monopoly on the dung deposited by strays and earn their living by selling it to housewives. . . .

During droughts and famines, farmers are severely tempted to kill or sell their livestock. Those who succumb to this temptation seal their doom, even if they survive the drought, for when the rains come, they will be unable to plow their fields. I want to be even more emphatic: Massive slaughter of cattle under the duress of famine constitutes a much greater threat to aggregate welfare than any likely miscalculation by particular farmers concerning the usefulness of their animals during normal times. It seems probable that the sense of unutterable profanity elicited by cow slaughter has its roots in the excruciating contradiction between immediate needs and long-term conditions of survival. Cow love with its sacred symbols and holy doctrines protects the farmer against calculations that are "rational" only in the short term. To Western experts it looks as if "the Indian farmer would rather starve to death than eat his cow.". . . They don't realize that the farmer would rather eat his cow than starve, but that he will starve if he does eat it. . . .

Do I mean to say that cow love has no effect whatsoever on . . . the agricultural system? No. What I am saying is that cow love is an active element in a complex, finely articulated material and cultural order. Cow love mobilizes the latent capacity of human beings to persevere in a low-energy ecosystem in which there is little room for waste or indolence. Cow love contributes to the adaptive resilience of the human population by preserving temporarily dry or barren but still useful animals; by discouraging the growth of an energy-expensive beef industry; by protecting cattle that fatten in the public domain or at landlord's expense; and by preserving the recovery potential of the cattle population during droughts and famines. . . .

Wastefulness is more a characteristic of modern agribusiness than of traditional peasant economies. . . .

Automobiles and airplanes are faster than oxcarts, but they do not use energy more efficiently. In fact, more calories go up in useless heat and smoke during a single day of traffic jams in the United States than is wasted by all the cows of India during an entire year. The comparison is even less favorable when we consider the fact that the stalled vehicles are burning up irreplaceable reserves of petroleum that it took the earth tens of millions of years to accumulate. If you want to see a real sacred cow, go out and look at the family car.

CRITICAL-THINKING QUESTIONS

1. What evidence does Harris offer to support his argument that defining the cow as sacred is a necessary strategy for human survival in India?
2. If survival strategies make sense when we take a close look at them, why do they become so "encased" in elaborate cultural explanations?
3. Does India's recognition of the sacred cow help or hurt that nation's natural environment?
4. Following Harris's logic, can you think of reasons that people in some parts of the world (the Middle East, for instance) do not eat pork?

12

Manifesto of the Communist Party

Karl Marx and Friedrich Engels

Society

CLASSIC

CONTEMPORARY

CROSS-CULTURAL

Karl Marx, collaborating with Friedrich Engels, produced the "Manifesto" in 1848. This document is a well-known statement about the origin of social conflict in the process of material production. The ideas of Marx and Engels have been instrumental in shaping the political lives of more than one-fifth of the world's population, and, of course, they have been instrumental in the development of the social-conflict paradigm in sociology.

BOURGEOIS AND PROLETARIANS[1]

The history of all hitherto existing society[2] is the history of class struggles.

Freeman and slave, patrician and plebeian, lord and serf, guild-master[3] and journeyman, in a word, oppressor and oppressed, stood in constant opposition to one another, carried on an uninterrupted, now hidden, now open fight, a fight that each time ended, either in a revolutionary reconstitution of society at large, or in the common ruin of the contending classes.

In the earlier epochs of history, we find almost everywhere a complicated arrangement of society into various orders, a manifold gradation of social rank. In ancient Rome we have patricians, knights, plebeians, slaves; in the Middle Ages, feudal lords, vassals, guild-masters, journeymen, apprentices, serfs; in almost all of these classes, again, subordinate gradations.

The modern bourgeois society that has sprouted from the ruins of feudal society has not done away with class antagonisms. It has but established new classes, new conditions of oppression, new forms of struggle in place of the old ones.

Our epoch, the epoch of the bourgeoisie, possesses, however, this distinctive feature; it has simplified the class antagonisms. Society as a whole is more and more splitting up into two great hostile camps, into two great classes directly facing each other: Bourgeoisie and Proletariat.

From the serfs of the Middle Ages sprang the chartered

Source: From *Manifesto of the Communist Party,* Part I, by Karl Marx and Friedrich Engels.

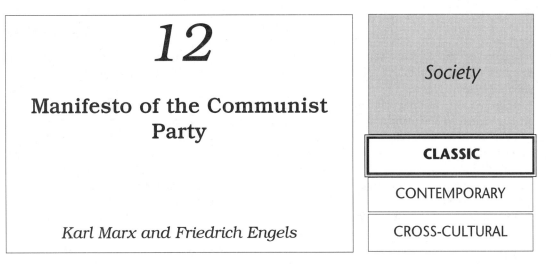

burghers of the earliest towns. From these burgesses the first elements of the bourgeoisie were developed.

The discovery of America, the rounding of the Cape, opened up fresh ground for the rising bourgeoisie. The East Indian and Chinese markets, the [colonization] of America, trade with the colonies, the increase in the means of exchange and in commodities generally, gave to commerce, to navigation, to industry, an impulse never before known, and thereby, to the revolutionary element in the tottering feudal society, a rapid development.

The feudal system of industry, under which industrial production was monopolized by close guilds, now no longer sufficed for the growing wants of the new markets. The manufacturing system took its place. The guild-masters were pushed on one side by the manufacturing middle class; division of labor between the different corporate guilds vanished in the face of division of labor in each single workshop.

Meantime the markets kept ever growing, the demand, ever rising. Even manufacture no longer sufficed. Thereupon, steam and machinery revolutionized industrial production. The place of manufacture was taken by the giant, Modern Industry, the place of the industrial middle class, by industrial millionaires, the leaders of whole industrial armies, the modern bourgeois.

Modern industry has established the world-market, for which the discovery of America paved the way. This market has given an immense development to commerce, to navigation, to communication by land. This development has, in its turn, reacted on the extension of industry; and in proportion as industry, commerce, navigation, railways extended, in the same proportion the bourgeoisie developed, increased its capital, and pushed into the background every class handed down from the Middle Ages.

We see, therefore, how the modern bourgeoisie is itself the product of a long course of development, of a series of revolutions in the modes of production and of exchange.

Each step in the development of the bourgeoisie was accompanied by a corresponding political advance of that class. An oppressed class under the sway of the feudal nobility, an armed and self-governing association in the mediaeval commune,[4] here independent urban republic (as in Italy and Germany), there taxable "third estate" of the monarchy (as in France), afterwards, in the period of manufacture proper, serving either the semi-feudal or the absolute monarchy as a counterpoise against the nobility, and, in fact, cornerstone of the great monarchies in general, the bourgeoisie has at last, since the establishment of modern industry and of the world-market, conquered for itself, in the modern representative State, exclusive political sway. The executive of the modern State is but a committee for managing the common affairs of the whole bourgeoisie.

The bourgeoisie, historically, has played a most revolutionary part.

The bourgeoisie, wherever it has got the upper hand, has put an end to all feudal, patriarchal, idyllic relations. It has pitilessly torn asunder the motley feudal ties that bound man to his "natural superiors," and has left remaining no other nexus between man and man than naked self-interest, than callous "cash payment." It has drowned the most heavenly ecstasies of religious fervour, of chivalrous enthusiasm, of philistine sentimentalism, in the icy water of egotistical calculation. It has resolved personal worth into exchange value, and in place of the numberless indefeasible chartered freedoms, has set up that single, unconscionable freedom—Free Trade. In one word, for exploitation, veiled by religious and political illusions, it has substituted naked, shameless, direct, brutal exploitation.

The bourgeoisie has stripped of its halo every occupation hitherto honoured and looked up to with reverent awe. It has converted the physician, the lawyer, the priest, the poet, the man of science, into its paid [wage-laborers].

The bourgeoisie has torn away from the family its sentimental veil, and has reduced the family relation to a mere money relation.

The bourgeoisie has disclosed how it came to pass that the brutal display of vigour in the Middle Ages, which reactionists so much admire, found its fitting complement in the most slothful indolence. It has been the first to show what man's activity can bring about. It has accomplished wonders far surpassing Egyptian pyramids, Roman aqueducts, and Gothic cathedrals; it has conducted expeditions that put in the shade all former Exoduses of nations and crusades.

The bourgeoisie cannot exist without constantly revolutionizing the instruments of production, and thereby the relations of production, and with them the whole relations of society. Conservation of the old modes of production in unaltered form, was, on the contrary, the first condition of existence for all earlier industrial classes. Constant revolutionizing of production, uninterrupted disturbance of all social conditions, everlasting uncertainty and agitation distinguish the bourgeois epoch from all earlier ones. All fixed, fast-frozen relations, with their train of ancient and venerable prejudices and opinions, are swept away, all new-formed ones become antiquated before they can ossify. All that is solid melts into air, all that is holy is profaned, and man is at last compelled to face with sober senses, his real conditions of life, and his relations with his kind.

The need of a constantly expanding market for its products chases the bourgeoisie over the whole surface of the globe. It must nestle everywhere, settle everywhere, establish [connections] everywhere.

The bourgeoisie has through its exploitation of the world-market given a cosmopolitan character to production and consumption in every country. To the great chagrin of reactionists, it has drawn from under the feet of industry the national ground on which it stood. All old-established national industries have been destroyed or are daily being destroyed. They are dislodged by new industries, whose introduction becomes a life and death question for all civilised nations, by industries that no longer work up indigenous raw material, but raw material drawn from the remotest zones; industries whose products are consumed, not only at home, but in every quarter of the globe. In place of the old wants, satisfied by the productions of the country, we find new wants, requiring for their satisfaction the products of distant lands and climes. In place of the old local and national seclusion and self-sufficiency, we have intercourse in every direction, universal interdependence of nations. And as in material, so also in intellectual production. The intellectual creations of individual nations become common property. National one-sidedness and narrow-mindedness become more and more impossible, and from the numerous national and local literatures there arises a world-literature.

The bourgeoisie, by the rapid improvement of all instruments of production, by the immensely facilitated means of communication, draws all, even the most barbarian, nations into civilization. The cheap prices of its commodities are the heavy artillery with which it batters down all Chinese walls, with which it forces the barbarians' intensely obstinate hatred of foreigners to capitulate. It compels all nations, on pain of extinction, to adopt the bourgeois mode of production; it compels them to introduce what it calls civilization into their midst, i.e., to become bourgeois themselves. In a word, it creates a world after its own image.

The bourgeoisie has subjected the country to the rule of the towns. It has created enormous cities, has greatly increased the urban population as compared with the rural, and has thus rescued a considerable part of the population from the idiocy of rural life. Just as it has made the country dependent on the towns, so it has made barbarian and semi-barbarian countries dependent on the civilised ones, nations of peasants on nations of bourgeois, the East on the West.

The bourgeoisie keeps more and more doing away with the scattered state of the population, of the means of production, and of property. It has agglomerated population, centralized means of production, and has concentrated property in a few hands. The necessary consequence of this was political centralization. Independent, or but loosely connected provinces, with separate interests, laws, governments and systems of taxation, became lumped together in one nation, with one government, one code of laws, one national class-interest, one frontier and one customs-tariff.

The bourgeoisie, during its rule of scarce one hundred years, has created more massive and more colossal productive forces than have all preceding generations together. Subjection of Nature's forces to man, machinery, application of chemistry to industry and agriculture, steam-navigation, railways, electric telegraphs, clearing of whole continents for cultivation, canalization of rivers, whole populations conjured out of the ground—what earlier century had even a presentiment that such productive forces slumbered in the lap of social labor?

We see then: The means of production and of exchange on whose foundation the bourgeoisie built itself up, were generated in feudal society. At a certain stage in the development of these means of production and of exchange, the conditions under which feudal society produced and exchanged, the feudal organization of agriculture and manufacturing industry, in one word, the feudal relations of property became no longer compatible with the already developed productive forces; they became so many fetters. They had to burst asunder; they were burst asunder.

Into their places stepped free competition, accompanied by a social and political constitution adapted to it, and by the economical and political sway of the bourgeois class.

A similar movement is going on before our own eyes. Modern bourgeois society with its relations of production, of exchange and of property, a society that has conjured up such gigantic means of production and of exchange, is like the sorcerer, who is no longer able to control the powers of the nether world whom he has called up by his spells. For many a decade past the history of industry and commerce is but the history of the revolt of modern productive forces against modern conditions of production, against the property relations that are the conditions for the existence of the bourgeoisie and of its rule. It is enough to mention the commercial crises that by their periodical return put on its trial, each time more threateningly, the existence of the entire bourgeois society. In these crises a great part not only of the existing products, but also of the previously created productive forces, are periodically destroyed. In these crises there breaks out an epidemic that, in all earlier epochs, would have seemed an absurdity—the epidemic of overproduction. Society suddenly finds itself put back into a state of momentary barbarism; it appears as if a famine, a universal war of devastation had cut off the supply of every means of subsistence; industry and commerce seem to be destroyed; and why? Because there is too much civilization, too much means of subsistence, too much industry, too much commerce. The productive forces at the disposal of society no longer tend to further the development of the conditions of bourgeois property; on the contrary, they have become too powerful for these conditions, by which they are fettered, and so soon as they overcome these fetters, they bring disorder into the whole of bourgeois society, endanger the existence of bourgeois property. The conditions of bourgeois society are too narrow to comprise the wealth created by them. And how does the bourgeoisie get over these crises? On the one hand by enforced destruction of a mass of productive forces; on the other, by the conquest of new markets, and by the more thorough exploitation of the old ones. That is to say, by paving the way for more extensive and more destructive crises, and by diminishing the means whereby crises are prevented.

The weapons with which the bourgeoisie felled feudalism to the ground are now turned against the bourgeoisie itself.

But not only has the bourgeoisie forged the weapons that bring death to itself; it has also called into existence the men who are to wield those weapons—the modern working class—the proletarians.

In proportion as the bourgeoisie, i.e., capital, is developed, in the same proportion is the proletariat, the modern working class, developed, a class of laborers, who live only so long as they find work, and who find work only so long as their labor increases capital. These laborers, who must sell themselves piecemeal, are a commodity, like every other article of commerce, and are consequently exposed to all the vicissitudes of competition, to all the fluctuations of the market.

Owing to the extensive use of machinery and to division of labor, the work of the proletarians has lost all individual character, and, consequently, all charm for the workman. He becomes an appendage of the machine, and it is only the most simple, most monotonous and most easily acquired knack that is required of him. Hence, the cost of production of a workman is restricted, almost entirely, to the means of subsistence that he requires for his maintenance, and for the propagation of his race. But the price of a commodity, and also of labor, is equal to its cost of production. In proportion, therefore, as the repulsiveness of the work increases, the wage decreases. Nay more, in proportion as the use of machinery and division of labor increases, in the same proportion the burden of toil also increases, whether by prolongation of the working hours, by increase of the work enacted in a given time, or by increased speed of the machinery, etc.

Modern industry has converted the little workshop of the patriarchal master into the great factory of the industrial capitalist. Masses of laborers, crowded into the factory, are organized like soldiers. As privates of the industrial army they are placed under the command of a perfect hierarchy of officers and sergeants. Not only are they the slaves of the bourgeois class, and of the bourgeois State, they are daily and hourly enslaved by the machine, by the over-looker, and, above all, by the individual bourgeois manufacturer himself. The more openly this despotism proclaims gain to be its end and aim, the more petty, the more hateful and the more embittering it is.

The less the skill and exertion or strength implied in manual labor, in other words, the more modern industry becomes developed, the more is the labor of men superseded by that of women. Differences of age and sex have no longer any distinctive social validity for the working class. All are instruments of labor, more or less expensive to use, according to their age and sex.

No sooner is the exploitation of the laborer by the manufacturer, so far, at an end, that he receives his wages in cash, than he is set upon by the other portions of the bourgeoisie, the landlord, the shopkeeper, the pawnbroker, etc.

The lower strata of the middle class—the small tradespeople, shopkeepers, and retired tradesmen generally, the handicraftsmen and peasants—all these sink gradually into the proletariat, partly because their diminutive capital does not suffice for the scale on which Modern Industry is carried on, and is swamped in the competition with the large capitalists, partly because their specialised skill is rendered worthless by new methods of production. Thus the proletariat is recruited from all classes of the population.

The proletariat goes through various stages of development. With its birth begins its struggle with the bourgeoisie. At first the contest is carried on by individual laborers, then by the workpeople of a factory, then by the operatives of one trade, in one locality, against the individual bourgeois who directly exploits them. They direct their attacks not against the bourgeois conditions of production, but against the instruments of production themselves; they destroy imported wares that compete with their labor, they smash to pieces machinery, they set factories ablaze, they seek to restore by force the vanished status of the workman of the Middle Ages.

At this stage the laborers still form an incoherent mass scattered over the whole country, and broken up by their mutual competition. If anywhere they unite to form more compact bodies, this is not yet the consequence of their own active union, but of the union of the bourgeoisie, which class, in order to attain its own political ends, is compelled to set the whole proletariat in motion, and is moreover yet, for a time, able to do so. At this stage, therefore, the proletarians do not fight their enemies, but the enemies of their enemies, the remnants of absolute monarchy, the landowners, the non-industrial bourgeois, the petty bourgeoisie. Thus the whole historical movement is concentrated in the hands of the bourgeoisie; every victory so obtained is a victory for the bourgeoisie.

But with the development of industry the proletariat not only increases in number, it becomes concentrated in greater masses, its strength grows, and it feels that strength more. The various interests and conditions of life within the ranks of the proletariat are more and more equalized, in proportion as machinery obliterates all distinctions of labor, and nearly everywhere reduces wages to the same low level. The growing competition among the bourgeois, and the resulting commercial crises, make the wages of the workers ever more fluctuating. The unceasing improvement of machinery, ever more rapidly developing, makes their livelihood more and more precarious; the collisions between individual workmen and individual bourgeois take more and more the character of collisions between two classes. Thereupon the workers begin to form combinations (Trades' Unions) against the bourgeois; they club together in order to keep up the rate of wages; they found permanent associations in order to make provision beforehand for these occasional revolts. Here and there the contest breaks out into riots.

Now and then the workers are victorious, but only for a time. The real fruit of their battles lies, not in the immediate result, but in the ever expanding union of the workers. This union is helped on by the improved means of communication that are created by modern industry, and that place the workers of different localities in contact with one another. It was just this contact that was needed to centralize the numerous local struggles, all of the same character, into one national struggle between classes. But every class struggle is a political struggle. And that union, to attain which the burghers of the Middle Ages, with their miserable highways, required centuries, the modern proletarians, thanks to railways, achieve in a few years.

This organization of the proletarians into a class, and consequently into a political party, is continually being upset again by the competition between the workers themselves. But it ever rises up again, stronger, firmer, mightier. It compels legislative recognition of particular interests of the workers, by taking advantage of the divisions among the bourgeoisie itself. Thus the ten-hours'-bill in England was carried.

Altogether collisions between the classes of the old society further, in many ways, the course of development of the proletariat. The bourgeoisie finds itself involved in a constant battle. At first with the aristocracy; later on, with those portions of the bourgeoisie itself, whose interests have become antagonistic to the progress of industry; at all times, with the bourgeoisie of foreign countries. In all these battles it sees itself compelled to appeal to the proletariat, to ask for its help, and thus, to drag it into the political arena. The bourgeoisie itself, therefore, supplies the proletariat with its own elements of political and general education, in other words, it furnishes the proletariat with weapons for fighting the bourgeoisie.

Further, as we have already seen, entire sections of the ruling classes are, by the advance of industry, precipitated into the proletariat, or are at least threatened in their conditions of existence. These also supply the proletariat with fresh elements of enlightenment and progress.

Finally, in times when the class-struggle nears the decisive hour, the process of dissolution going on within the ruling class, in fact within the whole range of old society, assumes such a violent, glaring character, that a small section of the ruling class cuts itself adrift, and joins the revolutionary class, the class that holds the future in its hands. Just as, therefore, at an earlier period, a section of the nobility went over to the bourgeoisie, so now a portion of the bourgeoisie goes over to the proletariat, and in particular, a portion of the bourgeois ideologists, who have raised themselves to the level of comprehending theoretically the historical movements as a whole.

Of all the classes that stand face to face with the bourgeoisie today, the proletariat alone is a really revolutionary class. The other classes decay and finally disappear in the face of modern industry; the proletariat is its special and essential product.

The lower-middle class, the small manufacturer, the shopkeeper, the artisan, the peasant, all these fight against the bourgeoisie, to save from extinction their existence as fractions of the middle class. They are therefore not revolutionary, but conservative. Nay more, they are reactionary, for they try to roll back the wheel of history. If by chance they are revolutionary, they are so, only in view of their impending transfer into the proletariat, they thus defend not their present, but their future interests, they desert their own standpoint to place themselves at that of the proletariat.

The "dangerous class," the social scum, that passively rotting mass thrown off by the lowest layers of old society, may, here and there, be swept into the movement by a proletarian revolution; its conditions of life, however, prepare it far more for the part of a bribed tool of reactionary intrigue.

In the conditions of the proletariat, those of old society at large are already virtually swamped. The proletarian is without property; his relation to his wife and children has no longer anything in common with the bourgeois family-relations; modern industrial labor, modern subjection to capital, the same in England as in France, in America as in Germany, has stripped him of every trace of national character. Law, morality, religion, are to him so many bourgeois prejudices, behind which lurk in ambush just as many bourgeois interests.

All the preceding classes that got the upper hand sought to fortify their already acquired status by subjecting at large to their conditions of appropriation. The proletarians cannot become masters of the productive forces of society, except by abolishing their own previous mode of appropriation, and thereby also every other previous mode of appropriation. They have nothing of their own to secure and to fortify; their mission is to destroy all previous securities for, and insurances of, individual property.

All previous historical movements were movements of minorities, or in the interest of minorities. The proletarian movement is the self-conscious, independent movement of the immense majority, in the interest of the immense majority. The proletariat, the lowest stratum of our present society, cannot stir, cannot raise itself up, without the whole superincumbent strata of official society being sprung into the air.

Though not in substance, yet in form, the struggle of the proletariat with the bourgeoisie is at first a national struggle. The proletariat of each country must, of course, first of all settle matters with its own bourgeoisie.

In depicting the most general phases of the development of the proletariat, we traced the more or less veiled civil war, raging within existing society, up to the point where that war breaks out into open revolution, and where the violent overthrow of the bourgeoisie, lays the foundation for the sway of the proletariat.

Hitherto, every form of society has been based, as we have already seen, on the antagonism of oppressing and oppressed classes. But in order to oppress a class, certain conditions must be assured to it under which it can, at least, continue its slavish existence. The serf, in the period of serfdom, raised himself to membership in the commune, just as the petty bourgeois, under the yoke of feudal absolutism, managed to develop into a bourgeois. The modern laborer, on the contrary, instead of rising with the progress of industry, sinks deeper and deeper below the conditions of existence of his own class. He becomes a pauper, and pauperism develops more rapidly than population and wealth. And here it becomes evident, that the bourgeoisie is unfit any longer to be the ruling class in society, and to impose its conditions of existence upon society as an overriding law. It is unfit to rule, because it is incompetent to assure an existence to its slave within his slavery, because it cannot help letting him sink into such a state, that it has to feed him, instead of being fed by him. Society can no longer live under this bourgeoisie, in other words, its existence is no longer compatible with society.

The essential condition for the existence, and for the sway of the bourgeois class, is the formation and augmentation of capital; the condition for capital is wage-labor. Wage-labor rests exclusively on competition between the laborers. The advance of industry, whose involuntary promoter is the bourgeoisie, replaces the isolation of the laborers, due to competition, by their involuntary combination, due to association. The development of modern industry, therefore, cuts from under its feet the very foundation on which the bourgeoisie produces and appropriates products. What the bourgeoisie therefore produces, above all, are its own grave-diggers. Its fall and the victory of the proletariat are equally inevitable.

CRITICAL-THINKING QUESTIONS

1. What are the distinguishing factors of "class conflict"? How does this differ from other kinds of conflict, as between individuals or nations?
2. Why do Marx and Engels argue that understanding society in the present requires investigating the society of the past?
3. On what grounds did Marx and Engels *praise* industrial capitalism? On what grounds did they *condemn* the system?

NOTES

1. By *bourgeoisie* is meant the class of modern capitalists, owners of the means of social production and employers of wage-labor. By *proletariat,* the class of modern wage-laborers who, having no means of production of their own, are reduced to selling their labor-power in order to live.

2. That is, all written history. In 1847, the prehistory of society, the social organization existing previous to recorded history, was all but unknown. Since then, Haxthausen discovered common ownership of land in Russia. Maurer proved it to be the social foundation from which all Teutonic races started in history, and by and by village communities were found to be, or to have been, the primitive form of society everywhere from India to Ireland. The inner organization of this primitive Communistic society was laid bare, in its typical form, by Morgan's crowning discovery of the true nature of the gens and its relation to the tribe. With the dissolution of these primaeval communities society begins to be differentiated into separate and finally antagonistic classes. I have attempted to retrace this process of dissolution in "Der Ursprung der Familie, des Privateigenthums und des Staats," 2d ed. Stuttgart 1886.

3. Guild-master, that is, a full member of a guild, a master within, not a head of, a guild.

4. "Commune" was the name taken, in France, by the nascent towns even before they had conquered from their feudal lords and masters, local self-government and political rights as "the Third Estate." Generally speaking, for the economical development of the bourgeoisie, England is here taken as the typical country, for its political development, France.

13

Society

CLASSIC

CONTEMPORARY

CROSS-CULTURAL

Gemeinschaft and Gesellschaft

Ferdinand Tönnies

The German sociologist Ferdinand Tönnies (1855–1936) described patterns of change by contrasting two types of social living: Gemeinschaft and Gesellschaft. In simple terms, Gemeinschaft is rooted in the rural, kinship-based life of the past; Gesellschaft, by contrast, finds its clearest expression in the commercial world of today's large, anonymous cities.

[A] relationship . . . and also the resulting association is conceived of either as real and organic life—this is the essential characteristic of the Gemeinschaft (community); or as imaginary and mechanical structure—this is the concept of Gesellschaft (society). . . .

All intimate, private, and exclusive living together, so we discover, is understood as life in Gemeinschaft (community). Gesellschaft (society) is public life—it is the world itself. In Gemeinschaft with one's family, one lives from birth on, bound to it in weal and woe. One goes into Gesellschaft as one goes into a strange country. A young man is warned against bad Gesellschaft, but the expression bad Gemeinschaft violates the meaning of the word. Lawyers may speak of domestic (*häusliche*) Gesellschaft, thinking only of the legalistic concept of social association; but the domestic Gemeinschaft, or home life with its immeasurable influence upon the human soul, has been felt by everyone who ever shared it. Likewise, a bride or groom knows that he or she goes into marriage as a complete Gemeinschaft of life (*communio totius vitae*). A Gesellschaft of life would be a contradiction in and of itself. One keeps or enjoys another's Gesellschaft, but not his Gemeinschaft in this sense. One becomes a part of a religious Gemeinschaft; religious Gesellschaften (associations or societies), like any other groups formed for given purposes, exist only in so far as they, viewed from without, take their places among the institutions of a political body or as they represent conceptual elements of a theory; they do not touch upon the religious Gemeinschaft as such. There exists a Gemeinschaft of language, of folkways or mores, or of beliefs; but, by way of contrast, Gesellschaft exists in the realm of business, travel, or sciences. So of special importance are the commercial Gesellschaften; whereas, even though a certain familiarity and Gemeinschaft may exist among business partners, one could indeed hardly

Source: From *Community and Society* by Ferdinand Tönnies. Copyright © 1957 Michigan State University Press. Reprinted with permission.

speak of commercial Gemeinschaft. To make the word combination "joint-stock Gemeinschaft" would be abominable. On the other hand, there exists a Gemeinschaft of ownership in fields, forest, and pasture. The Gemeinschaft of property between man and wife cannot be called Gesellschaft of property. Thus many differences become apparent.

Gemeinschaft is old; Gesellschaft is new as a name as well as a phenomenon. . . . [S]ays Bluntschli (*Staatswörterbuch IV*), "Wherever urban culture blossoms and bears fruits, Gesellschaft appears as its indispensable organ. The rural people know little of it." On the other hand, all praise of rural life has pointed out that the Gemeinschaft among people is stronger there and more alive; it is the lasting and genuine form of living together. In contrast to Gemeinschaft, Gesellschaft is transitory and superficial. Accordingly, Gemeinschaft should be understood as a living organism, Gesellschaft as a mechanical aggregate and artifact. . . .

The Gemeinschaft by blood, denoting unity of being, is developed and differentiated into Gemeinschaft of locality, which is based on a common habitat. A further differentiation leads to the Gemeinschaft of mind, which implies only cooperation and coordinated action for a common goal. Gemeinschaft of locality may be conceived as a community of physical life, just as Gemeinschaft of mind expresses the community of mental life. In conjunction with the others, this last type of Gemeinschaft represents the truly human and supreme form of community. Kinship Gemeinschaft signifies a common relation to, and share in, human beings themselves, while in Gemeinschaft of locality such a common relation is established through collective ownership of land; and, in Gemeinschaft of mind, the common bond is represented by sacred places and worshiped deities. All three types of Gemeinschaft are closely interrelated in space as well as in time. They are, therefore, also related in all such single phenomena and in their development, as well as in general human culture and its history. Wherever human beings are related through their wills in an organic manner and affirm each other, we find one or another of the three types of Gemeinschaft. Either the earlier type involves the later one, or the later type has developed to relative independence from some earlier one. It is, therefore, possible to deal with (1) kinship, (2) neighborhood, and (3) friendship as definite and meaningful derivations of these original categories. . . .

The theory of the Gesellschaft deals with the artificial construction of an aggregate of human beings which superficially resembles the Gemeinschaft in so far as the individuals live and dwell together peacefully. However, in the Gemeinschaft they remain essentially united in spite of all separating factors, whereas in the Gesellschaft they are essentially separated in spite of all uniting factors. In the Gesellschaft, as contrasted with the Gemeinschaft, we find no actions that can be derived from a priori and necessarily existing unity; no actions, therefore, which manifest the will and the spirit of the unity even if performed by the individual; no actions which, in so far as they are performed by the individual, take place on behalf of those united with him. In the Gesellschaft such actions do not exist. On the contrary, here everybody is by himself and isolated, and there exists a condition of tension against all others. Their spheres of activity and power are sharply separated, so that everybody refuses to everyone else contact with and admittance to his sphere; i.e., intrusions are regarded as hostile acts. Such a negative attitude toward one another becomes the normal and always underlying relation of these power-endowed individuals, and it characterizes the Gesellschaft in the condition of rest; nobody wants to grant and produce anything for another individual, nor will he be inclined to give ungrudgingly to another individual, if it be not in exchange for a gift or labor equivalent that he considers at least equal to what he has given. . . .

. . . In Gesellschaft every person strives for that which is to his own advantage and he affirms the actions of others only in so far as and as long as they can further his interest. Before and outside of convention and also before and outside of each special contract, the relation of all to all may therefore be conceived as potential hostility or latent war. Against this condition, all agreements of the will stand out as so many treaties and peace pacts. This conception is the only one which does justice to all facts of business and trade where all rights and duties can be reduced to mere value and definitions of ability to deliver. Every theory of pure private law or law of nature understood as pertaining to the Gesellschaft has to be considered as being based upon this conception.

CRITICAL-THINKING QUESTIONS

1. Describe the essential features of Gemeinschaft and Gesellschaft in order to clearly distinguish the two organizational types.

2. Why does Tönnies link Gemeinschaft to kinship, neighborhood, and friendship? How is Gesellschaft linked to commerce?

3. Based on reading this selection, do you think Tönnies found one type of social organization preferable to the other? If so, which one? Why?

Society

CLASSIC

CONTEMPORARY

CROSS-CULTURAL

14

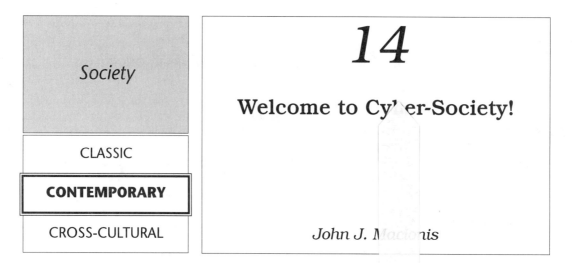

Welcome to Cyber-Society!

John J. Macionis

Just as the Industrial Revolution began to change society two centuries ago, so the Information Revolution is transforming our lives today. Sociology emerged to explore the character of modern, industrial society. To remain vital, the discipline now looks to the coming postmodern, postindustrial age we call "cyber-society." In what ways might new information technology reshape the economy, culture, and social stratification? This article offers some observations and informed speculation about the society of the twenty-first century.

More than two centuries ago, the onset of the Industrial Revolution ushered in the modern era. Then, clever scientists and enterprising business owners devised the means, first, to harness water power and, soon after, to generate steam from coal furnaces. The result—an unprecedented flow of power—greatly surpassed the flexing of animals' muscles and brought to life large machinery.

The age of factories was at hand. The Industrial Revolution changed virtually every dimension of social life, sparking unprecedented urban growth, reshaping the nature of work, and gradually raising living standards.

The second half of the twentieth century has witnessed the unfolding of another technological transformation—the Information Revolution—that marks our entry into the postindustrial age. At its core, the postindustrial (or postmodern) society brings a new focus to production. Industrial technology was geared to producing *things;* now, by contrast, we employ new information technology to manipulate *symbols* and to generate *ideas.*

The key to the Information Revolution is the computer. U.S. engineers first went "on line" fifty years ago when they switched on room-sized machines stuffed with vacuum tubes and wires. Despite its giant size, this early computer actually did no more than today's ten-dollar hand-held calculator. Since then, increasingly sophisticated computers have steadily moved to the center of our way of life to perform a host of complex tasks quickly and easily. In 2000, all new vehicles, the vast majority of businesses, and about one-half of U.S. households were outfitted with one or more computers. As computers proliferate—and as they become more powerful, smaller, and more portable—they are rewriting the rules of social life in the twenty-first century just as monstrous machines defined the era now coming to an end.

This article was written for this volume. Thanks to Glenna Huls and Howard Sacks for contributing ideas.

THE INTERNET: RIDING THE INFORMATION HIGHWAY

Once computers were a reality, the logical next task was linking them so people could communicate. This is the essential purpose of the Internet, often dubbed the "information superhighway."[1]

The origins of this worldwide network seem right out of the 1960s cold war film *Dr. Strangelove.* Back then, government officials and scientists were trying to imagine how to run the country after an atomic attack, which, they assumed, would quickly knock out telephones and eliminate television. Their brilliant solution was devising a communication system that no enemy could target, because it would have no central headquarters, no one in charge, and no main power switch. The Internet began as an unregulated, electronic web intended to link people throughout the country in one vast network.

By 1985, the federal government was installing high-speed data lines around the country and the Internet was about to be born. As the network continues to expand, thousands of government offices, as well as colleges and universities, and millions of private homes are now online, and all share in the cost of its operation. Especially during the 1990s, other countries joined in this technological revolution. In 2000, 175 (of 191) countries around the world (and perhaps 150 million people) were connected by the largest network in history. And, as time goes on, the number of Internet computer sites will continue to increase rapidly.

What is available on the Internet? Far more than anyone could ever list in a single directory. Popular activities include electronic mail (start a cyber-romance with a pen pal, or even send a message to the president of the United States: **www.president@whitehouse.gov**), checking out ideas for sociology papers and projects (**www.prenhall.com/macionis** or **www.TheSociologyPage.com**), participating in discussion groups or receiving newsletters on a wide range of topics, or searching libraries across the campus or around the world for books or other information. The excitement of the Internet lies in the fact that, given no formal rules for its use, its potential defies the imagination.

How will the Information Revolution and the proliferation of the Internet transform the shape of society? Given that the social sciences have a limited ability to predict the future, the answer is necessarily a matter of informed speculation. But, based on current trends and a little sociological imagination, we can offer a general sketch of the cyber-society of the twenty-first century.

THE ECONOMY: FROM MAKING THINGS TO PROCESSING SYMBOLS

The Industrial Revolution altered the focus of production from securing raw materials to manufacturing (in economic terms, from the primary to secondary sectors of the economy). Today, the Information Revolution is shifting production from goods to services, so that more and more work involves manipulating symbols.[2]

In the twenty-first century, not only the character of work but also its location has changed. Industrial technology concentrated workers, drawing people from countless small towns and villages toward the factories, in the process forging great cities. Today, a countertrend has begun, with information technology allowing employees to decentralize, living and working where they choose. In other words, while most of yesterday's workers labored in a factory or an office, more and more of today's employees work in the home, the car, or wherever they can "log on" (which, with cellular technology, is virtually anywhere).

CULTURE: AN EMERGING INDUSTRY

As our society has moved into the business of generating and manipulating symbols, culture itself has become big business. As it expands, this culture industry will ensure that our way of life will change more rapidly. The Information

Revolution promises that symbols—words, sounds, and images—will be generated at an unprecedented rate and spread rapidly across the nation and around the world.

Perhaps the key trend is that more and more of the cultural symbols that frame our lives are *new and intentionally created.* Historically, sociologists have characterized culture as a way of life transmitted over time from generation to generation. This traditional view envisions culture as rooted deep in our collective memory, and passed over the centuries from one generation to the next. From this historical view, culture comes to us as a largely intact body of knowledge, skills, and attitudes, something authentically our own because it belonged to our ancestors.

But in our cyber-society, more and more cultural symbols are new, intentionally generated by composers, entertainers, writers, teachers, filmmakers, and others who work within the burgeoning information economy. It is unlikely that we will soon leave behind heroes rooted in our national history—George Washington, Abigail Adams, Betsy Ross, Davy Crockett, Daniel Boone, Abraham Lincoln, Harriet Tubman, and Martin Luther King, Jr. Yet today's children will probably grow up more and more preoccupied with *virtual culture,* elements that spring from the mind of a contemporary culture-maker. The defining mark of virtual culture is that it is a new creation that we encounter on a screen: on television, in the movies, or through computer cyber-space. Today's "heroes" include Teletubbies, Pokémon, Star Wars characters, and a continuous flow of Disney creations. Certainly, at least some of these cultural icons embody values that have shaped our past. But few of them have any historical existence and almost all of them have come into being for the singular purpose of commercial gain.

And "virtual reality" may also redefine standards of truth. In the twenty-first century, assessing the veracity of cultural elements is becoming more difficult. Digital imagery, for example, now allows photographers to combine and manipulate pictures to show anything, making fiction "real." Moreover, computer animation enables movie producers to do the same, placing long-dead actors in contemporary scenes or showing humans interacting with lifelike dinosaurs. In short, we will struggle to assess how "real" virtual reality actually is.

More broadly, members of a cyber-society will have to recognize that they share responsibility for their collective way of life. That is, we will need to ask, "Who is creating this kind of culture? And for what purposes?"

SOCIALIZATION: ON THE SCREEN

Changes in culture will almost certainly bring about changes in socialization. Television has transformed how we learn our ways of life, evident from the fact that young people spend more time watching TV than they do talking to their parents (APA, 1993). Now, screens are not just for television and videos; harnessed to computers, they connect, entertain, and educate us. Indeed, the greater power of the computer to engage us lies in the fact that, unlike television, which demands passive viewing, the computer is interactive. This interactive capacity will place computers at the center of both entertainment and education in cyber-society.

Moreover, new information technology will continue to shift the center of socialization from the family to other sources of virtual culture. In other words, continuing the trend that began with the spread of television in the 1950s, children in cyber-society may well be socialized less and less by their parents. Cyber-socialization can certainly entertain and instruct, but we are left to wonder how well it will impart moral lessons and meet the emotional needs of our children.

SOCIAL INTERACTION: YOU COULD BE ANYWHERE

New information technology is eroding the importance of place in our lives. Edison's telephone greatly extended human "reach"; however, with sound tied to wires, Edison knew exactly where his call ended up. Today's cellular technology allows a person to key in a number and reach another person who could be, quite literally, anywhere on earth—at home or in a car or on a hiking trail or well above the earth, flying eight miles high. Similarly, with electronic messages traveling at almost the speed of light, computers take only seconds to connect us to Internet sites that are scattered everywhere around the world.

That new information technology will bring us into contact with more people than ever before seems indisputable. Yet, cyber-society may also become more impersonal as a diminishing share of our human "contacts" involve face-to-face interaction.

SOCIAL STRATIFICATION: "CYBER-SOPHISTICATES" VERSUS THE "CYBER-CLUELESS"?

The Industrial Revolution greatly transformed social stratification from a feudal caste system to a more fluid and ability-based class system. The Information Revolution promises to amplify this trend. New technology typically creates a class of superrich people, those who create and control the emerging form of production. Just as industrialists Andrew Carnegie and John D. Rockefeller amassed great fortunes a century ago, so Microsoft's Bill Gates (this country's richest individual in 2000 with a net worth approaching $100 billion) heads an elite that has profited handsomely by developing new information technology.

But, at the lower end of the class hierarchy, the shift to an information-based economy is defining a new underclass. People who lacked industrial skills a century ago were left out of the opportunities created by the machine age; similarly today's workers who lack symbolic skills are beginning to find themselves at the margins of the job market.

RACE AND ETHNICITY: DOES VIRTUAL REALITY COME IN COLORS?

And what of racial and ethnic dimensions of social inequality? By spreading information widely and rapidly, we might expect the cultural assimilation of new immigrants to proceed more quickly than ever.

Then, too, electronic forms of communication tend to be racially and ethnically neutral—that is, one cannot readily tell the race or ethnicity of an individual by reading e-mail, as one usually can in face-to-face interaction. Might this factor, too, encourage social contact (albeit, impersonal) among people of all racial and ethnic categories?

But an important counterpoint to such arguments is the issue of access. Will the fact that e-mail is colorblind amount to much if minorities, in general, have less financial means to ensure access to this new technology? Today, for example, a personal computer operates in only 25 percent of African American households—half the share of white households so equipped.

The access question also holds at a global level. In control of new information technology, rich societies such as the United States will project their culture more furiously than ever. Will representatives of each of the world's three or four thousand cultural systems be able to use the Internet to project *their* way of life? Or will they be eventual recipients of a cultural stream originating elsewhere?

GENDER: AN ANDROGYNOUS AGE?

As industrial societies mature, the social barriers that divide the lives of men and women begin to break down. Several factors animate this trend: The use of machinery lessens the need to perform heavy physical labor (a key reason that, traditionally, the workplace was defined as a man's world), while birth control technology greatly reduces fertility (one reason the home was defined as a woman's world). Add to these facts the broadening of women's political rights as well as expanding educational opportunities for women and we can appreciate the remarkable change in gender roles witnessed over the course of the twentieth century.

The Information Revolution promises to continue this trend toward gender equality. For one thing, production in cyber-society is centered not on making or moving *things* but on manipulating *ideas*—an activity that favors neither men nor women. Second, when people communicate through e-mail and other electronic channels, a person's sex—obvious in face-to-face interaction—is obscured. Third, cyber-work is not rigidly linked to place—people use computer technology as readily in the home as they do in the office. Fourth, cyber-work is compatible with flexible schedules—production is a matter of completing tasks, not punching timeclocks. Such a trend may lessen the traditional tension people face between pursuing their careers and caring for younger (or older) family members.

An additional fact is worth noting: The management of "culture" historically has been placed within the domain of women. That is, women took the lead in transmitting culture to children just as they were community leaders in the arts. The fact that "culture" was defined as feminine probably reflected a bias toward such matters in an industrial age preoccupied with masculine "things." But as culture itself becomes the central product of cyber-society, will women come to occupy more and more positions of economic power?

POLITICS: ELECTRONS KNOW NO NATIONAL BOUNDARIES

The onset of the industrial age was marked by the formation of the nation-state. Perhaps, then, we should not be surprised that, in the cyber-society of the twenty-first century, the concept of the nation-state is being drained of some of its meaning. Businesses are becoming global, with multinational organizations taking charge of both producing and distributing goods and services.

Will a world able to communicate ever more broadly and rapidly remain divided into almost 200 distinct political systems? No one should expect radical political change in the short term. But it seems all but inevitable that the pace of political activity—both within nations and among them—will increase with significant, long-term transformation in the world political structure.

Even today, new information technology is calling into question the concept of citizenship. For example, imagine a group of employees in a Mexico City office building who log onto computers and, traveling the "information superhighway," connect to a U.S. bank in Manhattan where they process transactions throughout the day. Are these "electronic immigrants" part of the labor force of Mexico or the United States?

HIGHER EDUCATION: THE VIRTUAL CAMPUS

The twentieth century witnessed a remarkable expansion of formal education in the United States. In 1900, many states had yet to require any schooling of their young people. By contrast, almost half of today's youngsters will complete some postsecondary school degree.

Initially, industrialization demanded that schools teach the "three Rs" (reading, 'riting, and 'rithmetic) to ensure a basically literate labor force capable of operating machinery. Today, however, the postindustrial, information economy demands much more in the way of learning.

Cyber-society promises not simply to demand more education, but to fundamentally transform learning itself, especially at the college level. Conventionally, attending college has demanded that one live on or near a campus, study in libraries, read assigned books, and attend classes. Yet, computer-based technology renders all of these things expendable. In 1996, for example, the governors of ten western states cooperated to launch the first "virtual university." Enrolling in the new Western Governors' University is accomplished online; students (who may never meet each other or their instructors face to face) read assignments from databases, send in term papers using e-mail, and use their keyboards to participate in discussion sessions. Will graduates display their diplomas on computer screens?

The appeal of online learning largely hinges on its promise of greater access—to students who are physically disabled and cannot navigate a traditional campus, who have responsibilities that keep them in the home, or who cannot afford the rising costs of conventional higher education. But whether online learning can match what is gained from various forms of personal interaction with faculty and other students remains, for the present, in doubt.

SUMMING UP: TECHNOLOGY SHAPES SOCIETY

Here, we have offered only a brief sketch of some of the transformations that new information technology may bring to U.S. society in the twenty-first century. Prediction of this kind is, of course, risky business. But history clearly demonstrates that technological revolutions begin with specific inventions (whether the steam engine or the computer) that unleash changes that ripple throughout a social system in many profound and often unexpected ways.

We stand at the beginning of a new era, defined by a new kind of productive economy, able only to guess at its long-term significance. Yet, there can be little doubt that revolutionary change is at hand. One key responsibility of we who live in the century, then, is to decide how (and, even, if) new information technology should be employed.

CRITICAL-THINKING QUESTIONS

1. As we enter cyber-society, what, if any, changes would you expect to the physical shape and social character of cities? Why?
2. Overall, do you think cyber-society will improve or degrade the quality of life for most people? In what ways? Why?
3. Do you think people living a century ago were able to imagine how the automobile would change society? How well can we imagine how computers will change society in the twenty-first century?

NOTES

1. The exponentially increasing numbers of people logging onto the Internet has overwhelmed existing telephone lines and resulted in long delays in transmitting information. For the short term, at least, the "information superhighway" may remain more of a "dirt road."

2. In 1900, 80 percent of the U.S. labor force were farmers or factory workers; in 2000, about 80 percent are service workers who engage in symbolic activity with other people.

REFERENCE

APA. 1993. *Violence and youth: Psychology's response.* Washington, D.C.: American Psychological Association.

Society

CLASSIC

CONTEMPORARY

CROSS-CULTURAL

15

The Amish: A Small Society

John A. Hostetler

Some 100,000 Old Order Amish live in the rolling farmland of Pennsylvania, Ohio, Indiana, and southern Ontario. These descendants of sixteenth-century Germans, who fled persecution for their religious beliefs, constitute a distinctive "small society" that keeps the larger world at arm's length. This description of the Amish suggests the extent of cultural diversity within North America and raises questions about why some people would reject the "advantages" that many others take for granted.

Small communities, with their distinctive character—where life is stable and intensely human—are disappearing. Some have vanished from the face of the earth, others are dying slowly, but all have undergone changes as they have come into contact with an expanding machine civilization. The merging of diverse peoples into a common mass has produced tension among members of the minorities and the majority alike.

The Old Order Amish, who arrived on American shores in colonial times, have survived in the modern world in distinctive, viable, small communities. They have resisted the homogenization process more successfully than others. In planting and harvest time one can see their bearded men working the fields with horses and their women hanging out the laundry in neat rows to dry. Many American people have seen Amish families, with the men wearing broad-brimmed black hats and the women in bonnets and long dresses, in railway depots or bus terminals. Although the Amish have lived with industrialized America for over two and a half centuries, they have moderated its influence on their personal lives, their families, communities, and their values.

The Amish are often perceived by other Americans to be relics of the past who live an austere, inflexible life dedicated to inconvenient and archaic customs. They are seen as renouncing both modern conveniences and the American dream of success and progress. But most people have no quarrel with the Amish for doing things the old-fashioned way. Their conscientious objection was tolerated in wartime, for after all, they are meticulous farmers who practice the virtues of work and thrift.

. . . The Amish are a church, a community, a spiritual union, a conservative branch of Christianity, a religion, a community whose members practice simple and austere living, a familistic entrepreneuring system, and an adaptive human community. . . .

Source: From *Amish Society,* 3rd ed., by John A. Hostetler (Baltimore: The Johns Hopkins University Press, 1980), pp. 3–12. Reprinted with permission.

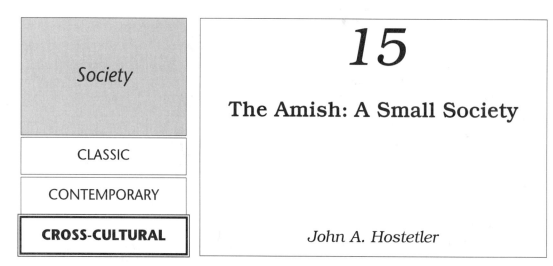

The Amish are in some ways a little commonwealth, for their members claim to be ruled by the law of love and redemption. The bonds that unite them are many. Their beliefs, however, do not permit them solely to occupy and defend a particular territory. They are highly sensitive in caring for their own. They will move to other lands when circumstances force them to do so.

Commonwealth implies a place, a province, which means any part of a national domain that geographically and socially is sufficiently unified to have a true consciousness of its unity. Its inhabitants feel comfortable with their own ideas and customs, and the "place" possesses a sense of distinction from other parts of the country. Members of a commonwealth are not foot-loose. They have a sense of productivity and accountability in a province where "the general welfare" is accepted as a day-to-day reality. Commonwealth has come to have an archaic meaning in today's world, because when groups and institutions become too large, the sense of commonwealth or the common good is lost. Thus it is little wonder that the most recent dictionaries of the American English language render the meaning of commonwealth as "obsolescent." In reality, the Amish are in part a commonwealth. There is, however, no provision for outcasts.

It may be argued that the Amish have retained elements of wholesome provincialism, a saving power to which the world in the future will need more and more to appeal. Provincialism need not turn to ancient narrowness and ignorance, confines from which many have sought to escape. A sense of province or commonwealth, with its cherished love of people and self-conscious dignity, is a necessary basis for relating to the wider world community. Respect for locality, place, custom, and local idealism can go a long way toward checking the monstrous growth of consolidation in the nation and thus help to save human freedom and individual dignity.

. . . Anthropologists, who have compared societies all over the world, have tended to call semi-isolated peoples "folk societies," "primitives," or merely "simple societies." These societies constitute an altogether different type in contrast to the industrialized, or so-called civilized, societies.

The "folk society," as conceptualized by Robert Redfield,[1] is a small, isolated, traditional, simple, homogeneous society in which oral communication and conventionalized ways are important factors in integrating the whole life. In such an ideal-type society, shared practical knowledge is more important than science, custom is valued more than critical knowledge, and associations are personal and emotional rather than abstract and categoric.

Folk societies are uncomfortable with the idea of change. Young people do what the old people did when they were young. Members communicate intimately with one another, not only by word of mouth but also through custom and symbols that reflect a strong sense of belonging to one another. A folk society is *Gemeinschaft*-like; there is a strong sense of "we-ness." Leadership is personal rather than institutionalized. There are no gross economic inequalities. Mutual aid is characteristic of the society's members. The goals of life are never stated as matters of doctrine, but neither are they questioned. They are implied by the acts that constitute living in a small society. Custom tends to become sacred. Behavior is strongly patterned, and acts as well as cultural objects are given symbolic meaning that is often pervasively religious. Religion is diffuse and all-pervasive. In the typical folk society, planting and harvesting are as sacred in their own ways as singing and praying.

The folk model lends itself well to understanding the tradition-directed character of Amish society. The heavy weight of tradition can scarcely be explained in any other way. The Amish, for example, have retained many of the customs and small-scale technologies that were common in rural society in the nineteenth century. Through a process of syncretism, Amish religious values have been fused with an earlier period of simple country living when everyone farmed with horses and on a scale where family members could work together. The Amish exist as a folk or "little" community in a rural subculture within the modern state. . . . The outsider who drives through an

Amish settlement cannot help but recognize them by their clothing, farm homes, furnishings, fields, and other material traits of culture. Although they speak perfect English with outsiders, they speak a dialect of German among themselves.

Amish life is distinctive in that religion and custom blend into a way of life. The two are inseparable. The core values of the community are religious beliefs. Not only do the members worship a deity they understand through the revelation of Jesus Christ and the Bible, but their patterned behavior has a religious dimension. A distinctive way of life permeates daily life, agriculture, and the application of energy to economic ends. Their beliefs determine their conceptions of the self, the universe, and man's place in it. The Amish world view recognizes a certain spiritual worth and dignity in the universe in its natural form. Religious considerations determine hours of work and the daily, weekly, seasonal, and yearly rituals associated with life experience. Occupation, the means and destinations of travel, and choice of friends and mate are determined by religious considerations. Religious and work attitudes are not far distant from each other. The universe includes the divine, and Amish society itself is considered divine insofar as the Amish recognize themselves as "a chosen people of God." The Amish do not seek to master nature or to work against the elements, but try to work with them. The affinity between Amish society and nature in the form of land, terrain, and vegetation is expressed in various degrees of intensity.

Religion is highly patterned, so one may properly speak of the Amish as a tradition-directed group. Though allusions to the Bible play an important role in determining their outlook on the world, and on life after death, these beliefs have been fused with several centuries of struggling to survive in community. Out of intense religious experience, societal conflict, and intimate agrarian experience, a mentality has developed that prefers the old rather than the new. While the principle seems to apply especially to religion, it has also become a charter for social behavior. "The old is the best, and the new is of the devil" has become a prevalent mode of thought. By living in closed communities where custom and a strong sense of togetherness prevail, the Amish have formed an integrated way of life and a folklike culture. Continuity of conformity and custom is assured and the needs of the individual from birth to death are met within an integrated and shared system of meanings. Oral tradition, custom, and conventionality play an important part in maintaining the group as a functioning whole. To the participant, religion and custom are inseparable. Commitment and culture are combined to produce a stable human existence.

. . . A century ago, hardly anyone knew the Amish existed. A half-century ago they were viewed as an obscure sect living by ridiculous customs, as stubborn people who resisted education and exploited the labor of their children. Today the Amish are the unwilling objects of a thriving tourist industry on the eastern seaboard. They are revered as hard-working, thrifty people with enormous agrarian stamina, and by some, as islands of sanity in a culture gripped by commercialism and technology run wild.

CRITICAL-THINKING QUESTIONS

1. Does this description of the Amish way of life make you think about your own way of life in different terms? How?
2. Why would the Amish reject technological advances, which most members of our society hold to be invaluable?
3. What might the majority of the U.S. population learn from the Amish?

NOTE

1. Robert Redfield, "The Folk Society," *American Journal of Sociology,* 52 (Jan. 1947), 293–308. See also his book *The Little Community* (Chicago: University of Chicago Press, 1955).

16

The Self

George Herbert Mead

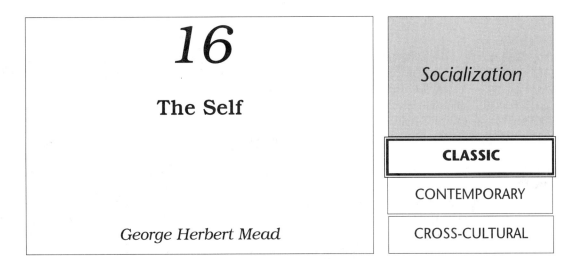

Socialization

CLASSIC

CONTEMPORARY

CROSS-CULTURAL

The self is not the body but arises in social experience. Explaining this insight is perhaps the greatest contribution of George Herbert Mead. Mead argues that the basic shape of our personalities is derived from the social groupings in which we live. Note, too, that even the qualities that distinguish each of us from others emerge only within a social community.

In our statement of the development of intelligence we have already suggested that the language process is essential for the development of the self. The self has a character which is different from that of the physiological organism proper. The self is something which has a development; it is not initially there, at birth, but arises in the process of social experience and activity, that is, develops in the given individual as a result of his relations to that process as a whole and to other individuals within that process. . . .

We can distinguish very definitely between the self and the body. The body can be there and can operate in a very intelligent fashion without there being a self involved in the experience. The self has the characteristic that it is an object to itself, and that characteristic distinguishes it from other objects and from the body. It is perfectly true that the eye can see the foot, but it does not see the body as a whole. We cannot see our backs; we can feel certain portions of them, if we are agile, but we cannot get an experience of our whole body. There are, of course, experiences which are somewhat vague and difficult of location, but the bodily experiences are for us organized about a self. The foot and hand belong to the self. We can see our feet, especially if we look at them from the wrong end of an opera glass, as strange things which we have difficulty in recognizing as our own. The parts of the body are quite dis-

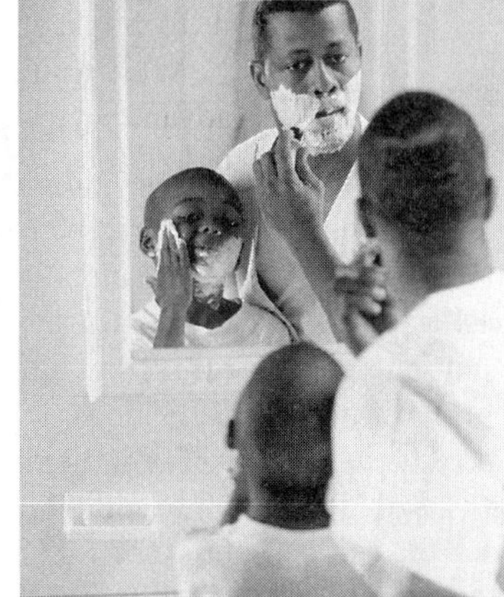

Source: From *Mind, Self and Society: From the Standpoint of a Social Behaviorist* by George Herbert Mead (Chicago: University of Chicago Press, 1934), pp. 135–42, 144, 149–56, 158, 162–64.

tinguishable from the self. We can lose parts of the body without any serious invasion of the self. The mere ability to experience different parts of the body is not different from the experience of a table. The table presents a different feel from what the hand does when one hand feels another, but it is an experience of something with which we come definitely into contact. The body does not experience itself as a whole, in the sense in which the self in some way enters into the experience of the self.

It is the characteristic of the self as an object to itself that I want to bring out. This characteristic is represented in the word "self," which is a reflexive, and indicates that which can be both subject and object. This type of object is essentially different from other objects, and in the past it has been distinguished as conscious, a term which indicates an experience with, an experience of, one's self. It was assumed that consciousness in some way carried this capacity of being an object to itself. In giving a behavioristic statement of consciousness we have to look for some sort of experience in which the physical organism can become an object to itself.[1]

When one is running to get away from someone who is chasing him, he is entirely occupied in this action, and his experience may be swallowed up in the objects about him, so that he has, at the time being, no consciousness of self at all. We must be, of course, very completely occupied to have that take place, but we can, I think, recognize that sort of a possible experience in which the self does not enter. We can, perhaps, get some light on that situation through those experiences in which in very intense action there appear in the experience of the individual, back of this intense action, memories and anticipations. Tolstoi as an officer in the war gives an account of having pictures of his past experience in the midst of his most intense action. There are also the pictures that flash into a person's mind when he is drowning. In such instances there is a contrast between an experience that is absolutely wound up in outside activity in which the self as an object does not enter, and an activity of memory and imagination in which the self is the principal object. The self is then entirely distinguishable from an organism that is surrounded by things and acts with reference to things, including parts of its own body. These latter may be objects like other objects, but they are just objects out there in the field, and they do not involve a self that is an object to the organism. This is, I think, frequently overlooked. It is that fact which makes our anthropomorphic reconstructions of animal life so fallacious. How can an individual get outside himself (experientially) in such a way as to become an object to himself? This is the essential psychological problem of selfhood or of self-consciousness; and its solution is to be found by referring to the process of social conduct or activity in which the given person or individual is implicated. The apparatus of reason would not be complete unless it swept itself into its own analysis of the field of experience; or unless the individual brought himself into the same experiential field as that of the other individual selves in relation to whom he acts in any given social situation. Reason cannot become impersonal unless it takes an objective, noneffective attitude toward itself; otherwise we have just consciousness, not *self*-consciousness. And it is necessary to rational conduct that the individual should thus take an objective, impersonal attitude toward himself, that he should become an object to himself. For the individual organism is obviously an essential and important fact or constituent element of the empirical situation in which it acts; and without taking objective account of itself as such, it cannot act intelligently, or rationally.

The individual experiences himself as such, not directly, but only indirectly, from the particular standpoints of other individual members of the same social group, or from the generalized standpoint of the social group as a whole to which he belongs. For he enters his own experience as a self or individual, not directly or immediately, not by becoming a subject to himself, but only insofar as he first becomes an object to himself just as other individuals are objects to him or in his experience; and he becomes an object to himself only by taking the attitudes of other individuals toward himself within a social environment or context of experience and behavior in which both he and they are involved.

The importance of what we term "communication" lies in the fact that it provides a form of behavior in which the organism or the individual may become an object to himself. It is that sort of communication which we have been discussing—not communication in the sense of the cluck of the hen to the chickens, or the bark of a wolf to the pack, or the lowing of a cow, but communication in the sense of significant symbols, communication which is directed not only to others but also to the individual himself. So far as that type of communication is a part of behavior it at least introduces a self. Of course, one may hear without listening; one may see things that he does not realize; do things that he is not really aware of. But it is where one does respond to that which he addresses to another and where that response of his own becomes a part of his conduct, where he not only hears himself but responds to himself, talks and replies to himself as truly as the other person replies to him, that we have behavior in which the individuals become objects to themselves. . . .

The self, as that which can be an object to itself, is essentially a social structure, and it arises in social experience. After a self has arisen, it in a certain sense provides for itself its social experiences, and so we can conceive of an absolutely solitary self. But it is impossible to conceive of a self arising outside of social experience. When it has arisen we can think of a person in solitary confinement for the rest of his life, but who still has himself as a companion, and is able to think and to converse with himself as he had communicated with others. That process to which I have just referred, of responding to one's self as another responds to it, taking part in one's own conversation with others, being aware of what one is saying and using that awareness of what one is saying to determine what one is going to say thereafter—that is a process with which we are all familiar. We are continually following up our own address to other persons by an understanding of what we are saying, and using that understanding in the direction of our continued speech. We are finding out what we are going to say, what we are going to do, by saying and doing, and in the process we are continually controlling the process itself. In the conversation of gestures what we say calls out a certain response in another and that in turn changes our own action, so that we shift from what we started to do because of the reply the other makes. The conversation of gestures is the beginning of communication. The individual comes to carry on a conversation of gestures with himself. He says something, and that calls out a certain reply in himself which makes him change what he was going to say. One starts to say something, we will presume an unpleasant something, but when he starts to say it he realizes it is cruel. The effect on himself of what he is saying checks him; there is here a conversation of gestures between the individual and himself. We mean by significant speech that the action is one that affects the individual himself, and that the effect upon the individual himself is part of the intelligent carrying-out of the conversation with others. Now we, so to speak, amputate that social phase and dispense with it for the time being, so that one is talking to one's self as one would talk to another person.[2]

This process of abstraction cannot be carried on indefinitely. One inevitably seeks an audience, has to pour himself out to somebody. In reflective intelligence one thinks to act, and to act solely so that this action remains a part of a social process. Thinking becomes preparatory to social action. The very process of thinking is, of course, simply an inner conversation that goes on, but it is a conversation of gestures which in its completion implies the expression of that which one thinks to an audience. One separates the significance of what he is saying to others from the actual speech and gets it ready before saying it. He thinks it out, and perhaps writes it in the form of a book; but it is still a part of social intercourse in which one is addressing other persons and at the same time addressing one's self, and in which one controls the address to other persons by the response made to one's own gesture. That the person should be responding to himself is necessary to the self, and it is this sort of social conduct which provides behavior within which that self appears. I know of no other form of behavior than the linguistic in which the individual is an object to himself, and, so far as I can see, the individual is not a self in the reflexive sense unless he is an object to himself. It is this fact that gives a critical importance to communication, since this is a type of behavior in which the individual does so respond to himself.

We realize in everyday conduct and experience that an individual does not mean a great deal of what he is doing and saying. We frequently say that such an individual is not himself. We come away from an interview with a realization that we have left out important things, that there are parts of the self that did not get into what was said. What determines the amount of the self that gets into communication is the social experience itself. Of course, a good deal of the self does not need to get expression. We carry on a whole series of different relationships to different people. We are one thing to one man and another thing to another. There are parts of the self which exist only for the self in relationship to itself. We divide ourselves up in all sorts of different selves with reference to our acquaintances. We discuss politics with one and religion with another. There are all sorts of different selves answering to all sorts of different social reactions. It is the social process itself that is responsible for the appearance of the self; it is not there as a self apart from this type of experience.

A multiple personality is in a certain sense normal, as I have just pointed out. . . .

The unity and structure of the complete self reflects the unity and structure of the social process as a whole; and each of the elementary selves of which it is composed reflects the unity and structure of one of the various aspects of that process in which the individual is implicated. In other words, the various elementary selves which constitute, or are organized into, a complete self are the various aspects of the structure of that complete self answering to the various aspects of the structure of the social process as a whole; the structure of the complete self is thus a reflection of the complete social process. The organization and unification of a social group is identical with the organization and unification of any one of the selves arising within the social process in which that group is engaged, or which it is carrying on.[3]

. . . Another set of background factors in the genesis of the self is represented in the activities of play and the game. . . . We find in children . . . imaginary companions which a good many children produce in their own experience. They organize in this way the responses which they call out in other persons and call out also in themselves. Of course, this playing with an imaginary companion is only a peculiarly interesting phase of ordinary play. Play in this sense, especially the stage which precedes the organized games, is a play at something. A child plays at being a mother, at being a teacher, at being a policeman; that is, it is taking different roles, as we say. We have something that suggests this in what we call the play of animals: A cat will play with her kittens, and dogs play with each other. Two dogs playing with each other will attack and defend, in a process which if carried through would amount to an actual fight. There is a combination of responses which checks the depth of the bite. But we do not have in such a situation the dogs taking a definite role in the sense that a child deliberately takes the role of another. This tendency on the part of children is what we are working with in the kindergarten where the roles which the children assume are made the basis for training. When a child does assume a role he has in himself the stimuli which call out that particular response or group of responses. He may, of course, run away when he is chased, as the dog does, or he may turn around and strike back just as the dog does in his play. But that is not the same as playing at something. Children get together to "play Indian." This means that the child has a certain set of stimuli that call out in itself the responses that they would call out in others, and which answer to an Indian. In the play period the child utilizes his own responses to these stimuli which he makes use of in building a self. The response which he has a tendency to make to these stimuli organizes them. He plays that he is, for instance, offering himself something, and he buys it; he gives a letter to himself and takes it away; he addresses himself as a parent, as a teacher; he arrests himself as a policeman. He has a set of stimuli which call out in himself the sort of responses they call out in others. He takes this group of responses and organizes them into a certain whole. Such is the simplest form of being another to one's self. It involves a temporal situation. The child says something in one character and responds in another character, and then his responding in another character is a stimulus to himself in the first character, and so the conversation goes on. A certain organized structure arises in him and in his other which replies to it, and these carry on the conversation of gestures between themselves.

If we contrast play with the situation in an organized game, we note the essential difference that the child who plays in a game must be ready to take the attitude of everyone else involved in that game, and that these different roles must have a definite relationship to each other. Taking a very simple game such as hide-and-seek, everyone with the exception of the one who is hiding is a person who is hunting. A child does not require more than the person who is hunted and the one who is hunting. If a child is playing in the first sense he just goes on playing, but there is no basic organization gained. In that early stage he passes from one to another just as a whim takes him. But in a game where a number of individuals are involved, then the child taking one role must be ready to take the role of everyone else. If he gets in a ball game he must have the responses of each position involved in his own position. He must know what everyone else is going to do in order to carry out his own play. He has to take all of these roles. They do not all have to be present in consciousness at the same time, but at some moments he has to have three or four individuals present in his own attitude, such as the one who is going to throw the ball, the one who is going to catch it, and so on. These responses must be, in some degree, present in his own make-up. In the game, then, there is a set of responses of such others so organized that the attitude of one calls out the appropriate attitudes of the other.

This organization is put in the form of the rules of the game. Children take a great interest in rules. They make rules on the spot in order to help themselves out of difficulties. Part of the enjoyment of the game is to get these rules. Now, the rules are the set of responses which a particular attitude calls out. You can demand a certain response in others if you take a certain attitude. These responses are all in yourself as well. There you get an organized set of such responses as that to which I have referred, which is something more elaborate than the roles found in play. Here there is just a set of responses that follow on each other indefinitely. At such a stage we speak of a child as not yet having a fully developed self. The child responds in a fairly intelligent fashion to the immediate stimuli that come to him, but they are not organized. He does not organize his life as we would like to have him do, namely, as a whole. There is just a set of responses of the type of play. The child reacts to a certain stimulus, and the reaction is in himself that is called out in others, but he is not a whole self. In his game he has to have an organization of these roles; otherwise he cannot play the game. The game represents the passage in the life of the child from taking the role of others in play to the organized part that is essential to self-consciousness in the full sense of the term.

. . . The fundamental difference between the game and play is that in the former the child must have the attitude of all the others involved in that game. The attitudes of the other players which the participant assumes organize into a sort of unit, and it is that organization which controls the response of the individual. The illustration used was of a person playing baseball. Each one of his own acts is determined by his assumption of the action of the others who are playing the game. What he does is controlled by his being everyone else on that team, at least insofar as those attitudes affect his own particular response. We get then an "other" which is an organization of the attitudes of those involved in the same process.

The organized community or social group which gives to the individual his unity of self may be called "the generalized other." The attitude of the generalized other is the attitude of the whole community.[4] Thus, for example, in the case of such a social group as a ball team, the team is the generalized other insofar as it enters—as an organized process or social activity—into the experience of any one of the individual members of it.

If the given human individual is to develop a self in the fullest sense, it is not sufficient for him merely to take the attitudes of other human individuals toward himself and toward one another within the human social process, and to bring that social process as a whole into his individual experience merely in these terms: He must also, in the same way that he takes the attitudes of other individuals toward himself and toward one another, take their attitudes toward the various phases or aspects of the common social activity or set of social undertakings in which, as members of an organized society or social group, they are all engaged; and he must then, by generalizing these individual attitudes of that organized society or social group itself, as a whole, act toward different social projects which at any given time it is carrying out, or toward the various larger phases of the general social process which constitutes its life and of which these projects are specific manifestations. This getting of the broad activities of any given social whole or organized society as such within the experiential field of any one of the individuals involved or included in that whole is, in other words, the essential basis and prerequisite of the fullest development of that individual's self: Only insofar as he takes the attitudes of the organized social group to which he belongs toward the organized, cooperative social activity or set of such activities in which that group as such is engaged, does he develop a complete self or possess the sort of complete self he has developed. And on the other hand, the complex cooperative processes and activities and institutional functionings of organized human society are also possible only insofar as every individual involved in them or belonging to that society can take the general attitudes of all other such individuals with reference to these processes and activities and institutional functionings, and to the organized social whole of experiential relations and interactions thereby constituted—and can direct his own behavior accordingly.

It is in the form of the generalized other that the social process influences the behavior of the individuals involved in it and carrying it on, i.e., that the community exercises control over the conduct of its individual members; for it is in this form that the social process or community enters as a determining factor into the individual's thinking. In abstract thought the individual takes the attitude of the generalized other[5] toward himself, without reference to its expression in any particular other individuals; and in concrete thought he takes that attitude insofar as it is expressed in the attitudes toward his behavior of those other individuals with whom he is involved in the given social situation or act. But only by taking the attitude of the generalized other toward himself, in one or another of these ways, can he think at all; for only thus can thinking—or the internalized conversation of gestures which constitutes thinking—occur. And only through the taking by individuals of the attitude or attitudes of the generalized other toward themselves is the existence of a universe of discourse, as that system of common or social meanings which thinking presupposes at its context, rendered possible.

. . . I have pointed out, then, that there are two general stages in the full development of the self. At the first of these stages, the individual's self is considered simply by an organization of the particular attitudes of other individuals toward himself and toward one another in the specific social acts in which he participates with them. But at the second stage in the full development of the individual's self that self is constituted not only by an organization of these particular individual attitudes, but also by an organization of the social attitudes of the generalized other or the social group as a whole to which he belongs. . . . So the self reaches its full development by organizing these individual attitudes of others into the organized social or group attitudes, and by thus becoming an individual reflection of the general systematic pattern of social or group behavior in which it and the others are all involved—a pattern which enters as a whole into the individual's experience in terms of these organized group attitudes which, through the mechanism of his central nervous system, he takes toward himself, just as he takes the individual attitudes of others.

. . . A person is a personality because he belongs to a community, because he takes over the institutions of that community into his own conduct. He takes its language as a medium by which he gets his personality, and then through a process of taking the different roles that all the others furnish he comes to get the attitude of the members of the community. Such, in a certain sense, is the structure of a man's personality. There are certain common responses which each individual has toward certain common things, and insofar as those common responses are awakened in the individual when he is affecting other persons he arouses his own self. The structure, then, on which the self is built is this response which is common to all, for one has to be a member of a community to be a self. Such responses are abstract attitudes, but they constitute just what we term a man's character. They give him what we term his principles, the acknowledged attitudes of all members of the community toward what are the values of that community. He is putting himself in the place of the generalized other, which represents the organized responses of all the members of the group. It is that which guides conduct controlled by principles, and a person who has such an organized group of responses is a man who we say has character, in the moral sense.

. . . I have so far emphasized what I have called the structures upon which the self is constructed, the framework of the self, as it were. Of course we are not only what is common to all: Each one of the selves is different from everyone else; but there has to be such a common structure as I have sketched in order that we may be members of a community at all. We cannot be ourselves unless we are also members in whom there is a community of attitudes which control the attitudes of all. We cannot have rights unless we have common attitudes. That which we have acquired as self-conscious persons makes us such members of society and gives us selves. Selves can only exist in definite relationships to other selves. No hard-and-fast line can be drawn between our own selves and the selves of others, since our own selves exist and enter as such into our experience only insofar as the selves of others exist and enter as such into our experience also. The individual possesses a self only in relation to the selves of the other members of his social group; and the structure of his self expresses or reflects the general behavior pattern of this social group to which he belongs, just as does the structure of the self of every other individual belonging to this social group.

CRITICAL-THINKING QUESTIONS

1. How does Mead distinguish between body and the self? What makes this a radically *social* view of the self?

2. How is the self both a subject and an object to itself? How is the ability to assume "the role of the other" vital to our humanity?

3. The idea that socialization produces conformity is easy to understand, but how does Mead argue that individual distinctiveness is also a result of social experience?

NOTES

1. Man's behavior is such in his social group that he is able to become an object to himself, a fact which constitutes him a more advanced product of evolutionary development than are the lower animals. Fundamentally it is this social fact—and not his alleged possession of a soul or mind with which he, as an individual, has been mysteriously and supernaturally endowed, and with which the lower animals have not been endowed—that differentiates him from them.

2. It is generally recognized that the specifically social expressions of intelligence, or the exercise of what is often called "social intelligence," depend upon the given individual's ability to take the roles of, or "put himself in the place of," the other individuals implicated with him in given social situations; and upon his consequent sensitivity to their attitudes toward himself and toward one another. These specifically social expressions of intelligence, of course, acquire unique significance in terms of our view that the whole nature of intelligence is social to the very core—that this putting of one's self in the places of others, this taking by one's self of their roles or attitudes, is not merely one of the various aspects or expressions of intelligence or intelligent behavior, but is the very essence of its character. Spearman's "X factor" in intelligence—the unknown factor which, according to him, intelligence contains—is simply (if our social theory of intelligence is correct) this ability of the intelligent individual to take the attitude of the other, or the attitudes of others, thus realizing the significations or grasping the meanings of the symbols or gestures in terms of which thinking proceeds; and thus being able to carry on with himself the internal conversation with these symbols or gestures which thinking involves.

3. The unity of the mind is not identical with the unity of the self. The unity of the self is constituted by the unity of the entire relational pattern of social behavior and experience in which the individual is implicated, and which is reflected in the structure of the self; but many of the aspects or features of this entire pattern do not enter into consciousness, so that the unity of the mind is in a sense an abstraction from the more inclusive unity of the self.

4. It is possible for inanimate objects, no less than for other human organisms, to form parts of the generalized and organized—the completely socialized—other for any given human individual, insofar as he responds to such objects socially or in a social fashion (by means of the mechanism of thought, the internalized conversation of gestures). Any thing—any object or set of objects, whether animate or inanimate, human or animal, or merely physical—toward which he acts, or to which he responds, socially, is an element in what for him is the generalized other; by taking the attitudes of which toward himself he becomes conscious of himself as an object or individual, and thus develops a self or personality. Thus, for example, the cult, in its primitive form, is merely the social embodiment of the relation between the given social group or community and its physical environment—an organized social means, adopted by the individual members of that group or community, of entering into social relations with that environment, or (in a sense) of carrying on conversations with it; and in this way that environment becomes part of the total generalized other for each of the individual members of the given social group or community.

5. We have said that the internal conversation of the individual with himself in terms of words or significant gestures—the conversation which constitutes the process or activity of thinking—is carried on by the individual from the standpoint of the "generalized other." And the more abstract that conversation is, the more abstract thinking happens to be, the further removed is the generalized other from any connection with particular individuals. It is especially in abstract thinking, that is to say, that the conversation involved is carried on by the individual with the generalized other, rather than with any particular individuals. Thus it is, for example, that abstract concepts are concepts stated in terms of the attitudes of the entire social group or community; they are stated on the basis of the individual's consciousness of the attitudes of the generalized other toward them, as a result of his taking these attitudes of the generalized other and then responding to them. And thus it is also that abstract propositions are stated in a form which anyone—any other intelligent individual—will accept.

17

Socialization and Television Violence

George Gerbner

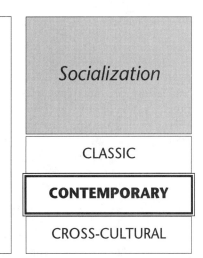

Socialization

CLASSIC

CONTEMPORARY

CROSS-CULTURAL

Through socialization we acquire the attitudes, beliefs, and values of our culture and learn the social and interpersonal skills needed to function effectively in society. Socialization is a lifelong process. Although our families play a critical role, the family itself is shaped by such external forces as government, business, and the media. In this selection, George Gerbner shows how being awash in television violence affects both children's and adults' attitudes and behavior. The toll of such socialization, Gerbner argues, includes increased aggression, desensitization to violence, and developing a "mean world syndrome."

Humankind may have had more bloodthirsty eras, but none as filled with *images* of violence as the present. We are awash in a tide of violent representations such as the world has never seen. Images of expertly choreographed brutality drench our homes. There is no escape from the mass-produced mayhem pervading the life space of ever larger areas of the world.

The television overkill has drifted out of democratic reach since it was first reported by the National Association of Educational Broadcasters in 1951. The first Congressional hearings were held by Senator Estes Kefauver's Subcommittee on Juvenile Delinquency in 1954. Through several more rounds of hearings in the 1960s and 1970s, despite the accumulation of critical research results, despite condemnation by government commissions and virtually all medical, law enforcement, parents', educational, and other organizations, and in the face of international embarrassment, violence has saturated the airways for the nearly thirty years we have been tracking it in our ongoing Cultural Indicators project[1] (Gerbner et al., 1993).

Broadcasters are licensed to serve "the public interest, convenience, and necessity." They are also paid to deliver a receptive audience to their business sponsors. Few industries are as public relations conscious as television. What compels them to endure public humiliation, risk the threat of repressive legislation and invite charges of undermining health, security, and the social order? The answer is not popularity.

The usual rationalization that television violence "gives the audience what it wants" is disingenuous. As the trade knows well, and as we shall see, violence is not highly rated. But there is no free market or box office for television programs through which audiences could express their wants.

Source: From "Television Violence: The Power and the Peril," by George Gerbner, in *Gender, Race, and Class in Media: A Text-Reader,* ed. Gail Dines and Jean M. Humez, pp. 547–57.

Unlike other media use, viewing is a ritual; people watch by the clock and not by the program. Ratings are determined more by the time of the program, the lead-in (previous program), and what else is on at the same time than by their quality or other attractions. Therefore, ratings are important because they set the price the advertiser pays for "buying" viewers available to the set at a certain time, but they have limited use as indicators of popularity. And even to the limited extent that a few violent programs may have a larger share of a certain time slot and can, therefore, extract a higher price for commercials, the incremental profits are hardly worth the social, institutional, and political damage they exact. Why would the business establishment subsidize its own undoing?

Therefore, it is clear that something is wrong with the way the problem has been posed and addressed. Either the damage is not what it is commonly assumed to be, or television violence must have some driving force and utility other than popularity, or both. Indeed it is both, and more.

The usual question—"Does television violence incite real-life violence?"—is itself a symptom rather than diagnostic tool of the problem. It obscures and, despite its alarming implications and intent, trivializes the issues involved.

Television violence must be understood as a complex scenario and an indicator of social relationships. It has both utility and consequences other than those usually considered in media and public discussion. And it is driven by forces other than free expression and audience demand.

Whatever else it does, violence in drama and news demonstrates power. It portrays victims as well as victimizers. It intimidates more than it incites. It paralyzes more than it triggers action. It defines majority might and minority risk. It shows one's place in the "pecking order" that runs society.

Violence is but the tip of the iceberg of a massive underlying connection to television's role as universal storyteller and an industry dependent on global markets. These relationships have not yet been recognized and integrated into any theory or regulatory practice. Television has been seen as one medium among many rather than as the mainstream of the cultural environment in which most children grow up and learn. Traditional regulatory and public interest conceptions are based on the obsolete assumption that the number of media outlets determines freedom and diversity of content. Today, however, a handful of global conglomerates can own many outlets in all media, deny entry to new and alternative perspectives, and homogenize content. The common carrier concept of access and protection applicable to a public utility like the telephone also falls short when the issue is not so much the number of channels and individual access to them but the centralized mass production of stories to grow on.

Let us, then, preview the task of broadening a discourse that has gone on too long in a narrow and shallow groove. Violence on television is an integral part of a system of global marketing. It dominates an increasing share of the world's screens despite its relative lack of popularity in any country. Its consequences go far beyond inciting aggression. The system inhibits the portrayal of diverse dramatic approaches to conflict, depresses independent television production, deprives viewers of more popular choices, victimizes some and emboldens others, heightens general intimidation, and invites repressive postures by politicians that exploit the widespread insecurities it itself generates.

The First Amendment to the U.S. Constitution forbade the only censors its authors knew—government—from interfering with the freedom of their press. Since then large conglomerates, virtual private governments, have imposed their formulas of overkill on media they own. Therefore, raising the issue of overkill directs attention to the controls that in fact abridge creative freedom, dominate markets, and constrain democratic cultural policy.

Behind the problem of television violence is the critical issue of who makes cultural policy on whose behalf in the electronic age. The debate about violence creates an opportunity to move the larger cultural policy issue to center stage, where it has been in other democracies for some time.

The convergence of communication technologies concentrates control over the most widely shared messages and images. Despite all the technocratic fantasies about hundreds of channels, and with antiviolence posturing filling the mass media, it is rare to encounter discussion of the basic issue of who makes cultural policy. In the absence of such discussion, cultural policy is made on private and limited grounds by an invisible corporate directorate whose members are unknown, unelected, and accountable only to their clients.

We need to ask the kinds of questions that can place the discussion of television violence as a cultural policy issue in a useful perspective. For example, What creative sources and resources will provide what mix of content moving on the "electronic superhighway" into every home? Who will tell the stories and for what underlying purpose? How can we assure survival of alternative perspectives, regardless of profitability and selling power?

There are no clear answers to these questions because, for one thing, they have not yet been placed on the agenda of public discourse. It will take organization, deliberation, and exploration to develop an approach to answering them. What follows, then, is an attempt to draw from our research answers to some questions that can help develop such an approach. We will be asking, What is unique about television and about violence on television? What systems of "casting" and "fate" dominate its representations of life? What conceptions of reality do these systems cultivate? Why does violence play such a prominent, pervasive, and persistent role in them? And, finally, how can we as a society deal with the overkill while, at the same time, enhancing rather than further curtailing cultural freedom and diversity?

THE NEW CULTURAL ENVIRONMENT

Nielsen figures show that, today, an American child is born into a home in which television is on an average of over seven hours a day. For the first time in human history, most of the stories about people, life, and values are told not by parents, schools, churches, or others in the community who have something to tell but by a group of distant conglomerates that have something to sell.

Television, the mainstream of the new cultural environment, has brought about a radical change in the way children grow up, learn, and live in our society. Television is a relatively nonselectively used ritual; children are its captive audience. Most people watch by the clock and not by the program. The television audience depends on the time of the day and the day of the week more than on the program. Other media require literacy, growing up, going out, and selection based on some previously acquired tastes, values, and predispositions. Traditional media research assumed such selectivity. But there are no "previously acquired tastes, values, and predispositions" with television. Viewing starts in infancy and continues throughout life.

Television helps to shape from the outset the predispositions and selections that govern the use of other media. Unlike other media, television requires little or no attention; its repetitive patterns are absorbed in the course of living. They become part and parcel of the family's style of life, but they neither stem from nor respond to its particular and selective needs and wants. It is television itself that cultivates the tastes, values, and predisposition that guide future selection of other media. That is why television has a major impact on what movies, magazines, newspapers, and books can be sold best in the new cultural environment.

The roles children grow into are no longer homemade, handcrafted, community inspired. They are products of a complex, integrated, and globalized manufacturing and marketing system. Television violence, defined as overt physical action that hurts or kills (or threatens to do so), is an integral part of that system. A study of "The Limits of Selective Viewing" (Sun, 1989) found that, on the whole, prime-time television presents a relatively small set of common themes, and violence pervades most of them.

Now, representations of violence are not necessarily undesirable. There is blood in fairy tales, gore in mythology, murder in Shakespeare. Not all violence is alike. In some contexts, violence can be a legitimate and even necessary cultural expression. Individually crafted, historically inspired, sparingly and selectively used expressions of symbolic violence can indicate the tragic costs of deadly compulsions. However, such a tragic sense of violence has been swamped by "happy violence" produced on the dramatic assembly line. This happy violence is cool, swift, painless, and often spectacular, even thrilling, but usually sanitized. It always leads to a happy ending. After all, it is designed to entertain and not to upset; it must deliver the audience to the next commercial in a receptive mood.

The majority of network viewers have little choice of thematic context or cast of character types and virtually no chance of avoiding violence. Nor has the proliferation of channels led to greater diversity of actual viewing (see, for example, Gerbner, 1993; Gerbner et al., 1993; Morgan & Shanahan, 1991). If anything, the dominant dramatic patterns penetrate more deeply into viewer choices through more outlets managed by fewer owners airing programs produced by fewer creative sources.

MESSAGE SYSTEM ANALYSIS

My conclusions are based on the findings of our Cultural Indicators project (CI) that began in 1967. CI is based at the University of Pennsylvania's Annenberg School for Communication. It is a cumulative database and an ongoing research project that relates recurrent features of the world of television to media policy and viewer conceptions of reality. By 1994 its computer archive contained observations on 2,816 programs and 34,882 characters coded according to many thematic, demographic, and action categories. The study is directed by this author in collaboration with Michael Morgan at the University of Massachusetts at Amherst and Nancy Signorielli at the University of Delaware.

CI is a three-pronged research effort: "Message system analysis" is the annual monitoring of television program content; "institutional policy analysis" looks at the economic and political bases of media decision making; "cultivation analysis" is an assessment of the long-range consequences of exposure to television's systems of messages.

Message system analysis is the study of the content of television programs. It includes every dramatic (fictional) program in each annual sample. It provides an unusual view of familiar territory. It is not a view of individual programs but an aggregate picture of the world of television, a bird's-eye view of what large communities of viewers absorb over long periods of time.

The role of violence in that world can be seen in our analysis of prime-time network programs and characters. Casting and fate, the demography of that world, are the important building blocks of the storytelling process. They have presented a stable pattern over the almost thirty years of monitoring network television drama and coding every speaking character in each year's sample. Middle-class white male characters dominate in numbers and power. Women play one out of three characters. Young people and the elderly make up one-third and one-fifth, respectively, of their actual proportions of the population. Most other minorities are even more underrepresented. That cast sets the stage for stories of conflict, violence, and the projection of white male prime-of-life power. Most of those who are underrepresented are also those who, when portrayed, suffer the worst fate.

The average viewer of prime-time television drama (serious as well as comedic) sees in a typical week an average of twenty-one criminals arrayed against an army of forty-one public and private law enforcers. There are fourteen doctors, six nurses, six lawyers, and two judges to handle them. An average of 150 acts of violence and about fifteen murders entertain them and their children every week, and that does not count cartoons and the news. Those who watch over three hours a day (more than half of all viewers) absorb much more.

About one of three (31 percent) of all characters and more than half (52 percent) of major characters are involved in violence either as victims or as victimizers (or both) in any given week. The ratio of violence to victimization defines the price to be paid for committing violence. When one group can commit violence with relative impunity, the price it pays for violence is relatively low. When another group suffers more violence than it commits, the price is high.

In the total cast of prime-time characters, defined as all speaking parts regardless of the importance of the role, the average "risk ratio" (number of victims per ten violents) is 12. Violence is an effective victimizer—and characterizer. Its distribution is not random; the calculus of risk is not evenly distributed. Women, children, poorer and older people, and some minorities pay a higher price for violence than do males in the prime of life. The price paid in victims for every ten violents is 15 for boys, 16 for girls, 17 for young women, 18.5 for lower class characters, and over 20 for elderly characters.

Violence takes on an even more defining role for major characters. It involves more than half of all major characters (58 percent of men and 41 percent of women). Most likely to be involved either as perpetrators or victims, or both, are characters portrayed as mentally ill (84 percent), characters with mental or other disability (70 percent), young adult males (69 percent), and Latino/Hispanic Americans (64 percent). Children, lower class, and mentally ill or otherwise disabled characters, pay the highest price—13 to 16 victims for every ten perpetrators.

Lethal victimization extends the pattern. About 5 percent of all characters and 10 percent of major characters are involved in killing (kill or get killed or both). Being Latino/Hispanic or lower class means bad trouble: They are the most likely to kill and be killed. Being poor, old, Hispanic, or a woman of color means double trouble, a disproportionate chance of being killed; they pay the highest relative price for taking another's life.

Among major characters, for every ten "good" (positively valued) men who kill, about four are killed. But for every ten "good" women who kill, six are killed, and for every ten women of color who kill, seventeen are killed. Older women characters get involved in violence only to be killed.

We calculated a violence "pecking order" by ranking the risk ratios of the different groups. Women, children, young people, lower class, disabled, and Asian Americans are at the bottom of the heap. When it comes to killing, older and Latino/Hispanic characters also pay a higher than average price. In other words, hurting and killing by most majority groups extracts a tooth for a tooth. But minority groups tend to pay a higher price for their show of force. That imbalance of power is, in fact, what makes them minorities even when, as is the case for women, they are a numerical majority.

CULTIVATION ANALYSIS: THE "LESSONS" OF TELEVISION

What are the consequences? These representations are not the sole or necessarily even the main determinants of what people think or do. But they are the most pervasive, inescapable, and policy-directed common and stable cultural contributions to what large communities absorb over long periods of time. We use the term *cul-*

tivation to distinguish the long-term cultivation of assumptions about life and values from short-term "effects" that are usually assessed by measuring change as a consequence of exposure to certain messages. With television, one cannot take a measure before exposure and only rarely without exposure. Television tends to cultivate and confirm stable conceptions about life. Cultivation analysis measures these "lessons" as it explores whether those who spend more time with television are more likely than comparable groups of lighter viewers to perceive the real world in ways that reflect the most common and repetitive features of the television world (see Morgan & Signorielli, 1990, for a detailed discussion of the theoretical assumptions and methodological procedures of cultivation analysis).

The systemic patterns in television content that we observe through message system analysis provide the basis for formulating survey questions about people's conceptions of social reality. These questions form the basis of surveys administered to large and representative national samples of respondents. The surveys include questions about fear of crime, trusting other people, walking at night in one's own neighborhood, chances of victimization, inclination to aggression, and so on. Respondents in each sample are divided into those who watch the most television, those who watch a moderate amount, and those who watch the least. Cultivation is assessed by comparing patterns of responses in the three viewing groups (light, medium, and heavy) while controlling for important demographic and other characteristics, such as education, age, income, gender, newspaper reading, neighborhood, and so on.

These surveys indicate that long-term regular exposure to violence-laden television tends to make an independent contribution (e.g., in addition to all other factors) to the feeling of living in a mean and gloomy world. The lessons range from aggression to desensitization and to a sense of vulnerability and dependence.

The symbolic overkill takes its toll on all viewers. However, heavier viewers in every subgroup express a greater sense of apprehension than do light viewers in the same groups. They are more likely than comparable groups of light viewers to overestimate their chances of involvement in violence; to believe that their neighborhoods are unsafe; to state that fear of crime is a very serious personal problem; and to assume that crime is rising, regardless of the facts of the case. Heavy viewers are also more likely to buy new locks, watchdogs, and guns "for protection." It makes no difference what they watch because only light viewers watch more selectively; heavy viewers watch more of everything that is on the air. Our studies show that they cannot escape watching violence (see, for example, Gerbner et al., 1993; Sun, 1989).

Moreover, viewers who see members of their own group underrepresented but overvictimized seem to develop a greater sense of apprehension, mistrust, and alienation, what we call the "mean world syndrome." Insecure, angry people may be prone to violence but are even more likely to be dependent on authority and susceptible to deceptively simple, strong, hard-line postures. They may accept and even welcome repressive measures such as more jails, capital punishment, harsher sentences—measures that have never reduced crime but never fail to get votes—if that promises to relieve their anxieties. That is the deeper dilemma of violence-laden television.

THE STRUCTURAL BASIS OF TELEVISION VIOLENCE

Formula-driven violence in entertainment and news is not an expression of freedom, viewer preference, or even crime statistics. The frequency of violence in the media seldom, if ever, reflects the actual occurrence of crime in a community. It is, rather, the product of a complex manufacturing and marketing machine.

Mergers, consolidation, conglomerization, and globalization speed the machine. "Studios are clipping productions and consolidating operations, closing off gateways for newcomers," notes the trade paper *Variety* on the front page of its August 2, 1993, issue. The number of major studios declines while their share of domestic and global markets rises. Channels proliferate while investment in new talent drops, gateways close, and creative sources shrink.

Concentration brings denial of access to new entries and alternative perspectives. It places greater emphasis on dramatic ingredients most suitable for aggressive international promotion. Having fewer buyers for their products forces program producers into deficit financing. That means that most producers cannot break even on the license fees they receive for domestic airings. They are forced into syndication and foreign sales to make a profit. They need a dramatic ingredient that requires no translation, "speaks action" in any language, and fits any culture. That ingredient is violence. (Sex is second but, ironically, it runs into more inhibitions and restrictions.)

Syndicators demand *action* (the code word for violence) because it "travels well around the world," said the producer of *Die Hard 2* (which killed 264 compared to 18 in *Die Hard 1*). "Everyone understands an action movie. If I tell a joke, you may not get it but if a bullet goes through the window, we all know how to hit the floor, no matter the language" (quoted in Auletta, 1993). Our analysis shows that violence dominates U.S. exports. We compared 250 U.S. programs exported to 10 countries with 111 programs shown in the United States during the same year. Violence was the main theme of 40 percent of home-shown and 49 percent of exported programs. Crime-action series composed 17 percent of home-shown and 46 percent of exported programs.

The rationalization for all that is that violence "sells." But what does it sell, to whom, and at what price? There is no evidence that, other factors being equal, violence per se is giving most viewers, countries, and citizens "what they want." The most highly rated programs are usually not violent. The trade paper *Broadcasting & Cable* (Editorial, 1993) editorialized that "the most popular programming is hardly violent as anyone with a passing knowledge of Nielsen ratings will tell you." The editorial added that "Action hours and movies have been the most popular exports for years" (p. 66)—that is, with the exporters, not with audiences. In other words, violence may help sell programs cheaply to broadcasters in many countries despite the dislike of their audiences. But television audiences do not buy programs, and advertisers, who do, pay for reaching the available audience at the least cost.

We compared data from over 100 violent and the same number of nonviolent prime-time programs stored in the CI database. The average Nielsen rating of the violent sample was 11.1; the same for the nonviolent sample was 13.8. The share of viewing households in the violent and nonviolent samples was 18.9 and 22.5, respectively. The amount and consistency of violence in a series further increased the gap. Furthermore, the nonviolent sample was more highly rated than the violent sample for each of the five seasons studied.

However, despite their low average popularity, what violent programs lose on general domestic audiences they more than make up by grabbing the younger viewers that advertisers want to reach and by extending their reach to the global market hungry for a cheap product. Even though, typically, these imports are also less popular abroad than quality shows produced at home, their extremely low cost, compared to local production, makes them attractive to the broadcasters who buy them.

Of course, some violent movies, video games, and other spectacles do attract sizable audiences. But those audiences are small compared to the home audience for television. They are the selective retail buyers of what television dispenses wholesale. If only a small proportion of television viewers growing up with the violent overkill become addicted to it, they can make many movies and games spectacularly successful.

PUBLIC RESPONSE AND ACTION

Most television viewers suffer the violence daily inflicted on them with diminishing tolerance. Organizations of creative workers in media, health professionals, law enforcement agencies, and virtually all other media-oriented professional and citizen groups have come out against "gratuitous" television violence. A March 1985 Harris survey showed that 78 percent disapprove of violence they see on television. A Gallup poll of October, 1990, found 79 percent in favor of "regulating" objectionable content in television. A *Times-Mirror* national poll in 1993 showed that Americans who said they were "personally bothered" by violence in entertainment shows jumped to 59 percent from 44 percent in 1983. Furthermore, 80 percent said entertainment violence was "harmful" to society, compared with 64 percent in 1983.

Local broadcasters, legally responsible for what goes on the air, also oppose the overkill and complain about loss of control. *Electronic Media* reported on August 2, 1993, the results of its own survey of 100 general managers across all regions and in all market sizes. Three of four said there is too much needless violence on television; 57 percent would like to have "more input on program content decisions."

The Hollywood Caucus of Producers, Writers, and Directors, speaking for the creative community, said in a statement issued in August, 1993:

> We stand today at a point in time when the country's dissatisfaction with the quality of television is at an all-time high, while our own feelings of helplessness and lack of power, in not only choosing material that seeks to enrich, but also in our ability to execute to the best of our ability, is at an all-time low.

Far from reflecting creative freedom, the marketing of formula violence restricts freedom and chills originality. The violence formula is, in fact, a de facto censorship extending the dynamics of domination, intimidation, and repression domestically and globally. Much of the typical political and legislative response exploits the anxieties that violence itself generates and offers remedies ranging from labeling and advisories to even more censorship.

There is a liberating alternative. It exists in various forms in most other democratic countries. It is public participation in making decisions about cultural investment and cultural policy. Independent grassroots citizen organization and action can provide the broad support needed for loosening the global marketing noose around the necks of producers, writers, directors, actors, and journalists.[2]

More freedom from violent and other inequitable and intimidating formulas, not more censorship, is the effective and acceptable way to increase diversity and reduce the dependence of program producers on the violence formula, and to reduce television violence to its legitimate role and proportion. The role of Congress, if any, is to turn its antitrust and civil rights oversight on the centralized and globalized industrial structures and marketing strategies that impose violence on creative people and foist it on the children and adults of the world. It is high time to develop a vision of the right of children to be born into a reasonable, free, fair, diverse, and nonthreatening cultural environment. It is time for citizen involvement in cultural decisions that shape our lives and the lives of our children.

CRITICAL-THINKING QUESTIONS

1. We often hear that television violence "gives viewers what they want." Why, according to Gerbner, are such statements "disingenuous"? Do viewers want more television violence? Do local broadcasters? What about Hollywood's writers, producers, and directors?

2. What are the messages that television violence sends about race, sex, age, and socioeconomic status? What are some of the consequences of

these messages? Can you think of other messages that television violence sends besides those discussed by Gerbner?

3. What solutions does Gerbner suggest to decrease television violence? What other remedies would *you* recommend at either the local or national level?

NOTES

1. Cultural Indicators is a database and a research project that relates recurrent features of the world of television to viewer conceptions of reality. Its cumulative computer archive contains observations on over 3,000 programs and 35,000 characters coded according to many thematic, demographic, and action categories. These form the basis for the content analyses cited in the references. The study is conducted at the University of Pennsylvania's Annenberg School for Communication in collaboration with Michael Morgan at the University of Massachusetts at Amherst and Nancy Signorielli at the University of Delaware. Thanks for research assistance are due to Mariaeleana Bartezaghi, Cynthia Kandra, Robin Kim, Amy Nyman, and Nejat Ozyegin.

2. One such alternative is the Cultural Environment Movement (CEM). CEM is a nonprofit educational corporation, an umbrella coalition of independent media, professional, labor, religious, health-related, women's, and minority groups opposed to private corporate as well as government censorship. CEM is working for freedom from stereotyped formulas and for investing in a freer and more diverse cultural environment. It can be reached by writing to Cultural Environment Movement, P.O. Box 31847, Philadelphia, PA 19104.

REFERENCES

Broadcasting & Cable, 1993. Editorial (September 20), 66.

AULETTA, K. 1993. What won't they do? *The New Yorker,* (May 17), 45–46.

GERBNER, G. 1993. "Miracles" of communication technology: Powerful audiences, diverse choices, and other fairy tales. In *Illuminating the blind spots,* ed. J. Wasko. New York: Ablex.

GERBNER, G., L. GROSS, M. MORGAN, and N. SIGNORIELLI. 1993. Growing up with television: The cultivation perspective. In *Media effects: Advances in theory and research,* eds. J. Bryant and D. Zillman. Hillsdale, N.J.: Lawrence Erlbaum.

MORGAN, M., and J. SHANAHAN. 1991. Do VCRs change the TV picture?: VCRs and the cultivation process. *American Behavioral Scientist,* 35(2): 122–35.

MORGAN, M., and N. SIGNORIELLI. 1990. Cultivation analysis: Conceptualization and methodology. In *Cultivation analysis: New directions in media effects research*, eds. N. Signorielli and M. Morgan, 13–33. Newbury Park, Calif.: Sage.

SUN, L. 1989. *Limits of selective viewing: An analysis of "diversity" in dramatic programming.* Unpublished master's thesis, the Annenberg School for Communication, University of Pennsylvania, Philadelphia.

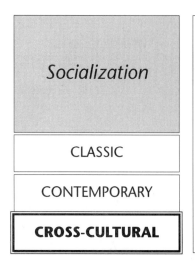

Socialization

CLASSIC

CONTEMPORARY

CROSS-CULTURAL

18

Parents' Socialization of Children in Global Perspective

D. Terri Heath

One of the most important functions of the family worldwide is the socialization of children. Although parents might receive help from others (such as relatives, neighbors, and professional caregivers), most communities expect parents themselves to raise their children to be productive and responsible adults. Across vastly different cultural environments, D. Terri Heath shows the universal importance of closeness with parents in affecting "the academic achievement, psychological well-being, substance use and juvenile delinquency, and general behavior of children worldwide."

THE BENEFITS OF CLOSE PARENT–YOUTH RELATIONSHIPS IN ADOLESCENCE

This article . . . [describes] how a positive relationship between parents and children later enhances the life satisfaction and psychological well-being of older youths and protects them from juvenile delinquency and substance abuse. As the cross-cultural examples illustrate, youth who perceive a close relationship with their parents exhibit more positive outcomes in each of these four areas. Life satisfaction and psychological well-being are described first, followed by illustrative cross-cultural examples. Next is a description of the impact of close parent–child relationships and their protective value on the substance abuse and juvenile delinquency of adolescents. Relevant, illustrative cross-cultural examples conclude this section.

Life satisfaction is a subjective measure of an individual's perception of his/her quality of life. Rather than objective measures of income, education, accumulation of wealth, and home ownership, life satisfaction is the level of individual satisfaction each person perceives in his/her own life: that which is privately known and privately evaluated. A multitude of factors influence life satisfaction, and because it is a personal evaluation, these factors differ for individuals. A study of life satisfaction among Hong Kong adolescents illustrates the profound effects peers and parents can exert on an adolescent's life satisfaction.

Psychological well-being is a measure of multiple submissions: self-esteem, locus of control, anxiety, loneliness, and sociability. Persons who exhibit high self-esteem, an internal locus of control, low anxiety and loneliness, and high sociability are considered to have strong psychological well-being. Just as with life satisfaction, many factors can influence psychological well-being, but

Source: From *Families in Multicultural Perspective,* eds. Bron B. Ingoldsby and Suzanna Smith, pp. 161–86. Copyright © 1995 Guilford Press, NY. Reprinted by permission of Guilford Press.

this section focuses specifically on the association between strong relationships with parents and positive outcomes for youth and young adults.

Hong Kong

Adolescence is a transitional period in the life cycle. Associations with family and peers are changing, and adolescents often feel increased pressure to succeed in social relationships outside their families. Their level of attachment, identification, and frequency of consultation with parents relative to that with peers influences the life satisfaction of adolescents in general and, specifically, their satisfaction with school, family, and others. Hong Kong, on the south coast of China, is heavily influenced by current political and economic changes in China. Chinese culture, with its emphasis on family and community over individual independence, continues to play a significant role in the culture of Hong Kong. Because the orientation of adolescents toward their peers and parents has important implications for their satisfaction with life, Hong Kong offers a unique look at this relationship in a rapidly developing society. In a study of 1,906 students, ages thirteen to sixteen, adolescents who were more oriented toward their parents, as well as those who were more oriented toward their peers, were equally satisfied with school, their acceptance by others, the government, and the media. However, those adolescents who are most oriented toward their parents were additionally satisfied with life in general, their families, and the environment (Man, 1991). Man (1991) concludes that "in a predominantly Chinese society like Hong Kong, the family remains a highly important determinant of the adolescents' life satisfaction" (p. 363).

Iran

Parents continue to influence the lives of their children as young adults through parental interactions, guidance, and shared history. When young adults are dissatisfied with their parents, their adult psychological well-being appears to be negatively influenced. When Iranian students, ages seventeen to thirty-nine, studying at universities in Iran and the United States were asked about their childhood dissatisfactions with their parents, an interesting pattern emerged. Those adults who perceived the most childhood dissatisfaction with parents were most likely to experience current loneliness, anxiety, external locus of control, misanthropy, neurosis, and psychosis when compared to adults who scored low on the dissatisfaction scale. They were also more likely to experience lower self-esteem and lower sociability, as well as decreased satisfaction with peer relationships, than were adults who had perceptions of childhood satisfaction with parents (Hojat, Borenstein, & Shapurian, 1990). There were no differences between the Iranian students studying at U.S. universities and those studying at Iranian institutions. The authors conclude that when a child's needs for closeness, attachment, and intimacy are not fulfilled to the child's satisfaction in early childhood, the result can be adult dissatisfactions with peer relationships and decreased psychological well-being in adulthood.

Puerto Rico

Can a child's need for closeness and intimacy be adequately fulfilled when the parents of the child are either alcohol dependent or mentally ill? By comparing three groups of children—those with an alcoholic parent, with a mentally ill parent, and with other parents without obvious diagnoses—researchers in Puerto Rico believe that children and adolescents, ages four to sixteen, with alcoholic or mentally ill parents are more likely than other children to be exposed to adverse family environments, such as stressful life events, marital discord, and family dysfunction. In addition, the children in these families were more maladjusted than were children in families without a diagnosed parent, according to reports by psychiatrists, parents, and the children themselves

(Rubio-Stipec et al., 1991). (However, the teachers of these three groups of children were unable to detect differences in child behavior, probably because 43 percent of them rated their familiarity with the child as "not good.") It appears from this research that children of alcoholic or mentally ill parents suffer negative consequences during childhood, and these consequences are readily apparent to psychiatrists, their parents, and even the children themselves.

In many cultures, adolescence is a period of rapid psychological growth and a shift in orientation from parents to peers. Adolescents move through this period from childhood at the beginning to adulthood at the end. Most choose educational and career paths during this period. Many choose marriage partners. They move from residing with their parents to residing with peers, with spouses, or by themselves. Because this is a time of such change, some adolescents cope with the transitions by engaging in problematic behaviors (e.g., drug and alcohol abuse and juvenile delinquency). This section presents some of the factors that contribute to problematic behaviors for youth in Canada and three subcultures in the United States: Native America, white, and Hispanic.

Canada

Social control theorists contend that adolescent alcohol consumption is influenced by the degree to which youth are influenced by peers more than parents. A study of alcohol consumption by Canadian eleventh and twelfth graders demonstrates this relationship (Mitic, 1990). Students were divided into three groups: (1) those who drank only with their parents, (2) those who drank only with their peers, and (3) those who drank both with and without their parents. The consumption rates of this last group were further divided into the amount of drinking with and without parents. As might be expected, students who drank only with parents consumed the least amount of alcohol. Those who drank with both parents and peers consumed the most alcohol and drank more heavily when they were with peers. It appears that what parents model for their children regarding alcohol consumption has only a small influence in the youths' consumption behaviors when the parents are not present.

Hispanics and Whites in the United States

Researchers found that Hispanic and white youth (ages nine to seventeen) in the United States are also significantly influenced in their drug and alcohol consumption by their relationships with friends and parents. For white and Hispanic adolescents who used either licit substances (e.g., cigarettes and alcohol), marijuana, or other illicit substances (e.g., cocaine, heroin, and prescription drugs used for recreational purposes), the single most important influence was the percentage of friends who used marijuana. Those youths who had higher percentages of friends who used marijuana were more likely to use each category of drug (licit, marijuana, and other illicit) than were youths who had fewer friends who used marijuana; this is equally true for both Hispanic and white youth. Although both users and abstainers were more affiliated with their parents than their peers, users were more strongly influenced by their peers; more likely to disregard parental objections to their friends; more likely to believe that their friends, rather than their parents, understand them best; and more likely to respect the ideas of their friends in difficult situations. The only cultural difference was that, in general, Hispanic youths respected their parents' views more than did white youths, regardless of whether they used or abstained from drugs and alcohol (Coombs, Paulson, & Richardson, 1991). Coombs et al. conclude that "youths having viable relationships with parents are less involved with drugs and drug-oriented peers" (p. 87).

Ojibway Native Americans

Delinquent behavior represents a dysfunctional response to stressors and strains in adolescence. On Native American reservations in the United States, an orientation toward parents and tribal elders appears to protect some youth from these negative behaviors. High percentages of Native American Ojibway adolescents, ages twelve to eighteen, reported inappropriate or illegal activities, such as using alcohol (85 percent), stealing something (70 percent), skipping school (64 percent), smoking marijuana (53 percent), and intentional damage to property (45 percent). However, those who spent more time with their family in chores, recreation, family discussions, and meals were less involved in negative behaviors. As expected, those youth who spent more time in activities away from their families—such as listening alone to the radio, and partying with drugs and alcohol—were at greatest risk for delinquent behaviors and court adjudications (Zitzow, 1990). Ojibway youths who spent more time in activities with parents and tribal elders were less likely to engage in delinquent behaviors resulting in court adjudications.

Summary

This last section focuses on how close parent–youth relationships are associated with the life satisfaction, psychological well-being, lack of substance use, and absence of delinquent behavior in adolescents. Without exception, adolescents in all six studies benefit from increased involvement with healthy parents. Parental involvement enhanced life satisfaction among adolescents in Hong Kong and contributed to psychological well-being among Iranian college students and Puerto Rican youths. The presence of parents was associated with less alcohol consumption among Canadian adolescents, a strong bond with parents was associated with less drug consumption by Hispanic and white youth in the United States, and spending time with parents and tribal elders was associated with less involvement in delinquent behaviors for Native American adolescents in the United States.

CONCLUSION

In reviewing the literature on cross-cultural research on parent–child relations for this chapter, a clear trend became increasingly apparent. When parents are more involved and/or have greater expectations of their children's behavior, children demonstrate better outcomes. As is apparent from the illustrative examples, greater parental involvement is an active involvement, not a passive one. It is acquired not simply by the amount of time parents and children spend together but rather by how the time is spent. An involved parent is not one who spends the majority of the day near his/her child but rarely interacting with the child. It is, instead, the parent who uses opportunities to share activities such as teaching the child a local trade, reading together, or fostering a close, supportive relationship through companionship. This active, involved parent appears much more likely to rear a successful child. Illustrative cross-cultural examples presented here of high-quality interaction between parents and children, such as spending time reading together in Great Britain, establishing firm limits and offering support in China, and engaging adolescents in activities with parents and tribal elders in the United States, has been associated with better child outcomes. These patterns emerged even when examining parent–son versus parent–daughter relations, relationships among family members in developing versus developed countries, or parent–child relationships in families that resided in Western cultures versus Eastern ones. . . .

CRITICAL-THINKING QUESTIONS

1. According to Heath, are there greater differences or similarities across cultures in the relationship between parent–child closeness and adolescent behavior?
2. What are some of the factors that contribute to the problematic behavior of adolescents both cross-culturally and within subcultures in the United States?

3. What does Heath mean by "parental involvement"? What other variables might also have an impact on parent–child relationships that are not discussed in this section?

REFERENCES

COOMBS, R. H., M. J. PAULSON, and M.A. RICHARDSON. 1991. Peer versus parental influence in substance use among Hispanic and Anglo children and adolescents. *Journal of Youth and Adolescence,* 20(1): 73–88.

HOJAT, M., B. D. BORENSTEIN, and R. SHAPURIAN. 1990. Perception of childhood dissatisfaction with parents and selected personality traits in adulthood. *Journal of General Psychology,* 117(3): 241–53.

MAN, P. 1991. The influence of peers and parents on youth life satisfaction in Hong Kong. *Social Indicators Research*, 24(4): 347–65.

MITIC, W. 1990. Parental versus peer influence on adolescents' alcohol consumption. *Psychological Reports*, 67: 1273–74.

RUBIO-STIPEC, M., H. BIRD, G. CANINO, and M. ALEGRIA. 1991. Children of alcoholic parents in the community. *Journal of Studies on Alcohol,* 52(1): 78–88.

ZITZOW, D. 1990. Ojibway adolescent time spent with parents/elders as related to delinquency and court adjudication experiences. *American Indian and Alaska Native Mental Health Research,* 4(1): 53–63.

19

The Dyad and the Triad

Georg Simmel

Social Interaction in Everyday Life

CLASSIC

CONTEMPORARY

CROSS-CULTURAL

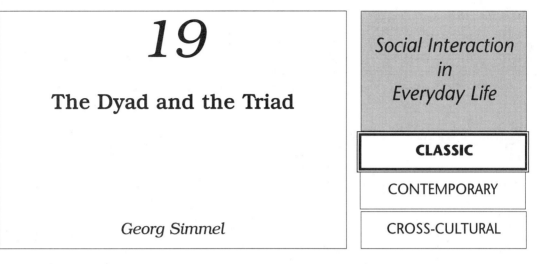

Sometimes called the "Freud of sociology," Georg Simmel explored many of the intricate details of everyday life with a keen perceptiveness. In this selection, Simmel describes the distinctive qualities of human relationships with two members (the dyad) and three members (the triad).

THE DYAD

Everyday experiences show the specific character that a relationship attains by the fact that only two elements participate in it. A common fate or enterprise, an agreement or secret between two persons, ties each of them in a very different manner than if even only three have a part in it. This is perhaps most characteristic of the secret. General experience seems to indicate that this minimum of two, with which the secret ceases to be the property of the one individual, is at the same time the maximum at which its preservation is relatively secure. . . .

The social structure here rests immediately on the one and on the other of the two, and the secession of either would destroy the whole. The dyad, therefore, does not attain that super-personal life which the individual feels to be independent of himself. As soon, however, as there is a sociation of three, a group continues to exist even in case one of the members drops out.

. . . Neither of the two members can hide what he has done behind the group, nor hold the group responsible for what he has failed to do. Here the forces with which the group surpasses the individual—indefinitely and partially, to be sure, but yet quite perceptibly—cannot compensate for individual inadequacies, as they can in larger groups. There are many respects in which two

Source: Reprinted and abridged with the permission of The Free Press, a Division of Simon & Schuster, from *The Sociology of Georg Simmel*, translated and edited by Kurt H. Wolff.

united individuals accomplish more than two isolated individuals. Nevertheless, the decisive characteristic of the dyad is that each of the two must actually accomplish something, and that in case of failure only the other remains—not a super-individual force, as prevails in a group even of three.

. . . Precisely the fact that each of the two knows that he can depend only upon the other and on nobody else, gives the dyad a special consecration—as is seen in marriage and friendship, but also in more external associations, including political ones, that consist of two groups. In respect to its sociological destiny and in regard to any other destiny that depends on it, the dyadic element is much more frequently confronted with All or Nothing than is the member of the larger group.

THE TRIAD VERSUS THE DYAD

This peculiar closeness between two is most clearly revealed if the dyad is contrasted with the triad. For among three elements, each one operates as an intermediary between the other two, exhibiting the twofold function of such an organ, which is to unite and to separate. Where three elements, A, B, C, constitute a group, there is, in addition to the direct relationship between A and B, for instance, their indirect one, which is derived from their common relation to C. . . . Discords between two parties which they themselves cannot remedy, are accommodated by the third or by absorption in a comprehensive whole.

Yet the indirect relation does not only strengthen the direct one. It may also disturb it. No matter how close a triad may be, there is always the occasion on which two of the three members regard the third as an intruder. The reason may be the mere fact that he shares in certain moods which can unfold in all their intensity and tenderness only when two can meet without distraction: The sensitive union of two is always irritated by the spectator. It may also be noted how extraordinarily difficult and rare it is for three people to attain a really uniform mood—when visiting a museum, for instance, or looking at a landscape—and how much more easily such a mood emerges between two. . . .

The sociological structure of the dyad is characterized by two phenomena that are absent from it. One is the intensification of relation by a third element, or by a social framework that transcends both members of the dyad. The other is any disturbance and distraction of pure and immediate reciprocity. In some cases it is precisely this absence which makes the dyadic relationship more intensive and strong. For, many otherwise undeveloped, unifying forces that derive from more remote psychical reservoirs come to life in the feeling of exclusive dependence upon one another and of hopelessness that cohesion might come from anywhere but immediate interaction. Likewise, they carefully avoid many disturbances and dangers into which confidence in a third party and in the triad itself might lead the two. This intimacy, which is the tendency of relations between two persons, is the reason why the dyad constitutes the chief seat of jealousy.

CRITICAL-THINKING QUESTIONS

1. Why do most people find their greatest experience of intimacy in a dyad?
2. What features of the dyad make this form of interaction unstable?
3. What are the characteristic strengths of the triad? What about weaknesses?
4. How might Simmel explain the common observation that "Two's company; three's a crowd"?

20

The Presentation of Self

Erving Goffman

Social Interaction in Everyday Life

CLASSIC

CONTEMPORARY

CROSS-CULTURAL

Face-to-face interaction is a complex process by which people both convey and receive information about each other. In this selection, Erving Goffman presents basic observations about how everyone tries to influence how others perceive them. In addition, he suggests ways in which people can evaluate how honestly others present themselves.

When an individual enters the presence of others, they commonly seek to acquire information about him or to bring into play information about him already possessed. They will be interested in his general socioeconomic status, his conception of self, his attitude toward them, his competence, his trustworthiness, etc. Although some of this information seems to be sought almost as an end in itself, there are usually quite practical reasons for acquiring it. Information about the individual helps to define the situation, enabling others to know in advance what he will expect of them and what they may expect of him. Informed in these ways, the others will know how best to act in order to call forth a desired response from him.

For those present, many sources of information become accessible and many carriers (or "sign-vehicles") become available for conveying this information. If unacquainted with the individual, observers can glean clues from his conduct and appearance which allow them to apply their previous experience with individuals roughly similar to the one before them or, more important, to apply untested stereotypes to him. They can also assume from past experience that only individuals of a particular kind are likely to be found in a given social setting. They can rely on what the individual says about himself or on documentary evidence he provides as to who and what he is. If they know, or know of, the individual by virtue of experience prior to the interaction, they can rely on assumptions as to the persistence and generality of psychological traits as a means of predicting his present and future behavior.

However, during the period in which the individual is in the immediate presence of the others, few events may occur which directly provide the others with the conclusive information they will need if they are to direct wisely their own activity. Many crucial facts lie beyond the time and place

Source: From *The Presentation of Self in Everyday Life* by Erving Goffman, copyright © 1959 by Erving Goffman, Bantam Doubleday Dell Publishing Group, Inc. Reprinted with permission.

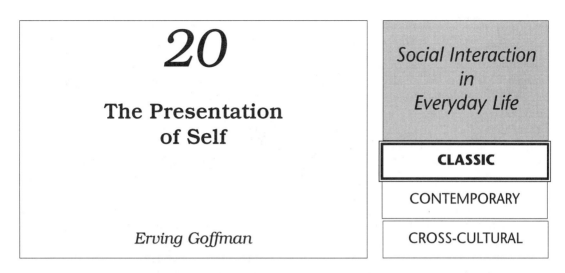

of interaction or lie concealed within it. For example, the "true" or "real" attitudes, beliefs, and emotions of the individual can be ascertained only indirectly, through his avowals or through what appears to be involuntary expressive behavior. Similarly, if the individual offers the others a product or service, they will often find that during the interaction there will be no time and place immediately available for eating the pudding that the proof can be found in. They will be forced to accept some events as conventional or natural signs of something not directly available to the senses. In Ichheiser's terms,[1] the individual will have to act so that he intentionally or unintentionally *expresses* himself, and the others will in turn have to be *impressed* in some way by him.

The expressiveness of the individual (and therefore his capacity to give impressions) appears to involve two radically different kinds of sign activity: the expression that he *gives,* and the expression that he *gives off.* The first involves verbal symbols or their substitutes which he uses admittedly and solely to convey the information that he and the others are known to attach to these symbols. This is communication in the traditional and narrow sense. The second involves a wide range of action that others can treat as symptomatic of the actor, the expectation being that the action was performed for reasons other than the information conveyed in this way. As we shall have to see, this distinction has an only initial validity. The individual does of course intentionally convey misinformation by means of both of these types of communication, the first involving deceit, the second feigning.

. . . Let us now turn from the others to the point of view of the individual who presents himself before them. He may wish them to think highly of him, or to think that he thinks highly of them, or to perceive how in fact he feels toward them, or to obtain no clear-cut impression; he may wish to ensure sufficient harmony so that the interaction can be sustained, or to defraud, get rid of, confuse, mislead, antagonize, or insult them. Regardless of the particular objective which the individual has in mind and of his motive for having this objective, it will be in his interests to control the conduct of the others, especially their responsive treatment of him. This control is achieved largely by influencing the definition of the situation which the others come to formulate, and he can influence this definition by expressing himself in such a way as to give them the kind of impression that will lead them to act voluntarily in accordance with his own plan. Thus, when an individual appears in the presence of others, there will usually be some reason for him to mobilize his activity so that it will convey an impression to others which it is in his interests to convey. Since a girl's dormitory mates will glean evidence of her popularity from the calls she receives on the phone, we can suspect that some girls will arrange for calls to be made, and Willard Waller's finding can be anticipated:

> It has been reported by many observers that a girl who is called to the telephone in the dormitories will often allow herself to be called several times, in order to give all the other girls ample opportunity to hear her paged.[2]

Of the two kinds of communication—expressions given and expressions given off—this report will be primarily concerned with the latter, with the more theatrical and contextual kind, the nonverbal, presumably unintentional kind, whether this communication be purposely engineered or not. As an example of what we must try to examine, I would like to cite at length a novelistic incident in which Preedy, a vacationing Englishman, makes his first appearance on the beach of his summer hotel in Spain:

> But in any case he took care to avoid catching anyone's eye. First of all, he had to make it clear to those potential companions of his holiday that they were of no concern to him whatsoever. He stared through them, round them, over them—eyes lost in space. The beach might have been empty. If by chance a ball was thrown his way, he looked surprised; then let a smile of amusement lighten his face (Kindly Preedy), looked round dazed to see that there *were* people on the beach, tossed it back with a smile to himself and not a smile *at* the people, and then resumed carelessly his nonchalant survey of space.

But it was time to institute a little parade, the parade of the Ideal Preedy. By devious handlings he gave any who wanted to look a chance to see the title of his book—a Spanish translation of Homer, classic thus, but not daring, cosmopolitan too—and then gathered together his beach-wrap and bag into a neat sand-resistant pile (Methodical and Sensible Preedy), rose slowly to stretch at ease his huge frame (Big-Cat Preedy), and tossed aside his sandals (Carefree Preedy, after all).

The marriage of Preedy and the sea! There were alternative rituals. The first involved the stroll that turns into a run and a dive straight into the water, thereafter smoothing into a strong splashless crawl towards the horizon. But of course not really to the horizon. Quite suddenly he would turn on to his back and thrash great white splashes with his legs, somehow thus showing that he could have swum further had he wanted to, and then would stand up a quarter out of water for all to see who it was.

The alternative course was simpler, it avoided the cold-water shock and it avoided the risk of appearing too high-spirited. The point was to appear to be so used to the sea, the Mediterranean, and this particular beach, that one might as well be in the sea as out of it. It involved a slow stroll down and into the edge of the water—not even noticing his toes were wet, land and water all the same to *him!*—with his eyes up at the sky gravely surveying portents, invisible to others, of the weather (Local Fisherman Preedy).[3]

The novelist means us to see that Preedy is improperly concerned with the extensive impressions he feels his sheer bodily action is giving off to those around him. We can malign Preedy further by assuming that he has acted merely in order to give a particular impression, that this is a false impression, and that the others present receive either no impression at all, or, worse still, the impression that Preedy is affectedly trying to cause them to receive this particular impression. But the important point for us here is that the kind of impression Preedy thinks he is making is in fact the kind of impression that others correctly and incorrectly glean from someone in their midst. . . .

There is one aspect of the others' response that bears special comment here. Knowing that the individual is likely to present himself in a light that is favorable to him, the others may divide what they witness into two parts; a part that is relatively easy for the individual to manipulate at will, being chiefly his verbal assertions, and a part in regard to which he seems to have little concern or control, being chiefly derived from the expressions he gives off. The others may then use what are considered to be the ungovernable aspects of his expressive behavior as a check upon the validity of what is conveyed by the governable aspects. In this a fundamental asymmetry is demonstrated in the communication process, the individual presumably being aware of only one stream of his communication, the witnesses of this stream and one other. For example, in Shetland Isle one crofter's wife, in serving native dishes to a visitor from the mainland of Britain, would listen with a polite smile to his polite claims of liking what he was eating; at the same time she would take note of the rapidity with which the visitor lifted his fork or spoon to his mouth, the eagerness with which he passed food into his mouth, and the gusto expressed in chewing the food, using these signs as a check on the stated feelings of the eater. The same woman, in order to discover what one acquaintance (A) "actually" thought of another acquaintance (B), would wait until B was in the presence of A but engaged in conversation with still another person (C). She would then covertly examine the facial expressions of A as he regarded B in conversation with C. Not being in conversation with B, and not being directly observed by him, A would sometimes relax usual constraints and tactful deceptions, and freely express what he was "actually" feeling about B. This Shetlander, in short, would observe the unobserved observer.

Now given the fact that others are likely to check up on the more controllable aspects of behavior by means of the less controllable, one can expect that sometimes the individual will try to exploit this very possibility, guiding the impression he makes through behavior felt to be reliably informing.[4] For example, in gaining admission to a tight social circle, the participant observer may not only wear an accepting look while listening to an informant, but may also be careful to wear the same look when observing the informant talking to others; observers of the observer will then not as easily discover where he actually stands. A specific illustration may be cited from Shetland Isle. When a neighbor dropped in to have a cup of tea, he would ordinarily wear at least a hint of an expectant warm smile as he passed through the door into the cottage. Since lack of physical obstructions outside the cottage and lack of light within it usually made it possible to observe the visitor unobserved as he approached the house, islanders sometimes took pleasure in watching the visitor drop whatever expression he was manifesting and replace it with a sociable one just before reaching the door. However, some visitors, in appreciating that this examination was occurring, would blindly adopt a social face a long distance from the house, thus ensuring the projection of a constant image.

This kind of control upon the part of the individual reinstates the symmetry of the communication process, and sets the stage for a kind of information game—a potentially infinite cycle of concealment, discovery, false revelation, and rediscovery. It should be added that since the others are likely to be relatively unsuspicious of the presumably unguided aspects of the individual's conduct, he can gain much by controlling it. The others of course may sense that the individual is manipulating the presumably spontaneous aspects of his behavior, and seek in this very act of manipulation some shading of conduct that the individual has not managed to control. This again provides a check upon the individual's behavior, this time his presumably uncalculated behavior, thus re-establishing the asymmetry of the communication process. Here I would like only to add the suggestion that the arts of piercing an individual's effort at calculated unintentionality seem better developed than our capacity to manipulate our own behavior, so that regardless of how many steps have occurred in the information game, the witness is likely to have the advantage over the actor, and the initial asymmetry of the communication process is likely to be retained. . . .

In everyday life, of course, there is a clear understanding that first impressions are important. Thus, the work adjustment of those in service occupations will often hinge upon a capacity to seize and hold the initiative in the service relation, a capacity that will require subtle aggressiveness on the part of the server when he is of lower socioeconomic status than his client. W. F. Whyte suggests the waitress as an example:

> The first point that stands out is that the waitress who bears up under pressure does not simply respond to her customers. She acts with some skill to control their behavior. The first question to ask when we look at the customer relationship is, "Does the waitress get the jump on the customer, or does the customer get the jump on the waitress?" The skilled waitress realizes the crucial nature of this question. . . .
>
> The skilled waitress tackles the customer with confidence and without hesitation. For example, she may find that a new customer has seated himself before she could clear off the dirty dishes and change the cloth. He is now leaning on the table studying the menu. She greets him, says, "May I change the cover, please?" and, without waiting for an answer, takes his menu away from him so that he moves back from the table, and she goes about her work. The relationship is handled politely but firmly, and there is never any question as to who is in charge.[5]

When the interaction that is initiated by "first impressions" is itself merely the initial interaction in an extended series of interactions involving the same participants, we speak of "getting off on the right foot" and feel that it is crucial that we do so. Thus, one learns that some teachers take the following view:

> You can't ever let them get the upper hand on you or you're through. So I start out tough. The first day I get a new class in, I let them know who's boss. . . . You've got to start off tough, then you can ease up as you go along. If you start out easy-going, when you try to get tough, they'll just look at you and laugh.[6]

. . . In stressing the fact that the initial definition of the situation projected by an individual tends to provide a plan for the cooperative activity that follows—in stressing this action point of view—we must not overlook the crucial fact that any projected definition of the situation also has a distinctive moral character. It is this moral character of projections that will chiefly concern us in this report. Society is organized on the principle that any individual who possesses certain social characteristics has a moral right to expect that others will value and treat him in an appropriate way. Connected with this principle is a second, namely that an individual who implicitly or explicitly signifies that he has certain social characteristics ought in fact to be what he claims he is. In consequence, when an individual projects a definition of the situation and thereby makes an implicit or explicit claim to be a person of a particular kind, he automatically exerts a moral demand upon the others, obliging them to value and treat him in the manner that persons of his kind have a right to expect. He also implicitly foregoes all claims to be things he does not appear to be[7] and hence foregoes the treatment that would be appropriate for such individuals. The others find, then, that the individual has informed them as to what is and as to what they *ought* to see as the "is."

One cannot judge the importance of definitional disruptions by the frequency with which they occur, for apparently they would occur more frequently were not constant precautions taken. We find that preventive practices are constantly employed to avoid these embarrassments and that corrective practices are constantly employed to compensate for discrediting occurrences that have not been successfully avoided. When the individual employs these strategies and tactics to protect his own projections, we may refer to them as "defensive practices"; when a participant employs them to save the definition of the situation projected by another, we speak of "protective practices" or "tact." Together, defensive and protective practices comprise the techniques employed to safeguard the impression fostered by an individual during his presence before others. It should be added that while we may be ready to see that no fostered impression would survive if defensive practices were not employed, we are less ready perhaps to see that few impressions could survive if those who received the impression did not exert tact in their reception of it.

In addition to the fact that precautions are taken to prevent disruption of projected definitions, we may also note that an intense interest in these disruptions comes to play a significant role in the social life of the group. Practical jokes and social games are played in which embarrassments which are to be taken unseriously are purposely engineered.[8] Fantasies are created in which devastating exposures occur. Anecdotes from the past—real, embroidered, or fictitious—are told and retold, detailing disruptions which occurred, almost occurred, or occurred and were admirably resolved. There seems to be no grouping which does not have a ready supply of these games, reveries, and cautionary tales, to be used as a source of humor, a catharsis for anxieties, and a sanction for inducing individuals to be modest in their claims and reasonable in their projected expectations. The individual may tell himself through dreams of getting into impossible positions. Families tell of the time a guest got his dates mixed and arrived when neither the house nor anyone in it was ready for him. Journalists tell of times when an all-too-meaningful misprint occurred, and the paper's assumption of objectivity or decorum was humorously discredited. Public servants tell of times a client ridiculously misunderstood form instructions, giving answers which implied an unanticipated and bizarre definition of the situation.[9] Seamen, whose home away from home is rigorously he-man, tell stories of coming back home and inadvertently asking mother to "pass the fucking butter."[10] Diplomats tell of the time a near-sighted queen asked a republican ambassador about the health of his king.[11]

To summarize, then, I assume that when an individual appears before others he will have many motives for trying to control the impression they receive of the situation.

CRITICAL-THINKING QUESTIONS

1. How does the "presentation of self" contribute to a definition of a situation in the minds of participants? How does this definition change over time?

2. Apply Goffman's approach to the classroom. What are the typical elements of the instructor's presentation of self? A student's presentation of self?

3. Can we evaluate the validity of people's presentations? How?

NOTES

1. Gustav Ichheiser, "Misunderstandings in Human Relations," supplement to *The American Journal of Sociology* 55 (Sept., 1949), 6–7.

2. Willard Waller, "The Rating and Dating Complex," *American Sociological Review* 2, 730.

3. William Sansom, *A Contest of Ladies* (London: Hogarth, 1956), pp. 230–32.

4. The widely read and rather sound writings of Stephen Potter are concerned in part with signs that can be engineered to give a shrewd observer the apparently incidental cues he needs to discover concealed virtues the gamesman does not in fact possess.

5. W. F. Whyte, "When Workers and Customers Meet," chap. 7, *Industry and Society,* ed. W. F. Whyte (New York: McGraw-Hill, 1946), pp. 132–33.

6. Teacher interview quoted by Howard S. Becker, "Social Class Variations in the Teacher-Pupil Relationship," *Journal of Educational Sociology* 25, 459.

7. This role of the witness in limiting what it is the individual can be has been stressed by Existentialists, who see it as a basic threat to individual freedom. See Jean-Paul Sartre, *Being and Nothingness,* trans. Hazel E. Barnes (New York: Philosophical Library, 1956), pp. 365ff.

8. Goffman, op. cit., pp. 319–27.

9. Peter Blau, "Dynamics of Bureaucracy" (Ph.D. dissertation, Department of Sociology, Columbia University, forthcoming, University of Chicago Press), pp. 127–29.

10. Walter M. Beattie, Jr., "The Merchant Seaman" (unpublished M.A. Report, Department of Sociology, University of Chicago, 1950), p. 35.

11. Sir Frederick Ponsonby, *Recollections of Three Reigns* (New York: Dutton, 1952), p. 46.

21

You Just Don't Understand: Women and Men in Conversation

Deborah Tannen

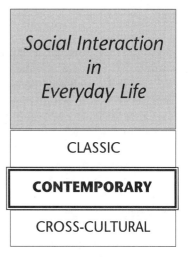

Social Interaction in Everyday Life

CLASSIC

CONTEMPORARY

CROSS-CULTURAL

Many men and women complain with frustration that they communicate on different "wave lengths." Deborah Tannen, a sociolinguist, explains why men and women often talk past each other in a host of everyday situations.

I was sitting in a suburban living room, speaking to a women's group that had invited men to join them for the occasion of my talk about communication between women and men. During the discussion, one man was particularly talkative, full of lengthy comments and explanations. When I made the observation that women often complain that their husbands don't talk to them enough, this man volunteered that he heartily agreed. He gestured toward his wife, who had sat silently beside him on the couch throughout the evening, and said, "She's the talker in our family."

Everyone in the room burst into laughter. The man looked puzzled and hurt. "It's true," he explained. "When I come home from work, I usually have nothing to say, but she never runs out. If it weren't for her, we'd spend the whole evening in silence." Another woman expressed a similar paradox about her husband: "When we go out, he's the life of the party. If I happen to be in another room, I can always hear his voice above the others. But when we're home, he doesn't have that much to say. I do most of the talking."

Who talks more, women or men? According to the stereotype, women talk too much. Linguist Jennifer Coates notes some proverbs:

> A woman's tongue wags like a lamb's tail.
>
> Foxes are all tail and women are all tongue.
>
> The North Sea will sooner be found wanting in water than a woman be at a loss for a word.

Throughout history, women have been punished for talking too much or in the wrong way. Linguist Connie Eble lists a variety of physical punishments used in Colonial America: Women were strapped to ducking stools and held underwater until they nearly drowned, put into the stocks with signs pinned to them, gagged, and silenced by a cleft stick applied to their tongues.

Though such institutionalized corporal punishments have given way to informal, often psychological ones, modern stereotypes are not

Source: Pp. 279–88 from *You Just Don't Understand* by Deborah Tannen.

much different from those expressed in the old proverbs. Women are believed to talk too much. Yet study after study finds that it is men who talk more at meetings, in mixed-group discussions, and in classrooms where girls or young women sit next to boys or young men. For example, communications researchers Barbara and Gene Eakins tape recorded and studied seven university faculty meetings. They found that, with one exception, men spoke more often and, without exception, spoke for a longer time. The men's turns ranged from 10.66 to 17.07 seconds, while the women's turns ranged from 3 to 10 seconds. In other words, the women's longest turns were still shorter than the men's shortest turns.

When a public lecture is followed by questions from the floor, or a talk show host opens the phones, the first voice to be heard asking a question is almost always a man's. And when they ask questions or offer comments from the audience, men tend to talk longer. Linguist Marjorie Swacker recorded question-and-answer sessions at academic conferences. Women were highly visible as speakers at the conferences studied; they presented 40.7 percent of the papers at the conferences studied and made up 42 percent of the audiences. But when it came to volunteering and being called on to ask questions, women contributed only 27.4 percent. Furthermore, the women's questions, on the average, took less than half as much time as the men's. (The mean was 23.1 seconds for women, 52.7 for men.) This happened, Swacker shows, because men (but not women) tended to preface their questions with statements, ask more than one question, and follow up the speaker's answer with another question or comment.

I have observed this pattern at my own lectures, which concern issues of direct relevance to women. Regardless of the proportion of women and men in the audience, men almost invariably ask the first question, more questions, and longer questions. In these situations, women often feel that men are talking too much. I recall one discussion period following a lecture I gave to a group assembled in a bookstore. The group was composed mostly of women, but most of the discussion was being conducted by men in the audience. At one point, a man sitting in the middle was talking at such great length that several women in the front rows began shifting in their seats and rolling their eyes at me. Ironically, what he was going on about was how frustrated he feels when he has to listen to women going on and on about topics he finds boring and unimportant.

RAPPORT-TALK AND REPORT-TALK

Who talks more, then, women or men? The seemingly contradictory evidence is reconciled by the difference between what I call *public* and *private speaking.* More men feel comfortable doing "public speaking," while more women feel comfortable doing "private" speaking. Another way of capturing these differences is by using the terms *report-talk* and *rapport-talk.*

For most women, the language of conversation is primarily a language of rapport: a way of establishing connections and negotiating relationships. Emphasis is placed on displaying similarities and matching experiences. From childhood, girls criticize peers who try to stand out or appear better than others. People feel their closest connections at home, or in settings where they *feel* at home—with one or a few people they feel close to and comfortable with—in other words, during private speaking. But even the most public situations can be approached like private speaking.

For most men, talk is primarily a means to preserve independence and negotiate and maintain status in a hierarchical social order. This is done by exhibiting knowledge and skill, and by holding center stage through verbal performance such as storytelling, joking, or imparting information. From childhood, men learn to use talking as a way to get and keep attention. So they are more comfortable speaking in larger groups made up of people they know less well—in the broadest sense, "public speaking." But even the most private situations can be approached like public speaking, more like giving a report than establishing rapport.

PRIVATE SPEAKING: THE WORDY WOMAN AND THE MUTE MAN

What is the source of the stereotype that women talk a lot? Dale Spender suggests that most people feel instinctively (if not consciously) that women, like children, should be seen and not heard, so any amount of talk from them seems like too much. Studies have shown that if women and men talk equally in a group, people think the women talked more. So there is truth to Spender's view. But another explanation is that men think women talk a lot because they hear women talking in situations where men would not: on the telephone; or in social situations with friends, when they are not discussing topics that men find inherently interesting; or, like the couple at the women's group, at home alone—in other words, in private speaking.

Home is the setting for an American icon that features the silent man and the talkative woman. And this icon, which grows out of the different goals and habits I have been describing, explains why the complaint most often voiced by women about the men with whom they are intimate is "He doesn't talk to me"—and the second most frequent is "He doesn't listen to me."

A woman who wrote to Ann Landers is typical:

> My husband never speaks to me when he comes home from work. When I ask, "How did everything go today?" he says, "Rough . . ." or "It's a jungle out there." (We live in Jersey and he works in New York City.)
>
> It's a different story when we have guests or go visiting. Paul is the gabbiest guy in the crowd—a real spellbinder. He comes up with the most interesting stories. People hang on every word. I think to myself, "Why doesn't he ever tell *me* these things?"
>
> This has been going on for thirty-eight years. Paul started to go quiet on me after ten years of marriage. I could never figure out why. Can you solve the mystery?
>
> —The Invisible Woman

Ann Landers suggests that the husband may not want to talk because he is tired when he comes home from work. Yet women who work come home tired too, and they are nonetheless eager to tell their partners or friends everything that happened to them during the day and what these fleeting, daily dramas made them think and feel.

Sources as lofty as studies conducted by psychologists, as down to earth as letters written to advice columnists, and as sophisticated as movies and plays come up with the same insight: Men's silence at home is a disappointment to women. Again and again, women complain, "He seems to have everything to say to everyone else, and nothing to say to me."

The film *Divorce American Style* opens with a conversation in which Debbie Reynolds is claiming that she and Dick Van Dyke don't communicate, and he is protesting that he tells her everything that's on his mind. The doorbell interrupts their quarrel, and husband and wife compose themselves before opening the door to greet their guests with cheerful smiles.

Behind closed doors, many couples are having conversations like this. Like the character played by Debbie Reynolds, women feel men don't communicate. Like the husband played by Dick Van Dyke, men feel wrongly accused. How can she be convinced that he doesn't tell her anything, while he is equally convinced he tells her everything that's on his mind? How can women and men have such different ideas about the same conversations?

When something goes wrong, people look around for a source to blame: either the person they are trying to communicate with ("You're demanding, stubborn, self-centered") or the group that the other person belongs to ("All women are demanding"; "All men are self-centered"). Some generous-minded people blame the relationship ("We just can't communicate"). But underneath, or overlaid on these types of blame cast outward, most people believe that something is wrong with them.

If individual people or particular relationships were to blame, there wouldn't be so many different people having the same problems. The real problem is conversational style. Women and men have different ways of talking. Even with the best intentions, trying to settle the problem through talk can only make things worse if it is ways of talking that are causing trouble in the first place. . . .

"TALK TO ME!"

Women's dissatisfaction with men's silence at home is captured in the stock cartoon setting of a breakfast table at which a husband and wife are sitting: He's reading a newspaper; she's glaring at the back of the newspaper. In a Dagwood strip, Blondie complains, "Every morning all he sees is the newspaper! I'll bet you don't even know I'm here!" Dagwood reassures her, "Of course I know you're here. You're my wonderful wife and I love you very much." With this, he unseeingly pats the paw of the family dog, which the wife has put in her place before leaving the room. The cartoon strip shows that Blondie is justified in feeling like the woman who wrote to Ann Landers: invisible.

Another cartoon shows a husband opening a newspaper and asking his wife, "Is there anything you would like to say to me before I begin reading the newspaper?" The reader knows that there isn't—but that as soon as he begins reading the paper, she will think of something. The cartoon highlights the difference in what women and men think talk is for: To him, talk is for information. So when his wife interrupts his reading, it must be to inform him of something that he needs to know. This being the case, she might as well tell him what she thinks he needs to know before he starts reading. But to her, talk is for interaction. Telling things is a way to show involvement, and listening is a way to show interest and caring. It is not an odd coincidence that she always thinks of things to tell him when he is reading. She feels the need for verbal interaction most keenly when he is (unaccountably, from her point of view) buried in the newspaper instead of talking to her.

Yet another cartoon shows a wedding cake that has, on top, in place of the plastic statues of bride and groom in tuxedo and gown, a breakfast scene in which an unshaven husband reads a newspaper across the table from his disgruntled wife. The cartoon reflects the enormous gulf between the romantic expectations of marriage, represented by the plastic couple in traditional wedding costume, and the often disappointing reality represented by the two sides of the newspaper at the breakfast table—the front, which he is reading, and the back, at which she is glaring.

These cartoons, and many others on the same theme, are funny because people recognize their own experience in them. What's not funny is that many women are deeply hurt when men don't talk to them at home, and many men are deeply frustrated by feeling they have disappointed their partners, without understanding how they failed or how else they could have behaved.

Some men are further frustrated because, as one put it, "When in the world am I supposed to read the morning paper?" If many women are incredulous that many men do not exchange personal information with their friends, this man is incredulous that many women do not bother to read the morning paper. To him, reading the paper is an essential part of his morning ritual, and his whole day is awry if he doesn't get to read it. In his words, reading the newspaper in the morning is as important to him as putting on makeup in the morning is to many women he knows. Yet many women, he observed, either don't subscribe to a paper or don't read it until they get home in the evening. "I find this very puzzling," he said. "I can't tell you how often I have picked up a woman's morning newspaper from her front door in the evening and handed it to her when she opened the door for me."

To this man (and I am sure many others), a woman who objects to his reading the morning paper is trying to keep him from doing something essential and harmless. It's a violation of his independence—his freedom of action. But when a woman who expects her partner to talk to her is disappointed that he doesn't, she perceives his behavior as a failure of intimacy: He's keeping things from her; he's lost interest in her; he's pulling away. A woman I will call Rebecca, who is generally quite happily married, told me that this is the one source of serious dissatisfaction with her husband, Stuart. Her term for his taciturnity is *stinginess of spirit.* She tells him what she is thinking, and he listens silently. She asks him what he is thinking, and he takes a long time to answer, "I don't know." In frustration she challenges, "Is there nothing on your mind?"

For Rebecca, who is accustomed to expressing her fleeting thoughts and opinions as they come to her, *saying* nothing means *thinking* nothing. But Stuart does not assume that his passing thoughts are worthy of utterance. He is not in the habit of uttering his fleeting ruminations, so just as Rebecca "naturally" speaks her thoughts, he "naturally" dismisses his as soon as they occur to him. Speaking them would give them more weight and significance than he feels they merit. All her life she has had practice in verbalizing her thoughts and feelings in private conversations with people she is close to; all his life he has had practice in dismissing his and keeping them to himself. . . .

PUBLIC SPEAKING: THE TALKATIVE MAN AND THE SILENT WOMAN

So far I have been discussing the private scenes in which many men are silent and many women are talkative. But there are other scenes in which the roles are reversed. Returning to Rebecca and Stuart, we saw that when they are home alone, Rebecca's thoughts find their way into words effortlessly, whereas Stuart finds he can't come up with anything to say. The reverse happens when they are in other situations. For example, at a meeting of the neighborhood council or the parents' association at their children's school, it is Stuart who stands up and speaks. In that situation, it is Rebecca who is silent, her tongue tied by an acute awareness of all the negative reactions people could have to what she might say, all the mistakes she might make in trying to express her ideas. If she musters her courage and prepares to say something, she needs time to formulate it and then waits to be recognized by the chair. She cannot just jump up and start talking the way Stuart and some other men can.

Eleanor Smeal, president of the Fund for the Feminist Majority, was a guest on a call-in radio talk show, discussing abortion. No subject could be of more direct concern to women, yet during the hour-long show, all the callers except two were men. Diane Rehm, host of a radio talk show, expresses puzzlement that although the audience for her show is evenly split between women and men, 90 percent of the callers to the show are men. I am convinced that the reason is not that women are uninterested in the subjects discussed on the show. I would wager that women listeners are bringing up the subjects they heard on *The Diane Rehm Show* to their friends and family over lunch, tea, and dinner. But fewer of them call in because to do so would be putting themselves on display, claiming public attention for what they have to say, catapulting themselves onto center stage.

I myself have been the guest on innumerable radio and television talk shows. Perhaps I am unusual in being completely at ease in this mode of display. But perhaps I am not unusual at all, because, although I am comfortable in the role of invited expert, I have never called in to a talk show I was listening to, although I have often had ideas to contribute. When I am the guest, my position of authority is granted before I begin to speak. Were I to call in, I would be claiming that right on my own. I would have to establish my credibility by explaining who I am, which might seem self-aggrandizing, or not explain who I am and risk having my comments ignored or not valued. For similar reasons, though I am comfortable lecturing to groups numbering in the thousands, I rarely ask questions following another lecturer's talk, unless I know both the subject and the group very well.

My own experience and that of talk show hosts seems to hold a clue to the difference in women's and men's attitudes toward talk: Many men are more comfortable than most women in using talk to claim attention. And this difference lies at the heart of the distinction between report-talk and rapport-talk.

CRITICAL-THINKING QUESTIONS

1. In general, who talks more, men or women? Who talks longer?
2. What is the difference between "report-talk" and "rapport-talk"? Between "private speaking" and "public speaking"?
3. In your opinion, is it possible to avoid some of the conflicts between report-talk and rapport-talk by developing a *shared* conversational style between men and women? Or is this unlikely?

22

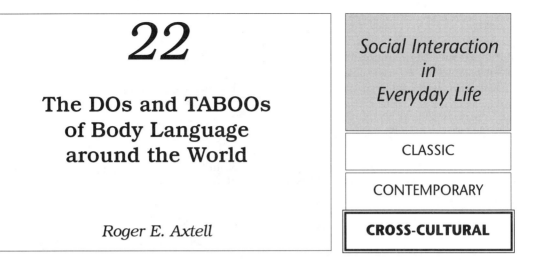

The DOs and TABOOs of Body Language around the World

Roger E. Axtell

Social Interaction in Everyday Life

CLASSIC

CONTEMPORARY

CROSS-CULTURAL

In a world that grows smaller every year, it is easy to offend others simply by being ourselves—gestures that we take as innocent may be seen by someone else as deeply insulting. This selection suggests the extent of the problem and, in an age of global business dealings, the need to cultivate cultural sensitivity.

THREE GREAT GAFFES OR ONE COUNTRY'S GOOD MANNERS, ANOTHER'S GRAND FAUX PAS

In Washington they call protocol "etiquette with a government expense account." But diplomacy isn't just for diplomats. How you behave in other people's countries reflects on more than you alone. It also brightens—or dims—the image of where you come from and whom you work for. The Ugly American about whom we used to read so much may be dead, but here and there the ghost still wobbles out of the closet.

Three well–traveled Americans tell how even an old pro can sometimes make the wrong move in the wrong place at the wrong time.

A Partner in One of New York's Leading Private Banking Firms

When the board chairman is Lo Win Hao, do you smile brightly and say, "How do you do, Mr. Hao?" or "Mr. Lo"? Or "Mr. Win"?

I traveled nine thousand miles to meet a client and arrived with my foot in my mouth. Determined to do things right, I'd memorized the names of the key men I was to see in Singapore. No easy job, inasmuch as the names all came in threes. So, of course, I couldn't resist showing off that I'd done my homework. I began by addressing top man Lo Win Hao with plenty of well placed Mr. Hao's—and sprinkled the rest of my remarks with a Mr. Chee this and a Mr. Woon that. Great show. Until a note was passed to me from one man I'd met before, in New York. Bad news. "Too friendly too soon, Mr. Long," it said. Where diffidence is next to godliness, there I was, calling a roomful of VIPs, in effect, Mr. Ed and Mr. Charlie. I'd remembered everybody's name—but forgotten that in Chinese the surname comes *first* and the given name *last.*

Source: From *DOs and TABOOs around the World*, 3rd ed., by Roger Axtell.

An Associate in Charge of Family Planning for an International Human Welfare Organization

The lady steps out in her dazzling new necklace and everybody dies laughing. (Or what not to wear to Togo on a Saturday night.)

From growing up in Cuba to joining the Peace Corps to my present work, I've spent most of my life in the Third World. So nobody should know better than I how to dress for it. Certainly one of the silliest mistakes an outsider can make is to dress up in "native" costume, whether it's a sari or a sombrero, unless you really know what you're doing. Yet, in Togo, when I found some of the most beautiful beads I'd ever seen, it never occurred to me not to wear them. While I was up-country, I seized the first grand occasion to flaunt my new find. What I didn't know is that locally the beads are worn not at the neck but at the waist—to hold up a sort of loincloth under the skirt. So, into the party I strutted, wearing around my neck what to every Togolese eye was part of a pair of underpants.

An Account Executive at an International Data Processing and Electronics Conglomerate

Even in a country run by generals, would you believe a runny nose could get you arrested?

A friend and I were coming into Colombia on business after a weekend in the Peruvian mountains touring Machu Picchu. What a sight that had been. And what a head cold the change in temperature had given my friend. As we proceeded through customs at the airport, he was wheezing and blowing into his handkerchief like an active volcano. Next thing I knew, two armed guards were lockstepping him through a door. I tried to intercede before the door slammed shut, but my spotty Spanish failed me completely. Inside a windowless room with the guards, so did his. He shouted in English. They shouted in Spanish. It was beginning to look like a bad day in Bogotá when a Colombian woman who had seen what happened burst into the room and finally achieved some bilingual understanding. It seems all that sniffling in the land of the infamous coca leaf had convinced the guards that my friend was waltzing through their airport snorting cocaine.

CUDDLY ETHNOCENTRICS

If only the world's customs inspectors could train their German shepherds to sniff out the invisible baggage we all manage to slip with us into foreign countries. They are like secret little land mines of the mind. Set to go off at the slightest quiver, they can sabotage a five-minute stroll down the Champs-Élysées or a $5 million tractor sale to Beijing. Three of our most popular national take-alongs:

Why Don't They Speak English? For the same reason we don't speak Catalan or Urdu. The wonder, in fact, is that so many people do speak so many languages. Seldom is a Continental European fluent in fewer than three, often more. Africans grow up with language of the nation that once colonized theirs plus half a dozen different tribal dialects. Japan has three distinct Japanese languages, which even the lowliest street sweeper can understand. Middle Eastern businesspeople shift effortlessly from their native tongue(s) to Oxford English to Quai d'Orsay French. Yet most of the English-speaking world remains as cheerfully monolingual as Queen Victoria's parakeet. If there are any complaints, then, it is clear they should not be coming from the American/English-speaking traveler.

Take Me to Your Burger King. In Peoria a Persian does not go looking for pot-au-feu. Alone among travelers, Americans seem to embark like astronauts—sealed inside a cozy life-support system from home. Scrambled eggs. Rent-a-cars. Showers. TV. Nothing wrong with any of it back home, but to the rest of the universe it looks sadly like somebody trying to read a book with the cover closed. Experiment! Try the local specialties.

American Know-How to the Rescue! Our brightest ideas have taken root all over the world—from assembling lines in Düsseldorf to silicone chips in Osaka to hybrid grains that are helping to nourish the Third World. Nonetheless, bigger, smarter, and faster do not inevitably add up to better. Indeed, the desire to take on shiny new American ways has been the downfall of nations whose cultures were already rich in art and technology when North America was still a glacier. As important as the idea itself is the way it is presented.

A U.S. doctor of public health recently back from West Africa offers an example of how to make the idea fit the ideology. "I don't just pop over and start handing out antimalarial pills on the corner," she says. "First I visit with the village chief. After he gives his blessing, I move in with the local witch doctor. After she shows me her techniques and I show her mine—and a few lives are saved—maybe then we can get the first native to swallow the first pill."

This is as true at the high-tech level as at the village dispensary. "What is all this drinking of green tea before the meeting with Mitsubishi?" The American way is to get right down to business. Yet if you look at Mitsubishi's bottom line, you have to wonder if green tea is such a bad idea after all.

It should come as no surprise that people surrounded by oceans rather than by other people end up ethnocentric. Even our biggest fans admit that America often strikes the rest of the world as a sweet-but-spoiled little darling, wanting desperately to please, but not paying too much attention to how it is done. Ever since the Marshall Plan, we seemed to believe that *our* games and *our* rules were the only ones in town. Any town. And that all else was the Heart of Darkness.

Take this scene in a Chinese cemetery. Watching a Chinese reverently placing fresh fruit on a grave, an American visitor asked, "When do you expect your ancestors to get up and eat the fruit?" The Chinese replied, "As soon as your ancestors get up and smell the flowers."

HANDS ACROSS THE ABYSS

Our bad old habits are giving way to a new when-in-Rome awareness. Some corporations take it so seriously that they put employees into a crash course of overseas cultural immersion. AT&T, for instance, encourages—and pays for—the whole family of an executive on the way to a foreign assignment to enroll in classes given by experts in the mores and manners of other lands.

Among the areas that cry out loudest for international understanding are how to say people's names, eat, dress, and talk. Get those four basics right and the rest is a piece of kuchen.

Basic Rule #1: What's in a Name?

. . . The first transaction between even ordinary citizens—and the first chance to make an impression for better or worse—is, of course, an exchange of names. In America there usually is not very much to get wrong. And even if you do, so what?

Not so elsewhere. Especially in the Eastern Hemisphere, where name frequently denotes social rank or family status, a mistake can be an outright insult. So can switching to a given name without the other person's permission, even when you think the situation calls for it.

"What would you like me to call you?" is always the opening line of one overseas deputy director for an international telecommunications corporation. "Better to ask several times," he advises, "than to get it wrong." Even then, "I err on the side of formality until asked to 'Call me Joe.'" Another frequent traveler insists his company provide him with a list of key people he will meet, country by country, surnames underlined, to be memorized on the flight over.

Don't Trust the Rules. Just when you think you have broken the international name code, they switch the rules on you. Take Latin America. Most people's names are a combination of the father's and mother's, with only the father's name used in conversation. In the Spanish-speaking countries the father's name comes first. Hence, Carlos Mendoza-Miller is called Mr. Mendoza. *But* in Portuguese-speaking Brazil it is the other way around, with the mother's name first.

In the Orient the Chinese system of surname first, given name last does not always apply. The Taiwanese, many of whom were educated in missionary schools, often have a Christian first name, which comes before any of the others—as in Tommy Ho Chin, who should be called Mr. Ho or, to his friends, Tommy Ho. Also, given names are often officially changed to initials, and a Y.Y. Lang is Y.Y.; never mind what it stands for. In Korea, which of a man's names takes a Mr. is determined by whether he is his father's first or second son. Although in Thailand names run backwards, Chinese style, the Mr. is put with the *given* name, and to a Thai it is just as important to be called by his given name as it is for a Japanese to be addressed by his surname. With the latter, incidentally, you can in a very friendly relationship respond to his using *your* first name by dropping the Mr. and adding *san* to his last name, as in Ishikawa-san.

Hello. Are you still there? Then get ready for the last installment of the name game, which is to disregard all of the above—sometimes. The reason is that many Easterners who deal regularly with the West are now changing the order of their names to un-confuse us. So, while to one another their names remain the same, to us the given name may come before the surname. Then again, it may not.

The safest course remains: Ask.

Basic Rule #2: Eat, Drink, and Be Wary

. . . [M]ealtime is no time for a thanks-but-no-thanks response. Acceptance of what is on your plate is tantamount to acceptance of host, country, and company. So, no matter how tough things may be to swallow, swallow. Or, as one veteran globe-girdler puts it, "Travel with a cast-iron stomach and eat everything everywhere."

Tastiness Is in the Eye of the Beholder. Often, what is offered constitutes your host country's proudest culinary achievements. What would we Americans think of a Frenchman who refused a bite of homemade apple pie or sizzling sirloin? Squeamishness comes not so much from the thing itself as from our unfamiliarity with it. After all, an oyster has remarkably the same look and consistency as a sheep's eye, and at first encounter a lobster would strike almost anybody as more a creature from science fiction than something you dip in melted butter and pop into your mouth.

Incidentally, in Saudi Arabia sheep's eyes are a delicacy, and in China it's bear's paw soup.

Perhaps the ultimate in exotic dining abroad befell a family planning expert on a trip for an international human welfare organization. It was a newly emerged African country where the national dish—in fact, the *only* dish eleven months of the year—is yam. The visitor's luck, however, was to be there the *other* month, when gorillas come in from the bush to steal the harvest. Being the only available protein, gorilla meat is as prized as sirloin is over here, and the village guest of honor was served a choice cut. Proudly, a platter of the usual mashed yams was placed before her—but with a roast gorilla hand thrusting artfully up from the center.

Is there any polite way out besides the back door?

Most experienced business travelers say no, at least not before taking at least a few bites. It helps, though, to slice whatever the item is very thin. This way, you minimize the texture—gristly, slimy, etc.—and the reminder of whence it came. Or, "Swallow it quickly," as one traveler recommends. "I still can't tell you what sheep's eyeballs taste like." As for dealing with taste, the old canard that "it tastes just like chicken" is often mercifully true. Even when the "it" is rodent, snake—or gorilla.

Another useful dodge is not knowing what you are eating. What's for dinner? Don't ask. Avoid poking around in the kitchen or looking at English-language menus. Your host will be flattered that you are following his lead, and who knows? Maybe it really is chicken in that stew. . . .

Bottoms Up—or Down? Some countries seem to do it deliberately, some inadvertently, except for Islam, where they don't do it at all. Either way, getting visitors as tipsy as possible as fast as possible stands as a universal sign of hospitality, and refusal to play your part equals rebuff. Wherever you go, toasts are as reciprocal as handshakes: If one does, all do. "I don't drink, thank you" rarely gets you off gracefully. Neither does protesting that you must get up early. (So must everyone else.)

"I try to wangle a glass of wine instead of the local firewater," one itinerant American says. "The only trouble is, the wine is usually stronger than the hard stuff." Mao-tai, Chinese wine made from sorghum, is notorious for leaving the unsuspecting thoroughly shanghaied. The Georgian wine so popular in Russia is no ladylike little Chablis either. In Nordic lands proper form for the toast is to raise the glass in a sweeping arc from belt buckle to lips while locking stares with your host. It takes very few akvavit-with-beer-chasers before you both start seeing northern lights.

In Africa, where all the new countries were once old European colonies, it is often taken for granted that if you are white you must have whiskey or gin or whatever the colonials used to like. A traveler to a former French possession describes the dilemma of being served a large gourdful of Johnnie Walker Red at nine in the morning. The host was simply remembering how the French had always loved their Scotch. *When* they drank it and *how much* were details he had never noticed. Yet there was no saying no without giving offense. A few sips had to be taken and a promise made to finish the rest later.

Basic Rule #3: Clothes Can Also *Un*make the Man

. . . Wherever you are, what you wear among strangers should not look strange to *them*. Which does not mean, "When in Morocco wear djellabas," etc. It means wear what you look natural in—and know how to wear—that also fits in with your surroundings.

For example, a woman dressed in a tailored suit, even with high heels and flowery blouse, looks startlingly masculine in a country full of diaphanous saris. More appropriate, then, is a silky, loose-fitting dress in a bright color—as opposed to blue serge or banker's gray.

In downtown Nairobi, a safari jacket looks as out of place as in London. With a few exceptions (where the weather is just too steamy for it), the general rule everywhere is that for business, for eating out, even for visiting people at home, you should be very buttoned up: conservative suit and tie for men, dress or skirt-suit for women. To be left in the closet until you go on an outdoor sightseeing trek:

jeans, however haute couture
jogging shoes
tennis and T-shirts
tight-fitting sweaters (women)
open-to-the-navel shirts (men)
funny hats (both)

Where you *can* loosen up, it is best to do it the way the indigines do. In the Philippines men wear the barong tagalog—a loose, frilly, usually white or cream-colored shirt with tails out, no jacket or tie. In tropical Latin American countries the counterpart to the barong is called a *guayabera* and, except for formal occasions, is acceptable business attire. In Indonesia they wear *Batiks*—brightly patterned shirts that go tieless and jacketless everywhere. In Thailand the same is true for the collarless Thai silk shirt. In Japan dress is at least as formal as in Europe (dark suit and tie for a man, business suit or tailored dress for a woman) except at country inns (called *ryokans*), where even big-city corporations sometimes hold meetings. Here you are expected to wear a kimono. Not to daytime meetings but to dinner, no matter how formal. (Don't worry—the inn always provides the kimono.)

One thing you notice wherever you go is that polyester is the mark of the tourist. The less drip-dry you are, the more you look as if you have come to do serious business, even if it means multiple dry-cleaning bills along the way.

Take It Off or Put It On—Depending. What you do or do not wear can be worse than bad taste—ranging from insulting to unhygienic to positively sinful. Shoes are among the biggest offenders in the East, even if you wear a 5AAA. They are forbidden within Muslim mosques and Buddhist temples. Never wear them into Japanese homes or restaurants unless the owner insists, and in Indian and Indonesian homes, if the host goes shoeless, do likewise. And wherever you take your shoes off, remember to place them neatly together facing the door you came in. This is particularly important in Japan. . . .

In certain conservative Arab countries, the price for wearing the wrong thing can hurt more than feelings. Mullahs have been known to give a sharp whack with their walking sticks to any woman whom they consider immodestly dressed. Even at American-style hotels there, do not wear shorts, skirts above the knee, sleeveless blouses, or low necklines—much less a bikini at the pool. . . .

CRITICAL-THINKING QUESTIONS

1. Historically, people in the United States have been rather indifferent to the dangers of inadvertently offending others. Why do you think this has been the case?
2. Have you ever offended others—or been offended—in the way depicted by Axtell? If so, how? How did you and others respond?
3. Can the type of cultural conflict Axtell describes occur right here in the United States? How?

23

Primary Groups

Charles Horton Cooley

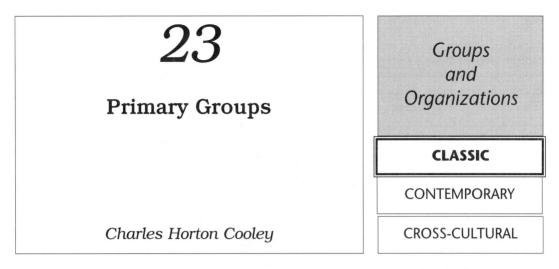

Charles Horton Cooley argues that human nature is a social *nature and is clearly expressed in group life. Cooley describes primary groups as "spheres of intimate association and cooperation" that are vital to the process of socialization.*

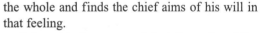

By primary groups I mean those characterized by intimate face-to-face association and cooperation. They are primary in several senses, but chiefly in that they are fundamental in forming the social nature and ideals of the individual. The result of intimate association, psychologically, is a certain fusion of individualities in a common whole, so that one's very self, for many purposes at least, is the common life and purpose of the group. Perhaps the simplest way of describing this wholeness is by saying that it is a "we"; it involves the sort of sympathy and mutual identification for which "we" is the natural expression. One lives in the feeling of the whole and finds the chief aims of his will in that feeling.

It is not to be supposed that the unity of the primary group is one of mere harmony and love. It is always a differentiated and usually a competitive unity, admitting of self-assertion and various appropriative passions; but these passions are socialized by sympathy, and come, or tend to come, under the discipline of a common spirit. The individual will be ambitious, but the chief object of his ambition will be some desired place in the thought of the others, and he will feel allegiance to common standards of service and fair play. So the boy will dispute with his fellows a place on the team, but above such disputes will place the common glory of his class and school.

The most important spheres of this intimate association and coopera-

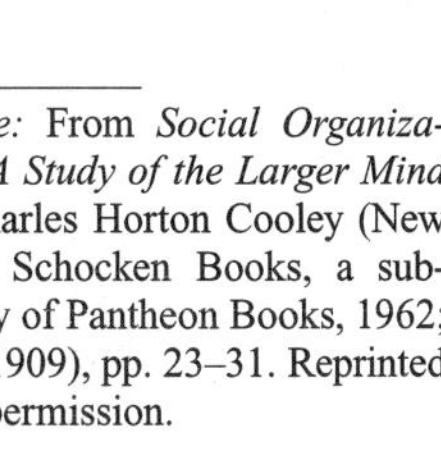

Source: From *Social Organization: A Study of the Larger Mind* by Charles Horton Cooley (New York: Schocken Books, a subsidiary of Pantheon Books, 1962; orig. 1909), pp. 23–31. Reprinted with permission.

tion—though by no means the only ones—are the family, the play-group of children, and the neighborhood or community group of elders. These are practically universal, belonging to all times and all stages of development; and are accordingly a chief basis of what is universal in human nature and human ideals. The best comparative studies of the family, such as those of Westermarck[1] or Howard,[2] show it to us as not only a universal institution, but as more alike the world over than the exaggeration of exceptional customs by an earlier school had led us to suppose. Nor can anyone doubt the general prevalence of play-groups among children or of informal assemblies of various kinds among their elders. Such association is clearly the nursery of human nature in the world about us, and there is no apparent reason to suppose that the case has anywhere or at any time been essentially different.

As regards play, I might, were it not a matter of common observation, multiply illustrations of the universality and spontaneity of the group discussion and cooperation to which it gives rise. The general fact is that children, especially boys after about their twelfth year, live in fellowships in which their sympathy, ambition, and honor are engaged even more often than they are in the family. Most of us can recall examples of the endurance by boys of injustice and even cruelty, rather than appeal from their fellows to parents or teachers—as, for instance, in the hazing so prevalent at schools, and so difficult, for this very reason, to suppress. And how elaborate the discussion, how cogent the public opinion, how hot the ambitions in these fellowships.

Nor is this facility of juvenile association, as is sometimes supposed, a trait peculiar to English and American boys; since experience among our immigrant population seems to show that the offspring of the more restrictive civilizations of the continent of Europe form self-governing play-groups with almost equal readiness. Thus Miss Jane Addams, after pointing out that the "gang" is almost universal, speaks of the interminable discussion which every detail of the gang's activity receives, remarking that "in these social folkmotes, so to speak, the young citizen learns to act upon his own determination."[3]

Of the neighborhood group it may be said, in general, that from the time men formed permanent settlements upon the land, down, at least, to the rise of modern industrial cities, it has played a main part of the primary, heart-to-heart life of the people. Among our Teutonic forefathers the village community was apparently the chief sphere of sympathy and mutual aid for the commons all through the "Dark" and Middle Ages, and for many purposes it remains so in rural districts at the present day. In some countries we still find it with all its ancient vitality, notably in Russia, where the *mir,* or self-governing village group, is the main theatre of life, along with the family, for perhaps 50 million peasants.

In our own life the intimacy of the neighborhood has been broken up by the growth of an intricate mesh of wider contacts which leaves us strangers to people who live in the same house. And even in the country the same principle is at work, though less obviously, diminishing our economic and spiritual community with our neighbors. How far this change is a healthy development, and how far a disease, is perhaps still uncertain.

Besides these almost universal kinds of primary association, there are many others whose form depends upon the particular state of civilization; the only essential thing, as I have said, being a certain intimacy and fusion of personalities. In our own society, being little bound by place, people easily form clubs, fraternal societies and the like, based on congeniality, which may give rise to real intimacy. Many such relations are formed at school and college, and among men and women brought together in the first instance by their occupations—as workmen in the same trade, or the like. Where there is a little common interest and activity, kindness grows like weeds by the roadside.

But the fact that the family and neighborhood groups are ascendant in the open and plastic time of childhood makes them even now incomparably more influential than all the rest.

Primary groups are primary in the sense that they give the individual his earliest and completest experience of social unity, and also in the sense that they do not change in the same degree as more elaborate relations, but form a comparatively permanent source out of which the latter are ever springing. Of course they are not independent of the larger society, but to some extent reflect its spirit; as the German family and the German school bear somewhat distinctly the print of German militarism. But this, after all, is like the tide setting back into creeks, and does not commonly go very far. Among the German, and still more among the Russian, peasantry are found habits of free cooperation and discussion almost uninfluenced by the character of the state; and it is a familiar and well-supported view that the village commune, self-governing as regards local affairs and habituated to discussion, is a very widespread institution in settled communities, and the continuator of a similar autonomy previously existing in the clan. "It is man who makes monarchies and establishes republics, but the commune seems to come directly from the hand of God."[4]

In our own cities the crowded tenements and the general economic and social confusion have sorely wounded the family and the neighborhood, but it is remarkable, in view of these conditions, what vitality they show; and there is nothing upon which the conscience of the time is more determined than upon restoring them to health.

These groups, then, are springs of life, not only for the individual but for social institutions. They are only in part moulded by special traditions, and, in larger degree, express a universal nature. The religion or government of other civilizations may seem alien to us, but the children or the family group wear the common life, and with them we can always make ourselves at home.

By human nature, I suppose, we may understand those sentiments and impulses that are human in being superior to those of lower animals, and also in the sense that they belong to mankind at large, and not to any particular race or time. It means, particularly, sympathy and the innumerable sentiments into which sympathy enters, such as love, resentment, ambition, vanity, hero-worship, and the feeling of social right and wrong.

Human nature in this sense is justly regarded as a comparatively permanent element in society. Always and everywhere men seek honor and dread ridicule, defer to public opinion, cherish their goods and their children, and admire courage, generosity, and success. It is always safe to assume that people are and have been human. . . .

To return to primary groups: The view here maintained is that human nature is not something existing separately in the individual, but a *group-nature* or *primary phase of society,* a relatively simple and general condition of the social mind. It is something more, on the one hand, than the mere instinct that is born in us—though that enters into it—and something else, on the other, than the more elaborate development of ideas and sentiments that makes up institutions. It is the nature which is developed and expressed in those simple, face-to-face groups that are somewhat alike in all societies; groups of the family, the playground, and the neighborhood. In the essential similarity of these is to be found the basis, in experience, for similar ideas and sentiments in the human mind. In these, everywhere, human nature comes into existence. Man does not have it at birth; he cannot acquire it except through fellowship, and it decays in isolation.

If this view does not recommend itself to common sense I do not know that elaboration will be of much avail. It simply means the application at this point of the idea that society and individuals are inseparable phases of a common whole, so that wherever we find an individual fact we may look for a social fact to go with it. If there is a universal nature in persons there must be something universal in association to correspond to it.

What else can human nature be than a trait of primary groups? Surely not an attribute of the separate individual—supposing there were any such thing—since its typical characteristics, such as affection, ambition, vanity, and resentment, are inconceivable apart from society. If it belongs, then, to man in association, what kind or degree of association is required to develop it? Evidently nothing elaborate, because elaborate phases of society are transient and diverse, while human nature is comparatively stable and universal. In short the family and neighborhood life is essential to its genesis and nothing more is.

Here as everywhere in the study of society we must learn to see mankind in psychical wholes, rather than in artificial separation. We must see and feel the communal life of family and local groups as immediate facts, not as combinations of something else. And perhaps we shall do this best by recalling our own experience and extending it through sympathetic observation. What, in our life, is the family and the fellowship; what do we know of the we-feeling? Thought of this kind may help us to get a concrete perception of that primary group-nature of which everything social is the outgrowth.

CRITICAL-THINKING QUESTIONS

1. Are primary groups necessarily devoid of conflict? How does Cooley address this issue?
2. Why does Cooley employ the term *primary* in his analysis? What are the characteristics of the implied opposite of primary groups: "secondary groups"?
3. What is Cooley's view of human nature? Why does he think that society cannot be reduced to the behavior of many distinct individuals?

NOTES

1. *The History of Human Marriage.*
2. *A History of Matrimonial Institutions.*
3. *Newer Ideals of Peace,* 177.
4. De Tocqueville, *Democracy in America,* vol. 1, chap 5.

24

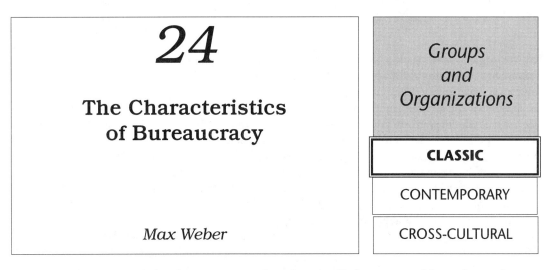

The Characteristics of Bureaucracy

Max Weber

Groups and Organizations

CLASSIC

CONTEMPORARY

CROSS-CULTURAL

According to Max Weber, human societies have historically been oriented by tradition of one kind or another. Modernity, in contrast, is marked by a different form of human consciousness: a rational world view. For Weber, there is no clearer expression of modern rationality than bureaucracy. In this selection, Weber identifies the characteristics of this organizational form.

Modern officialdom functions in the following specific manner:

I. There is the principle of fixed and official jurisdictional areas, which are generally ordered by rules, that is, by laws or administrative regulations. (1) The regular activities required for the purposes of the bureaucratically governed structure are distributed in a fixed way as official duties. (2) The authority to give the commands required for the discharge of these duties is distributed in a stable way and is strictly delimited by rules concerning the coercive means, physical, sacerdotal, or otherwise, which may be placed at the disposal of officials. (3) Methodical provision is made for the regular and continuous fulfillment of these duties and for the execution of the corresponding rights; only persons who have the generally regulated qualifications to serve are employed.

Source: From Max Weber: Essays in Sociology, by Max Weber, ed. H. H. Gerth and C. Wright Mills.

In public and lawful government these three elements constitute "bureaucratic authority." In private economic domination, they constitute bureaucratic "management." Bureaucracy, thus understood, is fully developed in political and ecclesiastical communities only in the modern state, and, in the private economy, only in the most advanced institutions of capitalism. Permanent and public office authority, with fixed jurisdiction, is not the historical rule but rather the exception. This is so even in large political structures such as those of the ancient Orient, the Germanic, and Mongolian empires of conquest, or of many feudal structures of state. In all these cases, the ruler executes the most important measures through personal trustees, table-companions, or court-servants. Their commissions and authority are not precisely delimited and are temporarily called into being for each case.

II. The principles of office hierarchy and of levels of graded authority mean a firmly ordered system of super- and subordination in which there is a supervision of the lower offices by the higher ones. Such a system offers the governed the possibility of appealing the decision of a lower office to its higher authority, in a definitely regulated manner. With the full development of the bureaucratic type, the office hierarchy is monocratically organized. The principle of hierarchical office authority is found in all bureaucratic structures: in state and ecclesiastical structures as well as in large party organizations and private enterprises. It does not matter for the character of bureaucracy whether its authority is called "private" or "public."

When the principle of jurisdictional "competency" is fully carried through, hierarchical subordination—at least in public office—does not mean that the "higher" authority is simply authorized to take over the business of the "lower." Indeed, the opposite is the rule. Once established and having fulfilled its task, an office tends to continue in existence and be held by another incumbent.

III. The management of the modern office is based upon written documents ("the files"), which are preserved in their original or draft form. There is, therefore, a staff of subaltern officials and scribes of all sorts. The body of officials actively engaged in a "public" office, along with the respective apparatus of material implements and the files, make up a "bureau." In private enterprise, "the bureau" is often called "the office."

In principle, the modern organization of the civil service separates the bureau from the private domicile of the official, and, in general, bureaucracy segregates official activity as something distinct from the sphere of private life. Public monies and equipment are divorced from the private property of the official. . . . In principle, the executive office is separated from the household, business from private correspondence, and business assets from private fortunes. The more consistently the modern type of business management has been carried through, the more are these separations the case. The beginnings of this process are to be found as early as the Middle Ages.

It is the peculiarity of the modern entrepreneur that he conducts himself as the "first official" of his enterprise, in the very same way in which the ruler of a specifically modern bureaucratic state spoke of himself as "the first servant" of the state. The idea that the bureau activities of the state are intrinsically different in character from the management of private economic offices is a continental European notion and, by the way of contrast, is totally foreign to the American way.

IV. Office management, at least all specialized office management—and such management is distinctly modern—usually presupposes a thorough and expert training. This increasingly holds for the modern executive and employee of private enterprises, in the same manner as it holds for the state official.

V. When the office is fully developed, official activity demands the full working capacity of the official, irrespective of the fact that his obligatory time in the bureau may be firmly delimited. In the normal case, this is only the product of a long development, in the public as well as in the private office. Formerly, in all cases, the normal state of affairs was reversed: Official business was discharged as a secondary activity.

VI. The management of the office follows general rules, which are more or less stable, more or less exhaustive, and which can be learned. Knowledge of these rules represents a special technical learning which the officials possess. It involves jurisprudence, or administrative or business management.

The reduction of modern office management to rules is deeply embedded in its very nature. The theory of modern public administration, for instance, assumes that the authority to order certain matters by decree—which has been legally granted to public authorities—does not entitle the bureau to regulate the matter by commands given for each case, but only to regulate the matter abstractly. This stands in extreme contrast to the regulation of all relationships through individual privileges and bestowals of favor, which is absolutely dominant in patrimonialism, at least insofar as such relationships are not fixed by sacred tradition.

All this results in the following for the internal and external position of the official.

I. Office holding is a "vocation." This is shown, first, in the requirement of a firmly prescribed course of training, which demands the entire capacity for work for a long period of time, and in the generally prescribed and special examinations which are prerequisites of employment. Furthermore, the position of the official is in the nature of a duty. This determines the internal structure of his relations, in the following manner: Legally and actually, office holding is not considered a source to be exploited for rents or emoluments, as was normally the case during the Middle Ages and frequently up to the threshold of recent times. . . . Entrances into an office, including one in the private economy, is considered an acceptance of a specific obligation of faithful management in return for a secure existence. It is decisive for the specific nature of modern loyalty to an office that, in the pure type, it does not establish a relationship to a *person,* like the vassal's or disciple's faith in feudal or in patrimonial relations and authority. Modern loyalty is devoted to impersonal and functional purposes. . . .

II. The personal position of the official is patterned in the following way:

(1) Whether he is in a private office or a public bureau, the modern official always strives and usually enjoys a distinct *social esteem* as compared with the governed. His social position is guaranteed by the prescriptive rules of rank order and, for the political official, by special definitions of the criminal code against "insults of officials" and "contempt" of state and church authorities.

The actual social position of the official is normally highest where, as in old civilized countries, the following conditions prevail: a strong demand for administration by trained experts; a strong and stable social differentiation, where the official predominantly derives from socially and economically privileged strata because of the social distribution of power; or where the costliness of the required training and status conventions are binding upon him. The possession of educational certificates—to be discussed elsewhere— are usually linked with qualification for office. Naturally, such certificates or patents enhance the "status element" in the social position of the official. . . .

Usually the social esteem of the officials as such is especially low where the demand for expert administration and the dominance of status conventions are weak. This is especially the case in the United States; it is often the case in new settlements by virtue of their wide fields for profit-taking and the great instability of their social stratification.

(2) The pure type of bureaucratic official is *appointed* by a superior authority. An official elected by the governed is not a purely bureaucratic figure. Of course, the formal existence of an election does not by itself mean that no appointment hides behind the election—in the state, especially, appointment by party chiefs. Whether or not this is the case does not depend upon legal statutes but upon the way in which the party mechanism functions. Once firmly organized, the parties can turn a formally free election into the mere acclamation of a candidate designated by the party chief. As a rule, however, a formally free election is turned into a fight, conducted according to definite rules, for votes in favor of one of two designated candidates. . . .

(3) Normally, the position of the official is held for life, at least in public bureaucracies; and this is increasingly the case for all similar structures. As a factual rule, *tenure for life* is presupposed, even where the giving of notice or periodic reappointment occurs. In contrast to the worker in a private enterprise, the official normally holds tenure. Legal or ac-

tual life-tenure, however, is not recognized as the official's right to the possession of office, as was the case with many structures of authority in the past. Where legal guarantees against arbitrary dismissal of transfer are developed, they merely serve to guarantee a strictly objective discharge of specific office duties free from all personal considerations. . . .

(4) The official receives the regular *pecuniary* compensation of a normally fixed *salary* and the old age security provided by a pension. The salary is not measured like a wage in terms of work done, but according to "status," that is, according to the kind of function (the "rank") and, in addition, possibly, according to the length of service. The relatively great security of the official's income, as well as the rewards of social esteem, make the office a sought-after position. . . .

(5) The official is set for a *"career"* within the hierarchical order of the public service. He moves from the lower, less important, and lower paid to the higher positions. The average official naturally desires a mechanical fixing of the conditions of promotion: if not of the offices, at least of the salary levels. He wants these conditions fixed in terms of "seniority," or possibly according to grades achieved in a developed system of expert examinations. . . .

CRITICAL-THINKING QUESTIONS

1. In what respects is bureaucracy impersonal? What are some of the advantages and disadvantages of this impersonality?

2. Through most of human history, kinship has been the foundation of social organization. Why is kinship missing from Weber's analysis of bureaucracy? On what other basis are people selected for bureaucratic positions?

3. Why does bureaucracy take a hierarchical form? Do you think formal organization must be hierarchical?

25

McJobs: McDonaldization and the Workplace

George Ritzer

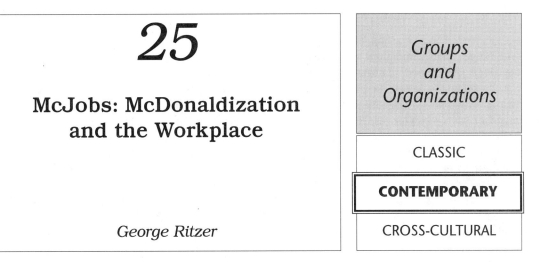

Groups and Organizations

CLASSIC

CONTEMPORARY

CROSS-CULTURAL

A decade ago, George Ritzer coined the term "McDonaldization" to refer to a set of organizational principles—including efficiency, uniformity, predictability, and control—that play an important part in today's society. Here, he describes the way McDonald's and similar organizations control not just their workers, but also their customers.

In recent years the spread of McDonaldized systems has led to the creation of an enormous number of jobs. Unfortunately, the majority of them can be thought of as McDonaldized jobs, or "McJobs." While we usually associate these types of positions with fast-food restaurants, and in fact there are many such jobs in that setting (over 2.5 million people worked in that industry in the United States in 1992 [Van Giezen, 1994]), McJobs have spread throughout much of the economy with the growing impact of McDonaldization on work settings which had previously experienced relatively little rationalization.

It is worth outlining some of the basic realities of employment in the fast-food industry in the United States since those jobs serve as a model for employment in other McDonaldized settings (Van Giezen, 1994). The large number of people employed in fast-food restaurants accounts for over 40 percent of the approximately 6 million people employed in restaurants of all types. Fast-food restaurants rely heavily on teenage employees—almost 70 percent of their employees are twenty years of age or younger. For many, the fast-food restaurant is likely to be their first employer. It is estimated that the first job for one of every fifteen workers was at McDonald's; one of every eight Americans has worked at McDonald's at some time in his or her life. The vast majority of employees are part-time workers: The average work week in the fast-food industry is 29.5 hours. There is a high turnover rate: Only slightly more than half the employees remain on the job for a year or more. Minorities are overrepresented in these jobs—almost two-thirds of employees are women and nearly a quarter are non-white. These are low-paid occupations, with many earning the minimum wage, or slightly more. As a result, these jobs are greatly affected by changes in the minimum wage: An upward revision has an important effect on the income of these workers. However, there is a real danger that many workers would lose their positions as a result of such increases, especially in economically marginal fast-food restaurants.[1]

Although the McDonaldization of society is manifest at all levels and in all realms of the social world, the work world has played a particularly pivotal role in this. On the one hand, it is the main source of many of the precursors of McDonaldization, including bureaucracies, scientific management, assembly lines, and so on. More contemporaneously, the kinds of jobs, work procedures, and organizing principles that have made McDonald's so successful have affected the way in which many businesses now organize much of their work. In fact, it could well be argued that the primary root of the McDonaldization of the larger society is the work world. On the other hand, the McDonaldization of the larger society has, in turn, served to further rationalize the work world. We thus have a self-reinforcing and enriching process that is speeding the growth and spread of McDonaldization.

The process of McDonaldization is leading to the creation of more and more McJobs.[2] The service sector, especially at its lower end, is producing an enormous number of jobs, most of them requiring little or no skill. There is no better example of this than the mountain of jobs being produced by the fast-food industry. However, new occupational creation is not the only source of McJobs: Many extant low-level jobs are being McDonaldized. More strikingly, large numbers of middle-level jobs are also being deskilled and transformed into McJobs.

McJobs are characterized by the five dimensions of McDonaldization. The jobs tend to involve a series of simple tasks in which the emphasis is on performing each as efficiently as possible. Second, the time associated with many of the tasks is carefully calculated and the emphasis on the quantity of time a task should take tends to diminish the quality of the work from the point of view of the worker. That is, tasks are so simplified and streamlined that they provide little or no meaning to the worker. Third, the work is predictable: employees do and say essentially the same things hour after hour, day after day. Fourth, many nonhuman technologies are employed to control workers and reduce them to robotlike actions. Some technologies are in place, and others are in development, that will lead to the eventual replacement of many of these "human robots" with computerized robots. Finally, the rationalized McJobs lead to a variety of irrationalities, especially the dehumanization of work. The result is the extraordinarily high turnover rate described above and difficulty in maintaining an adequate supply of replacements.[3]

The claim is usually made by spokespeople for McDonaldized systems that they are offering a large number of entry-level positions that help give employees basic skills they will need in order to move up the occupational ladder within such systems (and many of them do). This is likely to be true in the instances in which the middle-level jobs to which they move—for example shift leader, assistant manager, or manager of a fast-food restaurant—are also routinized and scripted. In fact, it turns out that this even holds for the positions held by the routinized and scripted instructors at [McDonald's training program at] Hamburger University who teach the managers, who teach the employees, and so on. However, the skills acquired in McJobs are not likely to prepare one for, help one to acquire, or help one to function well in, the far more desirable postindustrial occupations which are highly complex and require high levels of skill and education. Experience in routinized actions and scripted interactions do not help much when occupations require thought and creativity. . . .

At the cultural level, large numbers of people in the United States, and increasingly throughout much of the rest of the world, have come to value McDonaldization in general, as well as its fundamental characteristics. McDonaldization, as well as its various principles, has become part of our value system. That value system has, in turn, been translated into a series of principles that have been exported to, adopted by, and adapted to, a wide range of social settings. . . .

. . . For example, the behavior of customers at fast-food restaurants is being affected in much the same way as the behavior of those who work in those restaurants. . . .

The constraints on the behavior of employees and customers in McDonaldized systems are of both a structural and a cultural nature. Employees and customers find themselves in a variety of McDonaldized structures that demand that they behave in accord with the dictates of those structures. For example, the drive-through window associated with the fast-food restaurant (as well as other settings such as banks) structures both what customers in their cars and employees in their booths can and cannot do. They can efficiently exchange money for food, but their positions (in a car and a booth) and the press of other cars in the queue make any kind of personal interaction virtually impossible. Of course, many other kinds of behavior are either made possible, or prohibited, by such structures. In Giddens's (1984) terms, such structures are both enabling and constraining.

At a cultural level, both employees and customers are socialized into, and have internalized, the norms and values of working and living in a McDonaldized society. Employees are trained by managers or owners who are likely, themselves, to have been trained at an institution like McDonald's Hamburger University (Schaaf, 1991). Such institutions are as much concerned with inculcating norms and values as they are with the teaching of basic skills. For their part, customers are not required to attend Hamburger University, but they are "trained" by the employees themselves, by television advertisements, and by their own children who are often diligent students, teachers, and enforcers of the McDonald's way. This "training," like that of those employees who attend Hamburger University, is oriented not only to teaching the "skills" required to be a customer at a fast-food restaurant (e.g. how to queue up in order to order food), but also the norms and values of such settings as they apply to customers (e.g. customers are expected to dispose of their own debris; they are not expected to linger after eating). As a result of such formal and informal training, both employees and customers can be relied on to do what they are supposed to, and what is expected of them, with little or no personal supervision. . . .

. . . McJobs are not simply the deskilled jobs of our industrial past in new settings; they are jobs that have a variety of new and distinctive characteristics. . . . Industrial and McDonaldized jobs both tend to be highly routinized in terms of what people do on the job. However, one of the things that is distinctive about McDonaldized jobs, especially since so many of them involve work that requires interaction and communication, especially with consumers, is that what people *say* on the job is also highly routinized. To put this another way, McDonaldized jobs are tightly scripted: They are characterized by *both* routinized actions (for example, the way McDonald's hamburgers are to be put down on the grill and flipped [Love, 1986: 141–2]) and scripted interactions (examples include, "May I help you?"; "Would you like a dessert to go with your meal?"; "Have a nice day!"). Scripts are crucial because, as Leidner (1993) points out, many of the workers in McDonaldized systems are interactive service workers. This means that they not only produce goods and provide services, but they often do so in interaction with customers.

The scripting of interaction leads to new depths in the deskilling of workers. Not only have employee actions been deskilled; employees' ability to speak and interact with customers is now being limited and controlled. There are not only scripts to handle general situations, but also a range of subscripts to deal with a variety of contingencies. Verbal and interactive skills are being taken away from employees and built into the scripts in much the same way that manual skills were taken and built into various technologies. At one time distrusted in their ability to *do* the right thing, workers now find themselves no longer trusted to *say* the right thing. Once able to create distinctive interactive styles, and to adjust them to different circumstances, employees are now asked to follow scripts as mindlessly as possible. . . .

One very important, but rarely noted, aspect of the labor process in the fast-food restaurant and other McDonaldized systems is the extent to which customers are being led, perhaps even almost required, to perform a number of tasks without pay that were formerly performed by paid employees. For example, in the modern gasoline station the driver now does various things for free (pumps gas, cleans windows, checks oil, even pays through a computerized credit card system built into the pump) that were formerly done by paid attendants. In these and many other settings, McDonaldization has brought the customer *into* the labor process: The customer *is* the laborer! This has several advantages for employers such as lower (even nonexistent) labor costs, the need for fewer employees, and less trouble with personnel problems: Customers are far less likely to complain about a few seconds or minutes of tedious work than employees who devote a full work day to such tasks. Because of its advantages, as well as because customers are growing accustomed to and accepting of it, I think customers are likely to become even more involved in the labor process.

This is the most revolutionary development, at least as far as the labor process is concerned, associated with McDonaldization. As a result of this dramatic change, the analysis of the labor process must be extended to what customers do in McDonaldized systems. The distinction between customer and employee is eroding, or in postmodern terms "imploding," and one can envision more and more work settings in which customers are asked to do an increasing amount of "work." More dramatically, it is also likely that we will see more work settings in which there are no employees at all! In such settings customers, in interaction with nonhuman technologies, will do *all* of the human labor. A widespread example is the ATM in which customers (and the technology) do all of the work formerly done by bank tellers. More strikingly, we are beginning to see automated loan machines which dispense loans as high as $10,000 (Singletary, 1996). Again, customers and technologies do the work and, in the process, many loan-officer positions are eliminated. Similarly, the new automated gasoline pumps allow (or force) customers to do all of the required tasks; in some cases and at certain times (late at night) no employees at all are present.

In a sense, a key to the success of McDonaldized systems is that they have been able to supplement the exploitation of employees with the exploitation of customers. Lest we forget, Marx "put at the heart of his sociology—as no other sociology does—the theme of exploitation" (Worsley, 1982:115). In Marxian theory, the capitalists are seen as simply paying workers less than the value produced by the workers, and as keeping the rest for themselves. This dynamic continues in contemporary society, but capitalists have learned that they can ratchet up the level of exploitation not only by exploiting workers more, but also by exploiting a whole new group of people—consumers. In Marxian terms, customers create value in the tasks they perform for McDonaldized systems. And they are not simply paid less than the value they produce, they are paid *nothing at all*. In this way, customers are exploited to an even greater degree than workers. . . .

While no class within society is immune to McDonaldization, the lower classes are the most affected. They are the ones who are most likely to go to McDonaldized schools, live in inexpensive, mass-produced tract houses, and work in McDonaldized jobs. Those in the upper classes have much more of a chance of sending their children to non-McDonaldized schools, living in custom-built homes, and working in occupations in which they impose McDonaldization on others while avoiding it to a large degree themselves.

Also related to the social class issue . . . is the fact that the McDonaldization of a significant portion of the labor force does not mean that all, or even most, of the labor force is undergoing this process. In fact, the McDonaldization of some of the labor force is occurring at the same time that another large segment is moving in a postindustrial, that is, more highly skilled, direction (Hage & Powers, 1992). Being created in this sector of society are relatively high-status, well-paid occupations requiring high levels of education and training. In the main, these are far from McJobs and lack most, or all, of the dimensions discussed at the beginning of this [reading]. The growth of such postindustrial occupations parallels the concern in the labor process literature with flexible specialization occurring side by side with the deskilling of many other jobs. This points to a bifurcation in the class system. In spite of appearances, there is no contradiction here; McDonaldization and postindustrialization tend to occur in different sectors of the labor market. However, the spread of McJobs leads us to be dubious of the idea that we have moved into a new postindustrial era and have left behind the kind of deskilled jobs we associate with industrial society.

CRITICAL-THINKING QUESTIONS

1. Describe ways in which McDonaldization is evident in a number of familiar settings (not just the workplace, but perhaps shopping malls and even the college campus). What elements of McDonaldization can you find?
2. In what ways does a McDonaldized setting control not just workers but customers as well? Why do organizations want to control customers?
3. Why does McDonaldization seem to appeal to many people? Do you think this process is good for society as a whole or harmful? Why?

NOTES

This chapter combines a paper, "McJobs," published in Rich Feller and Garry Walz (eds.), *Career Transitions in Turbulent Times* (Greensboro, N.C.: ERIC/CASS Publications, 1996) and the Invited Plenary Address, International Labour Process Conference, Blackpool, England, April, 1995.

1. Although a study by Katz and Krueger (1992) indicates an employment *increase* accompanying a rise in the minimum wage.
2. As we will see below, other kinds of high-status, high-paying postindustrial occupations are also growing.
3. There are, of course, many other factors involved in turnover.

REFERENCES

GIDDENS, ANTHONY. 1984. *The constitution of society: Outline of the theory of structuration*. Berkeley, Calif.: University of California Press.

HAGE, JERALD, and CHARLES H. POWERS. 1992. *Post-industrial lives: Roles and relationships in the 21st century*. Newbury Park, Calif.: Sage.

LEIDNER, ROBIN. 1993. *Fast food, fast talk: Service work and the routinization of everyday life*. Berkeley, Calif.: University of California Press.

LOVE, JOHN. 1986. *McDonald's: Behind the arches*. Toronto: Bantam Books.

SCHAAF, DICK. 1994. Inside Hamburger University. *Training*, December: 18–24.

SINGLETARY, MICHELLE. 1996. Borrowing by the touch. *Washington Post*, 30 March: C1, C2.

VAN GIEZEN, ROBERT W. 1994. Occupational wages in the fast-food restaurant industry. *Monthly Labor Review*, August: 24–30.

WORSLEY, PETER. 1982. *Marx and Marxism*. Chichester: Ellis Horwood.

Groups and Organizations

CLASSIC

CONTEMPORARY

CROSS-CULTURAL

26

Japanese Etiquette and Ethics in Business

Boye De Mente

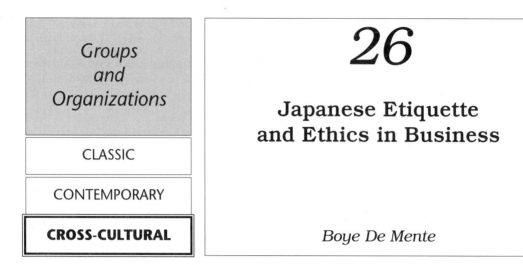

Businesses in different cultures vary in managerial style and organizational philosophy. Members of our society have a growing interest in the organizational practices of Japan, a nation that has had remarkable economic success in recent decades. Because the economies of Japan and the United States are increasingly linked, there are practical benefits to understanding the cultural patterns of this economic superpower.

SHU-SHIN KOYO *(IT'S FOR LIFE)*

Probably the most talked about and notorious facet of Japan's family-patterned company system is *shu-shin koyo* (shuu-sheen koe-yoe), or "lifetime employment," which applies, however, to only an elite minority of the nation's workers. Although a direct descendant of feudal Japan, when peasants and craftsmen were attached to a particular clan by birth, the lifetime employment system did not become characteristic of large-scale modern Japanese industry until the 1950s. In the immediate postwar period, losing one's job was tantamount to being sentenced to starvation. To prevent employees from being fired or arbitrarily laid off, national federation union leaders took advantage of their new freedom and the still weak position of industry to force adoption of the lifetime employment system by the country's major enterprises.

Under the lifetime employment system, all *permanent* employees of larger companies and government bureaus are, in practice, hired for life. These organizations generally hire only once a year, directly from schools. Well before the end of the school year, each company and government ministry or agency decides on how many new people it wants to bring in. The company or government bureau then invites students who are to graduate that year (in some cases only from certain universities) to take written and oral examinations for employment.

One company, for example, may plan on taking 200 university graduates as administrative trainees, and 500 junior and senior high school graduates for placement in blue-collar work. Since "permanent" employment is "for life," companies are careful to select candidates who have well-rounded personalities and are judged most likely to adjust to that particular company or agency's philosophy and "style."

Source: From *Japanese Etiquette and Ethics in Business,* 5th ed., by Boye De Mente (Lincolnwood, Ill.: NTC Business Books, 1987), pp. 71–81, 84–89, 91–97. Copyright © 1987. Reprinted with permission.

This method of employee selection is known as *Shikaku Seido* or "Personal Qualifications System." This means that new employees are selected on the basis of their education, character, personality, and family backgrounds; as opposed to work experience or technological backgrounds.

A larger Japanese company hiring new employees, as well as firms entering into new business tie-ups, are sometimes compared to *miai kekkon* or "arranged marriages." The analogy is a good one. Both employment and joint-venture affiliations are, in principle, for life. Therefore, both parties want to be sure not only of the short-term intentions of the potential partner but also of the character and personality—even if there are any "black sheep" in the family. Thus both prospective employee and potential business partner must undergo close scrutiny. When the Japanese commit themselves, the commitment is expected to be total.

Choosing employees on the basis of personal qualifications is especially important to Japanese supervisors and managers, because they personally cannot hire, fire, or hold back promotions. They must acquire and keep the trust, goodwill, and cooperation of their subordinates, and manage by example and tact.

Besides exercising control over employee candidates by allowing only students from certain universities to take their entrance examinations, many companies in Japan also depend upon well-known professors in specific universities to recommend choice candidates to them each year. The reputations of some professors, especially in the physical sciences, are often such that they can actually "parcel out" the best students from their graduating classes to top firms in their field.

NENKO JORETSU *(THE "MERIT OF YEARS")*

Once hired by a larger company, the permanent Japanese employee who is a university graduate is on the first rung of a pay/promotion escalator system that over the years will gradually and automatically take him to or near the upper management level. This is the famous (or infamous) *nenko joretsu* (nane-koe joe-ray-t'sue), "long-service rank" or seniority system, under which pay and promotions are primarily based on longevity.

Not surprisingly, the employee, at least in administrative areas, is considered more important than the job in the Japanese company system. As a result, job classifications on the administrative level may be clear enough, but specific duties of individuals tend to be ill-defined or not defined at all. Work is more or less assigned on a collective basis, and each employee tends to work according to his or her ability and inclinations. Those who are capable, diligent, and ambitious naturally do most of the work. Those who turn out to be lazy or incompetent are given tasks befitting their abilities and interests.

Young management trainees are switched from one job to another every two or three years, and in larger companies they are often transferred to other offices or plants. The reason for this is to expose them to a wide range of experiences so they will be more valuable to the company as they go up the promotion ladder. Individuals are "monitored" and informally rated, and eventually the more capable are promoted faster than the other members of their age group. The ones promoted the fastest usually become managing directors; and one of their number generally becomes president.

During the first twelve to fifteen years of employment, the most capable junior managers accrue status instead of more pay raises and faster promotions. If they prove to be equally capable in their personal relations with others, they are the ones who are eventually singled out to reach the upper levels of the managerial hierarchy.

The seniority system in Japanese companies takes ordinary, even incapable, people who have toed the company line and made no blunders, to the head of departments, and occasionally to the head of companies. But their limitations are recognized, and the department or company is run by competent people below them, with little or no damage to the egos of the less capable executives or to the overall harmony within the firm.

Each work-section of a Japanese company is three-layered, consisting of young, on-the-job trainees (a status that often lasts for several years); mature, experienced workers who carry most of the burden; and older employees whose productivity has fallen off due to their age.

Direct, specific orders do not set well with the members of these work-sections. Such orders leave them with the impression they are not trusted and that management has no respect for them. Even the lowest clerk or delivery boy in a company is very sensitive about being treated with respect. The Japanese say they prefer general "ambiguous" instructions. All that work-groups want from management "are goals and direction."

Because human relations are given precedence in the Japanese management system, great importance is attached to the "unity of employees" within each of these groups. The primary responsibility of the senior manager in a group is not to direct the people in their work but to make "adjustments" among them in order to maintain harmonious relations within the group.

"What is required of the ideal manager," say the Japanese, "is that he know how to adjust human relations rather than be knowledgeable about the operation of his department or the overall function of the company. In fact, the man who is competent and works hard is not likely to be popular with other members of his group and as a result does not make a good manager," they add.

Besides "appearing somewhat incompetent" as far as work is concerned while being skilled at preventing interemployee friction, the ideal Japanese manager has one other important trait. He is willing to shoulder all the responsibility for any mistakes or failings of his subordinates—hoping, of course, there will be no loss of face.

The efficient operation of this group system is naturally based on personal obligations and trust between the manager and his staff. The manager must make his staff obligated to him in order to keep their cooperation and in order to ensure that none of them will deliberately do anything or leave anything undone that would cause him embarrassment. Whatever knowledge and experience are required for the group to be productive is found among the manager's subordinates if he is weak in this area.

SEISHIN *(TRAINING IN SPIRIT)*

The Japanese associate productivity with employees having *seishin* (say-e-sheen), or "spirit," and being imbued with "Japanese morality." Company training, therefore, covers not only technical areas but also moral, philosophical, aesthetic, and political factors. Each of the larger companies has its own particular company philosophy and image, which are incorporated into its training and indoctrination programs. This is one of the prime reasons . . . major Japanese companies prefer not to hire older, experienced "outsiders"; it is assumed that they could not wholly accept or fit into the company mold.

ONJO SHUGI *("MOTHERING" EMPLOYEES)*

The amount of loyalty, devotion, and hard work displayed by most Japanese employees is in direct proportion to the paternalism, *onjo shugi* (own-joe shuu-ghee), of the company management system. The more paternalistic (maternalistic would seem to be a better word) the company, the harder working and the more devoted and loyal employees tend to be. Japanese-style paternalism includes the concept that the employer is totally responsible for the livelihood and well-being of all employees and must be willing to go all the way for an employee when the need arises.

The degree of paternalism in Japanese companies varies tremendously, with some of them literally practicing cradle-to-grave responsibility for employees and their families. Many managers thus spend a great deal of time participating in social events involving their staff members—births, weddings, funerals, and so on.

Fringe benefits make up a very important part of the income of most Japanese workers, and they include such things as housing or housing subsidies, transportation allowances, family allowances, child allowances, health services, free recreational facilities, educational opportunities, retirement funds, etc.

The wide range of fringe benefits received by Japanese employees is an outgrowth of spiraling inflation and an increasingly heavy income tax system during the years between 1945 and 1955. Companies first began serving employees free lunches. Then larger companies built dormitories, apartments, and houses. Eventually, recreational, educational, and medical facilities were added to employee benefits.

Japan's famous twice-a-year bonuses, *shoyo* (show-yoe), were originally regarded as a fringe benefit by employees and management, but workers and unions have long since considered them an integral part of wages. Unions prefer to call the bonuses *kimatsu teate* (kee-mot-sue tay-ah-tay), or "seasonal allowances." The bonuses, usually the equivalent of two to six or eight months of base wages, are paid in midsummer just before *Obon* (Oh-bone), a major Buddhist festival honoring the dead, and just before the end of the calendar year in December.

RINJI SAIYO *(THE OUTSIDERS)*

Not all employees of Japanese companies, including the larger ones, are hired for life or come under the *nenko joretsu* system of pay and promotion. There are two distinct categories of employees in most Japanese companies: those who are hired as permanent employees under the *shu-shin koyo* and *nenko joretsu* systems, and those hired under the *rinji saiyo* or "temporary appointment" system. The latter may be hired by the day or by the year, but they cannot be hired on contract for more than one year at a time. They are paid at a lower scale than permanent employees and may be laid off or fired at any time.

The *rinji saiyo* system of temporary employees is, of course, a direct outgrowth of the disadvantages of a permanent employment system, which at most is viable only in a booming, continuously growing economy.

The rapid internationalization of Japan's leading corporations is also having a profound effect on their policies regarding young Japanese who have graduated from foreign universities. Until the mid-1980s most Japanese companies simply would not consider hiring someone who had been partly or wholly educated abroad. Their rationale was that such people were no longer 100 percent Japanese and, therefore, would not fit into the training programs or the environment of Japanese companies.

Now a growing number of Japanese corporations with large international operations are looking for young people who have been educated abroad, speak a foreign language, and already have experience in living overseas. Ricoh, for example, now has a regular policy of hiring some of its annual crop of new employees from the group of Japanese students attending American universities.

Several Japanese employment agencies are now active among Japanese students in the U.S., providing them with information about job opportunities with Japanese companies overseas.

JIMUSHO NO HANA *("OFFICE FLOWERS")*

Women, mostly young, make up a highly visible percentage of Japan's labor force, particularly in offices (where they are often referred to as *jimusho no hana* or "office flowers") and in light manufacturing industries requiring precision handwork. Most of these young women are expected to leave the work force when they get married, but increasing numbers of them are staying on after marriage, at least until they begin having children, and are returning to the labor force after their children are raised.

Equally significant is that, little by little, women are beginning to cross the barrier between staff and management, and participate in the heady world of planning and decision-making.

While female managers are still generally confined to such industries as public relations, advertising, publishing, and retailing, economic and social pressures are gradually forcing other industries as well to begin thinking about desegregating their male-only management systems.

Another highly conspicuous phenomenon in Japan today is the growing number of women who head up their own successful companies in such areas as real estate, cosmetics, apparel, and the food business.

The world of Japanese business is still very much a male preserve, however, with many of the relationships and rituals that make up a vital part of daily business activity still closed to women. There are virtually no women in the numerous power groups, factions, clubs, and associations that characterize big business in Japan.

Foreign women who choose to do business in or with Japan face most of the same barriers that handicap Japanese women. They are unable to participate in the ritualistic after-work drinking and partying that are a major part of developing and maintaining effective business relations within the Japanese system. They cannot transcend their sex and be accepted as businesspersons first and foremost. They are unable to deal with other women on a managerial level in other companies simply because there generally are none.

They must also face the fact that most Japanese executives have had no experience in dealing with female managers, have no protocol for doing so, and are inclined to believe that women are not meant to be business managers in the first place.

This does not mean that foreign women cannot successfully engage in business in Japan, but they must understand the barriers, be able to accept them for what they are, and work around them. If they come on strong, as women or as managers, to Japanese businessmen who are traditionally oriented, they will most likely fail. They must walk a much finer line than men.

At the same time, a foreign woman who is both attractive and really clever in knowing how to use her femininity to manipulate men can succeed in Japan where others fail. This approach can be especially effective if the woman concerned is taken under the wing of an older, powerful Japanese businessman who likes her and takes a personal interest in her success.

Perhaps the most important lesson the foreign businesswoman in Japan must learn is that the Japanese regard business as a personal matter, and believe that the personal element must be satisfied before any actual business transpires. This means she must go through the process of establishing emotional rapport with her male Japanese counterparts, and convince them that she is a knowledgeable, experienced, trustworthy, and dependable business person.

It is often difficult for foreign men to develop this kind of relationship with Japanese businessmen, particularly when language is a problem, so the challenge to foreign women who want to do business in Japan (unless they go just as buyers or artists, etc.) is formidable.

The type of foreign woman who is most likely to do well in the Japanese environment is one who has a genuine affinity for the language and the culture, and appreciates both the opportunities and challenges offered by the situation. She must also have an outstanding sense of humor, be patient, and be willing to suppress some of her rational, liberal feelings.

RINGI SEIDO
(PUTTING IT IN WRITING)

In addition to the cooperative-work approach based on each employee contributing according to his or her ability and desire, many large Japanese companies divide and diversify management responsibility by a system known as *ringi seido* (reen-ghee say-ee-doe), which means, more or less, "written proposal system." This is a process by which management decisions are based on proposals made by lower level managers, and it is responsible for the "bottom-up" management associated with many Japanese companies.

Briefly, the *ringi* system consists of proposals written by the initiating section or department that are circulated horizontally and vertically to all layers of management for approval. Managers and executives who approve of the proposal stamp the document with their *hanko* (hahn-koe) name seals in the prescribed place. Anyone who disapproves either passes the document on without stamping it or puts his seal on it sideways or upside down to indicate conditional approval.

When approval is not unanimous, higher executives may send the document back with recommendations that more staff work be done on it or that the opinions of those who disapprove be taken into consideration. Managers may attach comments to the proposal if they wish.

In practice, the man who originates a *ringi-sho* (written proposal document) informally consults with other managers before submitting it for official scrutiny. He may work for weeks or months in his efforts to get the idea approved unofficially. If he runs into resistance, he will invariably seek help from colleagues who owe him favors. They in turn will approach others who are obligated to them.

The efficiency and effectiveness of the *ringi seido* varies with the company. In some it is little more than a formality, and there is pressure from the top to eliminate the system altogether. In other companies the system reigns supreme, and there is strong opposition to any talk of eliminating it. The system is so deeply entrenched in both the traditional management philosophy of the Japanese and the aspirations and ambitions of younger managers that it will no doubt be around for a long time.

The foreign businessman negotiating with a Japanese company should be aware that his proposals may be the subject of one or more *ringi-sho* which not only takes up a great deal of time (they must be circulated in the proper chain-of-status order), it also exposes them to the scrutiny of as many as a dozen or more individuals whose interests and attitudes may differ.

Whether or not a *ringi* proposal is approved by the president is primarily determined by who has approved it by the time it gets to him. If all or most of the more important managers concerned have stamped the *ringi-sho,* chances are the president will also approve it.

While this system is cumbersome and slow, generally speaking it helps build and maintain a cooperative spirit within companies. In addition, it assures that when a policy change or new program is initiated, it will have the support of the majority of managers.

As can be seen from the still widespread use of the *ringi seido,* top managers in many Japanese companies are not always planners and decision-makers. Their main function is to see that the company operates smoothly and efficiently as a team, to see that new managers are nurtured within the system, and to "pass judgment" on proposals made by junior managers.

NEMAWASHI *(BEHIND THE SCENES)*

Just as the originator of a *ringi* proposal will generally not submit it until he is fairly sure it will be received favorably, Japanese managers in general do not, unlike their foreign counterparts, hold formal meetings to discuss subjects and make decisions. They meet to agree formally on what has already been decided in informal discussions behind the scenes.

These informal discussions are called *nemawashi* (nay-mah-wah-she) or "binding up the roots"—to make sure a plant's roots are protected when it is transplanted.

Nemawashi protocol does not require that all managers who might be concerned be consulted. But agreement must always be obtained from the "right" person—meaning the individual in the department, division, or upper echelon of the company management—who really exercises power. . . .

MIBUN *(THE RIGHTS HAVE IT)*

Everybody in Japan has his or her *mibun* (me-boon), "personal rights" or "station in life," and every *bun* has its special rights and responsibilities. There are special rights and special restrictions applying to managers only, to students only, to teachers only, to workers only, etc. The restrictions of a particular category are usually clear-cut and are intended to control the behavior of the people within these categories at all times—for example, the office employee even when he is not working or the student when he isn't in school.

The traditional purpose of the feudalistic *mibun* concept was to maintain harmony within and between different categories of people. A second purpose was to prevent anyone from bringing discredit or shame upon his category or his superiors.

A good example of the *mibun* system at work was once told by Konosuke Matsushita, founder of the huge Matsushita Electric Company (Panasonic, National, etc.). At the age of ten, Matsushita was apprenticed to a bicycle shop, which meant that he was practically a slave, forced to work from five in the morning until bedtime.

In addition to his regular duties, Matsushita had to run to a tobacco store several times a day for customers who came into the bicycle shop. Before he could go, however, he had to wash. After several months of this, he hit upon the idea of buying several packs of cigarettes at one time, with his own meager savings, so that when a customer asked for tobacco, he not only could hand it to him immediately but also profit a few *sen* on each pack, since he received a discount by buying twenty packs at a time.

This pleased not only the bicycle shop customers but also Matsushita's master, who complimented him highly on his ingenuity. A few days later, however, the master of the shop told him that all the other workers were complaining about his enterprise and that he would have to stop it and return to the old system.

It was not within the *bun* of a mere flunky to demonstrate such ability.

The aims of foreign businessmen are often thwarted because they attempt to get things done by Japanese whose *bun* does not allow them to do whatever is necessary to accomplish the desired task. Instead of telling the businessmen they cannot do it or passing the matter on to someone who can, there is a tendency for the individual to wait a certain period, or until they are approached again by the businessmen, then announce that it is impossible.

In any dealings with a Japanese company, it is especially important to know the *bun* of the people representing the firm. The Japanese businessman who does have individual authority is often buttressed behind subordinates whose *bun* are strictly limited. If the outsider isn't careful, a great deal of time can be wasted on the wrong person.

It is the special freedoms or "rights" of the *bun* system that cause the most trouble. As is natural everywhere, the Japanese minimize the responsibilities of their *bun* and emphasize the rights, with the result that there are detailed and well-known rules outlining the rights of each category, but few rules covering the responsibilities.

As one disillusioned bureaucrat-turned-critic put it, "The rights of government and company bureaucrats tend to be limitless, while responsibilities are ignored or passed on to underlings. The underlings in turn say they are powerless to act without orders from above—or that it isn't their responsibility." The same critic also said that the only ability necessary to become a bureaucrat was that of escaping responsibility without being criticized.

A story related by a former editor of one of Japan's better known intellectual magazines illustrates how the *mibun* system penetrates into private life. While still an editor with the magazine, Mr. S went out one night for a few drinks with a very close writer-friend. While they were drinking, another writer, the noted Mr. D, came into the bar and joined them.

Mr. S continues: "I was not 'in charge' of Mr. D in my publishing house and didn't know him very well, but according to Japanese etiquette I should have bowed to him, paid him all kinds of high compliments, and told him how much I was obligated to him. But it was long after my working hours and I was enjoying a drink with a friend who was also a writer, so I just bowed and paid little attention to him.

"At this, Mr. D became angry and commanded me in a loud voice to go home. I refused to move, and he began shouting curses at me. I shouted back at him that I was drinking with a friend and it was none of his business, but he continued to abuse me loudly until my friend finally managed to quiet him down. Of course, I would have been fired the next day except that my friend was able to keep Mr. D from telling the directors of my company."

In doing business with a Japanese firm, it is important to find out the rank of each individual you deal with so you can determine the extent of his *bun*. It is also vital that you know the status of his particular section or department, which has its own ranking within the company.

There are other management characteristics that make it especially difficult for the uninitiated foreigner to deal with Japanese companies, including barriers to fast, efficient communication between levels of management within the companies. Everything must go through the proper chain of command, in a carefully prescribed, ritualistic way. If any link in this vertical chain is missing—away on business or sick—routine communication usually stops there. The ranking system does not allow Japanese management to delegate authority or responsibility to any important extent. Generally, one person cannot speak for another.

In fact, some Japanese observers have begun criticizing the consensus system of business and political management, saying its absolute power represents a major threat to Japan in that it prevents rapid decision-making and often makes it impossible for the Japanese to react swiftly enough to either problems or opportunities.

HISHOKAN *(WHERE ARE ALL THE SECRETARIES?)*

As most Western businessmen would readily admit, they simply could not get along without their secretaries. In many ways, secretaries are as important, if not more so, than the executives themselves. In Japan only the rare businessman has a secretary whose role approximates the function of the Western secretary.

The reason for the scarcity of secretaries in Japan is many-fold. The style of Japanese management—the collective work-groups, decision-making by consensus, face-to-face communication, and the role of the manager as harmony-keeper instead of director—practically precludes the secretarial function. Another factor is the language itself, and the different language levels demanded by the subordinate-superior system. Japanese does not lend itself to clear, precise instructions because of the requirements of etiquette. It cannot be transcribed easily or quickly, either in shorthand or by typewriter—although the appearance of Japanese-language computers in the early 1980s [began] to change that.

As a result, the Japanese are not prepared psychologically or practically for doing business through or with secretaries. The closest the typical Japanese company comes to having secretaries in the American sense are receptionists—usually pretty, young girls who are stationed at desks in building lobbies and in central floor and hall areas. They announce visitors who arrive with appointments and try to direct people who come in on business without specific appointments to the right section or department. When a caller who has never had any business with the company, and has no appointment, appears at one of the reception desks, the girl usually tries to line him up with someone in the General Affairs (*Somu Bu*) Department.

Small Japanese companies and many departments in larger companies do not have receptionists. In such cases, no specific individual is responsible for greeting and taking care of callers. The desks nearest the door are usually occupied by the lowest ranking members in the department, and it is usually up to the caller to get the attention of one of them and make his business known.

SHIGOTO *(IT'S NOT THE SLOT)*

The importance of face-to-face meetings in the conduct of business in Japan has already been mentioned. Regular, personal contact is also essential in maintaining "established relations" (the ability to *amaeru*) with business contacts. The longer two people have known each other and the more often they personally meet, the firmer this relationship.

This points up a particular handicap many foreign companies operating in Japan inadvertently impose on themselves by switching their personnel every two, three, or four years. In the normal course of business in Japan, it takes at least two years and sometimes as many as five years before the Japanese begin to feel like they really know their foreign employer, supplier, client, or colleague.

It also generally takes the foreign businessman transferred to Japan anywhere from one to three years or so to learn enough to really become effective in his job. Shortly afterward, he is transferred, recalled to the head office, is fired, or quits, and is replaced by someone else.

American businessmen in particular tend to pay too little attention to the disruption caused by personnel turnover, apparently because they think more in terms of the "position" or "slot" being filled by a "body" that has whatever qualifications the job calls for. Generally speaking, they play down the personality and character of the person filling the position and often do not adequately concern themselves with the role of human relations in business.

This, of course, is just the opposite of the Japanese way of doing things, and it accounts for a great deal of the friction that develops between Japanese and Westerners in business matters. . . .

SEKININ SHA
(FINDING WHERE THE BUCK STOPS)

In Western countries there is almost always one person who has final authority and responsibility, and it is easy to identify this person. All you have to do is ask, "Who is in charge?" In Japanese companies, however, no one individual is in charge. Both authority and responsibility are dispersed among the managers as a group. The larger the company, the more people are involved. When there are mistakes or failures, Japanese management does not try to single out any individual to blame. They try to focus on the cause of the failing in an effort to find out why it happened. In this way, the employee who made the mistake (if one individual was involved) does not lose face, and all concerned have an opportunity to learn a lesson.

Ranking Japanese businessmen advise that it is difficult to determine who has real authority and who makes final decisions in a Japanese company. Said a Sony director: "Even a top executive must consult his colleagues before he 'makes' a decision because he has become a high executive more by his seniority than his leadership ability. To keep harmony in his company he must act as a member of a family." Sony's co-founder Akio Morita adds that because of this factor, the traditional concept of promotion by seniority may not have much of a future in Japan. He agrees, however, that it is not something that can be changed in a short period of time.

In approaching a Japanese company about a business matter, it is therefore almost always necessary to meet and talk with the heads of several sections and departments on different occasions. After having gone through this procedure, you may still not get a clear-cut response from anyone, particularly if the various managers you approached have not come to a favorable consensus among themselves. It is often left up to you to synthesize the individual responses you receive and draw your own conclusions.

It is always important and often absolutely essential that the outsider (foreign or Japanese) starting a new business relationship with a Japanese company establish good rapport with each level of management in the company. Only by doing so can the outsider be sure his side of the story, his needs and expectations, will get across to all the necessary management levels.

Earle Okumura, a Los Angeles-based consultant, and one of the few Americans who is bilingual and bicultural and has had extensive business experience in Japan, suggests the following approach to establishing "lines of communication" with a Japanese company when the project concerns the introductions of new technology to be used by the Japanese firm:

Step I. Ask a director or the head of the Research and Development [R&D] Department to introduce you to the *kacho* (section chief) who is going to be directly in charge of your project within his department. Take the time to develop a personal relationship with the *kacho* (eating and drinking with him, etc.) then ask him to tell you exactly what you should do, and how you should go about trying to achieve and maintain the best possible working relationship with the company.

Step II. Ask the R&D *kacho,* with whom you now have at least the beginning of an *amae* relationship, to introduce you to his counterparts in the Production Department, Quality Control, and Sales Departments, etc., and go through the same get-acquainted process with each of them, telling them about yourself, your company, and your responsibilities. In all of these contacts, care must be taken not to pose any kind of threat or embarrassment to the different section managers.

Step III. After you have established a good, working relationship with the various *kacho* concerned, thoroughly explained your side of the project, and gained an understanding of their thinking, responsibilities, and capabilities, the third step is to get an appointment with the managing director or president of the company for a relaxed, casual conversation about policies, how much you appreciate being able to work with his company, and the advantages that should accrue to both parties as a result of the joint venture.

Do not, Okumura cautions, get involved in trying to pursue details of the project with the managing director or president. He will most likely not be familiar with them and, in any event, will be more concerned about your reliability, sincerity, and ability to deal with the company.

Before an American businessman commits himself to doing business with another company, he checks out the company's assets, technology, financial stability, etc. The Japanese businessman is first interested in the character and quality of the people in the other company and secondarily interested in its facilities and finances. The Japanese put more stock in goodwill and the quality of interpersonal relationships in their business dealings.

MIZU SHOBAI *(THE "WATER BUSINESS")*

Mizu shobai (Mee-zoo show-bye), literally "water business," is a euphemism for the so-called entertainment trade—which is another euphemism for the hundreds of thousands of bars, cabarets, night clubs, "soap houses" (formerly known as Turkish baths), hotspring spas, and geisha inns that flourish in Japan. The term *mizu* is applied to this area of Japanese life because, like pleasure, water sparkles and soothes, then goes down the drain or evaporates into the air (and the business of catering to fleshly pleasures was traditionally associated with hot baths). *Shobai* or "business" is a very appropriate word, because the *mizu shobai* is one of the biggest businesses in Japan, employing some 5 million men and women.[1]

Drinking and enjoying the companionship of attractive young women in *mizu shobai* establishments is an important part of the lives of Japanese businessmen. There are basically two reasons for their regular drinking. First, ritualistic drinking developed into an integral part of religious life in ancient times, and from there it was carried over into social and business life.

Thus, for centuries, no formal function or business dealing of any kind has been complete without a drinking party (*uchiage*) (uu-chee-ah-gay) to mark the occasion. At such times, drinking is more of a duty than anything else. Only a person who cannot drink because of some physical condition or illness is normally excused.

The second reason for the volume of customary drinking that goes on in Japan is related to the distinctive subordinate-superior relationships between people and to the minutely prescribed etiquette that prevents the Japanese from being completely informal and frank with each other *except when drinking.*

Because the Japanese must be so circumspect in their behavior at all "normal" times, they believe it is impossible to really get to know a person without drinking with him. The sober person, they say, will always hold back and not reveal his true character. They feel ill at ease with anyone who refuses to drink with them at a party or outing. They feel that refusing to drink indicates a person is arrogant, excessively proud, and unfriendly. The ultimate expression of goodwill, trust, and humility is to drink to drunkenness with your coworkers and with close or important business associates in general. Those who choose for any reason not to go all the way must simulate drunkenness in order to fulfill the requirements of the custom.

Enjoying the companionship of pretty, young women has long been a universal prerogative of successful men everywhere. In Japan it often goes further than that. It has traditionally been used as an inducement to engage in business as well as to seal bargains, probably because it is regarded as the most intimate activity men can share.

When the Japanese businessman offers his Western guest or client intimate access to the charms of attractive and willing young women—something that still happens regularly—he is not "pandering" or engaging in any other "nasty" practice. He is merely offering the Western businessman a form of hospitality that has been popular in Japan since ancient times. In short, Japanese businessmen do openly and without guilt feelings what many Western businessmen do furtively.

The foreign businessman who "passes" when offered the opportunity to indulge in this honorable Japanese custom, either before or after a bargain is struck, may be regarded as foolish or prudish for letting the opportunity go by, but he is no longer likely to be accused of insincerity.

Many Westerners find it difficult to join in wholeheartedly at the round of parties typically held for them by their Japanese hosts, especially if it is nothing more than a drinking party at a bar or cabaret. Westerners have been conditioned to intersperse their drinking with jokes, boasting, and long-winded opinions—supposedly rational—on religion, politics, business, or what-have-you.

Japanese businessmen, on the other hand, do not go to bars or clubs at night to have serious discussions. They go there to relax emotionally and physically—to let it all hang out. They joke, laugh, sing, dance, and make short, rapid-fire comments about work, their superiors, personal problems, and so on; but they do not have long, deep discussions.

When the otherwise reserved and carefully controlled Japanese businessman does relax in a bar, cabaret, or at a drinking party, he often acts—from a Western viewpoint—like a high school kid "in his cups" for the first time.

At a reception given by a group of American dignitaries at one of Tokyo's leading hotels, my table partner was the chief of the research division of the Japanese company being honored. The normally sober and distinguished scientist had had a few too many by the time the speeches began, and he was soon acting in the characteristic manner of the Japanese drunk. All during the speeches he giggled, sang, burped, and whooped it up, much to the embarrassment of both sides.

Most Japanese businessmen, particularly those in lower and middle management, drink regularly and have developed an extraordinary capacity to drink heavily night after night and keep up their day-to-day work. Since they drink to loosen up and enjoy themselves, to be hospitable and to get to know their drinking partners, they are suspicious of anyone who drinks and remains formal and sober. They call this "killing the *sake,*" with the added connotation that it also kills the pleasure.

During a boisterous drinking bout in which they sing and dance and trade risqué banter with hostesses or geisha, Japanese businessmen often sober up just long enough to have an important business exchange with a guest or colleague and then go back to the fun and games.

Foreign businessmen should be very cautious about trying to keep up with their Japanese hosts at such drinking rituals. It is all too common to see visiting businessmen being returned to their hotels well after midnight, sodden drunk. The key to this important ceremony is to drink moderately and simulate drunkenness.

In recent years, inflation has dimmed some of the nightly glow from geisha houses, the great cabarets, the bars, and the "in" restaurants in Japan's major cities. The feeling is also growing that the several billion dollars spent each year in the *mizu shobai* is incompatible with Japan's present-day needs. But like so many other aspects of Japanese life, the *mizu shobai* is deeply embedded in the overall socioeconomic system, as well as in the national psyche. It is not about to disappear in the foreseeable future.

Most of the money spent in the *mizu shobai* comes from the so-called *Sha-Yo Zoku* (Shah-Yoe Zoe-kuu), "Expense-Account Tribe"—the large number of salesmen, managers, and executives who are authorized to entertain clients, prospects, and guests at company expense. Japanese companies are permitted a substantial tax write-off for entertainment expenses to begin with, and most go way beyond the legal limit (based on their capital), according to both official and unofficial sources.

CRITICAL-THINKING QUESTIONS

1. Akio Morita, a founder of Sony Corporation, once commented that Japanese companies look more like social organizations than business enterprises (De Mente, 1987: 61). What evidence in this selection can be used to assess this observation?
2. How do Japanese business organizations differ from the ideal model of Western bureaucracy described by Max Weber (in Reading 24)?
3. What elements of Japanese business organizations explain the relatively slow entry of women into the work force, and especially into management positions?

NOTE

1. For more about the subject of *mizu shobai,* see *Bachelor's Japan* by Boye De Mente. Rutland, Vt.: Tuttle, 1967 (©1962).

REFERENCE

De Mente, B. 1987. *Japanese etiquette and ethics in business*. Lincolnwood, Ill.: NTC Business Books.

Deviance

CLASSIC

CONTEMPORARY

CROSS-CULTURAL

27

The Functions of Crime

Emile Durkheim

Common sense leads us to view crime, and all kinds of deviance, as pathological*—that is, as harmful to social life. Despite the obvious social costs of crime, however, Durkheim argues that crime is* normal *because it is part of all societies. Furthermore, he claims that crime makes important contributions to the operation of a social system.*

. . . Crime is present not only in the majority of societies of one particular species but in all societies of all types. There is no society that is not confronted with the problem of criminality. Its form changes; the acts thus characterized are not the same everywhere; but, everywhere and always, there have been men who have behaved in such a way as to draw upon themselves penal repression. . . . There is, then, no phenomenon that presents more indisputably all the symptoms of normality, since it appears closely connected with the conditions of all collective life. To make of crime a form of social morbidity would be to admit that morbidity is not something accidental, but, on the contrary, that in certain cases it grows out of the fundamental constitution of the living organism; it would result in wiping out all distinction between the physiological and the pathological. No doubt it is possible that crime itself will have abnormal forms, as, for example, when its rate is unusually high. This excess is, indeed, undoubtedly morbid in nature. What is normal, simply, is the existence of criminality. . . .

Here we are, then, in the presence of a conclusion in appearance quite paradoxical. Let us make no mistake. To classify crime among the phenomena of normal sociology is not to say merely that it is an inevitable, although regrettable, phenomenon, due to the incorrigible wickedness of men; it is to

Source: Reprinted with permission of The Free Press, a Division of Simon & Schuster, from *The Rules of Sociological Method* by Emile Durkheim, translated by S. A. Solovan and John H. Mueller. Edited by George E. G. Catlin.

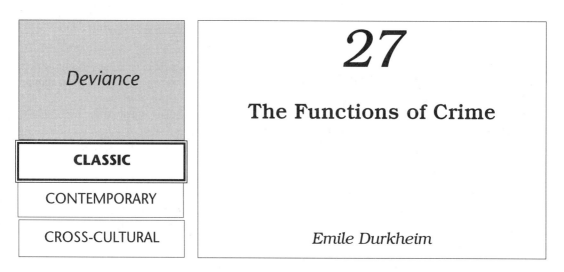

affirm that it is a factor in public health, an integral part of all healthy societies. This result is, at first glance, surprising enough to have puzzled even ourselves for a long time. Once this first surprise has been overcome, however, it is not difficult to find reasons explaining this normality and at the same time confirming it.

In the first place crime is normal because a society exempt from it is utterly impossible. Crime, we have shown elsewhere, consists of an act that offends certain very strong collective sentiments. In a society in which criminal acts are no longer committed, the sentiments they offend would have to be found without exception in all individual consciousnesses, and they must be found to exist with the same degree as sentiments contrary to them. Assuming that this condition could actually be realized, crime would not thereby disappear; it would only change its form, for the very cause which would thus dry up the sources of criminality would immediately open up new ones.

Indeed, for the collective sentiments which are protected by the penal law of a people at a specified moment of its history to take possession of the public conscience or for them to acquire a stronger hold where they have an insufficient grip, they must acquire an intensity greater than that which they had hitherto had. The community as a whole must experience them more vividly, for it can acquire from no other source the greater force necessary to control these individuals who formerly were the most refractory. For murderers to disappear, the horror of bloodshed must become greater in those social strata from which murderers are recruited; but, first it must become greater throughout the entire society. Moreover, the very absence of crime would directly contribute to produce this horror; because any sentiment seems much more respectable when it is always and uniformly respected.

One easily overlooks the consideration that these strong states of the common consciousness cannot be thus reinforced without reinforcing at the same time the more feeble states, whose violation previously gave birth to mere infraction of convention—since the weaker ones are only the prolongation, the attenuated form, of the stronger. Thus robbery and simple bad taste injure the same single altruistic sentiment, the respect for that which is another's. However, this same sentiment is less grievously offended by bad taste than by robbery; and since, in addition, the average consciousness has not sufficient intensity to react keenly to the bad taste, it is treated with greater tolerance. That is why the person guilty of bad taste is merely blamed, whereas the thief is punished. But, if this sentiment grows stronger, to the point of silencing in all consciousnesses the inclination which disposes man to steal, he will become more sensitive to the offenses which, until then, touched him but lightly. He will react against them, then, with more energy; they will be the object of greater opprobrium, which will transform certain of them from the simple moral faults that they were and give them the quality of crimes. For example, improper contracts, or contracts improperly executed, which only incur public blame or civil damages, will become offenses in law.

Imagine a society of saints, a perfect cloister of exemplary individuals. Crimes, properly so called, will there be unknown; but faults which appear venial to the layman will create there the same scandal that the ordinary offense does in ordinary consciousnesses. If, then, this society has the power to judge and punish, it will define these acts as criminal and will treat them as such. For the same reason, the perfect and upright man judges his smallest failings with a severity that the majority reserve for acts more truly in the nature of an offense. Formerly, acts of violence against persons were more frequent than they are today, because respect for individual dignity was less strong. As this has increased, these crimes have become more rare; and also, many acts violating this sentiment have been introduced into the penal law which were not included there in primitive times.[1] . . .

Crime is, then, necessary; it is bound up with the fundamental conditions of all social life, and by that very fact it is useful, because these conditions of which it is a part are themselves indispensable to the normal evolution of morality and law.

Indeed, it is no longer possible today to dispute the fact that law and morality vary from one social type to the next, nor that they change within the same type if the conditions of life are modified. But, in order that these transformations may be possible, the collective sentiments at the basis of morality must not be hostile to change, and consequently must have but moderate energy. If they were too strong, they would no longer be plastic. Every pattern is an obstacle to new patterns, to the extent that the first pattern is inflexible. The better a structure is articulated, the more it offers a healthy resistance to all modification; and this is equally true of functional, as of anatomical, organization. If there were no crimes, this condition could not have been fulfilled; for such a hypothesis presupposes that collective sentiments have arrived at a degree of intensity unexampled in history. Nothing is good indefinitely and to an unlimited extent. The authority which the moral conscience enjoys must not be excessive; otherwise no one would dare criticize it, and it would too easily congeal into an immutable form. To make progress, individual originality must be able to express itself. In order that the originality of the idealist whose dreams transcend his century may find expression, it is necessary that the originality of the criminal, who is below the level of his time, shall also be possible. One does not occur without the other.

Nor is this all. Aside from this indirect utility, it happens that crime itself plays a useful role in this evolution. Crime implies not only that the way remains open to necessary changes but that in certain cases it directly prepares these changes. Where crime exists, collective sentiments are sufficiently flexible to take on a new form, and crime sometimes helps to determine the form they will take. How many times, indeed, it is only an anticipation of future morality—a step toward what will be! According to Athenian law, Socrates was a criminal, and his condemnation was no more than just. However, his crime, namely, the independence of his thought, rendered a service not only to humanity but to his country. . . .

From this point of view the fundamental facts of criminality present themselves to us in an entirely new light. Contrary to current ideas, the criminal no longer seems a totally unsociable being, a sort of parasitic element, a strange and unassimilable body, introduced into the midst of society. On the contrary, he plays a definite role in social life.

CRITICAL-THINKING QUESTIONS

1. On what grounds does Durkheim argue that crime should be considered a "normal" element of society?
2. Why is a society devoid of crime an impossibility?
3. What are the functional consequences of crime and deviance?

NOTE

1. Calumny, insults, slander, fraud, etc.

28

Deviance

CLASSIC

CONTEMPORARY

CROSS-CULTURAL

On Being Sane in Insane Places

*David L. Rosenhan**

How do we know precisely what constitutes "normality" or mental illness? Conventional wisdom suggests that specially trained professionals have the ability to make reasonably accurate diagnoses. In this research, however, David Rosenhan provides evidence to challenge this assumption. What is—or is not—"normal" may have much to do with the labels that are applied to people in particular settings.

If sanity and insanity exist, how shall we know them?

The question is neither capricious nor itself insane. However much we may be personally convinced that we can tell the normal from the abnormal, the evidence is simply not compelling. It is commonplace, for example, to read about murder trials wherein eminent psychiatrists for the defense are contradicted by equally eminent psychiatrists for the prosecution on the matter of the defendant's sanity. More generally, there are a great deal of conflicting data on the reliability, utility, and meaning of such terms as "sanity," "insanity," "mental illness," and "schizophrenia." Finally, as early as 1934, [Ruth] Benedict suggested that normality and abnormality are not universal.[1] What is viewed as normal in one culture may be seen as quite aberrant in another. Thus, notions of normality and abnormality may not be quite as accurate as people believe they are.

To raise questions regarding normality and abnormality is in no way to question the fact that some behaviors are deviant or odd. Murder is deviant. So, too, are hallucinations. Nor does raising such questions deny the existence of the personal anguish that is often associated with "mental illness." Anxiety and depression exist. Psychological suffering exists. But normality and abnormality, sanity and insanity, and the diagnoses that flow from them may be less substantive than many believe them to be.

At its heart, the question of whether the sane can be distinguished from the insane (and whether degrees of insanity can be distinguished from each other) is a simple matter: Do the salient characteristics that lead to diagnoses reside in the patients themselves or in the environments and contexts in which observers find them? From Bleuler, through Kretchmer, through

*I thank W. Mischel, E. Orne, and M. S. Rosenhan for comments on an earlier draft of this manuscript.

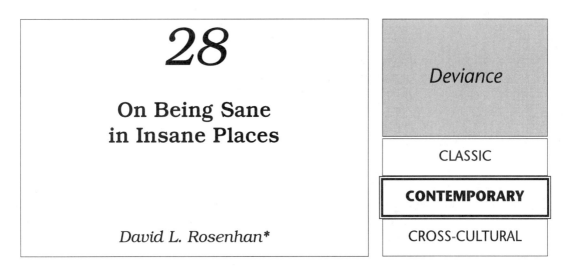

Source: Reprinted with permission from "On Being Sane in Insane Places" by David L. Rosenhan from *Science*, Vol. 179 (January 1973), pp. 250–58.

the formulators of the recently revised *Diagnostic and Statistical Manual* of the American Psychiatric Association, the belief has been strong that patients present symptoms, that those symptoms can be categorized, and, implicitly, that the sane are distinguishable from the insane. More recently, however, this belief has been questioned. Based in part on theoretical and anthropological considerations, but also on philosophical, legal, and therapeutic ones, the view has grown that psychological categorization of mental illness is useless at best and downright harmful, misleading, and pejorative at worst. Psychiatric diagnoses, in this view, are in the minds of the observers and are not valid summaries of characteristics displayed by the observed.

Gains can be made in deciding which of these is more nearly accurate by getting normal people (that is, people who do not have, and have never suffered, symptoms of serious psychiatric disorders) admitted to psychiatric hospitals and then determining whether they were discovered to be sane and, if so, how. If the sanity of such pseudopatients were always detected, there would be prima facie evidence that a sane individual can be distinguished from the insane context in which he is found. Normality (and presumably abnormality) is distinct enough that it can be recognized wherever it occurs, for it is carried within the person. If, on the other hand, the sanity of the pseudopatients were never discovered, serious difficulties would arise for those who support traditional modes of psychiatric diagnosis. Given that the hospital staff was not incompetent, that the pseudopatient had been behaving as sanely as he had been outside of the hospital, and that it had never been previously suggested that he belonged in a psychiatric hospital, such an unlikely outcome would support the view that psychiatric diagnosis betrays little about the patient but much about the environment in which an observer finds him.

This article describes such an experiment. Eight sane people gained secret admission to twelve different hospitals. Their diagnostic experiences constitute the data of the first part of this article; the remainder is devoted to a description of their experiences in psychiatric institutions. Too few psychiatrists and psychologists, even those who have worked in such hospitals, know what the experience is like. They rarely talk about it with former patients, perhaps because they distrust information coming from the previously insane. Those who have worked in psychiatric hospitals are likely to have adapted so thoroughly to the settings that they are insensitive to the impact of that experience. And while there have been occasional reports of researchers who submitted themselves to psychiatric hospitalization, these researchers have commonly remained in the hospitals for short periods of time, often with the knowledge of the hospital staff. It is difficult to know the extent to which they were treated like patients or like research colleagues. Nevertheless, their reports about the inside of the psychiatric hospital have been valuable. This article extends those efforts.

PSEUDOPATIENTS AND THEIR SETTINGS

The eight pseudopatients were a varied group. One was a psychology graduate student in his twenties. The remaining seven were older and "established." Among them were three psychologists, a pediatrician, a psychiatrist, a painter, and a housewife. Three pseudopatients were women, five were men. All of them employed pseudonyms, lest their alleged diagnoses embarrass them later. Those who were in mental health professions alleged another occupation in order to avoid the special attentions that might be accorded by staff, as a matter of courtesy or caution, to ailing colleagues.[2] With the exception of myself (I was the first pseudopatient and my presence was known to the hospital administrator and chief psychologist and, so far as I can tell, to them alone), the presence of pseudopatients and the nature of the research program was not known to the hospital staffs.[3]

The settings were similarly varied. In order to generalize the findings, admission into a variety of hospitals was sought. The twelve hospitals in the sample were located in five different states on the East and West coasts. Some were old and shabby, some were quite new. Some were research-oriented, others not. Some had good staff-patient ratios, others were quite understaffed. Only one was a strictly private hospital. All of the others were supported by state or federal funds or, in one instance, by university funds.

After calling the hospital for an appointment, the pseudopatient arrived at the admissions office complaining that he had been hearing voices. Asked what the voices said, he replied that they were often unclear, but as far as he could tell they said "empty," "hollow," and "thud." The voices were unfamiliar and were of the same sex as the pseudopatient. The choice of these symptoms was occasioned by their apparent similarity to existential symptoms. Such symptoms are alleged to arise from painful concerns about the perceived meaninglessness of one's life. It is as if the hallucinating person were saying, "My life is empty and hollow." The choice of these symptoms was also determined by the *absence* of a single report of existential psychoses in the literature.

Beyond alleging the symptoms and falsifying name, vocation, and employment, no further alterations of person, history, or circumstances were made. The significant events of the pseudopatient's life history were presented as they had actually occurred. Relationships with parents and siblings, with spouse and children, with people at work and in school, consistent with the aforementioned exceptions, were described as they were or had been. Frustrations and upsets were described along with joys and satisfactions. These facts are important to remember. If anything, they strongly biased the subsequent results in favor of detecting sanity, since none of their histories or current behaviors were seriously pathological in any way.

Immediately upon admission to the psychiatric ward, the pseudopatient ceased simulating *any* symptoms of abnormality. In some cases, there was a brief period of mild nervousness and anxiety, since none of the pseudopatients really believed that they would be admitted so easily. Indeed, their shared fear was that they would be immediately exposed as frauds and greatly embarrassed. Moreover, many of them had never visited a psychiatric ward; even those who had, nevertheless had some genuine fears about what might happen to them. Their nervousness, then, was quite appropriate to the novelty of the hospital setting, and it abated rapidly.

Apart from that short-lived nervousness, the pseudopatient behaved on the ward as he "normally" behaved. The pseudopatient spoke to patients and staff as he might ordinarily. Because there is uncommonly little to do on a psychiatric ward, he attempted to engage others in conversation. When asked by staff how he was feeling, he indicated that he was fine, that he no longer experienced symptoms. He responded to instructions from attendants, to calls for medication (which was not swallowed), and to dining-hall instructions. Beyond such activities as were available to him on the admissions ward, he spent his time writing down his observations about the ward, its patients, and the staff. Initially these notes were written "secretly," but as it soon became clear that no one much cared, they were subsequently written on standard tablets of paper in such public places as the dayroom. No secret was made of these activities.

The pseudopatient, very much as a true psychiatric patient, entered a hospital with no foreknowledge of when he would be discharged. Each was told that he would have to get out by his own devices, essentially by convincing the staff that he was sane. The psychological stresses associated with hospitalization were considerable, and all but one of the pseudopatients desired to be discharged almost immediately after being admitted. They were, therefore, motivated not only to behave sanely, but to be paragons of cooperation. That their behavior was in no way disruptive is confirmed by nursing reports, which have been obtained on most of the patients. These reports uniformly indicate that the patients were "friendly," "cooperative," and "exhibited no abnormal indications."

THE NORMAL ARE NOT DETECTABLY SANE

Despite their public "show" of sanity, the pseudopatients were never detected. Admitted, except in one case, with a diagnosis of schizophrenia,[4] each was discharged with a diagnosis of schizophrenia "in remission." The label "in remission" should in no way be dismissed as a formality, for at no time during any hospitalization had any question been raised about any pseudopatient's simulation. Nor are there any indications in the hospital records that the pseudopatient's status was suspect. Rather, the evidence is strong that, once labeled schizophrenic, the pseudopatient was stuck with that label. If the pseudopatient was to be discharged, he must naturally be "in remission"; but he was not sane, nor, in the institution's view, had he ever been sane.

The uniform failure to recognize sanity cannot be attributed to the quality of the hospitals, for, although there were considerable variations among them, several are considered excellent. Nor can it be alleged that there was simply not enough time to observe the pseudopatients. Length of hospitalization ranged from seven to fifty-two days, with an average of nineteen days. The pseudopatients were not, in fact, carefully observed, but this failure clearly speaks more to traditions within psychiatric hospitals than to lack of opportunity.

Finally, it cannot be said that the failure to recognize the pseudopatients' sanity was due to the fact that they were not behaving sanely. While there was clearly some tension present in all of them, their daily visitors could detect no serious behavioral consequences—nor, indeed, could other patients. It was quite common for the patients to "detect" the pseudopatients' sanity. During the first three hospitalizations, when accurate counts were kept, 35 of a total of 118 patients on the admissions ward voiced their suspicions, some vigorously. "You're not crazy. You're a journalist, or a professor [referring to the continual note-taking]. You're checking up on the hospital." While most of the patients were reassured by the pseudopatient's insistence that he had been sick before he came in but was fine now, some continued to believe that the pseudopatient was sane throughout his hospitalization. The fact that the patients often recognized normality when staff did not raises important questions.

Failure to detect sanity during the course of hospitalization may be due to the fact that physicians operate with a strong bias toward what statisticians call the type 2 error. This is to say that physicians are more inclined to call a healthy person sick (a false positive, type 2) than a sick person healthy (a false negative, type 1). The reasons for this are not hard to find: It is clearly more dangerous to misdiagnose illness than health. Better to err on the side of caution, to suspect illness even among the healthy.

But what holds for medicine does not hold equally well for psychiatry. Medical illnesses, while unfortunate, are not commonly pejorative. Psychiatric diagnoses, on the contrary, carry with them personal, legal, and social stigmas. It was therefore important to see whether the tendency toward diagnosing the sane insane could be reversed. The following experiment was arranged at a research and teaching hospital whose staff had heard these findings but doubted that such an error could occur in their hospital. The staff was informed that at some time during the following three months, one or more pseudopatients would attempt to be admitted into the psychiatric hospital. Each staff member was asked to rate each patient who presented himself at admissions or on the ward according to the likelihood that the patient was a pseudopatient. A 10-point scale was used, with a 1 and 2 reflecting high confidence that the patient was a pseudopatient.

Judgments were obtained on 193 patients who were admitted for psychiatric treatment. All staff who had had sustained contact with or primary responsibility for the patient—attendants, nurses, psychiatrists, physicians, and psychologists—were asked to make judgments. Forty-one patients were alleged, with high confidence, to be pseudopatients by at least one member of the staff. Twenty-three were considered suspect by at least one psychiatrist. Nineteen were suspected by one psychiatrist *and* one other staff member. Actually, no genuine pseudopatient (at least from my group) presented himself during this period.

The experiment is instructive. It indicates that the tendency to designate sane people as insane can be reversed when the stakes (in this case, prestige and diagnostic acumen) are high. But what can be said of the nineteen people who were suspected of being "sane" by one psychiatrist and another staff member? Were these people truly "sane," or was it rather the case that in the course of avoiding the type 2 error the staff tended to make more errors of the first sort—calling the crazy "sane"? There is no way of knowing. But one thing is certain: Any diagnostic process that lends itself so readily to massive errors of this sort cannot be a very reliable one.

THE STICKINESS OF PSYCHODIAGNOSTIC LABELS

Beyond the tendency to call the healthy sick—a tendency that accounts better for diagnostic behavior on admission than it does for such behavior after a lengthy period of exposure—the data speak to the massive role of labeling in psychiatric assessment. Having once been labeled schizophrenic, there is nothing the pseudopatient can do to overcome the tag. The tag profoundly colors others' perceptions of him and his behavior.

From one viewpoint, these data are hardly surprising, for it has long been known that elements are given meaning by the context in which they occur. Gestalt psychology made this point vigorously, and Asch[5] demonstrated that there are "central" personality traits (such as "warm" versus "cold") which are so powerful that they markedly color the meaning of other information in forming an impression of a given personality. "Insane," "schizophrenic," "manic-depressive," and "crazy" are probably among the most powerful of such central traits. Once a person is designated abnormal, all of his other behaviors and characteristics are colored by that label. Indeed, that label is so powerful that many of the pseudopatients' normal behaviors were overlooked entirely or profoundly misinterpreted. Some examples may clarify this issue.

Earlier I indicated that there were no changes in the pseudopatient's personal history and current status beyond those of name, employment, and, where necessary, vocation. Otherwise, a veridical description of personal history and circumstances was offered. Those circumstances were not psychotic. How were they made consonant with the diagnosis of psychosis? Or were those diagnoses modified in such a way as to bring them into accord with the circumstances of the pseudopatient's life, as described by him?

As far as I can determine, diagnoses were in no way affected by the relative health of the circumstances of a pseudopatient's life. Rather, the reverse occurred: The perception of his circumstances was shaped entirely by the diagnosis. A clear example of such translation is found in the case of a pseudopatient who had had a close relationship with his mother but was rather remote from his father during his early childhood. During adolescence and beyond, however, his father became a close friend, while his relationship with his mother cooled. His present relationship with his wife was characteristically close and warm. Apart from occasional angry exchanges, friction was minimal. The children had rarely been spanked. Surely there is nothing especially pathological about such a history. Indeed, many readers may see a similar pattern in their own experiences, with no markedly deleterious consequences. Observe, however, how such a history was translated in the psychopathological context, this from the case summary prepared after the patient was discharged:

> This white thirty-nine-year-old male . . . manifests a long history of considerable ambivalence in close relationships, which begins in early childhood. A warm relationship with his mother cools during his adolescence. A distant relationship to his father is described as becoming very intense. Affective stability is absent. His attempts to control emotionality with his wife and children are punctuated by angry outbursts and, in the case of the children, spankings. And while he says that he has several good friends, one senses considerable ambivalence embedded in those relationships also. . . .

The facts of the case were unintentionally distorted by the staff to achieve consistency with a popular theory of the dynamics of a schizophrenic reaction. Nothing of an ambivalent nature had been described in relations with parents, spouse, or friends. To the extent that ambivalence could be inferred, it was probably not greater than is found in all human relationships. It is true the pseudopatient's relationships with his parents changed over time, but in the ordinary context that would hardly be remarkable—indeed, it might very well be expected. Clearly, the meaning ascribed to his verbalizations (that is, ambivalence, affective instability) was determined by the diagnosis: schizophrenia. An entirely different meaning would have been ascribed if it were known that the man was "normal."

All pseudopatients took extensive notes publicly. Under ordinary circumstances, such behavior would have raised questions in the minds of observers, as, in fact, it did among patients. Indeed, it seemed so certain that the notes would elicit suspicion that elaborate precautions were taken to remove them from the ward each day. But the precautions proved needless. The closest any staff member came to questioning these notes occurred when one pseudopatient asked his physician what kind of medication he was receiving and began to write down the response. "You needn't write it," he was told gently. "If you have trouble remembering, just ask me again."

If no questions were asked of the pseudopatients, how was their writing interpreted? Nursing records for three patients indicate that the writing was seen as an aspect of their pathological behavior. "Patient engages in writing behavior" was the daily nursing comment on one of the pseudopatients who was never questioned about his writing. Given that the patient is in the hospital, he must be psychologically disturbed. And given that he is disturbed, continuous writing must be a behavioral manifestation of that disturbance, perhaps a subset of the compulsive behaviors that are sometimes correlated with schizophrenia.

One tacit characteristic of psychiatric diagnosis is that it locates the sources of aberration within the individual and only rarely within the complex of stimuli that surrounds him. Consequently, behaviors that are stimulated by the environment are commonly misattributed to the patient's disorder. For example, one kindly nurse found a pseudopatient pacing the long hospital corridors. "Nervous, Mr. X?" she asked. "No, bored," he said.

The notes kept by pseudopatients are full of patient behaviors that were misinterpreted by well-intentioned staff. Often enough, a patient would go "berserk" because he had, wittingly or unwittingly, been mistreated by, say, an attendant. A nurse coming upon the scene would rarely inquire even cursorily into the environmental stimuli of the patient's behavior. Rather, she assumed that his upset derived from his pathology, not from his present interactions with other staff members. Occasionally, the staff might assume that the patient's family (especially when they had recently visited) or other patients had stimulated the outburst. But never were the staff found to assume that one of themselves or the structure of the hospital had anything to do with a patient's behavior. One psychiatrist pointed to a group of patients who were sitting outside the cafeteria entrance half an hour before lunchtime. To a group of young residents he indicated that such behavior was characteristic of the oral-acquisitive nature of the syndrome. It seemed not to occur to him that there were very few things to anticipate in a psychiatric hospital besides eating.

A psychiatric label has a life and an influence of its own. Once the impression has been formed that the patient is schizophrenic, the expectation is that he will continue to be schizophrenic. When a sufficient amount of time has passed, during which the patient has done nothing bizarre, he is considered to be in remission and available for discharge. But the label endures beyond discharge, with the unconfirmed expectation that he will behave as a schizophrenic again. Such labels, conferred by mental health professionals, are as influential on the patient as they are on his relatives and friends, and it should not surprise anyone that the diagnosis acts on all of them as a self-fulfilling prophecy. Eventually, the patient himself accepts the diagnosis, with all of its surplus meanings and expectations, and behaves accordingly.

The inferences to be made from these matters are quite simple. Much as Zigler and Phillips have demonstrated that there is enormous overlap in the symptoms presented by patients who have been variously diagnosed,[6] so there is enormous overlap in the behaviors of the sane and the insane. The sane are not "sane" all of the time. We lose our tempers "for no good reason." We are occasionally depressed or anxious, again for no good reason. And we may find it difficult to get along with one or another person—again for no reason that we can specify. Similarly, the insane are not always insane. Indeed, it was the impression of the pseudopatients while living with them that they were sane for long periods of time—that the bizarre behaviors upon which their diagnoses were allegedly predicated constituted only a small fraction of their total behavior. If it makes no sense to label ourselves permanently depressed on the basis of an occasional depression, then it takes better evidence than is presently available to label all patients insane or schizophrenic on the basis of bizarre behaviors or cognitions. It seems more useful, as Mischel[7] has pointed out, to limit our discussions to *behaviors,* the stimuli that provoke them, and their correlates.

It is not known why powerful impressions of personality traits, such as "crazy" or "insane," arise. Conceivably, when the origins of and stimuli that give rise to a behavior are remote or unknown, or when the behavior strikes us as immutable, trait labels regarding the *behaver* arise. When, on the other hand, the origins and stimuli are known and available, discourse is limited to the behavior itself. Thus, I may hallucinate because I am sleeping, or I may hallucinate because I have ingested a peculiar drug. These are termed sleep-induced hallucinations, or dreams, and drug-induced hallucinations, respectively. But when the stimuli to my hallucinations are unknown, that is called craziness, or schizophrenia—as if that inference were somehow as illuminating as the others.

THE EXPERIENCE OF PSYCHIATRIC HOSPITALIZATION

The term "mental illness" is of recent origin. It was coined by people who were humane in their inclinations and who wanted very much to raise the station of (and the public's sympathies toward) the psychologically disturbed from that of witches and "crazies" to one that was akin to the physically ill. And they were at least partially successful, for the treatment of the mentally ill *has* improved considerably over the years. But while treatment has improved, it is doubtful that people really regard the mentally ill in the same way that they view the physically ill. A broken leg is something one recovers from, but mental illness allegedly endures forever. A broken leg does not threaten the observer, but a crazy schizophrenic? There is by now a host of evidence that attitudes toward the mentally ill are characterized by fear, hostility, aloofness, suspicion, and dread. The mentally ill are society's lepers.

That such attitudes infect the general population is perhaps not surprising, only upsetting. But that they affect the professionals—attendants, nurses, physicians, psychologists, and social workers—who treat and deal with the mentally ill is more disconcerting, both because such attitudes are self-evidently pernicious and because they are unwitting. Most mental health professionals would insist that they are sympathetic toward the mentally ill, that they are neither avoidant nor hostile. But it is more likely that an exquisite ambivalence characterizes their relations with psychiatric patients, such that their avowed impulses are only part of their entire attitude. Negative attitudes are there too and can easily be detected. Such attitudes should not surprise us. They are the natural offspring of the labels patients wear and the places in which they are found.

Consider the structure of the typical psychiatric hospital. Staff and patients are strictly segregated. Staff have their own living space, including their dining facilities, bathrooms, and assembly places. The glassed quarters that contain the professional staff, which the pseudopatients came to call "the cage," sit out on every dayroom. The staff emerge primarily for caretaking purposes—to give medication, to conduct a therapy or group meeting, to instruct or reprimand a patient. Otherwise, staff keep to themselves, almost as if the disorder that afflicts their charges is somehow catching.

So much is patient-staff segregation the rule that, for four public hospitals in which an attempt was made to measure the degree to which staff and patients mingle, it was necessary to use "time out of the staff cage" as the operational measure. While it was not the case that all time spent out of the cage was spent mingling with patients (attendants, for example, would occasionally emerge to watch television in the dayroom), it was the only way in which one could gather reliable data on time for measuring.

The average amount of time spent by attendants outside of the cage was 11.3 percent (range, 3 to 52 percent). This figure does not represent only time spent mingling with patients, but also includes time spent on such chores as folding laundry, supervising patients while they shave, directing ward cleanup, and sending patients to off-ward activities. It was the relatively rare attendant who spent time talking with patients or playing games with them. It proved impossible to obtain a "percent mingling time" for nurses, since the amount of time they spent out of the cage was too brief. Rather, we counted instances of emergence from the cage. On the average, daytime nurses emerged from the cage 11.5 times per shift, including instances when they left the ward entirely (range, 4 to 39 times). Late afternoon and night nurses were even less available, emerging on the average 9.4 times per shift (range, 4 to 41 times). Data on early morning nurses, who arrived usually after midnight and departed at 8 A.M., are not available because patients were asleep during most of this period.

Physicians, especially psychiatrists, were even less available. They were rarely seen on the wards. Quite commonly, they would be seen only when they arrived and departed, with the remaining time being spent in their offices or in the cage. On the average, physicians emerged on the ward 6.7 times per day (range, 1 to 17 times). It proved difficult to make an accurate estimate in this regard, since physicians often maintained hours that allowed them to come and go at different times.

The hierarchical organization of the psychiatric hospital has been commented on before, but the latent meaning of that kind of organization is worth noting again. Those with the most power have least to do with patients, and those with the least power are most involved with them. Recall, however, that the acquisition of role-appropriate behaviors occurs mainly through the observation of others, with the most powerful having the most influence. Consequently, it is understandable that attendants not only spend more time with patients than do any other members of the staff—that is required by their station in the hierarchy—but also, insofar as they learn from their superiors' behavior, spend as little time with patients as they can. Attendants are seen mainly in the cage, which is where the models, the action, and the power are.

I turn now to a different set of studies, these dealing with staff response to patient-initiated contact. It has long been known that the amount of time a person spends with you can be an index of your significance to him. If he initiates and maintains eye contact, there is reason to believe that he is considering your requests and needs. If he pauses to chat or actually stops and talks, there is added reason to infer that he is individuating you. In four hospitals, the pseudopatient approached the staff member with a request which took the following form: "Pardon me, Mr. [or Dr. or Mrs.] X, could you tell me when I will be eligible for grounds privileges?" (or ". . . when I will be presented at the staff meeting?" or ". . . when I am likely to be discharged?"). While the content of the question varied according to the appropriateness of the target and the pseudopatient's (apparent) current needs the form was always a courteous and relevant request for information. Care was taken never to approach a particular member of the staff more than once a day, lest the staff member become suspicious or irritated. . . . [R]emember that the behavior of the pseudopatients was neither bizarre nor disruptive. One could indeed engage in good conversation with them.

. . . Minor differences between these four institutions were overwhelmed by the degree to which staff avoided continuing contacts that patients had initiated. By far, their most common response consisted of either a brief response to the question, offered while they were "on the move" and with head averted, or no response at all.

The encounter frequently took the following bizarre form: (pseudopatient) "Pardon me, Dr. X. Could you tell me when I am eligible for grounds privileges?" (physician) "Good morning, Dave. How are you today?" (Moves off without waiting for a response.) . . .

POWERLESSNESS AND DEPERSONALIZATION

Eye contact and verbal contact reflect concern and individuation; their absence, avoidance and depersonalization. The data I have presented do not do justice to the rich daily encounters that grew up around matters of depersonalization and avoidance. I have records of patients who were beaten by staff for the sin of having initiated verbal contact. During my own experience, for example, one patient was beaten in the presence of other patients for having approached an attendant and [telling] him, "I like you." Occasionally, punishment meted out to patients for misdemeanors seemed so excessive that it could not be justified by the most radical interpretations of psychiatric canon. Nevertheless, they appeared to go unquestioned. Tempers were often short. A patient who had not heard a call for medication would be roundly excoriated, and the morning attendants would often wake patients with, "Come on, you m—f—s, out of bed!"

Neither anecdotal nor "hard" data can convey the overwhelming sense of powerlessness which invades the individual as he is continually exposed to the depersonalization of the psychiatric hospital. It hardly matters *which* psychiatric hospital—the excellent public ones and the very plush private hospital were better than the rural and shabby ones in this regard, but again, the features that psychiatric hospitals had in common overwhelmed by far their apparent differences.

Powerlessness was evident everywhere. The patient is deprived of many of his legal rights by dint of his psychiatric commitment. He is shorn of credibility by virtue of his psychiatric label. His freedom of movement is restricted. He cannot initiate contact with the staff, but may only respond to such overtures as they make. Personal privacy is minimal. Patient quarters can be entered and possessions examined by any staff member, for whatever reason. His personal history and anguish is available to any staff member (often including the "grey lady" and "candy striper" volunteer) who chooses to read his folder, regardless of their therapeutic relationship to him. His personal hygiene and waste evacuation are often monitored. The water closets may have no doors.

At times, depersonalization reached such proportions that pseudopatients had the sense that they were invisible, or at least unworthy of account. Upon being admitted, I and other pseudopatients took the initial physical examinations in a semipublic room, where staff members went about their own business as if we were not there.

On the ward, attendants delivered verbal and occasionally serious physical abuse to patients in the presence of other observing patients, some of whom (the pseudopatients) were writing it all down. Abusive behavior, on the other hand, terminated quite abruptly when other staff members were known to be coming. Staff are credible witnesses. Patients are not.

A nurse unbuttoned her uniform to adjust her brassiere in the presence of an entire ward of viewing men. One did not have the sense that she was being seductive. Rather, she didn't notice us. A group of staff persons might point to a patient in the dayroom and discuss him animatedly, as if he were not there.

One illuminating instance of depersonalization and invisibility occurred with regard to medications. All told, the pseudopatients were administered nearly 2100 pills, including Elavil, Stelazine, Compazine, and Thorazine, to name but a few. (That such a variety of medications should have been administered to patients presenting identical symptoms is itself worthy of note.) Only two were swallowed. The rest were either pocketed or deposited in the toilet. The pseudopatients were not alone in this. Although I have no precise records on how many patients rejected their medications, the pseudopatients frequently found the medications of other patients in the toilet before they deposited their own. As long as they were cooperative, their behavior and the pseudopatients' own in this matter, as in other important matters, went unnoticed throughout.

Reactions to such depersonalization among pseudopatients were intense. Although they had come to the hospital as participant observers and were fully aware that they did not "belong," they nevertheless found themselves caught up in and fighting the process of depersonalization. Some examples: A graduate student in psychology asked his wife to bring his textbooks to the hospital so he could "catch up on his homework"—this despite the elaborate precautions taken to conceal his professional association. The same student, who had trained for quite some time to get into the hospital, and who had looked forward to the experience, "remembered" some drag races that he had wanted to see on the weekend and insisted that he be discharged by that time. Another pseudopatient attempted a romance with a nurse. Subsequently, he informed the staff that he was applying for admission to graduate school in psychology and was very likely to be admitted, since a graduate professor was one of his regular hospital visitors. The same person began to engage in psychotherapy with other patients—all of this as a way of becoming a person in an impersonal environment.

THE SOURCES OF DEPERSONALIZATION

What are the origins of depersonalization? I have already mentioned two. First are attitudes held by all of us toward the mentally ill—including those who treat them—attitudes characterized by fear, distrust, and horrible expectations on the one hand, and benevolent intentions on the other. Our ambivalence leads, in this instance as in others, to avoidance.

Second, and not entirely separate, the hierarchical structure of the psychiatric hospital facilitates depersonalization. Those who are at the top have least to do with patients, and their behavior inspires the rest of the staff. Average daily contact with psychiatrists, psychologists, residents and physicians combined ranged from 3.9 to 25.1 minutes, with an overall mean of 6.8 (six pseudopatients over a total of 129 days of hospitalization). Included in this average are time spent in the admissions interview, ward meetings in the presence of a senior staff member, group and individual psychotherapy contacts, case presentation conferences, and discharge meetings. Clearly, patients do not spend much time in interpersonal contact with doctoral staff. And doctoral staff serve as models for nurses and attendants.

There are probably other sources. Psychiatric installations are presently in serious financial straits. Staff shortages are pervasive, staff time at a premium. Something has to give, and that something is patient contact. Yet, while financial stresses are realities, too much can be made of them. I have the impression that the psychological forces that result in depersonalization are much stronger than the fiscal ones and that the addition of more staff would not correspondingly improve patient care in this regard. The incidence of staff meetings and the enormous amount of recordkeeping on patients, for example, have not been as substantially reduced as has patient contact. Priorities exist, even during hard times. Patient contact is not a significant priority in the traditional psychiatric hospital, and fiscal pressures do not account for this. Avoidance and depersonalization may.

Heavy reliance upon psychotropic medication tacitly contributes to depersonalization by convincing staff that treatment is indeed being conducted and that further patient contact may not be necessary. Even here, however, caution needs to be exercised in understanding the role of psychotropic drugs. If patients were powerful rather than powerless, if they were viewed as interesting individuals rather than diagnostic entities, if they were socially significant rather than social lepers, if their anguish truly and wholly compelled our sympathies and concerns, would we not *seek* contact with them, despite the availability of medications? Perhaps for the pleasure of it all?

THE CONSEQUENCES OF LABELING AND DEPERSONALIZATION

Whenever the ratio of what is known to what needs to be known approaches zero, we tend to invent "knowledge" and assume that we understand more than we actually do. We seem unable to acknowledge that we simply don't know. The needs for diagnosis and remediation of behavioral and emotional problems are enormous. But rather than acknowledge that we are just embarking on understanding, we continue to label patients "schizophrenic," "manic-depressive," and "insane," as if in those words we had captured the essence of understanding. The facts of the matter are that we have known for a long time that diagnoses are often not useful or reliable, but we have nevertheless continued to use them. We now know that we cannot distinguish insanity from sanity. It is depressing to consider how that information will be used.

Not merely depressing, but frightening. How many people, one wonders, are sane but not recognized as such in our psychiatric institutions? How many have been needlessly stripped of their privileges of citizenship, from the right to vote and drive to that of handling their own accounts? How many have feigned insanity in order to avoid the criminal consequences of their behavior, and, conversely, how many would rather stand trial than live interminably in a psychiatric hospital—but are wrongly thought to be mentally ill? How many have been stigmatized by well-intentioned, but nevertheless erroneous, diagnoses? On the last point, recall again that a "type 2 error" in psychiatric diagnosis does not have the same consequences it does in medical diagnosis. A diagnosis of cancer that has been found to be in error is cause for celebration. But psychiatric diagnoses are rarely found to be in error. The label sticks, a mark of inadequacy forever.

Finally, how many patients might be "sane" outside the psychiatric hospital but seem insane in it—not because craziness resides in them, as it were, but because they are responding to a bizarre setting, one that may be unique to institutions which harbor nether people? Goffman[8] calls the process of socialization to such institutions "mortification"—an apt metaphor that includes the processes of depersonalization that have been described here. And while it is impossible to know whether the pseudopatients' responses to these processes are characteristic of all inmates—they were, after all, not real patients—it is difficult to believe that these processes of socialization to a psychiatric hospital provide useful attitudes or habits of response for living in the "real world."

SUMMARY AND CONCLUSIONS

It is clear that we cannot distinguish the sane from the insane in psychiatric hospitals. The hospital itself imposes a special environment in which the meanings of behavior can easily be misunderstood. The consequences to patients hospitalized in such an environment—the powerlessness, depersonalization, segregation, mortification, and self-labeling—seem undoubtedly countertherapeutic.

I do not, even now, understand this problem well enough to perceive solutions. But two matters seem to have some promise. The first concerns the proliferation of community mental health facilities, of crisis intervention centers, of the human potential movement, and of behavior therapies that, for all of their own problems, tend to avoid psychiatric labels, to focus on specific problems and behaviors, and to retain the individual in a relatively nonpejorative environment. Clearly, to the extent that we refrain from sending the distressed to insane places, our impressions of them are less likely to be distorted. (The risk of distorted perceptions, it seems to me, is always present, since we are much more sensitive to an individual's behaviors and verbalizations than we are to the subtle contextual stimuli that often promote them. At issue here is a matter of magnitude. And, as I have shown, the magnitude of distortion is exceedingly high in the extreme context that is a psychiatric hospital.)

The second matter that might prove promising speaks to the need to increase the sensitivity of mental health workers and researchers to the Catch-22 position of psychiatric patients. Simply reading materials in this area will be of help to some such workers and researchers. For others, directly experiencing the impact of psychiatric hospitalization will be of enormous use. Clearly, further research into the social psychology of such total institutions will both facilitate treatment and deepen understanding.

I and the other pseudopatients in the psychiatric setting had distinctly negative reactions. We do not pretend to describe the subjective experiences of true patients. Theirs may be different from ours, particularly with the passage of time and the necessary process of adaptation to one's environment. But we can and do speak to the relatively more objective indices of treatment within the hospital. It could be a mistake, and a very unfortunate one, to consider that what happened to us derived from malice or stupidity on the part of the staff. Quite the contrary, our overwhelming impression of them was of people who really cared, who were committed and who were uncommonly intelligent. Where they failed, as they sometimes did painfully, it would be more accurate to attribute those failures to the environment in which they, too, found themselves than to personal callousness. Their perceptions and behavior were controlled by the situation, rather than being motivated by a malicious disposition. In a more benign environment, one that was less attached to global diagnosis, their behaviors and judgments might have been more benign and effective.

CRITICAL-THINKING QUESTIONS

1. How does this research illustrate the basic ideas of labeling theory in sociology?
2. Once the "patients" were admitted to the hospitals, how was their subsequent behavior understood in terms of the label "mentally ill"? Did the label of mental illness disappear at the point at which the "patients" were discharged from the hospitals?
3. What, if any, ethical issues are raised by the way in which this research was conducted?

NOTES

1. R. Benedict, *Journal of General Psychology* 10 (1934), 59.

2. Beyond the personal difficulties that the pseudopatient is likely to experience in the hospital, there are legal and social ones that, combined, require considerable attention before entry. For example, once admitted to a psychiatric institution, it is difficult, if not impossible, to be discharged on short notice, state law to the contrary notwithstanding. I was not sensitive to these difficulties at the outset of the project, nor to the personal and situational emergencies that can arise, but later a writ of habeas corpus was prepared for each of the entering pseudopatients and an attorney was kept "on call" during every hospitalization. I am grateful to John Kaplan and Robert Bartels for legal advice and assistance in these matters.

3. However distasteful such concealment is, it was a necessary first step to examining these questions. Without concealment, there would have been no way to know how valid these experiences were; nor was there any way of knowing whether whatever detections occurred were a tribute to the diagnostic acumen of the staff or to the hospital's rumor network. Obviously, since my concerns are general ones that cut across individual hospitals and staffs, I have respected their anonymity and have eliminated clues that might lead to their identification.

4. Interestingly, of the twelve admissions, eleven were diagnosed as schizophrenic and one, with the identical symptomatology, as manic-depressive psychosis. This diagnosis has a more favorable prognosis, and it was given by the only private hospital in our sample. On the relations between social class and psychiatric diagnosis, see A. B. Hollingshead and F. C. Redlich, *Social Class and Mental Illness: A Community Study* (New York: John Wiley, 1958).

5. S. E. Asch, *Journal of Abnormal Social Psychology* 41(1946); *Social Psychology* (Englewood Cliffs, N.J.: Prentice-Hall, 1952).

6. E. Zigler and L. Phillips, *Journal of Abnormal Social Psychology* 63 (1961), 69. See also R. K. Freudenberg and J. P. Robertson, *American Medical Association Archives of Neurological Psychiatry* 76 (1956), 14.

7. W. Mischel, *Personality and Assessment* (New York: John Wiley, 1968).

8. E. Goffman, *Asylums* (Garden City, N.Y.: Doubleday, 1961).

Deviance

CLASSIC

CONTEMPORARY

CROSS-CULTURAL

29

The Code of the Streets

Elijah Anderson

In this reading, sociologist Elijah Anderson explores the cultural differences that exist in our inner cities. Alongside mainstream cultural values, he explains, exists a "code of the streets," which leads some young people to engage in crime and violence. From this point of view, crime is not so much a matter of breaking the rules as it is playing by a different set of rules.

Of all the problems besetting the poor inner-city black community, none is more pressing than that of interpersonal violence and aggression. It wreaks havoc daily with the lives of community residents and increasingly spills over into downtown and residential middle-class areas. Muggings, burglaries, carjackings, and drug-related shootings, all of which may leave their victims or innocent bystanders dead, are now common enough to concern all urban and many suburban residents. The inclination to violence springs from the circumstances of life among the ghetto poor—the lack of jobs that pay a living wage, the stigma of race, the fallout from rampant drug use and drug trafficking, and the resulting alienation and lack of hope for the future.

Simply living in such an environment places young people at special risk of falling victim to aggressive behavior. Although there are often forces in the community which can counteract the negative influences, by far the most powerful being a strong, loving, "decent" (as inner-city residents put it) family committed to middle-class values, the despair is pervasive enough to have spawned an oppositional culture, that of "the streets," whose norms are often consciously opposed to those of mainstream society. These two orientations—decent and street—socially organize the community, and their coexistence has important consequences for residents, particularly children growing up in the inner city. Above all, this environment means that even youngsters whose home lives reflect mainstream values—and the majority of homes in the community do—must be able to handle themselves in a street-oriented environment.

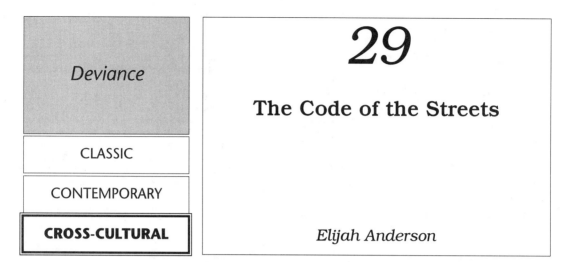

This is because the street culture has evolved what may be called a code of the streets, which amounts to a set of informal rules governing interpersonal public behavior, including violence. The rules prescribe both a proper comportment and a proper way to respond if challenged. They regulate the use of violence and so allow those who are inclined to aggression to precipitate violent encounters in an approved way. The rules have been established and are enforced mainly by the street-oriented, but on the streets the distinction between street and decent is often irrelevant; everybody knows that if the rules are violated, there are penalties. Knowledge of the code is thus largely defensive; it is literally necessary for operating in public. Therefore, even though families with a decency orientation are usually opposed to the values of the code, they often reluctantly encourage their children's familiarity with it to enable them to negotiate the inner-city environment.

At the heart of the code is the issue of respect—loosely defined as being treated "right," or granted the deference one deserves. However, in the troublesome public environment of the inner city, as people increasingly feel buffeted by forces beyond their control, what one deserves in the way of respect becomes more and more problematic and uncertain. This in turn further opens the issue of respect to sometimes intense interpersonal negotiation. In the street culture, especially among young people, respect is viewed as almost an external entity that is hard-won but easily lost, and so must constantly be guarded. The rules of the code in fact provide a framework for negotiating respect. The person whose very appearance—including his clothing, demeanor, and way of moving—deters transgressions feels that he possesses, and may be considered by others to possess, a measure of respect. With the right amount of respect, for instance, he can avoid "being bothered" in public. If he is bothered, not only may he be in physical danger but he has been disgraced or "dissed" (disrespected). Many of the forms that dissing can take might seem petty to middle-class people (maintaining eye contact for too long, for example), but to those invested in the street code, these actions become serious indications of the other person's intentions. Consequently, such people become very sensitive to advances and slights, which could well serve as warnings of imminent physical confrontation.

This hard reality can be traced to the profound sense of alienation from mainstream society and its institutions felt by many poor inner-city black people, particularly the young. The code of the streets is actually a cultural adaptation to a profound lack of faith in the police and the judicial system. The police are most often seen as representing the dominant white society and not caring to protect inner-city residents. When called, they may not respond, which is one reason many residents feel they must be prepared to take extraordinary measures to defend themselves and their loved ones against those who are inclined to aggression. Lack of police accountability has in fact been incorporated into the status system: The person who is believed capable of "taking care of himself" is accorded a certain deference, which translates into a sense of physical and psychological control. Thus the street code emerges where the influence of the police ends and personal responsibility for one's safety is felt to begin. Exacerbated by the proliferation of drugs and easy access to guns, this volatile situation results in the ability of the street-oriented minority (or those who effectively "go for bad") to dominate the public spaces.

DECENT AND STREET FAMILIES

Although almost everyone in poor inner-city neighborhoods is struggling financially and therefore feels a certain distance from the rest of America, the decent and the street family in a real sense represent two poles of value orientation, two contrasting conceptual categories. The labels "decent" and "street," which the residents themselves use, amount to evaluative judgments that confer status on local residents. The labeling is often the result of a social contest among individuals and families of the neighborhood. Individuals of the two orientations often coexist in the same extended family. Decent residents judge themselves to be so while judging others to be of the street, and street individuals often present themselves as decent, drawing distinctions between themselves and other people. In addition, there is quite a bit of circumstantial behavior—that is, one person may at different times exhibit both decent and street orientations, depending on the circumstances. Although these designations result from so much social jockeying, there do exist concrete features that define each conceptual category.

Generally, so-called decent families tend to accept mainstream values more fully and attempt to instill them in their children. Whether married couples with children or single-parent (usually female) households, they are generally "working poor" and so tend to be better off financially than their street-oriented neighbors. They value hard work and self-reliance and are willing to sacrifice for their children. Because they have a certain amount of faith in mainstream society, they harbor hopes for a better future for their children, if not for themselves. Many of them go to church and take a strong interest in their children's schooling. Rather than dwelling on the real hardships and inequities facing them, many such decent people, particularly the increasing number of grandmothers raising grandchildren, see their difficult situation as a test from God and derive great support from their faith and from the church community.

Extremely aware of the problematic and often dangerous environment in which they reside, decent parents tend to be strict in their child-rearing practices, encouraging children to respect authority and walk a straight moral line. They have an almost obsessive concern about trouble of any kind and remind their children to be on the lookout for people and situations that might lead to it. At the same time, they are themselves polite and considerate of others, and teach their children to be the same way. At home, at work, and in church, they strive hard to maintain a positive mental attitude and a spirit of cooperation.

So-called street parents, in contrast, often show a lack of consideration for other people and have a rather superficial sense of family and community. Though they may love their children, many of them are unable to cope with the physical and emotional demands of parenthood, and find it difficult to reconcile their needs with those of their children. These families, who are more fully invested in the code of the streets than the decent people are, may aggressively socialize their children into it in a normative way. They believe in the code and judge themselves and others according to its values.

In fact the overwhelming majority of families in the inner-city community try to approximate the decent-family model, but there are many others who clearly represent the worst fears of the decent family. Not only are their financial resources extremely limited, but what little they have may easily be misused. The lives of the street-oriented are often marked by disorganization. In the most desperate circumstances people frequently have a limited understanding of priorities and consequences, and so frustrations mount over bills, food, and, at times, drink, cigarettes, and drugs. Some tend toward self-destructive behavior; many street-oriented women are crack-addicted ("on the pipe"), alcoholic, or involved in complicated relationships with men who abuse them. In addition, the seeming intractability of their situation, caused in large part by the lack of well-paying jobs and the persistence of racial discrimination, has engendered deep-seated bitterness and anger in many of the most desperate and poorest blacks, especially young people. The need both to exercise a measure of control and to lash out at somebody is often reflected in the adults' relations with their children At the least, the frustrations of persistent poverty shorten the fuse in such people—contributing to a lack of patience with anyone, child or adult, who irritates them.

In these circumstances a woman—or a man, although men are less consistently present in children's lives—can be quite aggressive with children, yelling at and striking them for the least little infraction of the rules she has set down. Often little if any serious explanation follows the verbal and physical punishment. This response teaches children a particular lesson. They learn that to solve any kind of interpersonal problem one must quickly resort to hitting or other violent behavior. Actual peace and quiet, and also the appearance of calm, respectful children conveyed to her neighbors and friends, are often what the young mother most desires, but at times she will be very aggressive in trying to get them. Thus she may be quick to beat her children, especially if they defy her law, not because she hates them but because this is the way she knows to control them. In fact, many street-oriented women love their children dearly. Many mothers in the community subscribe to the notion that there is a "devil in the boy" that must be beaten out of him or that socially "fast girls need to be whupped." Thus much of what borders on child abuse in the view of social authorities is acceptable parental punishment in the view of these mothers.

Many street-oriented women are sporadic mothers whose children learn to fend for themselves when necessary, foraging for food and money any way they can get it. The children are sometimes employed by drug dealers or become addicted themselves. These children of the street, growing up with little supervision, are said to "come up hard." They often learn to fight at an early age, sometimes using short-tempered adults around them as role models. The street-oriented home may be fraught with anger, verbal disputes, physical aggression, and even mayhem. The children observe these goings-on, learning the lesson that might makes right. They quickly learn to hit those who cross them, and the dog-eat-dog mentality prevails. In order to survive, to protect oneself, it is necessary to marshal inner resources and be ready to deal with adversity in a hands-on way. In these circumstances physical prowess takes on great significance.

In some of the most desperate cases, a street-oriented mother may simply leave her young children alone and unattended while she goes out. The most irresponsible women can be found at local bars and crack houses, getting high and socializing with other adults. Sometimes a troubled woman will leave very young children alone for days at a time. Reports of crack addicts abandoning their children have become common in drug-infested inner-city communities. Neighbors or relatives discover the abandoned children, often hungry and distraught over the absence of their mother.

After repeated absences, a friend or relative, particularly a grandmother, will often step in to care for the young children, sometimes petitioning the authorities to send her, as guardian of the children, the mother's welfare check, if the mother gets one. By this time, however, the children may well have learned the first lesson of the streets: Survival itself, let alone respect, cannot be taken for granted; you have to fight for your place in the world.

CAMPAIGNING FOR RESPECT

These realities of inner-city life are largely absorbed on the streets. At an early age, often even before they start school, children from street-oriented homes gravitate to the streets, where they "hang"—socialize with their peers. Children from these generally permissive homes have a great deal of latitude and are allowed to "rip and run" up and down the street. They often come home from school, put their books down, and go right back out the door. On school nights eight- and nine-year-olds remain out until nine or ten o'clock (and teenagers typically come in whenever they want to). On the streets they play in groups that often become the source of their primary social bonds. Children from decent homes tend to be more carefully supervised and are thus likely to have curfews and to be taught how to stay out of trouble.

When decent and street kids come together, a kind of social shuffle occurs in which children have a chance to go either way. Tension builds as a child comes to realize that he must choose an orientation. The kind of home he comes from influences but does not determine the way he will ultimately turn out—although it is unlikely that a child from a thoroughly street-oriented family will easily absorb decent values on the streets. Youths who emerge from street-oriented families but develop a decency orientation almost always learn those values in another setting—in school, in a youth group, in church. Often it is the result of their involvement with a caring "old head" (adult role model).

In the street, through their play, children pour their individual life experiences into a common knowledge pool, affirming, confirming, and elaborating on what they have observed in the home and matching their skills against those of others. And they learn to fight. Even small children test one another, pushing and shoving, and are ready to hit other children over circumstances not to their liking. In turn, they are readily hit by other children, and the child who is toughest prevails. Thus the violent resolution of disputes, the hitting and cursing, gains social reinforcement. The child in effect is initiated into a system that is really a way of campaigning for respect.

In addition, younger children witness the disputes of older children, which are often resolved through cursing and abusive talk, if not aggression or outright violence. They see that one child succumbs to the greater physical and mental abilities of the other. They are also alert and attentive witnesses to the verbal and physical fights of adults, after which they compare notes and share their interpretations of the event. In almost every case the victor is the person who physically won the altercation, and this person often enjoys the esteem and respect of onlookers. These experiences reinforce the lessons the children have learned at home: Might makes right, and toughness is a virtue, while humility is not. In effect they learn the social meaning of fighting. When it is left virtually unchallenged, this understanding becomes an ever more important part of the child's working conception of the world. Over time the code of the streets becomes refined.

Those street-oriented adults with whom children come in contact—including mothers, fathers, brothers, sisters, boyfriends, cousins, neighbors, and friends—help them along in forming this understanding by verbalizing the messages they are getting through experience: "Watch your back." "Protect yourself." "Don't punk out." "If somebody messes with you, you got to pay them back." "If someone disses you, you got to straighten them out." Many parents actually impose sanctions if a child is not sufficiently aggressive. For example, if a child loses a fight and comes home upset, the parent might respond, "Don't you come in here crying that somebody beat you up; you better get back out there and whup his ass. I didn't raise no punks! Get back out there and whup his ass. If you don't whup his ass, I'll whup your ass when you come home." Thus the child obtains reinforcement for being tough and showing nerve.

While fighting, some children cry as though they are doing something they are ambivalent about. The fight may be against their wishes, yet they may feel constrained to fight or face the consequences—not just from peers but also from caretakers or parents, who may administer another beating if they back down. Some adults recall receiving such lessons from their own parents and justify repeating them to their children as a way to toughen them up: Looking capable of taking care of oneself as a form of self-defense is a dominant theme among both street-oriented and decent adults who worry about the safety of their children. There is thus at times a convergence in their child-rearing practices; although the rationales behind them may differ.

SELF-IMAGE BASED ON "JUICE"

By the time they are teenagers, most youths have either internalized the code of the streets or at least learned the need to comport themselves in accordance with its rules, which chiefly have to do with interpersonal communication. The code revolves around the presentation of self. Its basic requirement is the display of a certain predisposition to violence. Accordingly, one's bearing must send the unmistakable if sometimes subtle message to "the next person" in public that one is capable of violence and mayhem when the situation requires it, that one can take care of oneself. The nature of this communication is largely determined by the demands of the circumstances but can include facial expressions, gait, and verbal expressions—all of which are geared mainly to deterring aggression. Physical appearance, including clothes, jewelry, and grooming, also plays an important part in how a person is viewed; to be respected, it is important to have the right look.

Even so, there are no guarantees against challenges, because there are always people around looking for a fight to increase their share of respect—or "juice," as it is sometimes called on the street. Moreover, if a person is assaulted, it is important, not only in the eyes of his opponent but also in the eyes of his "running buddies," for him to avenge himself. Otherwise he risks being "tried" (challenged) or "moved on" by any number of others. To maintain his honor he must show he is not someone to be "messed with" or "dissed." In general, the person must "keep himself straight" by managing his position of respect among others; this involves in part his self-image, which is shaped by what he thinks others are thinking of him in relation to his peers.

Objects play an important and complicated role in establishing self-image. Jackets, sneakers, gold jewelry, reflect not just a person's taste, which tends to be tightly regulated among adolescents of all social classes, but also a willingness to possess things that may require defending. A boy wearing a fashionable, expensive jacket, for example, is vulnerable to attack by another who covets the jacket and either cannot afford to buy one or wants the added satisfaction of depriving someone else of his. However, if the boy forgoes the desirable jacket and wears one that isn't "hip," he runs the risk of being teased and possibly even assaulted as an unworthy person. To be allowed to hang with certain prestigious crowds, a boy must wear a different set of expensive clothes—sneakers and athletic suit—every day. Not to be able to do so might make him appear socially deficient. The youth comes to covet such items—especially when he sees easy prey wearing them.

In acquiring valued things, therefore, a person shores up his identity—but since it is an identity based on having things, it is highly precarious. This very precariousness gives a heightened sense of urgency to staying even with peers, with whom the person is actually competing. Young men and women who are able to command respect through their presentation of self—by allowing their possessions and their body language to speak for them—may not have to campaign for regard but may, rather, gain it by the force of their manner. Those who are unable to command respect in this way must actively campaign for it—and are thus particularly alive to slights.

One way of campaigning for status is by taking the possessions of others. In this context, seemingly ordinary objects can become trophies imbued with symbolic value that far exceeds their monetary worth. Possession of the trophy can symbolize the ability to violate somebody—to "get in his face," to take something of value from him, to "dis" him, and thus to enhance one's own worth by stealing someone else's. The trophy does not have to be something material. It can be another person's sense of honor, snatched away with a derogatory remark. It can be the outcome of a fight. It can be the imposition of a certain standard, such as a girl's getting herself recognized as the most beautiful. Material things, however, fit easily into the pattern. Sneakers, a pistol, even somebody else's girlfriend, can become a trophy. When a person can take something from another and then flaunt it, he gains a certain regard by being the owner, or the controller, of that thing. But this display of ownership can then provoke other people to challenge him. This game of who controls what is thus constantly being played out on inner-city streets, and the trophy—extrinsic or intrinsic, tangible or intangible—identifies the current winner.

An important aspect of this often violent give-and-take is its zero-sum quality. That is, the extent to which one person can raise himself up depends on his ability to put another person down. This underscores the alienation that permeates the inner-city ghetto community. There is a generalized sense that very little respect is to be had, and therefore everyone competes to get what affirmation he can of the little that is available. The craving for respect that results gives people thin skins. Shows of deference by others can be highly soothing, contributing to a sense of security, comfort, self-confidence, and self-respect. Transgressions by others which go unanswered diminish these feelings and are believed to encourage further transgressions. Hence one must be ever vigilant against the transgressions of others or even *appearing* as if transgressions will be tolerated. Among young people, whose sense of self-esteem is particularly vulnerable, there is an especially heightened concern with being disrespected. Many inner-city young men in particular crave respect to such a degree that they will risk their lives to attain and maintain it.

The issue of respect is thus closely tied to whether a person has an inclination to be violent, even as a victim. In the wider society people may not feel required to retaliate physically after an attack, even though they are aware that they have been degraded or taken advantage of. They may feel a great need to defend themselves *during* an attack, or to behave in such a way as to deter aggression (middle-class people certainly can and do become victims of street-oriented youths), but they are much more likely than street-oriented people to feel that they can walk away from a possible altercation with their self-esteem intact. Some people may even have the strength of character to flee, without any thought that their self-respect or esteem will be diminished.

In impoverished inner-city black communities, however, particularly among young males and perhaps increasingly among females, such flight would be extremely difficult. To run away would likely leave one's self-esteem in tatters. Hence people often feel constrained not only to stand up and at least attempt to resist during an assault but also to "pay back"—to seek revenge—after a successful assault on their person. This may include going to get a weapon or even getting relatives involved. Their very identity and self-respect, their honor, is often intricately tied up with the way they perform on the streets during and after such encounters. This outlook reflects the circumscribed opportunities of the inner-city poor. Generally people outside the ghetto have other ways of gaining status and regard, and thus do not feel so dependent on such physical displays.

BY TRIAL OF MANHOOD

On the street, among males these concerns about things and identity have come to be expressed in the concept of "manhood." Manhood in the inner city means taking the prerogatives of men with respect to strangers, other men, and women—being distinguished as a man. It implies physicality and a certain ruthlessness. Regard and respect are associated with this concept in large part because of its practical application: If others have little or no regard for a person's manhood, his very life and those of his loved ones could be in jeopardy. But there is a chicken-and-egg aspect to this situation: One's physical safety is more likely to be jeopardized in public *because* manhood is associated with respect. In other words, an existential link has been created between the idea of manhood and one's self-esteem, so that it has become hard to say which is primary. For many inner-city youths, manhood and respect are flip sides of the same coin; physical and psychological well-being are inseparable, and both require a sense of control, of being in charge.

The operating assumption is that a man, especially a real man, knows what other men know—the code of the streets. And if one is not a real man, one is somehow diminished as a person, and there are certain valued things one simply does not deserve. There is thus believed to be a certain justice to the code, since it is considered that everyone has the opportunity to know it. Implicit in this is that everybody is held responsible for being familiar with the code. If the victim of a mugging, for example, does not know the code and so responds "wrong," the perpetrator may feel justified even in killing him and may feel no remorse. He may think, "Too bad, but it's his fault. He should have known better."

So when a person ventures outside, he must adopt the code—a kind of shield, really—to prevent others from "messing with" him. In these circumstances it is easy for people to think they are being tried or tested by others even when this is not the case. For it is sensed that something extremely valuable is at stake in every interaction, and people are encouraged to rise to the occasion, particularly with strangers. For people who are unfamiliar with the code—generally people who live outside the inner city—the concern with respect in the most ordinary interactions can be frightening and incomprehensible. But for those who are invested in the code, the clear object of their demeanor is to discourage strangers from even thinking about testing their manhood. And the sense of power that attends the ability to deter others can be alluring even to those who know the code without being heavily invested in it—the decent inner-city youths. Thus a boy who has been leading a basically decent life can, in trying circumstances, suddenly resort to deadly force.

Central to the issue of manhood is the widespread belief that one of the most effective ways of gaining respect is to manifest "nerve." Nerve is shown when one takes another person's possessions (the more valuable the better), "messes with" someone's woman, throws the first punch, "gets in someone's face," or pulls a trigger. Its proper display helps on the spot to check others who would violate one's person and also helps to build a reputation that works to prevent future challenges. But since such a show of nerve is a forceful expression of disrespect toward the person on the receiving end, the victim may be greatly offended and seek to retaliate with equal or greater force. A display of nerve, therefore, can easily provoke a life-threatening response, and the background knowledge of that possibility has often been incorporated into the concept of nerve.

True nerve exposes a lack of fear of dying. Many feel that it is acceptable to risk dying over the principle of respect. In fact, among the hardcore street-oriented, the clear risk of violent death may be preferable to being "dissed" by another. The youths who have internalized this attitude and convincingly display it in their public bearing are among the most threatening people of all, for it is commonly assumed that they fear no man. As the people of the community say, "They are the baddest dudes on the street." They often lead an existential life that may acquire meaning only when they are faced with the possibility of imminent death. Not to be afraid to die is by implication to have few compunctions about taking another's life. Not to be afraid to die is the quid pro quo of being able to take somebody else's life—for the right reasons, if the situation demands it. When others believe this is one's position, it gives one a real sense of power on the streets. Such credibility is what many inner-city youths strive to achieve, whether they are decent or street-oriented, both because of its practical defensive value and because of the positive way it makes them feel about themselves. The difference between the decent and the street-oriented youth is often that the decent youth makes a conscious decision to appear tough and manly; in another setting—with teachers, say, or at his part-time job—he can be polite and deferential. The street-oriented youth, on the other hand, has made the concept of manhood a part of his very identity; he has difficulty manipulating it—it often controls him.

GIRLS AND BOYS

Increasingly, teenage girls are mimicking the boys and trying to have their own version of "manhood." Their goal is the same—to get respect, to be recognized as capable of setting or maintaining a certain standard. They try to achieve this end in the ways that have been established by the boys, including posturing, abusive language, and the use of violence to resolve disputes, but the issues for the girls are different. Although conflicts over turf and status exist among the girls, the majority of disputes seem rooted in assessments of beauty (which girl in a group is "the cutest"), competition over boyfriends, and attempts to regulate other people's knowledge of and opinions about a girl's behavior or that of someone close to her, especially her mother.

A major cause of conflicts among girls is "he say, she say." This practice begins in the early school years and continues through high school. It occurs when "people," particularly girls, talk about others, thus putting their "business in the streets." Usually one girl will say something negative about another in the group, most often behind the person's back. The remark will then get back to the person talked about. She may retaliate or her friends may feel required to "take up for" her. In essence this is a form of group gossiping in which individuals are negatively assessed and evaluated. As with much gossip, the things said may or may not be true, but the point is that such imputations can cast aspersions on a person's good name. The accused is required to defend herself against the slander, which can result in arguments and fights, often over little of real substance. Here again is the problem of low self-esteem, which encourages youngsters to be highly sensitive to slights and to be vulnerable to feeling easily "dissed." To avenge the dissing, a fight is usually necessary.

Because boys are believed to control violence, girls tend to defer to them in situations of conflict. Often if a girl is attacked or feels slighted, she will get a brother, uncle, or cousin to do her fighting for her. Increasingly, however, girls are doing their own fighting and are even asking their male relatives to teach them how to fight. Some girls form groups that attack other girls or take things from them. A hard-core segment of inner-city girls inclined toward violence seems to be developing. As one thirteen-year-old girl in a detention center for youths who have committed violent acts told me, "To get people to leave you alone, you gotta fight. Talking don't always get you out of stuff." One major difference between girls and boys: Girls rarely use guns. Their fights are therefore not life-or-death struggles. Girls are not often willing to put their lives on the line for "manhood." The ultimate form of respect on the male-dominated inner-city street is thus reserved for men.

"GOING FOR BAD"

In the most fearsome youths such a cavalier attitude toward death grows out of a very limited view of life. Many are uncertain about how long they are going to live and believe they could die violently at any time. They accept this fate; they live on the edge. Their manner conveys the message that nothing intimidates them; whatever turn the encounter takes, they maintain their attack—rather like a pit bull, whose spirit many such boys admire. The demonstration of such tenacity "shows heart" and earns their respect.

This fearlessness has implications for law enforcement. Many street-oriented boys are much more concerned about the threat of "justice" at the hands of a peer than at the hands of the police. Moreover, many feel not only that they have little to lose by going to prison but that they have something to gain. The toughening-up one experiences in prison can actually enhance one's reputation on the streets. Hence the system loses influence over the hard core who are without jobs, with little perceptible stake in the system. If mainstream society has done nothing *for* them, they counter by making sure it can do nothing *to* them.

At the same time, however, a competing view maintains that true nerve consists in backing down, walking away from a fight, and going on with one's business. One fights only in self-defense. This view emerges from the decent philosophy that life is precious, and it is an important part of the socialization process common in decent homes. It discourages violence as the primary means of resolving disputes and encourages youngsters to accept nonviolence and talk as confrontational strategies. But "if the deal goes down," self-defense is greatly encouraged. When there is enough positive support for this orientation, either in the home or among one's peers, then nonviolence has a chance to prevail. But it prevails at the cost of relinquishing a claim to being bad and tough; and therefore sets a young person up as at the very least alienated from street-oriented peers and quite possibly a target of derision or even violence.

Although the nonviolent orientation rarely overcomes the impulse to strike back in an encounter, it does introduce a certain confusion and so can prompt a measure of soul-searching, or even profound ambivalence. Did the person back down with his respect intact or did he back down only to be judged a "punk"—a person lacking manhood? Should he or she have acted? Should he or she have hit the other person in the mouth? These questions beset many young men and women during public confrontations. What is the "right" thing to do? In the quest for honor, respect, and local status—which few young people are uninterested in—common sense most often prevails, which leads many to opt for the tough approach, enacting their own particular versions of the display of nerve. The presentation of oneself as rough and tough is very often quite acceptable until one is tested. And then that presentation may help the person pass the test, because it will cause fewer questions to be asked about what he did and why. It is hard for a person to explain why he lost the fight or why he backed down. Hence many will strive to appear to "go for bad," while hoping they will never be tested. But when they are tested, the outcome of the situation may quickly be out of their hands, as they become wrapped up in the circumstances of the moment.

AN OPPOSITIONAL CULTURE

The attitudes of the wider society are deeply implicated in the code of the streets. Most people in inner-city communities are not totally invested in the code, but the significant minority of hard-core street youths who are have to maintain the code in order to establish reputations, because they have—or feel they have—few other ways to assert themselves. For these young people the standards of the street code are the only game in town. The extent to which some children—particularly those who through upbringing have become most alienated and those lacking in strong and conventional social support—experience, feel, and internalize racist rejection and contempt from mainstream society may strongly encourage them to express contempt for the more conventional society in turn. In dealing with this contempt and rejection, some youngsters will consciously invest themselves and their considerable mental resources in what amounts to an oppositional culture to preserve themselves and their self-respect. Once they do, any respect they might be able to garner in the wider system pales in comparison with the respect available in the local system; thus they often lose interest in even attempting to negotiate the mainstream system.

At the same time, many less alienated young blacks have assumed a street-oriented demeanor as a way of expressing their blackness while really embracing a much more moderate way of life;

they, too, want a nonviolent setting in which to live and raise a family. These decent people are trying hard to be part of the mainstream culture, but the racism, real and perceived, that they encounter helps to legitimate the oppositional culture. And so on occasion they adopt street behavior. In fact, depending on the demands of the situation, many people in the community slip back and forth between decent and street behavior,

A vicious cycle has thus been formed. The hopelessness and alienation many young inner-city black men and women feel, largely as a result of endemic joblessness and persistent racism, fuels the violence they engage in. This violence serves to confirm the negative feelings many whites and some middle-class blacks harbor toward the ghetto poor, further legitimating the oppositional culture and the code of the streets in the eyes of many poor young blacks. Unless this cycle is broken, attitudes on both sides will become increasingly entrenched, and the violence, which claims victims black and white, poor and affluent, will only escalate.

CRITICAL-THINKING QUESTIONS

1. Describe the major elements of what Anderson calls "the code of the streets." How does this "code" oppose mainstream values?
2. How is "the code of the streets" a product of the disadvantages, social isolation, and racism faced by many inner-city people?
3. Why do most inner-city people—even those who are poor—reject the street code?

Sexuality

CLASSIC

CONTEMPORARY

CROSS-CULTURAL

30

Understanding Sexual Orientation

Alfred C. Kinsey, Wardell B. Pomeroy, and Clyde E. Martin

In 1948, Alfred Kinsey and his colleagues published the first modern study of sexuality in the United States—and raised plenty of eyebrows. For the first time, people began talking openly about sex, questioning many common stereotypes. Here Kinsey reports his finding that sexual orientation is not a matter of clear-cut differences between heterosexuals and homosexuals, but is better described as a continuum by which most people combine elements of both.

THE HETEROSEXUAL-HOMOSEXUAL BALANCE

Concerning patterns of sexual behavior, a great deal of the thinking done by scientists and laymen alike stems from the assumption that there are persons who are "heterosexual" and persons who are "homosexual" that these two types represent antitheses in the sexual world, and that there is only an insignificant class of "bisexuals" who occupy an intermediate position between the other groups. It is implied that every individual is innately—inherently—either heterosexual or homosexual. It is further implied that from the time of birth one is fated to be one thing or the other, and that there is little chance for one to change his pattern in the course of a lifetime.

It is quite generally believed that one's preference for a sexual partner of one or the other sex is correlated with various physical and mental qualities, and with the total personality which makes a homosexual male or female physically, psychically, and perhaps spiritually distinct from a heterosexual individual. It is generally thought that these qualities make a homosexual person obvious and recognizable to anyone who has a sufficient understanding of such matters. Even psychiatrists discuss "the homosexual personality"

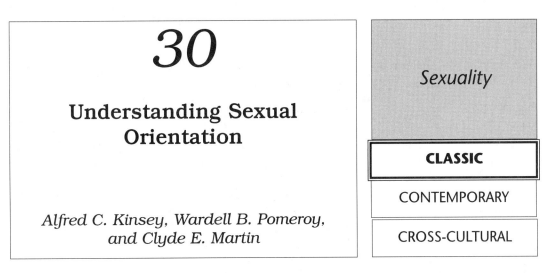

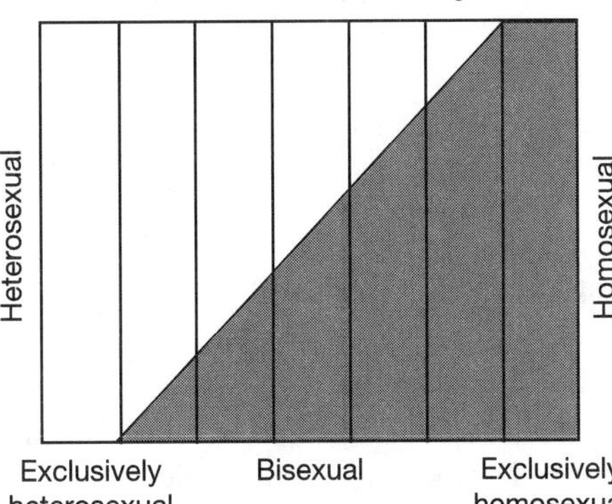

Source: From *Sexual Behavior in the Human Male* by Alfred C. Kinsey, Wardell B. Pomeroy, and Clyde E. Martin. Philadelphia: W. B. Saunders Company, 1948, pp. 636–39.

and many of them believe that preferences for sexual partners of a particular sex are merely secondary manifestations of something that lies much deeper in the totality of that intangible which they call the personality.

It is commonly believed, for instance, that homosexual males are rarely robust physically, are uncoordinated or delicate in their movements, or perhaps graceful enough but not strong and vigorous in their physical expression. Fine skins, high-pitched voices, obvious hand movements, a feminine carriage of the hips, and peculiarities of walking gaits are supposed accompaniments of a preference for a male as a sexual partner. It is commonly believed that the homosexual male is artistically sensitive, emotionally unbalanced, temperamental to the point of being unpredictable, difficult to get along with, and undependable in meeting specific obligations. In physical characters there have been attempts to show that the homosexual male has a considerable crop of hair and less often becomes bald, has teeth which are more like those of the female, a broader pelvis, larger genitalia, and a tendency toward being fat, and that he lacks a linea alba. The homosexual male is supposed to be less interested in athletics, more often interested in music and the arts, more often engaged in such occupations as bookkeeping, dress design, window display, hairdressing, acting, radio work, nursing, religious service, and social work. The converse to all of these is supposed to represent the typical heterosexual male. Many a clinician attaches considerable weight to these things in diagnosing the basic heterosexuality or homosexuality of his patients. The characterizations are so distinct that they seem to leave little room for doubt that homosexual and heterosexual represent two very distinct types of males. . . .

It should be pointed out that scientific judgments on this point have been based on little more than the same sorts of impressions which the general public has had concerning homosexual persons. But before any sufficient study can be made of such possible correlations between patterns of sexual behavior and other qualities in the individual, it is necessary to understand the incidences and frequencies of the homosexual in the population as a whole, and the relation of the homosexual activity to the rest of the sexual pattern in each individual's history.

The histories which have been available in the present study make it apparent that the heterosexuality or homosexuality of many individuals is not an all-or-none proposition. It is true that there are persons in the population whose histories are exclusively heterosexual, both in regard to their overt experience and in regard to their psychic reactions. And there are individuals in the population whose histories are exclusively homosexual, both in experience and in psychic reactions. But the record also shows that there is a considerable portion of the population whose members have combined, within their individual histories, both homosexual and heterosexual experience and/or psychic responses. There are some whose heterosexual experiences predominate, there are some whose homosexual experiences predominate, there are some who have had quite equal amounts of both types of experience.

Some of the males who are involved in one type of relation at one period in their lives may have only the other type of relation at some later period. There may be considerable fluctuation of patterns from time to time. Some males may be involved in both heterosexual and homosexual activities within the same period of time. For instance, there are some who engage in both heterosexual and homosexual activities in the same year, or in the same month or week, or even in the same day. There are not a few individuals who engage in group activities in which they may make simultaneous contact with partners of both sexes.

Males do not represent two discrete populations, heterosexual and homosexual. The world is not to be divided into sheep and goats. Not all things are black nor all things white. It is a fundamental of taxonomy that nature rarely deals with discrete categories. Only the human mind invents categories and tries to force facts into separated pigeon-holes. The living world is a continuum in each and every one of its aspects. The sooner we learn this concerning human sexual behavior the sooner we shall reach a sound understanding of the realities of sex.

CRITICAL-THINKING QUESTIONS

1. Why do you think people have long thought of heterosexuality and homosexuality as opposite and mutually exclusive (that is, only in terms of "exclusively heterosexual" or "exclusively homosexual" in the figure on page 165)?

2. Kinsey suggests that anyone's sexual orientation may well change over time. Do you agree? Why or why not?

3. Why do people tend to label someone with any degree of homosexual experience as a "homosexual"? (After all, we don't do the same in the case of any heterosexual experience.)

Sexuality

CLASSIC

CONTEMPORARY

CROSS-CULTURAL

31

Sex in America: How Many Partners Do We Have?

Robert T. Michael, John H. Gagnon, Edward O. Laumann, and Gina Kolata

Sex is a topic at once very familiar and little understood. This selection is part of a broad study of sexuality in the United States that produced some surprising findings. Despite the common belief that our society has become "free and easy" when it comes to sex, the typical individual has fewer sexual partners than most people think.

Sometimes, the myths about sex contain a grain of truth. The common perception is that Americans today have more sexual partners than they did just a decade or two ago. That, it turns out, is correct. A third of Americans who are over age fifty have had five or more sexual partners in their lifetime. But half of all Americans aged thirty to fifty have had five or more partners even though being younger, they had fewer years to accumulate them.

Still, when we ask older or younger people how many partners they had in the past year, the usual reply is zero or one. Something must have changed to make younger people accumulate more partners over a lifetime, yet sustain a pattern of having no partners or only one in any one year. The explanation is linked to one of our most potent social institutions and how it has changed.

That institution is marriage, a social arrangement so powerful that nearly everyone participates. About 90 percent of Americans have married by the time they are thirty, and a large majority spends much of their adulthood as part of a wedded couple. And marriage, we find, regulates sexual behavior with remarkable precision. No matter what they did before they wed, no matter how many partners they had, the sexual lives of married people are similar. Despite the popular myth that there is a great deal of adultery in marriage, our data and other reliable studies do not find it. Instead, a vast majority are faithful while the marriage is intact. . . .

So, yes, many young people probably are having sexual intercourse with a fair number of partners. But that stops with marriage. The reason that people now have more sexual partners over their lifetimes is that they are spending a longer period sexually active, but unmarried. The period has lengthened from both ends and in the middle. The average age at which people have their first sexual intercourse has crept down and the average

---

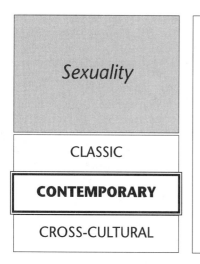

age at which people marry for the first time has edged up. And people are more likely to divorce now, which means they have time between marriages when they search for new partners once again.

To draw these conclusions, we looked at our respondents' replies to a variety of questions. First, we asked people when they first had heterosexual intercourse. Then, we asked what happens between the time when people first have intercourse and when they finally marry. How many partners do they have? Do they have more than one partner at any one time or do they have their partners in succession, practicing serial monogamy? We asked how many people divorced and how long they remained unmarried. Finally, we asked how many partners people had in their lifetimes.

In our analyses of the numbers of sex partners, we could not separately analyze patterns for gay men and lesbians. That is because homosexuals are such a small percentage of our sample that we do not have enough people in our survey to draw valid conclusions about this aspect of sexual behavior.

If we are going to look at heterosexual partners from the beginning, from the time that people first lose their virginity, we plunge headfirst into the maelstrom of teenage sex, always a turbulent subject, but especially so now, in the age of AIDS.

While society disputes whether to counsel abstinence from sexual intercourse or to pass out condoms in high schools, it also must grapple with a basic question: Has sexual behavior among teenagers changed? Are more having sexual intercourse and at younger ages, or is the overheated rhetoric a reaction to fears, without facts? The answer is both troubling and reassuring to the majority of adults who prefer teenagers to delay their sexual activity—troubling because most teenagers are having intercourse, but reassuring because sexual intercourse tends to be sporadic during the teen years.

We saw a steadily declining age at which teenagers first had sexual intercourse. Men and women born in the decade 1933–1942 had sex at an average age of about eighteen. Those born

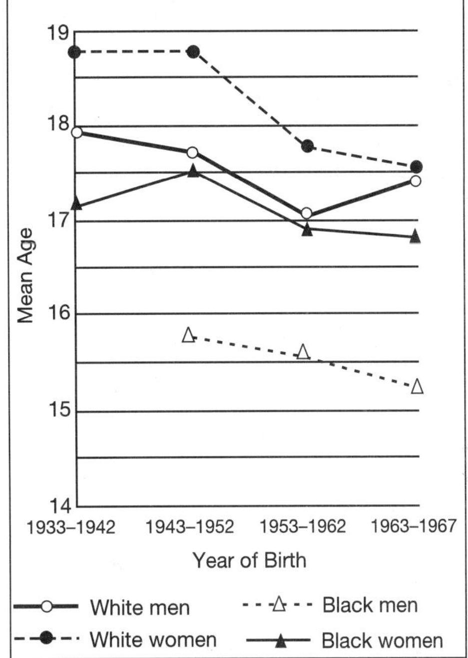

FIGURE 1 Mean Age at First Intercourse

Note: This includes respondents who had vaginal intercourse no later than age twenty-five and who have reached their twenty-fifth birthday by the date of the interview. Missing line segments indicate insufficient number of cases for a particular category (less than 30). Whites computed from cross-section sample; blacks computed from cross-section and the over-sample.

twenty to thirty years later have an average age at first intercourse that is about six months younger, as seen in Figure 1. The figure also indicates that the men report having sex at younger ages than the women. It also shows that blacks report a younger age at first intercourse than whites.

Another way to look at the age at first intercourse is illustrated in Figure 2. The figure shows the proportions of teenagers and young adults who experienced sexual intercourse at each age from twelve to twenty-five. To see at what age half the people had intercourse, for example, follow the . . . horizontal line that corresponds to a cumulative frequency of 50 percent. It shows that half of all black men had intercourse by the time they were fifteen, half of all Hispanic men

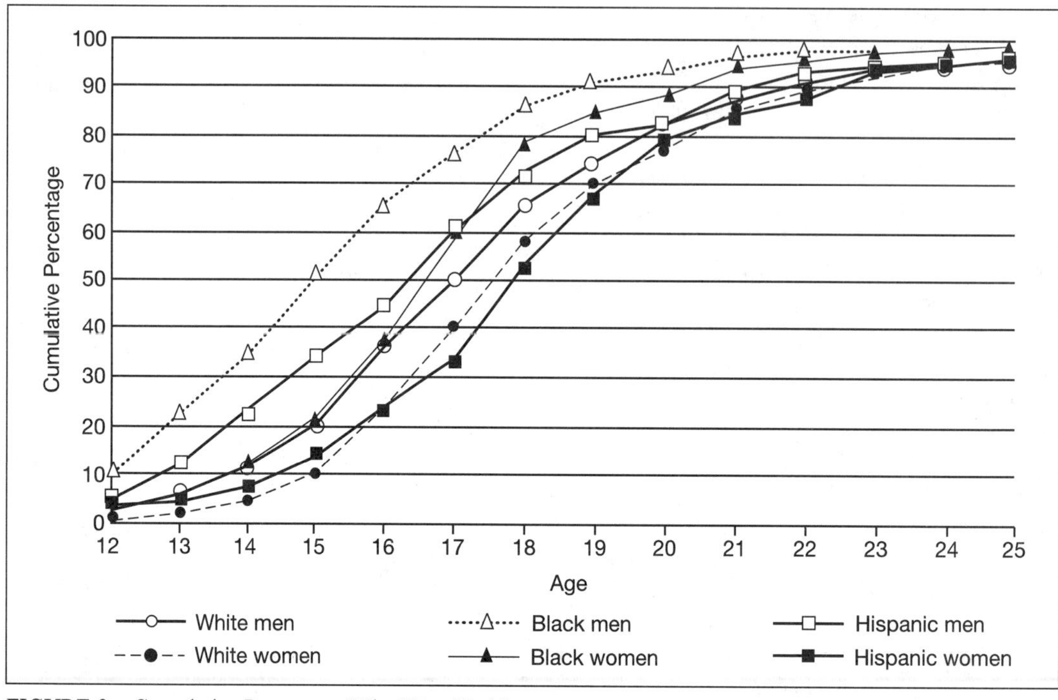

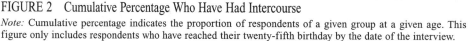

FIGURE 2 Cumulative Percentage Who Have Had Intercourse

Note: Cumulative percentage indicates the proportion of respondents of a given group at a given age. This figure only includes respondents who have reached their twenty-fifth birthday by the date of the interview.

had intercourse by the time they were about sixteen and a half, half of all black women had intercourse by the time they were nearly seventeen, and half the white women and half the Hispanic women had intercourse by the time they were nearly eighteen. By age twenty-two, about 90 percent of each group had intercourse.

The patterns are crystal clear. About half the teenagers of various racial and ethnic groups in the nation have begun having intercourse with a partner in the age range of fifteen to eighteen, and at least four out of five have had intercourse by the time their teenage years are over. Since the average age of marriage is now in the mid-twenties, few Americans wait until they marry to have sex.

Our data, in fact, show that the proportion of women who were either virgins when they turned twenty or had had sexual intercourse with only one person declined from 84 percent, among women born in 1933 to 1942, to about 50 percent for those born after 1953. . . .

The proportion of women who were virgins has traditionally been somewhat higher than the proportion of men who had had no sexual intercourse by age twenty, but that gender difference has disappeared. . . .

It's a change that built up for years, making it sometimes hard to appreciate just how profound it is. Stories of what sex among the unmarried was like decades ago can be startling. Even people who were no longer teenagers, and who were engaged, felt overwhelming social pressure to refrain from intercourse before marriage. . . .

In addition to having intercourse at younger ages, many people also are marrying later—a change that is the real legacy of the late 1960s and early 1970s. This period was not, we find, a sexual revolution, a time of frequent sex with many partners for all. Instead, it was the beginning of a profound change in the sexual life course, providing the second reason why Americans have accumulated more partners now than in decades past.

Since the 1960s, the route to the altar is no longer so predictable as it used to be. In the first half of the twentieth century, almost everyone who married followed the same course: dating, love, a little sexual experimentation with one partner, sometimes including intercourse, then marriage and children. It also was a time when there was a clear and accepted double standard—men were much more likely to have had intercourse with several women before marrying than women were to have had intercourse with several men.

At the dawn of the millennium, we are left with a nation that still has this idealized heterosexual life course but whose actual course has fragmented in the crucial years before marriage. Some people still marry at eighteen, others at thirty, leading to very different numbers of sexual partners before marriage. Social class plays a role, with less-educated people marrying earlier than better-educated people. Blacks tend to marry much later than whites, and a large number of blacks do not marry at all.

But a new and increasingly common pattern has emerged: affection or love and sex with a number of partners, followed by affection, love, and cohabitation. This cycles back to the sexual marketplace, if the cohabitation breaks up, or to marriage. Pregnancy can occur at any of these points, but often occurs before either cohabitation or marriage. The result is that the path toward marriage, once so straight and narrow, has begun to meander and to have many side paths, one of which is being trodden into a well-traveled lane.

That path is the pattern of living together before marriage. Like other recent studies, ours shows a marked shift toward living together rather than marriage as the first union of couples. With an increase in cohabitation, the distinctions among having a steady sexual partner, a live-in sexual partner, and a marriage have gotten more fuzzy. This shift began at the same time as talk of a sexual revolution. Our study shows that people who came of age before 1970 almost invariably got married without first living together, while the younger people seldom did. But, we find, the average age at which people first move in with a partner—either by marrying, or living together—has remained nearly constant, around age twenty-two for men and twenty for women. The difference is that now that first union is increasingly likely to be a cohabitation. . . .

With the increase in cohabitation, people are marrying later, on average. The longer they wait, however, the more likely they are to live with a sexual partner in the meantime. Since many couples who live together break up within a short time and seek a new partner, the result has been an increase in the average number of partners that people have before they marry. . . .

Finally, we can look at divorce rates, another key social change that began in the 1960s and that has led to increasing numbers of partners over a lifetime. Our data show this divorce pattern, as do many other data sets in the United States. For example, we can look at how likely it is that a couple will be divorced by the tenth anniversary of their marriage. For people born between 1933 and 1942, the chance was about one in five. For those born between 1943 and 1952, the chance was one in three. For those born between 1953 and 1962, the chance was closer to 38 percent. Divorced people as a group have more sexual partners than people who remain married and they are more likely, as a group, to have intercourse with a partner and live with a partner before they marry again.

These three social trends—earlier first intercourse, later marriage, and more frequent divorce—help explain why people now have more sexual partners over their lifetimes.

To discern the patterns of sexual partnering, we asked respondents how many sexual partners they had. We could imagine several scenarios. People could find one partner and marry. Or they could have sex with several before marrying. Or they could live with their partners first and then marry. Or they could simply have lots of casual sex, never marrying at all or marrying but also having extramarital sex.

Since our respondents varied in age from eighteen to fifty-nine, the older people in the study, who married by their early twenties, would have been married by the time the turbulent 1960s and 1970s came around. Their premarital behavior would be a relic from the past, telling us how much intercourse people had in the days before sex became so public an issue. The younger people in our study can show us whether there is a contrast between the earlier days and the decades after a sexual revolution was proclaimed. We can ask if they have more partners, if they have more than one sexual partner at a time, and if their sexual behavior is markedly different from that of the older generations that preceded them.

Most young people today show no signs of having very large numbers of partners. More than half the men and women in America who were eighteen to twenty-four in 1992 had just one sex partner in the past year and another 11 percent had none in the last year. In addition, studies in Europe show that people in the United Kingdom, France, and Finland have sexual life courses that are virtually the same as the American life course. The picture that emerges is strikingly different from the popular image of sexuality running out of control in our time.

In fact, we find, nearly all Americans have a very modest number of partners, whether we ask them to enumerate their partners over their adult lifetime or in the past year. The number of partners varies little with education, race, or religion. Instead, it is determined by marital status or by whether a couple is living together. Once married, people tend to have one and only one partner, and those who are unmarried and living together are almost as likely to be faithful.

Our data for the United States are displayed in Table 1.

The right-hand portion of Table 1 tells how many sexual partners people had since they turned eighteen. Very few, just 3 percent, had no partners, and few, just 9 percent, had a total of more than twenty partners.

The oldest people in our study, those aged fifty-five to fifty-nine, were most likely to have had just one sexual partner in their lifetimes—40 percent said they had had only one. This reflects the earlier age of marriage in previous generations and the low rate of divorce among these older couples. Many of the men were married by age twenty-two and the women by age twenty.

The left-hand portion of Table 1 shows the number of sexual partners that people had in the past twelve months. These are the data that show how likely people are to remain faithful to their sexual partner, whether or not they are married. Among married people, 94 percent had one partner in the past year. Couples who were living together were almost as faithful. Seventy-five percent of people who had never married but were living together had one partner in the past year. Eighty percent of people who were previously married and were cohabiting when we questioned them had one partner in the past year. Two-thirds of the single people who were not living with a partner had no partners or only one in the past year. Only a few percent of the population had as many as five partners for sexual intercourse in the past year, and many of these were people who were never married and were not living with anyone. They were mostly young and mostly male. . . .

One way to imagine the patterns of sexual partners is to think of a graph, with the vertical axis showing numbers of partners and the horizontal axis showing a person's age. The graph will be a series of blips, as the person finds partners, interspersed with flat regions where the person has no partners or when the person has just one steady partner. When the person marries, the line flattens out at a height of one, indicating that the individual has only one partner. If the marriage breaks up, the graph shows a few more blips until the person remarries, and then it flattens out again.

TABLE 1 Number of Sex Partners in Past Twelve Months and since Age Eighteen

	Sex partners past twelve months				*Sex partners since age eighteen*					
	0	*1*	*2 to 4*	*5+*	*0*	*1*	*2 to 4*	*5 to 10*	*10 to 20*	*21+*
Total	12%	71%	14%	3%	3%	26%	30%	22%	11%	9%
Gender										
Men	10	67	18	5	3	20	21	23	16	17
Women	14	75	10	2	3	31	36	20	6	3
Age										
18–24	11	57	24	9	8	32	34	15	8	3
25–29	6	72	17	6	2	25	31	22	10	9
30–34	9	73	16	2	3	21	29	25	11	10
35–39	10	77	11	2	2	19	30	25	14	11
40–44	11	75	13	1	1	22	28	24	14	12
45–49	15	75	9	1	2	26	24	25	10	14
50–54	15	79	5	0	2	34	28	18	9	9
55–59	32	65	4	0	1	40	28	15	8	7
Marital status										
Never married, noncohabiting	25	38	28	9	12	15	29	21	12	12
Never married, cohabiting	1	75	20	5	0	25	37	16	10	13
Married	2	94	4	1	0	37	28	19	9	7
Divorced, separated, widowed, noncohabiting	31	41	26	3	0	11	33	29	15	12
Divorced, separated, widowed, cohabiting	1	80	15	3	0	0	32	44	12	12
Education										
Less than high school	16	67	15	3	4	27	36	19	9	6
High school graduate or equivalent	11	74	13	3	3	30	29	20	10	7
Some college, vocational	11	71	14	4	2	24	29	23	12	9
Finished college	12	69	15	4	2	24	26	24	11	13
Master's/advanced degree	13	74	10	3	4	25	26	23	10	13
Current Religion										
None	11	68	13	7	3	16	29	20	16	16
Mainline Protestant	11	73	13	2	2	23	31	23	12	8
Conservative Protestant	13	70	14	3	3	30	30	20	10	7
Catholic	12	71	13	3	4	27	29	23	8	9
Jewish	3	75	18	3	0	24	13	30	17	17
Other religion	15	70	12	3	3	42	20	16	8	13
Race/Ethnicity										
White	12	73	12	3	3	26	29	22	11	9
Black	13	60	21	6	2	18	34	24	11	11
Hispanic	11	69	17	2	4	35	27	17	8	9
Asian	15	77	8	0	6	46	25	14	6	3
Native American	12	76	10	2	5	28	35	23	5	5

Note: Row percentages total 100 percent.

For an individual, the graph is mostly flat, punctuated by a few areas of blips. But if we superimposed everyone's graph on top of each other, we would have a sort of supergraph that looked like it was all blips. That, in essence, is what has led to the widespread impression that everyone is having lots of partners. We see the total picture—lots of sex in the population—without realizing that each individual spends most of his or her life with only one partner.

These findings give no support to the idea of a promiscuous society or of a dramatic sexual revolution reflected in huge numbers of people with multiple casual sex partners. The finding on which our data give strong and quite amazing evidence is not that most people do, in fact, form a partnership, or that most people do, in fact, ultimately get married. That fact also was well documented in many previous studies. Nor is it news that more recent marriages are much less stable than marriages that began thirty years ago. That fact, too, was reported by others before us. But we add a new fact, one that is not only important but that is striking.

Our study clearly shows that no matter how sexually active people are before and between marriages, no matter whether they lived with their sexual partners before marriage or whether they were virgins on their wedding day, marriage is such a powerful social institution that, essentially, married people are nearly all alike—they are faithful to their partners as long as the marriage is intact. It does not matter if the couple were high-school sweethearts who married after graduation day or whether they are in their thirties, marrying after each had lived with several others. Once married, the vast majority have no other sexual partner; their past is essentially erased. Marriage remains the great leveler.

We see this, for example, when we ask about fidelity in marriage. More than 80 percent of women and 65 to 85 percent of men of every age report that they had no partners other than their spouse while they were married. . . .

The marriage effect is so dramatic that it swamps all other aspects of our data. When we report that more than 80 percent of adult Americans age eighteen to fifty-nine had zero or one sexual partner in the past year, the figure might sound ludicrous to some young people who know that they and their friends have more than one partner in a year. But the figure really reflects the fact that most Americans in that broad age range are married and are faithful. And many of the others are cohabiting, and they too are faithful. Or they are without partners altogether, a situation that is especially likely for older women. . . . We find only 3 percent of adults had five or more partners in the past year. Half of all adult Americans had three or fewer partners over their lifetimes.

CRITICAL-THINKING QUESTIONS

1. What single factor seems to do more than any other to limit the typical person's number of sexual partners?
2. Were you surprised that half of U.S. adults have had three or fewer sexual partners over their lifetimes? Why do we tend to think of our society as much more sexually active?
3. What has changed with regard to sexuality in the United States over the course of the last fifty years? What has stayed pretty much the same?

32

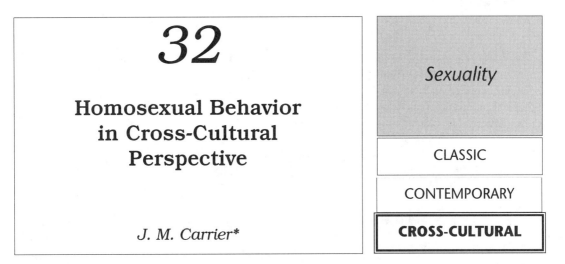

Homosexual Behavior in Cross-Cultural Perspective

*J. M. Carrier**

Sexuality

CLASSIC

CONTEMPORARY

CROSS-CULTURAL

Although sexuality is a biological process, the meaning *of sexuality is culturally variable. Carrier shows that attitudes toward homosexuality are far from uniform around the world. Some societies are quite accommodating about sexual practices that other societies punish harshly.*

The available cross-cultural data clearly show that the ways in which individuals organize their sexual behavior vary considerably between societies (Westermarck, 1908; Ford & Beach, 1951; Broude & Greene, 1976). Although biological and psychological factors help explain variations of sexual behavior between individuals within a given society, intercultural variations in patterns of human sexual behavior are mainly related to social and cultural differences occurring between societies around the world. The purpose of this chapter is to consider what kinds of variations in homosexual behavior occur between societies, and to determine which sociocultural factors appear to account for the variance of the behavior cross-culturally.[1]

THE CROSS-CULTURAL DATA

Data available on homosexual behavior in most of the world's societies, past or present, are meager. Much is known about the dominant middle-class white populations of the United States, England, and northern European countries where most scientific research on human sexual behavior has been done, but very little is known about homosexual behavior in the rest of the world. The lack of knowledge stems from the irrational fear and prejudice surrounding the study of human sexual behavior, and from the difficulties associated with the collection of information on a topic that is so personal and highly regulated in most societies.

Most of the cross-cultural information on sexual behavior has been gathered by Western anthropologists. The quality of the information collected and published, however, varies consid-

* The author is particularly indebted to Evelyn Hooker for her invaluable comments and criticism; and to the Gender Identity Research Group at UCLA for an early critique of the ideas presented in this paper.

erably. Based on a survey of the literature, Marshall and Suggs (1971) report that: "Sexual behavior is occasionally touched upon in anthropological publications but is seldom the topic of either articles or monographs by anthropologists." Broude and Greene (1976), after coding the sexual attitudes and practices in 186 societies using the Human Relations Area Files, note:[2]

> . . . information of any sort on sexual habits and beliefs is hard to come by. . . . when data do exist concerning sexual attitudes and practices, they are often sketchy and vague; what is more, such information is usually suspect in terms of its reliability, either because of distortions on the part of the subjects or because of biases introduced by the ethnographer. . . .

Cross-cultural data on homosexual behavior is further complicated by the prejudice of many observers who consider the behavior unnatural, dysfunctional, or associated with mental illness, and by the fact that in many of the societies studied the behavior is stigmatized and thus not usually carried out openly. Under these circumstances, the behavior is not easily talked about. At the turn of the twentieth century such adjectives as disgusting, vile, and detestable were still being used to describe homosexual behavior; and even in the mid-1930s some anthropologists continued to view the behavior as unnatural. In discussing sodomy with some of his New Guinea informants, Williams (1936), for example, asked them if they "had ever been subjected to an unnatural practice." With the acceptance of the view in the mid-1930s that homosexual behavior should be classified as a mental illness (or at best dysfunctional), many anthropologists replaced "unnatural" with the medical model. This model still finds adherents among researchers at present, especially those in the branch of anthropology referred to as psychological anthropology.

Because of the prejudice with which many researchers and observers approached the subject, statements about the reported absence of homosexual behavior, or the limited extent of the behavior where reported, should be viewed with some skepticism. Mead (1961) suggests that statements of this kind "can only be accepted with the greatest caution and with very careful analysis of the personality and training of the investigator." She further notes that: "Denials of a practice cannot be regarded as meaningful if that practice is verbally recognized among a given people, even though a strong taboo exists against it."

This chapter will mainly utilize the published research findings of empirical studies which have considered homosexual behavior in some detail. It will examine homosexual behavior in preliterate, peasant, and complex modern societies in all the major geographical regions of the world.[3] Where necessary, these findings will be supplemented with information found in accounts given by travelers, missionaries, and novelists.

SOCIOCULTURAL FACTORS

A number of sociocultural factors help explain variations of homosexual behavior between societies. Two of the most important are: cultural attitudes and proscriptions related to cross-gender behavior, and availability of sexual partners.[4] The latter is in turn related to such variables as segregation of sexes prior to marriage, expectations with respect to virginity, age at marriage, and available economic resources and/or distribution of income.

Cross-Gender and Homosexual Behavior

Different expectations for male persons as opposed to female persons are culturally elaborated from birth onward in every known society. Although behavioral boundaries between the sexes may vary culturally, male persons are clearly differentiated from female persons; and progeny is assured by normative societal rules which correlate male and female gender roles with sexual behavior, marriage, and the family. There is a general expectation in every society that a majority of adult men and women will cohabit and produce the next generation. Social pressure is thus applied in the direction of marriage. The general rule is that one should not remain single.

The cross-cultural data on human sexual behavior suggest that a significant relationship exists between much of the homosexual behavior reported cross culturally and the continuing need of societies to deal with cross-gender behavior. Feminine male behavior, and the set of anxieties associated with its occurrence in the male part of the population, appears to have brought about more elaborate cultural responses temporally and spatially than has masculine female behavior. There are no doubt many reasons why this is so, but it appears to be related in general to the higher status accorded men than women in most societies; and, in particular, to the defense role that men have historically played in protecting women and children from outsiders.

Societies in which homosexual behavior can be linked to cultural responses to cross-gender behavior may be categorized according to the type of response made. Three major cultural types have been identified: those societies which make a basic accommodation to cross-gender behavior, those societies which outlaw the behavior as scandalous and/or criminal, and those societies which neither make an accommodation to such behavior nor outlaw it but instead have a cultural formulation which tries to ensure that cross-gender behavior does not occur.

Accommodating Societies

Societies making an accommodation to cross-gender behavior in one form or another have been reported in many different parts of the world. Munroe et al. (1969), for example, put together a list of societies having what they call "institutionalized male transvestism . . . the permanent adoption by males of aspects of female dress and/or behavior in accordance with customary expectations within a given society." Their list includes Indian societies in North and South America, island societies in Polynesia and Southeast Asia, and preliterate and peasant societies in mainland Asia and Africa. Although reported for both sexes, male cross-gender behavior appears in the literature more often than female.

A folk belief exists in some of these societies that in every generation a certain number of individuals will play the gender role of the opposite sex, usually beginning at or prior to puberty and often identified at a very early age. The Mohave Indians of the American Southwest, for example, used to hold the following belief—typical of many Indian societies in North America—about cross-gender behavior of both sexes:

> Ever since the world began at the magic mountain . . . it was said that there would be transvestites. In the beginning, if they were to become transvestites, the process started during their intrauterine life. When they grew up they were given toys according to their sex. They did not like these toys however. (Devereux, 1937)

In southern Mexico one group of Zapotec Indians believes that "effeminate males" are born not made: "Typical comments include: But what can we do; he was born that way; he is like God made him. A related belief also exists that . . . it is a thing of the blood" (Royce, 1973). In Tahiti, the belief exists that there is at least one cross-gender behaving male, called a *māhū* in all villages: "When one dies then another substitutes . . . God arranges it like this. It isn't allowed (that there should be) two *māhū* in one place" (Levy, 1973).

Cross-gender behavior is accepted in other societies because it is believed that some supernatural event makes people that way prior to birth, or that the behavior is acquired through some mystical force or dream after birth. In India, for example, the following belief exists about the *Hijadās,* cross-gender behaving males thought to be impotent at birth who later have their genitals removed:

> When we ask a *Hijadā* or an ordinary man in Gujarat "Why does a man become a *Hijadā*?" the usual reply is "One does not become a *Hijadā* by one's own will; it is only by the command of the *mātā* that one becomes a *Hijadā*." The same idea is found in a myth

about the origin of the *Hijadās*. It is said that one receives the *mātā's* command either in dreams or when one sits in meditation before her image. (Shah, 1961)

Among the Chukchee of northeastern Asia, a role reversal was accepted because of an unusual dream or vision:

> Transformation takes place by the command of the *ka'let* (spirits) usually at the critical age of early youth when shamanistic inspiration first manifests itself. (Bogores, 1904)

Among the Lango in Africa:

> A number of Lango men dress as women, simulate menstruation, and become one of the wives of other males. They are believed to be impotent and to have been afflicted by some supernatural agency. (Ford & Beach, 1951)

Although not necessarily accepted gladly, the various folk beliefs make the behavior acceptable, and a certain number of cross-gender behaving individuals are to be expected in every generation. Expectations about the extent to which the opposite gender role is to be played, however, appear to have changed over time with acculturation. Affected individuals in the past often were required to make a public ritualized change of gender and cross-dress and behave in accordance with their new identity. Among the Mohave, for example, there was an initiation ceremony and it was important for the initiate "to duplicate the behavior pattern of his adopted sex and make 'normal' individuals of his anatomic sex feel toward him as though he truly belonged to his adopted sex" (Devereux, 1937). The *māhū* in Tahiti were described in the latter part of the eighteenth century as follows:

> These men are in some respects like the Eunichs [sic] in India but are not castrated. They never cohabit with women but live as they do. They pick their beard out and dress as women, dance and sing with them and are as effeminate in their voice. (Morrison, 1935)

Affected individuals in most societies at present are allowed a choice as to the extent they want to play the role; e.g., how far they want to identify with the opposite sex, whether they want to cross-dress or not, etc. Levy (1973) notes, for example, that in Tahiti: "Being a *māhū* does not now usually entail actually dressing as a woman." The North American Indian societies who used to have initiation ceremonies discontinued them long ago; and, although expectations about cross-gender behaving individuals persist, only remnants of the original belief system are remembered currently. They continue, however, to be tolerant and "there apparently is no body of role behavior aimed at humiliating boys who are feminine or men who prefer men sexually" (Stoller, 1976).

The link between cross-gender behavior and homosexual behavior is the belief that there should be concordance between gender role and sexual object choice. When a male behaves like a female, he should be expected therefore to want a male sexual partner and to play the female sex role—that is, to play the insertee role in anal intercourse or fellatio. The same concordance should be expected when a female behaves like a male. As a result of beliefs about concordance, it is important to note that a society may not conceptualize the sexual behavior or its participants as "homosexual."

There is some evidence in support of this linking of gender role and homosexual behavior in societies making an accommodation and providing a social role for cross-gender behaving individuals. Kroeber (1940), for example, concluded from his investigations that: "In most of primitive northern Asia and North America, men of homosexual trends adopted women's dress, work, and status, and were accepted as nonphysiological but institutionalized women." Devereux's Mohave informants said that the males who changed their gender role to female had male husbands and that both anal intercourse and fellatio were practiced, with the participants playing the appropriate gender sex role. The informants noted the same concordance for females who behaved like males.

Unfortunately, the anthropological data do not always make clear whether cultural expectations in a given society were for concordance between gender role and erotic object; or, in terms of actual behavior, how many cross-gender behaving individuals chose same sex, opposite sex, or both sexes as erotic objects. In the paper I just quoted, Kroeber also concluded: "How far invert erotic practices accompanied the status is not always clear from the data, and it probably varied. At any rate, the North American attitude toward the berdache stresses not his erotic life but his social status; born a male, he became accepted as a woman socially."

Many anthropologists and other observers confounded their findings by assuming an equivalence between "transvestite" and "homosexual."[5] Thus, when an informant described cross-gender behavior, they may have concluded without foundation that a same-sex erotic object choice was part of the behavior being described, and that they were eliciting information on "homosexuals." Angelino and Shedd (1955) provide supporting evidence. They reviewed the literature on an often used anthropological concept, berdache, and concluded that the "term has been used in an exceedingly ambiguous way, being used as a synonym for homosexualism, hermaphroditism, transvestism, and effeminism." They also note that the meaning of berdache changed over time; going from kept boy/male prostitute, to individuals who played a passive role in sodomy, to males who played a passive sex role and cross-dressed.

In spite of the confusion between "transvestite" and "homosexual," the available data suggest that in many of the societies providing a social role for cross-gender behavior, the selection of sexual partners was based on the adopted gender role; and, though they might be subjected to ridicule, neither partner in the sexual relationship was penalized for the role played.

The *māhū* role in Tahiti provides a contemporary look at how one Polynesian society continues to provide a social role for cross-gender behavior. According to Levy (1973), villagers in his area of study do not agree on the sexual behavior of the *māhū*—some "believe that *māhū* do not generally engage in homosexual intercourse." Information from both *māhū* and *non-māhū* informants, however, leads to the conclusion that probably a majority of the *māhūs* prefer adolescent males with whom they perform "ote moa" (literally, "penis sucking"). The following are some aspects of the role and the community response to it:

> It is said to be exclusive. Its essential defining characteristic is "doing woman's work," that is, a role reversal which is *publicly demonstrated*—either through clothes or through other public aspects of women's role playing. Most villagers approve of, and are pleased by, the role reversal. But homosexual behavior is a covert part of the role, and it is disapproved by many villagers. Men who have sexual relations with the *māhū* . . . do not consider themselves abnormal. Villagers who know of such activities may disapprove, but they do not label the partners as unmanly. The *māhū* is considered as a substitute woman for the partner. A new word, *raerae,* which reportedly originated in Papeete, is used by some to designate nontraditional types of homosexual behavior. (Levy, 1973)

It should also be noted that in Levy's village of study *māhūs* were the only adult men reported to be engaging in homosexual intercourse.

Another contemporary example of a social role for cross-gender behavior is the *Hijadā* role provided cross-gender behaving males in northwestern India. Given slightly different names by different observers (*Hijarās, Hinjrās,* and *Hijirās*), these males appear to be playing the same role. There is general agreement on the fact that they cross-dress, beg alms, and collect dues at special ceremonies where they dance and sing as women. There is a considerable difference of opinion, however, as to whether they engage in homosexual intercourse or in any sexual activity for that matter. From the available data, it appears that they live mostly in towns in communes, with each commune having a definite jurisdiction of villages and towns "where its members can beg alms and collect dues" (Shah, 1961). They are also reported to live separately by themselves. From the findings of Carstairs (1956) and Shah (1961), one can at least conclude that the *Hijadās* living alone are sexually active:

> Carstairs is wrong in considering all the Hijadās as homosexual, but there seems to be some truth in his information about the homosexuality of the Deoli Hijadā (Note: Deoli is the village of Carstairs' study.) Faridi and Mehta also note that some Hijadās practice "sodomy." This, however, is not institutionalized homosexuality. (Shah, 1961)

The finding by Opler (1960) that "they cannot carry on sexual activities and do not marry" may apply to the majority of *Hijadās* living in communes. The question of what kind of sexual behavior the *Hijadās* practice, if any, cannot be answered definitively with the data available. That they are still a viable group in India is confirmed by a recent Associated Press release:

> About 2000 eunuchs dressed in brightly colored saris and other female garb were converging on this northern town from all over India this weekend for a private convention of song, dance and prayer.
>
> Local reaction to the gathering was mixed. "They're perverts," commented a local peanut vendor. "We should have nothing to do with them. They should be run out of town."
>
> A New Delhi social worker . . . said they sometimes supplement their income as paid lovers of homosexuals. (Excerpts from AP, February 6, 1979)

Disapproving Societies

Societies in which cross-gender behavior produces strong emotional negative reactions in large segments of the population tend to have the following commonalities: (1) negative reactions produced by the behavior are essentially limited to the male part of the population and relate mainly to effeminate males; (2) cross-gender behavior is controlled by laws which prohibit cross-dressing, and by laws and public opinion which consider other attributes associated with the behavior as scandalous; (3) gender roles are sharply dichotomized; and (4) a general belief exists that anyone demonstrating cross-gender behavior is homosexual.

A number of complex modern and peasant societies in the Middle East, North Africa, southern Europe, and Central and South America have the commonalities listed. The author's research in Mexico (Carrier, 1976 and 1977) illustrates how homosexual behavior in these societies appears to be linked to social responses to cross-gender behavior. The comments that follow are limited to male homosexual behavior. Female homosexuality is known to exist in these societies, but too little is known about the behavior to be included in the discussion.

Mexican Homosexual Behavior. The Mexican mestizo culture places a high value on manliness. One of the salient features of the society is thus a sharp delimitation between the roles played by males and females. Role expectations in general are for the male to be dominant and independent and for the female to be submissive and dependent. The continued sharp boundary between male and female roles in Mexico appears to be due in part to a culturally defined hypermasculine ideal model of manliness, referred to under the label *machismo*. The ideal female role is generally believed to be the reciprocal of the macho (male) role.[6]

As a consequence of the high status given manliness, Mexican males from birth onward are expected to behave in as manly a way as possible. Peñalosa (1968) sums it up as follows: "Any signs of feminization are severely repressed in the boy." McGinn (1966) concludes: "The young Mexican boy may be severely scolded for engaging in feminine activities, such as playing with dolls or jacks. Parents verbally and physically punish feminine traits in their male children." The importance of manly behavior continues throughout the life span of Mexican males.

One result of the sharp dichotomization of male and female gender roles is the widely held belief that effeminate males basically prefer to play the female role rather than the male. The link between male effeminacy and homosexuality is the additional belief that as a result of this role preference effeminate males are sexually interested only in masculine males with whom they play the passive sex role. Although the motivations of males participating in homosexual encounters are without question diverse and complex, the fact remains that in Mexico cultural pressure is brought to bear on effeminate males to play the passive insertee role in sexual intercourse, and a kind of de facto cultural approval is given (that is, no particular stigma is attached to) masculine males who want to play the active insertor role in homosexual intercourse.

The beliefs linking effeminate males with homosexuality are culturally transmitted by a vocabulary which provides the appropriate labels, by homosexually oriented jokes and word games (*albures*), and by the mass media. The links are established at a very early age. From early childhood on, Mexican males are made aware of the labels used to denote male homosexuals and the connection is always clearly made that these homosexual males are guilty of unmanly effeminate behavior.

The author's data also support the notion that prior to puberty effeminate males in Mexico are targeted as sexual objects for adolescent and adult males, and are expected to play the passive insertee sex role in anal intercourse. Following the onset of puberty, they continue to be sexual targets for other males because of their effeminacy. The consensus of my effeminate respondents in Mexico is that regardless of whether they are at school, in a movie theater, on the downtown streets, in a park, or in their own neighborhood, they are sought out and expected to play the anal passive sex role by more masculine males. As one fourteen-year-old respondent put it, in response to the question of where he had looked for sexual contacts during the year prior to the interview: "I didn't have to search for them . . . they looked for me."

The other side of the coin is represented by masculine male participants in homosexual encounters. Given the fact that effeminate males in Mexico are assumed homosexual and thus considered available as sexual outlets, how do the cultural factors contribute to the willingness of masculine males to play the active insertor sex role? The available data suggest that, insofar as the social variables are concerned, their willingness to participate in homosexual encounters is due to the relatively high level of sexual awareness that exists among males in the society, to the lack of stigmatization of the insertor sex role, and to the restraints that may be placed on alternative sexual outlets by available income and/or by marital status. The only cultural proscriptions are that "masculine" males should not play the passive sex role and should not be exclusively involved with homosexual intercourse.

The passive sex role is by inference—through the cultural equivalence of effeminacy with homosexuality—prescribed for "effeminate" males. It becomes a self-fulfilling prophecy of the society that effeminate males (a majority?) are eventually, if not from the beginning, pushed toward exclusively homosexual behavior. Some do engage in heterosexual intercourse, and some marry and set up households; but these probably are a minority of the identifiably effeminate males among the mestizos of the Mexican population.

Brazilian Homosexual Behavior. Both Young (1973) and Fry (1974) note the relationship between cross-gender behavior and homosexuality in Brazil:

> Brazilians are still pretty hung-up about sexual roles. Many Brazilians believe in the *bicha/bofe* (femme/butch) dichotomy and try to live by it. In Brazil, the average person doesn't even recognize the existence of the masculine homosexual. For example, among working-class men, it is considered all right to fuck a *bicha,* an accomplishment of sorts, just like fucking a woman. (Young, 1973)
>
> In the simplest of terms, a male is a man until he is assumed or proved to have "given" in which case he becomes a *bicha.* With very few exceptions, males who "eat" *bichas* are not classified as anything other than "real men." Under this classificatory scheme they differ in no way from males who restrict themselves to "eating" females. (Note: the male who gives is an insertee, the one who eats is an insertor.) (Fry, 1974)

Southern European Homosexual Behavior. Contemporary patterns of male homosexual behavior in Greece appear similar to those observed by the author in Mexico. An American anthropologist who collected data on homosexual behavior in Greece while working there on an archaeological project (Bialor, 1975) found, for example, that preferences for playing one sex role or the other (anal insertor or anal insertee) appear to be highly developed among Greek males. Little or no stigma is attached to the masculine male who plays the active insertor role. The social setting in modern Greece also appears to be strikingly similar to that in modern Mexico. Karlen (1971) describes it as follows:

> The father spends his spare time with other men in cafes; society is a male club, and there all true companionship lies. Women live separate, sequestered lives. Girls' virginity is carefully protected, and the majority of homicides are committed over the "honor" of daughters and sisters. In some Greek villages a woman does not leave her home unaccompanied by a relative between puberty and old age. Women walk the street, even in Athens, with their eyes down; a woman who looks up when a man speaks to her is, quite simply, a whore. The young male goes to prostitutes and may carry on homosexual connections; it is not unusual for him to marry at thirty having had no sexual experience save with prostitutes and male friends. (p. 16)

In an evaluation of the strategy of Turkish boys' verbal dueling rhymes, Dundes, Leach, and Ozkok (1972) make the following observations about homosexual behavior in Turkey:

> It is extremely important to note that the insult refers to *passive* homosexuality, not to homosexuality in general. In this context there is nothing insulting about being the active homosexual. In a homosexual relationship, the active phallic aggressor gains status; the passive victim of such aggression loses status. It is important to play the active role in a homosexual relationship; it is shameful and demeaning to be forced to take the passive role.

Moroccan Homosexual Behavior. The author does not know of any formal studies of homosexual behavior in Morocco. The available information suggests, however, that contemporary patterns of homosexual behavior in Morocco are similar to those in Mexico; that is, as long as Moroccan males play the active, insertor sex role in the relationship, there is never any question of their being considered homosexual. Based on his field work in Morocco shortly after the turn of the century, Westermarck (1908) believed that "a very large proportion of the men" in some parts of the country were involved in homosexual activity. He also noted that: "In Morocco active pederasty is regarded with almost complete indifference, whilst the passive sodomite, if a grown-up individual, is spoken of with scorn. Dr. Polak says the same of the Persians." Contemporary patterns of homosexual behavior in the Islamic Arab countries of North Africa are probably similar to those in Morocco. . . .

DISCUSSION

Heterosexual intercourse, marriage, and the creation of a family are culturally established as primary objectives for adults living in all of the societies discussed above. Ford & Beach (1951) concluded from their cross-cultural survey that "all known cultures are strongly biased in favor of copulation between males and females as contrasted with alternative avenues of sexual expression." They further note that this viewpoint is biologically adaptive in that it favors perpetuation of the species and social group, and that societies favoring other nonreproductive forms of sexual expression for adults would not be likely to survive for many generations.

Homosexual intercourse appears to be the most important alternative form of sexual expression utilized by people living around the world. All cultures have established rules and regulations that govern the selection of a sexual partner or partners. With respect to homosexual behavior, however, there appear to be greater variations of the rules and regulations. And male homosexual behavior generally appears to be more regulated by cultures than female homosexual behavior. This difference may be the result of females being less likely than males to engage in homosexual activity; but it may also just be the result of a lack of data on female as compared with male homosexual behavior cross-culturally.

Exclusive homosexuality, however, because of the cultural dictums concerning marriage and the family, appears to be generally excluded as a sexual option even in those societies where homosexual behavior is generally approved. For example, the two societies where all male individuals are free to participate in homosexual activity if they choose, Siwan and East Bay, do not sanction exclusive homosexuality.[7] Although nearly all male members of these two societies are reported to engage in extensive homosexual activities, they are not permitted to do so exclusively over their adult life span. Davenport (1965) reports "that East Bay is a society which permits men to be either heterosexual or bisexual in their behavior, but denies the possibility of the exclusively homosexual man." He notes that "they have no concept and therefore no word for the exclusive homosexual." There are not much data available on the Siwans, but it has been reported that whether single or married Siwan males "are expected to have both homosexual and heterosexual affairs" (Ford & Beach, 1951).

In East Bay there are two categories of homosexual relationships. One category appears similar to that found in a number of Melanesian societies; an older man plays the active (insertor) sex role in anal intercourse with younger boys "from seven to perhaps eleven years of age." Davenport notes:

> The man always plays the active role, and it is considered obligatory for him to give the boy presents in return for accommodating him. A man would not engage his own son in such a relationship, but fathers do not object when friends use their young sons in this way, provided the adult is kind and generous. (p. 200)

The other category is between young single men of the same age group who play both sex roles in anal intercourse. The young men, however, "are not regarded as homosexual lovers. They are simply friends or relatives, who, understanding each other's needs and desires, accommodate one another thus fulfilling some of the obligations of kinship and friendship." This category may be related to several social factors which limit heterosexual contacts of young single men. First, the population is highly masculine with a male/female ratio of 120:100 in the fifteen- to twenty-five-year-old age group. Second, females have historically been brought in as wives for those who could afford the bride price. Third, sexual relations between unmarried individuals and adultery are forbidden. Both relationships are classed as larcenies and "only murder carries a more severe punishment." At first marriage a bride is expected to be a virgin. Chastity is highly valued in that it indicates adultery is less likely to occur after marriage. And fourth, there is "an extensive system for separating the sexes by what amounts to a general social avoidance between men and women in all but a few situations." From early adolescence on, unmarried men and boys sleep and eat in the men's house; and married men spend much of their time there during the day. Davenport notes that both masturbation and anal copulation are socially approved and regarded as substitutes for heterosexual intercourse by members of the society. Female homosexual activity is not reported in East Bay.

Among Siwan males the accepted homosexual relationship is "between a man and a boy but not between adult men or between two young boys" (Bullough, 1976). They are reported to practice anal intercourse with the adult man always playing the active (insertor) sex role. In this society, boys are more valued than girls. Allah (1917) reports that

> . . . bringing up of a boy costs very little whereas the girl needs ornaments, clothing, and stains. Moreover the boy is a very fruitful source of profit for the father, not for the work he does, but because he is hired by his father to another man to be used as a catamite. Sometimes two men exchange their sons. If they are asked about this, they are not ashamed to mention it.

Homosexual activity is not reported for Siwan females.

The way in which cross-gender behavior is linked to homosexual behavior, and the meaning ascribed to the "homosexual" behavior by participants and significant others, differ between the three categories of societies identified in this study. What is considered homosexuality in one culture may be considered appropriate behavior within prescribed gender roles in another, a homosexual act only on the part of one participant in another, or a ritual act involving growth and masculinity in still another. Care must therefore be taken when judging sexual behavior cross-culturally with such culture-bound labels as "homosexual" and "homosexuality."

From a cultural point of view, deviations from sexual mores in a given society appear most likely to occur as a result of the lack of appropriate sexual partners and/or a result of conditioning in approved sexual behavior which is limited by age or ritual (for example, where homosexual intercourse is only appropriate for a certain age group and/or ritual time period and inappropriate thereafter). Homosexual activity initiated by sociocultural variables may over time through interaction with personality variables, produce an outcome not in accordance with the sexual mores of the society.

The findings presented in this chapter illustrate the profound influence of culture on the structuring of individual patterns of sexual behavior. Whether from biological or psychological causation, cross-gender behaving individuals in many societies must cope with a cultural formulation which equates their behavior with homosexual activity and thus makes it a self-fulfilling prophecy that they become homosexually involved. There are also individuals in many societies who might *prefer* to be exclusively homosexual but are prevented from doing so by cultural edicts. From whatever causes that homosexual impulses originate, whether they be biological or psychological, culture provides an additional dimension that cannot be ignored.

CRITICAL-THINKING QUESTIONS

1. What type of society tends to be accepting of homosexuality? What kind of society is disapproving of this sexual orientation? Why?
2. What insights can be drawn from this article that help to explain violence and discrimination directed toward gay people in U.S. society?
3. Are data about sexuality easily available to researchers? Why not?

NOTES

1. Homosexual behavior or activity will be used here to describe sexual behavior between individuals of the same sex; it may have nothing to do with sexual object choice or sexual orientation of the individual involved. Additionally, the terms "sex role" and "gender role" will be used to describe different behavioral phenomena. As Hooker (1965) points out, they "are often used interchangeably, and with resulting confusion." Following her suggestion the term "sex role," when homosexual practices are described, will refer to typical sexual performance only. "The gender connotations (M-F) of these performances need not then be implicitly assumed." The term "gender role" will refer to the expected attitudes and behavior that distinguish males from females.

2. The Human Relations Area Files (HRAF) contain information on the habits, practices, customs, and behavior of populations in hundreds of societies around the world. These files utilize accounts given not only by anthropologists but also by travelers, writers, missionaries, and explorers. Most cross-cultural surveys of sexual behavior, like those of Ford & Beach and Broude & Greene, have been based on HRAF information. A major criticism of the HRAF information on sexual behavior relates to the difficulty of assessing the reliability of the data collected in different time periods by different people with varying amounts of scientific training as observers.

3. "Preliterate" refers to essentially tribal societies that do not have a written language; "peasant" refers to essentially agrarian literate societies; and "complex modern" refers to highly industrialized societies.

4. In one of the first scholarly surveys of homosexual behavior done by an anthropologist, Westermarck (1908) concluded that: "A very important cause of homosexual practices is absence of the other sex."

5. The confounding of transvestism with homosexuality still occurs. For example, Minturn, Grosse, and Haider (1969) coded male homosexuality with transvestism in a recent study of the patterning of sexual beliefs and behavior, "because it is often difficult to distinguish between the two practices, and because they are assumed to be manifestations of the same psychological processes and to have similar causes."

6. The roles described represent the normative cultural ideals of the mestizoized national culture. Mestizos are Mexican nationals of mixed Indian and Spanish ancestry. They make up a large majority of the population, and their culture is the dominant one.

7. Both societies are small, each totaling less than 1,000 inhabitants. The Siwans live in an oasis in the Libyan desert. The people of East Bay (a pseudonym) live in a number of small coastal villages in an island in Melanesia.

REFERENCES

ALLAH, M. 1917. Siwan customs. *Harvard African Studies,* 1:7.

ANGELINO, A., and C. SHEDD. 1955. A note on berdache. *American Anthropologist,* 57:121–25.

ASSOCIATED PRESS. 1979. Eunuchs gather for convention in India. *Panipat,* February 6, 1979.

BIALOR, P. 1975. Personal communication.

BOGORES, W. 1904. The Chukchee. *Memoirs of American Museum of Natural History,* 2: 449–51.

BROUDE, G., and S. GREENE. 1976. Cross-cultural codes on twenty sexual attitudes and practices. *Ethnology,* 15(4):410–11.

BULLOUGH, V. 1976. *Sexual variance in society and history,* 22–49. New York: John Wiley.

CARRIER, J. 1976. Cultural factors affecting urban Mexican male homosexual behavior. *Archives of Sexual Behavior,* 5(2):103–24.

———. 1977. Sex-role preference as an explanatory variable in homosexual behavior. *Archives of Sexual Behavior,* 6(1):53–65.

CARSTAIRS, G. 1956. Hinjra and Jiryan: Two derivatives of Hindu attitudes to sexuality. *British Journal of Medical Psychology,* 2:129–32.

DAVENPORT, W. 1965. Sexual patterns and their regulation in a society of the southwest Pacific. In *Sex and behavior,* 164–207. New York: John Wiley.

DEVEREUX, G. 1937. Institutionalized homosexuality of the Mohave Indians. In *The problem of homosexuality in modern society,* 183–226. New York: E. P. Dutton.

DUNDES, A., J. LEACH, and B. OZKOK. 1972. The strategy of Turkish boys' verbal dueling. In *Directions in sociolinguistics: The ethnography of communication.* New York: Holt.

FORD, C .S., and F. A. BEACH. 1951. *Patterns of sexual behavior.* New York: Harper & Row.

FRY, P. 1974. Male homosexuality and Afro-Brazilian possession cults. Unpublished paper presented to Symposium on Homosexuality in Crosscultural Perspective, 73rd Annual Meeting of the American Anthropological Association, Mexico City.

HOOKER, E. 1965. An empirical study of some relations between sexual patterns and gender identity in male homosexuals. In *Sex research: New developments,* 24–25. New York: Holt.

KARLEN, A. 1971. *Sexuality and homosexuality: A new view.* New York: W. W. Norton.

KROEBER, A. 1940. Psychosis or social sanction. *Character and Personality,* 8:204–15. Reprinted in *The nature of culture,* 313. Chicago: University of Chicago Press, 1952.

LEVY, R. 1973. *Tahitians.* Chicago: University of Chicago Press.

MARSHALL, D., and R. SUGGS. 1971. *Human sexual behavior,* 220–21. New York: Basic Books.

MCGINN, N. 1966. Marriage and family in middle-class Mexico. *Journal of Marriage and Family Counseling,* 28:305–13.

MEAD, M. 1961. Cultural determinants of sexual behavior. In *Sex and internal secretions,* 1433–79. Baltimore: Williams & Wilkins.

MINTURN, L., M. GROSSE, and S. HAIDER. 1969. Cultural patterning of sexual beliefs and behavior. *Ethnology,* 8(3):3.

MORRISON, J. 1935. *The journal of James Morrison.* London: Golden Cockeral Press.

MUNROE, R., J. WHITING, and D. HALLY. 1969. Institutionalized male transvestism and sex distinctions. *American Anthropologist,* 71:87–91.

OPLER, M. 1960. The Hijarā (hermaphrodites) of India and Indian national character: A rejoinder. *American Anthropologist,* 62(3):505–11.

PEÑALOSA, F. 1968. Mexican family roles. *Journal of Marriage and Family Counseling,* 30:680–89.

ROYCE, A. 1973. Personal communication.

SHAH, A. 1961. A note on the Hijadās of Gujarat. *American Anthropologist,* 63(6):1325–30.

STOLLER, R. 1976. Two feminized male American Indians. *Archives of Sexual Behavior,* 5(6):536.

WESTERMARCK, E. 1908. On homosexual love. In *The origin and development of the moral ideas.* London: Macmillan.

WILLIAMS, F. 1936. *Papuans of the trans-fly.* London: Oxford University Press.

YOUNG, A. 1973. Gay gringo in Brazil. In *The gay liberation book,* eds. L. Richmond and G. Noguera, 60–67. San Francisco: Ramparts Press.

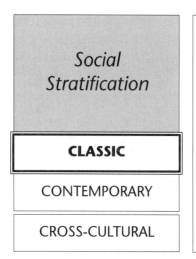

33

Some Principles of Stratification

Kingsley Davis and Wilbert E. Moore with a response by Melvin Tumin

Why is some degree of social stratification found everywhere? This selection outlines what has become known as the "Davis and Moore thesis": Social stratification is a consequence of the fact that some social positions are more important to the operation of a social system than others. The selection is followed by a critical response by Melvin Tumin, who suggests a number of ways in which social stratification is dysfunctional *for society.*

Starting from the proposition that no society is "classless," or unstratified, an effort is made to explain, in functional terms, the universal necessity which calls forth stratification in any social system. Next, an attempt is made to explain the roughly uniform distribution of prestige as between the major types of positions in every society. Since, however, there occur between one society and another great differences in the degree and kind of stratification, some attention is also given to the varieties of social inequality and the variable factors that give rise to them. . . .

Throughout, it will be necessary to keep in mind one thing—namely, that the discussion relates to the system of positions, not to the individuals occupying those positions. It is one thing to ask why different positions carry different degrees of prestige, and quite another to ask how certain individuals get into those positions. Although, as the argument will try to show, both questions are related, it is essential to keep them separate in our thinking. Most of the literature on stratification has tried to answer the second question (particularly with regard to the ease or difficulty of mobility between strata) without tackling the first. The first question, however, is logically prior and, in the case of any particular individual or group, factually prior.

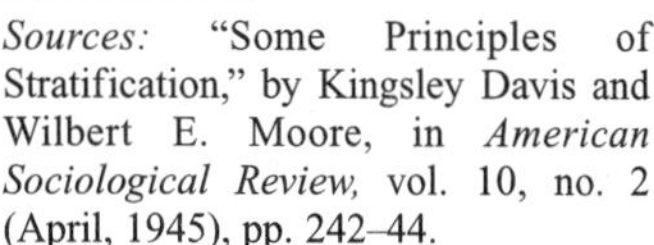

Sources: "Some Principles of Stratification," by Kingsley Davis and Wilbert E. Moore, in *American Sociological Review,* vol. 10, no. 2 (April, 1945), pp. 242–44.

"Some Principles of Stratification: A Critical Analysis," by Melvin Tumin, in *American Sociological Review,* vol. 18, no. 4 (Aug., 1953), pp. 387–93. Reprinted with permission.

THE FUNCTIONAL NECESSITY OF STRATIFICATION

Curiously, however, the main functional necessity explaining the universal presence of stratification is precisely the requirement faced by any society of placing and motivating individuals in the social structure. As a functioning mechanism a society must somehow distribute its members in social positions and induce them to perform the duties of these positions. It must thus concern itself with motivation at two different levels: to instill in the proper individuals the desire to fill certain positions, and, once in these positions, the desire to perform the duties attached to them. Even though the social order may be relatively static in form, there is a continuous process of metabolism as new individuals are born into it, shift with age, and die off. Their absorption into the positional system must somehow be arranged and motivated. This is true whether the system is competitive or noncompetitive. A competitive system gives greater importance to the motivation to achieve positions, whereas a noncompetitive system gives perhaps greater importance to the motivation to perform the duties of the positions; but in any system both types of motivation are required.

If the duties associated with the various positions were all equally pleasant to the human organism, all equally important to societal survival, and all equally in need of the same ability or talent, it would make no difference who got into which positions, and the problem of social placement would be greatly reduced. But actually it does make a great deal of difference who gets into which positions, not only because some positions are inherently more agreeable than others, but also because some require special talents or training and some are functionally more important than others. Also, it is essential that the duties of the positions be performed with the diligence that their importance requires. Inevitably, then, a society must have, first, some kind of rewards that it can use as inducements, and, second, some way of distributing these rewards differentially according to positions. The rewards and their distribution become a part of the social order, and thus give rise to stratification.

One may ask what kind of rewards a society has at its disposal in distributing its personnel and securing essential services. It has, first of all, the things that contribute to sustenance and comfort. It has, second, the things that contribute to humor and diversion. And it has, finally, the things that contribute to self respect and ego expansion. The last, because of the peculiarly social character of the self, is largely a function of the opinion of others, but it nonetheless ranks in importance with the first two. In any social system all three kinds of rewards must be dispensed differentially according to positions.

In a sense the rewards are "built into" the position. They consist in the "rights" associated with the position, plus what may be called its accompaniments or perquisites. Often the rights, and sometimes the accompaniments, are functionally related to the duties of the position. (Rights as viewed by the incumbent are usually duties as viewed by other members of the community.) However, there may be a host of subsidiary rights and perquisites that are not essential to the function of the position and have only an indirect and symbolic connection with its duties, but which still may be of considerable importance in inducing people to seek the positions and fulfill the essential duties.

If the rights and perquisites of different positions in a society must be unequal, then the society must be stratified, because that is precisely what stratification means. Social inequality is thus an unconsciously evolved device by which societies insure that the most important positions are conscientiously filled by the most qualified persons. Hence every society, no matter how simple or complex, must differentiate persons in terms of both prestige and esteem, and must therefore possess a certain amount of institutionalized inequality.

It does not follow that the amount or type of inequality need be the same in all societies. This is largely a function of factors that will be discussed presently.

THE TWO DETERMINANTS OF POSITIONAL RANK

Granting the general function that inequality subserves, one can specify the two factors that determine the relative rank of different positions. In general those positions convey the best reward, and hence have the highest rank, which (a) have the greatest importance for the society and (b) require the greatest training or talent. The first factor concerns function and is a matter of relative significance; the second concerns means and is a matter of scarcity.

Differential Functional Importance. Actually a society does not need to reward positions in proportion to their functional importance. It merely needs to give sufficient reward to them to insure that they will be filled competently. In other words, it must see that less essential positions do not compete successfully with more essential ones. If a position is easily filled, it need not be heavily rewarded, even though important. On the other hand, if it is important but hard to fill, the reward must be high enough to get it filled anyway. Functional importance is therefore a necessary but not a sufficient cause of high rank being assigned to a position.[1]

Differential Scarcity of Personnel. Practically all positions, no matter how acquired, require some form of skill or capacity for performance. This is implicit in the very notion of position, which implies that the incumbent must, by virtue of his incumbency, accomplish certain things.

There are, ultimately, only two ways in which a person's qualifications come about: through inherent capacity or through training. Obviously, in concrete activities both are always necessary, but from a practical standpoint the scarcity may lie primarily in one or the other, as well as in both. Some positions require innate talents of such high degree that the persons who fill them are bound to be rare. In many cases, however, talent is fairly abundant in the population but the training process is so long, costly, and elaborate that relatively few can qualify. Modern medicine, for example, is within the mental capacity of most individuals, but a medical education is so burdensome and expensive that virtually none would undertake it if the position of the M.D. did not carry a reward commensurate with the sacrifice.

If the talents required for a position are abundant and the training easy, the method of acquiring the position may have little to do with its duties. There may be, in fact, a virtually accidental relationship. But if the skills required are scarce by reason of the rarity of talent or the costliness of training, the position, if functionally important, must have an attractive power that will draw the necessary skills in competition with other positions. This means, in effect, that the position must be high in the social scale—must command great prestige, high salary, ample leisure, and the like.

How Variations Are to Be Understood. Insofar as there is a difference between one system of stratification and another, it is attributable to whatever factors affect the two determinants of differential reward—namely, functional importance and scarcity of personnel. Positions important in one society may not be important in another, because the conditions faced by the societies, or their degree of internal development, may be different. The same conditions, in turn, may affect the question of scarcity; for in some societies the stage of development, or the external situation, may wholly obviate the necessity of certain kinds of skill or talent. Any particular system of stratification, then, can be understood as a product of the special conditions affecting the two aforementioned grounds of differential reward.

CRITICAL RESPONSE BY MELVIN TUMIN

The fact of social inequality in human society is marked by its ubiquity and its antiquity. Every known society, past and present, distributes its scarce and demanded goods and services unequally. And there are attached to the positions which command unequal amounts of such goods and services certain highly morally-toned evaluations of their importance for the society.

The ubiquity and the antiquity of such inequality has given rise to the assumption that there must be something both inevitable and positively functional about such social arrangements. . . . Clearly, the truth or falsity of such an assumption is a strategic question for any general theory of social organization. It is therefore most curious that the basic premises and implications of the assumption have only been most casually explored by American sociologists. . . .

Let us take [the Davis and Moore] propositions and examine them *seriatim.*

(1) *Certain positions in any society are more functionally important than others and require special skills for their performance.*

The key term here is "functionally important." The functionalist theory of social organization is by no means clear and explicit about this term. The minimum common referent is to something known as the "survival value" of a social structure. This concept immediately involves a number of perplexing questions. Among these are: (a) the issue of minimum versus maximum survival, and the possible empirical referents which can be given to those terms; (b) whether such a proposition is a useless tautology since any *status quo* at any given moment is nothing more and nothing less than everything present in the *status quo.* In these terms, all acts and structures must be judged positively functional in that they constitute essential portions of the *status quo*; (c) what kind of calculus of functionality exists which will enable us, at this point in our development, to add and subtract long and short range consequences, with their mixed qualities, and arrive at some summative judgment regarding the rating an act or structure should receive on a scale of greater or lesser functionality? At best, we tend to make primarily intuitive judgments. Often enough, these judgments involve the use of value-laden criteria, or, at least, criteria which are chosen in preference to others not for any sociologically systematic reasons but by reason of certain implicit value preferences. . . .

A generalized theory of social stratification must recognize that the prevailing system of inducements and rewards is only one of many variants in the whole range of possible systems of motivation which, at least theoretically, are capable of working in human society. It is quite conceivable, of course, that a system of norms could be institutionalized in which the idea of threatened withdrawal of services, except under the most extreme circumstances, would be considered as absolute moral anathema. In such a case, the whole notion of relative functionality, as advanced by Davis and Moore, would have to be radically revised.

(2) *Only a limited number of individuals in any society have the talents which can be trained into the skills appropriate to these positions (i.e., the more functionally important positions).*

The truth of this proposition depends at least in part on the truth of proposition 1 above. It is, therefore, subject to all the limitations indicated above. But for the moment, let us assume the validity of the first proposition and concentrate on the question of the rarity of appropriate talent.

If all that is meant is that in every society there is a *range* of talent, and that some members of any society are by nature more talented than others, no sensible contradiction can be offered, but a question must be raised here regarding the amount of sound knowledge present in any society concerning the presence of talent in the population.

For, in every society there is some demonstrable ignorance regarding the amount of talent present in the population. *And the more rigidly stratified a society is, the less chance does that society have of discovering any new facts about the talents of its members.* Smoothly working and stable systems of stratification, wherever found, tend to build-in obstacles to the further exploration of the range of available talent. This is especially true in those societies where the opportunity to discover talent in any one generation varies with the differential resources of the parent generation. Where, for instance, access to education depends upon the wealth of one's parents, and where wealth is differentially distributed, large segments of the population are likely to be deprived of the chance even to *discover* what are their talents.

Whether or not differential rewards and opportunities are functional in any one generation, it is clear that if those differentials are allowed to be socially inherited by the next generation, then the stratification system is specifically dysfunctional for the discovery of talents in the next generation. In this fashion, systems of social stratification tend to limit the chances available to maximize the efficiency of discovery, recruitment and training of "functionally important talent."

. . . In this context, it may be asserted that there is some noticeable tendency for elites to restrict further access to their privileged positions, once they have sufficient power to enforce such restrictions. This is especially true in a culture where it is possible for an elite to contrive a high demand and a proportionately higher reward for its work by restricting the numbers of the elite available to do the work. The recruitment and training of doctors in modern United States is at least partly a case in point. . . .

(3) *The conversion of talents into skills involves a training period during which sacrifices of one kind or another are made by those undergoing the training.*

Davis and Moore introduce here a concept, "sacrifice," which comes closer than any of the rest of their vocabulary of analysis to being a direct reflection of the rationalizations, offered by the more fortunate members of a society, of the rightness of their occupancy of privileged positions. It is the least critically thought-out concept in the repertoire, and can also be shown to be least supported by the actual facts.

In our present society, for example, what are the sacrifices which talented persons undergo in the training period? The possibly serious losses involve the surrender of earning power and the cost of the training. The latter is generally borne by the parents of the talented youth undergoing training, and not by the trainees themselves. But this cost tends to be paid out of income which the parents were able to earn generally by virtue of *their* privileged positions in the hierarchy of stratification. That is to say, the parents' ability to pay for the training of their children is part of the differential *reward* they, the parents, received for their privileged positions in the society. And to charge this sum up against sacrifices made by the youth is falsely to perpetrate a bill or a debt already paid by the society to the parents. . . .

What tends to be completely overlooked, in addition, are the psychic and spiritual rewards which are available to the elite trainees by comparison with their age peers in the labor force. There is, first, the much higher prestige enjoyed by the college student and the professional-school student as compared with persons in shops and offices. There is, second, the extremely highly valued privilege of having greater opportunity for self-development. There is, third, all the psychic gain involved in being allowed to delay the assumption of adult responsibilities such as earning a living and supporting a family. There is, fourth, the access to leisure and freedom of a kind not likely to be experienced by the persons already at work.

If these are never taken into account as rewards of the training period it is not because they are not concretely present, but because the emphasis in American concepts of reward is almost exclusively placed on the material returns of positions. The emphases on enjoyment, entertainment, ego enhancement, prestige and esteem are introduced only when the differentials in these which accrue to the skilled positions need to be justified. If these other rewards were taken into account, it would be much more difficult to demonstrate that the training period, as presently operative, is really sacrificial. Indeed, it might turn out to be the case that even at this point in their careers, the elite trainees were being differentially rewarded relative to their age peers in the labor force. . . .

(4) *In order to induce the talented persons to undergo these sacrifices and acquire the training, their future positions must carry an inducement value in the form of differential, i.e., privileged and disproportionate access to the scarce and desired rewards which the society has to offer.*

Let us assume, for the purposes of the discussion, that the training period is sacrificial and the talent is rare in every conceivable human society. There is still the basic problem as to whether the allocation of differential rewards in scarce and desired goods and services is the only or the most efficient way of recruiting the appropriate talent to these positions.

For there are a number of alternative motivational schemes whose efficiency and adequacy ought at least to be considered in this context. What can be said, for instance, on behalf of the motivation which De Man called "joy in work," Veblen termed "instinct for workmanship" and which we latterly have come to identify as "intrinsic work satisfaction"? Or, to what extent could the motivation of "social duty" be institutionalized in such a fashion that self-interest and social interest come closely to coincide? Or, how much prospective confidence can be placed in the possibilities of institutionalizing "social service" as a widespread motivation for seeking one's appropriate position and fulfilling it conscientiously?

Are not these types of motivations, we may ask, likely to prove most appropriate for precisely the "most functionally important positions"? Especially in a mass industrial society, where the vast majority of positions become standardized and routinized, it is the skilled jobs which are likely to retain most of the quality of "intrinsic job satisfaction" and be most readily identifiable as socially serviceable. Is it indeed impossible then to build these motivations into the socialization pattern to which we expose our talented youth? . . .

(5) *These scarce and desired goods consist of rights and perquisites attached to, or built into, the positions and can be classified into those things which contribute to (a) sustenance and comfort; (b) humor and diversion; (c) self-respect and ego expansion.*

(6) *This differential access to the basic rewards of the society has as a consequence the differentiation of the prestige and esteem which various strata acquire. This may be said, along with the rights and perquisites, to constitute institutionalized social inequality, i.e., stratification.*

With the classification of the rewards offered by Davis and Moore there need be little argument. Some question must be raised, however, as to whether any reward system, built into a general stratification system, must allocate equal amounts of all three types of reward in order to function effectively, or whether one type of reward may be emphasized to the virtual neglect of others. This raises the further question regarding which type of emphasis is likely to prove most effective as a differential inducer. Nothing in the known facts about human motivation impels us to favor one type of reward over the other, or to insist that all three types of reward must be built into the positions in comparable amounts if the position is to have an inducement value.

It is well known, of course, that societies differ considerably in the kinds of rewards they emphasize in their efforts to maintain a reasonable balance between responsibility and reward. There are, for instance, numerous societies in which the conspicuous display of differential economic advantage is considered extremely bad taste. In short, our present knowledge commends to us the possibility of considerable plasticity in the way in which different types of rewards can be structured into a functioning society. This is to say, it cannot yet be demonstrated that it is *unavoidable* that differential prestige and esteem shall accrue to positions which command differential rewards in power and property.

What does seem to be unavoidable is that differential prestige shall be given to those in any society who conform to the normative order as against those who deviate from that order in a way judged immoral and detrimental. On the assumption that the continuity of a society depends on the continuity and stability of its normative order, some such distinction between conformists and deviants seems inescapable.

It also seems to be unavoidable that in any society, no matter how literate its tradition, the older, wiser and more experienced individuals who are charged with the enculturation and socialization of the young must have more power than the young, on the assumption that the task of effective socialization demands such differential power.

But this differentiation in prestige between the conformist and the deviant is by no means the same distinction as that between strata of individuals each of which operates *within* the normative order, and is composed of adults. . . .

(7) *Therefore, social inequality among different strata in the amounts of scarce and desired goods, and the amounts of prestige and esteem which they receive, is both positively functional and inevitable in any society.*

If the objections which have heretofore been raised are taken as reasonable, then it may be stated that the only items which any society *must* distribute unequally are the power and property necessary for the performance of different tasks. If such differential power and property are viewed by all as commensurate with the differential responsibilities, and if they are culturally defined as *resources* and not as rewards, then no differentials in prestige and esteem need follow.

Historically, the evidence seems to be that every time power and property are distributed unequally, no matter what the cultural definition, prestige and esteem differentiations have tended to result as well. Historically, however, no systematic effort has ever been made, under propitious circumstances, to develop the tradition that each man is as socially worthy as all other men so long as he performs his appropriate tasks conscientiously. While such a tradition seems utterly utopian, no known facts in psychological or social science have yet demonstrated its impossibility or its dysfunctionality for the continuity of a society. The achievement of a full institutionalization of such a tradition seems far too remote to contemplate. Some successive approximations at such a tradition, however, are not out of the range of prospective social innovation.

What, then, of the "positive functionality" of social stratification? Are there other, negative, functions of institutionalized social inequality which can be identified, if only tentatively? Some such dysfunctions of stratification have already been suggested in the body of this paper. Along with others they may now be stated, in the form of provisional assertions, as follows:

1. Social stratification systems function to limit the possibility of discovery of the full range of talent available in a society. This results from the fact of unequal access to appropriate motivation, channels of recruitment, and centers of training.
2. In foreshortening the range of available talent, social stratification systems function to set limits upon the possibility of expanding the productive resources of the society, at least relative to what might be the case under conditions of greater equality of opportunity.
3. Social stratification systems function to provide the elite with the political power necessary to procure acceptance and dominance of an ideology which rationalizes the *status quo*, whatever it may be, as "logical," "natural" and "morally right." In this manner, social stratification systems function as essentially conservative influences in the societies in which they are found.
4. Social stratification systems function to distribute favorable self-images unequally throughout a population. To the extent that such favorable self-images are requisite to the development of the creative potential inherent in men, to that extent stratification systems function to limit the development of this creative potential.
5. To the extent that inequalities in social rewards cannot be made fully acceptable to the less privileged in a society, social stratification systems function to encourage hostility, suspicion, and distrust among the various segments of a society and thus to limit the possibilities of extensive social integration.
6. To the extent that the sense of significant membership in a society depends on one's place on the prestige ladder of the society, social stratification systems function to distribute unequally the sense of significant membership in the population.

7. To the extent that loyalty to a society depends on a sense of significant membership in the society, social stratification systems function to distribute loyalty unequally in the population.
8. To the extent that participation and apathy depend upon the sense of significant membership in the society, social stratification systems function to distribute the motivation to participate unequally in a population.

Each of the eight foregoing propositions contains implicit hypotheses regarding the consequences of unequal distribution of rewards in a society in accordance with some notion of the functional importance of various positions. These are empirical hypotheses, subject to test. They are offered here only as exemplary of the kinds of consequences of social stratification which are not often taken into account in dealing with the problem. They should also serve to reinforce the doubt that social inequality is a device which is uniformly functional for the role of guaranteeing that the most important tasks in a society will be performed conscientiously by the most competent persons.

The obviously mixed character of the functions of social inequality should come as no surprise to anyone. If sociology is sophisticated in any sense, it is certainly with regard to its awareness of the mixed nature of any social arrangement, when the observer takes into account long- as well as short-range consequences and latent as well as manifest dimensions.

CRITICAL-THINKING QUESTIONS

1. Why do Davis and Moore argue that all societies attach greater rewards to some positions than to others?
2. Does the "Davis and Moore thesis" justify social stratification as it presently exists in the United States (or anywhere else)?
3. In what ways does Tumin argue that social stratification is *dysfunctional* for a social sys-tem?

NOTE

1. Unfortunately, functional importance is difficult to establish. To use the position's prestige to establish it, as is often unconsciously done, constitutes circular reasoning from our point of view. There are, however, two independent clues: (a) the degree to which a position is functionally unique, there being no other positions that can perform the same function satisfactorily; and (b) the degree to which other positions are dependent on the one in question. Both clues are best exemplified in organized systems of positions built around one major function. Thus in most complex societies the religious, political, economic, and educational functions are handled by distinct structures not easily interchangeable. In addition each structure possesses many different positions, some clearly dependent on, if not subordinate to, others. In sum, when an institutional nucleus becomes differentiated around one main function, and at the same time organizes a large portion of the population into its relationships, *key* positions in it are of the highest functional importance. The absence of such specialization does not prove functional unimportance, for the whole society may be relatively unspecialized; but it is safe to assume that the more important functions receive the first and clearest structural differentiation.

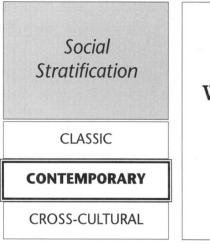

Social Stratification

CLASSIC

CONTEMPORARY

CROSS-CULTURAL

34

Who Has How Much and Why

Andrew Hacker

While many economists and politicians have applauded the expansion of the U.S. economy during the 1990s, a number of sociologists point out that income inequality is greater now than it was in the 1960s: The rich have gotten richer, the middle class has been shrinking, and the working class is barely surviving. In this selection, Andrew Hacker explains why he believes that, in terms of income and wealth, the United States is one of the most stratified nations in the industrialized world.

YES, THE RICH ARE GETTING RICHER

John F. Kennedy defended the importance of business prosperity by arguing that "a rising tide lifts all boats." It was a deft figure of speech: We imagine tugboats, tankers, and superliners all together on the high water.

However, recent decades have failed to validate Kennedy's thesis. Of course, there can be no denying that the tide of wealth in America has swelled. Between 1976 and 1996, the amount of money in the hands of America's households rose from $2.9 trillion to $4.8 trillion, after the 1976 figure is adjusted to 1996-value dollars. All told, the income of the average household went from $39,415 to $47,123, also in constant dollars, resulting in a twenty-year gain of 19.6 percent.

[Table 1] shows how various segments of the society fared during those two decades. Its figures, which come from annual Census Bureau surveys, simply divide the total number of households into five equal groups, ranging from the poorest to the best-off. So in 1996, each fifth contained 20.2 million homes, consisting of families or of individuals living alone or together. Thus the incomes of those in the middle fifth ranged from $27,760 to $44,006, with an average of $35,486. The Census also specifies the incomes of the richest 5 percent of all households. Lastly, figures are given for the share of all household income received by each segment. Thus in 1996, the middle fifth ended up with 15.1 percent of the total, or $719 billion from the $4.8 trillion.

Clearly, all boats did not rise equally with this tide. Here were the twenty-year percentage increases—and one decrease—in the average income for each of the quintiles and also for the top 5 percent:

Source: Reprinted with the permission of Scribner, a Division of Simon & Schuster from *Money* by Andrew Hacker.

Richest 5%	+59.9%	Middle 20%	+5.3%
Top 20%	+35.4%	Fourth 20%	+4.5%
Second 20%	+12.4%	Bottom 20%	–0.9%

While all segments of the population enjoyed an increase in income, the top fifth did thirteen times better than the fourth fifth. And measured by their shares of the aggregate, not just the bottom fifth but the three above it all ended up losing ground. Indeed, the overall share received by those segments, comprising four of every five households, dropped from 56.7 percent to 51.0 percent. At the same time, the average income of the richest 5 percent rose from a comfortable $126,131 to an affluent $201,684.

. . . Two factors intertwine. On the one hand, more of the 1996 households had two or more incomes coming in. Thus the $115,514 average for the top fifth could represent, say, $72,035 from one spouse and $43,479 from the other. But it is noteworthy that while there were also more dual earnings down in the fourth quintile, their income average rose by only $601 during the two decades.

The second factor is that 1976 to 1996 saw the creation of more high individual incomes at one end of the scale and more low incomes at the other. Thus the proportion of men earning more than $50,000—again, computed in constant dollars—grew from 14.9 percent to 17.6 percent. But overall, the median income for men dropped from $24,898 to $23,834, due to declining wages for those in the bottom tiers. All indications are that these disparities will continue in the decades ahead.

CHANGING STATES

If income disparities are on the rise, they are also being compressed. . . . In 1960, income in the richest state (Connecticut) was 2.6 times that of the poorest state (Mississippi). By 1996, the gap (Alaska versus West Virginia) had been reduced to a ratio of 2.0. And if the 1996 comparison stays with the contiguous states (New Jersey versus West Virginia), the richest-poorest ratio declines to 1.8.

Closing the gap has nurtured a national homogeneity. This is illustrated vividly in the shopping mall, which has emerged as America's most distinctive institution. Set down in malls in New Hampshire or New Mexico, we would be hard pressed to say where in the country we are. All have Gaps and Radio Shacks, multiplexes playing the same movies, and though food markets may have regional names, their merchandise is much the same.

Mobility also plays a role. The 1990 Census reported that over half the residents of New Hampshire, Florida, Wyoming, Nevada, Oregon, Arizona, Colorado, California, and Alaska had

Table 1 How Households Divided the Nation's Income, 1976 and 1996 (in 1996-value dollars)

1976			*1996*	
Share of All Income	*Segment Average*	*Household Segments*	*Segment Average*	*Share of All Income*
43.3%	$85,335	Top 20%	$115,514	49.0%
24.8%	$48,876	Second 20%	$54,922	23.2%
17.1%	$33,701	Middle 20%	$35,486	15.1%
10.4%	$20,496	Fourth 20%	$21,097	9.0%
4.4%	$8,672	Bottom 20%	$8,596	3.7%
100.0%	$39,416	All Households	$47,123	100.0%
16.0%	$126,131	Richest 5%	$201,684	21.4%

been born elsewhere. And by now, Maryland, Idaho, Delaware, Washington, Virginia, and New Mexico are likely to have joined the list. New arrivals adapt quite easily, since each year sees more Americans sharing common attitudes and attributes.

Among the more striking developments has been the economic rise of the South. In 1960, the six poorest states were all from that region, while by 1996 only three were. Indeed, household income doubled in Arkansas, Mississippi, and South Carolina. Among the losers, Ohio dropped to nine places behind Virginia, and New York's income fell below the national median [see Table 2].

WOMEN AND CHILDREN LAST?

All parents want their children to have a good start in life, and one underpinning is a family budget ample enough to provide a range of opportunities. Yet a rising proportion of children are growing up in homes without the means even for basic necessities.

In 1995, a third of all youngsters lived in homes with incomes of less than $25,000, and one in five were in homes where the income was below $15,000. At issue is what is required for growing up in modern America. More often than not, low incomes bring inferior local schools and inadequate exposure to the manners demanded by the wider world. As a result, millions of American children are deprived of a chance to develop whatever promise they have. Of course, poverty is not the only factor. We all know of youngsters, especially from immigrant families—who move far beyond the world of their parents. Still, two causes of the increased impoverishment of children should be singled out.

Of America's 70.3 million children aged eighteen or under, 31.3 percent are living with only one parent, or with a relative other than a parent, or in a foster home. The 68.7 percent with both of their parents in their home is an all-time low. In 1970, for example, the proportion was 85.2 percent. While it can be questioned whether two parents are necessary for a child's optimal development, the fact remains that single parents earn a lot less money. For two-parent families, the median income is $49,969, almost double the $26,990 for the relatively small group of single fathers and more than three times the $16,235 for single mothers. (The two-parent and one-parent families do not differ much in size. Those with two parents average 1.49 children; and those with single mothers average 1.34.) Nor is childhood poverty due only to marital breakups. Among today's single mothers, an all-time high of 35.6 percent have never been married. In 1970, the proportion was 7.1 percent.

Racial disparities are also reflected in the changing composition of families. As [Table 3] shows, even when black children are raised by two parents, their households are twice as likely as white two-parent homes to have incomes under $15,000. While the $43,946 median income for two-parent black families is fairly

Table 2 A Dozen Gainers and Losers

Gainers' Rank	*1960*	*1996*	*Losers' Rank*	*1960*	*1996*
Wisconsin	14th	7th	Michigan	5th	13th
Colorado	20th	6th	Ohio	7th	23rd
Iowa	30th	24th	New York	9th	27th
Virginia	34th	14th	Indiana	16th	26th
Georgia	40th	31st	New Mexico	25th	49th
North Carolina	46th	28th	West Virginia	37th	50th

Table 3 The Coming Generation: Incomes of Families Where Children Are Being Raised

Incomes of White Families	*All White Families*	*Two Parents (76.3%)*	*Mother Only (18.7%)**
Over $40,000	54.0%	65.0%	15.6%
$15,000–$40,000	32.6%	29.3%	42.6%
Under $15,000	13.4%	5.7%	41.8%
White Median	$43,091	$50,594	$18,099
Per Black $1,000	$1,901	$1,151	$1,393
Incomes of Black Families	*All Black Families*	*Two Parents (39.7%)*	*Mother Only (54.0%)**
Over $40,000	28.1%	55.9%	8.5%
$15,000–$40,000	36.6%	35.3%	36.0%
Under $15,000	35.3%	8.8%	55.5%
Black Median	$22,671	$43,946	$12,989
Per White $1,000	$526	$869	$718

*The remaining 6.3 percent of black children and 5.0 percent of white children are living with their fathers or with other relatives or are in foster care.

close to the $50,594 for whites, the overall black median is only 52.6 percent of the white figure. Moreover, the typical black woman who is raising children on her own must make do with $12,989, compared with $18,099 for the white single mother. These figures suggest that the United States disproportionately denies opportunities to black children. Stated another way, one reason why America's children are not being allowed to show their true talents is that many of them are of African origin.

THE SALARY SPECTRUM

[Table 4] does not list the incomes of corporate chairmen, medical school professors, or investment firm partners. . . . This table records the wages and salaries of full-time workers in forty-two typical occupations.

Despite its reputation as a high-wage economy, the midpoint pay for America's full-time workers in 1996 was a rather modest $25,480, not really enough to give a family a middle-class living standard. The median for the 51.9 million employed men was $28,964, and for the 39.0 million women it was $21,736. (So an average working couple might bring in $50,700, which explains why there are so many dual-earner households.) The table's figures raise several questions and suggest some partial answers.

Women as a group are paid less, but is that because they are clustered in lower-wage occupations? The earnings of bank tellers, hairdressers, and sewing-machine operators suggest that this is the case. Yet the pay for nurses and elementary school teachers—jobs traditionally held by women—have surpassed that of many occupations dominated by men. (Teachers' unions tend to remain strong, while those of construction workers have lost much of their dominant force.) Moreover, each year finds more women in better-paid positions such as pharmacists, financial managers, and college professors.

Indeed, women now account for 38.9 percent of all pharmacists, compared with 12.1 percent in 1970. For insurance adjusters, the respective figures are 71.9 percent and 29.6 percent. And women now make up 54.2 percent of the nation's

Table 4 Median Pay for Full-time Wage and Salary Workers, 1996 (with percentage of women in each occupation)

Above National Median			*Below National Median*		
	Earnings[1]	*Women*[2]		*Earnings*	*Women*
Lawyers (salaried)	$59,748	35.3%	Printing operators	$25,168	11.0%
Pharmacists	$51,584	38.9%	Automotive mechanics	$24,856	0.9%
Engineers	$49,348	8.6%	Flight attendants	$21,684	81.4%
Computer analysts	$46,332	28.3%	Secretaries	$21,112	98.5%
College faculty	$45,240	38.0%	Factory assemblers	$19,656	42.0%
Financial managers	$40,664	55.4%	Taxicab drivers	$19,448	8.4%
Computer programmers	$40,144	30.1%	Data entry keyers	$19,032	86.2%
Architects	$39,520	19.4%	Meat cutters	$19,032	21.7%
Registered nurses	$36,244	91.5%	Telephone operators	$18,876	88.9%
High school teachers	$36,244	54.8%	Security guards	$17,316	19.6%
Journalists	$35,776	50.0%	Bakers	$17,004	38.8%
Police officers	$34,684	12.4%	Bank tellers	$16,380	90.7%
Elementary school teachers	$34,424	82.8%	Bartenders	$16,120	54.2%
Librarians	$34,320	82.9%	Janitors and cleaners	$15,652	27.6%
Electricians	$31,772	2.2%	Hairdressers	$15,184	88.3%
Realtors	$31,460	51.3%	Garage workers	$14,352	3.3%
Electronic repairers	$31,304	5.5%	Waiters and waitresses	$14,092	70.1%
Motor vehicle salespeople	$30,836	8.8%	Hotel clerks	$13,884	71.2%
Designers	$30,784	48.0%	Cooks and chefs	$13,728	35.2%
Clergy	$27,768	11.5%	Laundry workers	$13,208	70.3%
Insurance adjusters	$26.312	71.9%	Sewing machine operators	$13,208	83.0%

[1]All workers, median earnings: $25,480
[2]Median percentage of women: 42.9%

bartenders, as against 21.1 percent twenty-six years earlier. Yet these shifts do not always bring better earnings. When insurance adjuster was mainly a man's occupation, it paid well for inspecting dented cars and burned-out buildings. Today, most are women who tap claims into computers.

Many of the amenities we desire depend on a supply of low-wage workers. This is clearly the case with those who launder our linen and park our cars. But it is also true of hotel clerks, most of whom are young people who haven't yet chosen a long-term career. Waiters and waitresses also tend to be younger or are older women bringing in a household's second income. Sewing-machine operators, many of whom are recent immigrants, often labor under third-world conditions. Were they to demand more than their current pay, their employers would probably send their work to an actual third-world country.

ARE WE STILL NUMBER ONE?

For most of the twentieth century, the United States has led the world in industrial production, technological innovation, and personal standards of living. In 1970, for example, America ranked first in per capita output. Our nearest rivals were Sweden, Canada, Denmark, and Switzerland, which like us had escaped being World War II battlegrounds. At that time, even advanced countries such as the Netherlands and Britain were only half as productive as the United States. Yet there were signs that change was under way: A once bomb-scarred Germany had risen to sixth place.

The per capita figures for 1995, the most recent at this writing, show dramatic changes. The United States has fallen to sixth place [see Table 5], a sad descent considering that its primacy once seemed beyond challenge. Three

Table 5 Per Capita Gross Domestic Product and Purchasing Power (per $1,000 for the United States)

	GDP per Capita, 1970		*GDP per Capita, 1995*		*Purchasing Power, 1995*	
1.	UNITED STATES	$1,000	Switzerland	$1,506	UNITED STATES	$1,000
2.	Sweden	$857	Japan	$1,469	Switzerland	$958
3.	Canada	$776	Norway	$1,158	Japan	$819
4.	Denmark	$663	Denmark	$1,108	Norway	$813
5.	Switzerland	$662	Germany	$1,020	Belgium	$803
6.	Germany*	$641	UNITED STATES	$1,000	Austria	$788
7.	Norway	$622	Austria	$997	Denmark	$787
8.	France	$613	France	$926	Canada	$783
9.	Australia	$572	Belgium	$916	France	$779
10.	Belgium	$556	Netherlands	$890	Germany	$744
11.	Netherlands	$497	Sweden	$880	Netherlands	$739
12.	United Kingdom	$450	Finland	$763	Italy	$736
13.	Austria	$409	Canada	$718	United Kingdom	$714
14.	Japan	$404	Italy	$705	Sweden	$687
15.	Italy	$365	United Kingdom	$693	Finland	$658

*West Germany only.

other countries—Austria, France, and Belgium—were less than $100 behind America in per capita GDP. Most striking is that in the quarter-century, Japan tripled its per capita production. Although Sweden and the United Kingdom dropped in the rankings, their output still improved while America's was treading water.

Perhaps embarrassed by the GDP measure, which gave the United States sixth place, American economists devised an alternative gauge. This index computes "personal purchasing power" for each country, by noting differing price levels. Example: While hourly wages in Britain and America are quite similar ($9.37 versus $9.56), the same basket of goods in Britain costs 42.2 percent more. With this new formula, the United States is once again number one, but not because our economy is more innovative or efficient. Prices are lower here due to a combination of choice and circumstance.

Other countries raise much of their public revenue from some variant of a "value-added tax," which is factored into the price of purchases. This charge tends to be "invisible" since it is seldom put on price tags or sales slips. But it clearly raises prices, as can be seen by what a gallon of gasoline costs here and abroad: Austria, $3.13; Italy, $3.46; Norway, $3.79, Japan, $4.14; United States, $1.24. Other counties tax themselves to provide funds for social services and public amenities. Americans have chosen lower taxes and prices and reduced levels of benefits.

America is the world's largest market, measured by the amount of money available for shopping. With one dominant language, national advertising media, and familiar brand names, economies of scale can be reflected in reduced prices. We have also mastered the delivery of bargains at complexes such as Price Cosco and Wal-Mart, and via mail from Lands' End and L. L. Bean. Other countries are beginning to build supermarkets and shopping centers, but they are still well behind America.

So, yes, the United States has the world's highest living standard—if gauged by the sums we devote to personal purchases. But being the leader in consumption is not necessarily a cause for congratulation. If production is what creates national wealth and the prospect of a prosperous future, America is no longer first and is unlikely to regain its primacy.

CRITICAL-THINKING QUESTIONS

1. What data does Hacker offer to support his argument that, in the United States, the rich are getting richer and the poor are getting poorer? Why does he predict that such disparities will continue?

2. According to Hacker, how do geographical mobility, sex, race, marital status, and occupation affect families' socioeconomic status?

3. How would you explain the increasing social stratification in the United States?

35

Women's Poverty in Africa

Social Stratification

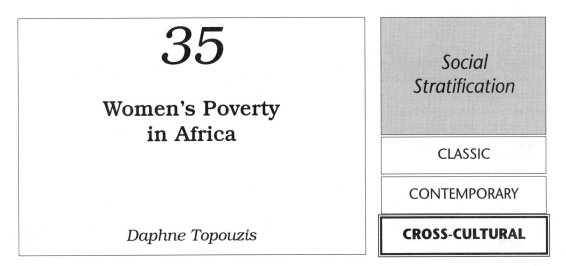

CLASSIC

CONTEMPORARY

CROSS-CULTURAL

Daphne Topouzis

The concept "feminization of poverty" refers to the increasing share of poor people who are women. Poverty is growing faster in Africa than in any other part of the world. In this article, Daphne Topouzis discusses why the poorest of the poor in African countries are women and their dependent families. Note the interplay among economic, social, political, and environmental factors that create a "vicious circle of poverty" that will be difficult for even the most well-intentioned policies to break.

An alarming trend with potentially devastating economic, social, and environmental consequences is developing across Africa, with evidence showing that nearly two-thirds of Africa's fast-growing, poverty-stricken population consists of women. The picture becomes bleaker considering that between 1970 and 1985, the number of Africans living in abject poverty rose by 75 percent to about 270 million, or half the population of the continent, according to the International Labor Organization.

Poor shelter, malnutrition, disease, illiteracy, overwork, a short life expectancy, and high maternal and infant mortality rates mark the lives of the poorest of poor women and their dependent families. Poverty is growing faster in Africa than in any other part of the world. Even more alarming, perhaps, is the fact that the feminization of poverty is becoming increasingly structural, advancing well beyond the reach of policy-makers and development projects. As a result, it is becoming virtually impossible for women to escape the cycle of crushing poverty in which they are entrenched.

If this trend is not reversed, however, about 400 million Africans will be living in absolute poverty by 1995, argues the newly released United Nations Development Programme *1990 Human Development Report,* and up to 260 million could be women.

The feminization of poverty is only beginning to be recognized as a pressing problem in Africa and elsewhere in the world, and there are as yet no statistical indicators or figures available to help identify the magnitude of the crisis. At best, studies on poverty refer to it in passing, but more often, they fail to appreciate the ramifications of this shift in the pattern of poverty on overall economic development.

The reasons behind the increasing concentration of poverty among women in Africa are as

Source: From "The Feminization of Poverty," by Daphne Topouzis, from *Africa Report,* July/August, 1990, pp. 60–63,

varied as they are complex. A combination of prolonged drought and the debt crisis have triggered large-scale male migrations to the cities, leaving one-third of all rural households headed by women. In some regions of sub-Saharan Africa, up to 43 percent of all households are headed by women, according to the U.N. *1989 World Survey on Women in Development.*

This phenomenon is transforming the family structure and socioeconomic fabric of African societies across the continent, placing additional financial burdens on already poor and overworked women. Women heads of households tend to have more dependents, fewer breadwinning family members, and restricted access to productive resources. "Female members of a poor household are often worse off than male members because of gender-based differences in the distribution of food and other entitlements within the family," adds the *1990 Human Development Report.*

The poverty crisis has been further aggravated by ill-fated agricultural policies or a neglect of agriculture by national governments, rapid population growth, and pressure on land available for cultivation—all of which have contributed to declining productivity and food consumption in many African countries. Between 1980 and 1985, per capita income in Africa declined by 30 percent, taking into account the negative terms of trade. The first victims of food shortages and famine tend to be women with young children, which is not surprising, considering that just under half of all African women and 63 percent of pregnant women suffer from anemia.

The adverse effects of the economic recession and remedial structural adjustment programs should be added to the list of factors that have contributed to the impoverishment of women. Structural adjustment has in many cases increased unemployment in the cities, and women are again the first to be laid off in the formal sector. Austerity measures have also decreased women's purchasing power and removed subsidies on basic foodstuffs. Thus, already overworked women have no choice but to work even longer hours to keep their families afloat, often at the expense of caring for their children and their own health. According to the U.N. Fund for Population Activity's *State of the World Population 1990,* rural African women tend to have more children in order to lighten their load with food production.

And last but not least, armed conflicts in Sudan, Ethiopia, Angola, Mozambique, and civil unrest in several other countries have left thousands of women widowed, displaced, or abandoned to a life of permanent emergency as refugees: An estimated two-thirds of the 5 million adult refugee population on the continent are women. "When armies march, there is no harvest," reads one African saying. As a result, women refugees often become almost totally dependent on relief from international organizations whose resources for them are currently on the decline.

THE PLIGHT OF RURAL WOMEN

From near food self-sufficiency in 1970, Africa over the past two decades has witnessed a marked decline in food production and consumption per person, while real per capita access to resources has decreased accordingly. African women, who produce, process, and market over 75 percent of the food, suffer greater deprivations than men and continue to be ignored by national policy-makers and international aid organizations.

Thus, even though the past two years have seen bumper crops in many Sahelian countries, women farmers have not benefited from this, and the poorest among them are still unable to grow enough food to sustain their families. One of the reasons is that, as a whole, they remain excluded from access to improved technology, credit, extension services, and land. Landless, unskilled, and illiterate rural women often live precarious lives on the edge of impoverishment, regardless of how hard they work.

Women in developing countries work twice as many hours as men for one-tenth of the income. In East Africa, women spend up to sixteen hours every day growing, processing, and preparing food, gathering fuel and water, and performing other household chores, in addition to caring for their children and the extended family. In Malawi, women put in twice as many hours as men cultivating maize, the main cash crop, and the same number of hours in cotton, in addition to doing all the housework.

In South Africa's homelands, women walk from three to five miles every other day to collect fuelwood weighing up to sixty-five pounds, according to *Apartheid's Environmental Toll,* a report released by Worldwatch Institute in Washington, D.C. Environmental degradation affects women directly, as they have to walk longer distances to fetch fuelwood and water. In turn, impoverished women—most of whom live in ecologically fragile areas—have little alternative but to continue degrading their environment in order to survive. Poverty, overpopulation, and environmental degradation are not only inextricably linked, but they continually reinforce one another.

URBAN WOMEN IN "PINK COLLAR JOBS"

Women are still a minority in the public sector in Africa: In Benin and Togo, 21 percent of public sector employees are women, while in Tanzania, their share in formal employment was 15.6 percent in 1983. Poor urban women have little professional training. As a result, they are reduced to low-wage, low-status, or "pink collar," jobs, which include clerical, teaching, and social services. In Kenya, 78.9 percent of the female work force in the service sector is employed in pink collar jobs, while only 6.1 percent is employed in high-paying jobs. The economic crisis has had a profound effect on these women, with unemployment rising by 10 percent annually in the period 1980–1985. In Botswana and Nigeria, the rate of unemployment among young women under twenty was 44 percent and 42 percent respectively in 1987, as opposed to males of the same age group, at 23.5 and 22.2 percent. For those who retained their jobs, wages were often slashed by one-third.

The vast majority of urban women work in the informal sector where earnings are meager, and there is no legal protection or job security: In Ghana, 85 percent of all employment in trade in 1970 was accounted for by women; in Nigeria, 94 percent of the street food vendors are women. These women earn substantially less than their male counterparts and often live on the edge of poverty, so that a slight deterioration in economic conditions, such as price rises of essential foodstuffs, can directly threaten their survival, as well as that of their families. In Dar es Salaam, argues the *1990 Human Development Report,* poor women had to cut back from three meals a day to two. In extreme cases, poor urban women have resorted to begging, prostitution, and other illicit activities in order to survive.

STRUCTURAL ADJUSTMENT

Structural adjustment programs prescribed by international financial institutions have largely failed to integrate women into economic development and have imposed drastic cuts in education and health services, thereby exacerbating existing inequalities and marginalizing women further. A recent study conducted by a group of experts set up by the Commonwealth Ministers Responsible for Women, entitled *Engendering Adjustment for the 1990s,* argues that women in developing countries "have been at the epicenter of the crisis and have borne the brunt of the adjustment efforts."

Particularly alarming is the fact that for the first time in many years, maternal and infant mortality rates are beginning to rise and girls' school enrollments are starting to fall. "If you educate a man, you simply educate an individual, but if you educate a woman, you educate a family," said J. E. Aggrey, a Ghanaian educator. Few, however. have taken this message seriously: Illiteracy in Africa is four times as high among women as among men, and the higher the level of education, the lower the percentage of girls. In Côte d'Ivoire, 82 women among 707 students completed university studies in 1983. In thirteen out of eighteen African countries for which figures are available, expenditure per pupil in primary school decreased dramatically, up to 40 percent, between 1980 and 1984/5.

Women's health has also suffered severe setbacks as a result of structural adjustment programs. In Nigeria, where health fees and social service subsidies were slashed, health care and food costs have spiralled by 400 to 600 percent, according to a recent report in *West Africa.* About 75,000 women die each year from causes related to pregnancy or childbirth in Nigeria alone—that is, one woman every seven minutes, according to the same source. In Benin, Cameroon, Nigeria, Malawi, Mali, and Mozambique, one out of five fifteen-year-old women dies before she reaches forty-five years of age for reasons related to pregnancy and childbirth.

WOMEN IN DEVELOPMENT

Between 1965 and 1986, women were neglected by development planners largely due to misconceptions and misdirected efforts and as a result, hardly benefited from development aid, argued a 1988 World Bank report. Thus, it was taken for granted that all households are male-headed, that women do not work, and that by increasing the income of a household, everyone will benefit. Rural development projects geared toward women tended to emphasize training and health, hygiene, nutrition, and child care, neglecting to help women improve their capabilities as farmers. Women were barred from access to credit and improved technology because it was the men who were addressed as the real producers.

A case in point is the Sedhiou Project in Senegal, which provided credit to cooperatives but refused female membership. In a British-funded cotton growing project in Bura, Kenya, women have no access to plots where they can grow food, and malnutrition has increased among their children; at an integrated rural development project in Zambia, women have little time to grow food and care for their families because they have to work long hours on their husbands' cash crop, to mention but a few examples.

The devastating drought, famines, and the economic crisis of the 1980s pressured African governments and development organizations into recognizing the vital role women play in economic development. Most African governments now have a ministry, bureau, or department dealing with women's affairs and some legislative adjustments have been made to improve the socioeconomic status of women. These initiatives, however, have not reached the most vulnerable and impoverished of women, not least because their needs are multisectoral and are unlikely to be met by a single government department, while being ignored or given token recognition by other ministries.

In essence, women's economic contributions remain largely overlooked and equitable development strategies have yet to be translated into effective plans of action. In many countries, African women still cannot own the land they cultivate or get access to credit. In Lesotho, women lack the most basic legal and social rights: They cannot sign contracts, borrow money, or slaughter cattle without their husbands' consent.

Sustainable development has to become synonymous with equitable development, and economic recovery will only come about if the feminization of poverty is tackled as an economic and social problem rather than as a purely developmental or exclusively a women's problem. There are some encouraging initiatives in Ghana, Tanzania, and Nigeria, where farmers' cooperatives are obtaining loans for poor women from local banks.

However, a formidable task awaits national governments and development workers: Access to productive resources such as land, capital, and technology, fair wages, training, and education and basic health care are essential conditions if African women are to break out of the vicious circle of poverty and underdevelopment. Equally pressing, however, are policy-making and legislative reforms to combat discrimination against women and change male attitudes regarding women's contributions to social and economic life.

CRITICAL-THINKING QUESTIONS

1. What are the reasons for the "feminization of poverty" in many African countries?
2. In 1970, most Africans were self-sufficient in food production and consumption. Why has this self-sufficiency decreased dramatically in the last two decades?
3. How have attitudes *about* women shaped economic and educational policies *toward* women?

Gender

CLASSIC

CONTEMPORARY

CROSS-CULTURAL

36

Sex and Temperament in Three Primitive Societies

Margaret Mead

The work of anthropologist Margaret Mead laid the foundation for much of our contemporary sociological research and debate on gender. Are "masculine" and "feminine" traits innate or learned? Do men and women differ because of nature (heredity) or nurture (socialization)? Based on her studies of three "primitive peoples" in New Guinea, Margaret Mead argues that cultural conditioning is more important than biology in shaping women's and men's behavior.

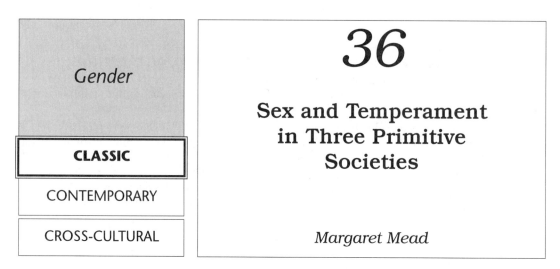

We have now considered in detail the approved personalities of each sex among three primitive peoples. We found the Arapesh—both men and women—displaying a personality that, out of our historically limited preoccupations, we would call maternal in its parental aspects, and feminine in its sexual aspects. We found men, as well as women, trained to be cooperative, unaggressive, responsive to the needs and demands of others. We found no idea that sex was a powerful driving force either for men or for women. In marked contrast to these attitudes, we found among the Mundugumor that both men and women developed as ruthless, aggressive, positively sexed individuals, with the maternal cherishing aspects of personality at a minimum. Both men and women approximated to a personality type that we in our culture would find only in an undisciplined and very violent male. Neither the Arapesh nor the Mundugumor profit by a contrast between the sexes; the Arapesh ideal is the mild, responsive man married to the mild, responsive woman; the Mundugumor ideal is the violent aggressive man married to the violent aggressive woman. In the third tribe, the Tchambuli, we found a genuine reversal of the sex attitudes of our own culture, with the woman the dominant, impersonal, managing partner, the man the less responsible and the emotionally dependent person. These three situations suggest, then, a very defi-

Source: From *Sex and Temperament in Three Primitive Societies*, pp. 279–88, by Margaret Mead,

nite conclusion. If those temperamental attitudes which we have traditionally regarded as feminine—such as passivity, responsiveness, and a willingness to cherish children—can so easily be set up as the masculine pattern in one tribe, and in another be outlawed for the majority of women as well as for the majority of men, we no longer have any basis for regarding such aspects of behaviour as sex-linked. And this conclusion becomes even stronger when we consider the actual reversal in Tchambuli of the position of dominance of the two sexes, in spite of the existence of formal patrilineal institutions.

The material suggests that we may say that many, if not all, of the personality traits which we have called masculine or feminine are as lightly linked to sex as are the clothing, the manners, and the form of head-dress that a society at a given period assigns to either sex. When we consider the behaviour of the typical Arapesh man or woman as contrasted with the behaviour of the typical Mundugumor man or woman, the evidence is overwhelmingly in favour of the strength of social conditioning. In no other way can we account for the almost complete uniformity with which Arapesh children develop into contented, passive, secure persons, while Mundugumor children develop as characteristically into violent, aggressive, insecure persons. Only to the impact of the whole of the integrated culture upon the growing child can we lay the formation of the contrasting types. There is no other explanation of race, or diet, or selection that can be adduced to explain them. We are forced to conclude that human nature is almost unbelievably malleable, responding accurately and contrastingly to contrasting cultural conditions. The differences between individuals who are members of different cultures, like the differences between individuals within a culture, are almost entirely to be laid to differences in conditioning, especially during early childhood, and the form of this conditioning is culturally determined. Standardized personality differences between the sexes are of this order, cultural creations to which each generation, male and female, is trained to conform. There remains, however, the problem of the origin of these socially standardized differences.

While the basic importance of social conditioning is still imperfectly recognized—not only in lay thought, but even by the scientist specifically concerned with such matters—to go beyond it and consider the possible influence of variations in hereditary equipment is a hazardous matter. The following pages will read very differently to one who has made a part of his thinking a recognition of the whole amazing mechanism of cultural conditioning—who has really accepted the fact that the same infant could be developed into a full participant in any one of these three cultures—than they will read to one who still believes that the minutiae of cultural behaviour are carried in the individual germ-plasm. If it is said, therefore, that when we have grasped the full significance of the malleability of the human organism and the preponderant importance of cultural conditioning, there are still further problems to solve, it must be remembered that these problems come *after* such a comprehension of the force of conditioning; they cannot precede it. The forces that make children born among the Arapesh grow up into typical Arapesh personalities are entirely social, and any discussion of the variations which do occur must be looked at against this social background.

With this warning firmly in mind, we can ask a further question. Granting the malleability of human nature, whence arise the differences between the standardized personalities that different cultures decree for all of their members, or which one culture decrees for the members of one sex as contrasted with the members of the opposite sex? If such differences are culturally created, as this material would most strongly suggest that they are, if the new-born child can be shaped with equal ease into an unaggressive Arapesh or an aggressive Mundugumor, why do these striking contrasts occur at all? If the clues to the different personalities decreed for men and women in

Tchambuli do not lie in the physical constitution of the two sexes—an assumption that we must reject both for the Tchambuli and for our own society—where can we find the clues upon which the Tchambuli, the Arapesh, the Mundugumor, have built? Cultures are manmade, they are built of human materials; they are diverse but comparable structures within which human beings can attain full human stature. Upon what have they built their diversities?

We recognize that a homogeneous culture committed in all of its gravest institutions and slightest usages to a cooperative, unaggressive course can bend every child to that emphasis, some to a perfect accord with it, the majority to an easy acceptance, while only a few deviants fail to receive the cultural imprint. To consider such traits as aggressiveness or passivity to be sex-linked is not possible in the light of the facts. Have such traits, then, as aggressiveness or passivity, pride or humility, objectivity or a preoccupation with personal relationships, an easy response to the needs of the young and the weak or a hostility to the young and the weak, a tendency to initiate sex-relations or merely to respond to the dictates of a situation or another person's advances—have these traits any basis in temperament at all? Are they potentialities of all human temperaments that can be developed by different kinds of social conditioning and which will not appear if the necessary conditioning is absent?

When we ask this question we shift our emphasis. If we ask why an Arapesh man or an Arapesh woman shows the kind of personality that we have considered in the first section of this book, the answer is: Because of the Arapesh culture, because of the intricate, elaborate, and unfailing fashion in which a culture is able to shape each new-born child to the cultural image. And if we ask the same question about a Mundugumor man or woman, or about a Tchambuli man as compared with a Tchambuli woman, the answer is of the same kind. They display the personalities that are peculiar to the cultures in which they were born and educated. Our attention has been on the differences between Arapesh men and women as a group and Mundugumor men and women as a group. It is as if we had represented the Arapesh personality by a soft yellow, the Mundugumor by a deep red, while the Tchambuli female personality was deep orange, and that of the Tchambuli male, pale green. But if we now ask whence came the original direction in each culture, so that one now shows yellow, another red, the third orange and green by sex, then we must peer more closely. And leaning closer to the picture, it is as if behind the bright consistent yellow of the Arapesh, and the deep equally consistent red of the Mundugumor, behind the orange and green that are Tchambuli, we found in each case the delicate, just discernible outlines of the whole spectrum, differently overlaid in each case by the monotone which covers it. This spectrum is the range of individual differences which lie back of the so much more conspicuous cultural emphases, and it is to this that we must turn to find the explanation of cultural inspiration, of the source from which each culture has drawn.

There appears to be about the same range of basic temperamental variation among the Arapesh and among the Mundugumor, although the violent man is a misfit in the first society and a leader in the second. If human nature were completely homogeneous raw material, lacking specific drives and characterized by no important constitutional differences between individuals, then individuals who display personality traits so antithetical to the social pressure should not reappear in societies of such differing emphases. If the variations between individuals were to be set down to accidents in the genetic process, the same accidents should not be repeated with similar frequency in strikingly different cultures, with strongly contrasting methods of education.

But because this same relative distribution of individual differences does appear in culture after culture, in spite of the divergence between the cultures, it seems pertinent to offer a hypothesis to explain upon what basis the personalities of men and women have been differently standardized so often in the history of the human race. This hypothesis is an extension of that advanced by Ruth Benedict in her *Patterns of Culture.* Let us assume that there are definite temperamental differences between human beings which if not entirely hereditary at least are established on a hereditary base very soon after birth. (Further than this we cannot at present narrow the matter.) These differences finally embodied in the character structure of adults, then, are the clues from which culture works, selecting one temperament, or a combination of related and congruent types, as desirable, and embodying this choice in every thread of the social fabric—in the care of the young child, the games the children play, the songs the people sing, the structure of political organization, the religious observance, the art and the philosophy.

Some primitive societies have had the time and the robustness to revamp all of their institutions to fit one extreme type, and to develop educational techniques which will ensure that the majority of each generation will show a personality congruent with this extreme emphasis. Other societies have pursued a less definitive course, selecting their models not from the most extreme, most highly differentiated individuals, but from the less marked types. In such societies the approved personality is less pronounced, and the culture often contains the types of inconsistencies that many human beings display also; one institution may be adjusted to the uses of pride, another to a casual humility that is congruent neither with pride nor with inverted pride. Such societies, which have taken the more usual and less sharply defined types as models, often show also a less definitely patterned social structure. The culture of such societies may be likened to a house the decoration of which has been informed by no definite and precise taste, no exclusive emphasis upon dignity or comfort or pretentiousness or beauty, but in which a little of each effect has been included.

Alternatively, a culture may take its clues not from one temperament, but from several temperaments. But instead of mixing together into an inconsistent hotchpotch the choices and emphases of different temperaments, or blending them together into a smooth but not particularly distinguished whole, it may isolate each type by making it the basis for the approved social personality for an age-group, a sex-group, a caste-group, or an occupational group. In this way society becomes not a monotone with a few discrepant patches of an intrusive colour, but a mosaic, with different groups displaying different personality traits. Such specializations as these may be based upon any facet of human endowment—different intellectual abilities, different artistic abilities, different emotional traits. So the Samoans decree that all young people must show the personality trait of unaggressiveness and punish with opprobrium the aggressive child who displays traits regarded as appropriate only in titled middle-aged men. In societies based upon elaborate ideas of rank, members of the aristocracy will be permitted, even compelled, to display a pride, a sensitivity to insult, that would be deprecated as inappropriate in members of the plebeian class. So also in professional groups or in religious sects some temperamental traits are selected and institutionalized, and taught to each new member who enters the profession or sect. Thus the physician learns the bedside manner, which is the natural behaviour of some temperaments and the standard behaviour of the general practitioner in the medical profession; the Quaker learns at least the outward behaviour and the rudiments of meditation, the capacity for which is not necessarily an innate characteristic of many of the members of the Society of Friends.

So it is with the social personalities of the two sexes. The traits that occur in some members of each sex are specially assigned to one sex, and disallowed in the other. The history of the social definition of sex-differences is filled with such arbitrary arrangements in the intellectual and artistic field, but because of the assumed congruence between physiological sex and emotional endowment we have been less able to recognize that a similar arbitrary selection is being made among emotional traits also. We have assumed that because it is convenient for a mother to wish to care for her child, this is a trait with which women have been more generously endowed by a carefully teleological process of evolution. We have assumed that because men have hunted, an activity requiring enterprise, bravery, and initiative, they have been endowed with these useful attitudes as part of their sex-temperament.

Societies have made these assumptions both overtly and implicitly. If a society insists that warfare is the major occupation for the male sex, it is therefore insisting that all male children display bravery and pugnacity. Even if the insistence upon the differential bravery of men and women is not made articulate, the difference in occupation makes this point implicitly. When, however, a society goes further and defines men as brave and women as timorous, when men are forbidden to show fear and women are indulged in the most flagrant display of fear, a more explicit element enters in. Bravery, hatred of any weakness, of flinching before pain or danger—this attitude which is so strong a component of *some human* temperaments has been selected as the key to masculine behaviour. The easy unashamed display of fear or suffering that is congenial to a different temperament has been made the key to feminine behaviour.

Originally two variations of human temperament, a hatred of fear or willingness to display fear, they have been socially translated into inalienable aspects of the personalities of the two sexes. And to that defined sex-personality every child will be educated, if a boy, to suppress fear, if a girl, to show it. If there has been no social selection in regard to this trait, the proud temperament that is repelled by any betrayal of feeling will display itself, regardless of sex, by keeping a stiff upper lip. Without an express prohibition of such behaviour the expressive unashamed man or woman will weep, or comment upon fear or suffering. Such attitudes, strongly marked in certain temperaments, may by social selection be standardized for everyone, or outlawed for everyone, or ignored by society, or made the exclusive and approved behaviour of one sex only.

Neither the Arapesh nor the Mundugumor have made any attitude specific for one sex. All of the energies of the culture have gone towards the creation of a single human type, regardless of class, age, or sex. There is no division into age-classes for which different motives or different moral attitudes are regarded as suitable. There is no class of seers or mediums who stand apart drawing inspiration from psychological sources not available to the majority of the people. The Mundugumor have, it is true, made one arbitrary selection, in that they recognize artistic ability only among individuals born with the cord about their necks, and firmly deny the happy exercise of artistic ability to those less unusually born. The Arapesh boy with a tinea infection has been socially selected to be a disgruntled, antisocial individual, and the society forces upon sunny cooperative children cursed with this affliction a final approximation to the behaviour appropriate to a pariah. With these two exceptions no emotional role is forced upon an individual because of birth or accident. As there is no idea of rank which declares that some are of high estate and some of low, so there is no idea of sex-difference which declares that one sex must feel differently from the other. One possible imaginative social construct, the attribution of different personalities to different members of the community classified into sex-, age-, or caste-groups, is lacking.

When we turn however to the Tchambuli, we find a situation that while bizarre in one respect, seems nevertheless more intelligible in another. The Tchambuli have at least made the point of sex-difference; they have used the obvious fact of sex as an organizing point for the formation of social personality, even though they seem to us to have reversed the normal picture. While there is reason to believe that not every Tchambuli woman is born with a dominating, organizing, administrative temperament, actively sexed and willing to initiate sex-relations, possessive, definite, robust, practical and impersonal in outlook, still most Tchambuli girls grow up to display these traits. And while there is definite evidence to show that all Tchambuli men are not, by native endowment, the delicate responsive actors of a play staged for the women's benefit, still most Tchambuli boys manifest this coquettish play-acting personality most of the time. Because the Tchambuli formulation of sex-attitudes contradicts our usual premises, we can see clearly that Tchambuli culture has arbitrarily permitted certain human traits to women, and allotted others, equally arbitrarily, to men.

CRITICAL-THINKING QUESTIONS

1. How do female and male personality traits differ among the Arapesh, the Mundugumor, and the Tchambuli?

2. How does Mead explain these differences? What does she mean, for example, when she states that "human nature is unbelievably malleable to cultural conditions"?

3. Most people in the United States still describe men as aggressive, strong, confident, and ambitious while characterizing women as emotional, talkative, romantic, and nurturing. Does this mean that biology is more important than environment in shaping our personality and behavior?

Gender

CLASSIC

CONTEMPORARY

CROSS-CULTURAL

37

How Subtle Sex Discrimination Works

Nijole V. Benokraitis

There are many forms of sex discrimination. Blatant sex discrimination is typically intentional, quite visible, and easily documented. Covert sex discrimination is hidden, purposeful, and difficult to prove. This selection discusses subtle sex discrimination—behavior, often unnoticed, that people have internalized as "normal," "natural," or customary.

Subtle sex discrimination refers to the unequal and harmful treatment of women that is typically less visible and obvious than blatant sex discrimination. It is often not noticed because most people have internalized subtle sexist behavior as "normal," "natural," or acceptable. Subtle sex discrimination can be relatively innocent or manipulative, intentional or unintentional, well-meaning or malicious. Subtle sex discrimination is difficult to document because many people do not perceive it as serious or harmful. In addition, subtle sex discrimination is often more complex than it appears: What is discrimination to many women may not seem discriminatory to many men or even women. . . .

Source: "How Subtle Sex Discrimination Works," by Nijole V. Benokraitis, from "Sex Discrimination in the 21st Century" by Nijole V. Benokraitis from *Subtle Sexism: Current Practices and Prospects for Change*, ed. Nijole Benokraitis, pp. 11, 14–24, copyright © 1997, Sage Publications, Inc. Reprinted by permission of Sage Publications, Inc.

CONDESCENDING CHIVALRY

Condescending chivalry refers to superficially courteous behavior that is protective and paternalistic, but treats women as subordinates. Sometimes the chivalry is well-intentioned because it "protects" women from criticism. For example, "A male boss will haul a guy aside and just kick ass if the [male] subordinate performs badly in front of a client" but may not say anything to a female subordinate (Fraker, 1984). Not providing such criticism may seem benevolent in the short term, but it will handicap an employee's performance in the long run. . . .

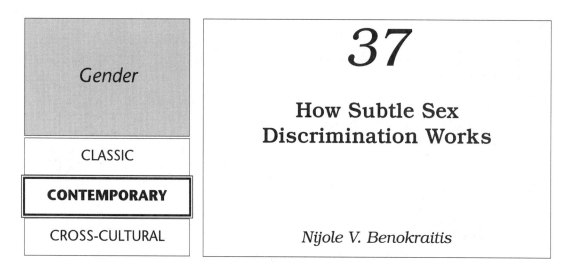

Thus, chivalrous behavior can signal status inequality. According to some researchers, outmoded attitudes—on the parts of both men and women—are preventing many qualified women from breaking into top jobs as school superintendents. Unlike their male counterparts, female candidates still get such questions from school board members as "How would your husband feel about your moving?" "Can you deal with a district where the administrators are mostly men?" and "Can you handle tough discipline problems?" According to researchers, the oppressive chivalry continues after a woman is hired. Female school superintendents often face greater scrutiny, for example, when it comes to such "masculine" tasks as finances and maintenance issues (see Nakashima, 1996).

SUPPORTIVE DISCOURAGEMENT

Supportive discouragement refers to a form of subtle sex discrimination where women receive mixed messages about their abilities, intelligence, or accomplishments. One form of supportive discouragement involves encouraging women to succeed in general but not rewarding their actual achievements because the latter may not reflect traditionally male interests:

> . . . [H]aving served on several search committees, I'm aware of how often feminist (or even woman-topic) dissertations are dismissed as "jargony," "trendy," etc. . . . I'm not really sure if feminism is still seen as a "fly-by-night" sort of discipline, but the accusation is a difficult one to argue because the people who make it will assure you until they're blue in the face (or you are) that they would love to hire a woman, are not opposed to feminism, etc. But it's only "this" dissertation, you see, they are opposed to. . . . (E-mail correspondence, 1996)

Another form of supportive discouragement encourages women to be ambitious and successful but places numerous obstacles in their paths, which either limit or derail the progress. Consider the following example from a colleague in the United Kingdom:

> One of the largest departments in our College is the Access department which offers part-time courses for people with no formal qualifications who wish to enter higher education or return to work. I would say that about 70 percent of these students are female and intend to go into teaching or similar work. The College refuses to implement a crèche or other day-care on the basis that it would be too expensive; staffing would cost almost nothing as the College runs courses for Nursery Nurses, childcare workers, etc. This despite the fact that of the people who are offered places on the Access course and turn it down, 80 percent give lack of child care as the main reason. Of this 80 percent, 92 percent are women. The courses are also run in some of the worst accommodations on site—"temporary" buildings which have been there for about twenty years and which are in a terrible state. The Chemistry department (not many women here) has, however, had at least three major renovations in the last ten years. It certainly makes clear to the many women on the Access course the opinion the College management has of their relative importance. (E-mail correspondence, 1996)

FRIENDLY HARASSMENT

Friendly harassment refers to sexually oriented behavior that, at face value, looks harmless or even playful. If it creates discomfort, embarrassment, or humiliation, however, it is a form of subtle discrimination. According to some female students at Stanford Medical School, for example, it is in such traditionally male-taught courses as those in surgery and internal medicine that many women encounter the most offensive sexual jokes. A fourth-year student said that many of her days "are spent fending off stupid little comments," many of them sexual, from male residents and doctors. She hesitated to complain, however, because good evaluations from professors are essential to get a good residency (Gose, 1995).

When women don't laugh at "stupid little jokes," moreover, they are often accused of not having a sense of humor:

> In response to a question from a friend of mine (a female graduate student) regarding how to comport herself at a job interview, a male faculty adviser responds, "Just flirt!" When I recount the incident to a male friend (junior faculty in another field at another institution), he responds: "Maybe it was a joke. Lighten up!" The primary sexism of the first remark gets echoed in the secondary sexism of the second remark, which trivializes the offense and the indignation ["no sense of humor"]. (E-mail correspondence, 1996)

Humor and jokes serve a number of functions: They reinforce group solidarity; define the defiant/outsider group; educate; save face; ingratiate; express caring for others; provide a safety valve for discussing taboo topics; maintain status inequality; silence or embarrass people; and provide tension release, hostility, and anger toward any group that is seen as marginal, inferior, or threatening. A single joke can serve several of these functions.

Although women's humor can be a powerful tool for changing stereotypes about females, much of men's sexual humor expresses male dominance over women, negates their personhood, and tries to silence women: "There are whole categories of jokes about women for which there are no male parallels: prostitute jokes, mother-in-law jokes, dumb blonde jokes, woman driver jokes, Jewish mother jokes" (Crawford, 1995:138). Women often don't laugh at many of these jokes not because they don't have a sense of humor, but because the "jokes" are hostile, aggressive, and demeaning. . . .

SUBJECTIVE OBJECTIFICATION

Subjective objectification refers to a form of subtle sex discrimination that treats women as children, possessions, or sex objects. Women are often punished like children—their "allowances" may be taken away, they may be forbidden to associate with their friends, their physical mobility may be limited, they may be given curfews, or they may be threatened with punishment similar to that of children. . . .

Our culture is continuously bombarded with images of women as little more than sexual body parts. The Media Action Alliance, which publishes the *Action Agenda* newsletter, is constantly filled with examples of posters, ads, videos, and other media materials that glorify violence against women and exploitation of women's bodies. It has been estimated that the average teenager sees between 1,900 and 2,400 sex-related messages per year on television alone (Brown, Childers, & Waszik, 1990). Many of the images, including those in films targeted at adolescents, treat women's bodies as trophies: Boys compete to be the first to "score," to achieve the most sexual conquests, and to "make it" with the sexiest teenage girls (see Whatley, 1994).

A frightening result of such competition can include rape and other sexual assaults on women. Consider the "Spur Posse" case in California. In 1993 eight members of a suburban high school, many of them top athletes at the school, created a clique called the "Spur Posse." Their primary goal was to "score" with as many girls as possible. They kept track of the girls with whom they had intercourse, and some bragged that their individual tallies ran into the sixties. In at least seven cases, girls from ten to sixteen years old said they had been raped. Some of the parents condoned their sons' behavior. One father, in fact, boasted to reporters that the assaults were not rape but indicators of his son's virility and sexual prowess (Seligmann, 1993).

This bizarre perception of women as possessions and trophies follows many boys into adulthood. According to Brooks (1995:3–4), what he refers to as "the Centerfold Syndrome" represents "one of the most malignant forces in contemporary relationships between men and women." One of the elements of the Centerfold Syndrome is objectification:

> Women become objects as men become objectifiers. As the culture has granted men the right and privilege of looking at women, women have been expected to accept the role of stimulators of men's visual interest, with their bodies becoming objects that can be lined up, compared, and rated. . . . Objective physical aspects are critical: Size, shape, and harmony of body parts are more important than a woman's human qualities. . . . Men talk of their attraction to women in dehumanizing terms based on the body part of their obsession—"I'm a leg man," or "I'm an ass man." (pp. 3–4)

Brooks notes that one of the most harmful effects of such objectification is that real women become more complicated, less appealing, and even ugly: "Stretch marks, varicose veins, sagging breasts, and cellulite-marked legs, common phenomena for real female bodies, may be viewed as repugnant by men who see women as objects" (p. 5). As a result, Centerfold Syndrome men may be sexually and emotionally inexpressive with the most important women in their lives.

RADIANT DEVALUATION

Although women are less likely to be openly maligned or insulted than in the past, they are devalued more subtly but just as effectively. Often, the devaluation is done in glowing terms:

> A psychologist, one of the most popular instructors in her college, said she would get good teaching evaluations from her male chair but that the positive review would be couched in sex-stereotypical rather than professional terms—she was described as being "mama-ish" and as having a "charming" approach to teaching. Being "mama-ish" and "charming" are *not* the criteria used by tenure and promotion committees. (Benokraitis & Feagin, 1995:102)

On a much broader scale, some scholars contend that the most recent devaluations have focused on antifeminist intellectual harassment through the use of "vilification and distortion or even violence to repress certain areas of research and forms of inquiry" (Clark et al., 1996:x). Attacks on feminists and feminist scholarship are nothing new. What has changed, however, is that much of the "newest wave of antifeminism cloaks itself in the vestments of feminism: the new antifeminists are women who, claiming to be feminists themselves, now maintain they are rescuing the women's movement from those who have led it astray" (Ginsburg & Lennox, 1996:170). Many of these devaluators have impressive academic credentials, are articulate, have been supported by conservative corporate foundations, and have found a receptive audience in the mainstream media and many publishing companies, which see antifeminism as a "hot commodity" because it is so profitable. Blaming feminism for such (real or imagined) ailments as the deterioration of relationships between the sexes and the presumed dissolution of the family—especially when the criticism comes from well-educated, self-proclaimed feminists—sells a lot of books.

LIBERATED SEXISM

Liberated sexism refers to the process that, at face value, appears to be treating women and men equally but that, in practice, increases men's freedom while placing greater burdens on women. One of the best examples of liberated sexism is work overloads both within the home and at the job site. Since the 1970s, increasing numbers of women have found themselves with two jobs—one inside and one outside the home. Ironically, women working these "double days" are often referred to as "liberated women." But liberated from what?

Shared parenting reflects more rhetoric than reality. In a national study, Bianchi (1990) found that more than 60 percent of divorced fathers either did not visit their children, or did not visit them and had no telephone or mail contact with them over a one-year period. Employed mothers with preschool-age children spend twenty-four hours more a week in child-care activities than do their husbands. Because the husband's job typically takes priority over his wife's (his salary is usually much higher), nearly nine out of ten mothers care for their children when they are sick, compared with only one out of ten working fathers (DeStefano & Colasanto, 1990). Although in one survey 56 percent of male employees said they were interested in flexible work schedules that would allow them more family time, in reality fewer than 1 percent take advantage of the unpaid paternity leaves that some 30 percent of companies offer today. The Family and Medical Leave Act, which was signed into law by President Clinton in 1993, allows workers of employers with fifty or more employees to take up to twelve weeks of unpaid leave following the birth or adoption of a child. Most men fear the career repercussions of taking paternity leaves or can't afford unpaid leaves financially, however (see Sommer, 1994). . . .

CONSIDERATE DOMINATION

Men often occupy preeminent positions and control important decision-making functions. . . . Men's dominance is built into our language, laws, and customs in both formal and informal ways. The dominance is accepted because it has been internalized and is often portrayed as "collegial," authoritative, or mutually beneficial.

Most of us take for granted that the expert and dominant cast of characters in the media are men. The media routinely ignore women or present them as second-class citizens. A recent survey of the front-page stories of twenty national and local newspapers found that although women make up 52 percent of the population, they show up just 13 percent of the time in the prime news spots. Even the stories about breast implants quoted men more often than women. Two-thirds of the bylines on front pages were male, and three-quarters of the opinions on op-ed pages were by men. Fewer than a third of the photographs on front pages featured women. Since the old "women's sections" are now more unisex and focus on both men and women, news about and by women has lost space even in these lifestyle sections (Goodman, 1992; see also Overholser, 1996).

Television news is not much better. In a study of the content of evening news programs on CBS, NBC, and ABC, Rakow and Kranich (1991) found that women as on-camera sources of information were used in less than 15 percent of the cases. When women did speak, they were usually passive reactors to public events as housewife or wife of the man in the news rather than participants or experts. Even in critical analyses of issues that affect more women than men, women may not appear on the screen. For example, a lengthy story on CBS on welfare reform did not use any women or feminist sources. . . .

COLLEGIAL EXCLUSION

One of the most familiar forms of subtle sexism is collegial exclusion, whereby women are made to feel invisible or unimportant through physical, social, or professional isolation. When Hall and Sandler's pamphlet, "The Classroom Climate: A Chilly One for Women?" was published in 1982, it was an instant success. Among other reasons, Sandler and Hall articulated the feelings that many women had experienced in higher education of being ignored, not having female role models, or being excluded from classroom discussions and activities. Since then, many studies have documented women's exclusion from classroom discourse, textbooks, and other academic activities (see, for example, Ginorio, 1995; Lewis, 1990; Maher & Tetreault, 1994; Peterson & Kroner, 1992).

Although there has been greater awareness of exclusion, it's not evident that there has been much change since 1982. At Stanford Medical School, for example, "The male body has been used as the standard, and the woman's body has been seen as a variation on that theme," says a third-year female student. Several women once heard a professor dismiss the clitoris with five words: "like the penis, just shorter" (Gose, 1995:A50). At Yale and American University law schools, female students' complaints are strikingly similar to those that Hall and Sandler described in 1982: Women feel their speech is stifled in class; professors respond more positively to comments by men, even if a woman voiced the same idea first; male students, even friends, ignore women's comments on legal issues and talk around them; male students and faculty devalue women's opinions; and men don't hear what women say (Torry, 1995).

When I asked the subscribers of the Women's Studies e-mail discussion list if they or someone they knew had ever experienced subtle sexism, many of the responses (from both the United States and Europe) described collegial exclusion. Here are a few examples:

> Just got back from a national conference and heard a female college president relate her experiences at meetings with other college presidents in the state. She was the only female present at the meetings and found that her suggestions/insights were ignored by her male colleagues. However, when the same suggestions later came from one of them, they were acknowledged. She finally took to writing her suggestions on the chalkboard. They couldn't be ignored that way—or at least not for long.
>
> There was a series of women-only staff development meetings set up by one of the more senior women (there are few), but the "only" time that could be found for this was on Monday at 6:00 p.m. Other staff development meetings are held at lunchtime with time off for anybody who wants to go.
>
> Women often feel they're isolated. . . . Many women begin with great promise but are demoralized and cut off from support . . . I'm referring to women who are cut off from support in ways it's hard to explain . . . often the only women in their departments . . . although some are in departments with other untenured women but the Old White Guys have the power. [The women] often are lacking a real (feminist) community. . . .

CRITICAL-THINKING QUESTIONS

1. Why are the various categories of subtle sex discrimination presented as oxymorons? How does subtle sexism differ from more blatant forms of discrimination?
2. Can you identify situations in which you have experienced subtle sex discrimination? Have you ever discriminated in this way against others?
3. What are the individual and organizational costs of subtle sex discrimination? What remedies might be effective in decreasing this form of inequality?

REFERENCES

Benokraitis, N. V., and J. R. Feagin. 1995. *Modern sexism: Blatant, subtle, and covert discrimination.* Englewood Cliffs, N.J.: Prentice Hall.

Bianchi, S. 1990. America's children: Mixed prospects. *Population Bulletin,* 45:3–41.

Brooks, G. R. 1995. *The centerfold syndrome: How men can overcome objectification and achieve intimacy with women.* San Francisco, Calif.: Jossey-Bass.

Brown, J. D., K. W. Childers, and C. S. Waszik. 1990. Television and adolescent sexuality. *Journal of Adolescent Health Care,* 11:62–70.

Clark, V., S. N. Garner, M. Higonnet, and K. H. Katrak, eds. 1996. *Antifeminism in the academy.* New York: Routledge.

Crawford, M. 1995. *Talking difference: On gender and language.* Thousand Oaks, Calif.: Sage.

DeStefano, L., and D. Colasanto. 1990. Unlike 1975, today most Americans think men have it better. *Gallup Poll Monthly,* (February):25–36.

Fraker, S. 1984. Why top jobs elude female executives. *Fortune,* (April 16):46.

Ginorio, A. B. 1995. *Warming the climate for women in academic science.* Washington, D.C.: Association of American Colleges and Universities.

Ginsburg, E., and S. Lennox. 1996. Antifeminism in scholarship and publishing. In *Antifeminism in the academy,* eds. V. Clark, S. N. Garner, M. Higonnet, and K. H. Katrak, 169–200. New York: Routledge.

Goodman, E. 1992. A woman's place is in the paper. *Baltimore Sun,* (April 7):15A.

Gose, B. 1995. Women's place in medicine. *Chronicle of Higher Education,* (November 3):A49.

Lewis, M. 1990. Interrupting patriarchy: Politics, resistance, and transformation in the feminist classroom. *Harvard Educational Review,* 60:472.

Maher, F. A., and M. K. T. Tetreault. 1994. *The feminist classroom.* New York: Basic Books.

Nakashima, E. 1996. When it comes to top school jobs, women learn it's tough to get ahead. *Washington Post,* (April 21):B1, B5.

Overholser, G. 1996. Front page story: Women. *Washington Post,* (April 21):C6.

Peterson, S. B., and T. Kroner. 1992. Gender biases in textbooks for introductory psychology and human development. *Psychology of Women Quarterly,* 16:17–36.

Rakow, L. F., and K. Kranich. 1991. Woman as sign in television news. *Journal of Communication,* 41:8–23.

Seligmann, J. 1993. A town's divided loyalties. *Newsweek,* (April 12):29.

Sommer, M. 1994. Welcome cribside, Dad. *Christian Science Monitor,* (June 28):19.

TORRY, S. 1995. Voice of concern grows louder on gender bias issue. *Washington Post,* (November 20):7.

WHATLEY, M. H. 1994. Keeping adolescents in the picture: Construction of adolescent sexuality in textbook images and popular films. In *Sexual culture and the construction of adolescent identities*, ed. J. M. Irvine, 183–205. Philadelphia: Temple University Press.

38

Women in Today's World

Naomi Neft and Ann D. Levine

Gender

CLASSIC

CONTEMPORARY

CROSS-CULTURAL

Many scholars date the emergence of the modern women's movement to eighteenth-century Europe, when a number of individual women, including Mary Wollstonecraft, publicly defied the widely held view that women were innately inferior to men and should be subject to men's control. Since then, and especially during the last three decades. women in the Western world have taken significant steps to enhance women's rights. As Naomi Neft and Ann D. Levine show, however, progress has been slow. Improving the lives of women and girls across the globe still remains a pressing priority.

Women throughout the world today live longer, healthier lives, are better educated, enjoy more job opportunities, and earn higher salaries than ever before. In many countries around the globe there are more women than men in college and more women than ever in top-level leadership roles, both in business and in public life. The past several decades have witnessed tremendous improvements in women's literacy, longevity, education and employment opportunities, and general standard of living. And as women's lives have gotten better, their families have become better educated, better nourished, healthier, and more productive. Where women thrive, communities and nations thrive.

GLOBAL GENDER GAPS

Yet progress has not always been even, and some parts of the world have suffered recent reversals. There are many places in the world where women's average life expectancy is less than fifty years and where the great majority of women can neither read nor write. And in country after country, women constitute the majority of the poor, accounting for more than 70 percent of the world's 1.3 billion people living in poverty.

Despite having made many great strides in attaining women's rights and improving their lives, all too often girls and women find that their access to education, employment, health care, political influence, and sometimes even food or life itself is limited solely because of their gender. In some parts of the world, it is not uncommon for a fetus to be aborted or a baby killed for no other reason than because she is female. Around the world, millions of women live in societies where centuries-old social and religious laws, customs, and traditions have created insurmountable barriers to education, jobs, and health care, as well as depriving women of most of their political and civil rights. And where women have limited

Source: From *Where Women Stand* by Naomi Neft and Ann D. Levine.

access to schooling, health care, and economic opportunities, their families tend to be larger, poorer, less educated, and debilitated by malnutrition and disease.

Although female enrollment in school is higher than ever and literacy rates are rising:

- Women make up nearly two-thirds of the world's 960 million illiterates.
- In primary school, enrollment rates for girls are about equal to boys', yet girls' dropout rates are higher and girls account for two-thirds of the 100 million children who drop out of primary school in the first four years.
- Female students are still enrolled mostly in the courses traditionally regarded as suitable for women: home economics, humanities, education, and the arts.
- Women teachers predominate in preschools and primary schools, are a minority in colleges and universities, and rarely attain the rank of full professor.

Although more women than ever are working outside the home and make up one-third of the world's labor force, they:

- Are concentrated in the least skilled and the lowest paying jobs.
- Occupy less than 6 percent of top management positions.
- Work overwhelmingly more in part-time jobs than men and are thus often not eligible for maternity, health insurance, and other benefits.
- Generally earn one-half to three-quarters of men's wages.
- Usually have higher unemployment rates than men and take longer to find new jobs.
- Tend to be the last ones hired, the first ones fired.

Although most women have the right to marry whom they choose and have legal access to divorce and inheritance rights, there are still parts of the world where:

- A husband is the legal head of the household, with complete authority over his wife and children.
- A married woman cannot work, obtain a passport, buy or sell property, secure a bank loan, or open a bank account without her husband's permission.
- A widow is entitled to only a small fraction of her husband's estate, and customary law may even award the entire estate to the husband's family, leaving her destitute.
- Adultery is defined differently for women and men (a woman may be guilty if she has been unfaithful only once, a man only if he keeps a mistress).

Although women throughout the world are healthier than ever and their life expectancy rates are rising:

- There are seventeen countries where women's average life expectancy is less than fifty years.
- In some countries, particularly where sons are favored over daughters, it is not unusual for baby girls to die of neglect or even to be killed by their parents.
- Over half a million women around the world die from pregnancy-related causes every year, while another 15 million suffer serious long-term complications.
- 70,000 to 200,000 women, including teenage girls, die every year as a result of unsafe, illegal abortions.
- Women now account for nearly half of all new cases of HIV infection.

Although many countries have enacted laws specifically aimed at prohibiting acts of violence against women:

- In some societies, physical abuse of wives is an accepted part of marriage.
- In most countries, marital rape is not considered a crime.
- The great majority of rapes and other assaults are never reported, let alone prosecuted, and when convictions do occur, sentences are often light.
- In some Islamic countries, women are beaten and sometimes even killed for not wearing the traditional Muslim head covering.
- In war-torn countries around the globe, thousands of women and girls are victims of mass rape and torture.

Although women make up about half the world's electorate:

- Only five countries, all in Europe, have national legislatures with 30 percent or more female members.
- Sweden is the only country with more women than men in its cabinet.

- Only five countries currently have women leaders.
- There is still one country—Kuwait—where only men can vote.

WHERE TODAY'S WOMEN LIVE

There are slightly more than 2.8 billion females in the world today, and about half of them live in just six countries: China, India, the United States, Indonesia, Brazil, and Russia. Women constitute just under half the global population—there are 98.6 females for every 100 males.

While women outlive men almost everywhere, there are thirty-nine countries where males outnumber females [see Table 1]. Countries with larger female populations tend to be the developed ones, such as Canada, the United States, and many European nations, where people live longer and more women than men survive to old age.

The relatively few countries where men outnumber women tend to be those where life expectancy for both sexes is fairly short. Nature dictates that more boys are born than girls—about 105 boys for every 100 girls—but because survival rates are usually greater for girls, females generally soon equal and eventually outnumber the males. Thus, countries where overall life expectancy is short—such as Afghanistan, Bangladesh, China, India, Pakistan, and many Middle Eastern countries—have larger male populations. (In some oil-producing

Table 1 Sex Ratios Worldwide (number of females per 100 males)

Females	*Country*	*Females*	*Country*
117	Ukraine	104	Burundi
114	Belarus	104	Congo
114	Latvia	104	El Salvador
113	Russia	104	Haiti
112	Estonia	104	Slovakia
111	Georgia	104	Switzerland
111	Lithuania	104	United Kingdom
110	Moldova	103	Angola
108	Cambodia	103	Canada
107	Austria	103	Chad
107	Hungary	103	Greece
107	Portugal	103	Japan
106	Central African Republic	103	Korea, North
106	Croatia	103	Laos
106	Czech Republic	103	Mali
106	Finland	103	Sierra Leone
106	Germany	103	Spain
106	Italy	103	Sweden
106	Kazakhstan	103	Turkmenistan
106	Slovenia	103	Vietnam
105	Azerbaijan	102	Argentina
105	France	102	Benin
105	Kyrgyzstan	102	Bolivia
105	Lebanon	102	Burkina Faso
105	Nicaragua	102	Chile
105	Poland	102	Colombia
105	Puerto Rico	102	Denmark
105	United States	102	Israel
105	Uruguay	102	Madagascar
104	Armenia	102	Malawi
104	Belgium	102	Mauritania
104	Bulgaria	102	Mozambique

(continued)

Females	*Country*	*Females*	*Country*
102	Netherlands	99	Ecuador
102	New Zealand	99	Eritrea
102	Niger	99	Guinea
102	Nigeria	99	Peru
102	Norway	99	Sudan
102	Romania	99	Venezuela
102	Rwanda	98	Costa Rica
102	Somalia	98	Guatemala
102	Tanzania	98	Honduras
102	Thailand	98	Korea, South
102	Togo	98	Liberia
102	Trinidad and Tobago	98	Macedonia
102	Uzbekistan	98	Malaysia
102	Yemen	98	Paraguay
102	Yugoslavia	98	Syria
102	Zaire	98	Tunisia
102	Zambia	97	Dominican Republic
101	Bosnia-Herzegovina	97	Egypt
101	Brazil	97	Iran
101	Cameroon	97	Ivory Coast
101	Ghana	97	Kuwait
101	Indonesia	97	Panama
101	Mexico	97	Philippines
101	Myanmar	97	Singapore
101	South Africa	96	Iraq
101	Sri Lanka	96	Turkey
101	Tajikistan	95	Afghanistan
101	Uganda	95	Albania
101	Zimbabwe	95	China
100	Algeria	95	Jordan
100	Australia	95	Nepal
100	Ethiopia	94	Bangladesh
100	Ireland	94	Taiwan
100	Jamaica	93	India
100	Kenya	92	Libya
100	Morocco	92	Pakistan
100	Senegal	81	Saudi Arabia
99	Cuba	52	United Arab Emirates

countries of the Middle East, such as Saudi Arabia and the United Arab Emirates, the sex ratio is further affected by the large numbers of male immigrant workers.) And in those countries that also favor sons over daughters, this natural sex imbalance is skewed even further by the abortion of a disproportionate number of female fetuses and higher death rates among female infants and young girls. Among the countries with such "missing" girls are Bangladesh, China, India, Pakistan, and to a lesser extent Egypt, Nepal, South Korea, and Turkey. . . .

Emergence of Modern Feminism

By the seventeenth century a few women had started speaking out for women's rights, especially for educational opportunities, but it was not until the eighteenth century that the seeds of modern feminism were sown. With the intellectual movement known as the Enlightenment came many democratic ideas and values, including the rights of the individual. Yet most women were untouched by the social, political, and economic rights that the Enlightenment conferred on men. Even as feudalism disintegrated as a social system, feudal relations of power persisted in marriage: Wives were still regarded as the property of their husbands.

The first major feminist work was Mary Wollstonecraft's *A Vindication of the Rights of Woman,* published in Britain [in] 1792. It argued for increased educational opportunities for women as well as political equality with men. Gradually, women in many countries started to organize to advance their own concerns, which usually included such issues as educational opportunities, the right to work, and laws pertaining to divorce and child custody.

The Struggle to Vote

Over the next two centuries women made tremendous strides toward equality with men. The single most important and most arduous struggle during this period was the fight for women's suffrage, which originated in Western Europe and spread, ironically, largely through colonization, around the globe.

In many countries, women attained the right to vote only after years of difficult struggle. In most Western countries, the women's suffrage movement grew out of decades of women's increasing public involvement in social issues, such as the abolition of slavery and the temperance movement. By the mid-1800s many of the women who had been active in these movements started banding together in a campaign for women's rights, especially the right to vote. In Britain and the United States, as the movement for suffrage gained momentum, it sometimes grew militant and even violent.

Despite these efforts, by the dawn of the twentieth century only one country had granted its female citizens the right to vote. In 1893 New Zealand granted women equal voting rights with men. It took nearly a decade for the next country to follow suit: In 1902 Australia granted women the right to vote in federal elections, even though some states still barred them from voting in local elections. Finland (1906), Norway (1913), Denmark (1915), and a host of other European countries followed in quick succession.

In 1918 Canada became the first North American country to extend the franchise to women, followed by the United States in 1920. Ecuador, in 1928, was the first South American country to grant women's suffrage, and in 1931 Sri Lanka became the first Asian country to do so, followed by Thailand in 1932. The first African country to grant women the right to vote was Senegal in 1945. Cameroon and Liberia followed in 1946.

Following World War II the process greatly accelerated, and today practically every woman in the world has the right to vote. In only a small handful of countries—Bahrain, Brunei, Kuwait, Oman, Qatar, Saudi Arabia, and United Arab Emirates are women still denied access to the ballot box. However, it should be noted that in all of these countries except Kuwait, men cannot vote either. And in Kuwait, for many years voting was strictly limited to literate, native-born males whose families had lived in the country since 1920. It was not until the mid-1990s that the government extended voting rights to naturalized male citizens and their sons. Although a separate law granting women the right to vote was under consideration at the same time, it was never adopted.

In a few countries, including Russia and China, women's suffrage was adopted practically overnight as part of a national revolution that granted equal political rights to women and men. Elsewhere, suffrage was often achieved only after many years of struggle, and sometimes it came in stages. In several countries women were first allowed to vote in local elections, later on a national level. In Chile, for example, women could vote in municipal elections as early as 1931 but had to wait until 1949 to cast their ballots in legislative and presidential elections.

In other countries, voting rights were first limited to certain groups of women, defined by age, education, or other criteria. The United Kingdom, for example, first extended voting rights to women in 1918, but only to women over the age of thirty. It was not until 1928 that the franchise was extended to all women over twenty-one, finally giving them complete voting equality with men. In Belgium a 1919 law granted national voting rights to widows or mothers of servicemen and civilians killed during World War I, as well as to women who had been political prisoners. Only in 1948 was the franchise extended to all women. In Portugal a 1931 law gave voting rights to women who had completed secondary or higher education, whereas men were required only to know how to read and write. It was not until 1976 that full equality was achieved. In South Africa voting rights were granted to white women in 1930, to Indian and colored women and men in 1983, and to African women and men in 1994.

New Wave of Feminism

In many countries, once suffrage was attained, women's movements began diminishing in strength as well as size, and it was not until the 1960s that a new wave of feminism emerged. By this time several factors—lower infant mortality rates, rising life expectancy, and the introduction of modern contraceptives—had given women more control over their lives and greater freedom from childbearing responsibilities.

At the same time, rising inflation was propelling more women into the labor force, and by 1970 women constituted 40 percent or more of the work force in more than a dozen developed countries, among them Canada, Denmark, France, the United Kingdom, and the United States. The blatant discrimination these women encountered reinvigorated the older feminist organizations; it also inspired a new generation of women's groups that were concerned largely with women's rights in general and employment discrimination in particular. In the United States and parts of Europe, this resurgence became known as the women's liberation movement and much attention was given to consciousness raising, that is, making women more aware of their common problems.

Today's Issues

As the feminist movement gained momentum in many countries, it grew stronger, earned greater acceptance, and broadened its scope to encompass a wider range of issues. Today almost every country has a wide array of women's organizations—some dealing with the broad issue of women's rights, others focusing on specific concerns such as abortion, sexual harassment, violence against women, or the problems of immigrant or minority women. In poorer countries women's groups concentrate more on obtaining adequate food and health care, gaining legal rights and educational opportunities, and improving their economic status, for example through gaining easier access to credit.

Although progress on many fronts has been fairly steady over the past several decades, the recent marked growth of religious fundamentalism has begun to pose a serious threat to women's rights in many countries. While fundamentalist movements within Catholicism, evangelical Protestantism, Judaism, and Hinduism have had serious repercussions in some parts of the world, none has had such a far-reaching effect on women as the worldwide resurgence of the various forms of Islamic fundamentalism. One of the most militant and repressive of these movements has taken hold in Afghanistan, where a fundamentalist force known as Taliban has imposed strict Islamic law. Afghani women, who once enjoyed a number of rights and freedoms, are now being forced to observe *purdah*, the practice of keeping women in seclusion and prohibiting them from seeing any men other than their relatives. In public they must be accompanied by a male relative and must always be swathed in the traditional *burqua*, a head-to-toe covering with only a netted opening for the wearer's eyes. In addition, girls can no longer attend school and women may not work outside the home except in hospitals or clinics—and even then only with female patients. By late 1996, the Taliban force had captured over two-thirds of the country. Militant Islamic groups have also emerged in Algeria, Egypt, Iran, Somalia, and Turkey, where they have attacked and even killed women who were not wearing the traditional head covering. They have also closed shelters for battered women and revised schoolbooks to emphasize their interpretation of Islamic teachings, including those aspects that restrict women.

In some of the Eastern European countries that have recently undergone a transition from communism to democracy, a resurgence of the Roman Catholic Church has been a critical factor in curtailing women's access to abortion. In Poland in 1993, the church lobbied successfully to greatly restrict the country's liberal abortion law and keep sex education out of the classroom. Three years later a revised law reinstated sex education and somewhat liberalized the country's abortion rules although it was still far from the abortion-on-demand policy that existed under communism.

Other setbacks for women, especially in the area of employment, are evident in those parts of the world currently suffering drastic economic downturns. Women are bearing the brunt of these crises, suffering high levels of unemployment coupled with cutbacks in child care and other government services. And in the many war-torn nations of the world, such as Bosnia, Cambodia, Croatia, Liberia, Peru, Rwanda, Somalia, and Uganda, it is estimated that women and children account for about 70 percent of all civilian fatalities. Whether a conflict is with another country or an internal ethnic, religious, or civil war, women and girls are often prime targets, and those who survive suffer the many devastating effects of armed conflict: torture, mass rape, broken families, and the loss of homes and property.

CRITICAL-THINKING QUESTIONS

1. Describe the gender gaps around the world in literacy, employment, inheritance rights, violence against women, and political leadership.
2. Because life expectancy rates are generally higher for females than for males, why do many Middle Eastern countries have much larger male populations?
3. Why do Neft and Levine describe women's suffrage as "the single most important and most arduous struggle" for women's rights during the last two centuries? Are there any countries in the world where women are still denied the right to vote?

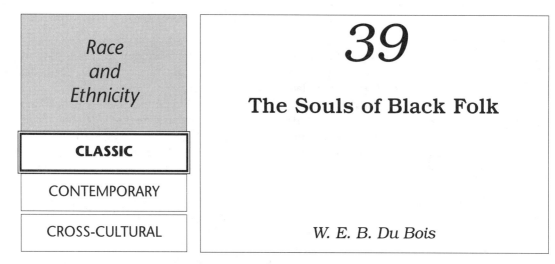

Race and Ethnicity

CLASSIC

CONTEMPORARY

CROSS-CULTURAL

39

The Souls of Black Folk

W. E. B. Du Bois

W. E. B. Du Bois, a pioneering U.S. sociologist and the first African American to receive a doctorate from Harvard University, describes how a color-conscious society casts black people as "strangers in their own homes." One result, Du Bois explains, is that African Americans develop a "double consciousness," seeing themselves as Americans but always gazing back at themselves through the eyes of the white majority, as people set below and apart by color.

Between me and the other world there is ever an unasked question: unasked by some through feelings of delicacy; by others through the difficulty of rightly framing it. All, nevertheless, flutter round it. They approach me in a half-hesitant sort of way, eye me curiously or compassionately, and then, instead of saying directly, How does it feel to be a problem? they say, I know an excellent colored man in my town; or, I fought at Mechanicsville; or, Do not these Southern outrages make your blood boil? At these I smile, or am interested, or reduce the boiling to a simmer, as the occasion may require. To the real question, How does it feel to be a problem? I answer seldom a word.

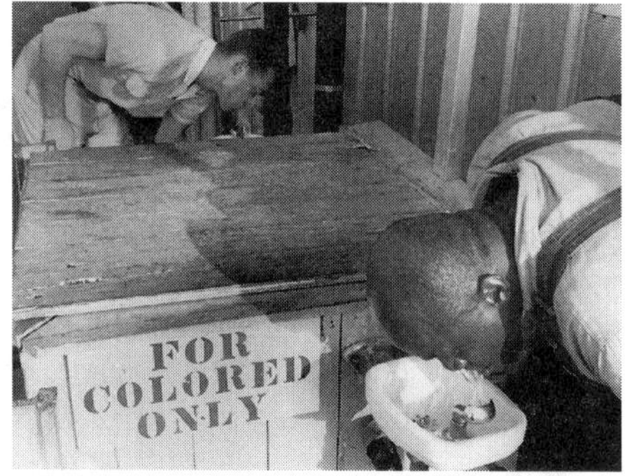

And yet, being a problem is a strange experience—peculiar even for one who has never been anything else, save perhaps in babyhood and in Europe. It is in the early days of rollicking boyhood that the revelation first bursts upon one, all in a day, as it were. I remember well when the shadow swept across me. I was a little thing, away up in the hills of New England, where the dark Housatonic winds between Hoosac and Taghkanic to the sea. In a wee wooden schoolhouse, something put it into the boys' and girls' heads to buy gorgeous visiting-cards—ten cents a package—and exchange. The exchange was merry, till one girl, a tall newcomer, refused my card—refused it peremptorily, with a glance. Then it dawned upon me with a certain suddenness that I was different from the others; or like, mayhap, in

Source: From *The Souls of Black Folk* by W. E. B. Du Bois (New York: Penguin, 1982; orig. 1903), pp. 43–53.

heart and life and longing, but shut out from their world by a vast veil. I had thereafter no desire to tear down that veil, to creep through; I held all beyond it in common contempt, and lived above it in a region of blue sky and great wandering shadows. That sky was bluest when I could beat my mates at examination-time, or beat them at a foot-race, or even beat their stringy heads. Alas, with the years all this fine contempt began to fade; for the words I longed for, and all their dazzling opportunities, were theirs, not mine. But they should not keep these prizes, I said; some, all, I would wrest from them. Just how I would do it I could never decide: by reading law, by healing the sick, by telling the wonderful tales that swam in my head—some way. With other black boys the strife was not so fiercely sunny: Their youth shrunk into tasteless sycophancy, or into silent hatred of the pale world about them and mocking distrust of everything white; or wasted itself in a bitter cry, Why did God make me an outcast and a stranger in mine own house? The shades of the prison-house closed round about us all: walls strait and stubborn to the whitest, but relentlessly narrow, tall, and unscalable to sons of night who must plod darkly on in resignation, or beat unavailing palms against the stone, or steadily, half hopelessly, watch the streak of blue above.

After the Egyptian and Indian, the Greek and Roman, the Teuton and Mongolian, the Negro is a sort of seventh son, born with a veil, and gifted with second-sight in this American world—a world which yields him no true self-consciousness, but only lets him see himself through the revelation of the other world. It is a peculiar sensation, this double-consciousness, this sense of always looking at one's self through the eyes of others, of measuring one's soul by the tape of a world that looks on in amused contempt and pity. One ever feels his twoness—an American, a Negro; two souls, two thoughts, two unreconciled strivings; two warring ideals in one dark body, whose dogged strength alone keeps it from being torn asunder.

The history of the American Negro is the history of this strife, this longing to attain self-conscious manhood, to merge his double self into a better and truer self. In this merging he wishes neither of the older selves to be lost. He would not Africanize America, for America has too much to teach the world and Africa. He would not bleach his Negro soul in a flood of white Americanism, for he knows that Negro blood has a message for the world. He simply wishes to make it possible for a man to be both a Negro and an American, without being cursed and spit upon by his fellows, without having the doors of Opportunity closed roughly in his face.

This, then, is the end of his striving: to be a coworker in the kingdom of culture, to escape both death and isolation, to husband and use his best powers and his latent genius. These powers of body and mind have in the past been strangely wasted, dispersed, or forgotten. The shadow of a mighty Negro past flits through the tale of Ethiopia the Shadowy and of Egypt the Sphinx. Through history, the powers of single black men flash here and there like falling stars, and die sometimes before the world has rightly gauged their brightness. Here in America, in the few days since Emancipation, the black man's turning hither and thither in hesitant and doubtful striving has often made his very strength to lose effectiveness, to seem like absence of power, like weakness. And yet it is not weakness—it is the contradiction of double aims. The double-aimed struggle of the black artisan on the one hand to escape white contempt for a nation of mere hewers of wood and drawers of water, and on the other hand to plough and nail and dig for a poverty-stricken horde—could only result in making him a poor craftsman, for he had but half a heart in either cause. By the poverty and ignorance of his people, the Negro minister or doctor was tempted toward quackery and demagogy; and by the criticism of the other world, toward ideals that made him ashamed of his lowly tasks. The would-be black *savant* was confronted by the paradox that the knowledge his people needed was a twice-told tale to his white neighbors, while the knowledge which would teach the white world was Greek to his own flesh and blood. The innate love of harmony and beauty that set the ruder souls of his people a-dancing and a-singing raised but confusion and doubt in the soul of the black artist; for the beauty revealed to him was the soul-beauty of a race which his larger audience despised, and he could not articulate the message of another people. This waste of double aims, this seeking to satisfy two unreconciled ideals, has wrought sad havoc with the courage and faith and deeds of ten thousand thousand people, has sent them often wooing false gods and invoking false means of salvation, and at times has even seemed about to make them ashamed of themselves.

Away back in the days of bondage they thought to see in one divine event the end of all doubt and disappointment; few men ever worshipped Freedom with half such unquestioning faith as did the American Negro for two centuries. To him, so far as he thought and dreamed, slavery was indeed the sum of all villainies, the cause of all sorrow, the root of all prejudice; Emancipation was the key to a promised land of sweeter beauty than ever stretched before the eyes of wearied Israelites. In song and exhortation swelled one refrain—Liberty; in his tears and curses the God he implored had Freedom in his right hand. At last it came, suddenly, fearfully, like a dream. With one wild carnival of blood and passion came the message in his own plaintive cadences:

> Shout, O children!
> Shout, you're free!
> For God has bought your liberty!

Years have passed away since then,—ten, twenty, forty; forty years of national life, forty years of renewal and development, and yet the swarthy spectre sits in its accustomed seat at the Nation's feast. In vain do we cry to this our vastest social problem:

> Take any shape but that, and my firm nerves
> Shall never tremble!

The Nation has not yet found peace from its sins; the freedman has not yet found in freedom his promised land. Whatever of good may have come in these years of change, the shadow of a deep disappointment rests upon the Negro people—a disappointment all the more bitter because the unattained ideal was unbounded save by the simple ignorance of a lowly people.

The first decade was merely a prolongation of the vain search for freedom, the boon that seemed ever barely to elude their grasp, like a tantalizing will-o'-the-wisp, maddening and misleading the headless host. The holocaust of war, the terrors of the Ku-Klux Klan, the lies of carpet-baggers, the disorganization of industry, and the contradictory advice of friends and foes, left the bewildered serf with no new watchword beyond the old cry for freedom. As the time flew, however, he began to grasp a new idea. The ideal of liberty demanded for its attainment powerful means, and these the Fifteenth Amendment gave him. The ballot, which before he had looked upon as a visible sign of freedom, he now regarded as the chief means of gaining and perfecting the liberty with which war had partially endowed him. And why not? Had not votes made war and emancipated millions? Had not votes enfranchised the freedmen? Was anything impossible to a power that had done all this? A million black men started with renewed zeal to vote themselves into the kingdom. So the decade flew away, the revolution of 1876 came, and left the half-free serf weary, wondering, but still inspired. Slowly but steadily, in the following years, a new vision began gradually to replace the dream of political power—a powerful movement, the rise of another ideal to guide the unguided, another pillar of fire by night after a clouded day. It was the ideal of "book-learning"; the curiosity, born of compulsory ignorance, to know and test the power of the cabalistic letters of the white man, the longing to know. Here at last seemed to have been discovered the mountain path to Canaan; longer than the highway of Emancipation and law, steep and rugged, but straight, leading to heights high enough to overlook life.

Up the new path the advance guard toiled, slowly, heavily, doggedly; only those who have watched and guided the faltering feet, the misty minds, the dull understandings, of the dark pupils of these schools know how faithfully, how piteously, this people strove to learn. It was weary work. The cold statistician wrote down the inches of progress here and there, noted also where here and there a foot had slipped or some one had fallen. To the tired climbers, the horizon was ever dark, the mists were often cold, the Canaan was always dim and far away. If, however, the vistas disclosed as yet no goal, no resting-place, little but flattery and criticism, the journey at least gave leisure for reflection and self-examination; it changed the child of Emancipation to the youth with dawning self-consciousness, self-realization, self-respect. In those sombre forests of his striving his own soul rose before him, and he saw himself, darkly as through a veil; and yet he saw in himself some faint revelation of his power, of his mission. He began to have a dim feeling that, to attain his place in the world, he must be himself, and not another. For the first time he sought to analyze the burden he bore upon his back, that dead-weight of social degradation partially masked behind a half-named Negro problem. He felt his poverty; without a cent, without a home, without land, tools, or savings, he had entered into competition with rich, landed, skilled neighbors. To be a man is hard, but to be a poor race in a land of dollars is the very bottom of hardships. He felt the weight of his ignorance, not simply of letters, but of life, of business, of the humanities; the accumulated sloth and shirking and awkwardness of decades and centuries shackled his hands and feet. Nor was his burden all poverty and ignorance. The red stain of bastardy, which two centuries of systematic legal defilement of Negro women had stamped upon his race, meant not only the loss of ancient African chastity, but also the hereditary weight of a mass of corruption from white adulterers, threatening almost the obliteration of the Negro home.

A people thus handicapped ought not to be asked to race with the world, but rather allowed to give all its time and thought to its own social problems. But alas! while sociologists gleefully count his bastards and his prostitutes, the very soul of the toiling, sweating black man is darkened by the shadow of a vast despair. Men call the shadow prejudice, and learnedly explain it as the natural defence of culture against barbarism, learning against ignorance, purity against crime, the "higher" against the "lower" races. To which the Negro cries Amen! and swears that to so much of this strange prejudice as is founded on just homage to civilization, culture, righteousness, and progress, he humbly bows and meekly does obeisance. But before that nameless prejudice that leaps beyond all this he stands helpless, dismayed, and well-nigh speechless; before that personal disrespect and mockery, the ridicule and systematic humiliation, the distortion of fact and wanton license of fancy, the cynical ignoring of the better and the boisterous welcoming of the worse, the all-pervading desire to inculcate disdain for everything black, from Toussaint to the devil—before this there rises a sickening despair that would disarm and discourage any nation save that black host to whom "discouragement" is an unwritten word.

But the facing of so vast a prejudice could not but bring the inevitable self-questioning, self-disparagement, and lowering of ideals which ever accompany repression and breed in an atmosphere of contempt and hate. Whisperings and portents came borne upon the four winds: Lo! we are diseased and dying, cried the dark hosts; we cannot write, our voting is vain; what need of education, since we must always cook and serve? And the Nation echoed and enforced this self-criticism saying: Be content to be servants, and nothing more; what need of higher culture for half-men? Away with the black man's ballot, by force or fraud—and behold the suicide of a race! Nevertheless, out of the evil came something of good—the more careful adjustment of education to real life, the clearer perception of the Negroes' social responsibilities, and the sobering realization of the meaning of progress.

So dawned the time of *Sturm und Drang:* Storm and stress today rocks our little boat on the mad waters of the world-sea; there is within and without the sound of conflict, the burning of body and rending of soul; inspiration strives with doubt, and faith with vain questionings. The bright ideals of the past—physical freedom, political power, the training of brains and the training of hands—all these in turn have waxed and waned, until even the last grows dim and overcast. Are they all wrong, all false? No, not that, but each alone was over-simple and incomplete—the dreams of a credulous race-childhood, or the fond imaginings of the other world which does not know and does not want to know our power. To be really true, all these ideals must be melted and welded into one. The training of the schools we need today more than ever—the training of deft hands, quick eyes and ears, and above all the broader, deeper, higher culture of gifted minds and pure hearts. The power of the ballot we need in sheer self-defence—else what shall save us from a second slavery? Freedom, too, the long-sought, we still seek, the freedom of life and limb, the freedom to work and think, the freedom to love and aspire. Work, culture, liberty—all these we need, not singly but together, not successively but together, each growing and aiding each, and all striving toward that vaster ideal that swims before the Negro people, the ideal of human brotherhood, gained through the unifying ideal of Race; the ideal of fostering and developing the traits and talents of the Negro, not in opposition to or contempt for other races, but rather in large conformity to the greater ideals of the American Republic, in order that some day on American soil two world-races may give each to each those characteristics both so sadly lack. We the darker ones come even now not altogether empty-handed: There are today no truer exponents of the pure human spirit of the Declaration of Independence than the American Negroes; there is no true American music but the wild sweet melodies of the Negro slave, the American fairy tales and folklore are Indian and African; and, all in all, we black men seem the sole oasis of simple faith and reverence in a dusty desert of dollars and smartness. Will America be poorer if she replace her brutal dyspeptic blundering with light-hearted but determined Negro humility? or her coarse and cruel wit with loving jovial good-humor? or her vulgar music with the soul of the Sorrow Songs?

Merely a concrete test of the underlying principles of the great republic is the Negro Problem, and the spiritual striving of the freedmen's sons is in the travail of souls whose burden is almost beyond the measure of their strength, but who bear it in the name of an historic race, in the name of this the land of their fathers' fathers, and in the name of human opportunity.

CRITICAL-THINKING QUESTIONS

1. What does Du Bois mean by the "double consciousness" of African Americans?

2. Du Bois writes that people of color aspire to realizing a "better and truer self." What do you think he imagines such a self to be?

3. What are some of the reasons, according to Du Bois, that Emancipation (from slavery in 1863) brought disappointment to former slaves, at least in the short run?

4. Does this essay seem optimistic or pessimistic about the future of U.S. race relations? Why?

40

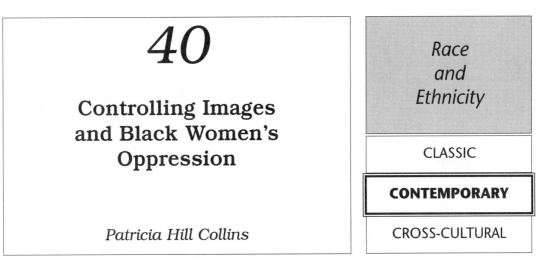

Controlling Images and Black Women's Oppression

Patricia Hill Collins

Race and Ethnicity

CLASSIC

CONTEMPORARY

CROSS-CULTURAL

As W. E. B. Du Bois (see Reading 39) noted, many victims of racial prejudice and stereotypes often experience inevitable self-questioning and self-disparagement. Recently, feminists have argued that women of color typically confront gendered racism—a combination of both *racism and sexism. In the following selection, Patricia Hill Collins shows how negative images of black women have provided an ideological justification for race, gender, and class inequality.*

"Black women emerged from slavery firmly enshrined in the consciousness of white America as 'Mammy' and the 'bad black woman,'" contends Cheryl Gilkes (1983:294). The dominant ideology of the slave era fostered the creation of four interrelated, socially constructed controlling images of Black womanhood, each reflecting the dominant group's interest in maintaining Black women's subordination. Given that both Black and white women were important to slavery's continuation, the prevailing ideology functioned to mask contradictions in social relations affecting all women. According to the cult of true womanhood, "true" women possessed four cardinal virtues: piety, purity, submissiveness, and domesticity. Elite white women and those of the emerging middle class were encouraged to aspire to these virtues. African American women encountered a different set of controlling images. The sexual ideology of the period as is the case today "confirmed the differing material circumstances of these two groups of women . . . by balancing opposing definitions of womanhood and motherhood, each dependent on the other for its existence" (Carby, 1987:25).

The first controlling image applied to African American women is that of the mammy—the faithful, obedient domestic servant. Created to justify the economic exploitation of house slaves and sustained to explain Black women's longstanding restriction to domestic service, the mammy image represents the normative yardstick used to evaluate all Black women's behavior. By loving, nurturing, and caring for her white children and "family" better than her own, the mammy symbolizes the dominant group's perception of the ideal Black female relationship to elite white male power. Even though she may be well loved and may wield considerable authority in her white "family," the mammy still knows her

Source: Copyright © 1990, 2000. From *Black Feminist Thought: Knowledge, Consciousness, and the Politics of Empowerment* by Patricia Hill Collins. Reproduced by permission of Taylor & Francis Inc./Routledge, Inc.

"place" as obedient servant. She has accepted her subordination.

Black women intellectuals have aggressively deconstructed the image of African American women as contented mammies by challenging traditional views of Black women domestics (Dill, 1980, 1988; Clark-Lewis, 1985; Rollins, 1985). Literary critic Trudier Harris's (1982) volume *From Mammies to Militants: Domestics in Black American Literature* investigates prominent differences in how Black women have been portrayed by others in literature and how they portray themselves. In her work on the difficulties faced by Black women leaders, Rhetaugh Dumas (1980) describes how Black women executives are hampered by being treated as mammies and penalized if they do not appear warm and nurturing. But despite these works, the mammy image lives on in scholarly and popular culture. Audre Lorde's account of a shopping trip offers a powerful example of its tenacity: "I wheel my two-year-old daughter in a shopping cart through a supermarket in . . . 1967, and a little white girl riding past in her mother's cart calls out excitedly, 'Oh look, Mommy, a baby maid!' " (1984:126).[1]

The mammy image is central to interlocking systems of race, gender, and class oppression. Since efforts to control African American family life require perpetuating the symbolic structures of racial oppression, the mammy image is important because it aims to shape Black women's behavior as mothers. As the members of African American families who are most familiar with the skills needed for Black accommodation, Black women are encouraged to transmit to their own children the deference behavior many are forced to exhibit in mammy roles. By teaching Black children their assigned place in white power structures, Black women who internalize the mammy image potentially become effective conduits for perpetuating racial oppression. In addition, employing mammies buttresses the racial superiority of white women employers and weds them more closely to their fathers, husbands, and sons as sources of elite white male power (Rollins, 1985).

The mammy image also serves a symbolic function in maintaining gender oppression. Black feminist critic Barbara Christian argues that images of Black womanhood serve as a reservoir for the fears of Western culture, "a dumping ground for those female functions a basically Puritan society could not confront" (1985:2). Juxtaposed against the image of white women promulgated through the cult of true womanhood, the mammy image as the Other symbolizes the oppositional difference of mind/body and culture/nature thought to distinguish Black women from everyone else. Christian comments on the mammy's gender significance: "All the functions of mammy are magnificently physical. They involve the body as sensuous, as funky, the part of women that white southern America was profoundly afraid of. Mammy, then, harmless in her position of slave, unable because of her all-giving nature to do harm, is needed as an image, a surrogate to contain all those fears of the physical female" (1985:2). The mammy image buttresses the ideology of the cult of true womanhood, one in which sexuality and fertility are severed. "Good" white mothers are expected to deny their female sexuality and devote their attention to the moral development of their offspring. In contrast, the mammy image is one of an asexual woman, a surrogate mother in blackface devoted to the development of a white family.

No matter how loved they were by their white "families," Black women domestic workers remained poor because they were economically exploited. The restructured post–World War II economy in which African American women moved from service in private homes to jobs in the low-paid service sector has produced comparable economic exploitation. Removing Black women's labor from African American families and exploiting it denies Black extended family units the benefits of either decent wages or Black women's unpaid labor in their homes. Moreover, many white families in both the middle class and working class are able to maintain their class position because they have long used Black women as a source of cheap labor (Rollins, 1985; Byerly, 1986). The mammy image is designed to mask this economic exploitation of social class (King, 1973).

For reasons of economic survival, African American women may play the mammy role in paid work settings. But within African American communities these same women often teach their own children something quite different. Bonnie Thornton Dill's (1980) work on child-rearing patterns among Black domestics show that while the participants in her study showed deference behavior at work, they discouraged their children from believing that they should be deferent to whites and encouraged their children to avoid domestic work. Barbara Christian's analysis of the mammy in Black slave narratives reveals that, "unlike the white southern image of mammy, she is cunning, prone to poisoning her master, and not at all content with her lot" (1985:5).

The fact that the mammy image cannot control Black women's behavior as mothers is tied to the creation of the second controlling image of Black womanhood. Though a more recent phenomenon, the image of the Black matriarch fulfills similar functions in explaining Black women's placement in interlocking systems of race, gender, and class oppression. Ironically, Black scholars such as William E. B. Du Bois (1969) and E. Franklin Frazier (1948) described the connections among higher rates of female-headed households in African American communities, the importance that women assume in Black family networks, and the persistence of Black poverty. However, neither scholar interpreted Black women's centrality in Black families as a *cause* of African American social class status. Both saw so-called matriarchal families as an *outcome* of racial oppression and poverty. During the eras when Du Bois and Frazier wrote, the oppression of African Americans was so total that control was maintained without the controlling image of matriarch. But what began as a muted theme in the works of these earlier Black scholars grew into a full-blown racialized image in the 1960s, a time of significant political and economic mobility for African Americans. Racialization involves attaching racial meaning to a previously racially unclassified relationship, social practice, or group (Omi & Winant, 1986). Prior to the 1960s, female-headed households were certainly higher in African American communities, but an ideology racializing female-headedness as a causal feature of Black poverty had not emerged. Moreover, "the public depiction of Black women as unfeminine, castrating matriarchs came at precisely the same moment that the feminist movement was advancing its public critique of American patriarchy" (Gilkes, 1983:296).

While the mammy typifies the Black mother figure in white homes, the matriarch symbolizes the mother figure in Black homes. Just as the mammy represents the "good" Black mother, the matriarch symbolizes the "bad" Black mother. The modern Black matriarchy thesis contends that African American women fail to fulfill their traditional "womanly" duties (Moynihan, 1965). Spending too much time away from home, these working mothers ostensibly cannot properly supervise their children and are a major contributing factor to their children's school failure. As overly aggressive, unfeminine women, Black matriarchs allegedly emasculate their lovers and husbands. These men, understandably, either desert their partners or refuse to marry the mothers of their children. From an elite white male standpoint, the matriarch is essentially a failed mammy, a negative stigma applied to those African American women who dared to violate the image of the submissive, hard-working servant.

Black women intellectuals examining the role of women in African American families discover few matriarchs and even fewer mammies (Hale, 1980; Myers, 1980; Sudarkasa, 1981; Dill, 1988). Instead they portray African American mothers as complex individuals who often show tremendous strength under adverse conditions. In *A Raisin in the Sun*, the first play presented on Broadway written by a Black woman, Lorraine Hansberry (1959) examines the struggles of widow Lena Younger to actualize her dream of purchasing a home for her family. In *Brown Girl, Brownstones*, novelist Paule Marshall (1959) presents Mrs. Boyce, a Black mother negotiating a series of relationships with her husband, her daughters, the women in her community, and the work she must perform outside her home. Ann Allen Shockley's *Loving Her* (1974) depicts the struggle of a lesbian mother trying to balance her needs for self-actualization with the pressures of child-rearing in the homophobic community. Like these fictional analyses, Black women's scholarship on Black single mothers also challenges the matriarchy thesis (Ladner, 1972; McCray, 1980; Lorde, 1984; McAdoo, 1985; Brewer, 1988).

Like the mammy, the image of the matriarch is central to interlocking systems of race, gender, and class oppression. Portraying African American women as matriarchs allows the dominant group to blame Black women for the success or failure of Black children. Assuming that Black poverty is passed on intergenerationally via value transmission in families, an elite white male standpoint suggests that Black children lack the attention and care allegedly lavished on white, middle-class children and that this deficiency seriously retards Black children's achievement. Such a view diverts attention from the political and economic inequality affecting Black mothers and children and suggests that anyone can rise from poverty if he or she only received good values at home. Those African Americans who remain poor are blamed for their own victimization. Using Black women's performance as mothers to explain Black economic subordination links gender ideology to explanations of class subordination.

The source of the matriarch's failure is her inability to model appropriate gender behavior. In the post–World War II era, increasing numbers of white women entered the labor market, limited their fertility, and generally challenged their prescribed roles in white patriarchal institutions. The image of the Black matriarch emerged at that time as a powerful symbol for both Black and white women of what can go wrong if white patriarchal power is challenged. Aggressive, assertive women are penalized—they are abandoned by their men, end up impoverished, and are stigmatized as being unfeminine.

The image of the matriarch also supports racial oppression. Much social science research implicitly uses gender relations in African American communities as one putative measure of Black cultural disadvantage. For example, the Moynihan Report (1965) contends that slavery destroyed Black families by creating reversed roles for men and women. Black family structures are seen as being deviant because they challenge the patriarchal assumptions underpinning the construct of the ideal "family." Moreover, the absence of Black patriarchy is used as evidence for Black cultural inferiority (Collins, 1989). Black women's failure to conform to the cult of true womanhood can then be identified as one fundamental source of Black cultural deficiency. Cheryl Gilkes posits that the emergence of the matriarchal image occurred as a counterideology to efforts by African Americans and women who were confronting interlocking systems of race, gender, and class oppression: "The image of dangerous Black women who are also deviant castrating mothers divided the Black community at the critical period in the Black liberation struggle and created a wider gap between the worlds of Black and white women at a critical period in women's history" (1983:297).

Taken together, images of the mammy and the matriarch place African American women in an untenable position. For Black women workers in domestic work and other occupations requiring long hours and/or substantial emotional labor, becoming the ideal mammy means precious time and energy spent away from husbands and children. But being employed when Black men have difficulty finding steady work exposes African American women to the charge that Black women emasculate Black men by failing to be submissive, dependent, "feminine" women. Moreover, Black women's financial contributions to Black family well-being have also been cited as evidence supporting the matriarchy thesis (Moynihan, 1965). Many Black women are the sole support of their families, and labeling these women "matriarchs" erodes their self-confidence and ability to confront oppression. In essence, African American women who must work are labeled mammies, then are stigmatized again as matriarchs for being strong figures in their own homes.

A third, externally defined, controlling image of Black womanhood—that of the welfare mother—appears tied to Black women's increasing dependence on the post–World War II welfare state. Essentially an updated version of the breeder women image created during slavery, this image provides an ideological justification for efforts to harness Black women's fertility to the needs of a changing political economy.

During slavery the breeder woman image portrayed Black women as more suitable for having children than white women. By claiming that Black women were able to produce children as easily as animals, this objectification of Black women as the Other provided justification for interference in the reproductive rights of enslaved Africans. Slaveowners wanted enslaved Africans to "breed" because every slave child born represented a valuable unit of property, another unit of labor, and, if female, the prospects for more slaves. The externally defined, controlling image of the breeder woman served to justify slaveowner intrusion into Black women's decisions about fertility (King, 1973; Davis, 1981).

The post–World War II political economy has offered African Americans rights not available in former historical periods. (Fusfeld & Bates, 1984; Wilson, 1987). African Americans have successfully acquired basic political and economic protections from a greatly expanded welfare state, particularly Social Security, Aid to Families with Dependent Children, unemployment compensation, affirmative action, voting rights, antidiscrimination legislation, and the minimum wage. In spite of sustained opposition by Republican administrations in the 1980s, these programs allow many African Americans to reject the subsistence-level, exploitative jobs held by their parents and grandparents. Job export, deskilling, and increased use of illegal immigrants have all been used to replace the loss of cheap, docile Black labor (Braverman, 1974; Gordon et al., 1982; Nash & Fernandez-Kelly, 1983). The large numbers of undereducated, unemployed African Americans, most of whom are women and children, who inhibit inner cities cannot be forced to work. From the standpoint of the dominant group, they no longer represent cheap labor but instead signify a costly threat to political and economic stability.

Controlling Black women's fertility in such a political economy becomes important. The image of the welfare mother fulfills this function by labeling as unnecessary and even dangerous to the values of the country the fertility of women who are not white and middle class. A closer look at this controlling image reveals that it shares some important features with its mammy and matriarch counterparts. Like the matriarch, the welfare mother is labeled a bad mother. But unlike the matriarch, she is not too aggressive—on the contrary, she is not aggressive enough. While the matriarch's unavailability contributed to her children's poor socialization, the welfare mother's accessibility is deemed the problem. She is portrayed as being content to sit around and collect welfare, shunning work and passing on her bad values to her offspring. The image of the welfare mother represents another failed mammy, one who is unwilling to become "de mule uh de world."

The image of the welfare mother provides ideological justifications for interlocking systems of race, gender, and class oppression. African Americans can be racially stereotyped as being lazy by blaming Black welfare mothers for failing to pass on the work ethic. Moreover, the welfare mother has no male authority figure to assist her. Typically portrayed as an unwed mother, she violates one cardinal tenet of Eurocentric masculinist thought: She is a woman alone. As a result, her treatment reinforces the dominant gender ideology positing that a woman's true worth and financial security should occur through heterosexual marriage. Finally, in the post–World War II political economy, one of every three African American families is officially classified as poor. With such high levels of Black poverty, welfare state policies supporting poor Black mothers and their children have become increasingly expensive. Creating the controlling image of the welfare mother and stigmatizing her as the cause of her own poverty and that of African American communities shifts the angle of vision away from structural sources of poverty and blames the victims themselves. The image of the welfare mother thus provides ideological justification for the dominant group's interest in limiting the fertility of Black mothers who are seen as producing too many economically unproductive children (Davis, 1981).

The fourth controlling image—the Jezebel, whore, or sexually aggressive woman—is central in the nexus of elite white male images of Black womanhood because efforts to control Black women's sexuality lie at the heart of Black women's oppression. The image of Jezebel originated under slavery when Black women were portrayed as being, to use Jewelle Gomez's words, "sexually aggressive wet nurses" (Clarke et al., 1983:99). Jezebel's function was to relegate all Black women to the category of sexually aggressive women, thus providing a powerful rationale for the widespread sexual assaults by white men typically reported by Black slave women (Davis, 1981; Hooks, 1981; White, 1985). Yet Jezebel served another function. If Black slave women could be portrayed as having excessive sexual appetites, then increased fertility should be the expected outcome. By suppressing the nurturing that African American women might give their own children which would strengthen Black family networks, and by forcing Black women to work in the field or "wet nurse" white children, slaveowners effectively tied the controlling images of Jezebel and Mammy to the economic exploitation inherent in the institution of slavery.

The fourth image of the sexually denigrated Black woman is the foundation underlying elite white male conceptualizations of the mammy, matriarch, and welfare mother. Connecting all three is the common theme of Black women's sexuality. Each image transmits clear messages about the proper links among female sexuality, fertility, and Black women's roles in the political economy. For example, the mammy, the only somewhat positive figure, is a desexed individual. The mammy is typically portrayed as overweight, dark, and with characteristically African features—in brief, as an unsuitable sexual partner for white men. She is asexual and therefore is free to become a surrogate mother to the children she acquired not through her own sexuality. The mammy represents the clearest example of the split between sexuality and motherhood present in Eurocentric masculinist thought. In contrast, both the matriarch and the welfare mother are sexual beings. But their sexuality is linked to their fertility, and this link forms one fundamental reason they are negative images. The matriarch represents the sexually aggressive woman, one who emasculates Black men because she will not permit them to assume roles as Black patriarchs. She refuses to be passive and thus is stigmatized. Similarly, the welfare mother represents a woman of low morals and uncontrolled sexuality, factors identified as the cause of her impoverished state. In both cases Black female control over sexuality and fertility is conceptualized as antithetical to elite white male interests.

Taken together, these four prevailing interpretations of Black womanhood form a nexus of elite white male interpretations of Black female sexuality and fertility. Moreover, by meshing smoothly with systems of race, class, and gender oppression, they provide effective ideological justifications for racial oppression, the politics of gender subordination, and the economic exploitation inherent in capitalist economies. . . .

CRITICAL-THINKING QUESTIONS

1. Describe the four negative images of Black women. How have these images reinforced an "interlocking system" of Black women's oppression?
2. Collins argues that the controlling images "are designed to make racism, sexism, and poverty appear to be natural, normal, and an inevitable part of everyday life." Do you agree or disagree with this statement? Support your position.
3. Do women of other categories (such as Asians, Latinas, and Native Americans) face similar or different stereotypes?

NOTE

1. Brittan and Maynard (1984) note that ideology (1) is common sense and obvious; (2) appears natural, inevitable, and universal; (3) shapes lived experience and behavior; (4) is sedimented in people's consciousness; and (5) consists of a system of ideas embedded in the social system as a whole. This example captures all dimensions of how racism and sexism function ideologically. The status of Black woman as servant is so "common sense" that even a child knows it. That the child saw a Black female child as a baby maid speaks to the naturalization dimension and to the persistence of controlling images in individual consciousness and the social system overall.

REFERENCES

BRAVERMAN, H. 1974. *Labor and monopoly capital.* New York: Monthly Review Press.

BREWER, R. 1988. Black women in poverty: Some comments on female-headed families. *Signs,* 13(2): 331–39.

BRITTAN, A., and M. MAYNARD. 1984. *Sexism, racism and oppression.* New York: Basil Blackwell.

BYERLY, V. 1986. *Hard times cotton mills girls.* Ithaca, N.Y.: Cornell University Press.

CARBY, H. 1987. *Reconstructing womanhood: The emergence of the Afro-American woman novelist.* New York: Oxford.

CHRISTIAN, B. 1985. *Black feminist criticism, perspectives on black women writers.* New York: Pergamon.

CLARKE, C., J. L. GOMEZ, E. HAMMONDS, B. JOHNSON, and L. POWELL. 1983. Conversations and questions: Black women on black women writers. *Conditions: Nine,* 3(3):88–137.

CLARK-LEWIS, E. 1985. *"This work had a' end": The transition from live-in to day work.* Southern Women: The Intersection of Race, Class and Gender. Working Paper #2 Memphis, Tenn.: Center for Research on Women, Memphis State University.

COLLINS, P. H. 1989. A comparison of two works on black family life. *Signs,* 14(4):875–84.

DAVIS, A. Y. 1981. *Women, race and class.* New York: Random House.

DILL, B. T. 1980. 'The means to put my children through': Child-rearing goals and strategies among black female domestic servants. In *The Black woman,* ed. L. F. Rodgers-Rose, 107–23. Beverly Hills, Calif.: Sage.

———. 1988a. 'Making your job good yourself': Domestic service and the construction of personal dignity. In *Women and the politics of empowerment,* eds. A. Bookman and S. Morgen, 33–52. Philadelphia: Temple University Press.

———. 1988b. Our mothers' grief: Racial ethnic women and the maintenance of families. *Journal of Family History,* 13(4):415–31.

DU BOIS, W. E. B. 1969. *The Negro American family.* New York: Negro Universities Press.

DUMAS, R. G. 1980. Dilemmas of Black females in leadership. In *The Black woman,* ed. L. F. Rodgers-Rose, 203–15. Beverly Hills, Calif.: Sage.

FRAZIER, E. F. 1948. *The Negro family in the United States.* New York: Dryden Press.

FUSFELD, D. R., and T. BATES. 1984. *The political economy of the urban ghetto.* Carbondale: Southern Illinois University Press.

GILKES, C. T. 1983. From slavery to social welfare: Racism and the control of Black women. In *Class, race, and sex: The dynamics of control,* eds. A. Swerdlow and H. Lessinger, 288–300. Boston: G. K. Hall.

GORDON, D. M., R. EDWARDS, and M. REICH. 1982. *Segmented work, divided workers.* New York: Cambridge University Press.

HALE, J. 1980. The Black woman and child rearing. In *The Black woman,* ed. L. F. Rodgers-Rose, 79–88. Beverly Hills, Calif.: Sage.

HANSBERRY, L. 1959. *A raisin in the sun.* New York: Signet.

HARRIS, T. 1982. *From mammies to militants: Domestics in Black American literature.* Philadelphia: Temple University Press.

HOOKS, B. 1981. *Ain't I a woman: Black women and feminism.* Boston: South End Press.

KING, M. 1973. The politics of sexual stereotypes. *Black Scholar,* 4(6–7):12–23.

LADNER, J. 1972. *Tomorrow's tomorrow.* Garden City, N.Y.: Doubleday.

LORDE, A. 1984. *Sister outsider.* Trumansberg, N.Y.: The Crossing Press.

MARSHALL, P. 1959. *Brown girl, brownstones*. New York: Avon.

MCADOO, H. P. 1985. Strategies used by Black single mothers against stress. *Review of Black political economy*, 14(2–3):153–66.

MCCRAY, C. A. 1980. The Black woman and family roles. In *The Black woman*, ed. L. F. Rodgers-Rose, 67–78. Beverly Hills, Calif.: Sage.

MOYNIHAN, D. P. 1965. *The negro family: The case for national action*. Washington, D.C.: GPO.

MYERS, L. W. 1980. *Black women: Do they cope better?* Englewood Cliffs, N.J.: Prentice Hall.

NASH, J., and M. P. FERNANDEZ-KELLY, eds. 1983. *Women, men and the international division of labor.* Albany: State University of New York.

OMI, M., and H. WINANT. 1986. *Racial formation in the United States: From the 1960s to the 1980s.* New York: Routledge.

ROLLINS, J. 1985. *Between women: Domestics and their employers*. Philadelphia: Temple University Press.

SHOCKLEY, A. A. 1974. *Loving her*. Tallahassee, Fla.: Naiad Press.

SUDARKASA, N. 1981. Interpreting the African heritage in Afro-American family organization. In *Black families*, ed. H. P. McAdoo, 37–53. Beverly Hills, Calif.: Sage.

WHITE, D. G. 1985. *Ar'n't I a woman? Female slaves in the plantation south*. New York: W. W. Norton.

WILSON, W. J. 1987. *The truly disadvantaged: The inner city, the underclass, and public policy.* Chicago: University of Chicago Press.

41

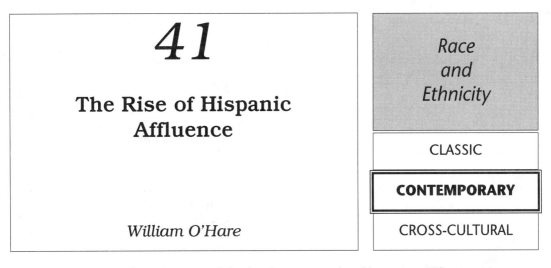

The Rise of Hispanic Affluence

William O'Hare

Race and Ethnicity

CLASSIC

CONTEMPORARY

CROSS-CULTURAL

Social scientists have documented the disadvantages endured by various U.S. minorities. Yet no minority is internally homogeneous. Although, taken as a whole, Hispanics receive only two-thirds of the average U.S. income, the number of affluent Hispanic households grew sharply during the 1980s.

The mainstream media usually portray America's Hispanics as a group of impoverished, newly arrived immigrants from Mexico or Central America. The truth is more complex. A significant share of the Hispanic community has moved into affluence since 1970, and upscale Hispanic households are one of the nation's fastest-growing market segments.

Affluence means different things to different people, but most analyses put households with annual incomes of $50,000 or more in the affluent category. The number of Hispanic* households with an income of $50,000 or more (in 1988 dollars) grew from 191,000 in 1972 to 638,000 in 1988, a 234 percent increase.

Most of this increase occurred during the 1980s. The number of affluent Hispanic households grew by only 129,000 between 1972 and 1980, then gained 318,000 between 1980 and 1988. More than 2.6 million Hispanics live in these 638,000 affluent households.

In 1972, 7.2 percent of Hispanic households were affluent. That share grew to 8.2 percent by 1980 and 10.8 percent in 1988. It is a higher proportion than the share of black households that are affluent (9.8 percent) but much lower than the figure for whites (23.2 percent). And only 1.3 percent of Hispanic households are in the super-affluent category, with annual incomes of more than $100,000.

A DIFFERENT MARKET

Among all Hispanic households, average income is low because the average incomes of recent immigrants are so low. However, the averages obscure the rapid growth of affluent Hispanics. Upscale Hispanics represent a growing but often underserved consumer market.

*In this article, the terms *black* and *white* refer to non-Hispanic blacks and non-Hispanic whites.

Source: From *American Demographics,* vol. 12, no. 8, August 1990, pp. 40–43. Reprinted with permission.

TABLE 1 Affluent Americans: A Comparison of Wealthy Hispanics and Whites

Demographic	*Affluent Hispanics*	*Affluent Whites*
Age		
15–24	10%	7%
25–44	54	40
45–64	25	25
65 and older	11	28
Marital Status		
Married	78	82
Widowed	3	3
Divorced/separated	11	7
Never married	8	8
Education		
Less than high school	19	6
High school graduate	28	27
1–3 years college	25	19
College graduate	29	48
Household Size		
1 person	3	6
2 people	19	33
3 or more people	78	61
Tenure		
Owner	74	86
Renter	26	14
Region		
Northeast	18	26
Midwest	9	24
South	30	30
West	42	20
Metropolitan Status		
Central city	36	24
Suburbs	61	60
Rural	4	15

Note: Distribution of affluent Hispanics and affluent non-Hispanic whites by selected characteristics of householder, 1988.

Source: Current Population Survey, March 1989, Bureau of the Census.

Affluent Hispanics are similar to other affluent groups in some respects, but their differences are important. Like most affluent households, Hispanics achieve affluence by having multiple paychecks. Of the 11.9 million Hispanic workers reported by the Census Bureau in 1988, only 211,000, or 1.8 percent, individually made more than $50,000. Of these, 84 percent were men. Of the 638,000 Hispanic households that were affluent in 1988, 504,000 of them were married couples.

Hispanic households tend to be larger than white households, and affluent Hispanics are no exception. Seventy-eight percent of affluent Hispanic households include three or more people, compared with only 61 percent of white households. One-third of white households contain just two people, and 6 percent are people who live alone, compared with only 19 percent and 3 percent of affluent Hispanic households.

Affluent Hispanics are more likely than affluent whites to be young adults, and they are less likely to be aged sixty-five or older. Fifty-four percent of affluent Hispanics are aged twenty-five to forty-four, for example, compared with only 40 percent of affluent whites. Twenty-eight percent of affluent whites are aged sixty-five or older, compared with 11 percent of affluent Hispanics. This reflects the younger age structure of the Hispanic population in general.

Education is a powerful influence on the affluence of Hispanic households, but the average educational level of affluent Hispanics is still less than that of affluent whites. Almost half (48 percent) of affluent white householders have at least a four-year college degree, compared with only 29 percent of affluent Hispanic householders. Fully 19 percent of affluent Hispanic householders are high school dropouts, versus just 6 percent of whites.

WHERE THEY LIVE

Location is one of the major differences between affluent Hispanics and other affluent groups. Forty-two percent of all affluent Hispanic households are in the West, compared with only 20 percent of affluent white households. Only 9 percent of affluent Hispanics live in the Midwest, compared with one-quarter of affluent whites.

Affluent Hispanics are also twice as likely as affluent whites to live in a large metropolitan area. One-third of affluent Hispanics live in metropolitan areas of 1 million or more, partly because so many live in Los Angeles. While 15 percent of affluent whites live in nonmetropolitan areas, only 4 percent of affluent Hispanics live outside of metros.

Within metropolitan areas, affluent Hispanics are much more likely than affluent whites to live in the central city. About 60 percent of both Hispanic and white affluent households are in the suburbs of large cities. But 36 percent of affluent Hispanics live in the central cities, compared with 24 percent of whites. This may explain why only about three-quarters of affluent Hispanics are homeowners, compared with 86 percent of affluent whites.

The latest reliable data on affluent Hispanics within specific metropolitan areas are from the 1980 census. To locate pockets of affluence in the nation's metropolitan areas, I examined the share of Hispanic households with incomes of $35,000 or more in 1979, which is roughly equivalent to an income of $50,000 or more in 1988. This analysis revealed that the metropolitan areas where Hispanic households are most likely to be affluent are not the areas with the largest Hispanic populations. In fact, the share of Hispanic households with 1979 incomes of $35,000 or more was lower in metropolitan areas where Hispanics made up a large share of the total population.

At the top of the list is Honolulu where more than one-quarter of all Hispanic households had incomes of more than $35,000 in 1980. Honolulu is followed by Washington, D.C., Detroit, and Nassau-Suffolk, New York. Despite Miami's relatively affluent Cuban community, that metropolitan area ended up ninth in this ranking. And almost all of the metros at the bottom of the list are heavily Hispanic and located in the Southwest. In Brownsville-McAllen, Texas, and Visalia, California, fewer than 4 percent of Hispanic households had 1979 incomes of $35,000 or more.

TABLE 2 Concentrations of Affluent Hispanics

Metropolitan Area	*Percent Affluent*	*Metropolitan Area*	*Percent Affluent*
1. Honolulu, HI	25.3%	22. Tucson, AZ	7.5%
2. Washington, DC-MD-VA	24.6	23. Phoenix, AZ	7.2
3. Detroit, MI	18.7	24. Albuquerque, NM	7.1
4. Nassau-Suffolk, NY	15.8	25. Philadelphia, PA-NJ	7.1
5. San Francisco-Oakland, CA	15.1	26. Austin, TX	6.5
6. San Jose, CA	14.8	27. Boston-Lowell-Brockton-Lawrence-Haverhill, MA	6.5
7. Anaheim-Santa Ana-Garden Grove, CA	14.2	28. Salinas-Seaside-Monterey, CA	6.3
8. New Orleans, LA	13.2	29. Stockton, CA	6.3
9. Miami, FL	11.5	30. Corpus Christi, TX	6.1
10. Houston, TX	11.3	31. Laredo, TX	5.7
11. Chicago, IL	10.9	32. Jersey City, NJ	5.5
12. Oxnard-Simi Valley-Ventura, CA	10.2	33. Bakersfield, CA	5.5
13. Newark, NJ	9.8	34. Bergen-Passaic, NJ	5.1
14. Tampa-St. Petersburg, FL	9.8	35. San Antonio, TX	4.8
15. Denver-Boulder, CO	9.3	36. New York, NY-NJ	4.7
16. Sacramento, CA	9.1	37. Fresno, CA	4.7
17. Los Angeles-Long Beach, CA	8.7	38. El Paso, TX	4.6
18. Santa Barbara-Santa Maria-Lompoc, CA	8.6	39. Las Cruces, NM	4.2
19. Riverside-San Bernardino-Oakland, CA	8.3	40. McAllen-Pharr-Edinburg, TX	3.6
20. San Diego, CA	8.2	41. Brownsville-Harlingen-San Benito, TX	3.5
21. Dallas-Fort Worth, TX	8.1	42. Visalia-Tulare-Porterville, CA	3.3

Notes: Percent of Hispanic households with incomes of $50,000 or more in 1989 dollars, in selected metropolitan areas, 1979 ($50,000 in 1989 dollars is roughly equivalent to $35,000 in 1979). Ranking is based on unrounded percentages.

Source : 1980 census.

The number of affluent Hispanics is growing because Hispanics are becoming a larger share of our population, and also because an ever-growing share of Hispanics are moving up in U.S. society. Like other groups, most affluent Hispanic households are married couples where both husband and wife work. But affluent Hispanics are heavily concentrated in the West, in large (1 million plus) metropolitan areas, and in central cities. . . .

CRITICAL-THINKING QUESTIONS

1. How affluent are Hispanics compared to whites? Compared to African Americans?
2. In what respects do affluent Hispanics differ from affluent whites?
3. What evidence supports the conclusion that Hispanics have improved their social position in recent decades? What evidence leads to the conclusion that they have not?

42

A Comeback for American Indians

C. Matthew Snipp

Race and Ethnicity

CLASSIC

CONTEMPORARY

CROSS-CULTURAL

When European settlers arrived in the early 1600s, some 18 million Indians lived in North America, speaking approximately 300 languages. By 1900, only a fraction of Indians had survived military slaughter, enslavement, forced labor, land confiscation, coerced mass migration, and European diseases such as influenza, measles, smallpox, and typhus. Yet, as C. Matthew Snipp shows in this reading, since 1980 the American Indian population has "staged a surprising comeback" due to higher birth rates, a higher life expectancy, and better health services.

In 1915, the Census Bureau predicted that so-called "full-blooded" American Indians would eventually disappear from the U.S. population. Famine, malnutrition, and disease contributed to a low level of fertility among American Indians in the early 1900s.

The Census Bureau may have been justified in its gloomy prediction back then: The American Indian population had dwindled from perhaps as many as 5 to 7 million to as few as a quarter-million by 1890. However, as the century progressed, a remarkable event took place. Instead of disappearing, the American Indian population staged a surprising comeback.

The numbers are hard to pin down, in part because of methodological problems such as changing census definitions for urban areas, procedural changes in the census, and compositional changes in the American Indian population—including changes in the numbers of people identifying themselves as American Indian. Because interracial persons have a variety of options about how they identify themselves, population numbers may swell or decline depending on how multiracial persons are inclined to affiliate with or disassociate from a particular group. In recent decades, the American Indian population has increased substantially because large numbers of persons have chosen to "switch" the racial background they report in the census (see Table 1).

However, when the numbers are adjusted for these factors, a trend becomes clear: Throughout the first half of this century, growth in the American Indian population gathered momentum, starting slowly at first, and then gradually increasing in numbers over the decades.

Despite the signs of renewed vigor in the American Indian population, no one could have predicted the spectacular growth in the American

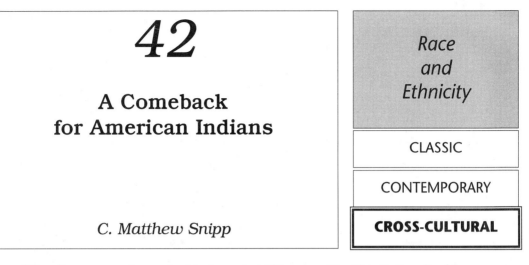

Source: From "A Demographic Comeback for American Indians" by C. Matthew Snipp, in *Population Today* 24 (November, 1996), pp. 4–5. © 1996. Originally from *Changing Numbers, Changing Needs: American Indian Demography and Public Health*, eds., Gary Sandefur, Ronald R. Findfuss, and Barney Cohen, September 1996. Reprinted by permission of the National Academy Press.

Table 1 American Indian and Alaska Native Population Growth, 1970, 1980, and 1990

	1970	*1980*	*1990*
American Indian/Alaska native	792,730	1,423,045*	1,959,234
Total U.S. population	203,302,000	226,546,000	248,718,000

*Changes in census definitions, census procedures, and the composition of the American Indian population (due to variations in the numbers of people self-identifying as American Indian) may account for the large increase in the American Indian population between 1970 and 1980.

Source: U.S. Bureau of the Census, *General Population Characteristics, United States, 1990*; and *Statistical Abstract of the United States, 1995.*

Indian population since 1950. In the second half of the twentieth century, the American Indian population has increased fivefold to almost 2 million in 1990. At least in the short term, there are few reasons to expect this trend to reverse itself.

HIGH BIRTH AND MORTALITY RATES

The American Indian population has a markedly higher birth rate than either the black or the white population. Throughout the 1980s, the crude birth rate for the white population hovered around 15 per 1,000 population. For the same period, the rate for blacks remained between 21 to 22 per 1,000 population. Even using conservative estimates, the American Indian birth rate exceeded both these groups, ranging from a low of 25.5 in 1981 to a high of 27.9 in 1992.

American Indian women begin their childbearing at a relatively early age. About 45 percent have their first child as teenagers. In contrast, only about 21 percent of white women begin childbearing in their teens. In addition, the fertility of American Indians residing on reservations was noticeably higher than American Indian couples living in urban areas. American Indian fertility now resembles the fertility of other low-income groups.

The American Indian population also has a substantially higher mortality rate than the white population. The American Indian mortality rate ranged between 21.0 and 22.9 deaths per 1,000 population between 1980 and 1990, compared to an almost steady rate of 9 white deaths per 1,000 for the same period.

American Indians have lived shorter lives than whites in the past, but more recent numbers show this trend to be equalizing. In the period 1972–1974, the life expectancy of American Indians was 61 years, and for whites, 72 years—an 18 percent gap. In 1988, life expectancy for American Indians was 72 years, and 76 years for whites, a much narrower difference of 6 percent.

Alcoholism continues to be a major cause of death in the American Indian population. In the years 1989–1991, the American Indian mortality rate from alcohol-related diseases was 51.8 per 100,000 population, 630 percent higher than the total U.S. rate of 7.1 per 100,000 population.

Suicide is also a significant cause of death compared to other population groups. In 1989–1991, the suicide rate for American Indians was 16.5 per 100,000 population, higher than the rate of 11.5 per 100,000 population for the rest of the United States.

American Indians under age forty-five have staggering rates of mortality compared to whites of the same age. American Indians ages fifteen to twenty-four have a death rate from all causes of 221 per 100,000 persons. This rate is 133 percent higher than the death rate of whites of the same age. A majority of these deaths (85 percent) were the result of accidents, suicide, and homicide. Suicides are 172 percent higher for young American Indian adults than for young whites, and homicides kill nearly three times more American Indians than whites per capita. However, accidents—especially car accidents—are the true scourge of American Indians at this age.

THE PARADOX OF LOW INFANT DEATHS

High levels of socioeconomic distress are frequently accompanied by high levels of infant mortality. Poor areas have limited access to medical care, pre- and neonatal care, and good maternal nutrition. But here, American Indians are an anomaly. Although American Indians are among the poorest groups in American society—32 percent have incomes below the poverty threshold—they have relatively low infant mortality rates. In 1984, infant mortality for American Indians was 11 deaths per 1,000 live births, somewhat higher than the white rate of 8.5 per 1,000 live births, but far lower than the 18 per 1,000 rate for blacks. In relative terms, however, American Indian infant mortality is still about 29 percent higher than the rate for whites. Indeed, there is evidence that all American Indian deaths, including infants, may be under-reported.

The Indian Health Service provides essential services to pregnant women and newborns. Without this care, it is likely that American Indians would have much larger numbers of infant deaths, and have infant mortality rates more closely resembling those found in other impoverished groups.

RESIDENCE: RESERVATION, URBAN, AND RURAL

One-third of all American Indians live on reservations, which are usually very small communities. Of the 279 recognized reservations, only eighteen had populations of 5,000 or more in 1990. The largest in area, the Navajo reservation is also the most populous with 143,000 residents in 1990. It is nearly thirteen times larger than the next largest reservation, Pine Ridge Sioux in South Dakota, which had a 1990 population of 11,182.

These reservations have grown substantially in the past two decades, more than doubling in population size. Yet in relative terms, they represent a slowly declining share of the total American Indian population.

The American Indian population has experienced rapid and recent urbanization, but still is concentrated in rural areas. About three-quarters of the American Indian population is found in the West and in rural areas. Relatively few are in New England or the Southeast. Nearly half of the population was located outside of metropolitan areas in 1990.

MEETING THE CHALLENGES OF THE NEXT CENTURY

Once on the brink of extinction, the American Indian population has rebounded in a dramatic way. At least numerically, the existence of the American Indian population is assured for the foreseeable future. Yet, American Indians' future vitality will depend on more than growth alone. Tribal leaders and others concerned with the future well-being of American Indians must find innovative ways to provide for their material needs and ensure their cultural survival. As American Indians move into the next century, meeting the many challenges of preserving cultural traditions and improving economic well-being will, more than numbers alone, be the foundation for sustaining the place of American Indians within American society.

CRITICAL-THINKING QUESTIONS

1. Why is the exact number of American Indians "hard to pin down"?

2. Although the life expectancy rates of American Indians have increased, mortality rates are still higher than those of the white population. What are the major causes of death among American Indians? Why do you think the death rate is so high?

3. What does Snipp mean when he says that "American Indians' future vitality will depend on more than growth alone"? What other factors might be important in ensuring American Indians' cultural survival?

43

The Tragedy of Old Age in America

Robert N. Butler

Aging and the Elderly

CLASSIC

CONTEMPORARY

CROSS-CULTURAL

The United States has often been described as a "youth culture," in which youth is a measure of personal worth. In this selection, Robert Butler explores the U.S. view of the elderly, which he finds to be fraught with myths and prejudices. He argues that these not only hurt elderly people but also disadvantage everyone.

What is it like to be old in the United States? What will our own lives be like when we are old? Americans find it difficult to think about old age until they are propelled into the midst of it by their own aging and that of relatives and friends. Aging is the neglected stepchild of the human life cycle. Though we have begun to examine the socially taboo subjects of dying and death, we have leaped over that long period of time preceding death known as old age. In truth, it is easier to manage the problem of death than the problem of living as an old person. Death is a dramatic, one-time crisis while old age is a day-by-day and year-by-year confrontation with powerful external and internal forces, a bittersweet coming to terms with one's own personality and one's life.

Those of us who are not old barricade ourselves from discussions of old age by declaring the subject morbid, boring, or in poor taste. Optimism and euphemism are other common devices. People will speak of looking forward to their "retirement years." The elderly are described respectfully as "senior citizens," "golden agers," "our elders," and one hears of old people who are considered inspirations and examples of how to "age well" or "gracefully." There is the popularly accepted opinion that Social Security and pensions provide a comfortable and reliable flow of funds so the elderly have few financial worries. Medicare has lulled the population into reassuring itself that the once terrible financial burdens

Source: From *Why Survive? Being Old in America* by Robert N. Butler, M.D., pp. 1–2, 6–12, 15–16, copyright © 1975 by Robert N. Butler, M.D., HarperCollins Publishers, Inc. Reprinted with permission of HarperCollins Publishers, Inc.

of late-life illnesses are now eradicated. Advertisements and travel folders show relaxed, happy, well-dressed older people enjoying recreation, travel, and their grandchildren. If they are no longer living in the old family home, they are pictured as delighted residents of retirement communities with names like Leisure World and Sun City, with lots of grass, clean air, and fun. This is the American ideal of the "golden years" toward which millions of citizens are expectantly toiling through their workdays.

But this is not the full story. A second theme runs through the popular view of old age. Our colloquialisms reveal a great deal: Once you are old you are "fading fast," "over the hill," "out to pasture," "down the drain," "finished," "out of date," an "old crock," "fogy," "geezer," or "biddy." One hears children saying they are afraid to get old, middle-aged people declaring they want to die after they have passed their prime, and numbers of old people wishing they were dead.

What can we possibly conclude from these discrepant points of view? Our popular attitudes could be summed up as a combination of wishful thinking and stark terror. We base our feelings on primitive fears, prejudice, and stereotypes rather than on knowledge and insight. In reality, the way one experiences old age is contingent upon physical health, personality, earlier-life experiences, the actual circumstances of late-life events (in what order they occur, how they occur, when they occur), and the social supports one receives: adequate finances, shelter, medical care, social roles, religious support, recreation. All of these are crucial and interconnected elements which together determine the quality of late life. . . .

MYTHS AND STEREOTYPES ABOUT THE OLD

In addition to dealing with the difficulties of physical and economic survival, older people are affected by the multitude of myths and stereotypes surrounding old age:

> An older person thinks and moves slowly. He does not think as he used to or as creatively. He is bound to himself and to his past and can no longer change or grow. He can learn neither well nor swiftly and, even if he could, he would not wish to. Tied to his personal traditions and growing conservatism, he dislikes innovations and is not disposed to new ideas. Not only can he not move forward, he often moves backward. He enters a second childhood caught up in increasing egocentricity and demanding more from his environment than he is willing to give to it. Sometimes he becomes an intensification of himself, a caricature of a lifelong personality. He becomes irritable and cantankerous, yet shallow and enfeebled. He lives in his past; he is behind the times. He is aimless and wandering of mind, reminiscing and garrulous. Indeed, he is a study in decline, the picture of mental and physical failure. He has lost and cannot replace friends, spouse, job, status, power, influence, income. He is often stricken by diseases which, in turn, restrict his movement, his enjoyment of food, the pleasures of well-being. He has lost his desire and capacity for sex. His body shrinks, and so too does the flow of blood to his brain. His mind does not utilize oxygen and sugar at the same rate as formerly. Feeble, uninteresting, he awaits his death, a burden to society, to his family and to himself.

In its essentials, this view I have sketched approximates the picture of old age held by many Americans. As in all clichés, stereotypes, and myths there are bits of truth. But many of the current views of old age represent confusions, misunderstandings, or simply a lack of knowledge about old age. Others may be completely inaccurate or biased, reflecting prejudice or outright hostility. Certain prevalent myths need closer examination.

The Myth of "Aging"

The idea of chronological aging (measuring one's age by the number of years one has lived) is a kind of myth. It is clear that there are great differences in the rates of physiological, chronological, psychological, and social aging within the person and from person to person. In fact, physiological indicators show a greater range from the mean in old age than in any other age group, and this is true of personality as well. Older people actually become more diverse rather than more similar with advancing years. There are extraordinarily "young" eighty-year-olds as well as "old" eighty-year-olds. Chronological age, therefore, is a convenient but imprecise indicator of physical, mental, and emotional status. For the purposes of this book old age may be considered to commence at the conventionally accepted point of sixty-five.

We do know that organic brain damage can create such extensive intellectual impairment that people of all types and personalities may become dull-eyed, blank-faced, and unresponsive. Massive destruction of the brain and body has a "leveling" effect which can produce increasing homogeneity among the elderly. But most older people do not suffer impairment of this magnitude during the greater part of their later life.

The Myth of Unproductivity

Many believe the old to be unproductive. But in the absence of diseases and social adversities, old people tend to remain productive and actively involved in life. There are dazzling examples like octogenarians Georgia O'Keeffe continuing to paint and Pope John XXIII revitalizing his church, and septuagenarians Duke Ellington composing and working his hectic concert schedule and Golda Meir acting as her country's vigorous Prime Minister. Substantial numbers of people become unusually creative for the first time in old age, when exceptional and inborn talents may be discovered and expressed. What is most pertinent to our discussion here, however, is the fact that many old people continue to contribute usefully to their families and community in a variety of ways, including active employment. The 1971 Bureau of Labor Statistics figures show 1,780,000 people over sixty-five working full time and 1,257,000 part time. Since society and business practice do not encourage the continued employment of the elderly, it is obvious that many more would work if jobs were available.

When productive incapacity develops, it can be traced more directly to a variety of losses, diseases, or circumstances than to that mysterious process called aging. Even then, in spite of the presence of severe handicaps, activity and involvement are often maintained.

The Myth of Disengagement

This is related to the previous myth and holds that older people prefer to disengage from life, to withdraw into themselves, choosing to live alone or perhaps only with their peers. Ironically, some gerontologists themselves hold these views. One study, *Growing Old: The Process of Disengagement*, presents the theory that mutual separation of the aged person from his society is a natural part of the aging experience. There is no evidence to support this generalization. Disengagement is only one of many patterns of reaction to old age.

The Myth of Inflexibility

The ability to change and adapt has little to do with one's age and more to do with one's lifelong character. But even this statement has to be qualified. One is not necessarily destined to maintain one's character in earlier life permanently. True, the endurance, the strength, and the stability in human character structure are remarkable and protective. But most, if not all, people change and remain open to change throughout the course of life, right up to its termination. The old notion, whether ascribed to Pope Alexander VI or Sigmund Freud, that character is laid down in final form by the fifth year of life can be confidently refuted. Change is the hallmark of living. The notion that older people become less responsive to innovation and change because of age is not supported by scientific studies of healthy older people living in the community or by everyday observations and clinical psychiatric experience.

A related cliché is that political conservatism increases with age. If one's options are constricted by job discrimination, reduced or fixed income, and runaway inflation, as older people's are, one may become conservative out of economic necessity rather than out of qualities innate in the psyche. Thus an older person may vote against the creation of better schools or an expansion of social services for tax reasons. His property—his home—may be his only equity, and his income is likely to be too low to weather increased taxes. A perfectly sensible self-interest rather than "conservatism" is at work here. Naturally, conservatives do exist among the elderly, but so do liberals, radicals, and moderates. Once again diversity rather than homogeneity is the norm.

The Myth of "Senility"

The notion that old people are senile, showing forgetfulness, confusional episodes, and reduced attention, is widely accepted. "Senility" is a popularized layman's term used by doctors and the public alike to categorize the behavior of the old. Some of what is called senile is the result of brain damage. But anxiety and depression are also frequently lumped within the same category of senility, even though they are treatable and often reversible. Old people, like young people, experience a full range of emotions, including anxiety, grief, depression, and paranoid states. It is all too easy to blame age and brain damage when accounting for the mental problems and emotional concerns of later life.

Drug tranquilization is another frequent, misdiagnosed, and potentially reversible cause of so-called senility. Malnutrition and unrecognized physical illnesses, such as congestive heart failure, may produce "senile behavior" by reducing the supply of blood, oxygen, and food to the brain. Alcoholism, often associated with bereavement, is another cause. Because it has been so convenient to dismiss all these manifestations by lumping them together under an improper and inaccurate diagnostic label, the elderly often do not receive the benefits of decent diagnosis and treatment.

Actual irreversible brain damage,[1] of course, is not a myth, and two major conditions create mental disorders. One is cerebral arteriosclerosis (hardening of the arteries of the brain); the other, unfortunately referred to as senile brain disease, is due to a mysterious dissolution of brain cells. Such conditions account for some 50 percent of the cases of major mental disorders in old age, and the symptoms connected with these conditions are the ones that form the basis for what has come to be known as senility. But, as I wish to emphasize again, similar symptoms can be found in a number of other conditions which *are* reversible through proper treatment.

The Myth of Serenity

In contrast to the previous myths, which view the elderly in a negative light, the myth of serenity portrays old age as a kind of adult fairyland Now at last comes a time of relative peace and serenity when people can relax and enjoy the fruits of their labors after the storms of active life are over. Advertising slogans, television, and romantic fiction foster the myth. Visions of carefree, cookie-baking grandmothers and rocking-chair grandfathers are cherished by younger generations. But, in fact, older persons experience more stresses than any other age group, and these stresses are often devastating. The strength of the aged to endure crisis is remarkable, and tranquility is an unlikely as well as inappropriate response under these circumstances. Depression, anxiety, psychosomatic illnesses, paranoia, garrulousness, and irritability are some of the internal reactions to external stresses.

Depressive reactions are particularly widespread in late life. To the more blatant psychotic depressions and the depressions associated with organic brain diseases must be added the everyday depressions that stem from long physical illness or chronic discomfort, from grief, despair, and loneliness, and from an inevitably lowered self-esteem that comes from diminished social and personal status.

Grief is a frequent companion of old age—grief for one's own losses and for the ultimate loss of one's self. Apathy and emptiness are a common sequel to the initial shock and sadness that come with the deaths of close friends and relatives. Physical disease and social isolation can follow bereavement.

Anxiety is another common feature. There is much to be anxious about; poverty, loneliness, and illness head the list. Anxiety may manifest itself in many forms: rigid patterns of thinking and behaving, helplessness, manipulative behavior, restlessness and suspiciousness, sometimes to the point of paranoid states.[2]

Anger and even rage may be seen:

> Mary Mack, 73, left her doctor's office irritable, depressed, and untreated. She was angry at the doctor's inattention. She charged that he simply regarded her as a complainer and did not take the necessary time to examine her carefully. She had received the same response from other doctors. Meanwhile her doctor entered the diagnosis in his file: hypochondriasis with chronic depression. No treatment was given. The prognosis was evidently considered hopeless.
>
> John Barber, an elderly black man, spent all his life working hard at low wages for his employers. When he was retired he literally went on strike. He refused to do anything. He would sit all day on his front porch, using his family as the substitute victim of his years of pent-up anger. He had always been seen as mild mannered. Now he could afford to let himself go into rages and describe in vicious detail what he was going to do to people. A social worker viewing his behavior declared to his family that he was "psychotic." But Mr. Barber was not insane; he was angry.

AGEISM—THE PREJUDICE AGAINST THE ELDERLY

The stereotyping and myths surrounding old age can be explained in part by lack of knowledge and by insufficient contact with a wide variety of older people. But there is another powerful factor operating—a deep and profound prejudice against the elderly which is found to some degree in all of us. In thinking about how to describe this, I coined the word "ageism" in 1968:

> Ageism can be seen as a process of systematic stereotyping of and discrimination against people because they are old, just as racism and sexism accomplish thus with skin color and gender. Old people are categorized as senile, rigid in thought and manner, old-fashioned in morality and skills. . . . Ageism allows the younger generations to see older people as different from themselves; thus they subtly cease to identify with their elders as human beings.

Ageism makes it easier to ignore the frequently poor social and economic plight of older people. We can avoid dealing with the reality that our productivity-minded society has little use for nonproducers—in this case those who have reached an arbitrarily defined retirement age. We can also avoid, for a time at least, reminders of the personal reality of our own aging and death.

Ageism is manifested in a wide range of phenomena, both on individual and institutional levels—stereotypes and myths, outright disdain and dislike, or simply subtle avoidance of contact; discriminatory practices in housing, employment, and services of all kinds; epithets, cartoons, and jokes. At times ageism becomes an expedient method by which society promotes viewpoints about the aged in order to relieve itself of responsibility toward them. At other times ageism serves a highly personal objective, protecting younger (usually middle-aged) individuals—often at high emotional cost—from thinking about things they fear (aging, illness, death). . . .

Older people are not always victims, passive and fated by their environment. They, too, initiate direct actions and stimulate responses. They may exploit their age and its accompanying challenges to gain something they want or need, perhaps to their own detriment (for example, by demanding services from others and thus allowing their own skills to atrophy). Exploitation can backfire; excessive requests to others by an older person may be met at first, but as requests increase they are felt as demands—and may indeed be demands. Younger people who attempt to deal with a demanding older person may find themselves going through successive cycles of rage, guilt, and overprotectiveness without realizing they are being manipulated. In addition to his "age," the older person may exploit his diseases and his impairments, capitalizing upon his alleged helplessness. Invalids of all ages do this, but older people can more easily take on the appearance of frailty when others would not be allowed this behavior. Manipulation by older people is best recognized for what it is—a valuable clue that there is energy available which should be redirected toward greater benefit for themselves and others.

It must also be remembered that the old can have many prejudices against the young. These may be a result of their attractiveness, vigor, and sexual prowess. Older people may be troubled by the extraordinary changes that they see in the world around them and blame the younger generation. They may be angry at the brevity of life and begrudge someone the fresh chance of living out a life span which they have already completed.

Angry and ambivalent feelings flow, too, between the old and the middle-aged, who are caught up in the problems unique to their age and position within the life cycle. The middle-aged bear the heaviest personal and social responsibilities since they are called upon to help support—individually and collectively—both ends of the life cycle: the nurture and education of their young and the financial, emotional, and physical care of the old. Many have not been prepared for their heavy responsibilities and are surprised and overwhelmed by them. Frequently these responsibilities trap them in their careers or life styles until the children grow up or their parents die. A common reaction is anger at both the young and the old. The effects of financial pressures are seen primarily in the middle and lower economic classes. But the middle-aged of all classes are inclined to be ambivalent toward the young and old since both age groups remind them of their own waning youth. In addition—with reason—they fear technological or professional obsolescence as they see what has happened to their elders and feel the pressure of youth pushing its way toward their position in society. Furthermore, their responsibilities are likely to increase in the future as more and more of their parents and grandparents live longer life spans.

CRITICAL-THINKING QUESTIONS

1. Butler presents several "themes" that shape popular views of old age in the United States. What evidence of these do you find in the mass media? What about in your own attitudes and behavior toward elderly people?
2. Why do you think our society has developed views of aging that are not realistic?
3. How do the elderly themselves sometimes reinforce ageism?

NOTES

1. Human beings react in varying ways to brain disease just as they do to other serious threats to their persons. They may become anxious, rigid, depressed, and hypochondriacal. (Hypochondriasis comprises bodily symptoms or fear of diseases that are not due to physical changes but to emotional concerns. They are no less real simply because they do not have a physical origin.) These reactions can be ameliorated by sensitive, humane concern, talk, and understanding even though the underlying physical process cannot be reversed. Therefore, even the irreversible brain syndromes require proper diagnosis and treatment of their emotional consequences.

2. No less a thinker than Aristotle failed to distinguish between the intrinsic features of aging and the reaction of the elderly to their lives. He considered cowardice, resentment, vindictiveness, and what he called "senile avarice" to be intrinsic to late life. Cicero took a warmer and more positive view of old age. He understood, for example, "If old men are morose, troubled, fretful, and hard to please . . . these are faults of character and not of age." So he explained in his essay *"De Senectute."*

44

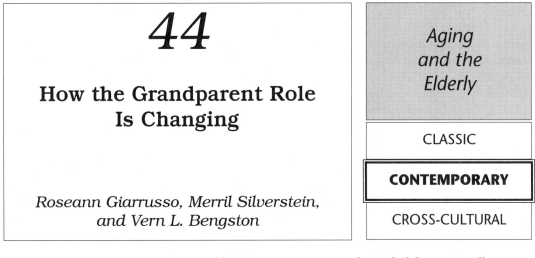

How the Grandparent Role Is Changing

Roseann Giarrusso, Merril Silverstein, and Vern L. Bengston

Aging and the Elderly

CLASSIC

CONTEMPORARY

CROSS-CULTURAL

As Reading 45 describes, our world is aging. Increasing numbers of adults—especially in Western nations—are now great-grandparents and even great-great-grandparents. Such unprecedented longevity suggests the growing importance of multigenerational family relations. In this reading, Roseann Giarrusso, Merril Silverstein, and Vern L. Bengston examine how our longevity has already affected intergenerational family structures and why grandparent-grandchild relationships will become more important.

Grandparenthood has changed over the past decades as demographic shifts have increased the complexity of family structures and roles. Increases in longevity, in divorce and remarriage rates, and in old-age migration have simultaneously produced new opportunities and new stresses for grandparents. The longevity revolution has increased the number of three-, four-, and five-generation families, thereby lengthening the time spent in the grandparent role and adding multiple roles of great- and great-great-grandparent. Increases in divorce and remarriage rates have resulted in a high proportion of blended families and step-grandparent relationships. Improved health, stable finances, and early retirement have made geographic mobility possible for retirees. How have these changes in family structure, composition, and living arrangements influenced the role of grandparents? What are the implications of these changes for the psychological well-being and resources available to grandparents?

In this [reading] we first examine how population aging and the changing structure of the intergenerational family highlights the increasing diversity in grandparenting and great-grandparenting styles. Second, we examine how divorce and remarriage in the middle generation influences grandparents' ability to enact their role when custodial parents act as gatekeepers to their children, and we underscore the need for research on grandparents rearing grandchildren in order to determine the psychological costs and rewards to caregiving grandparents. Third, we discuss how household arrangements and geographic mobility of grandparents and grandchildren jointly influence their relationship. We conclude with an overview of some research and policy implications that result from these complex family arrangements and emphasize the need for greater conceptual and theoretical development in grandparenting studies.

Source: Reprinted with permission from "Family Complexity and the Grandparent Role," by Roseann Giarrusso, Merril Silverstein, and Vern L. Bengston, *Generations*, 20:1, (Spring, 1996), pp. 17–23.

CHANGING INTERGENERATIONAL FAMILY STRUCTURES

Because of dramatic increases in average longevity over the past century, it has become more likely that grandparents, great-grandparents, and even great-great-grandparents will survive long enough to have relationships with grandchildren, great-grandchildren, or great-great-grandchildren. Where fewer than 50 percent of adolescents in 1900 had two or more grandparents alive, by 1976 that figure had grown to almost 90 percent (Uhlenberg, 1980). Thus, there is an unprecedented number of grandparents in American society today; more than three-quarters of adults can expect to become a grandparent (Barranti, 1985; Hagestad, 1985; Kivnick, 1982).

While historical increases in life expectancy have resulted in families with more generations alive simultaneously, reductions in fertility have resulted in smaller average family size (Bengtson & Tress, 1980; Uhlenberg, 1980; Watkins, Menken, & Bongaarts, 1987). Consequently, the shape of American families has gone from that of a pyramid, with larger numbers of young people at the base, to that of a beanpole. Three, four, and five generations of family members are increasingly present, but with fewer numbers being born in each subsequent generation than in previous eras (Bengston, Rosenthal, & Burton, 1990).

With fewer family members in each generation, existing *intergenerational* family relations take on added significance. Since there may be more *between*-generation kin than *within*-generation kin available in such a family structure, grandchildren may emerge as potentially more important sources of emotional meaning and practical support for grandparents than in the past. Thus, grandparenthood may be an increasingly significant social role for older people, offering valuable rewards. At the same time, it is important to consider whether a more involved grandparenthood also results in social, economic, and psychological costs—especially for grandparents who become "surrogate parents" for their grandchildren (Bengtson, Rosenthal, & Burton, 1995).

Elongation of multigenerational families also can occur from age-condensed family patterns: Teenage pregnancy can produce differences of less than twenty years between generations, leading to grandparenthood in one's twenties or thirties, over four or five generations. This kind of intergenerational structure is more common among ethnic minorities than among the white majority. In addition, higher rates of fertility, along with the tendency to include fictive kin in definitions of family, have created a paradox for minority grandparents: Although they have a larger kin network from which they may draw potential support, they also have a larger number of kin to whom they must *provide* support (Bengtson, Rosenthal, & Burton, 1995). . . .

Adult Grandchildren

Not only have relationships with grandparents, great-grandparents, and great-great-grandparents been a neglected topic of research, so too have relationships of grandparents with *adult* grandchildren. Most previous research has tended to focus only on pre-adult grandchildren or those living with the grandparent (Jendrek, 1994; Robertson, 1995). Given the growth recently of studies examining adult parent-child relations, it is surprising that only scant attention has been devoted to studying relationships between grandparents and adult grandchildren.

Because of increases in longevity over the past century, it has become more likely that a grandparent will not only survive, but live long enough to have *long-term* relationships with *adult* grandchildren. As the median age of first grandparenthood has remained relatively constant over the past century at forty-five years (Hagestad, 1985), gains in life expectancy imply that grandparents are spending many more years in the grandparent role: Among women, for example, this status can engage 50 percent of their lives, and the prevalence of grandparents who have adult grandchildren is historically unprecedented (Goldman, 1986). Farkas and Hogan (1994) examined intergenerational family structure in seven economically developed nations (including the United States) during the 1980s and found that more than half (50.6 percent) of people sixty-five years of age and older have a grandchild who is at least eighteen years old. Lawton, Silverstein, and Bengtson (1994) found a slightly higher percentage in a study of intergenerational relations in the United Stares conducted by the American Association of Retired Persons (AARP), with 56 percent of Americans sixty-five years of age and older having at least one adult grandchild.

In light of the recent expansion in adult grandchild-grandparent relations in the American population, it is unfortunate that little attention has been paid by large-scale survey researchers to these adult intergenerational relationships. For example, most of the major national surveys designed to study social aspects of aging ask no specific questions of older adults about their relationships with grandchildren (or great-grandchildren) or of younger adults about their relationships with grandparents.

Other scholarly analyses concerning the relationships of grandparents with pre-adult grandchildren suggest that grandparents are more involved with their younger grandchildren than ever before. Some researchers have speculated that the grandparent-grandchild bond may be even more significant in adult relations (Hagestad, 1981; Troll, 1980). As yet, however, the trajectory or life-course "career" of grandparent-grandchild relationships, and the contribution of "successful" grandparenting to quality of life of older adults, are issues that are unclear and remain unexamined. . . .

Diversity in the Styles of Grandparenting

Population aging has not only led to the long-term viability of grandparenthood; it has also led to an increasing diversity in the demographic characteristics of individuals holding the roles of grandparent and grandchild. Today grandparents may range in age from 30 to 110, and grandchildren range from newborns to retirees (Hagestad, 1985). With demographic diversity in grandparents has come a corresponding diversity in grandparenting styles (Bengtson, 1985). Consequently, some scholars have suggested that the role of grandparent is ill-defined, that it is a social status without clear normative expectations attached to it. Fischer and Silverman (1982) and Wood (1982) refer to the grandparent role as "tenuous" or "ambiguous," without clear prescriptions regarding the rights and duties of grandparents. In fact, there is no single "grandparent role," but there are multiple ways to be a grandparent. It is important not to confuse variance in styles of role enactment with lack of role definition. What is needed is a classification of the different types of grandparenting since there are a variety of reasons that grandparents do not perform the role in the same way.

Yet there has been little empirical research on the styles of grandparenting and the sources of diversity in those styles. In the only previous attempt to classify grandparent-grandchild relations, Cherlin and Furstenberg (1986) identified five types of grandparenting styles by cross-classifying grandparents on three relationship dimensions: exchange of services with grandchild, influence over grandchild, and frequency of contact with grandchild. They labeled these types as follows: (1) detached, (2) passive, (3) supportive, (4) authoritative, and (5) influential. Their analysis suggested that none of the five styles is dominant, and they conclude that grandparenting styles are quite diverse in contemporary American society.

However, Cherlin and Furstenberg's classification does not take into account several relevant dimensions of grandparent-grandchild relations. One of the most important issues related to grandparenting styles is the extent of bonds, solidarity, or connectedness in multigenerational relationships. The lives of grandparents or great-grandparents and their grandchildren and great-grandchildren are linked in a number of ways: through roles, through interactions, through sentiments, and through exchanges of support. Connectedness between grandparents and grandchildren can also be considered along more social-psychological dimensions. One approach is a typology of grandparenting styles based on six dimensions of intergenerational solidarity (Bengtson & Schrader, 1982) that are comprehensive in describing intergenerational relations and that have been widely used in empirical studies (Atkinson, Kivett, & Campbell, 1986; Roberts & Bengtson, 1990; Rossi & Rossi, 1990). These six dimensions are affection (emotional closeness), association (frequency of contact), consensus (agreement), normative quality (importance of familial obligations to members), structure (geographic proximity), and function (helping behavior).

Silverstein, Lawton, and Bengtson (1994) used data from the AARP national study of intergenerational linkages to create a typology of five categories of adult parent-child relations based on five of the six dimensions of intergenerational solidarity. They found five types of intergenerational relationships: (1) *tight-knit*—connected on all five dimensions of intergenerational solidarity; (2) *sociable*—connected only on associational, structural, affectional, and consensual dimensions of solidarity; (3) *cordial but distant*—connected only on affectional and consensual dimensions of solidarity; (4) *obligatory*—connected on associational, structural, and functional solidarity; and (5) *detached*—connected on none of the five dimensions of intergenerational solidarity. While these dimensions have been used to describe parent-child relations, the same five types of parenting styles may also characterize grandparenting styles and grandparent-grandchild relations—an issue awaiting future research development.

DIVORCE AND REMARRIAGE

The structure of American families has undergone profound changes as a result of increases in divorce and remarriage during the past decade. Such changes in family composition and living arrangements can interfere with grandparents' ability to perform their role. The parental generation mediates the grandparent-grandchild relationship, since they provide the opportunities for grandparents and grandchildren to socialize together (Barranti, 1985; Hagestad, 1985; Robertson, 1977). When the parents are divorced, the quality of the grandparent-grandchild relationship may suffer—or it may strengthen.

Divorce may weaken grandparent-grandchild relations on the noncustodial (usually paternal) side of the family but strengthen those relations on the custodial (usually maternal) side of the family (Clingempeel et al., 1992; Creasey, 1993; Matthews & Sprey, 1984). Custodial parents can effectively prevent the parents of an estranged spouse from seeing their grandchildren (Gladstone, 1989). Thus, divorce has a particularly harsh effect on the relationship between grandchildren and grandparents whose children have not been given custody. Even though all states now have grandparents' rights legislation, which gives grandparents the power to go to court to secure their right to visit their grandchildren (Wilson & DeShare, 1982), grandparent-grandchild association after divorce will probably become increasingly matrilineal. Further, if the divorced parent remarries, then step-grandparents may enter with a new role that is fraught with ambiguous expectations (Cherlin, 1978; Henry, Ceglian & Ostrander, 1993).

The greater their investment in the grandparent role, the more distress grandparents may feel when contact with grandchildren declines following the parental divorce (Myers & Perrin, 1993), and one would expect that reduced contact between grandparent and grandchild will have an enduring effect on the well-being of both generations. The long-term consequence of early parental divorce and remarriage for grandparents and adult grandchildren is a subject that requires further research investigation.

Future research should also examine possible positive outcomes of the increasing complexity of family arrangements; step-relationships, for example, may have taken on added importance. These changes in the family have led to the development of "latent kin networks" (Riley, Kahn, & Foner, 1994), which have the potential of being activated when needed. It is possible that such complex family arrangements have led to new definitions of family, making it necessary to test long-held assumptions about the primacy of biological relationships over other kinship forms. Step-children and step-grandchildren may represent untapped resources for family members in later life.

Most past research on step-relations has focused on the difficulties that exist between pre-adult step-children and their step-parents (Paisley, Ihinger-Tillman, & Lofquist, 1994). We know of no research on how these step-relations develop over the life course, as step-children, siblings, parents, grandparents, or great-grandparents age. When step-grandparents share many years of life with step-grandchildren, especially during the grandchildren's formative years, the intergenerational bonds that develop may equal or surpass those of biological relations—particularly in cases where custody arrangements preclude contact with biological grandchildren.

GRANDPARENTS AS SURROGATE PARENTS

Increasing numbers of grandparents are rearing their grandchildren because of divorce and other problems such as drug and alcohol addiction, AIDS, incarceration, and unemployment within the parental generation (Chalfie, 1994). Census figures estimate the number of grandchildren living with their grandparents (many without a parent present) to be as high as 3.4 million, with African American grandchildren being slightly more than three times more likely than their white counterparts to be in this type of living arrangement (U.S. Bureau of the Census, 1993). Grandparents caring for grandchildren is such a rapidly growing problem that AARP established the Grandparent Information Center in 1993, which in its first four months of operation received over 2,100 calls and requests for information from grandparents who are rearing a grandchild.

Only recently has research begun to address the role of the grandparents who assume direct, full-time caregiving responsibilities for their grandchildren (Burton, 1995; Chalfie, 1994; Shore & Hayslip, 1994). These studies indicate that caregiving grandparents experience a variety of stresses and strains for which there is little institutional support. They encounter difficulties in such matters as obtaining financial assistance, health insurance coverage, and housing, as well as in gaining legal rights to make decisions regarding the child's education and medical care (Chalfie, 1994). Minority caregiving grandparents, because they tend to have low incomes and multiple caregiving roles, may experience greater stress than similar white grandparents, putting them in "double-jeopardy" of experiencing psychological distress (Dowd & Bengtson, 1978). Many questions on caregiving grandparents need to be addressed in future research: What are the consequences of becoming a parent again in midlife? Does this responsibility lead to lower levels of psychological well-being, or an increase in intergenerational conflict? When grandparents become parents to their grandchildren, who takes over their previous function as safety net in times of family emergencies? And, while providing full-time care for a grandchild may be stressful, grandparent caregivers are also likely to obtain certain rewards and informal support from their intergenerational family relations (Burton, 1995). Future research needs to examine these benefits. . . .

GEOGRAPHIC MOBILITY AND HOUSEHOLD ARRANGEMENTS

Grandparent-grandchild relationships are obviously influenced by how close geographically the generations are to each other, since this factor structures opportunities for interaction (Baranowski, 1987). There is evidence that movement of older people to retirement communities reduces in-person contact between older people and their adult children (Silverstein & Zablotsky, in press), and, it may be concluded, with their grandchildren. Developmental approaches to late-life migration have found that return of the elderly to their home community or to the household of an adult child often follows a decline in functioning and death of a spouse (Litwak & Longino, 1988; Silverstein, 1995). However, the role of grandchildren in caregiving to their grandparents following such a move is not known and needs further study.

The role of parent as "gatekeeper" to grandchildren remains a critical factor in regulating grandparent contact. Remarriage of a divorced parent influences the amount of contact between grandparents and their grandchildren when the parent relocates (Gladstone, 1991). The number of adult children moving to the parental home (following divorce or unemployment) with young children in tow has swelled the number of generationally complex households with the older—grandparent—generation as the head of household. At the same time, after leaving the parental nest, adult grandchildren renegotiate their relationships with their grandparents—most commonly reducing the frequency of contact with them (Field & Minkler, 1988). A recent trend may moderate this residential transition: A "boomerang" generation of young adults is moving back to or never leaving the parental nest, to take advantage of a lower cost of living. The result is an increase in the number of three-generational households that have two adult generations. Young-adult "boomerangers" might maintain or strengthen their relationships with grandparents by virtue of living with parents who facilitate extended intergenerational involvement.

In immigrant families, acculturation of adult grandchildren, especially those in ethnic groups with traditional values and orientations, may serve to distance grandparents from their grandchildren. Does assimilation and loss of native language among native-born grandchildren result in reduced intergenerational cohesion with traditional grandparents? There is some evidence that acculturation—the adoption of mainstream values, language, and practices—does create a cultural gulf between generations in the Hispanic family. Schmidt and Padilla (1983) find that Spanish-language compatibility between grandparents and grandchildren predicts the amount of contact between them, underscoring the importance of cultural affinity in structuring intergenerational relations. Research also shows that the better the grandchild speaks the native language of the grandparent, the greater the tendency of grandchildren to live with grandparents (Perez, 1994). Yet, we are unaware of research that formally links acculturation to the propensity of adult grandchildren to move away from grandparents or to leave their ethnic enclave in pursuit of educational or employment opportunities. . . .

POLICY IMPLICATIONS

The results reviewed above concerning increasing family complexity and grandparent-grandchild relations raise new questions not only for researchers but also for program planners and policy makers as well. Recently implemented cuts to government health programs such as Medicare make it clear that federal and state government can go only so far in providing support for old-age dependencies. It is more important than ever to look for alternative solutions to the support and care of the growing population of aging Americans.

The most cost-effective solution may be to develop new programs and policies to shore up or strengthen intergenerational family ties. But before developing such programs, policy makers need to consider the increasing complexity of family arrangements. Successful programs would accommodate the diversity that characterizes the role of grandparent, and also revise traditional definitions of caregiving to conform with changes in the shape of the intergenerational family from pyramid to beanpole. Legislators are familiar with the concept of the "sandwich generation," wherein the middle generation is faced with caring for aging parents while simultaneously raising minor children. However, changes in family structure, coupled with increases in divorce, have resulted in a situation, unparalleled in human history, of fifty-five-year-old children caring for seventy-five-year-old parents and ninety-five-year-old grandparents while rearing adolescent grandchildren—a "club sandwich generation." Policy makers need to develop more programs that provide financial support in such situations—"dependent" care tax credits, for example.

Finally, policy makers must anticipate intergenerational conflict that might result from certain types of geographic mobility or household arrangements and should develop programs that could help families prevent such intergenerational conflicts.

CONCLUSION

In this article we have highlighted three social changes that have increased structural complexity in the intergenerational family, consequently expanding the varieties and contingencies of grandparent-grandchild relationships. Because of the almost exponential rise in the heterogeneity of grandparenting experiences and styles over the last several decades, the investigation of these relationships represents one of the most fertile areas of inquiry in family studies. We predict that social scientists and policy makers will continue to be challenged in their efforts to keep pace with rapid societal changes affecting this ever-evolving and increasingly disparate population of middle-aged and older adults. In the future, intergenerational family structures might become even more diverse. Coupled with shifts in social, political, and economic conditions, such family complexities make even more pressing the need for fresh theoretical perspectives, informed research designs, and innovative intervention strategies to address the needs of grandparents.

CRITICAL-THINKING QUESTIONS

1. What do Giarrusso and her colleagues mean when they say that the shape of U.S. families has gone from a "pyramid" to a "beanpole"? What are the rewards and costs for grandparents and grandchildren in terms of this changing family structure?
2. Some researchers speculate that grandparent-grandchild relationships in the future may be more significant than in the past. What are the reasons for such predictions? How do divorce, remarriage, and geographical mobility threaten the positive impact of such relationships?
3. Giarrusso and her colleagues propose several economic policies to strengthen intergenerational family ties. Do you think their suggestions are realistic? Also, what role, if any, can families play in addressing the needs of grandparents, adult children, and grandchildren that the authors address?

REFERENCES

ATKINSON, M. P., V. R. KIVETT, and R. T. CAMPBELL. 1986. Intergenerational solidarity: An examination of a theoretical model. *Journal of Gerontology*, 41:408–16.

BARANOWSKI, M. D. 1987. The grandfather-grandchild relationship: Patterns and meaning. Paper presented at 40th Annual Scientific Meeting of the Gerontological Society of America, Washington, D.C., Nov. 18–22.

BARRANTI, C. C. R. 1985. The grandparent/grandchild relationship: Family resources in an era of voluntary bonds. *Family Relations*, 34:343–52.

BENGTSON, V. L. 1985. Symbolism and diversity in the grandparenthood role. In *Grandparenthood*, V. L. Bengtson and J. F. Robertson, eds. Beverly Hills, Calif.: Sage.

BENGTSON, V. L., C. J. ROSENTHAL, and L. M. BURTON, 1990. Families and aging: Diversity and heterogeneity. In *Handbook of aging and the social sciences*, 3rd ed., eds. R. H. Binstock and L. K. George. San Diego, Calif.: Academic Press.

———. 1995. Paradoxes of families and aging. In *Handbook of aging and the social sciences*, 4th ed., eds. R. H. Binstock and L. K. George. San Diego, Calif.: Academic Press.

BENGTSON, V. L., and S. S. SCHRADER, 1982. Parent-child relations. In *Handbook of research instruments in social gerontology*, vol. 2, eds. D. Mangen and W. Peterson. Minneapolis: University of Minnesota Press.

BENGTSON, V. L., and J. TREAS. 1980. The changing family context of mental health and aging. In *Handbook of mental health and aging*, eds. J. E. Birren and B. Sloane. Englewood Cliffs, N.J.: Prentice-Hall.

BURTON, L. M. 1995. Early and on-time grandmotherhood in multigeneration Black families. Doctoral dissertation. University of Southern California.

CHALFIE, D. 1994. *Going it alone: A closer look at grandparents parenting grandchildren*. Washington, D.C.: AARP Women's Initiative.

CHERLIN, A. 1978. Remarriage as an incomplete institution. *American Journal of Sociology*, 84:634–50.

CHERLIN, A., and F. FURSTENBERG. 1986. *The new American grandparent: A place in the family*. New York: Basic Books.

CLINGEMPEEL, W. G., et al. 1992. Children's relationships with maternal grandparents: A longitudinal study of family structure and pubertal status effects. *Child Development*, 63:1404–22.

CREASEY, G. L. 1993. The association between divorce and late adolescent grandchildren's relations with grandparents. *Journal of Youth and Adolescence*, 22(5):513–29.

DOWD J. J., and V. L. BENGTSON. 1978. Aging in minority populations: An examination of the double jeopardy hypothesis. *Journal of Gerontology*, 33(3):427–36.

FARKAS, J. I., and D. P. HOGAN. 1994. The demography of changing intergenerational relationships. In *Adult intergenerational relations: Effects of societal change*, eds. V. L. Bengtson, K. W. Schaie, and L. M. Burton. New York: Springer.

FIELD, D., and M. MINKLER. 1988. Continuity and change in social support between young-old and old-old or very-old age. *Journal of Gerontology*, 43(4):100–6.

FISCHER, L. R., and J. SILVERMAN. 1982. Grandmothering as a tenuous role relationship. Paper presented at the Annual Meeting of the National Council on Family Relations, Detroit, Mich.

GLADSTONE, J. W. 1989. Grandmother-grandchild contact: The mediating influence of the middle generation following marriage breakdown and remarriage. *Canadian Journal on Aging*, 8:355–65.

———. 1991. An analysis of changes in grandparent-grandchild visitation following an adult child's remarriage. *Canadian Journal on Aging*, 10(2):113–26.

GOLDMAN, N. 1986. Effects of mortality levels on kinship. In *Consequences of mortality trends and differentials*. New York: United Nations.

HAGESTAD, G. O. 1981. Problems and promises in the social psychology of intergenerational relations. In *Stability and change in the family*, eds. R. Fogel et al., New York: Academic Press.

———. 1985. Continuity and connectedness. In *Grandparenthood*, eds. V. L. Bengtson and J. F. Robertson. Beverly Hills, Calif.: Sage.

HENRY, C. S., C. P. CEGLIAN, and D. L. OSTRANDER. 1993. The transition to step-grandparenthood. *Journal of Divorce and Remarriage*, 19:25–44.

JENDREK, M. P. 1994. Grandparents who parent their grandchildren: Circumstances and decisions. *Gerontologist*, 34(2):206–16.

KIVNICK, H. Q. 1982. Grandparenthood: An overview of meaning and mental health. *Gerontologist*, 22(1):59–66.

LAWTON, L., M. SILVERSTEIN, V. L. BENGTSON. 1994. Solidarity between generations in families. In *Hidden connections: Intergenerational linkages in American society*, eds. V. L. Bengtson and R. A. Harootyan. New York: Springer.

LITWAK, E., and C. F. LONGINO. 1988. Migration patterns among the elderly: A developmental perspective. *Gerontologist*, 27:266–72.

MATTHEWS, S., and J. SPREY. 1984. The impact of divorce on grandparenthood: An exploratory study. *Gerontologist*, 24:41–47.

MYERS, J. E., and PERRIN, N. 1993. Grandparents affected by parental divorce: A population at risk? *Journal of Counseling and Development*, 22:62–66.

PASLEY, K., M. IHINGER-TALLMAN, and A. LOFQUIST. 1994. Remarriage and step-families: Making progress in understanding. In *Stepparenting*, eds. K. Pasley and M. Ihinger-Tallman. Westport, Conn.: Greenwood Press.

PEREZ, L. 1994. The household structure of second-generation children: An exploratory study of extended family arrangements. *International Migration Review*, 28(4):736–47.

RILEY, M. W., R. L. KAHN, and A. FONER, eds. 1994. *Age and structural lag: Society's failure to provide meaningful opportunities in work, family and leisure*. New York: John Wiley.

ROBERTS, R. E. L., and V. L. BENGTSON. 1990. Is intergenerational solidarity a unidimensional construct? A second test of a formal model. *Journal of Gerontology: Social Sciences*, 45:S12–20.

ROBERTSON, J. F. 1977. Grandmotherhood: A study of role conceptions. *Journal of Marriage and the Family*, 39:165–74.

———. 1995. Grandparenting in an era of rapid change. In *Handbook of aging and the family*, eds. R. Blieszner and V. H. Bedford. Westport, Conn.: Greenwood Press.

ROSSI, A. S., and P. H. ROSSI. 1990. *Of human bonding: Parent-child relationships across the life course*. New York: Aldine de Gruyter.

SCHMIDT, A., and A. M. PADILLA. 1983. Grandparent-grandchild interaction in a Mexican American group. *Hispanic Journal of Behavioral Sciences*, 5(2):181–98.

SHORE, R. J., and B. HAYSLIP, JR. 1994. Custodial grandparenting: Implications for children's development. In *Redefining families: Implications for children's development*, eds. A. E. Gottfried and A. W. Gottfried. New York: Plenum Press.

SILVERSTEIN, M. 1995. Stability and change in temporal distance between the elderly and their children. *Demography*, 32(1):29–45.

SILVERSTEIN, M., L. LAWTON, and V. L. BENGTSON. 1994. Types of relations between parents and adult children. In *Hidden connections: Intergenerational linkages in American society*, eds. V. L. Bengtson and R. A. Harootyan. New York: Springer.

SILVERSTEIN, M., and D. ZABLOTSKY. In press. Health and social factors in retirement community migration. *Journal of Gerontology: Social Sciences*.

TROLL, L. E. 1980. Grandparenting. In *Aging in the 1980s: Psychological issues*, ed. L. W. Poon. Washington, D. C.: American Psychological Association.

UHLENBERG, P. 1980. Death and the family. *Journal of Family History*, 5(3):313–20.

U.S. BUREAU OF THE CENSUS. 1993. Marital status and living arrangements: March 1993. *Current Population Reports* (Series P-20, No. 478). Washington, D.C.: Government Printing Office.

WATKINS, S. C., J. A. MENKEN, and J. BONGAARTS. 1987. Demographic foundations of family change. *American Sociological Review*, 52:346–58.

WILSON, K. B., and M. R. DESHARE. 1982. The legal rights of grandparents: A preliminary discussion. *Gerontologist*, 22:67–71.

WOOD, V. 1982. Grandparenthood: An ambiguous role. *Generations*, 7(2):18–24.

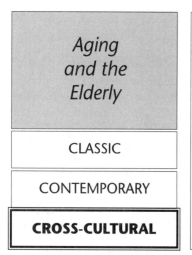

Aging and the Elderly

CLASSIC

CONTEMPORARY

CROSS-CULTURAL

45

Our Aging World

Frank B. Hobbs and Bonnie L. Damon

The average age in societies around the world is rising. Even now, demographers report, the eighty-and-over age group is the fastest-growing portion of the elderly population. Frank B. Hobbs and Bonnie L. Damon describe the growing number of elderly persons worldwide, compare the growth of the elderly population in developed and developing countries, and raise important questions about the future implications of our aging world.

POPULATION AGING IS WORLDWIDE

To set the aging of the United States in context it is useful to look at aging in the rest of the world. Fertility rates and infant and maternal mortality have declined in most nations. Also, mortality from infectious and parasitic diseases has declined. The world's nations generally have improved other aspects of health and education. All of these factors have interacted so that every major region in the world shows an increased proportion of the population that will be sixty-five or older by 2020.

There were 357 million persons aged sixty-five and over in the world in 1994 [see Table 1]. They represent 6 percent of the world's population. By the year 2000, there would be about 418 million elderly. The annual growth rate for the elderly was 2.8 percent in 1993–94 (compared with an average annual rate for the total world population of 1.6 percent). Such growth is expected to continue far into the twenty-first century.

Numerical growth of the elderly population is worldwide. It is occurring in both developed and developing countries. The average annual growth rate in 1993–94 of persons sixty-five years and over was 3.2 percent in developing countries compared with 2.3 percent in the developed world. In absolute numbers, from 1993 to 1994, the net balance of the world's elderly population (sixty-five years and over) increased by over 1,000 persons every hour. Of this increase, 63 percent occurred in developing countries.

Over half (55 percent) of the world's elderly lived in developing nations in 1994. These developing regions could be home to nearly two-thirds (65 percent) of the world's elderly by the year 2020. Thirty nations had elderly populations of at least 2 million in 1994. . . . Current population

Source: From *65+ in the United States.* U.S. Bureau of the Census, Current Population Reports, Special Studies, P23–190 (Washington, D.C.: Government Printing Office, 1996), pp. 24–27.

projections indicate there will be fifty-five such nations by 2020.

Among countries with more than 1 million population, Sweden has the highest proportion of people aged sixty-five and over, with 18 percent in 1994—about the same as the state of Florida. Sweden also has the highest proportion aged eighty and over with 5 percent. The Caribbean is the oldest of the major developing regions with 7 percent of its population sixty-five or older in 1994.

By 2020, the elderly will constitute from one-fifth to nearly one-fourth of the population of many European countries. For example, Census Bureau projections indicate that 23 percent of Germany's population would be elderly compared with 22 percent for Italy, Finland, Belgium, Croatia, Denmark, and Greece. The elderly population of twelve additional European countries with more than 1 million population will constitute at least one-fifth of the total country population. The United States would be 16 percent.

Japan's population age sixty-five and over is expected to grow dramatically in the coming decades. According to projections, the percentage of Japan's population that is elderly could grow from 14 percent (17.1 million) in 1994 to 17 percent (21.0 million) in 2000 and to 26 percent (32.2 million) by 2020. . . . This is a rapid rise in a short time. Japan's population eighty years and over also is projected to grow very rapidly, from 3 percent of their total population in 1994 to 7 percent by 2020. Already the Japanese are reducing retirement benefits and making other adjustments to prepare for the economic and social results of a rapidly aging society.

In 1994, the world had an estimated 61 million persons aged eighty or older. That number is expected to increase to 146 million by the year 2020. Persons eighty years and over constituted only 1 percent of the world's total population in 1994 and more than 20 percent of the world's elderly (28 percent in developed countries, 16 percent in developing nations).

DEVELOPED COUNTRIES NOW HAVE MOST OF THE WORLD'S OLDEST POPULATION

Although the developed countries of the world represented only 22 percent of the total world population in 1994, the majority of the world's population aged eighty and over live in developed countries. However, it is projected that by 2020, the majority will live in developing countries. For many nations, the eighty-and-over age group will be the fastest growing portion of the elderly population. In 2000, 26 percent of the elderly in the United States would be eighty or older, which, among countries with a population size of at least 5 million, would rank

Table 1 World Population by Age and Sex, 1994 and 2000

	Population (millions)			*Percentage of Total*			
Year and Age	*Both Sexes*	*Male*	*Female*	*Both Sexes*	*Male*	*Female*	*Males per 100 Females*
1994							
All ages	5,640	2,841	2,798	100.0%	100.0%	100.0%	101.5
Under 15 years . . .	1,790	917	873	31.7	32.3	31.2	105.1
15 to 64 years	3,492	1,771	1,722	61.9	62.3	61.5	102.9
65 years and over . .	357	153	204	6.3	5.4	7.3	75.2
2000							
All ages	6,161	3,103	3,057	100.0	100.0	100.0	101.5
Under 15 years . . .	1,877	962	915	30.5	31.0	29.9	105.2
15 to 64 years	3,866	1,959	1,907	62.7	63.1	62.4	102.8
65 years and over . .	418	182	236	6.8	5.9	7.7	77.1

Source: U.S. Bureau of the Census, International Data Base.

Table 2 Projected Population for Countries with More than One Million Persons Aged 80 Years and Over, 1994 and 2020

	Rank		*Population Aged 80 Years and Over (in thousands, based on rank in 1994)*	
Country/Area	*1994*	*2020*	*1994*	*2020*
China, Mainland	1	1	9,010	28,737
United States	**2**	**2**	**7,760**	**13,007**
India	3	3	4,021	12,639
Japan	4	4	3,597	9,362
Russia	5	5	3,317	7,191
Germany	6	6	3,313	5,889
France	7	8	2,563	3,754
United Kingdom	8	9	2,342	3,400
Italy	9	7	2,221	4,142
Ukraine	10	12	1,421	2,923
Spain	11	13	1,287	2,488
Brazil	*	10	*	3,132
Indonesia	*	11	*	3,034
Mexico	*	14	*	2,296
Poland	*	15	*	1,877
Turkey	*	16	*	1,751
Canada	*	17	*	1,595
Thailand	*	18	*	1,477
Pakistan	*	19	*	1,385
Romania	*	20	*	1,264
South Korea	*	21	*	1,221
Vietnam	*	22	*	1,199
Argentina	*	23	*	1,072
Iran	*	24	*	1,039

*Indicates population 80 years and over in 1994 was less than 1 million.

Source: U.S. Bureau of the Census, International Data Base.

sixth, behind Sweden, Denmark, Switzerland, Cuba, and the United Kingdom.

In 1994, China had the largest number of persons aged eighty or older followed by the United States [see Table 2]. Nine additional countries had over 1 million persons eighty years and over in 1994. By 2020, this list is expected to include thirteen additional countries, ten of which are developing countries. In many developing countries, the population eighty and over in 2020 is likely to at least quadruple from 1994. This highlights the problems governments may have in planning support services for this burgeoning population group.

The rapid growth of the oldest old has various health and economic implications for individuals, families, and governments throughout the world. The oldest old often have severe chronic health problems which demand special attention. The nature and duration of their illnesses are likely to produce a substantial need for prolonged care. Developing nations already have diluted resources. They are the most limited in being able to provide preventive measures and, in future years, supportive services. The United States and other countries face enormous investments and payments to maintain current levels of services for the oldest old.

CRITICAL-THINKING QUESTIONS

1. What are some of the reasons for the growth of aging populations worldwide?

2. In the 1990s, the majority of the world's population aged eighty and over lived in developed countries. How is this expected to change by

2020? As the average length of life continues to increase in both developed and developing countries, who, if anyone, is responsible for improving the quality of extended life?

3. Hobbs and Damon observe that "The United States and other countries face enormous investments and payments to maintain current levels of services for the old." What, specifically, are examples of such investments and payments? Who will pay for the necessary services for elderly populations—individuals? families? government? corporations? people in the labor force? others?

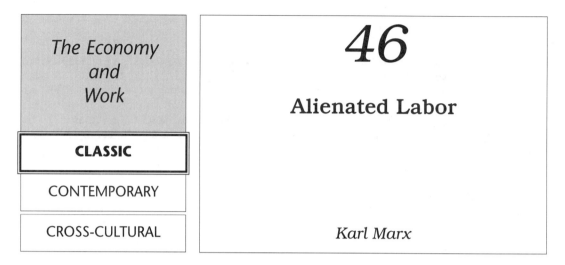

The Economy and Work

CLASSIC

CONTEMPORARY

CROSS-CULTURAL

46

Alienated Labor

Karl Marx

The human species, argues Karl Marx, is social by nature and expresses that social nature in the act of production. But within the capitalist economic system, Marx claims, the process of production does not affirm human nature but denies it. The result is what he terms "alienated labor."

. . . [We] have shown that the worker sinks to the level of a commodity, and to a most miserable commodity; that the misery of the worker increases with the power and volume of his production; that the necessary result of competition is the accumulation of capital in a few hands, and thus a restoration of monopoly in a more terrible form; and finally that the distinction between capitalist and landlord, and between agricultural laborer and industrial worker, must disappear, and the whole of society divide into the two classes of property *owners* and *propertyless* workers. . . .

Thus we have now to grasp the real connexion between this whole system of alienation—private property, acquisitiveness, the separation of labor, capital and land, exchange and competition, value and the devaluation of man, monopoly and competition—and the system of *money*. . . .

We shall begin from a *contemporary* economic fact. The worker becomes poorer the more wealth he produces and the more his production increases in power and extent. The worker becomes an ever cheaper commodity the more goods he creates. The *devaluation* of the human world increases in direct relation with the *increase in value* of the world of things. Labor does not only create goods; it also produces itself and the worker as a *commodity,* and indeed in the same proportion as it produces goods.

This fact simply implies that the object produced by labor, its product, now

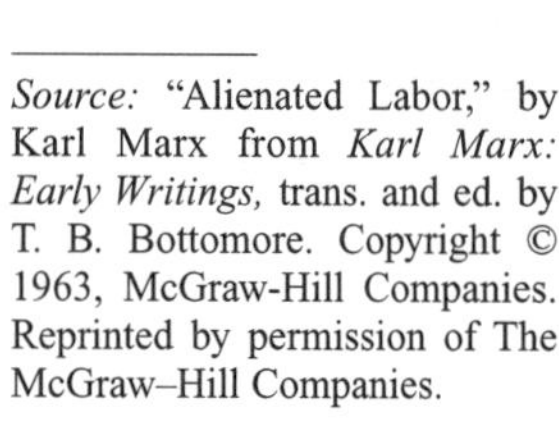

stands opposed to it as an *alien being,* as a *power independent* of the producer. The product of labor is labor which has been embodied in an object and turned into a physical thing; this product is an *objectification* of labor. The performance of work is at the same time its objectification. The performance of work appears in the sphere of political economy as a *vitiation*[1] of the worker, objectification as a *loss* and as *servitude to the object,* and appropriation as *alienation.*

So much does the performance of work appear as vitiation that the worker is vitiated to the point of starvation. So much does objectification appear as loss of the object that the worker is deprived of the most essential things not only of life but also of work. Labor itself becomes an object which he can acquire only by the greatest effort and with unpredictable interruptions. So much does the appropriation of the object appear as alienation that the more objects the worker produces the fewer he can possess and the more he falls under the domination of his product, of capital.

All these consequences follow from the fact that the worker is related to the *product of his labor* as to an *alien* object. For it is clear on this presupposition that the more the worker expends himself in work the more powerful becomes the world of objects which he creates in face of himself, the poorer he becomes in his inner life, and the less he belongs to himself. It is just the same as in religion. The more of himself man attributes to God the less he has left in himself. The worker puts his life into the object, and his life then belongs no longer to himself but to the object. The greater his activity, therefore, the less he possesses. What is embodied in the product of his labor is no longer his own. The greater this product is, therefore, the more he is diminished. The *alienation* of the worker in his product means not only that his labor becomes an object, assumes an *external* existence, but that it exists independently, *outside himself,* and alien to him, and that it stands opposed to him as an autonomous power. The life which he has given to the object sets itself against him as an alien and hostile force.

Let us now examine more closely the phenomenon of *objectification;* the worker's production and the *alienation* and *loss* of the object it produces, which is involved in it. The worker can create nothing without *nature,* without the *sensuous external world.* The latter is the material in which his labor is realized, in which it is active, out of which and through which it produces things.

But just as nature affords the *means of existence* of labor, in the sense that labor cannot *live* without objects upon which it can be exercised, so also it provides the *means of existence* in a narrower sense; namely the means of physical existence for the *worker* himself. Thus, the more the worker *appropriates* the external world of sensuous nature by his labor the more he deprives himself of *means of existence,* in two respects: First, that the sensuous external world becomes progressively less an object belonging to his labor or a means of existence of his labor, and secondly, that it becomes progressively less a means of existence in the direct sense, a means for the physical subsistence of the worker.

In both respects, therefore, the worker becomes a slave of the object; first, in that he receives an *object of work,* i.e. receives *work,* and secondly, in that he receives *means of subsistence.* Thus the object enables him to exist, first as a *worker* and secondly, as a *physical subject.* The culmination of this enslavement is that he can only maintain himself as a *physical subject* so far as he is a *worker,* and that it is only as a *physical subject* that he is a worker.

(The alienation of the worker in his object is expressed as follows in the laws of political economy: The more the worker produces the less he has to consume; the more value he creates the more worthless he becomes; the more refined his product the more crude and misshapen the worker; the more civilized the product the more barbarous the worker; the more powerful the work the more feeble the worker; the more the work manifests intelligence the more the worker declines in intelligence and becomes a slave of nature.)

Political economy conceals the alienation in the nature of labor insofar as it does not examine the direct relationship between the worker (*work*) *and production.* Labor certainly produces marvels for the rich but it produces privation for the worker. It produces palaces, but hovels for the worker. It produces beauty, but deformity for the worker. It replaces labor by machinery, but it casts some of the workers back into a barbarous kind of work and turns the others into machines. It produces intelligence, but also stupidity and cretinism for the workers.

The direct relationship of labor to its products is the relationship of the worker to the objects of his production. The relationship of property owners to the objects of production and to production itself is merely a *consequence* of this first relationship and confirms it. We shall consider this second aspect later.

Thus, when we ask what is the important relationship of labor, we are concerned with the relationship of the *worker* to production.

So far we have considered the alienation of the worker only from one aspect; namely, *his relationship with the products of his labor.* However, alienation appears not merely in the result but also in the *process of production,* within *productive activity* itself. How could the worker stand in an alien relationship to the product of his activity if he did not alienate himself in the act of production itself? The product is indeed only the *résumé* of activity, of production. Consequently, if the product of labor is alienation, production itself must be active alienation—the alienation of activity and the activity of alienation. The alienation of the object of labor merely summarizes the alienation in the work activity itself.

What constitutes the alienation of labor? First, that the work is *external* to the worker, that it is not part of his nature; and that, consequently, he does not fulfill himself in his work but denies himself, has a feeling of misery rather than well-being, does not develop freely his mental and physical energies but is physically exhausted and mentally debased. The worker, therefore, feels himself at home only during his leisure time, whereas at work he feels homeless. His work is not voluntary but imposed, *forced labor.* It is not the satisfaction of a need, but only a *means* for satisfying other needs. Its alien character is clearly shown by the fact that as soon as there is no physical or other compulsion it is avoided like the plague. External labor, labor in which man alienates himself, is a labor of self-sacrifice, of mortification. Finally, the external character of work for the worker is shown by the fact that it is not his own work but work for someone else, that in work he does not belong to himself but to another person. . . .

We arrive at the result that man (the worker) feels himself to be freely active only in his animal functions—eating, drinking and procreating, or at most also in his dwelling and in personal adornment—while in his human functions he is reduced to an animal. The animal becomes human and the human becomes animal.

Eating, drinking, and procreating are of course also genuine human functions. But abstractly considered, apart from the environment of human activities, and turned into final and sole ends, they are animal functions.

We have now considered the act of alienation of practical human activity, labor, from two aspects: (1) the relationship of the worker to the *product of labor* as an alien object which dominates him. This relationship is at the same time the relationship to the sensuous external world, to natural objects, as an alien and hostile world; (2) the relationship of labor to the *act of production* within *labor.* This is the relationship of the worker to his own activity as something alien and not belonging to him, activity as suffering (passivity), strength as powerlessness, creation as emasculation, the *personal* physical and mental energy of the worker, his personal life (for what is life but activity?), as an activity which is directed against himself, independent of him and not belonging to him. This is *self-alienation* as against the [afore]mentioned alienation of the *thing.*

We have now to infer a third characteristic of *alienated labor* from the two we have considered.

Man is a species-being not only in the sense that he makes the community (his own as well as those of other things) his object both practically and theoretically, but also (and this is simply another expression for the same thing) in the sense that he treats himself as the present, living species, as a *universal* and consequently free being.

Species-life, for man as for animals, has its physical basis in the fact that man (like animals) lives from inorganic nature, and since man is more universal than an animal so the range of inorganic nature from which he lives is more universal. Plants, animals, minerals, air, light, etc. constitute, from the theoretical aspect, a part of human consciousness as objects of natural science and art; they are man's spiritual inorganic nature, his intellectual means of life, which he must first prepare for enjoyment and perpetuation. So also, from the practical aspect, they form a part of human life and activity. In practice man lives only from these natural products, whether in the form of food, heating, clothing, housing, etc. The universality of man appears in practice in the universality which makes the whole of nature into his inorganic body: (1) as a direct means of life; and equally (2) as the material object and instrument of his life activity. Nature is the inorganic body of man; that is to say nature, excluding the human body itself. To say that man *lives* from nature means that nature is his *body* with which he must remain in a continuous interchange in order not to die. The statement that the physical and mental life of man, and nature, are interdependent means simply that nature is interdependent with itself, for man is a part of nature.

Since alienated labor (1) alienates nature from man; and (2) alienates man from himself, from his own active function, his life activity; so it alienates him from the species. It makes *species-life* into a means of individual life. In the first place it alienates species-life and individual life, and secondly, it turns the latter, as an abstraction, into the purpose of the former, also in its abstract and alienated form.

For labor, *life activity, productive life,* now appear to man only as *means* for the satisfaction of a need, the need to maintain his physical existence. Productive life is, however, species-life. It is life creating life. In the type of life activity resides the whole character of a species, its species-character; and free, conscious activity is the species-character of human beings. Life itself appears only as a *means of life.*

The animal is one with its life activity. It does not distinguish the activity from itself. It is *its activity.* But man makes his life activity itself an object of his will and consciousness. He has a conscious life activity. It is not a determination with which he is completely identified. Conscious life activity distinguishes man from the life activity of animals. Only for this reason is he a species-being. Or rather, he is only a self-conscious being, i.e., his own life is an object for him, because he is a species-being. Only for this reason is his activity free activity. Alienated labor reverses the relationship, in that man because he is a self-conscious being makes his life activity, his *being,* only a means for his *existence.*

CRITICAL-THINKING QUESTIONS

1. Does Marx argue that work is inevitably alienating? Why does work within a capitalist economy produce alienation?
2. In what different respects does labor within capitalism alienate the worker?
3. Based on this analysis, under what conditions do you think Marx would argue that labor is not alienating?

NOTE

1. Debasement.

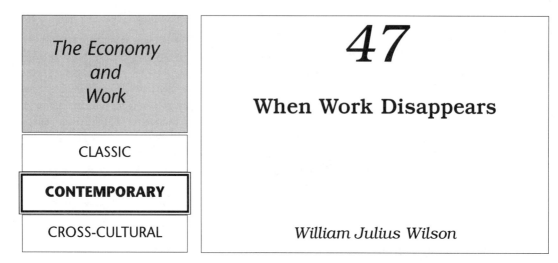

The Economy and Work

CLASSIC

CONTEMPORARY

CROSS-CULTURAL

47

When Work Disappears

William Julius Wilson

Many inner-city areas of the United States are facing catastrophic levels of poverty. Why? In this excerpt from a recent book, William Julius Wilson offers his assessment of the causes of urban decline and makes practical suggestions about how we can solve this pressing problem.

The disappearance of work in the ghetto cannot be ignored, isolated or played down. Employment in America is up. The economy has churned out tens of millions of new jobs in the last two decades. In that same period, joblessness among inner-city blacks has reached catastrophic proportions. Yet in this Presidential election year, the disappearance of work in the ghetto is not on either the Democratic or the Republican agenda. There is harsh talk about work instead of welfare but no talk of where to find it.

The current employment woes in the inner city continue to be narrowly defined in terms of race or lack of individual initiative. It is argued that jobs are widely available, that the extent of inner-city poverty is exaggerated. Optimistic policy analysts—and many African Americans—would prefer that more attention be devoted to the successes and struggles of the black working class and the expanding black middle class. This is understandable. These two groups, many of whom have recently escaped from the ghetto, represent a majority of the African American population. But ghetto joblessness still afflicts a substantial—and increasing—minority: It's a problem that won't go away on its own. If it is not addressed, it will have lasting and harmful consequences for the quality of life in the cities and, eventually, for the lives of all Americans. Solutions will have to be found—and those solutions are at hand.

For the first time in the twentieth century, a significant majority of adults in many inner-city neighborhoods are not working in a typical week. Inner cities have always featured high levels of poverty, but the current levels of joblessness in some neighborhoods are unprecedented. For example, in the famous black-belt neighborhood of Washington Park on Chicago's South Side, a majority of adults had jobs in 1950; by 1990, only one in three worked in a typical week. High neighborhood joblessness has a far more devas-

Source: From *When Work Disappears* by William Julius Wilson.

tating effect than high neighborhood poverty. A neighborhood in which people are poor but employed is different from a neighborhood in which people are poor and jobless. Many of today's problems in the inner-city neighborhoods—crime, family dissolution, welfare—are fundamentally a consequence of the disappearance of work.

What causes the disappearance of work? There are several factors, including changes in the distribution and location of jobs, and in the level of training and education required to obtain employment. Nor should we overlook the legacy of historic racial segregation. However, the public debate around this question is not productive because it seeks to assign blame rather than recognizing and dealing with the complex realities that have led to economic distress for many Americans. Explanations and proposed solutions to the problem are often ideologically driven.

Conservatives tend to stress the importance of values, attitudes, habits, and styles. In this view, group differences are reflected in the culture. The truth is, cultural factors do play a role; but other, more important variables also have to be taken into account. Although race is clearly a significant variable in the social outcomes of inner-city blacks, it's not the *only* factor. The emphasis on racial differences has obscured the fact that African Americans, whites, and other ethnic groups have many common values, aspirations, and hopes.

An elderly woman who has lived in one inner-city neighborhood on the South Side of Chicago for more than forty years reflects: "I've been here since March 11, 1953. When I moved in, the neighborhood was intact. It was intact with homes, beautiful homes, minimansions, with stores, Laundromats, with Chinese cleaners. We had drugstores. We had hotels. We had doctors over on 39th street. We had doctors' offices in the neighborhood. We had the middle class and upper middle class. It has gone from affluent to where it is today. And I would like to see it come back, that we can have some of the things we had. Since I came in young, and I'm a senior citizen now, I would like to see some of the things come back so I can enjoy them like we did when we first came in."

In the neighborhood of Woodlawn, on the South Side of Chicago, there were more than 800 commercial and industrial establishments in 1950. Today, it is estimated that only about 100 are left. In the words of Loïc Wacquant, a member of one of the research teams that worked with me over the last eight years: "The once-lively streets—residents remember a time, not so long ago, when crowds were so dense at rush hour that one had to elbow one's way to the train station—now have the appearance of an empty, bombed-out war zone. The commercial strip has been reduced to a long tunnel of charred stores, vacant lots littered with broken glass and garbage, and dilapidated buildings left to rot in the shadow of the elevated train line. At the corner of 63d Street and Cottage Grove Avenue, the handful of remaining establishments that struggle to survive are huddled behind wrought-iron bars. . . . The only enterprises that seem to be thriving are liquor stores and currency exchanges, those 'banks of the poor' where one can cash checks, pay bills and buy money orders for a fee."

The state of the inner-city public schools was another major concern expressed by our urban-poverty study respondents. The complaints ranged from overcrowded conditions to unqualified and uncaring teachers. Sharply voicing her views on these subjects, a twenty-five-year-old married mother of two children from a South Side census tract that just recently became poor stated: "My daughter ain't going to school here. She was going to a nursery school where I paid and of course they took the time and spent it with her, because they was getting the money. But the public schools, no! They are overcrowded and the teachers don't care."

A resident of Woodlawn who had left the neighborhood as a child described how she felt upon her return about the changes that had occurred: "I was really appalled. When I walked down 63d Street when I was younger, everything you wanted was there. But now, coming back as an adult with my child, those resources are just gone, completely. . . . And housing, everybody has moved, there are vacant lots everywhere."

Neighborhoods plagued by high levels of joblessness are more likely to experience low levels of social organization: The two go hand in hand. High rates of joblessness trigger other neighborhood problems that undermine social organization, ranging from crime, gang violence, and drug trafficking to family breakups. And as these controls weaken, the social processes that regulate behavior change.

Industrial restructuring has further accelerated the deterioration of many inner-city neighborhoods. Consider the fate of the West Side black community of North Lawndale in Chicago: Since 1960, nearly half of its housing stock has disappeared; the remaining units are mostly run-down or dilapidated. Two large factories anchored the economy of this neighborhood in its good days—the Hawthorne plant of Western Electric, which employed more than 43,000 workers, and an International Harvester plant with 14,000 workers. But conditions rapidly changed. Harvester closed its doors in the late 1960's. Sears moved most of its offices to the Loop in downtown Chicago in 1973. The Hawthorne plant gradually phased out its operations and finally shut down in 1984.

"Jobs were plentiful in the past," attested a twenty-nine-year-old unemployed black man who lives in one of the poorest neighborhoods on the South Side. "You could walk out of the house and get a job. Maybe not what you want, but you could get a job. Now, you can't find anything. A lot of people in this neighborhood, they want to work but they can't get work. A few, but a very few, they just don't want to work."

The more rapid the neighborhood deterioration, the greater the institutional disinvestment. In the 1960s and 1970s, neighborhoods plagued by heavy abandonment were frequently redlined (identified as areas that should not receive or be recommended for mortgage loans or insurance); this paralyzed the housing market, lowered property values and encouraged landlord abandonment.

As the neighborhood disintegrates, those who are able to leave depart in increasing numbers; among these are many working- and middle-class families. The lower population density in turn creates additional problems. Abandoned buildings increase and often serve as havens for crack use and other illegal enterprises that give criminals—mostly young blacks who are unemployed—footholds in the community. Precipitous declines in density also make it even more difficult to sustain or develop a sense of community. The feeling of safety in numbers is completely lacking in such neighborhoods.

Problems in the new poverty or high-jobless neighborhoods have also created racial antagonism among some of the high-income groups in the city. The high joblessness in ghetto neighborhoods has sapped the vitality of local businesses and other institutions and has led to fewer and shabbier movie theaters, bowling alleys, restaurants, public parks and playgrounds and other recreational facilities. When residents of inner-city neighborhoods venture out to other areas of the city in search of entertainment, they come into brief contact with citizens of markedly different racial or class backgrounds. Sharp differences in cultural style often lead to clashes.

Some behavior on the part of residents from socially isolated ghetto neighborhoods—for instance, the tendency to enjoy a movie in a communal spirit by carrying on a running conversation with friends and relatives or reacting in an unrestrained manner to what they see on the screen—is considered offensive by other groups, particularly black and white members of the middle class. Expressions of disapproval, either overt or with subtle hostile glances, tend to trigger belligerent responses from the ghetto residents, who then purposely intensify the behavior that is the source of irritation. The white and even the black middle-class moviegoers then exercise their option and exit, expressing resentment and experiencing intensified feelings of racial or class antagonism as they depart.

The areas surrendered in such a manner become the domain of the inner-city residents. Upscale businesses are replaced by fast-food chains and other local businesses that cater to the new clientele. White and black middle-class citizens complain bitterly about how certain areas of the central city have changed—and thus become "off-limits"—following the influx of ghetto residents.

The negative consequences are clear: Where jobs are scarce, many people eventually lose their feeling of connectedness to work in the formal economy; they no longer expect work to be a regular, and regulating, force in their lives. In the case of young people, they may grow up in an environment that lacks the idea of work as a central experience of adult life—they have little or no labor-force attachment. These circumstances also increase the likelihood that the residents will rely on illegitimate sources of income, thereby further weakening their attachment to the legitimate labor market.

A twenty-five-year-old West Side father of two who works two jobs to make ends meet condemned the attitude toward work of some inner-city black males:

> They try to find easier routes and had been conditioned over a period of time to just be lazy, so to speak. Motivation nonexistent, you know, and the society that they're affiliated with really don't advocate hard work and struggle to meet your goals such as education and stuff like that. And they see who's around them and they follow that same pattern, you know. . . . They don't see nobody getting up early in the morning, going to work or going to school all the time. The guys they be with don't do that . . . because that's the crowd that you choose—well, that's been presented to you by your neighborhood.

Work is not simply a way to make a living and support one's family. It also constitutes a framework for daily behavior because it imposes discipline. Regular employment determines where you are going to be and when you are going to be there. In the absence of regular employment, life, including family life, becomes less coherent. Persistent unemployment and irregular employment hinder rational planning in daily life, the necessary condition of adaptation to an industrial economy.

It's a myth that people who don't work don't want to work. One mother in a new poverty neighborhood on the South Side explained her decision to remain on welfare even though she would like to get a job:

> I was working and then I had two kids. And I'm struggling. I was making, like, close to $7 an hour. . . . I had to pay a baby-sitter. Then I had to deal with my kids when I got home. And I couldn't even afford medical insurance. . . . I was so scared, when my kids were sick or something, because I have been turned away from a hospital because I did not have a medical card. I don't like being on public aid and stuff right now. But what do I do with my kids when the kids get sick?

Working mothers with comparable incomes face, in many cases, even greater difficulty. Why? Simply because many low-wage jobs do not provide health-care benefits, and most working mothers have to pay for transportation and spend more for child care. Working mothers also have to spend more for housing because it is more difficult for them to qualify for housing subsidies. It is not surprising, therefore, that many welfare-reliant mothers choose not to enter the formal labor market. It would not be in their best economic interest to do so. Given the economic realities, it is also not surprising that many who are working in these low-wage jobs decide to rely on or return to welfare, even though it's not a desirable alternative for many of the black single mothers. As one twenty-seven-year-old welfare mother of three children from an impoverished West Side neighborhood put it: "I want to work. I do not work but I want to work. I don't want to just be on public aid."

As the disappearance of work has become a characteristic feature of the inner-city ghetto, so too has the disappearance of the traditional married-couple family. Only one-quarter of the black families whose children live with them in inner-city neighborhoods in Chicago are husband-wife families today, compared with three-quarters of the inner-city Mexican families, more than one-half of the white families and nearly one-half of the Puerto Rican families. And in census tracts with poverty rates of at least 40 percent, only 16.5 percent of the black families with children in the household are husband-wife families.

There are many factors involved in the precipitous decline in marriage rates and the sharp rise in single-parent families. The explanation most often heard in the public debate associates the increase of out-of-wedlock births and single-parent families with welfare. Indeed, it is widely assumed among the general public and reflected in the recent welfare reform that a direct connection exists between the level of welfare benefits and the likelihood that a young woman will bear a child outside marriage.

However, there is little evidence to support the claim that Aid to Families With Dependent Children plays a significant role in promoting out-of-wedlock births. Research examining the association between the generosity of welfare benefits and out-of-wedlock childbearing and teen-age pregnancy indicates that benefit levels have no significant effect on the likelihood that African American girls and women will have children outside marriage. Likewise, welfare rates have either no significant effect or only a small effect on the odds that whites will have children outside marriage. The rate of out-of-wedlock teen-age childbearing has nearly doubled since 1975—during years when the value of A.F.D.C., food stamps, and Medicaid fell, after adjusting for inflation. And the smallest increases in the number of out-of-wedlock births have not occurred in states that have had the largest declines in the inflation-adjusted value of A.F.D.C. benefits. Indeed, while the real value of cash welfare benefits has plummeted over the past twenty years, out-of-wedlock childbearing has increased, and postpartum marriages (marriages following the birth of a couple's child) have decreased as well.

It's instructive to consider the social differences between inner-city blacks and other groups, especially Mexicans. Mexicans come to the United States with a clear conception of a traditional family unit that features men as breadwinners. Although extramarital affairs by men are tolerated, unmarried pregnant women are "a source of opprobrium, anguish or great concern," as Richard P. Taub, a member of one of our research terms, put it. Pressure is applied by the kin of both parents to enter into marriage.

The family norms and behavior in inner-city black neighborhoods stand in sharp contrast. The relationships between inner-city black men and women, whether in a marital or nonmarital situation, are often fractious and antagonistic. Inner-city black women routinely say that black men are hopeless as either husbands or fathers and that more of their time is spent on the streets than at home.

The men in the inner city generally feel that it is much better for all parties to remain in a nonmarital relationship until the relationship dissolves rather than to get married and then have to get a divorce. A twenty-five-year-old unmarried West Side resident, the father of one child, expressed this view:

> Well, most black men feel now, why get married when you got six to seven women to one guy, really. You know, because there's more women out here mostly than men. Because most dudes around here are killing each other like fools over drugs or all this other stuff.

The fact that blacks reside in neighborhoods and are engaged in social networks and households that are less conducive to employment than those of other ethnic and racial groups in the inner city clearly has a negative effect on their search for work. In the eyes of employers in metropolitan Chicago, these differences render inner-city blacks less desirable as workers, and therefore are reluctant to hire them. The white chairman of a car transport company, when asked if there were differences in the work ethic of whites, blacks and Hispanics, responded with great certainty:

> Definitely! I don't think, I know: I've seen it over a period of thirty years. Basically, the Oriental is much more aggressive and intelligent and studious than the Hispanic. The Hispanics, except Cubans of course, they have the work ethnic [sic]. The Hispanics are *mañana, mañana, mañana*—tomorrow, tomorrow, tomorrow." As for native-born blacks, they were deemed "the laziest of the bunch.

If some employers view the work ethic of inner-city poor blacks as problematic, many also express concerns about their honesty, cultural attitudes and dependability—traits that are frequently associated with the neighborhoods in which they live. A white suburban retail drugstore manager expressed his reluctance to hire someone from a poor inner-city neighborhood. "You'd be afraid they're going to steal from you," he stated. "They grow up that way. They grow up dishonest and I guess you'd feel like, geez, how are they going to be honest here?"

In addition to qualms about the work ethic, character, family influences, cultural predispositions and the neighborhood milieu of ghetto residents, the employers frequently mentioned concerns about applicants' language skills and educational training. They "just don't have the language skills," stated a suburban employer. The president of an inner-city advertising agency highlighted the problem of spelling:

> I needed a temporary a couple months ago, and they sent me a black man. And I dictated a letter to him. He took shorthand, which was good. Something like 'Dear Mr. So-and-So, I am writing to ask about how your business is doing.' And then he typed the letter, and I read the letter, and it's 'I am writing to ax about your business.' Now you hear them speaking a different language and all that, and they say 'ax' for 'ask.' Well, I don't care about that, but I didn't say 'ax,' I said 'ask.'

Many inner-city residents have a strong sense of the negative attitudes that employers tend to have toward them. A thirty-three-year-old employed janitor from a poor South Side neighborhood had this observation: "I went to a couple jobs where a couple of the receptionists told me in confidence: 'You know what they do with these applications from blacks as soon as the day is over?' They say, 'We rip them and throw them in the garbage.'" In addition to concerns about being rejected because of race, the fears that some inner-city residents have of being denied employment simply because of their inner-city address or neighborhood are not unfounded. A welfare mother who lives in a large public housing project put it this way:

> Honestly, I believe they look at the address and the—your attitudes, your address, your surround—you know, your environment has a lot to do with your employment status. The people with the best addresses have the best chances. I feel so, I feel so.

It is instructive to study the fate of the disadvantaged in Europe. There, too, poverty and joblessness are on the increase; but individual deficiencies and behavior are not put forward as the culprits. Furthermore, welfare programs that benefit wide segments of the population like child care, children's allowances (an annual benefit per child), housing subsidies, education, medical care and unemployment insurance have been firmly institutionalized in many Western European democracies. Efforts to cut back on these programs in the face of growing joblessness have met firm resistance from working- and middle-class citizens.

My own belief is that the growing assault on welfare mothers is part of a larger reaction to the mounting problems in our nation's inner cities. When many people think of welfare they think of young, unmarried black mothers having babies. This image persists even though roughly equal numbers of black and white families received A.F.D.C. in 1994, and there were also a good many Hispanics on the welfare rolls.

Nevertheless, the rise of black A.F.D.C. recipients was said to be symptomatic of such larger problems as the decline in family values and the dissolution of the family. In an article published in *Esquire*, Pete Hamill wrote:

> The heart of the matter is the continued existence and expansion of what has come to be called the Underclass. . . . trapped in cycles of welfare dependency, drugs, alcohol, crime, illiteracy and disease, living in anarchic and murderous isolation in some of the richest cities on the earth. As a reporter, I've covered their miseries for more than a quarter of a century. . . . And in the last decade, I've watched this group of American citizens harden and condense, moving even further away from the basic requirements of a human life: work, family, safety, the law.

One has the urge to shout, "Enough is enough!"

What can be done? I believe that steps must be taken to galvanize Americans from all walks of life who are concerned about human suffering and the public policy direction in which we are now moving. We need to generate a public-private partnership to fight social inequality. The following policy frameworks provide a basis for further discussion and debate. Given the current political climate, these proposals might be dismissed as unrealistic. Nor am I suggesting that we can or should simply import the social policies of the Japanese, the Germans, or other Western Europeans. The question is how we Americans can address the problems of social inequality, including record levels of joblessness in the inner city, that threaten the very fabric of our society.

CREATE STANDARDS FOR SCHOOLS

Ray Marshall, former Secretary of Labor, points out that Japan and Germany have developed policies designed to increase the number of workers with "higher-order thinking skills." These policies require young people to meet high performance standards before they can graduate from secondary schools, and they hold each school responsible for meeting these standards.

Students who meet high standards are not only prepared for work but they are also ready for technical training and other kinds of postsecondary education. Currently, there are no mandatory academic standards for secondary schools in the United States. Accordingly, students who are not in college-preparatory courses have severely limited options with respect to pursuing work after high school. A commitment to a system of performance standards for every public school in the United States would be an important first step in addressing the huge gap in educational performance between the schools in advantaged and disadvantaged neighborhoods.

A system of at least local performance standards should include the kind of support that would enable schools in disadvantaged neighborhoods to meet the standards that are set. State governments, with federal support, not only would have to create equity in local school financing (through loans and scholarships to attract more high-quality teachers, increased support for teacher training and reforms in teacher certification) but would also have to insure that highly qualified teachers are more equitably distributed in local school districts.

Targeting education would be part of a national effort to raise the performance standards of all public schools in the United States to a desirable level, including schools in the inner city. The support of the private sector should be enlisted in this national effort. Corporations, local businesses, civic clubs, community centers and churches should be encouraged to work with the schools to improve computer-competency training.

IMPROVE CHILD CARE

The French system of child welfare stands in sharp contrast to the American system. In France, children are supported by three interrelated government programs, as noted by Barbara R. Bergmann, a professor of economics at American University: child care, income support, and medical care. The child-care program includes establishments for infant care, high-quality nursery schools (*écoles maternelles*), and paid leave for parents of newborns. The income-support program includes child-support enforcement (so that the absent parent continues to contribute financially to his or her child's welfare), children's allowances, and welfare payments for low-income single mothers. Finally, medical care is provided through a universal system of national health care financed by social security, a preventive-care system for children, and a group of public-health nurses who specialize in child welfare.

ESTABLISH CITY-SUBURBAN PARTNERSHIPS

If the other industrial democracies offer lessons for a long-term solution to the jobs problem involving relationships between employment, education, and family-support systems, they also offer another lesson: the importance of city-suburban integration and cooperation. None of the other industrialized democracies have allowed their city centers to deteriorate as has the United States.

It will be difficult to address growing racial tensions in American cities unless we tackle the problems of shrinking revenue and inadequate social services and the gradual disappearance of work in certain neighborhoods. The city has become a less desirable place in which to live, and the economic and social gap between the cities and suburbs is growing. The groups left behind compete, often along racial lines, for declining resources, including the remaining decent schools, housing, and neighborhoods. The rise of the new urban poverty neighborhoods has worsened these problems. Their high rates of joblessness and social disorganization have created problems that often spill over into other parts of the city. All of these factors aggravate race relations and elevate racial tensions.

Ideally, we would restore the federal contribution to city revenues that existed in 1980 and sharply increase the employment base. Regardless of changes in federal urban policy, however, the fiscal crises in the cities would be significantly eased if the employment base could be substantially increased. Indeed, the social dislocations caused by the steady disappearance of work have led to a wide range of urban social problems, including racial tensions. Increased employment would help stabilize the new poverty neighborhoods, halt the precipitous decline in density, and ultimately enhance the quality of race relations in urban areas.

Reforms put forward to achieve the objective of city-suburban cooperation range from proposals to create metropolitan governments to proposals for metropolitan tax-base sharing (currently in effect in Minneapolis-St. Paul), collaborative metropolitan planning, and the creation of regional authorities to develop solutions to common problems if communities fail to reach agreement. Among the problems shared by many metropolises is a weak public transit system. A commitment to address this problem through a form of city-suburban collaboration would benefit residents of both the city and the suburbs.

The mismatch between residence and the location of jobs is a problem for some workers in America because, unlike the system in Europe, public transportation is weak and expensive. It's a particular problem for inner-city blacks because they have less access to private automobiles and, unlike Mexicans, do not have a network system that supports organized car pools. Accordingly, they depend heavily on public transportation and therefore have difficulty getting to the suburbs, where jobs are more plentiful. Until public transit systems are improved in metropolitan areas, the creation of privately subsidized car-pool and van-pool networks to carry inner-city residents to the areas of employment, especially suburban areas, would be a relatively inexpensive way to increase work opportunities.

The creation of for-profit information and placement centers in various parts of the inner city not only could significantly improve awareness of the availability of employment in the metropolitan area but could also serve to refer workers to employers. These centers would recruit or accept inner-city workers and try to place them in jobs. One of their main purposes would be to make persons who have been persistently unemployed or out of the labor force "job ready."

REINTRODUCE THE W.P.A.

The final proposal under consideration here was advanced by the perceptive journalist Mickey Kaus of *The New Republic,* who has long been concerned about the growth in the number of welfare recipients. Kaus's proposal is modeled on the Works Progress Administration (W.P.A.), the large public-works program initiated in 1935 by President Franklin D. Roosevelt. The public-works jobs that Roosevelt had in mind included highway construction, slum clearance, housing construction, and rural electrification. As Kaus points out:

> In its eight-year existence, according to official records, the W.P.A. built or improved 651,000 miles of roads, 953 airports, 124,000 bridges and viaducts, 1,178,000 culverts, 8,000 parks, 18,000 playgrounds and athletic fields, and 2,000 swimming pools. It constructed 40,000 buildings (including 8,000 schools) and repaired 85,000 more. Much of New York City—including La Guardia Airport, F.D.R. Drive, plus hundreds of parks and libraries—was built by the W.P.A.

A neo-W.P.A. program of employment, for every American citizen over eighteen who wants it, would provide useful public jobs at wages slightly below the minimum wage. Like the work relief under Roosevelt's W.P.A., it would not carry the stigma of a cash dole. People would be earning their money. Although some workers in the W.P.A.-style jobs "could be promoted to higher-paying public service positions," says Kaus, most of them would advance occupationally by moving to the private sector. "If you have to work anyway," he says, "why do it for $4 an hour?"

Under Kaus's proposal, after a certain date, able-bodied recipients on welfare would no longer receive cash payments. However, unlike the welfare-reform bill that Clinton has agreed to sign, Kaus's plan would make public jobs available to those who move off welfare. Also, Kaus argues that to allow poor mothers to work, government-financed day care must be provided for their children if needed. But this service has to be integrated into the larger system of child care for other families in the United States to avoid creating a "day-care ghetto" for low-income children.

A W.P.A.-style jobs program will not be cheap. In the short run, it is considerably cheaper to give people cash welfare than it is to create public jobs. Including the costs of supervisors and materials, each subminimum-wage W.P.A.-style job would cost an estimated $12,000, more than the public cost of staying on welfare. That would represent $12 billion for every 1 million jobs created.

The solutions I have outlined were developed with the idea of providing a policy framework that could be easily adopted by a reform coalition. A broad range of groups would support the long-term solutions—the development of a system of national performance standards in public schools, family policies to reinforce the learning system in the schools, a national system of school-to-work transition, and the promotion of city-suburban integration and cooperation. The short-term solutions, which range from job information and placement centers to the creation of W.P.A.-style jobs, are more relevant to low-income people, but they are the kinds of opportunity-enhancing programs that Americans of all racial and class backgrounds tend to support.

Although my policy framework is designed to appeal to broad segments of the population, I firmly believe that if adopted, it would alleviate a good deal of the economic and social distress currently plaguing the inner cities. The immediate problem of the disappearance of work in many inner-city neighborhoods would be confronted. The employment base in these neighborhoods would be increased immediately by the newly created jobs, and income levels would rise because of the expansion of the earned-income tax credit. Programs like universal health care and day care would increase the attractiveness of low-wage jobs and "make work pay."

Increasing the employment base would have an enormous positive impact on the social organization of ghetto neighborhoods. As more people become employed, crime and drug use would subside; families would be strengthened and welfare receipt would decline significantly; ghetto-related culture and behavior, no longer sustained and nourished by persistent joblessness, would gradually fade. As more people became employed and gained work experience, they would have a better chance of finding jobs in the private sector when they became available. The attitudes of employers toward inner-city workers would change, partly because the employers would be dealing with job applicants who had steady work experience and would furnish references from their previous supervisors.

This is not to suggest that all the jobless individuals from the inner-city ghetto would take advantage of these employment opportunities. Some have responded to persistent joblessness by abusing alcohol and drugs, and these handicaps will affect their overall job performance, including showing up for work on time or on a consistent basis. But such people represent only a small proportion of inner-city workers. Most of them are ready, willing, able and anxious to hold a steady job.

The long-term solutions that I have advanced would reduce the likelihood that a new generation of jobless workers will be produced from the youngsters now in school and preschool. We must break the cycle of joblessness and improve the youngsters' preparation for the new labor market in the global economy.

My framework for long-term and immediate solutions is based on the notion that the problems of jobless ghettos cannot be separated from those of the rest of the nation. Although these solutions have wide-ranging application and would alleviate the economic distress of many Americans, their impact on jobless ghettos would be profound. Their most important contribution would be their effect on the children of the ghetto, who would be able to anticipate a future of economic mobility and harbor the hopes and aspirations that for so many of their fellow citizens help define the American way of life.

CRITICAL-THINKING QUESTIONS

1. According to Wilson, what is the primary cause of inner-city decline? How does his assessment differ from common notions about this problem?
2. Why have inner-city areas lost so many jobs over the last fifty years?
3. What solutions does Wilson offer? Do you agree with his approach? Why or why not?

The Economy and Work

CLASSIC

CONTEMPORARY

CROSS-CULTURAL

48

Maid in the U.S.A.

Mary Romero

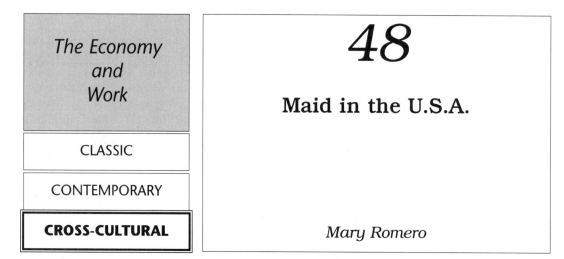

Domestic work—almost exclusively performed by women of color—is both underpaid and undervalued in our society. In this selection, Mary Romero describes some of the strategies Chicana domestics use to eliminate the demeaning aspects of their work, to define the relationships between themselves and employers in more equal terms, and to professionalize their jobs.

Although Chicanas consider flexibility, autonomy and independence the advantages of domestic service over other jobs, these characteristics are not inherent features. Domestics have to negotiate directly with employers to establish a flexible work schedule and autonomy on the job. An analysis of their work histories in domestic service reveals that Chicana domestics actively negotiate informal labor arrangements that include both strategies to eliminate the most oppressive aspects of the occupation and to develop instrumental employer-employee relationships aimed at professionalizing it. Unable to find employment offering job security, advancement, or benefits, Chicanas make calculated attempts to improve the occupation by minimizing employer control and personalism. . . .

NEGOTIATING SPECIFIC TASKS

In the informal labor arrangement, domestic and employer must verbally negotiate working conditions, including tasks, timing, technique, the length of the working day, and payment. When starting with a new employer, the domestic works one day, and if the employer is satisfied with her work, the two agree upon a work schedule and the specific tasks to be accomplished. Mrs. Rodriquez describes the ideal situation: "Once the person learns that you're going to do the job they just totally leave you to your own. It's like it's your own home." This ideal is similar to the informal arrangements Glenn reports.[1] However, half of the women I interviewed explain that the ideal situation is achieved after some supervision and negotiation. Such an experience is alluded to in Mrs. Portillo's explanation of why she left an employer: "I don't want somebody right behind me telling me what to do. I will not work like that and that's why I didn't stay any longer with this lady."

The priority of domestics in the informal labor arrangement is to negotiate a work structure that provides autonomy and independence. Autonomy on the job is created when the worker controls the planning and organization of the housework, as well as the work pace and method. Gaining autonomy also assures the worker that the parameters of the work are maintained. The ideal situation is to have the worker structuring the work, with the employer removed from direct supervision. Chicana domestics stated their desire for autonomy, using the common expression "being your own boss."

Fifteen of the Chicanas make a practice of carefully distinguishing specific tasks that are considered part of the agreement from other tasks that are undertaken only for additional pay. Although informal work arrangements frequently imply a set number of hours, the typical arrangement is referred to as "charging by the house." Mrs. Salazar explains the verbal contract:

> When you say you're going to clean a house, after you find out how big it is, you tell them [the employer] "I'll clean it for say sixty dollars." You're not saying how long you're going to be there. To me, that was just a contract between you and the customer and after awhile when you've been there awhile, you know how fast you can work and I was doing it in less than eight hours.

Mrs. Lopez expresses her preference for "charging by the house": "I never liked to work by the hour because if I would work by the hour the lady would just go crazy loading me up with work, with more work and more work to do."

Charging a flat rate also eliminates employers' attempts at speedup by adding more tasks and forcing the domestic to increase the work pace. Glenn also found that Japanese American domestics attempt to limit the amount of work by specifying tasks rather than time. Charging a flat rate is a significant change in the occupation, particularly in light of the broad range of physical and emotional labor domestics report. The list of tasks suggests that many employers purchase labor power rather than labor services; that is, workers are not hired simply to provide the labor service of cleaning the house but their labor is purchased for a certain amount of hours to do a variety of unspecified tasks. "Charging by the house" involves specifying the specific tasks and, thus, placing boundaries on the job description. . . .

Like the dialectic between employer and employee Glenn describes, there is an ongoing negotiation as the domestic attempts to maintain the agreement while the employer attempts to lengthen the work day or to add more tasks. For instance, Mrs. Tafoya recalls an incident in which an employer attempted to extract additional unpaid labor:

> I guess the niece came home. I knew the record player was playing and she was kinda—but I thought she was just tapping like you would tap [indicates with her hand on the table], you know. She was dancing and I guess the wax wasn't dry. She made a mess. I said to Mrs. Johnson [employer], I says I'm not going to clean that again. You get your niece to clean that. I did it once and it was beautiful. And I did it because nobody was here and I know that it would dry right. So if you want it redone you have your niece do it. And she says but you're getting paid for it. I says yea, I got paid for it and I did it.

By refusing to wax the floor over again, Mrs. Tafoya maintained the original labor arrangement.

Mrs. Sanchez gave an account that illustrates her attempt to place limits on the amount of work done and her efforts to maintain the original verbal contract. Mrs. Sanchez described a current problem she was having with an employer who is attempting to add more work. Mimicking the high-pitched voice of her employer, she repeated the employer's question: "Would you mind doing this? Would you mind doing that?" Mrs. Sanchez confided that she wanted to respond by saying, "Yes I do mind and I won't do it" but instead she said "Well, I'll do it this time." She expressed the importance of pointing out to the employer that the task would be done this time but was not to be expected in the future.

Another strategy Chicanas use to limit the work and reduce employers' efforts to extract unpaid labor involves developing a routine for handling "extras." The women describe preparing a monthly or bimonthly schedule for rotating particular tasks, such as cleaning the stove or refrigerator, and thereby avoid many special requests. Another common practice is to establish an understanding with the employer that if one task is added, another is eliminated. If the employer does not identify the tasks to be eliminated, the employee simply selects one and later explains that there was not enough time for both. Mrs. Garcia recalls learning this strategy from her cousin:

> My cousin said, "Do the same thing every time you come in, as far as changing the sheets, vacuum and dust, and window sills, pictures on the walls, and stuff like that unless they ask you to do something extra. Then, maybe don't clean the tile in the bathroom, or just do the windows that really need it, so you can have some time to do this other stuff that they wanted you to do extra." And she said, "Never do more than what they ask you to do, because if you do them you're not really getting paid for it." . . .

Chicana domestics, not unlike African American and Japanese American domestics, did not necessarily find an affective relationship the ingredient for a satisfying working relationship. In fact, the opposite is the case, because affective relationships provide more opportunities for exploitation. Frequently, close friendships result in fictitious kinship references, such as a younger employer adopting the domestic as a surrogate mother. Redefining the work obligation as a "family" obligation places the domestic in a difficult position. As Mrs. Portillo explains, the personal nature of the relationship creates an atmosphere conducive to manipulation: "Some people use their generosity to pressure you." Maintaining the conditions of the contract also becomes difficult because extra requests are made as if from a friend rather than from an employer. When employers use personalism as a means to extract additional labor, many domestics are able to increase their pay by threatening to quit. However, when they no longer feel in control, many choose to quit and find another employer.

MINIMIZING CONTACT WITH EMPLOYERS

Domestics commonly report conflict over the work process. In order to structure the work as a meaningful and nondegrading activity, domestics struggle to remove employers from control of decisions. When employers control the work process, domestics are reduced to unskilled labor and housecleaning becomes mindless hourly work. Furthermore, domestics strive to eliminate the rituals of deference and the stigma of servitude. Minimizing the contact with employers was the most successful strategy for gaining control over the work process.

Employers are reluctant to turn over the control of the process to the domestic. Instead they attempt to structure the work to be supervised and monitored. Chicanas report that some employers give detailed instructions on how to clean their homes; they specified washing the floor on hands and knees, using newspaper instead of paper towels on the windows, or even in which direction to scrub the wall. Mrs. Portillo, a retired domestic with thirty years of experience, expresses the frustration of working for an employer who retained control of the work process.

> I used to have one lady that used to work right along with me. I worked with her three years. I found it hard. I was taking orders. I'm not the type to want to take orders. I know what I'm going to do. I know what general housecleaning is.

Under supervised conditions, domestics find themselves simply taking orders, which reduces their work activity to quick, monotonous gestures.

Mrs. Sanchez voices the general consensus that the less interaction there is with employers, the better are the working conditions: "The conflicts have been mostly with people who stay at home and really just demand the impossible." Five domestics even commented that they selected employers on the basis of whether the employer worked outside the home.

Chicanas argue that working women are more appreciative of the housework done and are relieved to turn over the planning and execution of cleaning to the domestic. Unemployed women, on the other hand, are portrayed as "picky" and unwilling to relinquish control. Three domestics whom I interviewed suggested that unemployed women feel guilty because they are not doing the work themselves and thus retain control and responsibility for the housework. Mrs. Lucero's description represents the distinctions domestics make between working women and full-time homemakers:

> I think women that weren't working were the ones that always had something to complain about. The ones that did work were always satisfied. I've never come across a lady that works that has not been satisfied. Those that are home and have the time to do it themselves, and don't want to do it, they are the ones that are always complaining, you know, not satisfied, they always want more and more. You can't really satisfy them.

Working women tend to be ideal employers because they are rarely home and are unable to supervise.

The selection of employers is essential in maximizing the advantages of domestic service over other available jobs. For instance, Mrs. Gallegos explains that she selects jobs on the basis of the type of work that she wants to avoid: "Well, if I can help it, I don't like to do ovens. I hardly do that anymore. . . . I don't like to work for people who are very dirty either." Four characteristics that the woman most frequently mention as qualities of a good employer are trust, respect, the understanding that family responsibilities come before work, and the ability to maintain a system for housecleaning. Only employers who trust their employees will allow the worker to structure the housework. Such respect indicates that employers are not trying to affirm and enhance their status by establishing the domestic's inferior status. Most of the women felt that family obligations, such as a sick child, superseded the work obligation. Therefore, they sought employers who were willing to accommodate occasional changes in the schedule and did not threaten to fire the worker. Domestics prefer to work for employers who maintain the house between cleanings and are not "dirty." Bad employers are characterized as "constantly looking over their shoulder," expecting the domestic to pick up after the children, leaving too many notes, and adding extra tasks. Domestics control their work environments to a large degree by replacing undesirable employers with more compatible ones.

A high turnover rate has always been characteristic of contemporary domestic service. Nevertheless, if a good working arrangement is established, domestics continue with an employer for some time. Over half of the women in this study worked for the same employer for at least two-thirds of their work histories as domestics. The women with the most extensive domestic experience have very impressive records. For instance, Mrs. Portillo, a sixty-eight-year-old retired domestic, had the same employers for the entire thirty years of her employment. Another woman, Mrs. Rivas, a fifty-three-year-old domestic with thirty-two years of experience, had the same employer for twenty years. Two younger women, Mrs. Montoya, age thirty-three, and Mrs. Rivera, age thirty-two, both have twelve years of experience and have worked for the same employer for eleven years.

Half of the women stated that they consider the first couple of days with a new employer a time to decide whether to keep the employer. For instance, Mrs. Fernandez bases her decision to stay with a new employer on watching for signs of supervision and monitoring and unreasonable expectations.

> You can tell if they're [employers] going to trust you or not. If they're not overlooking—see, you know—over you all the time. If they start looking or saying "I don't want this moved or I don't want this done or be careful with this"—well, you know, you can be so careful but there's accidents happen. So if they start being picky I won't stay.

Mrs. Lopez classifies the type of employer by the attitude they expose in the first few minutes of their first encounter:

> I have had ladies that have said "I know you know what to do so I'll leave it to you" or they pull out their cleaning stuff and tell you "This is for this and this is for that" and I say "I know I've done this before." "Oh, ok. I'll let you do it."

Supervision and monitoring of workers not only function to control the work process but remind the worker of her subordinate position in society. Offering unsolicited advice about cleaning techniques—such as scrubbing floors on hands and knees rather than with a mop, or the safest way to bend while picking up the vacuum cleaner and moving heavy furniture—symbolizes a level of servitude. Asking a domestic to scrub floors on hands and knees—not a common practice of housewives today—is experienced as demeaning. The inferior status of the domestic is also evident in the employer's instructions on how to bend without themselves offering assistance.

BECOMING AN EXPERT

Another strategy used by Chicanas in the struggle to transform domestic service is to define themselves as expert cleaners or housekeepers. It is a unique strategy not reported among the African Americans studied by Rollins, Coley, or Dill or the Japanese Americans in Glenn's study.[2] This strategy attempts to transform the employee-employer relationship, creating an ideal situation in which employers turn over responsibility for the housework to the domestic. Establishing themselves as expert housecleaners involved defining a routine set of housework tasks and eliminating personal services such as babysitting, laundry, or ironing. Older Chicanas recalled babysitting, ironing, cooking and doing laundry, but in recent years they rarely do such tasks. Even younger Chicanas in their thirties, some with twelve years' experience, do ironing or laundry only for employers they started with ten years ago.

The importance of redefining social relationships in domestic service is most apparent in the woman's distinctions between the work they do and the maid's work. Mrs. Fernandez, a thirty-five-year-old domestic, indicates the distinction in the following account:

> They [the employer's children] started to introduce me to their friends as their maid. "This is our maid Angela." I would say "I'm not your maid. I've come to clean your house and a maid is someone who takes care of you and lives here or comes in every day and I come once a week and it is to take care of what you have messed up. I'm not your maid. I'm your housekeeper."

These Chicanas define their work as different from maid's work. Mrs. Montoya's statement illustrates the equation of personal services with maid's work:

> I figure I'm not there to be their personal maid. I'm there to do their housecleaning—their upkeep of the house. Most of the women I work for are professionals and so they feel it's not my job to run around behind them. Just to keep their house maintenance clean and that's all they ask.

Mrs. Rojas, a thirty-three-year-old domestic with twelve years of experience, equates deferential behavior with being a maid.

> One or two [employers] that I work for now have children that are snotty, you know they thought that I was their maid or they would treat me like a maid you know instead of a cleaning lady.

These workers resisted attempts by employers and their families to structure the work around rituals of deference and avoided doing the emotional labor attached to personal services.

The Chicanas interviewed consider themselves experts. They are aware of the broad range of knowledge that they have acquired from cleaning a variety of homes. This includes the removal of stains on various surfaces, tips for reorganizing the home, and the pros and cons of certain brands of appliances. A source of pride among the women was the fact that they had introduced a labor-saving device or tactic into the employer's home. Mrs. Garcia's experience in removing stains illustrates the assistance domestics give employers:

> They [employers] just wipe their stoves and then complain "this doesn't come off anymore." They never took a SOS pad or a scrub brush to scrub it off. They expect it just to come off because they wiped. . . . Their kitchen floors would have Kool-Aid stains or they would have it on the counters, so I would just pour Clorox on it and the Clorox would just bring it right up and they would say "But you'll ruin it!" "No it will be alright." "Are you sure?" I never ruined anything from helping them out. . . .

CREATING A BUSINESSLIKE ENVIRONMENT

As in other female-dominated occupations—such as nursing and teaching—private household workers lack authority and must therefore rely on the employers' cooperation to change the structure of the work and social relationships. Mrs. Rojas describes one woman she worked for who accepted her obligation as an employer and maintained the agreement to hire Mrs. Rojas every Wednesday.

> I use to work for her on Wednesday and she would be going on a trip away with her husband and stuff because he did a lot of out-of-state work and she would go with him and being that I was going to be there on Wednesday and she wasn't she'd pay me anyway so I got paid from her whether I went [to work] or not as long as it was her who was going to be gone and not an excuse from me or something. She is about the only one that ever did that.

This employer is unique because most employers in domestic service expect the domestic to keep a work schedule to clean their houses on a regular basis but do not accept the responsibility of providing the work they promised.

In another account about an employer's daughter expecting her to be subordinate, Mrs. Rojas illustrates the role some employers play in eliminating servitude aspects of the occupation:

> I told a young lady something about leaving her underclothes thrown around, and she asked me what was I there for? I went straight in, called her mother and told her the situation. Her mother came home from work and let the young lady have it. She [the mother] was thoroughly upset. I was not there to be her [the daughter's] personal maid and she was told that in no uncertain terms.

Analysis of the informal networks used by both employers and employees points to a key role in establishing a businesslike environment. The informal network between employers and employees socializes both the value of modernizing trends in the occupation. Chicana work histories revealed that, particularly for younger workers, the introduction of domestic service involved an informal apprenticeship program. Like the domestics interviewed in Coley's study, the new recruit accompanied a relative to work for several days or weeks until the new recruit decided she was ready to work alone. . . .

Although the Chicanas identified these training sessions as providing experience in cleaning, learning about new products or appliances, and discovering the pros and cons of structuring the work in particular ways, the most important function may have been the socialization of new recruits to expect certain working conditions and wages and to learn ways to negotiate with employers. . . .

CONCLUSION

Faced with limited job opportunities, Chicanas turn to domestic service and restructure the occupation to resemble a businesslike arrangement. Similarly to the union members in Coley's study, the Chicana household workers I interviewed define themselves as professional cleaners hired to do general housework. They urge their employers to turn over the planning along with the execution of the work. They consider themselves skilled laborers who are well able to schedule tasks, determine cleaning techniques, select the appropriate work materials, and set the work pace. Verbal agreements specified tasks to minimize supervision and increase the degree of autonomy. Eliminating the employer from a supervisory role also removes the worker from a subordinate position. Like the household worker's collective that Salzinger studied in the Bay area, Chicanas are "redefining domestic work as skilled labor, and on that basis struggling for increased pay and security and for autonomy and control over their work," and "they are in fact engaged in what in other contexts has been called a 'professionalization project.'"[3] Domestics' ability to select and change employers is the critical locus of autonomy and control in what would otherwise be a powerless, subservient position. Working for a different employer—and in many cases two to three employers—places Chicanas in a strong negotiating position.

Like other full-time domestics, Chicanas employed as day workers in private households are moving away from "wage work" and from selling their "labor time" toward a "flat rate" in which a "job" is exchanged for a specified amount of money. In this situation, any efficiency realized by the worker saves her time and can sometimes be converted into profit that will accrue to her. Chicanas are attempting to transform domestic work in the direction of the petit-bourgeois relation of customer-vendor rather than the preindustrial relation of mistress-servant or even the wage worker-employer relation of capitalism. This arrangement is most successful with employed housewives who readily accept the skills of domestics. The strategy to transform domestic service by selling labor services rather than labor power is also useful in eliminating potentially exploitative aspects of the domestic-mistress relationship. Strategies described by Chicanas in the study are consistent with the emergence of cleaning agencies that advertise expert and skilled labor.

Although there is a long history of attempts to organize maid's unions,[4] most private household workers are isolated from each other and struggle for better working conditions on an individual basis. Nevertheless, the goals of individual struggle have similarities with issues of collective action: raising wages; providing benefits such as paid vacations, holidays, sick leave, and worker's unemployment compensation; changing attitudes toward the occupation; and creating public awareness about the value of the labor.

CRITICAL-THINKING QUESTIONS

1. Why do domestic workers try to redefine their work on the basis of a contract rather than hourly work?
2. How do domestic workers negotiate specific tasks? minimize their contact with employers? create a businesslike environment?
3. Some observers argue that domestic work should be eliminated and all of us should "pick up after ourselves" instead of expecting others to do our dirty work. Do you agree or disagree?

NOTES

1. Evelyn Nakano Glenn, "Occupational Ghettoization: Japanese American Women and Domestic Service, 1905–1970," *Ethnicity* 7, 4 (1981), 352–86.

2. Soraya Moore Coley, "'And Still I Rise': An Exploratory Study of Contemporary Black Private Household Workers" (Ph.D. diss., Bryn Mawr College, 1981); Bonnie Thornton Dill, "Making Your Job Good Yourself: Domestic Service and the Construction of Personal Dignity," in *Women and the Politics of Empowerment*, ed. Ann Bookman and Sandra Morgen (Philadelphia: Temple University Press, 1988), pp. 33–52; Judith Rollins, *Between Women: Domestics and Their Employers* (Philadelphia: Temple University Press, 1985).

3. Leslie Salzinger, "A Maid by Any Other Name: The Transformation of 'Dirty Work' by Central American Immigrants," in *Ethnography Unbound: Power and Resistance in the Modern Metropolis*, ed. Michael Buraway et al. (Berkeley and Los Angeles: University of California Press, 1991), pp. 139–60.

4. Phyllis Palmer, *Domesticity and Dirt: Housewives and Domestic Servants in the United States, 1920–1945* (Philadelphia: Temple University Press, 1989).

49

The Power Elite

C. Wright Mills

Politics, Government, and the Military

CLASSIC

CONTEMPORARY

CROSS-CULTURAL

Conventional wisdom suggests that U.S. society operates as a democracy, guided by the "voice of the people." C. Wright Mills argues that above ordinary people—and even above many politicians—are "the higher circles," those who run the corporations, operate the military establishment, and manipulate the machinery of the state. It is this relative handful of people whom Mills calls "the power elite."

The powers of ordinary men are circumscribed by the everyday worlds in which they live, yet even in these rounds of job, family, and neighborhood they often seem driven by forces they can neither understand nor govern. "Great changes" are beyond their control, but affect their conduct and outlook nonetheless. The very framework of modern society confines them to projects not their own, but from every side, such changes now press upon the men and women of the mass society, who accordingly feel that they are without purpose in an epoch in which they are without power.

But not all men are in this sense ordinary. As the means of information and of power are centralized, some men come to occupy positions in American society from which they can look down upon, so to speak, and by their decisions mightily affect, the everyday worlds of ordinary men and women. They are not made by their jobs; they set up and break down jobs for thousands of others; they are not confined by simple family responsibilities; they can escape. They may live in many hotels and houses, but they are bound by no one community. They need not merely "meet the demands of the day and hour"; in some part, they create these demands, and cause others to meet them. Whether or not they profess their power, their technical and political experience of it far transcends that of the underlying population. What Jacob Burckhardt said of "great men,"

Source: From *The Power Elite* by C. Wright Mills. Copyright ©1956 by C. Wright Mills. Renewed 1984 by Yaraslava Mills. Used by permission of Oxford University Press, Inc.

most Americans might well say of their elite: "They are all that we are not."

The power elite is composed of men whose positions enable them to transcend the ordinary environments of ordinary men and women; they are in positions to make decisions having major consequences. Whether they do or do not make such decisions is less important than the fact that they do occupy such pivotal positions: Their failure to act, their failure to make decisions, is itself an act that is often of greater consequence than the decisions they do make. For they are in command of the major hierarchies and organizations of modern society. They rule the big corporations. They run the machinery of the state and claim its prerogatives. They direct the military establishment. They occupy the strategic command posts of the social structure, in which are now centered the effective means of the power and the wealth and the celebrity which they enjoy.

The power elite are not solitary rulers. Advisers and consultants, spokesmen and opinion-makers are often the captains of their higher thought and decision. Immediately below the elite are the professional politicians of the middle levels of power, in the Congress and in the pressure groups, as well as among the new and old upper classes of town and city and region. Mingling with them, in curious ways which we shall explore, are those professional celebrities who live by being continually displayed but are never, so long as they remain celebrities, displayed enough. If such celebrities are not at the head of any dominating hierarchy, they do often have the power to distract the attention of the public or afford sensations to the masses, or, more directly, to gain the ear of those who do occupy positions of direct power. More or less unattached, as critics of morality and technicians of power, as spokesmen of God and creators of mass sensibility, such celebrities and consultants are part of the immediate scene in which the drama of the elite is enacted. But that drama itself is centered in the command posts of the major institutional hierarchies.

The truth about the nature and the power of the elite is not some secret which men of affairs know but will not tell. Such men hold quite various theories about their own roles in the sequence of event and decision. Often they are uncertain about their roles, and even more often they allow their fears and their hopes to affect their assessment of their own power. No matter how great their actual power, they tend to be less acutely aware of it than of the resistances of others to its use. Moreover, most American men of affairs have learned well the rhetoric of public relations, in some cases even to the point of using it when they are alone, and thus coming to believe it. The personal awareness of the actors is only one of the several sources one must examine in order to understand the higher circles. Yet many who believe that there is no elite, or at any rate none of any consequence, rest their argument upon what men of affairs believe about themselves, or at least assert in public.

There is, however, another view: Those who feel, even if vaguely, that a compact and powerful elite of great importance does now prevail in America often base that feeling upon the historical trend of our time. They have felt, for example, the domination of the military event, and from this they infer that generals and admirals, as well as other men of decision influenced by them, must be enormously powerful. They hear that the Congress has again abdicated to a handful of men decisions clearly related to the issue of war or peace. They know that the bomb was dropped over Japan in the name of the United States of America, although they were at no time consulted about the matter. They feel that they live in a time of big decisions; they know that they are not making any. Accordingly, as they consider the present as history, they infer that at its center, making decisions or failing to make them, there must be an elite of power.

On the one hand, those who share this feeling about big historical events assume that there is an elite and that its power is great. On the other hand, those who listen carefully to the reports of men apparently involved in the great decisions often do not believe that there is an elite whose powers are of decisive consequence.

Both views must be taken into account, but neither is adequate. The way to understand the power of the American elite lies neither solely in recognizing the historic scale of events nor in accepting the personal awareness reported by men of apparent decision. Behind such men and behind the events of history, linking the two, are the major institutions of modern society. These hierarchies of state and corporation and army constitute the means of power; as such they are now of a consequence not before equaled in human history—and at their summits, there are now those command posts of modern society which offer us the sociological key to an understanding of the role of the higher circles in America.

Within American society, major national power now resides in the economic, the political, and the military domains. Other institutions seem off to the side of modern history, and, on occasion, duly subordinated to these. No family is as directly powerful in national affairs as any major corporation; no church is as directly powerful in the external biographies of young men in America today as the military establishment; no college is as powerful in the shaping of momentous events as the National Security Council. Religious, educational, and family institutions are not autonomous centers of national power; on the contrary, these decentralized areas are increasingly shaped by the big three, in which developments of decisive and immediate consequence now occur.

Families and churches and schools adapt to modern life; governments and armies and corporations shape it; and, as they do so, they turn these lesser institutions into means for their ends. Religious institutions provide chaplains to the armed forces where they are used as a means of increasing the effectiveness of its morale to kill. Schools select and train men for their jobs in corporations and their specialized tasks in the armed forces. The extended family has, of course, long been broken up by the industrial revolution, and now the son and the father are removed from the family, by compulsion if need be, whenever the army of the state sends out the call. And the symbols of all these lesser institutions are used to legitimate the power and the decisions of the big three.

The life-fate of the modern individual depends not only upon the family into which he was born or which he enters by marriage, but increasingly upon the corporation in which he spends the most alert hours of his best years; not only upon the school where he is educated as a child and adolescent, but also upon the state which touches him throughout his life; not only upon the church in which on occasion he hears the word of God, but also upon the army in which he is disciplined.

If the centralized state could not rely upon the inculcation of nationalist loyalties in public and private schools, its leaders would promptly seek to modify the decentralized educational system. If the bankruptcy rate among the top 500 corporations were as high as the general divorce rate among the 37 million married couples, there would be economic catastrophe on an international scale. If members of armies gave to them no more of their lives than do believers to the churches to which they belong, there would be a military crisis.

Within each of the big three, the typical institutional unit has become enlarged, has become administrative, and, in the power of its decisions, has become centralized. Behind these developments there is a fabulous technology, for as institutions, they have incorporated this technology and guide it, even as it shapes and paces their developments.

The economy—once a great scatter of small productive units in autonomous balance—has become dominated by two or three hundred giant corporations, administratively and politically interrelated, which together hold the keys to economic decisions.

The political order, once a decentralized set of several dozen states with a weak spinal cord, has become a centralized, executive establishment which has taken up into itself many powers previously scattered, and now enters into each and every cranny of the social structure.

The military order, once a slim establishment in a context of distrust fed by state militia, has become the largest and most expensive feature of government, and, although well-versed in smiling public relations, now has all the grim and clumsy efficiency of a sprawling bureaucratic domain.

In each of these institutional areas, the means of power at the disposal of decision makers have increased enormously; their central executive powers have been enhanced; within each of them modern administrative routines have been elaborated and tightened up.

As each of these domains becomes enlarged and centralized, the consequences of its activities become greater, and its traffic with the others increases. The decisions of a handful of corporations bear upon military and political as well as upon economic developments around the world. The decisions of the military establishment rest upon and grievously affect political life as well as the very level of economic activity. The decisions made within the political domain determine economic activities and military programs. There is no longer, on the one hand, an economy, and, on the other hand, a political order containing a military establishment unimportant to politics and to money-making. There is a political economy linked, in a thousand ways, with military institutions and decisions. On each side of the world-split running through central Europe and around the Asiatic rimlands, there is an ever-increasing interlocking of economic, military, and political structures. If there is government intervention in the corporate economy, so is there corporate intervention in the governmental process. In the structural sense, this triangle of power is the source of the interlocking directorate that is most important for the historical structure of the present.

The fact of the interlocking is clearly revealed at each of the points of crisis of modern capitalist society—slump, war, and boom. In each, men of decision are led to an awareness of the interdependence of the major institutional orders. In the nineteenth century, when the scale of all institutions was smaller, their liberal integration was achieved in the automatic economy, by an autonomous play of market forces, and in the automatic political domain, by the bargain and the vote. It was then assumed that out of the imbalance and friction that followed the limited decisions then possible a new equilibrium would in due course emerge. That can no longer be assumed, and it is not assumed by the men at the top of each of the three dominant hierarchies.

For given the scope of their consequences, decisions—and indecisions—in any one of these ramify into the others, and hence top decisions tend either to become coordinated or to lead to a commanding indecision. It has not always been like this. When numerous small entrepreneurs made up the economy, for example, many of them could fail and the consequences still remain local; political and military authorities did not intervene. But now, given political expectations and military commitments, can they afford to allow key units of the private corporate economy to break down in slump? Increasingly, they do intervene in economic affairs, and as they do so, the controlling decisions in each order are inspected by agents of the other two, and economic, military, and political structures are interlocked.

At the pinnacle of each of the three enlarged and centralized domains, there have arisen those higher circles which make up the economic, the political, and the military elites. At the top of the economy, among the corporate rich, there are the chief executives; at the top of the political order, the members of the political directorate; at the top of the military establishment, the elite of soldier-statesmen clustered in and around the Joint Chiefs of Staff and the upper echelon. As each of these domains has coincided with the others, as decisions tend to become total in their consequence, the leading men in each of the three domains of power—the warlords, the corporation chieftains, the political directorate—tend to come together, to form the power elite of America.

The higher circles in and around these command posts are often thought of in terms of what their members possess: They have a greater share than other people of the things and experiences that are most highly valued. From this point of view, the elite are simply those who have the most of what there is to have, which is generally held to include money, power, and prestige—as well as all the ways of life to which these lead. But the elite are not simply those who have the most, for they could not "have the most" were it not for their positions in the great institutions. For such institutions are the necessary bases of power, of wealth, and of prestige, and at the same time, the chief means of exercising power, of acquiring and retaining wealth, and of cashing in the higher claims for prestige.

By the powerful we mean, of course, those who are able to realize their will, even if others resist it. No one, accordingly, can be truly powerful unless he has access to the command of major institutions, for it is over these institutional means of power that the truly powerful are, in the first instance, powerful. Higher politicians and key officials of government command such institutional power; so do admirals and generals, and so do the major owners and executives of the larger corporations. Not all power, it is true, is anchored in and exercised by means of such institutions, but only within and through them can power be more or less continuous and important.

Wealth also is acquired and held in and through institutions. The pyramid of wealth cannot be understood merely in terms of the very rich; for the great inheriting families, as we shall see, are now supplemented by the corporate institutions of modern society: Every one of the very rich families has been and is closely connected—always legally and frequently managerially as well—with one of the multimillion-dollar corporations.

The modern corporation is the prime source of wealth, but, in latter-day capitalism, the political apparatus also opens and closes many avenues to wealth. The amount as well as the source of income, the power over consumer's goods as well as over productive capital, are determined by position within the political economy. If our interest in the very rich goes beyond their lavish or their miserly consumption, we must examine their relations to modern forms of corporate property as well as to the state; for such relations now determine the chances of men to secure big property and to receive high income.

Great prestige increasingly follows the major institutional units of the social structure. It is obvious that prestige depends, often quite decisively, upon access to the publicity machines that are now a central and normal feature of all the big institutions of modern America. Moreover, one feature of these hierarchies of corporation, state, and military establishment is that their top positions are increasingly interchangeable. One result of this is the accumulative nature of prestige. Claims for prestige, for example, may be initially based on military roles, then expressed in and augmented by an educational institution run by corporate executives, and cashed in, finally, in the political order, where, for General Eisenhower and those he represents, power and prestige finally meet at the very peak. Like wealth and power, prestige tends to be cumulative: The more of it you have, the more you can get. These values also tend to be translatable into one another: The wealthy find it easier than the poor to gain power; those with status find it easier than those without it to control opportunities for wealth.

If we took the 100 most powerful men in America, the 100 wealthiest, and the 100 most celebrated away from the institutional positions they now occupy, away from their resources of men and women and money, away from the media of mass communication that are now focused upon them—then they would be powerless and poor and uncelebrated. For power is not of a man. Wealth does not center in the person of the wealthy. Celebrity is not inherent in any personality. To be celebrated, to be wealthy, to have power requires access to major institutions, for the institutional positions men occupy determine in large part their chances to have and to hold these valued experiences.

The people of the higher circles may also be conceived as members of a top social stratum, as a set of groups whose members know one another, see one another socially and at business, and so, in making decisions, take one another into account. The elite, according to this conception, feel themselves to be, and are felt by others to be, the inner circle of "the upper social classes." They form a more or less compact social and psychological entity; they have become self-conscious members of a social class. People are either accepted into this class or they are not, and there is a qualitative split, rather than merely a numerical scale, separating them from those who are not elite. They are more or less aware of themselves as a social class and they behave toward one another differently from the way they do toward members of other classes. They accept one another, understand one another, marry one another, tend to work and to think if not together at least alike.

Now, we do not want by our definition to prejudge whether the elite of the command posts are conscious members of such a socially recognized class, or whether considerable proportions of the elite derive from such a clear and distinct class. These are matters to be investigated. Yet in order to be able to recognize what we intend to investigate, we must note something that all biographies and memoirs of the wealthy and the powerful and the eminent make clear: No matter what else they may be, the people of these higher circles are involved in a set of overlapping "crowds" and intricately connected "cliques." There is a kind of mutual attraction among those who "sit on the same terrace"—although this often becomes clear to them, as well as to others, only at the point at which they feel the need to draw the line; only when, in their common defense, they come to understand what they have in common, and so close their ranks against outsiders.

The idea of such ruling stratum implies that most of its members have similar social origins, that throughout their lives they maintain a network of informal connections, and that to some degree there is an interchangeability of position between the various hierarchies of money and power and celebrity. We must, of course, note at once that if such an elite stratum does exist, its social visibility and its form, for very solid historical reasons, are quite different from those of the noble cousinhoods that once ruled various European nations.

That American society has never passed through a feudal epoch is of decisive importance to the nature of the American elite, as well as to American society as a historic whole. For it means that no nobility or aristocracy, established before the capitalist era, has stood in tense opposition to the higher bourgeoisie. It means that this bourgeoisie has monopolized not only wealth but prestige and power as well. It means that no set of noble families has commanded the top positions and monopolized the values that are generally held in high esteem; and certainly that no set has done so explicitly by inherited right. It means that no high church dignitaries or court nobilities, no entrenched landlords with honorific accouterments, no monopolists of high army posts have opposed the enriched bourgeoisie and in the name of birth and prerogative successfully resisted its self-making.

But this does *not* mean that there are no upper strata in the United States. That they emerged from a "middle class" that had no recognized aristocratic superiors does not mean they remained middle class when enormous increases in wealth made their own superiority possible. Their origins and their newness may have made the upper strata less visible in America than elsewhere. But in America today there are in fact tiers and ranges of wealth and power of which people in the middle and lower ranks know very little and may not even dream. There are families who, in their well-being, are quite insulated from the economic jolts and lurches felt by the merely prosperous and those farther down the scale. There are also men of power who in quite small groups make decisions of enormous consequence for the underlying population. . . .

CRITICAL-THINKING QUESTIONS

1. What institutions form the "interlocking triangle" in Mills's analysis? Why does he think these are the most powerful social institutions?
2. Explain how Mills argues that the existence of a power elite is not a consequence of *people* per se but a result of the institutions of U.S. society.
3. Does the lack of an aristocratic history mean that power is dispersed throughout U.S. society?

Politics, Government, and the Military

CLASSIC

CONTEMPORARY

CROSS-CULTURAL

50

Pornography: Not a Moral Issue

Catharine A. MacKinnon

In conventional usage, the term "politics" evokes thoughts of campaigns and elections for office. Critics of the status quo, however, typically argue that various dimensions of everyday life are political insofar as some category of humanity wields power over others. Thus feminists contend that pornography—widely thought of as obscenity—is more correctly understood as a type of sexual politics *expressing male power over women. To Catharine MacKinnon, a leading feminist and lawyer, pornography is not a moral issue but an important political matter.*

A critique of pornography[1] is to feminism what its defense is to male supremacy. Central to the institutionalization of male dominance, pornography cannot be reformed or suppressed or banned. It can only be changed. The legal doctrine of obscenity, the state's closest approximation to addressing the pornography question, has made the First Amendment[2] into a barrier to this process. . . . Obscenity law is concerned with morality, specifically morals from the male point of view, meaning the standpoint of male dominance. The feminist critique of pornography is about politics, specifically politics from women's point of view, meaning the standpoint of the subordination of women to men.[3] Morality here means good and evil; politics means power and powerlessness. Obscenity is a moral idea; pornography is a political practice. Obscenity is abstract; pornography is concrete. The two concepts represent two entirely different things. Nudity, explicitness, excess of candor, arousal or excitement, prurience, unnaturalness—these qualities bother obscenity law when sex is depicted or portrayed. Abortion, birth control information, and treatments for "restoring sexual virility" (whose, do you suppose?) have also been included.[4] Sex forced on real women so that it can be sold at a profit to be forced on other real women; women's bodies trussed and maimed and raped and made into things to be hurt and obtained and accessed, and this presented as the nature of women; the coercion that is visible and the coercion that has become invisible—this and more bothers feminists about pornography. Obscenity as such probably does little harm,[5] pornography causes attitudes and behaviors of violence and discrimination that define the treatment and status of half of the population.[6] To make the legal and philosophical consequences of this distinction clear, I will describe the feminist critique of pornography, criticize the law of obscenity in terms of it, then discuss the criticism that

Source: From *Feminism Unmodified: Discourses on Life and Law* by Catharine A. MacKinnon (Cambridge: Harvard University Press, 1987), pp. 146–53, 162. Reprinted by permission of the author.

pornography "dehumanizes" women to distinguish the male morality of liberalism and obscenity law from a feminist political critique of pornography.[7] . . .

Pornography, in the feminist view, is a form of forced sex, a practice of sexual politics, an institution of gender inequality. In this perspective, pornography is not harmless fantasy or a corrupt and confused misrepresentation of an otherwise natural and healthy sexuality. Along with the rape and prostitution in which it participates, pornography institutionalizes the sexuality of male supremacy, which fuses the erotization of dominance and submission with the social construction of male and female.[8] Gender is sexual. Pornography constitutes the meaning of that sexuality. Men treat women as who they see women as being. Pornography constructs who that is. Men's power over women means that the way men see women defines who women can be. Pornography is that way.

In pornography, women desire dispossession and cruelty. Men, permitted to put words (and other things) in women's mouths, create scenes in which women desperately want to be bound, battered, tortured, humiliated, and killed. Or merely taken and used. This is erotic to the male point of view. Subjection itself, with self-determination ecstatically relinquished, is the content of women's sexual desire and desirability. Women are there to be violated and possessed, men to violate and possess them, either on screen or by camera or pen, on behalf of the viewer.

One can be for or against this pornography without getting beyond liberalism. The critical yet formally liberal view of Susan Griffin, for example, conceptualizes eroticism as natural and healthy but corrupted and confused by "the pornographic mind."[9] Pornography distorts Eros, which preexists and persists, despite male culture's pornographic "revenge" upon it. Eros is, unaccountably, *still there.* Pornography mistakes it, mis-images it, mis-represents it. There is no critique of *reality* here, only objections to how it is seen; no critique of that reality that pornography imposes on women's real lives, those lives that are so seamlessly *consistent* with the pornography that pornography can be credibly defended by saying it is only a mirror of reality.

Contrast this view with the feminist analysis of Andrea Dworkin, in which sexuality itself is a social construct, gendered to the ground. Male dominance here is not an artificial overlay upon an underlying inalterable substratum of uncorrupted essential sexual being. Sexuality free of male dominance will require *change,* not reconceptualization, transcendence, or excavation. Pornography is not imagery in some relation to a reality elsewhere constructed. It is not a distortion, reflection, projection, expression, fantasy, representation, or symbol either. It is sexual reality. Dworkin's *Pornography: Men Possessing Women*[10] presents a sexual theory of gender inequality of which pornography is a core constitutive practice. The way pornography produces its meaning constructs and defines men and women as such. Gender is what gender means.[11] It has no basis in anything other than the social reality its hegemony constructs. The process that gives sexuality its male supremacist meaning is therefore the process through which gender inequality becomes socially real.

In this analysis the liberal defense of pornography as human sexual liberation, as derepression—whether by feminists, lawyers, or neo-Freudians[12]—is a defense not only of force and sexual terrorism, but of the subordination of women. Sexual liberation in the liberal sense frees male sexual aggression in the feminist sense. What looks like love and romance in the liberal view looks a lot like hatred and torture in the feminist view. Pleasure and eroticism become violation. Desire appears as lust for dominance and submission. The vulnerability of women's projected sexual availability—that acting we are allowed: Asking to be acted upon—is victimization. Play conforms to scripted roles, fantasy expresses ideology—is not exempt from it—and admiration of natural physical beauty becomes objectification.

The experience of the (overwhelmingly) male audiences who consume pornography[13] is therefore not fantasy or simulation or catharsis[14] but sexual reality: the level of reality on which sex itself largely operates. To understand this, one does not have to notice that pornography models are real women to whom something real is being done,[15] nor does one have to inquire into the systematic infliction of pornographic sexuality upon women,[16] although it helps. The aesthetic of pornography itself, the *way* it provides what those who consume it want, is itself the evidence. When uncensored explicit—that is, the most pornographic—pornography tells all, all means what a distanced detached observer would report about who did what to whom. This is the turn-on. Why does observing sex objectively presented cause the male viewer to experience his own sexuality? Because his eroticism is, socially, a watched thing. . . . It is not that life and art imitate each other; in sexuality, they *are* each other.

The law of obscenity,[17] the state's primary approach[18] to its version of the pornography question, has literally nothing in common with this feminist critique. Their obscenity is not our pornography. One commentator has said, "Obscenity is not suppressed primarily for the protection of others. Much of it is suppressed for the purity of the 'community.' Obscenity, at bottom, is not a crime. Obscenity is a sin."[19] This is, on one level, literally accurate. Men are turned on by obscenity, including its suppression, the same way they are by sin. Animated by morality from the male standpoint, in which violation—of women and rules—is eroticized, obscenity law can be seen to proceed according to the interest of male power, robed in gender-neutral good and evil.

Morality in its specifically liberal form (although, as with most dimensions of male dominance, the distinction between left and right is more formal than substantive) revolves around a set of parallel distinctions that can be consistently traced through obscenity law. Even though the approach this law takes to the problem it envisions has shifted over time, its fundamental norms remain consistent: Public is opposed to private, in parallel with ethics and morality, and factual is opposed to valued determinations. Under male supremacy, these distinctions are gender-based: Female is private, moral, valued, subjective; male is public, ethical, factual, objective.[20] If such gendered concepts are constructs of the male experience, imposed from the male standpoint on society as a whole, liberal morality expresses male supremacist politics. That is, discourse conducted in terms of good and evil that does not expose the gendered foundations of these concepts proceeds oblivious to—and serves to disguise—the position of power that underlies, and is furthered by, that discourse. . . .

Reexamining the law of obscenity in light of the feminist critique of pornography that has become possible, it becomes clear that male morality sees as good that which maintains its power and sees as evil that which undermines or qualifies it or questions its absoluteness. Differences in the law over time—such as the liberalization of obscenity doctrine—reflect either changes in the group of men in power or shifts in their perceptions of the best strategy for maintaining male supremacy—probably some of both. But it must be made to work. The outcome, descriptively analyzed, is that obscenity law prohibits what it sees as immoral, which from a feminist standpoint tends to be relatively harmless, while protecting what it sees as moral, which from a feminist standpoint is often that which is damaging to women. So it, too, is a politics, only covertly so. What male morality finds evil, meaning threatening to its power, feminist politics tends to find comparatively harmless. What feminist politics identifies as central in our subordination—the erotization of dominance and submission—male morality tends to find comparatively harmless or defends as affirmatively valuable, hence protected speech.

In 1973 obscenity under law came to mean that which 'the average person applying contemporary community standards' would find that, . . .

taken as a whole, appeals to the prurient interest . . . [which] depicts or describes, in a patently offensive way, sexual conduct specifically defined by the applicable state law; and [which], taken as a whole, lacks serious literary, artistic, political, or scientific value."[21] Feminism doubts whether the average person, gender neutral, exists; has more questions about the content and process of definition of community standards than about deviations from them; wonders why prurience counts but powerlessness doesn't; why sensibilities are better protected from offense than women are from exploitation; defines sexuality, hence its violation and expropriation, more broadly than does any state law and wonders why a body of law that can't in practice tell rape from intercourse should be entrusted with telling pornography from anything less. The law of obscenity says that intercourse on street corners is not legitimized by the fact that the persons are "simultaneously engaged in a valid political dialogue."[22] But, in a feminist light, one sees that the requirement that a work be considered "as a whole" legitimizes something very like that on the level of publications like *Playboy.*[23] Experimental evidence is beginning to support what victims have long known: Legitimate settings diminish the injury perceived as done to the women whose trivialization and objectification it contextualizes.[24] Besides, if a woman is subjected, why should it matter that the work has other value?[25] Perhaps what redeems a work's value among men *enhances* its injury to women. Existing standards of literature, art, science, and politics are, in feminist light, remarkably consonant with pornography's mode, meaning, and message. Finally and foremost, a feminist approach reveals that although the content and dynamic of pornography are about women—about the sexuality of women, about women as sexuality—in the same way that the vast majority of "obscenities" refer specifically to women's bodies, our invisibility has been such that the law of obscenity has *never even considered pornography a women's issue.*[26]. . .

. . . [T]he law of obscenity has the same surface theme and the same underlying theme as pornography itself. Superficially both involve morality: rules made and transgressed for purposes of sexual arousal. Actually, both are about power, about the equation between the erotic and the control of women by men: *women* made and transgressed for purposes of sexual arousal. It seems essential to the kick of pornography that it be to some degree against the rules, but it is never truly unavailable or truly illegitimate. Thus obscenity law, like the law of rape, preserves the value of, without restricting the ability to get, that which it purports to both devalue and to prohibit. Obscenity law helps keep pornography sexy by putting state power—force, hierarchy—behind its purported prohibition on what men can have sexual access to. The law of obscenity is to pornography as pornography is to sex: a map that purports to be a mirror, a legitimization and authorization and set of directions and guiding controls that project themselves onto social reality while claiming merely to reflect the image of what is already there. Pornography presents itself as fantasy or illusion or idea, which can be good or bad as it is accurate or inaccurate, while it actually, *hence accurately,* distributes power. Liberal morality cannot deal with illusions that *constitute* reality because its theory of reality, lacking a substantive critique of the distribution of social power, cannot get behind the empirical world, truth by correspondence. On the surface, both pornography and the law of obscenity are about sex. In fact, it is the status of women that is at stake.

CRITICAL-THINKING QUESTIONS

1. According to MacKinnon, how does pornography involve constructing a definition of masculinity and femininity? What does it mean to suggest that reality is "gendered"?
2. What is the conventional understanding of pornography as a moral issue? Why does MacKinnon reject that as incorrect, as a male

supremacy analysis, and as inconsistent with the political goals of feminism?

3. Based on a reading of MacKinnon's article, why do conservatives often criticize feminism for "politicizing" everyday life?

NOTES

Many of the ideas in this essay were developed and refined in close collaboration with Andrea Dworkin. It is difficult at times to distinguish the contribution of each of us to a body of work that—through shared teaching, writing, speaking, organizing, and political action on every level—has been created together. I have tried to credit specific contributions that I am aware are distinctly hers. This text is mine; she does not necessarily agree with everything in it.

1. This speech as a whole is intended to communicate what I mean by pornography. The key work on the subject is Andrea Dworkin, *Pornography: Men Possessing Women* (1981). No definition can convey the meaning of a word as well as its use in context can. However, what Andrea Dworkin and I mean by pornography is rather well captured in our legal definition: "Pornography is the graphic sexually explicit subordination of women, whether in pictures or in words, that also includes one or more of the following: (1) women are presented dehumanized as sexual objects, things, or commodities; or (2) women are presented as sexual objects who enjoy pain or humiliation; or (3) women are presented as sexual objects who experience sexual pleasure in being raped; or (4) women are presented as sexual objects tied up or cut up or mutilated or bruised or physically hurt; or (5) women are presented in postures of sexual submission, servility, or display; or (6) women's body parts—including but not limited to vaginas, breasts, and buttocks—are exhibited, such that women are reduced to those parts; or (7) women are presented as whores by nature; or (8) women are presented being penetrated by objects or animals; or (9) women are presented in scenarios of degradation, injury, torture, shown as filthy or inferior, bleeding, bruised, or hurt in a context that makes these conditions sexual." Pornography also includes "the use of men, children, or transsexuals in the place of women." Pornography, thus defined, is discrimination on the basis of sex and, as such, a civil rights violation. This definition is a slightly modified version of the one passed by the Minneapolis City Council on December 30, 1983. Minneapolis, Minn., Ordinance amending Tit. 7, chs. 139 and 141, Minneapolis Code of Ordinances Relating to Civil Rights (Dec. 30, 1983). The ordinance was vetoed by the mayor, reintroduced, passed again, and vetoed again in 1984.

2. "Congress shall make no law . . . abridging the freedom of speech, or of the press . . ." U.S. Const. amend. I.

3. The sense in which I mean women's perspective as different from men's is like that of Virginia Woolf's reference to "the difference of view, the difference of standard" in her "George Eliot," 1 *Collected Essays* 204 (1966). Neither of us uses the notion of a gender difference to refer to something biological or natural or transcendental or existential. Perspective parallels standards because the social experience of gender is confined by gender. *See* Catharine A. MacKinnon, *Sexual Harassment of Working Women,* 107–41 (1979) . . . ; Virginia Woolf, *Three Guineas* (1938); *see also* Andrea Dworkin, "The Root Cause," in *Our Blood: Essays and Discourses on Sexual Politics,* 96 (1976). I do not refer to the gender difference here descriptively, leaving its roots and implications unspecified, so they could be biological, existential, transcendental, in any sense inherent, or social but necessary. I mean "point of view" as a view, hence a standard, that is imposed on women by force of sex inequality, which is a political condition. "Male," which is an adjective here, is a social and political concept, not a biological attribute; it is a status socially conferred upon a person because of a condition of birth. As I use "male," it has nothing whatever to do with inherency, preexistence, nature, inevitability, or body as such. Because it is in the interest of men to be male in the system we live under (male being powerful as well as human), they seldom question its rewards or even see it as a status at all.

4. Criminal Code, Can. Rev. Stat. chap. c-34, § 159(2)(c) and (d)(1970). People v. Sanger, 222 N.Y. 192, 118 N.E. 637 (1918).

5. *The Report of the Commission on Obscenity and Pornography* (1970) (majority report). The accuracy of the commission's findings is called into question by: (1) widespread criticism of the commission's methodology from a variety of perspectives, e.g., L. Sunderland, *Obscenity—The Court, the Congress and the President's Commission* (1975); Edward Donnerstein, "Pornography Commission Revisited: Aggression—Erotica and Violence against Women," 39 *Journal of Personality and Social Psychology* 269 (1980); Ann Garry, "Pornography and Respect for Women," 4 *Social Theory and Practice* 395 (Summer 1978); Irene Diamond, "Pornography and Repression," 5 *Signs: A Journal of Women in Culture and Society* 686 (1980); Victor Cline, "Another View: Pornography Effects, the State of the Art," in *Where Do You Draw the Line?* (V.B. Cline, ed. 1974); Pauline Bart and Margaret Jozsa, "Dirty Books, Dirty Films, and Dirty Data," in *Take Back the Night: Women on Pornography* 204 (Laura Lederer, ed. 1982); (2) the commission's tendency to minimize the significance of its own findings, *e.g.,* those by Donald Mosher on the differential effects of exposure by gender, and (3) the design of the commission's research. The commission did not focus on questions about gender, did its best to eliminate "violence" from its materials (so as not to overlap with the Violence Commission), and propounded unscientific theories such as Puritan guilt to explain women's negative responses to the materials.

Further, scientific causality is unnecessary to legally validate an obscenity regulation: "But, it is argued, there is no scientific data which conclusively demonstrate that exposure to obscene materials adversely affects men and women or their society. It is [urged] that, absent such a demonstration, any kind of state regulation is 'impermissible.' *We reject this argument.* It is not for us to resolve empirical uncertainties underlying state legislation, save in the exceptional case where that legislation plainly impinges upon rights protected by the Constitution itself. . . . Although there is no conclusive proof of a connection between antisocial behavior and obscene material, the legislature of Georgia could quite reasonably determine that such a connection does or might exist" Paris Adult Theatre I v. Slaton, 413 U.S. 49, 60–61 (1973) (Burger, J., for the majority) (emphasis added); see also Roth v. U.S., 354 U.S. 476, 501 (1957).

6. Some of the harm of pornography to women, as defined in note 1. . . , and as discussed in this talk, has been documented in empirical studies. Recent studies have found that exposure to pornography increases the willingness of normal men to aggress against women under laboratory conditions; makes both women and men substantially less able to perceive accounts of rape as accounts of rape; makes normal men more closely resemble convicted rapists psychologically; increases attitudinal measures that are known to correlate with rape, such as hostility toward women, propensity to rape, condoning rape, and predictions that one would rape or force sex on a woman if one knew one would not get caught; and produces other attitude changes in men, such as increasing the extent of their trivialization, dehumanization, and objectification of women. Diana E. H. Russell, "Pornography and Violence: What Does the New Research Say?" in Lederer, note [5] . . . , at 216; Neil M. Malamuth and Edward Donnerstein, eds., *Pornography and Sexual Aggression* (1984); Dolph Zillman, *The Connection between Sex and Aggression* (1984); J. V. P. Check, N. Malamuth, and R. Stille, "Hostility to Women Scale" (1983) (unpublished manuscript); Edward Donnerstein, "Pornography: Its Effects on Violence against Women," in Malamuth and Donnerstein, eds., *Pornography and Sexual Aggression* (1984); Neil M. Malamuth and J. V. P. Check, "The Effects of Mass Media Exposure on Acceptance of Violence against Women: A Field Experiment," 15 *Journal of Research in Personality* 436 (1981); Neil M. Malamuth, "Rape Proclivities among Males," 37 *Journal of Social Issues* 138 (1981); Neil M. Malamuth and Barry Spinner, "A Longitudinal Content Analysis of Sexual Violence in the Best-Selling Erotic Magazines," 16 *Journal of Sex Research* 226 (1980); Mosher, "Sex Callousness Towards Women," in 8 *Technical Report of the Commission on Obscenity and Pornography* 313 (1971); Dolph Zillman and J. Bryant, "Effects of Massive Exposure to Pornography," in Malamuth and Donnerstein, eds., *Pornography and Sexual Aggression* (1984).

7. The following are illustrative, not exhaustive, of the body of work I term the "feminist critique of pornography." Andrea Dworkin, note 1 . . . ; Dorchen Leidholdt, "Where Pornography Meets Fascism," *Win* (Mar. 15, 1983) at 18; George Steiner, "Night Words," in *The Case Against Pornography,* 227 (D. Holbrook, ed. 1973); Susan Brownmiller, *Against Our Will: Men, Women and Rape,* 394 (1975); Robin Morgan, "Pornography and Rape: Theory and Practice," in *Going Too Far,* 165 (Robin Morgan, ed. 1977); Kathleen Barry, *Female Sexual Slavery* (1979); *Against SadoMasochism: A Radical Feminist Analysis* (R. R. Linden, D. R. Pagano, D. E. H. Russell, and S. L. Star, eds. 1982), especially chapters by Ti-Grace Atkinson, Judy Butler, Andrea Dworkin, Alice Walker, John Stoltenberg, Audre Lorde, and Susan Leigh Star; Alice Walker, "Coming Apart," in Lederer, *Take Back the Night,* note [5] . . . , and other articles in that volume with the exception of the legal ones; Gore Vidal, "Women's Liberation Meets the Miller-Mailer-Manson Man," in *Homage to Daniel Shays: Collected Essays 1952–1972,* 389 (1972); Linda Lovelace and Michael McGrady, *Ordeal* (1980). Works basic to the perspective taken here are Kate Millett, *Sexual Politics* (1969) and Florence Rush, *The Best-Kept Secret: Sexual Abuse of Children* (1980). "Violent Pornography: Degradation of Women versus Right of Free Speech," 8 *New York University Review of Law and Social Change,* 181 (1978) contains both feminist and nonfeminist arguments.

8. [For more extensive discussions of this subject, *see* my prior work, especially "Feminism, Marxism, Method and the State: An Agenda for Theory," 7 *Signs: Journal of Women in Culture and Society* 515 (1982)], [hereinafter cited as *Signs* I].

9. Susan Griffin, *Pornography and Silence: Culture's Revenge against Nature* (1981), pp. 2–4, 251–65.

10. Dworkin, note 1.

11. *See also* Dworkin, note [3]. . . .

12. The position that pornography is sex—that [whenever] you think of sex you think of pornography—underlies nearly every treatment of the subject. In particular, nearly every nonfeminist treatment proceeds on the implicit or explicit assumption, argument, criticism, or suspicion that pornography is sexually liberating in some way, a position unifying an otherwise diverse literature. *See, e.g.,* D. H. Lawrence, "Pornography and Obscenity," in his *Sex, Literature and Censorship* 64 (1959); Hugh Hefner, "The Playboy Philosophy," *Playboy* (Dec. 1962), at 73, and *Playboy* (Feb. 1963), at 43; Henry Miller, "Obscenity and the Law of Reflection," in his *Remember to Remember,* 274, 286 (1947); Deirdre English, "The Politics of Porn: Can Feminists Walk the Line?" *Mother Jones* (April 1980), at 20; Jean Bethke Elshtain, "The Victim Syndrome: A Troubling Turn in Feminism," *The Progressive* (June 1982), at 42. To choose an example at random: "In opposition to the Victorian view that narrowly defines proper sexual function in a rigid way that is analogous to ideas of excremental regularity and moderation, pornography builds a model of plastic variety and joyful excess in sexuality. In opposition to the sorrowing Catholic dismissal of sexuality as an unfortunate and spiritually superficial concomitant of propagation, pornography affords the alternative idea of the independent status of sexuality as a profound and shattering ecstasy." David Richards, "Free Speech and Obscenity Law: Toward a Moral Theory of the First Amendment," 123 *University of Pennsylvania Law Review,* 45, 81 (1974) (footnotes omitted). *See also* F. Schauer, "Response: Pornography and the First Amendment," 40 *University of Pittsburgh Law Review,* 605, 616 (1979).

13. Spending time around adult bookstores, attending pornographic movies, and talking with pornographers (who, like all smart pimps, do some form of market research), as

well as analyzing the pornography itself in sex/gender terms, all confirm that pornography is for men. That women may attend or otherwise consume it does not make it any less for men, any more than the observation that mostly men consume pornography means that pornography does not harm women. *See* Martha Langelan, "The Political Economy of Pornography," *Aegis: Magazine on Ending Violence against Women* (Autumn 1981), at 5; J. Cook, "The X-Rated Economy," *Forbes* (Sept. 18, 1978), at 60. Personal observation reveals that most women tend to avoid pornography as much as possible—which is not very much, as it turns out.

14. The "fantasy" and "catharsis" hypotheses, together, assert that pornography cathects sexuality on the level of fantasy fulfillment. The work of Edward Donnerstein, particularly, shows that the opposite is true. The more pornography is viewed, the *more* pornography—and the more brutal pornography—is both wanted and required for sexual arousal. What occurs is not catharsis, but desensitization, requiring progressively more potent stimulation. See works cited note [6] . . . ; Murray Straus, "Leveling, Civility, and Violence in the Family," 36 *Journal of Marriage & The Family* (1974), 13.

15. Lovelace and McGrady, note [7] . . . , provides an account by one coerced pornography model. *See also* Andrea Dworkin, "Pornography's 'Exquisite Volunteers,' " *Ms.* (March 1981), at 65.

16. However, for one such inquiry, see Russell, note [6]. . . , at 228: A random sample of 930 San Francisco households found that 10 percent of women had at least once "been upset by anyone trying to get you to do what they'd seen in pornographic pictures, movies or books." Obviously, this figure could only include those who knew that the pornography was the source of the sex, so this finding is conservative. *See also* Diana E. H. Russell, *Rape in Marriage,* 27–41 (1983) (discussing the data base). The hearings Andrea Dworkin and I held for the Minneapolis City Council on the ordinance cited in note 1 produced many accounts of the use of pornography to force sex on women and children. *Public Hearings on Ordinances to Add Pornography as Discrimination against Women,* Committee on Government Operations, City Council, Minneapolis, Minn., Dec. 12–13, 1983. (Hereinafter cited as *Hearings.*)

17. To body of law ably encompassed and footnoted by William Lockhart and Robert McClure, "Literature, the Law of Obscenity and the Constitution," 38 *Minnesota Law Review,* 295 (1954) and "Censorship of Obscenity," 45 *Minnesota Law Review,* 5 (1960), I add only the most important cases since then: Stanley v. Georgia, 394 U.S. 557 (1969); U.S. v. Reidel, 402 U.S. 351 (1970); Miller v. California, 413 U.S. 15 (1973); Paris Adult Theatre I v. Slaton, 413 U.S. 49 (1973); Hamling v. U.S., 418 U.S. 87 (1973); Jenkins v. Georgia, 418 U.S. 153 (1973); U.S. v. 12 200-Ft. Reels of Super 8mm Film, 413 U.S. 123 (1973); Erznoznik v. City of Jacksonville, 422 U.S. 205 (1975); Splawn v. California, 431 U.S. 595 (1976); Ward v. Illinois, 431 U.S. 767 (1976); Lovisi v. Slayton, 539 F.2d 349 (4th Cir. 1976). *See also* New York v. Ferber, 458 U.S. 747 (1982).

18. For a discussion of the role of the law of privacy in supporting the existence of pornography, see Ruth Colker, "Pornography and Privacy: Towards the Development of a Group Based Theory for Sex Based Intrusions of Privacy," 1 *Law and Inequality: A Journal of Theory and Practice* (1983), 191.

19. Louis Henkin, "Morals and the Constitution: The Sin of Obscenity," 63 *Columbia Law Review,* 391, 395 (1963).

20. These parallels are discussed more fully in *Signs* II. It may seem odd to denominate "moral" as *female* here, since this article discusses male morality. Under male supremacy, men define things; I am describing that. Men define women *as* "moral." This is the male view of women. My analysis, a feminist critique of the male standpoint, terms "moral" the concept that pornography is about good and evil. This is *my* analysis of *them,* as contrasted with their attributions to women.

21. Miller v. California, 413 U.S. 15, 24 (1973).

22. Paris Adult Theatre I v. Slaton, 413 U.S. 49, 67 (1973). *See also* Miller v. California, 413 U.S. 15, 25 n.7 ("A quotation from Voltaire in the flyleaf of a book will not constitutionally redeem an otherwise obscene publication," quoting Kois v. Wisconsin, 408 U.S. 229, 231 [1972]).

23. Penthouse International v. McAuliffe, 610 F.2d 1353, 1362–73 (5th Cir. 1980). For a study in enforcement, *see* Coble v. City of Birmingham, 389 So.2d 527 (Ala. Ct. App. 1980).

24. Malamuth and Spinner, note [6] . . . (". . . the portrayal of sexual aggression within such 'legitimate' magazines as *Playboy* and *Penthouse* may have a greater impact than similar portrayals in hard-core pornography"); Neil M. Malamuth and Edward Donnerstein, "The Effects of Aggressive-Pornographic Mass Media Stimuli," 15 *Advances in Experimental Social Psychology* (1982), 103, 130.

25. Some courts, under the obscenity rubric, seem to have understood that the quality of artistry does not undo the damage. People v. Mature Enterprises, 343 N.Y.S.2d 911, 925 n. 14(N.Y. Sup. 1973) ("This court will not adopt a rule of law which states that obscenity is suppressible but that well-written or technically well produced obscenity is not," quoting, in part, People v. Fritch, 13 N.Y.2d 119, 126, 243 N.Y.S.2d, 1, 7, 192 N.E.2d 713 [1963]). More to the point of my argument here is Justice O'Connor's observation that "[t]he compelling interests identified in today's opinion . . . suggest that the Constitution might in fact permit New York to ban knowing distribution of works depicting minors engaged in explicit sexual conduct, regardless of the social value of the depictions. For example, a twelve-year-old child photographed while masturbating surely suffers the same psychological harm whether the community labels the photograph 'edifying' or 'tasteless.' The audience's appreciation of the depiction is simply irrelevant to New York's asserted interest in protecting children from psychological, emotional, and mental harm." New York v. Ferber, 458 U.S. 747, 774–75 (1982) (concurring). Put another way, how does it make a harmed child *not harmed* that what was produced by harming him is great art?

26. Women typically get mentioned in obscenity law only in the phrase, "women and men," used as a synonym for "people." At the same time, exactly who the victim of pornography is, has long been a great mystery. The few references to "exploitation" in obscenity litigation do not evoke a woman victim. For example, one reference to "a system of commercial exploitation of people with sadomasochistic sexual aberrations" concerned the customers of women dominatrixes, all of whom were men. State v. Von Cleef, 102 N.J. Super. 104, 245 A.2d 495, 505 (1968). The children at issue in *Ferber* were boys. Similarly, Justice Frankfurter invoked the "sordid exploitation of man's nature and impulses" in discussing his conception of pornography in Kingsley Pictures Corp. v. Regents, 360 U.S. 684, 692 (1958).

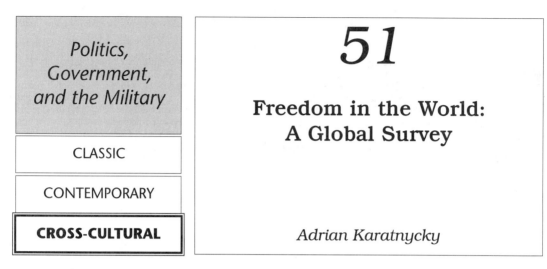

Politics, Government, and the Military

CLASSIC

CONTEMPORARY

CROSS-CULTURAL

51

Freedom in the World: A Global Survey

Adrian Karatnycky

This selection, prepared by the president of Freedom House, a human rights organization, provides a look at the extent of political freedom in the world during 1998–1999. Although the trend is positive, one-third of the world's people live without basic political rights.

MORE FREE COUNTRIES THAN EVER

Despite a year that saw violent civil war in the Republic of the Congo, attempts at ethnic cleansing in Kosovo, ethnic and political violence in Indonesia, and severe economic turbulence in many of the world's emerging markets, freedom made significant strides in 1998. As the year drew to a close, 88 of the world's 191 countries (46 percent) were rated as Free, meaning that they maintain a high degree of political and economic freedom and respect basic civil liberties. This was the largest number of Free countries on record, and represented a net gain of seven from last year—the second-largest increase in the twenty-six year history of the *Survey*. Another 53 countries (28 percent of the world total) were rated as Partly Free, enjoying more limited political rights and civil liberties, often in a context of corruption, weak rule of law, ethnic strife, or civil war. This represented a drop of four from the previous year. Finally, 50 countries (26 percent of the world total) that deny their citizens basic rights and civil liberties were rated as Not Free. This represented a drop of three from the previous year.

There were seven new entrants into the ranks of Free countries in 1998, including India, which had been rated as Partly Free since 1991, a year that saw the killing of former prime minister Rajiv Gandhi, intense labor strife, and an escalation of intercommunal violence resulting in thousands of deaths. India's return to the ranks of Free countries was the consequence of greater internal stability, fewer instances of intercommunal violence, and the peaceful democratic transfer of power to an opposition-led government. Other entrants into the ranks of Free countries were the Dominican Republic, where a democratically elected government has made efforts to strengthen the administration of jus-

Source: From *Freedom in the World: The Annual Survey of Political Rights and Civil Liberties, 1998–1999*, ed. Adrian Karatnycky (New York: Freedom House, 1999). Reprinted by permission of Freedom House.

FREEDOM IN THE WORLD, 1998–1999

The population of the world this year is estimated at 5,908.7 billion persons, who reside in 191 sovereign states and 61 related and disputed territories—a total of 252 entities. The level of political rights and civil liberties as shown comparatively by the Freedom House Survey is:

Free: 2,354.0 billion (39.84 percent of the world's population) live in 88 of the states and in 44 of the related and/or disputed territories.

Partly Free: 1,570.6 billion (26.59 percent of the world's population) live in 53 of the states and 4 of the related and/or disputed territories.

Not Free: 1,984.1 billion (33.58 percent of the world's population) live in 50 of the states and 13 of the related and/or disputed territories.

A Record of the Survey
(population in billions)

Survey Date		*Free*	*Partly Free*	*Not Free*	*World Population*
January '81		1,613.0 (35.90%)	970.9 (21.60%)	1,911.9 (42.50%)	4,495.8
January '83		1,665.4 (36.32%)	918.8 (20.04%)	2,000.2 (43.64%)	4,584.1
January '85		1,671.4 (34.85%)	1,117.4 (23.30%)	2,007.0 (41.85%)	4,795.8
January '87		1,842.5 (37.10%)	1,171.5 (23.60%)	1,949.9 (39.30%)	4,963.9
January '89		1,992.8 (38.86%)	1,027.9 (20.05%)	2,107.3 (41.09%)	5,128.0
January '90		2,034.4 (38.87%)	1,143.7 (21.85%)	2,055.9 (39.28%)	5,234.0
January '91		2,088.2 (39.23%)	1,485.7 (27.91%)	1,748.7 (32.86%)	5,322.6
January '92	(a)	1,359.3 (25.29%)	2,306.6 (42.92%)	1,708.2 (31.79%)	5,374.2
January '93		1,352.2 (24.83%1	2,403.3 (44.11%)	1,690.4 (31.06%)	5,446.0
January '94		1,046.2 (19.00%)	2,224.4 (40.41%)	2,234.6 (40.59%)	5,505.2
January '95		1,119.7 (19.97%)	2,243.4 (40.01%)	2,243.9 (40.02%)	5,607.0
January '96		1,114.5 (19.55%)	2,365.8 (41.49%)	2,221.2 (38.96%)	5.701.5
January '97		1,250.3 (21.67%)	2,260.1 (39.16%)	2,260.6 (39.17%)	5,771.0
January '98		1,266.0 (21.71%)	2,281.9 (39.12%)	2,284.6 (39.17%)	5,832.5
January '99	(b)	2,354.0 (39.84%)	1,570.6 (26.59%)	1,984.1 (33.58%)	5,908.7

(a) The large shift in the population figure between 1991 and 1992 is due to India's change from Free to Partly Free.
(b) The large shift in the population figure between 1998 and 1999 is due to India's change from Partly Free to Free.

tice; Ecuador, which recently concluded free and fair elections; Nicaragua, where improved relations between civilian authorities and a military formerly dominated by the Sandinistas contributed to the strengthening of democratic stability and where greater attention was paid to the problems of indigenous peoples on the country's Atlantic coast; Papua New Guinea, which saw a January 1998 peace agreement put an end to a destabilizing nine-year secessionist rebellion on Bougainville Island; Slovakia, where free and fair elections brought to power a government dominated by reformers; and Thailand, where the government of Prime Minister Chuan Leekpai has fostered increasing political accountability.

In addition, three countries formerly ranked as Not Free—Indonesia, Nigeria, and Sierra Leone—made tangible progress and are now rated as Partly Free. In Indonesia, the downfall of Suharto has led to the reemergence of political parties and civic groups and the promise of free elections. Although the country's economic crisis has sparked ethnic violence targeting the Chinese minority (and some violence has occurred during student demonstrations), some political controls have loosened, political parties and movements have begun to gain strength, and the media have become more outspoken. In Nigeria, the death of military dictator Sani Abacha has led to a political opening that holds out the promise of multiparty elections and already has seen the reemergence of public debate, a resurgence of political parties, the return of exiled leaders, relatively free and fair local elections, and the rise of an increasingly vibrant press. In Sierra Leone, the defeat of a military coup has put an end to chaos and violence and restored power to the country's democratically elected civilian authorities.

The Global Trend

	Free	*Partly Free*	*Not Free*
1988–1989	61	39	68
1993–1994	72	63	55
1998–1999	88	53	50

Tracking Democracy

	Number of Democracies
1988–1989	69
1993–1994	108
1998–1999	117

MORE FREE PEOPLE THAN EVER

As a result of the gains in freedom in 1998—especially in India, the world's most populous democracy—2.354 billion people (40 percent of the world's population) now live in Free societies, 1.570 billion (26.5 percent) live in countries that are Partly Free, and 1.984 billion (33.5 percent) live in Not Free countries. The proportion of the world's population living in freedom is the highest in the history of the *Survey*.

In addition to these shifts from one category to another, the 1998 survey recorded more modest improvements in freedom in twenty-one countries. Not all trends for the year were positive. The survey registered more modest declines in freedom in ten countries. These changes are reflected by upward or downward arrows, signifying improvements or declines in a country's score on the freedom scale. One country which registered worrying trends was Argentina, which suffered from the destabilizing effects of political sex scandals and efforts to blackmail political leaders.

Thirteen countries were judged to be the world's most repressive and have received Freedom House's lowest rating: scores of 7 for political rights and 7 for civil liberties. In these states, basic political rights and civil liberties are nonexistent, there is no free press, and independent civic life is suppressed. The most repressive countries, the "world's worst" in terms of freedom, include Iraq, North Korea, Cuba, and Sudan. The others are Afghanistan, Burma, Equatorial Guinea, Libya, Saudi Arabia, Somalia, Syria, Turkmenistan, and Vietnam. It is notable that of the thirteen least free states, three are one-party Marxist-Leninist states and eight are predominantly Islamic. The number of countries that received Freedom House's lowest rating (7,7) has declined from twenty-one at the close of 1994.

The *Survey of Freedom* also found that at the end of 1998 there were 117 electoral democracies, representing over 61 percent of the world's countries and nearly 55 percent of its population. The Freedom House roster of electoral democracies is based on a stringent standard requiring that all elected national authority must be the product of free and fair electoral processes. Thus, in the estimation of the *Survey*, neither Mexico (whose 1997 national legislative elections were judged free and fair, but whose last national presidential elections failed to meet that standard) nor Malaysia (whose governing United Malays National Organization enjoys huge and unfair advantages in national elections) qualifies as an electoral democracy. After a period in which electoral democracies increased dramatically from 69 in 1987, their number has remained stagnant at 117 since 1995.

The survey team identified five events that represented important gains for freedom in 1988 and five which signaled setbacks for freedom.

THE 13 WORST RATED COUNTRIES

Afghanistan
Burma
Cuba
Equatorial Guinea
Iraq
Korea, North
Libya
Saudi Arabia
Somalia
Sudan
Syria
Turkmenistan
Vietnam

THE WORST RATED RELATED TERRITORY

Kosovo (Yugoslavia)

THE WORST RATED DISPUTED TERRITORY

Tibet (China)

TOP FIVE GAINS FOR FREEDOM IN 1998

1. NIGERIA: Developments have moved in a promising direction since the death of the tyrannical General Abacha, with many civil liberties restored, political parties legalized, and national elections pledged for 1999. A good omen was the holding of local elections which were deemed free and fair.

2. INDONESIA: President Suharto's resignation has been accompanied by indications of changes towards electoral democracy and enhanced civil liberties. On the negative side has been mounting violence against the Chinese minority and bloody clashes between students and the army.

3. CORRUPTION ALERT: The governments of the United States and other leading democracies, along with the World Bank, are focusing increased attention on the role of corruption in undermining political and economic reform in transitional societies. A positive sign: Demands for improvements in the rule of law are increasingly being incorporated into decisions on foreign assistance.

4. FREEDOM ON THE NET: Several years ago China and other authoritarian regimes announced plans to control the Internet's political content. Those efforts have failed. In the future, the Internet will play a growing role in linking democratic forces within repressive societies and in building a global network of freedom activists.

5. DICTATORS BEWARE: Both current and former dictators had reason for concern. Though controversial, the effort to bring General Pinochet to justice sent a chilling message to tyrants around the world. Yugoslavia's Milosevic was under increased pressure, Indonesia's Suharto resigned, and Congo's Kabila traveled abroad only after securing assurance that he would not be arrested.

TOP FIVE SETBACKS FOR FREEDOM IN 1998

1. RUSSIA: The assassination of democracy advocate Galina Staravoitova was the most tragic development in a bad year for Russian reformers. With President Yeltsin enfeebled, a coalition of neo-Communists and hardline nationalists gained increased influence, and succeeded in bringing down a reformist government. A new government, dominated by former Communists, made little progress in stemming corruption or reviving the economy.

2. MALAYSIA: President Mahathir Mohamad responded to his country's economic decline in all the wrong ways: repressing political critics, tightening political control, and placing restrictions on the economy. Here is a prime example of everything that is wrong with "Asian values."

*3. **CONGO:*** Events moved from bad to worse in the Democratic Republic of Congo. President Kabila showed no sign of relaxing his repressive policies. Much of the country remained contested territory, with forces from a half dozen African nations pillaging the countryside and terrorizing the populace.

*4. **RELIGIOUS PERSECUTION:*** The persecution of religious minorities, especially Christians, remained a serious problem in a number of countries. Among the worst violators: Pakistan, Egypt, China, and Iran. Persecution was most serious in Sudan, where Christians and animists in the southern regions were killed, starved, and forced into exile by forces of the Moslem North.

*5. **NUCLEAR PROLIFERATION:*** The detonation of nuclear devices by India and Pakistan was a jolting reminder of the menace still posed by weapons of mass destruction. Other reasons to worry included Iraq's determination to rebuild its nuclear, chemical, and biological arsenal, North Korea's nuclear saber-rattling, and the role of Russian scientists in the development of weapons for Iran and other states.

ELECTORAL DEMOCRACY AND FREEDOM

Despite the emergence of electoral democracy as the world's predominant form of government, major violations of human rights and civil liberties remain the norm in a majority of countries containing some three-fifths of the world's population. This disjunction arises from the fact that many electoral democracies fall short of being Free. In an influential 1997 article in *Foreign Affairs*, Fareed Zakaria drew on Freedom House data underlining this fact to suggest that the world had entered an era characterized by "The Rise of Illiberal Democracy." Yet there are signs that electoral democracy eventually does have a positive effect on freedom. Particularly notable in the 1998 *Survey* was the growing respect for civil liberties in a number of electoral democracies. In fact, it appears that the trend to which political scientists were pointing had peaked in the first half of the 1990s—a period of rapid democratic expansion in the wake of the collapse of Marxist-Leninist regimes.

Freedom House's most current data suggest that, as the 1990s draw toward a close, we are observing a decline in the number of "illiberal democracies" and an increase in the number and proportion of the world's electoral democracies that are also liberal (i.e., Free) democracies. In 1995, for example, the *Survey* found there were 117 electoral democracies, of which 76 were rated Free (64.9 percent), 40 were judged to be Partly Free (over 34 percent), and one—war-ravaged Bosnia-Herzegovina—was Not Free. Today, out of 117 electoral democracies, 88 (over 75 percent) are Free, while the remaining 29 are Partly Free.

Since 1995, the electoral democracies that have seen a deepening climate of respect for political rights and civil liberties and thus have entered the ranks of Free countries include the Dominican Republic, El Salvador, Honduras, India, Mali, Nicaragua, Papua New Guinea, the Philippines, Romania, Taiwan, and Thailand. These gains have been partly offset by setbacks in some formerly Free electoral democracies, for a net gain of ten Free countries. Ecuador, Slovakia, and Venezuela have oscillated between the Free and Partly Free categories since 1995.

While electoral democracy allows space to emerge for competing political interests and holds out the promise of greater freedom and respect for human rights, the record of some electoral democracies remains marred by political restrictions and violations of civil liberties. Not all these Partly Free democracies suffer from an identical set of problems: Some have weak governments incapable of guaranteeing basic civil liberties in the face of violent political movements (Colombia and Georgia); others must contend with powerful and politically influential militaries (Turkey and Paraguay), or: internal security forces that can act with impunity (Brazil). Some are plagued by powerful oligarchic forces and/or the weak rule of law (Russia and Ukraine); in other cases, democratically elected leaders seek to centralize their power or to exercise power arbitrarily. Yet these phenomena should not obscure the overall global record: Most democratically elected leaders function within the context of effective checks and balances on their power, and most are able to marshal democratic legitimacy in their efforts to govern effectively and responsibly.

At the close of 1998, the Partly Free democracies were twenty-nine in number. The record of the *Survey* in recent years shows that precisely these flawed, Partly Free electoral democracies hold the greatest potential for the expansion of freedom. For where there is free electoral competition among political parties, there is also the possibility for open criticism of government policies and the airing of alternative viewpoints. Many new democracies are just beginning the arduous process of institutionalizing the rule of law; creating a vibrant civil society; instituting procedures that protect minority rights; fostering a sense of moderation and tolerance among competing political forces; developing economically and politically independent broadcast media; and ensuring effective civilian control over the police and the military. All this takes time. It should therefore come as no surprise that most new democracies make more rapid progress in the areas of political processes and political rights than in the area of civil liberties. Nonetheless, though complete freedom may be long in coming, citizens of Partly Free electoral democracies can at least engage in serious debate over public policy—a right rarely, if ever, enjoyed in non-democratic regimes. Some critics have suggested that electoral democracy leads to bad governance, increases instability, places ethnic minorities at peril and legitimizes efforts to suppress political opponents. But the record suggests otherwise. There are eighty-eight electoral democracies that successfully protect a broad range of political and civil rights. Moreover, even the twenty-nine electoral democracies that Freedom House rates as only Partly Free are not states that brutally suppress basic freedoms. Rather, they are generally countries in which civic institutions are weak, poverty is rampant, and intergroup tensions are acute. This is not surprising, as many such fragile democracies are emerging from protracted periods of intense civil strife, and some are building new states.

The *Survey* shows evidence of improvements in civil liberties in countries that had previously established democratic electoral practices. This sequence makes sense because free and fair elections take less time to implement than the more complex processes that produce the rule of law and a strong civil society. As the Freedom House data suggest, illiberal democracy tends toward liberal democracy so long as there is internal or external pressure for further reform. Moreover, the regular transfer of power between competing political elites, or even the prospect of such a transfer, appears to improve the chances for the deepening of civil liberties.

Clearly, some Partly Free (or illiberal) democracies lack respect for the rule of law, checks and balances among the branches of government, and protections for the rights of minorities. It is also true that in some circumstances (especially in multiethnic settings) open electoral processes can be occasions for the emergence of political demagogy directed against ethnic minorities. Indeed, almost three in ten electoral democracies fail adequately to safeguard basic freedoms for these sorts of reasons. At the same time, the *Survey of Freedom* suggests that, over the last twenty years, the emergence of electoral democracies has been the best indicator of subsequent progress in the areas of civil liberties and human rights.

ETHNICITY AND NATIONALISM

The Freedom House data also suggest that countries without a predominant ethnic majority are less successful in establishing open and democratic societies than ethnically homogeneous countries. For the purposes of making this comparison, we define countries in which over two-thirds of the population belong to a single ethnic group as mono-ethnic, and those without such a two-thirds majority as multiethnic.

According to this definition, 66 of the 88 Free countries (75 percent) are mono-ethnic, while 22 (25 percent) are multiethnic. Of the 114 countries in the world that possess a dominant ethnic group, 66 (58 percent) are Free, 22 (19 percent) are Partly Free, and 26 (23 percent) are Not Free. By contrast, among multiethnic countries only 22 of 77 (29 percent) are Free, 31 (40 percent) are Partly Free, and 24 (31 percent) are Not Free. A mono-ethnic country, therefore, is twice as likely to be Free as a multiethnic one.

A similar pattern can be found among the 117 electoral democracies, which include 77 mono-ethnic and 40 multiethnic countries. Of the 77 mono-ethnic democracies, 66 (86 percent) are Free, and 11 (14 percent) are Partly Free. Among multiethnic democracies, 22 (55 percent) are Free and 18 are Partly Free (45 percent). Thus multiethnic democracies are nearly two-and-a-half times more likely to be only Partly Free than are mono-ethnic ones.

In the face of ethnic conflicts in Africa, the former Yugoslavia, and elsewhere, many analysts have recently focused on the destructive power of contemporary nationalism. Yet the fact that nation-states appear to provide the most durable basis for political freedom and respect for civil liberties deserves greater attention. At the same time, while the survey suggests that democracies are more likely to be Free if they do not face significant ethnic cleavages, there also is compelling evidence that multiethnic societies can preserve a broad array of political and civil freedoms. Successful multiethnic societies include established democracies like Canada, Belgium, and Switzerland, as well as such new democracies as Estonia, Latvia, Mali, Namibia, and South Africa. India's return to the ranks of Free countries is an indication that, even in an ethnically charged environment, it is possible for multiethnic societies to establish a climate and framework of significant respect for personal freedoms, the rule of law, and the rights of religious and ethnic minorities.

The set of forty multiethnic electoral democracies merits closer investigation. Are there common characteristics among the Free multiethnic democracies? Is there a significant correlation between certain patterns of population distribution in multiethnic societies and greater freedom? Are homogeneous concentrations of particular ethnic groups more or less conducive to stability and freedom? Is the dispersion of ethnic minorities throughout a country more compatible with democratic stability and the expansion of freedom? Do different forms of state organization contribute to a higher degree of freedom? Are federal arrangements more or less conducive to the development of freedom? When are federal arrangements successful and when do they provoke ethnic conflict or separatism? Under what circumstances do federal arrangements break down? What is the effect of external diasporas and the forces of irredentism on the political development of multiethnic states?

It is clear that in some settings political appeals based on ethnicity make it impossible for democratic systems that feature a regular transfer of power to function. Yet the example of numerous free and democratic multiethnic societies shows that it is possible to transcend ethnic appeals in politics, to avert the permanent disenfranchisement of ethnic minorities, and to establish durable democracies.

In the aftermath of the Cold War, nationalism has come to be identified with violence and intolerance. The *Survey* makes clear, however, that nation-states—many of which are the products of nationalist ideas of state organization—tend to be more compatible with stable democratic rule and political freedom. Indeed, in the 1980s and 1990s, most successful ethnic struggles for national self-determination and even nationhood have been peaceful, involving mass protests, independent civic organization, strikes, and other forms of opposition activity. In the former Soviet bloc, such activism contributed to the downfall of oppressive regimes and the creation of a number of free and democratic states. Where nationalism has led to violence and bloody warfare, another factor has often been present—that of irredentism.

In several instances, ethnic and national aspirations to autonomy or independence have received military support from neighboring nation-states ruled by the very ethnic group that is seeking sovereignty or separation. In such cases (for example, Bosnia's Serb Republic; ethnically Armenian Nagorno-Karabakh in Azerbaijan; the Transdniester Republic in Moldova; to a lesser but considerable degree, the Kosovo Liberation Army; and the Rwandan-aided rebellions in the Republic of the Congo), what is at work may be support provided by an existing state seeking to extend its borders rather than the aspiration to create a new nation-state.

REGIONAL VARIATIONS

Democracy and freedom have been on the upswing since the mid-1970s. Clearly, this trend has been visible across all continents and in most cultures, underscoring that human liberty and democracy are not Western constructs, but universal aspirations. Yet while the expansion of democracy and freedom has been global, it has not everywhere proceeded at the same pace. There have been important geographical and cultural variations that deserve attention and deeper understanding.

At the close of 1998, democracy and freedom are the dominant trends in Western and East-Central Europe, in the Americas, and increasingly in the Asian-Pacific region. In the former Soviet Union the picture is decidedly more mixed, with the growth of freedom stalled and a number of countries evolving into dictatorships. In Africa, too, Free societies and electoral democracies remain a distinct minority. Moreover, there are no democracies or Free societies within the Arab world, and few in other predominantly Muslim societies.

Of the 53 countries in Africa, 9 are Free (17 percent), 21 are Partly Free (40 percent) and 23 are Not Free (43 percent). Only 17 African countries (less than one-third) are electoral democracies. As of the end of 1998, Lesotho's democracy fell, while at the same time, the *Survey* noted positive trends in Nigeria and Sierra Leone.

In Asia, 19 of the region's 38 countries are Free (50 percent), 9 are Partly Free (24 percent), and 10 are Not Free (26 percent). Despite the looming presence of Communist China and the rhetoric of "Asian values," 24 (63 percent) of the region's polities are electoral democracies.

In East-Central Europe and the former USSR, there are growing signs of a deepening chasm. In Central Europe and parts of Eastern Europe, including the Baltic states, democracy and freedom prevail; in the former USSR, however, progress toward the emergence of open societies has stalled or failed. Overall, 19 of the 27 post-Communist countries of East-Central Europe and the former USSR are electoral democracies. Ten of the region's states are Free, 11 are Partly Free, and 6 are Not Free. Of the 12 non-Baltic former Soviet republics, 7 countries are Partly Free, 5 are Not Free, and none are Free.

Among the 35 countries in the Americas, 31 are electoral democracies. Twenty-five states are rated as Free, 9 are Partly Free, and 1—Cuba—is Not Free.

In the Middle East (excluding North Africa), the roots of democracy and freedom are weakest. In this region there is only one Free country, Israel; there are three Partly Free states, Jordan, Kuwait, and Turkey; and there are ten countries that are Not Free. Israel and Turkey are the region's only two electoral democracies.

Western Europe is the preserve of Free countries and democracies, with all twenty-four states both free and democratic.

In addition to these regional breakdowns, Freedom House has examined the state of freedom and democracy in the Arab world. Among the sixteen states with an Arab majority, there are no Free countries, Three predominantly Arab states—Jordan, Kuwait, and Morocco—are Partly Free. There are no electoral democracies in the Arab world.

The *Survey* also reveals some interesting patterns in the relationship between cultures and political development. While there are broad differences within civilizations, and while democracy and human rights find expression in a wide array of cultures and beliefs, the *Survey* shows some important variations in the relationship between religious belief or tradition and political freedom.

Of the eighty-eight countries that are rated Free, seventy-nine are majority Christian by tradition or belief. Of the nine Free countries that are not majority Christian, one is Israel, often considered part of a Judeo-Christian tradition, and two others, Mauritius and South Korea, have significant Christian communities representing at least a third of their population. Of the six remaining Free countries, Mali is predominantly Muslim; nearly half of Taiwan's population is Buddhist; Mongolia and Thailand are chiefly Buddhist; Japan has a majority that observes both Buddhist and Shinto traditions; and India is predominantly Hindu.

While seventy-nine of the eighty-eight Free countries are predominantly Christian, just eleven of the sixty-seven countries with the poorest record in terms of political rights and civil liberties are predominantly Christian. By this indicator, a predominantly Christian country is nearly five-and-a-half times as likely to be Free and democratic as it is to be repressive and non-democratic. There is also a strong correlation between electoral democracy and Hinduism (India, Mauritius, and Nepal), and there are a significant number of Free countries among traditionally Buddhist societies and societies in which Buddhism is the most widespread faith (Japan, Mongolia, Taiwan, and Thailand).

At the close of the twentieth century, the Islamic world remains most resistant to the spread of democracy and civil liberties, especially the Arab countries. Only one country with a Muslim majority—Mali—is Free, fourteen are Partly Free, and twenty-eight are Not Free. Six countries with a predominantly Muslim population are electoral democracies: Albania, Bangladesh, Kyrgyzstan, Mali, Pakistan, and Turkey. Yet the year's trends also showed that the Islamic world is not completely resistant to the expansion of freedom. There was limited progress in Indonesia, the world's most populous Islamic county, and in Nigeria, where half the population is Muslim, there was momentum toward a democratic political opening.

Although we tend to think of civilizations and cultures as fixed and stable entities, it should be kept in mind that political transformations within civilizations can spread rapidly. For example, before the Third Wave of democratization was launched in the 1970s, the majority of predominantly Catholic countries were tyrannies; they included Latin America's oligarchies and military dictatorships, East-Central Europe's Marxist-Leninist states, Iberia's authoritarian-corporalist systems, and the Philippine dictatorship of Ferdinand Marcos. Social scientists speculated about the influence that Catholicism's hierarchical system of church authority might have on Catholic attitudes toward politics. Today, of course, most Catholic countries have become Free and democratic, and some would argue that it was precisely the internal discipline of the Catholic church which made possible the rapid spread of pro-democratic values following Vatican II and under the papacy of John Paul II.

THE GLOBAL EXPANSION OF FREEDOM

The last quarter century has seen a rapid expansion of democratic governance along with a more gradual expansion of civil society and civil liberties. There is little question that the *Survey's* findings reflect significant gains for human freedom at the dawn of a new millennium. Still, many of the new electoral democracies and newly Free countries remain fragile, and political reversals cannot be excluded. Moreover, there appears to be little forward momentum for democratic change and freedom in many of the Not Free countries. In particular, there is little evidence of progress toward democracy in the Arab world and in the world's remaining Marxist-Leninist states.

The global expansion of political and civic freedoms has coincided with the expansion of market-based economies. Indeed, on the basis of the Freedom House *Survey* and parallel efforts to monitor and assess global economic change, there is growing empirical evidence of the links between economic freedom and political freedom.[1]

Not only does economic freedom help establish the conditions for political freedom by promoting the growth of prosperous middle and working classes, but successful market economies appear to require political freedom as a barrier against economic cronyism, rent seeking, and other anticompetitive and inefficient practices. Open and democratically accountable societies and economies have also shown themselves capable of weathering economic setbacks—a likely consequence of their political legitimacy (rooted in democratic accountability) and economic legitimacy (rooted in property rights). Moreover, while open societies are not immune to corruption scandals, they have strong instruments for combating graft and bribery, including a free press, the separation of powers, alternations in power between various political elites, and independent judicial systems.

While the *Survey* can be used to examine broad trends, it is important that such trends not be equated with iron laws of history or be interpreted one-dimensionally. For example, while the *Survey* findings show that liberal economic change at times leads to liberal political reform, there are also numerous other cases where political openings lead the way to economic liberalization. The more careful conclusion from an examination of the twenty-six year record of the *Survey* is that both trends manifest themselves in close proximity to one another. Opposition to the dominance of the state in economic life is usually accompanied by opposition to the dominance of the state in personal life and in the life of civil society. Certainly, there appears to be growing awareness of this relationship, as indicated by the growing emphasis on democracy promotion in the foreign assistance policies of the advanced industrial democracies, and by the stress on issues of good governance and effective anticorruption regimes by multilateral donors like the World Bank.

POLICY IMPLICATIONS

What challenges issue from the *Survey's* findings? What are the policy implications?

The Freedom House findings make it clear that the world is becoming more free. This trend is mainly the consequence of the strengthening of the rule of law, of improvements in civilian control over militaries and police, the successful management of divisive group conflicts, and the growing effectiveness of civil society.

Most of this progress toward respect for political rights and civil liberties is unfolding in countries which have already undergone more limited democratic openings. The *Survey* finds that such societies over time grow receptive to a further deepening of freedom. This suggests that U.S. and international efforts to promote democratic transitions and to give some priority to material and technical assistance to democratic regimes are having a positive effect. But it also means that most progress is occurring in already Partly Free countries. This year, only a small number of Not Free countries registered meaningful progress. Moreover, after a decade of the rapid expansion of electoral democracies, the number of democracies in 1998, 117, is the same as the figure for 1994.

Yet while there is an extremely active and intelligently conceived U.S. policy to promote democratic transitions once limited political openings have occurred, far fewer resources are being directed at promoting democratic openings in the most repressive societies. For example, USAID efforts in closed societies focus mainly on limited technical assistance in support of modest economic reforms, rather than on support for democratic forces in these closed societies. Moreover, USAID does not devote significant resources to promoting political openings in closed societies. Such efforts are primarily undertaken by the independent, Congressionally funded National Endowment for Democracy.

While the United States has something approaching a consistent policy with regard to several rogue and pariah states that also violate basic human rights on a massive scale—Burma, Cuba, Iran, Iraq, Libya, and North Korea specifically—that policy mainly seeks to isolate these countries, and few resources are devoted to efforts that might actively promote change within them.

In the cases of some of the world's most important countries in which basic freedoms are broadly suppressed, U.S. policy consists of occasional—and at times muted—criticism of human rights violations and general expectations that the forces of economic change and trade will somehow inevitably lead to improvements in political and civil liberties. Among the countries in which there is little effort to promote democratic change are China, Vietnam, and—with the exception of the Palestinian National Authority—the Arab world.

Admittedly, some of the world's most closed societies (for example, North Korea) may be impervious to U.S. and other efforts to promote democratic ideas and foster the emergence of democratic movements. But the example of the collapse of communism in Central and Eastern Europe shows that totalitarian societies cannot forever withstand the pressures of an increasingly open and interdependent world.

Moreover, new technologies and the force of modest market-oriented change in some of the most repressive countries suggest that the capacity of the state to exert day-to-day control over information and private life is lessening, even if repression of political dissent is not.

OPENING UP CLOSED SOCIETIES

A comprehensive strategy to open up closed societies should be developed in cooperation with the nongovernmental sector. The mission of USAID should be expanded to allow it to be more active in fostering the development of the nongovernmental sector in closed countries. Aid and assistance for radio broadcasting, book publishing, contact with independent civic forces, and the transfer of information through the Internet should be expanded.

PROTECTING AGAINST REVERSALS

While 1998 saw the expansion of freedom in many parts of the world, forward momentum appears to have stalled in the twelve non-Baltic former republics of the Soviet Union, including Russia and Ukraine. Setbacks for reform and the weakening of reformist voices is likely a temporary phenomenon. It should not be seen as a signal to scale back drastically U.S. engagement. Rather, it requires a more efficient and precise deployment of resources oriented around assisting reformers in their efforts to win the political battle of ideas.

Reversals of democratic progress should meet with active diplomatic and nongovernmental initiatives. In a period of some economic turmoil and social difficulties in transitional societies, the preservation of gains for civil liberties and political rights must be an urgent priority for U.S. policymakers and the international democratic community.

ECONOMIC FREEDOM AND POLITICAL LIBERTY

The economic crisis that rocked emerging markets in 1998 has not resulted in a reversal of progress toward greater political and economic freedom. Indeed, economic difficulties have not led to a worldwide resurgence of statism. On the contrary, economic failures have rightly been identified with a lack of transparency, cronyism, and corruption. In short, the case for a link between more open and democratically accountable government and economic success is gaining greater credence. The acknowledgment of such a relationship appears to have played a key role in the political openings in Indonesia and Nigeria. The ability of democratic states like the Philippines, Thailand, South Korea, and Brazil to implement policies to address the looming economic crisis have also done much to convince the international financial community that democratic accountability and legitimacy of rule is an important instrument for political reform.

But international donors and financial institutions need to take more resolute policy steps to act on these trends. The changing attitude of some international financial and aid organizations is a positive sign. The World Bank, in particular, has been innovative in its efforts to introduce issues of governance, corruption, and transparency into its programming and to begin to reach out to civil society and nongovernmental groups.

There is growing understanding among some policymakers of the link between the functioning of an effective rule of law system—a system that requires the checks and balances of a free society, a free press, and democratic accountability—and effective economic performance.

INTERNATIONAL STRUCTURES

In 1998, the fiftieth anniversary of the Universal Declaration of Human Rights was celebrated and efforts were made to intensify international action against basic rights violations. There were welcome efforts to arrest and prosecute those guilty of genocide and war crimes, including those guilty of atrocities in Rwanda and in Bosnia.

Many countries—though not the United States, which, for convincing reasons, was opposed—voted to adopt a charter for a far-reaching International Criminal Court. Yet while international action to eradicate rights abuses can be helpful, it must be limited in scope. Above all, international structures should not jeopardize or weaken the ability of democratic states to act to preserve or to protect freedom. Regrettably, many of the provisions in the proposed Criminal Court would have just such an effect.

As the Freedom House findings suggest, freedom is making important gains around the world. Nevertheless, the majority of mankind still lives in societies in which many or all basic freedoms are violated, and in a majority of countries the rule of law is absent or weak. Any body that emerges from an international consensus that includes undemocratic and unfree states is likely to be problematic in its composition. Adequate safeguards must exist to prevent such a court from acting capriciously. The United States is right to object to the current form of the proposed international Criminal Court. A far better policy would be the promotion of new structures made up of the growing community of free and democratic countries that could coordinate cooperation on behalf of human rights and against genocide and war crimes.

CONCLUSIONS

The remarkable expansion of human freedom recorded in the twenty-six years of the *Survey of Freedom* has not proceeded in a straight line. It has featured reversals as well as gains. Therefore, nothing in the findings should suggest that the expansion of democracy and freedom is inevitable. Indeed, much of the progress the *Survey* has recorded is the byproduct of a growing and systematic collaboration between established and new democracies, between democracies and countries in transition, and between established civic groups operating in the context of freedom and their pro-democratic counterparts seeking to promote change in closed societies. The findings of the *Survey* in future years will depend in no small measure on the success of such collaboration and on the elaboration of effective U.S. government policies to extend freedom to parts of the world where it is largely absent.

CRITICAL-THINKING QUESTIONS

1. A sharp increase in world freedom came from change in what major nation of the world during 1998?
2. What is the longer-term trend in political rights and freedoms?
3. In which regions of the world is political freedom most widespread? In which is it least widespread?

NOTE

1. Recent comparisons of the relationship between political freedom and economic liberty conducted by Freedom House (Adrian Karatnycky, Alexander Motyl, and Charles Graybow, eds., *Nations in Transit 1998*, New Brunswick, N.J.: Transaction Books, 1998) and the Heritage Foundation (Bryan T. Johnson, "Comparing Economic Freedom and Political Freedom," in Bryan T. Johnson, Kim R. Homes, and Melanie Kirkpatrick. eds., *1999 Index of Economic Freedom*, Washington, D.C.: The Heritage Foundation and Dow Jones Company, Inc., 1999, 29–34), respectively, have found a high correlation between the two variables. According to the authors of *Nations in Transit 1998*, post-Communist countries that are consolidated democracies also tend to have consolidated their market economies. When these countries' performance with respect to political and economic freedom is related to economic growth, the study found that consolidated democracies and market economies averaged a growth rate of 4.7 percent in 1997, transitional polities and economies registered an average growth rate of 1.4 percent, and consolidated autocracies and statist economies in the region averaged close to a 3 percent drop in GDP. The study similarly found high correlations between more open political systems and lower levels of corruption. Moreover, societies with lower levels of corruption were significantly more successful in generating economic growth. The region's least corrupt countries, for example, grew at an average rate of 4.7 percent in 1997, while states registering high levels of corruption averaged a decline of nearly 1 percent. Researchers at the Heritage Foundation found a high degree of correlation between political rights and civil liberties (as measured by Freedom House) and economic freedom (as measured by the Heritage Foundation's surveys).

52

"His" and "Her" Marriage

Family

CLASSIC

CONTEMPORARY

CROSS-CULTURAL

Jessie Bernard

Social scientists have found that men and women are not joined at the hip by a wedding ceremony. Rather, their subsequent lives differ in terms of gender roles, power, and ways of communicating. Bernard was among the first sociologists to point out that marriage has a different meaning for women and men. As this selection shows, spouses rarely define reality in the same way, even with regard to simple routines such as sweeping the floor or mowing the lawn.

. . . [T]here is by now a very considerable body of well-authenticated research to show that there really are two marriages in every marital union, and that they do not always coincide.

"HIS" AND "HER" MARRIAGES

. . . [T]he differences in the marriages of husbands and wives have come under the careful scrutiny of a score of researchers. They have found that when they ask husbands and wives identical questions about the union, they often get quite different replies. There is usually agreement on the number of children they have and a few other such verifiable items, although not, for example, on length of premarital acquaintance and of engagement, on age at marriage, and interval between marriage and birth of first child. Indeed, with respect to even such basic components of the marriage as frequency of sexual relations, social interaction, household tasks, and decision making, they seem to be reporting on different marriages. As, I think, they are.

In the area of sexual relations, for example, Kinsey and his associates found different responses in from one- to two-thirds of the couples they studied. Kinsey interpreted these differences in terms of selective perception. In the generation he was studying, husbands wanted sexual relations oftener than the wives did, thus "the females may be overesti-

Edward Hopper (1882–1967), *Room in New York*, 1932. Oil on Canvas, 29 x 36 in. UNL-Sheldon Memorial Art Gallery & Sculpture Garden. F. M. Hall Collection, 1932. H-166.

Source: From *The Future of Marriage* by Jessie Bernard. Copyright © 1972. Reprinted with permission.

mating the actual frequencies" and "the husbands . . . are probably underestimating the frequencies." The differences might also have been vestiges of the probable situation earlier in the marriage when the desired frequency of sexual relations was about six to seven times greater among husbands than among wives. This difference may have become so impressed on the spouses that it remained in their minds even after the difference itself had disappeared or even been reversed. In a sample of happily married, middle-class couples a generation later, Harold Feldman found that both spouses attributed to their mates more influence in the area of sex than they did to themselves.

Companionship, as reflected in talking together, he found, was another area where differences showed up. Replies differed on three-fourths of all the items studied, including the topics talked about, the amount of time spent talking with each other, and which partner initiated conversation. Both partners claimed that whereas they talked more about topics of interest to their mates, their mates initiated conversations about topics primarily of interest to themselves. Harold Feldman concluded that projection in terms of needs was distorting even simple, everyday events, and lack of communication was permitting the distortions to continue. It seemed to him that "if these sex differences can occur so often among these generally well-satisfied couples, it would not be surprising to find even less consensus and more distortion in other less satisfied couples."

Although, by and large, husbands and wives tend to become more alike with age, in this study of middle-class couples, differences increased with length of marriage rather than decreased, as one might logically have expected. More couples in the later than in the earlier years, for example, had differing pictures in their heads about how often they laughed together, discussed together, exchanged ideas, or worked together on projects, and about how well things were going between them.

The special nature of sex and the amorphousness of social interaction help to explain why differences in response might occur. But household tasks? They are fairly objective and clear-cut and not all that emotion-laden. Yet even here there are his-and-her versions. Since the division of labor in the household is becoming increasingly an issue in marriage, the uncovering of differing replies in this area is especially relevant. Hard as it is to believe, Granbois and Willett tell us that more than half of the partners in one sample disagreed on who kept track of money and bills. On the question, who mows the lawn? more than a fourth disagreed. Even family income was not universally agreed on.

These differences about sexual relations, companionship, and domestic duties tell us a great deal about the two marriages. But power or decision making can cover all aspects of a relationship. The question of who makes decisions or who exercises power has therefore attracted a great deal of research attention. If we were interested in who really had the power or who really made the decisions, the research would be hopeless. Would it be possible to draw any conclusion from a situation in which both partners agree that the husband ordered the wife to make all the decisions? Still, an enormous literature documents the quest of researchers for answers to the question of marital power. The major contribution it has made has been to reveal the existence of differences in replies between husbands and wives.

The presence of such inconsistent replies did not at first cause much concern. The researchers apologized for them but interpreted them as due to methodological inadequacies; if only they could find a better way to approach the problem, the differences would disappear. Alternatively, the use of only the wife's responses, which were more easily available, was justified on the grounds that differences in one direction between the partners in one marriage compensated for differences in another direction between the partners in another marriage and thus canceled them out. As, indeed, they did. For when Granbois and Willett, two market researchers, analyzed the replies of husbands and wives separately, the overall picture was in fact the same for both wives and husbands. Such canceling out of differences in the total sample, however, concealed almost as much as it revealed about the individual couples who composed it. Granbois and Willett concluded, as Kinsey had earlier, that the "discrepancies . . . reflect differing perceptions on the part of responding partners." And this was the heart of the matter.

Differing reactions to common situations, it should be noted, are not at all uncommon. They are recognized in the folk wisdom embedded in the story of the blind men all giving different replies to questions on the nature of the elephant. One of the oldest experiments in juridical psychology demonstrates how different the statements of witnesses of the same act can be. Even in laboratory studies, it takes intensive training of raters to make it possible for them to arrive at agreement on the behavior they observe.

It has long been known that people with different backgrounds see things differently. We know, for example, that poor children perceive coins as larger than do children from more affluent homes. Boys and girls perceive differently. A good deal of the foundation for projective tests rests on the different ways in which individuals see identical stimuli. And this perception—or, as the sociologists put it, definition of the situation—is reality for them. In this sense, the realities of the husband's marriage are different from those of the wife's.

Finally, one of the most perceptive of the researchers, Constantina Safilios-Rothschild, asked the crucial question: Was what they were getting, even with the best research techniques, family sociology or wives' family sociology? She answered her own question: What the researchers who relied on wives' replies exclusively were reporting on was the wife's marriage. The husband's was not necessarily the same. There were, in fact, two marriages present:

> One explanation of discrepancies between the responses of husbands and wives may be the possibility of two "realities," the husband's subjective reality and the wife's subjective reality—two perspectives which do not always coincide. Each spouse perceives "facts" and situations differently according to his own needs, values, attitudes, and beliefs. An "objective" reality could possibly exist only in the trained observer's evaluation, if it does exist at all.

Interpreting the different replies of husbands and wives in terms of selective perception, projection of needs, values, attitudes, and beliefs, or different definitions of the situation, by no means renders them trivial or incidental or justifies dismissing or ignoring them. They are, rather, fundamental for an understanding of the two marriages, his and hers, and we ignore them at the peril of serious misunderstanding of marriage, present as well as future.

IS THERE AN OBJECTIVE REALITY IN MARRIAGE?

Whether or not husbands and wives perceive differently or define situations differently, still sexual relations are taking place, companionship is or is not occurring, tasks about the house are being performed, and decisions are being made every day by someone. In this sense, some sort of "reality" does exist. David Olson went to the laboratory to see if he could uncover it.

He first asked young couples expecting babies such questions as these: Which one of them would decide whether to buy insurance for the newborn child? Which one would decide the husband's part in diaper changing? Which one would decide whether the new mother would return to work or to school? When there were differences in the answers each gave individually on the questionnaire, he set up a situation in which together they had to arrive at a decision in his laboratory. He could then compare the results of the questionnaire with the results in the simulated situation. He found neither spouse's questionnaire response any more accurate than the other's; that is, neither conformed better to the behavioral "reality" of the laboratory than the other did.

The most interesting thing, however, was that husbands, as shown on their questionnaire response, perceived themselves as having more power than they actually did have in the laboratory "reality," and wives perceived that they had less. Thus, whereas three-fourths (73 percent) of the husbands overestimated their power in decision making, 70 percent of the wives underestimated theirs. Turk and Bell found similar results in Canada. Both spouses tend to attribute decision-making power to the one who has the "right" to make the decision. Their replies, that is, conform to the model of marriage that has characterized civilized mankind for millennia. It is this model rather than their own actual behavior that husbands and wives tend to perceive.

We are now zeroing in on the basic reality. We can remove the quotation marks. For there is, in fact, an objective reality in marriage. It is a reality that resides in the cultural—legal, moral, and conventional—prescriptions and proscriptions and, hence, expectations that constitute marriage. It is the reality that is reflected in the minds of the spouses themselves. The differences between the marriages of husbands and of wives are structural realities, and it is these structural differences that constitute the basis for the different psychological realities.

THE AUTHORITY STRUCTURE OF MARRIAGE

Authority is an institutional phenomenon; it is strongly bound up with faith. It must be believed in; it cannot be enforced unless it also has power. Authority resides not in the person on whom it is conferred by the group or society, but in the recognition and acceptance it elicits in others. Power, on the other hand, may dispense with the prop of authority. It may take the form of the ability to coerce or to veto; it is often personal, charismatic, not institutional. This kind of personal power is self-enforcing. It does not require shoring up by access to force. In fact, it may even operate subversively. A woman with this kind of power may or may not know that she possesses it. If she does know she has it, she will probably disguise her exercise of it.

In the West, the institutional structure of marriage has invested the husband with authority and backed it by the power of church and state. The marriages of wives have thus been officially dominated by the husband. Hebrew, Christian, and Islamic versions of deity were in complete accord on this matter. The laws, written or unwritten, religious or civil, which have defined the marital union have been based on male conceptions, and they have undergirded male authority.

Adam came first. Eve was created to supply him with companionship, not vice versa. And God himself had told her that Adam would rule over her; her wishes had to conform to his. The New Testament authors agreed. Women were created for men, not men for women; women were therefore commanded to be obedient. If they wanted to learn anything, let them ask their husbands in private, for it was shameful for them to talk in the church. They should submit themselves to their husbands, because husbands were superior to wives; and wives should be as subject to their husbands as the church was to Christ. Timothy wrapped it all up: "Let the woman learn in silence with all subjection. But I suffer not a woman to teach, nor to usurp authority over the man, but to be in silence." Male Jews continued for millennia to thank God three times a day that they were not women. And the Koran teaches women that men are naturally their superiors because God made them that way; naturally, their own status is one of subordination.

The state as well as the church had the same conception of marriage, assigning to the husband and father control over his dependents, including his wife. Sometimes this power was well-nigh absolute, as in the case of the Roman patria potestas—or the English common law, which flatly said, "The husband and wife are as one and that one is the husband." There are rules still lingering today with the same, though less extreme, slant. Diane B. Schulder has summarized the legal framework of the wife's marriage as laid down in the common law:

> The legal responsibilities of a wife are to live in the home established by her husband; to perform the domestic chores (cleaning, cooking, washing, etc.) necessary to help maintain that home; to care for her husband and children. . . . A husband may force his wife to have sexual relations as long as his demands are reasonable and her health is not endangered. . . . The law allows a wife to take a job if she wishes. However, she must see that her domestic chores are completed, and, if there are children, that they receive proper care during her absence.

A wife is not entitled to payment for household work; and some jurisdictions in the United States expressly deny payment for it. In some states, the wife's earnings are under the control of her husband, and in four, special court approval and in some cases husband's consent are required if a wife wishes to start a business of her own.

The male counterpart to these obligations includes that of supporting his wife. He may not disinherit her. She has a third interest in property owned by him, even if it is held in his name only. Her name is required when he sells property.

Not only divine and civil law but also rules of etiquette have defined authority as a husband's prerogative. One of the first books published in England was a *Boke of Good Manners,* translated from the French of Jacques Le Grand in 1487, which included a chapter on "How Wymmen Ought to Be Gouerned." The thirty-third rule of Plutarch's *Rules for Husbands and Wives* was that women should obey their husbands; if they "try to rule over their husbands they make a worse mistake than the husbands do who let themselves be ruled." The husband's rule should not, of course, be brutal; he should not rule his wife "as a master does his chattel, but as the soul governs the body, by feeling with her and being linked to her by affection." Wives, according to Richard Baxter, a seventeenth-century English divine, had to obey even a wicked husband, the only exception being that a wife need not obey a husband if he ordered her to change her religion. But, again, like Plutarch, Baxter warned that the husband should love his wife; his authority should not be so coercive or so harsh as to destroy love. Among his twelve rules for carrying out the duties of conjugal love, however, was one to the effect that love must not be so imprudent as to destroy authority.

As late as the nineteenth century, Tocqueville noted that in the United States the ideals of democracy did not apply between husbands and wives:

> Nor have the Americans ever supposed that one consequence of democratic principles is the subversion of marital power, or the confusion of the natural authorities in families. They hold that every association must have a head in order to accomplish its objective, and that the natural head of the conjugal association is man. They do not therefore deny him the right of directing his partner; and they maintain, that in the smaller association of husband and wife, as well as in the great social community, the object of democracy is to regulate and legalize the powers which are necessary, not to subvert all power.
>
> This opinion is not peculiar to men and contested by women; I never observed that the women of America consider conjugal authority as an unfortunate usurpation [by men] of their rights, nor that they thought themselves degraded by submitting to it. It appears to me, on the contrary, that they attach a sort of pride to the voluntary surrender of their own will, and make it their boast to bend themselves to the yoke, not to shake it off.

The point here is not to document once more the specific ways (religious, legal, moral, traditional) in which male authority has been built into the marital union—that has been done a great many times—but merely to illustrate how different (structurally or "objectively" as well as perceptually or "subjectively") the wife's marriage has actually been from the husband's throughout history.

THE SUBVERSIVENESS OF NATURE

The rationale for male authority rested not only on biblical grounds but also on nature or natural law, on the generally accepted natural superiority of men. For nothing could be more self-evident than that the patriarchal conception of marriage, in which the husband was unequivocally the boss, was natural, resting as it did on the unchallenged superiority of males.

Actually, nature, if not deity, is subversive. Power, or the ability to coerce or to veto, is widely distributed in both sexes, among women as well as among men. And whatever the theoretical or conceptual picture may have been, the actual, day-by-day relationships between husbands and wives have been determined by the men and women themselves. All that the institutional machinery could do was to confer authority; it could not create personal power, for such power cannot be conferred, and women can generate it as well as men. . . . Thus, keeping women in their place has been a universal problem, in spite of the fact that almost without exception institutional patterns give men positions of superiority over them.

If the sexes were, in fact, categorically distinct, with no overlapping, so that no man was inferior to any woman or any woman superior to any man, or vice versa, marriage would have been a great deal simpler. But there is no such sharp cleavage between the sexes except with respect to the presence or absence of certain organs. With all the other characteristics of each sex, there is greater or less overlapping, some men being more "feminine" than the average woman and some women more "masculine" than the average man. The structure of families and societies reflects the positions assigned to men and women. The bottom stratum includes children, slaves, servants, and outcasts of all kinds, males as well as females. As one ascends the structural hierarchy, the proportion of males increases, so that at the apex there are only males.

When societies fall back on the lazy expedient—as all societies everywhere have done—of allocating the rewards and punishments of life on the basis of sex, they are bound to create a host of anomalies, square pegs in round holes, societal misfits. Roles have been allocated on the basis of sex which did not fit a sizable number of both sexes—women, for example, who chafed at subordinate status and men who could not master superordinate status. The history of the relations of the sexes is replete with examples of such misfits. Unless a modus vivendi is arrived at, unhappy marriages are the result.

There is, though, a difference between the exercise of power by husbands and by wives. When women exert power, they are not rewarded; they may even be punished. They are "deviant." Turk and Bell note that "wives who . . . have the greater influence in decision making may experience guilt over this fact." They must therefore dissemble to maintain the illusion, even to themselves, that they are subservient. They tend to feel less powerful than they are because they *ought* to be.

When men exert power, on the other hand, they are rewarded; it is the natural expression of authority. They feel no guilt about it. The prestige of authority goes to the husband whether or not he is actually the one who exercises it. It is not often even noticed when the wife does so. She sees to it that it is not.

There are two marriages, then, in every marital union, his and hers. And his . . . is better than hers. The questions, therefore, are these: In what direction will they change in the future? Will one change more than the other? Will they tend to converge or to diverge? Will the future continue to favor the husband's marriage? And if the wife's marriage is improved, will it cost the husband's anything, or will his benefit along with hers?

CRITICAL-THINKING QUESTIONS

1. What evidence does Bernard offer to support her conclusion that there are "his" and "her" marriages rather than "our" marriage?
2. Does the traditional inequality of men and women support or undermine marital roles? How?
3. What are the consequences for marriage of the gradual process by which the two sexes are becoming more socially equal?

53

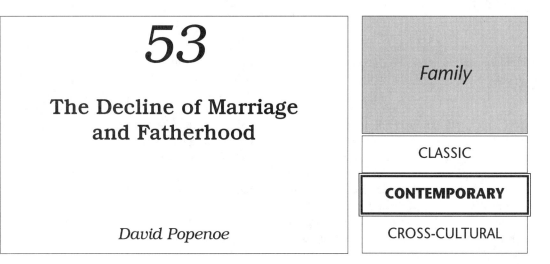

The Decline of Marriage and Fatherhood

Family

CLASSIC

CONTEMPORARY

CROSS-CULTURAL

David Popenoe

The American family has changed dramatically since the 1960s both in its structure and in many of its functions. Some social scientists feel that family life has improved because people have more choices today than in the past. Others maintain that many of the changes amount to a deterioration of the family and a breakdown of society itself. In this selection, David Popenoe argues that U. S. fathers are more removed from family life than ever before and that the "massive erosion" of marriage and fatherhood contribute to many of our social problems.

. . . While the new father has been emerging gradually for most of this century, it is only in the past thirty years that we have witnessed the enormous increase in absent fathers. In times past, many children were left fatherless through his premature death. Today, the fathers are still alive and out there somewhere; the problem is that they seldom see much, if anything, of their children.

The main reason for contemporary father absence is the dramatic decline of marriage. Divorce rates have skyrocketed in the past thirty years, and even more recently we have seen a veritable explosion in the rate of unwed motherhood. What this means, in human terms, is that about half of today's children will spend at least a portion of their growing-up years living apart from their fathers.

As a society, we can respond to this new fatherlessness in several ways. We can, as more and more of us seem to be doing, simply declare fathers to be unnecessary, superfluous. This is the response of "single parents by choice." It is the response of those who say that if daddies and mommies are expected to do precisely the same things in the home, why do we need both? It is the response of those who declare that unwed motherhood is a woman's right, or that single-parent families are every bit as good as two-parent families, or that divorce is generally beneficial for children.

In my view, these responses represent a human tragedy—for children, for women, for men, and for our society as a whole. I am writing this [reading] to tell you why. My main emphasis will be on children. I hope to convince you, especially those of you who rely on empirical evidence before you make up your mind, that the evidence is strong: Fathering is different from mothering; involved fathers are indispensable for the good of

---

Source: Reprinted and abridged with the permission of The Free Press, a division of Simon & Schuster, from *Life without Father* by David Popenoe. Copyright © 1996 by David Popenoe.

children and society; and our growing national fatherlessness is a disaster in the making.

THE DECLINE OF FATHERHOOD

The decline of fatherhood is one of the most basic, unexpected, and extraordinary social trends of our time. The trend can be captured in a single telling statistic: In just three decades, from 1960 to 1990, the percentage of children living apart from their biological fathers more than doubled, from 17 percent to 36 percent. If this rate continues, by the turn of the century nearly 50 percent of American children will be going to sleep each night without being able to say good night to their dads.

No one predicted this trend, few researchers or government agencies have monitored it, and it is not widely discussed, even today. But its importance to society is second to none. Father absence is a major force lying behind many of the attention-grabbing issues that dominate the news: crime and delinquency; premature sexuality and out-of-wedlock teen births; deteriorating educational achievement; depression, substance abuse, and alienation among teenagers; and the growing number of women and children in poverty. These issues all point to a profound deterioration in the well-being of children. Some experts have suggested, in fact, that the current generation of children and youth is the first in our nation's history to be less well-off—psychologically, socially, economically, and morally—than their parents were at the same age. Or as Senator Daniel Patrick Moynihan has observed, "the United States . . . may be the first society in history in which children are distinctly worse off than adults."[1]

Along with the growing father absence, our cultural view of fatherhood is changing. Few people have doubts about the fundamental importance of mothers. But fathers? More and more the question is being raised, are fathers really necessary? Many would answer no, or maybe not. And to the degree that fathers are still thought necessary, fatherhood is said by many to be merely a social role, as if men had no inherent biological predisposition whatsoever to acknowledge and to invest in their own offspring. If merely a social role, then perhaps anyone is capable of playing it. The implication is one of arbitrary substitutability. Not just biological fathers, but any competent actor who has studied the part can easily step in: mothers, partners, stepfathers, uncles and aunts, grandparents. Perhaps the script can even be rewritten and the role changed—or dropped.

FATHERS: ESSENTIAL BUT PROBLEMATIC

Across time and cultures, fathers have always been considered by societies to be essential—and not just for their sperm. Indeed, until today, no known society ever thought of fathers as potentially unnecessary. Biological fathers are everywhere identified, if possible, and play some role in their children's upbringing. Marriage and the nuclear family—mother, father, and children—are the most universal social institutions in existence. In no society has nonmarital childbirth been the cultural norm. To the contrary, a concern for the "legitimacy" of children is another cultural near universal: The mother of an illegitimate child virtually everywhere has been regarded as a social deviant, if not a social outcast, and her child has been stigmatized.

At the same time, being a father is universally problematic for men and for their societies in a way that being a mother is not. While mothers the world over bear and nurture their young with an intrinsic acknowledgment and, most commonly, acceptance of their role, taking on the role of father is often filled with conflict, tension, distance, and doubt. Across societies, fathers may or may not be closely engaged with their children, reside with the mother, or see their father role as highly important.

The source of this sex-role difference can be plainly stated. Men are not biologically as attuned to being committed fathers as women are to being committed mothers. Left culturally unregulated, men's sexual behavior can be promiscuous, their paternity casual, their commitment to families weak. Yet in virtually all societies, especially modern societies, both child and social well-being depend on high levels of paternal investment: the time, energy, and resources that fathers are willing to impart to their children.

That men are not perfectly attuned to fatherhood in biological terms is not to say that fathering behavior is foreign to the nature of men. Far from it. Evolutionary scientists tell us that the development of the fathering capacity and high paternal investments in offspring—features not common among our primate relatives—have been a source of enormous evolutionary advantage for human beings. Because human young are more dependent on adults for a longer period of their lives than any other species and human mothers require a great deal of help if their children are to survive, a key to human evolution was the capturing of male effort to the goal of childbearing. It is almost certainly the case that the human family is the oldest social institution, at heart a biological arrangement for raising children that has always involved fathers as well as mothers.

In recognition of the fatherhood problem—that fatherhood is essential but also somewhat problematic—human cultures have realized that sanctions are necessary if paternal investments are to be maximized. The main cultural carrier of sanctions is the institution of marriage, a major purpose of which is to hold men to the reproductive pair bond. Simply defined, marriage is a relationship within which a community socially approves and encourages sexual intercourse and the birth of children. It is society's way of signaling to would-be parents of children that their long-term relationship together is socially important. As evidenced by the vows of fidelity and permanence that almost universally are part of the wedding ceremony, an important purpose of marriage is to hold the man to the union. Margaret Mead once said, with the fatherhood problem strongly in mind, that there is no society in the world where men will stay married for very long unless culturally required to do so.

FATHERHOOD AND MARRIAGE

Today, because the great social complexity of modern societies requires longer periods of socialization and dependency for children than ever before, the need for adult investments in children has reached new heights. In order to succeed economically in an increasingly technological society, children must be highly educated. In order to succeed socially and psychologically in an increasingly complex and heterogeneous culture, children must have strong and stable attachments to adults. Nonfamily institutions can help with education, but family and close-kin groups are essential for socioemotional success. Parents and other close relatives are still the persons most likely to have the motivational levels necessary to provide the time and attention that children need to feel loved and special.

Yet at the time when the childrearing task is ever more demanding and male assistance with the task is ever more important, cultural sanctions holding men to marriage and children have dramatically weakened. Marriage, once both sacred and economically essential for survival, is today based solely on the fragile tie of affection for one's mate. And whereas the institution of marriage once legally bound a couple with a high degree of permanence, marriages can now be broken unilaterally on a whim.

The United States has by far the highest divorce rate in the industrialized world. The chance that a first marriage occurring today will end in divorce stands at around 50 percent—by some estimates as high as 60 percent. The chance in the middle of the last century was around 5 percent. In the past three decades alone, the divorce rate has doubled or tripled, depending upon how one calculates it.

Marriages are not only breaking up in large numbers, but the institution itself is in decline. The marriage rate is dropping. In place of marriage we are witnessing the rapid rise of nonmarital cohabitation, which by its very nature implies a lower level of commitment. More problematic still is the increase in "single parenting by choice."

There has emerged in the last decade or two a tendency for women to go it alone. It would be nice, many of these women report, if the perfect man came into the picture. But he is not around, so I am going to have a child anyway. This phenomenon was made culturally memorable by the *Murphy Brown* television episode in which Murphy decided to have a nonmarital child and that fact was celebrated nationwide. Like Murphy, but typically without her level of economic resources, more and more women report with each passing year that they, too, might have a child if they are unable to find the right man.

The lifestyle of the single parent, rather than being eschewed, is becoming socially accepted as part of a new wave of tolerance befitting the contemporary celebration of diversity. Even marriage and family-relations professionals have come to extol "alternative lifestyles." Textbooks that used to be entitled *Marriage and the Family* (read: married-father-included) are now entitled *Intimate Relationships* or the all-inclusive *Families*. The growth of unmarried mothers on welfare has raised some national ire, but many on the Left believe that there is a new national "right" for such mothers to have as many children as they want and immediately receive support for those children from taxpayers.

With this kind of cultural acceptance, it is little wonder that the percentage of out-of-wedlock births in America has increased 600 percent in just three decades, from 5 percent of all births in 1960 to 30 percent in 1991.[2] If the percentage keeps climbing at its current rate, 40 percent of all births (and 80 percent of minority births) will take place out of wedlock by the turn of the century.[3]

THE SHRINKING FATHER

Contemporary fatherhood faces an additional challenge. The father's role has shrunk drastically over the years. American fathers have been losing authority within the family and psychologically withdrawing from a direct role in childrearing almost since colonial times.

The Puritan father was a domestic patriarch; he was not only the family's chief provider and protector but also the moral authority and chief educator, at least of his older children. In the last century, however, the focus of the family turned to mothers. With the rise of a major new family form—what historians label "the modern nuclear family" but what most people today know as "the traditional family"—the father's main role became family breadwinner. Legally and socially fathers became the second parent, and their direct role in the home increasingly was marginalized. Finally, with the waning of the modern nuclear family in this century, even the breadwinner role has eroded.

Today men are being asked to return to domestic roles. Fathers are badly needed as comprehensive childrearers on an equal basis with mothers. Not only does this represent a radical shift from recent history, but increasingly men are asked to become major caretakers for infants and toddlers, a role they never before in history have had to embrace.

THE FATHERHOOD DEBATE

Could it be that the era of fatherhood is at an end, that the fatherhood problem can be resolved by simply getting rid of fathers and perhaps substituting someone or something else in their stead? Is there something new and different about modern societies that makes single parenthood a reasonable option and makes these societies increasingly immune from the age-old proscription against illegitimacy? Have we become so free and individualized and prosperous that the traditional social structures surrounding family life no longer have the importance that they have had in all of human history to date?

Positive answers to these questions have been forcefully argued. The argument contains these key elements:

- Women no longer need men for provision or protection, the traditional male family roles. For provision, most women now have independent access to the labor market; and if they don't, they have access to government-supported welfare programs. For protection, women have the police, and in any event it is usually their male partner from whom they must be protected.
- Both single mothers and their children have been unfairly stigmatized over the generations. This has been grossly unfair to mothers as well as to the children who did absolutely nothing to bring about their plight. Societies today are able, thankfully, to correct this age-old injustice.
- Male-female family life is inherently inequitable, a patriarchal institution wherein men have always dominated women. Men are selfish, irresponsible, psychologically untrustworthy, even intractable. If women are to achieve true equality, therefore, we must find some alternative to the nuclear family.
- Men frequently leave their wives and children in the lurch, especially in times of crisis, either through psychological withdrawal or outright desertion. It is safer for a woman never to begin counting on a man.
- It is not clear that fathers any longer provide something unique to their children. There is not much they do that mothers do not, or cannot, do just as well.

There is some truth, of course, to each of these points. Many women today are perfectly capable, in economic and other terms, of raising children by themselves. The traditional stigma against illegitimacy is something that few people want to bring back. There does seem to be some kind of inherent inequality between men and women, if nothing more than that men are bigger and stronger and more aggressive. The selfish, irresponsible male is not uncommon. And since some fathers and mothers do carry out the same childrearing activities, the question of why we need both is a reasonable one to ask.

But the aim of this [reading] is to try to convince you that this no-father argument is fundamentally wrong. If we continue down the path of fatherlessness, we are headed for social disaster.

FATHERS AND MOTHERS

It is the rare child who does not wish to grow up with both a father and a mother. We should ask the question, why do children have this desire? Despite their sometimes wanting candy for breakfast, children do have, after all, a certain wisdom about life. Is it simply that they don't want to be any different from their friends? Is it merely something they have been taught to say? I think not.

Every child comes into the world totally dependent upon adults, especially the parents to whom they were born. To a large extent children's life chances come from who cares for them and how they are cared for. Of course, children are surprisingly flexible and malleable; some can thrive in the most intolerable of circumstances. But this fact says nothing about the life chances for the multitude. I suspect that children instinctively realize that the world is made up almost equally of two sexes, that each sex possesses biological and psychological traits that balance and complement the other, and that each sex brings something unique and important to children's lives.

Whatever the basis for children's primal desire for a father and a mother, the weight of social science evidence strongly supports the rationality of their wish. In my many years as a functioning social scientist, I know of few other bodies of evidence whose weight leans so much in one direction as does the evidence about family structure: On the whole, two parents—a father and a mother— are better for the child than one parent.[4]

There are, to be sure, many complicating factors to the simple proposition that two parents are best. Family structure is only a gross approximation of what actually goes on within a family. We all know of a two-parent family that is the family from hell. A child can certainly be well-raised to adulthood by one loving parent who is wholly devoted to that child's well-being. But such problems and exceptions in no way deny the aggregate finding or generalization. After all, to take another much-publicized area of research, plenty of three-pack-a-day smokers live to a ripe old age and die of natural causes.

What does the social science evidence about family structure and child well-being actually show? Researchers Sara McLanahan and Gary Sandefur recently examined six nationally representative data sets containing over twenty-five thousand children from a variety of racial and social-class backgrounds. Their conclusion:

> Children who grow up with only one of their biological parents (nearly always the mother) are disadvantaged across a broad array of outcomes . . . they are twice as likely to drop out of high school, 2.5 times as likely to become teen mothers, and 1.4 times as likely to be idle—out of school and out of work—as children who grow up with both parents.[5]

Sure, you may say, that is because one-parent families are poorer. But here is the researchers' conclusion about the economic factor:

> Loss of economic resources accounts for about 50 percent of the disadvantages associated with single parenthood. Too little parental supervision and involvement and greater residential mobility account for most of the rest.[6]

Many other researchers . . . have come up with similar conclusions. The evidence covers the full range of possible effects, from crime to school achievement. Social analysts William A. Galston and Elaine Ciulla Kamark report, for example, that

> The relationship [between family structure and crime] is so strong that controlling for family configuration erases the relationship between race and crime and between low income and crime. This conclusion shows up again and again in the literature.[7]

Based on such evidence, a strong case can be made that paternal deprivation, in the form of the physical, economic, and emotional unavailability of fathers to their children, has become the most prevalent form of child maltreatment in America today.[8]

Is the missing ingredient in the single-parent family simply a second adult who can provide "parental supervision and involvement"? It is in part, but only in part. Consider this conclusion of McLanahan and Sandefur: "Children of stepfamilies don't do better than children of mothers who never remarry."[9]

The main missing ingredient in a growing number of families today, I shall argue, is the biological father. He can be replaced adequately here and there, and obviously not all biological fathers are good fathers, but in general males biologically unrelated to their children cannot be expected to have the same motivation and dedication to raising those children as males raising their own biological offspring. The incidence of sexual abuse among stepfathers, for example, is far higher than among biological fathers.

It is not my intent to stigmatize step- and adoptive parents. Those alternative family forms where parents are doing their job well deserve our deepest respect; those experiencing difficulties should be provided both compassion and tangible assistance. My point is this: Being a father is much more than merely fulfilling a social role. Engaged biological fathers care profoundly and selflessly about their own children; such fatherly love is not something that can easily be transferred or reduced to the learning of a script. Why many biological fathers themselves are now becoming disengaged from their children is, of course, a puzzling phenomenon . . .

FATHERHOOD, MARRIAGE, AND THE GOOD SOCIETY

Today in America the social order is fraying badly; we seem to be on a path to continuing social decline. The past three decades have seen steeply rising rates of crime, declining interpersonal and political trust, growing personal and corporate greed, deteriorating communities, and increasing confusion over moral issues.[10] I am referring not only to the situation of the inner city poor, with which most Americans have little contact, but to the overall quality of daily life. The average American seemingly has become more anxious, unsettled, and insecure.

Our societal decline can be phrased in terms of a failure of social values. People no longer conduct themselves, to the same extent as prior generations, according to the civic virtues of honesty, self-sacrifice, and personal responsibility. People have become strong on individual rights and weak on community obligations.[11] In our ever-growing pursuit of the self—self-expression, self-development, self-actualization, and self-fulfillment—the social has become increasingly problematic.

At the heart of the problem lies an erosion of personal relationships. People no longer trust others as they once did; they no longer feel the same sense of commitment and obligation to others. This is certainly not a new or original observation. The perceived erosion of "primary relationships" that is associated with modernity was one of the formative conceptions of the discipline of sociology in the last century.[12] But the early sociologists could not have known the great extent to which their conception would prove correct.

Fathers are one of the two most important role models in children's lives. Some children across America now go to bed each night worrying about whether their father will be there the next morning. Some wonder what ever happened to their father. Some think to themselves, who is my father? Is it a stretch to believe that the father-neglected or father-abandoned child is more likely to have a jaundiced view of such values as honesty, self-sacrifice, and personal responsibility, to say nothing of trust?

The decline of fatherhood and of marriage cuts at the heart of the kind of environment considered ideal for childrearing. Such an environment, according to a substantial body of knowledge, consists of an enduring two-parent family that engages regularly in activities together, has many of its own routines and traditions, and provides a great deal of quality contact time between adults and children. The children have frequent contact with relatives, active neighboring in a supportive setting, and contact with their parents' world of work. In addition, there is little concern on the part of children that their parents will break up. Finally, each of these ingredients comes together in the development of a rich family subculture that has lasting meaning and strongly promulgates such family values as responsibility, cooperation, and sharing.

In our society, as in all others so far as we know, the family is the seedbed of trusting and socially responsible personal relationships. The family is also, not coincidentally, the seedbed of those civic virtues that we are losing. Children do not hold such virtues as honesty and self-sacrifice at birth; these virtues must be purposefully taught and reinforced through close personal relationships and good example. Children learn many things, including values, through imitation or modeling. The more consistently caring and altruistic the parent is, the more likely it is the child will be so. If such virtues are not taught within the family, they normally are not taught at all.

What the decline of fatherhood and marriage in America really means, then, is that slowly, insidiously, and relentlessly our society has been moving in an ominous direction—toward the devaluation of children. There has been an alarming weakening of the fundamental assumption, long at the center of our culture, that children are to be loved and valued at the highest level of priority. Nothing could be more serious for our children or our future.

Our national response, therefore, should be the reestablishment of fatherhood and marriage as strong social and cultural realities. If we are to make progress toward a more just and humane society, a major national objective should be no less than this: to increase the proportion of children who are living with and cared for by their married, biological fathers and to decrease the proportion of children who are not.

CRITICAL-THINKING QUESTIONS

1. Why, according to Popenoe, have both fatherhood and marriage declined?
2. Do you agree that "If we continue down the path of fatherlessness, we are headed for social disaster"? Are there other possible reasons that help to explain such social problems as crime and delinquency, out-of-wedlock teen births, and deteriorating educational achievement?
3. What remedies does Popenoe propose to halt the United States' "path of continuing social decline"? Do you agree or disagree with his position? How, specifically, might his proposals be implemented?

NOTES

1. *The New York Times,* Sept. 25, 1986, p. C7.

2. U.S. Department of Health and Human Services, *Vital Statistics of the United States, 1991.* Vol. 1, *Natality* (Washington, DC: GPO, 1993). Among blacks, the increase has been from 23 percent to 68 percent.

3. Congressional testimony of Lee Rainwater, Harvard University. Cited in William J. Bennett, *The Index of Leading Cultural Indicators* (New York: Simon and Schuster, 1994), p. 47.

4. It should be noted that social science evidence is never conclusive, on this or any other matter. . . . The world is too complex; the scientific method can only imperfectly be applied to the study of human beings; researchers have biases; and people may not always be telling investigators the truth. These are but a few of the many problems endemic to the social sciences. The best use of the social science evidence is to help confirm or disconfirm. Does the evidence generally support a proposition or not? If it does, fine; if it does not, one had better have a good explanation as to why that proposition may still be true.

5. Sara S. McLanahan, "The Consequences of Single Motherhood," *The American Prospect,* 18 (1994), 48–58, esp. 49. Article is drawn from Sara McLanahan and Gary Sandefur, *Growing Up with a Single Parent,* (Cambridge, Mass.: Harvard University Press, 1994).

6. McLanahan, *Consequences,* p. 52.

7. Elaine Ciulla Kamark and William A. Galston, *Putting Children First: A Progressive Family Policy for the 1990s* (Washington, D.C.: Progressive Policy Institute, 1990), pp. 14–15.

8. See Henry B. Biller, *Fathers and Families: Paternal Factors in Child Development* (Westport, Conn.: Auburn House, 1993).

9. McLanahan, *Consequences,* p. 51.

10. Two general books on this topic are: James Lincoln Collier, *The Rise of Selfishness in America* (New York: Oxford University Press, 1991); and Art Carey, *The United States of Incompetence* (Boston: Houghton Mifflin, 1991). See also: Louis Harris, *Inside America,* (New York: Vintage Books, 1987); and William J. Bennett, *The Index of Leading Cultural Indicators* (New York: Simon & Schuster, 1994). In the light of such changes, some observers have called into question the very idea of social progress itself. See Christopher Lasch, *The True and Only Heaven* (New York: W. W. Norton, 1991).

11. Mary Ann Glendon, *Rights Talk: The Impoverishment of Political Discourse,* (New York: Free Press, 1991).

12. Robert A. Nisbet, *The Sociological Tradition.* (New York: Basic Books, 1966).

12 Ingoldsby

54

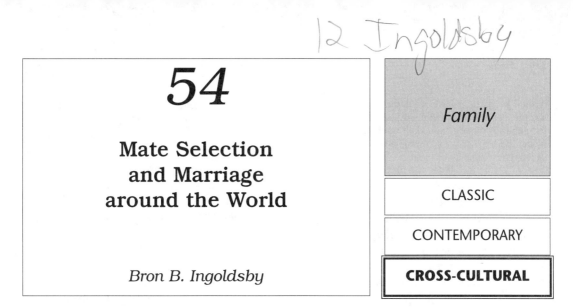

Mate Selection and Marriage around the World

Family

CLASSIC

CONTEMPORARY

CROSS-CULTURAL

Bron B. Ingoldsby

The institution of marriage is very popular throughout the world. Yet, how mates are chosen varies considerably from one culture to another. As Bron B. Ingoldsby shows, free-choice mate selection—which is common in Western countries—is not how couples have been paired with their prospective spouses in most other societies.

MATE SELECTION PROCEDURES

Historically, there have been three general approaches to choosing one's mate: marriage by capture, marriage by arrangement, and free-choice mate selection. I examine each of them in turn.

Marriage by Capture

Although it has probably never been the usual method of obtaining a wife, men have taken women by force in many times and places. This typically occurred in patriarchal societies in which women were often considered property. Often women were seized as part of the spoils of war, and other times a specific woman was forced into marriage because the man wanted her and could not afford the brideprice or obtain the permission of her parents. The capture and marriage of a woman was legal in England until the reign of Henry VII, who made it a crime to abduct an heiress (Fielding, 1942).

The ancient Hebrews would seize wives under certain circumstances. A dramatic example is recounted in the Old Testament (Judges, chapter 21), where it was arranged for young women to be kidnapped from two different areas to serve as wives so that the tribe of Benjamin would not die out after a war that they had lost.

There was also a formal procedure for dealing with wives captured in warfare:

> When thou goest forth to war against thine enemies, and the Lord thy God hath delivered them into thine hands, and thou has taken them captive, And seest among the captives a beautiful woman, and hast a desire unto her, that thou wouldest have her to thy wife; Then thou shalt bring her home to thine house; and she shall shave her head, and pare her nails; And she shall put the raiment of her captivity from off her, and shall remain in thine house, and bewail her father and her mother a full month: and after that thou shalt go in unto her, and be her husband, and she shall be thy wife. And

Source: "Mate Selection and Marriage," by Bron B. Ingoldsby, in *Families in Multicultural Perspective,* eds. Bron B. Ingoldsby and Suzanna Smith, pp. 143-57.

it shall be, if thou have no delight in her, then thou shalt let her go whither she will; but thou shalt not sell her at all for money, thou shalt not make merchandise of her, because thou has humbled her (Deuteronomy 21:10–14).

At least she was given time to get used to the idea and never sold into slavery! Fielding (1942) cites a number of different cultures, including the Australian aborigines, who frequently resorted to marriage by capture in the recent past. The Yąnomamö of Venezuela (an Amazonian tribe) are reported (Peters, 1987) to use capture as one of their mate selection options. One village is often raided by another for the specific purpose of finding wives. If a man captures a young, attractive female, he must be careful as other men from his own village will try to steal her from him.

In the popular musical *Seven Brides for Seven Brothers,* the concept of marriage by capture is acted out, and one of the songs is based on the historical incident of the rape of the Sabine women. There are many cultures that still have remnants of the old practice of marriage by capture in their wedding ceremonies. In each of them, the match is prearranged, but the husband pretends to take his bride by force, and she feigns resistance.

One example are the Roro of New Guinea. On the wedding day, the groom's party surrounds the bride's home and acts out an assault on it. The bride attempts to run away but is caught. Then a sham battle ensues, with the bride's mother leading the way and crying at the loss of her daughter when she is taken off to the groom (Fielding, 1942).

Marriage by Arrangement

It appears that the most common method of mate selection has been by arrangement. Typically, the parents, often with the aid of certain relatives or professional matchmakers, have chosen the spouse for their child. This form of mate choice is more common when extended kin groups are strong and important. Essentially, marriage is seen as of group, rather than individual, importance, and economics is often the driving force rather than love between the principals.

Arranged marriages have been considered especially important for the rulers of kingdoms and other nobility. Care had to be taken to preserve bloodlines, enhance wealth, and resolve political issues. It is believed, for instance, that the majority of King Solomon's 700 wives and 300 concubines were acquired for the purpose of political alliances.

Stephens (1963) identifies four major reasons that determine mate choice in societies in which marriages are arranged. The first is *price.* The groom's family may need to pay for the bride, with either money or labor. In some cultures, the situation is reversed, with the bride's family paying a dowry to the husband. In other cases, there is a direct exchange, where both families make payments to each other or simply trade women for each other's sons.

The second consideration is *social status.* That is, the reputation of the family from which the spouse for one's child will come is very important. A third determinant is any *continuous marriage arrangement.* This refers to a set pattern for mate selection, which is carried on from generation to generation. For instance, cousin marriages are preferred in many societies.

The final criteria for mate choice are *sororate and levirate* arrangements, which refer to second marriages and tend to be based on brideprice obligations. These terms are more fully explained later in the [reading]. Stephens also notes nineteen societies (including, for example, some large ones such as China and Renaissance Europe) that have practiced child betrothals or child marriages. This means that the marriage is arranged before puberty and can even be worked out before the child is born.

In addition to marriage by capture, the Yąnomamö also practice variety within arranged marriages. The ideal match is between cross-cousins, and the majority of unions fall into this category. Most betrothals are made before the girl is three years of age. Men initiate these arrangements at about the time they become hunters, which is shortly after they turn fifteen. Another acceptable form of mate selection is sister exchange. Two unrelated single males wish to acquire wives and have sisters who are not promised to anyone, so they simply trade sisters (Peters, 1987).

Some societies have provided an "out" for couples who have strong personal preferences that go against the arrangement of their families. This is to permit elopement. Stephens (1963) gives this account of the Iban of Borneo:

> When a young woman is in love with a man who is not acceptable to her parents, there is an old custom called *nunghop bui,* which permits him to carry her off to his own village. She will meet him by arrangement at the waterside, and step into his boat with a paddle in her hand, and both will pull away as fast as they can. If pursued he will stop every now and then to deposit some article of value on the bank, such as a gun, a jar, or a favor for the acceptance of her family, and when he has exhausted his resources he will leave his own sword. When the pursuers observe this they cease to follow, knowing he is cleared out. As soon as he reaches his own village he tidies up the house and spreads the mats, and when his pursuers arrive he gives them food to eat and toddy to drink, and sends them home satisfied. In the meanwhile he is left in possession of his wife. (p. 200)

Following is a detailed look at some of the specific mechanisms of arranged marriages.

Brideprice. Throughout much of human history, marriage has been seen as chiefly an economic transaction. As an old German saying goes, "It is not man that marries maid, but field marries field, vineyard marries vineyard, cattle marry cattle" (Tober, 1984, p. 12). The purpose of a brideprice is to compensate the family of the bride for the loss of her services. It is extremely common and is indicative of the value of women in those societies. Stephens (1963) reports that Murdock's World Ethnographic Sample yields the following breakdown on marriage payments:

Brideprice—260 societies
Bride service—75 societies
Dowry—24 societies
Gift or woman exchange—31 societies
No marriage payment—152 societies

This means that in 62 percent of the world's societies, a man must pay in order to marry a woman. The price is usually paid in animals, shell money, or other valuable commodities and often exceeds one's annual income. Some cultures prefer payment in service, often many years of labor to the bride's parents, or at least permit it for suitors who cannot afford to pay in goods. One famous example from the Old Testament is that of Jacob, who labored seven years for each of Laban's two daughters, Leah and Rachel.

Dowry. The dowry appears to be an inducement for a man to marry a particular woman and therefore relieve her family of the financial burden of caring for her. Although relatively rare, it is a sign of a culture that places a low value on women. Actually, the key purpose of a dowry is probably to stabilize a marriage, because it is not given to the husband but is something that the bride brings with her into the marriage. For example, in Cyprus before the time of English influence, the expected dowry was often a house. If the husband divorced his wife or mistreated her and she left him, the dowry went with her. Like modern-day wedding gifts, or the bride's trousseau, it was an investment in the marriage and intended to reduce the chances of a breakup (Balswick, 1975).

The dowry has been around for a long time. The Babylonian code of Hammurabi (1955 B.C.E.) clearly stated that the wife's property stayed with her if her husband divorced her and passed on to her children when she died. Ancient Greece and Rome also considered the dowry to be essential in any honorable marriage (Fielding, 1942).

Recent research in the southern Indian state of Kerala (Billig, 1992) differentiates between the traditional dowry and an actual "groomprice." Groomprice is money paid by the bride's family directly to the husband to use as he sees fit. In the 1950s and 1960s, rapid population growth resulted in more younger women looking for husbands a few (average of seven) years older than themselves. This surplus of potential brides increased the value of husbands. Popular revulsion for the groomprice has resulted in a decrease in the age difference (now five years), women lowering their social status expectations for their husband or increasing their own education, and a government outlawing of the practice.

Sororate and Levirate. These terms refer to marriage practices designed to control remarriages after the death of the first spouse. In cultures that practice the sororate, a sister replaces a deceased wife. Assume that a man has paid a good brideprice for his wife but some time later she becomes ill and dies. He has lost his wife and the brideprice. Therefore, to make good on the original bargain, the parents who received the brideprice provide the man with a new wife. This new wife is an unmarried sister or other close relative of the first wife. Here we see how marriage is often more of an economic transaction than it is a personal relationship.

Much more widely practiced has been the levirate. Under this system, it is the husband who dies, and his wife must be married to a brother of the deceased man. There are various reasons for this practice. One is that the wife belonged to her husband as part of his property and as such would be inherited along with the other possessions by a near relative. Another is that it is presumed that women need someone to take care of them, and brothers-in-law (which is the meaning of the Latin word *levir*) should assume that responsibility. It has been reported that the levirate has been practiced by the New Caledonians, the Mongols, the Afghans, the Abyssinians, the Hebrews, and the Hindus, as well as certain Native American and African tribes (Fielding, 1942).

The chief reason that the Hindus and Hebrews practiced the levirate was religious and had to do with the importance of having a son in the family. Hindu men needed a son to perform certain sacrifices, so if a man died before having one, a boy born to his former wife and brother would carry out those ceremonies in his name (Fielding, 1942).

For the Hebrews, it was also important that every man have a son, so that his name would not die out. There was a ritualized penalty for men who refused to marry their brother's widow and rear a son in his name:

> And if the man like not to take his brother's wife, then let his brother's wife go up to the gate unto the elders, and say, My husband's brother refuseth to raise up unto his brother a name in Israel, he will not perform the duty of my husband's brother. Then the elders of his city shall call him, and speak unto him: and if he stand to it, and say, I like not to take her; Then shall his brother's wife come in to him in the presence of the elders, and loose his shoe from his foot, and spit in his face, and shall answer and say, So shall it be done unto that man that will not build up his brother's house. (Deuteronomy 25:7–9).

The punishment for refusing to practice the levirate used to be more severe than the above-quoted ritual. In Genesis, chapter 38, we read of Judah's son Onan and how he was killed by the Lord for refusing to impregnate his dead older brother's wife. The book of Ruth in the Old Testament is also an excellent example of how the levirate worked. It is an account of how Naomi has no more sons for her daughter-in-law Ruth to marry, so she arranges for another male relative, Boaz, to take on the responsibility.

Matchmaking. There are various ways in which two young people can be brought together. Typically, the parents of both boys and girls will work out the details among themselves and then announce it to their children. The initial go-between in Turkey has been the boy's mother, who would inspect possibilities at the public baths and then give reports to her son (Tober, 1984). The popular musical *Fiddler on the Roof* is about father-arranged marriages. Often, hired go-betweens, or matchmakers, assist in making the arrangement. They might act as intermediaries between the families or suggest potential spouses. Checking for astrological or other religious signs and requirements could also be part of their job.

In the 1800s, bachelor pioneers in the American West would sometimes find a wife by ordering one from a mail-order catalog. Even today, many Asian families publish matrimonial want ads in search of a respectable spouse for their child (Tober, 1984). I recently found the following in the classified section of a Philippine newspaper:

> FOREIGNER: video match a decent friendship marriage consultant office introducing a beautiful single educated Filipina view friendship to marriage.
>
> LADIES: Australian European businessmen newly arrive in town sincerely willing to meet decent Filipina view friendship to marriage. Ambassador Hotel suite 216.

Computer dating services in the United States, Japan, and elsewhere manifest the continued utility of professional matchmaking, even in societies in which the individuals involved make the final decisions themselves. There are also magazines designed for singles that include matrimonial or relationship want ads.

There are immigrants to Western societies who are not comfortable with love-based unions and prefer to have their marriages arranged by their parents or through a mediator. It is estimated, for instance, that up to 90 percent of the marriages in the East Indian community in Edmonton, Alberta, are to some degree arranged (Jimenez, 1992). Some ethnic Indians return to the Indian subcontinent to find a spouse, whereas others allow their parents to find a match locally for them. Some place ads in newspapers such as *India Today* or *India Abroad,* which focus on desired background characteristics such as education, religion, and age. In deference to Western customs, the young people can veto any match that does not appeal to them, and a dowry is rarely accepted.

Free-Choice Mate Selection

. . . [L]ove gradually became the principal criterion for marriage in the Western world after the Renaissance. The shift from kinship and economic motives to personal ones in mate selection led to the conclusion that the individuals themselves, rather than their parents or others, were best qualified to make the decision. In societies in which the basic family unit is nuclear, both romantic love and free mate choice are more common. This is because extended kin groups are not important enough to see marriage as needing to be group controlled.

Even though free choice is the mate selection method of the modern United States, one should not conclude that it is the most common approach in the world. In a survey of forty societies, Stephens (1963) found only five in which completely free mate choice is permitted. An additional six allowed the young people to choose their spouse, but subject to parental approval. Twelve other cultures had a mix of arranged marriages and free-choice (usually subject to approval) unions, and the final sixteen allowed only arranged marriages.

Moreover, even free choice does not mean that one can marry anyone. All societies have marital regulations. The rule of *exogamy* declares that a person must marry outside his/her group. Typically, this means that certain relatives are unavailable as marriage partners. Exogamous rules are generally the same as the incest taboos of the society, which prohibit sexual intercourse between close blood relatives. Others go beyond that, however. In classical China, two people with the same surname could not marry even if there was no kinship relation (Hutter, 1981).

The rule of *endogamy* declares that a person must marry within his/her group. This rule applies social pressure to marry someone who is similar to oneself in important ways, including religion, race, or ethnic group; social class; and age. These factors have been found to be related to marital compatibility and are precisely the kinds of things considered by parents in arranged marriages. One reason why the divorce rate seems to be higher in free-choice societies may be that many couples ignore endogamy issues and allow romantic love to be practically the sole consideration in mate selection. There is a tendency for marriages to be fairly homogamous, however, even in free-mate-choice societies.

A final factor is *propinquity* (geographical nearness). It is, of course, impossible to marry someone who lives so far away from you that you never meet. At another level, however, this principle refers to a human tendency to be friends with people with whom it is convenient to interact. Let us say that you leave your hometown to attend college elsewhere. You left a boyfriend or girlfriend back at home and you also meet someone new at college. All other things being equal, which one will you marry? Generally, it will be the one at school simply because it is easier.

Some Examples. Free mate choice is on the rise in China today. However, it is very different from the courtship pattern in North America. Young people gather information about each other first and check for mutual suitability before going public with their relationship. In fact, dating follows, rather than precedes, the decision to marry. Typically, the couple knows each other for well over two years before marrying. This cautious approach is paying off, as the quality of these marriages seems to be higher than that of arranged unions (Liao & Heaton, 1992).

The Igbo are a people living in present-day Nigeria (Okonjo, 1992). About 55 percent of the Igbo have their marriages arranged, while the remaining 45 percent are in free-choice unions. Most of the latter are younger, indicating a move from arranged to free choice, which we see occurring throughout much of the world today. Regardless of type, premarital chastity is very highly valued among the Igbo.

As the Ibgo move to free mate choice based on love, their various arranged practices are falling into disfavor. Customs that are quickly disappearing include woman-to-woman marriage. In this situation, an older childless woman pays the brideprice to marry a younger female, usually a cousin. A male mate is chosen for the "wife" to have children with, but they belong to the older female spouse, who has the legal role of "husband."

Another way of securing an heir is *father-to-daughter* marriage. If a man has no sons, he may prohibit a daughter from marrying. She has children from a male mate (not the father) but her sons are considered her father's. Women whose husbands turn out to be impotent are allowed to have a lover from whom to have children, who are considered to be the legal husband's. Other arranged practices seldom practiced anymore are the levirate and child marriages.

CRITICAL-THINKING QUESTIONS

1. What four major issues influence mate choice in societies where marriages are arranged? What societal functions do the specific mechanisms of arranged marriages (such as brideprice, dowry, sororate, levirate, and matchmaking) fulfill?
2. Does marriage by free choice mean that a person can really marry *anyone?* What factors (or rules) considerably narrow the field of eligible mates in societies with free-choice mate selection?
3. What are the advantages and disadvantages of marrying for love (in free-choice societies) rather than economic or political considerations (in societies with arranged marriages)? Would marriages in North America be less likely to end in divorce if marriages were arranged?

REFERENCES

BALSWICK, J. 1975. The function of the dowry system in a rapidly modernizing society: The case of Cyprus. *International Journal of Sociology and the Family,* 5(2):158–167.

BILLIG, M. 1992. The marriage squeeze and the rise of groomprice in India's Kerala state. *Journal of Comparative Family Studies,* 23(2):197–216.

FIELDING, W. 1942. *Strange customs of courtship and marriage.* New York: New Home Library.

The Holy Bible. King James Version.

HUTTER, M. 1981. *The changing family: Comparative perspectives.* New York: Wiley.

JIMENEZ, M. 1992. Many Indo-Canadians follow age-old custom. *The Edmonton Journal.* (July 26):B3.

LIAO, C., and T. HEATON. 1992. Divorce trends and differentials in China. *Journal of Comparative Family Studies,* 23(3):413–429.

OKONJO, K. 1992. Aspects of continuity and change in mate selection among the Igbo west of the river Niger. *Journal of Comparative Family Studies,* 23(3): 339–360.

PETERS, J. 1987. Yąnomamö mate selection and marriage. *Journal of Comparative Family Studies,* 18(1):79–98.

STEPHENS, W. 1963. *The family in cross-cultural perspective.* New York: Holt, Rinehart & Winston.

TOBER, B. 1984. *The bride: A celebration.* New York: Harry N. Abrams.

Religion

CLASSIC

CONTEMPORARY

CROSS-CULTURAL

55

The Protestant Ethic and the Spirit of Capitalism

Max Weber

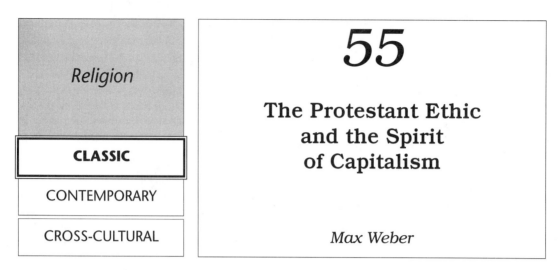

In perhaps his most well known treatise, Max Weber argues that a major factor in the development of the capitalist economic system was the distinctive world view of early, ascetic Protestantism, especially Calvinism and Puritanism. In this excerpt from his classic analysis, Weber explains that religious ideas about work and materials initially fostered capitalism's growth; ultimately, he concludes, capitalism was able to stand on its own without religious supports.

A product of modern European civilization, studying any problem of universal history, is bound to ask himself to what combination of circumstances the fact should be attributed that in Western civilization, and in Western civilization only, cultural phenomena have appeared which (as we like to think) lie in a line of development having *universal* significance and value. . . . All over the world there have been merchants, wholesale and retail, local and engaged in foreign trade. . . .

But in modern times the Occident has developed, in addition to this, a very different form of capitalism which has appeared nowhere else: the rational capitalistic organization of (formally) free labour. Only suggestions of it are found elsewhere. Even the organization of unfree labour reached a considerable degree of rationality only on plantations and to a very limited extent in the *Ergasteria* of antiquity. In the manors, manorial workshops, and domestic industries on estates with serf labour it was probably somewhat less developed. Even real domestic industries with free labour have definitely been proved to have existed in only a few isolated cases outside the Occident. . . .

Rational industrial organization, attuned to a regular market, and neither to political nor irrationally speculative opportunities for profit, is not, however, the only peculiarity of Western capitalism. The modern rational organization of the capitalistic enterprise would not have been possible without two

Source: From *The Protestant Ethic and the Spirit of Capitalism* by Max Weber, copyright © 1988, Prentice-Hall, Inc. Reprinted by permission.

other important factors in its development: the separation of business from the household, which completely dominates modern economic life, and closely connected with it, rational book-keeping. . . .

Hence in a universal history of culture the central problem for us is not, in the last analysis, even from a purely economic view-point, the development of capitalistic activity as such, differing in different cultures only in form: the adventurer type, or capitalism in trade, war, politics, or administration as sources of gain. It is rather the origin of this sober bourgeois capitalism with its rational organization of free labour. Or in terms of cultural history, the problem is that of the origin of the Western bourgeois class and of its peculiarities, a problem which is certainly closely connected with that of the origin of the capitalistic organization of labour, but is not quite the same thing. For the bourgeois as a class existed prior to the development of the peculiar modern form of capitalism, though, it is true, only in the Western hemisphere.

Now the peculiar modern Western form of capitalism has been, at first sight, strongly influenced by the development of technical possibilities. Its rationality is today essentially dependent on the calculability of the most important technical factors. But this means fundamentally that it is dependent on the peculiarities of modern science, especially the natural sciences based on mathematics and exact and rational experiment. On the other hand, the development of these sciences and of the technique resting upon them now receives important stimulation from these capitalistic interests in its practical economic application. It is true that the origin of Western science cannot be attributed to such interests. Calculation, even with decimals, and algebra have been carried on in India, where the decimal system was invented. But it was only made use of by developing capitalism in the West, while in India it led to no modern arithmetic or book-keeping. Neither was the origin of mathematics and mechanics determined by capitalistic interests. But the *technical* utilization of scientific knowledge, so important for the living conditions of the mass of people, was certainly encouraged by economic considerations, which were extremely favourable to it in the Occident. But this encouragement was derived from the peculiarities of the social structure of the Occident. We must hence ask, from *what* parts of that structure was it derived, since not all of them have been of equal importance?

Among those of undoubted importance are the rational structures of law and of administration. For modern rational capitalism has need, not only of the technical means of production, but of a calculable legal system and of administration in terms of formal rules. Without it adventurous and speculative trading capitalism and all sorts of politically determined capitalisms are possible, but no rational enterprise under individual initiative, with fixed capital and certainty of calculations. Such a legal system and such administration have been available for economic activity in a comparative state of legal and formalistic perfection only in the Occident. We must hence inquire where that law came from. Among other circumstances, capitalistic interests have in turn undoubtedly also helped, but by no means alone nor even principally, to prepare the way for the predominance in law and administration of a class of jurists specially trained in rational law. But these interests did not themselves create that law. Quite different forces were at work in this development. And why did not the capitalistic interests do the same in China or India? Why did not the scientific, the artistic, the political, or the economic development there enter upon that path of rationalization which is peculiar to the Occident?

For in all the above cases it is a question of the specific and peculiar rationalism of Western culture. . . . It is hence our first concern to work out and to explain genetically the special peculiarity of Occidental rationalism, and within this field that of the modern Occidental form. Every such attempt at explanation must, recognizing the fundamental importance of the economic factor, above all take account of the economic conditions. But at the same time the opposite correlation must not be left out of consideration. For though the development of economic rationalism is partly dependent on rational technique and law, it is at the same time determined by the ability and disposition of men to adopt certain types of practical rational conduct. When these types have been obstructed by spiritual obstacles, the development of rational economic conduct has also met serious inner resistance. The magical and religious forces, and the ethical ideas of duty based upon them, have in the past always been among the most important formative influences on conduct. In the studies collected here we shall be concerned with these forces.

Two older essays have been placed at the beginning which attempt, at one important point, to approach the side of the problem which is generally most difficult to grasp: the influence of certain religious ideas on the development of an economic spirit, or the *ethos* of an economic system. In this case we are dealing with the connection of the spirit of modern economic life with the rational ethics of ascetic Protestantism. Thus we treat here only one side of the causal chain. . . .

. . . [T]hat side of English Puritanism which was derived from Calvinism gives the most consistent religious basis for the idea of the calling. . . . For the saints' everlasting rest is in the next world; on earth man must, to be certain of his state of grace, "do the works of him who sent him, as long as it is yet day." Not leisure and enjoyment, but only activity serves to increase the glory of God according to the definite manifestations of His will.

Waste of time is thus the first and in principle the deadliest of sins. The span of human life is infinitely short and precious to make sure of one's own election. Loss of time through sociability, idle talk, luxury, even more sleep than is necessary for health, six to at most eight hours, is worthy of absolute moral condemnation. It does not yet hold, with Franklin, that time is money, but the proposition is true in a certain spiritual sense. It is infinitely valuable because every hour lost is lost to labour for the glory of God. Thus inactive contemplation is also valueless, or even directly reprehensible if it is at the expense of one's daily work. . . .

[T]he same prescription is given for all sexual temptation as is used against religious doubts and a sense of moral unworthiness: "Work hard in your calling." But the most important thing was that even beyond that labour came to be considered in itself the end of life, ordained as such by God. St. Paul's "He who will not work shall not eat" holds unconditionally for everyone. Unwillingness to work is symptomatic of the lack of grace.

Here the difference from the mediæval viewpoint becomes quite evident. Thomas Aquinas also gave an interpretation of that statement of St. Paul. But for him labour is only necessary *naturali ratione* for the maintenance of individual and community. Where this end is achieved, the precept ceases to have any meaning. Moreover, it holds only for the race, not for every individual. It does not apply to anyone who can live without labour on his possessions, and of course contemplation, as a spiritual form of action in the Kingdom of God, takes precedence over the commandment in its literal sense. Moreover, for the popular theology of the time, the highest form of monastic productivity lay in the increase of the *Thesaurus ecclesliæ* through prayer and chant.

. . . For everyone without exception God's Providence has prepared a calling, which he should profess and in which he should labour. And this calling is not, as it was for the Lutheran, a fate to which he must submit and which he must make the best of, but God's commandment to the individual to work for the divine glory. This seemingly subtle difference had far-reaching psychological consequences, and became connected with a further development of the providential interpretation of the economic order which had begun in scholasticism.

It is true that the usefulness of a calling, and thus its favour in the sight of God, is measured primarily in moral terms, and thus in terms of the importance of the goods produced in it for the community. But a further, and, above all, in practice the most important, criterion is found in private profitableness. For if that God, whose hand the Puritan sees in all the occurrences of life, shows one of His elect a chance of profit, he must do it with a purpose. Hence the faithful Christian must follow the call by taking advantage of the opportunity. "If God show you a way in which you may lawfully get more than in another way (without wrong to your soul or to any other), if you refuse this, and choose the less gainful way, you cross one of the ends of your calling, and you refuse to be God's steward, and to accept His gifts and use them for Him when He requireth it: you may labour to be rich for God, though not for the flesh and sin." . . .

The superior indulgence of the *seigneur* and the parvenu ostentation of the *nouveau riche* are equally detestable to asceticism. But, on the other hand, it has the highest ethical appreciation of the sober, middle-class, self-made man. "God blesseth His trade" is a stock remark about those good men who had successfully followed the divine hints. The whole power of the God of the Old Testament, who rewards His people for their obedience in this life, necessarily exercised a similar influence on the Puritan who . . . compared his own state of grace with that of the heroes of the Bible. . . .

Although we cannot here enter upon a discussion of the influence of Puritanism in all . . . directions, we should call attention to the fact that the toleration of pleasure in cultural goods, which contributed to purely aesthetic or athletic enjoyment, certainly always ran up against one characteristic limitation: They must not cost anything. Man is only a trustee of the goods which have come to him through God's grace. He must, like the servant in the parable, give an account of every penny entrusted to him, and it is at least hazardous to spend any of it for a purpose which does not serve the glory of God but only one's own enjoyment. What person, who keeps his eyes open, has not met representatives of this viewpoint even in the present? The idea of a man's duty to his possessions, to which he subordinates himself as an obedient steward, or even as an acquisitive machine, bears with chilling weight on his life. The greater the possessions the heavier, if the ascetic attitude toward life stands the test, the feeling of responsibility for them, for holding them undiminished for the glory of God and increasing them by restless effort. The origin of this type of life also extends in certain roots, like so many aspects of the spirit of capitalism, back into the Middle Ages. But it was in the ethic of ascetic Protestantism that it first found a consistent ethical foundation. Its significance for the development of capitalism is obvious.

This worldly Protestant asceticism, as we may recapitulate up to this point, acted powerfully against the spontaneous enjoyment of possessions; it restricted consumption, especially of luxuries. On the other hand, it had the psychological effect of freeing the acquisition of goods from the inhibitions of traditionalistic ethics. It broke the bonds of the impulse of acquisition in that it not only legalized it, but (in the sense discussed) looked upon it as directly willed by God. . . .

As far as the influence of the Puritan outlook extended, under all circumstances—and this is, of course, much more important than the mere encouragement of capital accumulation—it favoured the development of a rational bourgeois economic life; it was the most important, and above all the only consistent influence in the development of that life. It stood at the cradle of the modern economic man.

To be sure, these Puritanical ideals tended to give way under excessive pressure from the temptations of wealth, as the Puritans themselves knew very well. With great regularity we find the most genuine adherents of Puritanism among the classes which were rising from a lowly status, the small bourgeois and farmers while the *beati possi-*

dentes, even among Quakers, are often found tending to repudiate the old ideals. It was the same fate which again and again befell the predecessor of this worldly asceticism, the monastic asceticism of the Middle Ages. In the latter case, when rational economic activity had worked out its full effects by strict regulation of conduct and limitation of consumption, the wealth accumulated either succumbed directly to the nobility, as in the time before the Reformation, or monastic discipline threatened to break down, and one of the numerous reformations became necessary.

In fact the whole history of monasticism is in a certain sense the history of a continual struggle with the problem of the secularizing influence of wealth. The same is true on a grand scale of the worldly asceticism of Puritanism. The great revival of Methodism, which preceded the expansion of English industry toward the end of the eighteenth century, may well be compared with such a monastic reform. We may hence quote here a passage from John Wesley himself which might well serve as a motto for everything which has been said above. For it shows that the leaders of these ascetic movements understood the seemingly paradoxical relationships which we have here analysed perfectly well, and in the same sense that we have given them. He wrote:

> I fear, wherever riches have increased, the essence of religion has decreased in the same proportion. Therefore I do not see how it is possible, in the nature of things, for any revival of true religion to continue long. For religion must necessarily produce both industry and frugality, and these cannot but produce riches. But as riches increase, so will pride, anger, and love of the world in all its branches. How then is it possible that Methodism, that is, a religion of the heart, though it flourishes now as a green bay tree, should continue in this state? For the Methodists in every place grow diligent and frugal; consequently they increase in goods. Hence they proportionately increase in pride, in anger, in the desire of the flesh, the desire of the eyes, and the pride of life. So, although the form of religion remains, the spirit is swiftly vanishing away. Is there no way to prevent this—this continual decay of pure religion? We ought not to prevent people from being diligent and frugal; *we must exhort all Christians to gain all they can, and to save all they can; that is, in effect, to grow rich.*

As Wesley here says, the full economic effect of those great religious movements, whose significance for economic development lay above all in their ascetic educative influence, generally came only after the peak of the purely religious enthusiasm was past. Then the intensity of the search for the Kingdom of God commenced gradually to pass over into sober economic virtue; the religious roots died out slowly, giving way to utilitarian worldliness. Then, as Dowden puts it, as in *Robinson Crusoe,* the isolated economic man who carries on missionary activities on the side takes the place of the lonely spiritual search for the Kingdom of Heaven of Bunyan's pilgrim, hurrying through the market-place of Vanity. . . .

A specifically bourgeois economic ethic had grown up. With the consciousness of standing in the fullness of God's grace and being visibly blessed by Him, the bourgeois business man, as long as he remained within the bounds of formal correctness, as long as his moral conduct was spotless and the use to which he put his wealth was not objectionable, could follow his pecuniary interests as he would and feel that he was fulfilling a duty in doing so. The power of religious asceticism provided him in addition with sober, conscientious, and unusually industrious workmen, who clung to their work as to a life purpose willed by God.

Finally, it gave him the comforting assurance that the unequal distribution of the goods of this world was a special dispensation of Divine Providence, which in these differences, as in particular grace, pursued secret ends unknown to men. . . .

One of the fundamental elements of the spirit of modern capitalism, and not only of that but of all modern culture: Rational conduct on the basis of the idea of the calling, was born—that is what this discussion has sought to demonstrate—from the spirit of Christian asceticism. One has only to re-read the passage from Franklin, quoted at the beginning of this essay, in order to see that the essential elements of the attitude which was there called the spirit of capitalism are the same as what we have just shown to be the content of the Puritan worldly asceticism, only without the religious basis, which by Franklin's time had died away. . . .

Since asceticism undertook to remodel the world and to work out its ideals in the world, material goods have gained an increasing and finally an inexorable power over the lives of men as at no previous period in history. Today the spirit of religious asceticism—whether finally, who knows?—has escaped from the cage. But victorious capitalism, since it rests on mechanical foundations, needs its support no longer. The rosy blush of its laughing heir, the Enlightenment, seems also to be irretrievably fading, and the idea of duty in one's calling prowls about in our lives like the ghost of dead religious beliefs. Where the fulfilment of the calling cannot directly be related to the highest spiritual and cultural values, or when, on the other hand, it need not be felt simply as economic compulsion, the individual generally abandons the attempt to justify it at all. In the field of its highest development, in the United States, the pursuit of wealth, stripped of its religious and ethical meaning, tends to become associated with purely mundane passions, which often actually give it the character of sport.

No one knows who will live in this cage in the future, or whether at the end of this tremendous development entirely new prophets will arise, or there will be a great rebirth of old ideas and ideals, or, if neither, mechanized petrification, embellished with a sort of convulsive self-importance. For of the last stage of this cultural development, it might well be truly said: "Specialists without spirit, sensualists without heart; this nullity imagines that it has attained a level of civilization never before achieved."

But this brings us to the world of judgments of value and of faith, with which this purely historical discussion need not be burdened. . . .

Here we have only attempted to trace the fact and the direction of its influence to their motives in one, though a very important point. But it would also further be necessary to investigate how Protestant Asceticism was in turn influenced in its development and its character by the totality of social conditions, especially economic. The modern man is in general, even with the best will, unable to give religious ideas a significance for culture and national character which they deserve. But it is, of course, not my aim to substitute for a one-sided materialistic an equally one-sided spiritualistic causal interpretation of culture and of history. Each is equally possible, but each, if it does not serve as the preparation, but as the conclusion of an investigation, accomplishes equally little in the interest of historical truth.

CRITICAL-THINKING QUESTIONS

1. What are the distinctive characteristics of the religious orientation that Weber called the "Protestant ethic"? In what ways did they promote the development of the capitalist economic system?
2. In what respects do early Calvinists with a sense of "calling" differ from today's "workaholics"?
3. In what sense does Weber's analysis differ from the materialist orientation of Karl Marx (Reading 46), who suggested that productive forces shape the world of ideas?

Religion

CLASSIC

CONTEMPORARY

CROSS-CULTURAL

56

Culture Wars

James Davison Hunter

The religious conflict that has marked the United States throughout most of our history has now subsided. But, Hunter explains, today's "culture wars" over this nation's future direction are a moral crusade in which opposing sides are animated by a religious fervor.

. . . When we look all around the social and political landscape, we see a general harmony among the traditional faiths of the United States; by and large, Protestants get along well with Catholics, Christians get along better with Jews, and even the small number of religious cults are more of a curiosity than a source of widespread resentment and antagonism. If one can argue anything on the basis of scholarly study, it is that the predictions of the Enlightenment age are coming true after all.

But are they? Is the age of cultural and, in particular, religious conflict in America coming to a close?

The answer must be no. The reason is that cultural conflict is taking shape along new and in many ways unfamiliar lines.

Let me begin to make sense of the new lines of cultural warfare by first defining what I mean by "cultural conflict." I define cultural conflict very simply as political and social hostility rooted in different systems of moral understanding. The end to which these hostilities tend is the domination of one cultural and moral ethos over all others. Let it be clear, the principles and ideals that mark these competing systems of moral understanding are by no means trifling but always have a character of ultimacy to them. They are not merely attitudes that can change on a whim but basic commitments and beliefs that provide a source of identity, purpose, and togetherness for the people who live by them. It is for precisely this reason that political action rooted in these principles and ideals tends to be so passionate.

So what is new about the contemporary cultural conflict? . . . [T]he cultural hostilities dominant over the better part of American history have taken place *within* the boundaries of a larger biblical culture—among numerous Protestant groups, and Catholics and Jews—over such issues as doctrine,

---

Source: From *Culture Wars: The Struggle to Define America* by James Davison Hunter. Copyright © 1991 by BasicBooks, a division of HarperCollins Publishers, Inc. Reprinted by permission.

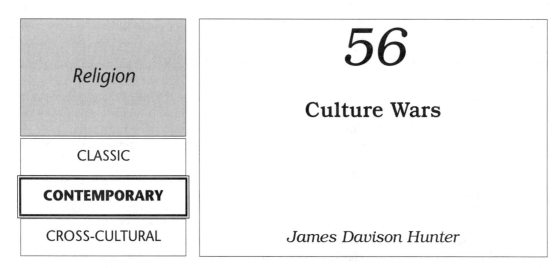

ritual observance, and religious organization. Underlying their disagreements, therefore, were basic agreements about the order of life in community and nation—agreements forged by biblical symbols and imagery. But the old arrangements have been transformed. . . . The older agreements have unraveled. The divisions of political consequence today are not theological and ecclesiastical in character but the result of differing worldviews. That is to say, they no longer revolve around specific doctrinal issues or styles of religious practice and organization but around our most fundamental and cherished assumptions about how to order our lives—our own lives and our lives together in this society. Our most fundamental ideas about who we are as Americans are now at odds.

Because this is a culture war, the nub of political disagreement today on the range of issues debated—whether abortion, child care, funding for the arts, affirmative action and quotas, gay rights, values in public education, or multiculturalism—can be traced ultimately and finally to the matter of moral authority. By moral authority I mean the basis by which people determine whether something is good or bad, right or wrong, acceptable or unacceptable, and so on. Of course, people often have very different ideas about what criteria to use in making moral judgments, but this is just the point. It is the commitment to different and opposing bases of moral authority and the world views that derive from them that creates the deep cleavages between antagonists in the contemporary culture war. As we will see, this cleavage is so deep that it cuts *across* the old lines of conflict, making the distinctions that long divided Americans—those between Protestants, Catholics, and Jews—virtually irrelevant.

At this point let me introduce a critical word of qualification. Though competing moral visions are at the heart of today's cultural war, these do not always take form in coherent, clearly articulated, sharply differentiated world views. Rather, these moral visions take expression as *polarizing impulses* or *tendencies* in American culture. It is important, in this light, to make a distinction between how these moral visions are institutionalized in different organizations and in public rhetoric, and how ordinary Americans relate to them. In truth, most Americans occupy a vast middle ground between the polarizing impulses of American culture. Many will obviously lean toward one side while many others will tilt toward the other. Some Americans may seem altogether oblivious to either. The point is that most Americans, despite their predispositions, would not embrace a particular moral vision wholly or uncritically. Where the polarizing tendencies in American culture tend to be sharpest is in the organizations and spokespeople who have an interest in promoting a particular position on a social issue. It is they who, perhaps unwittingly, give voice to the competing moral visions. (Even then, I might add, the world views articulated are often less than coherent!) These institutions possess tremendous power in the realm of public discourse. They almost seem to have a life of their own: an existence, power, and agenda independent of the people for whom they presumably speak.

POLARIZING IMPULSES: THE ORTHODOX AND THE PROGRESSIVE

To come right to the point, the cleavages at the heart of the contemporary culture war are created by what I would like to call *the impulse toward orthodoxy* and *the impulse toward progressivism.* The terms are imperfect, but each aspires to describe in shorthand a particular locus and source of moral truth, the fundamental (though perhaps subconscious) moral allegiances of the actors involved in the culture war as well as their cultural and political dispositions. Though the terms "orthodox" and "progressive" may be familiar to many, they have a particular meaning here that requires some elaboration.

Let me acknowledge, first off, that the words, orthodox and progressive, can describe specific doctrinal creeds or particular religious practices. Take orthodoxy. Within Judaism, orthodoxy is defined mainly by commitment to Torah and the community that upholds it; within Catholicism, orthodoxy is defined largely by loyalty to church teaching—the Roman Magisterium; and within Protestantism, orthodoxy principally means devotion to the complete and final authority of Scripture. Substantively, then, these labels can mean vastly different things within different religious traditions.

But I prefer to use the terms orthodox and progressive as *formal properties* of a belief system or world view. What is common to all three approaches to *orthodoxy,* for example (and what makes orthodoxy more of a formal property), *is the commitment on the part of adherents to an external, definable, and transcendent authority.* Such objective and transcendent authority defines, at least in the abstract, a consistent, unchangeable measure of value, purpose, goodness, and identity, both personal and collective. It tells us what is good, what is true, how we should live, and who we are. It is an authority that is sufficient for all time. . . .

Within cultural progressivism, by contrast, moral authority tends to be defined by the spirit of the modern age, a spirit of rationalism and subjectivism. Progressivist moral ideals tend, that is, to derive from and embody (though rarely exhaust) that spirit. From this standpoint, truth tends to be viewed as a process, as a reality that is ever unfolding. There are many distinctions that need to be made here. For example, what about those progressivists who still identify with a particular religious heritage? For them, one may note a strong tendency to translate the moral ideals of a religious tradition so that they conform to and legitimate the contemporary *zeitgeist.* In other words, what all *progressivist* world views share in common *is the tendency to resymbolize historic faiths according to the prevailing assumptions of contemporary life.* . . . The general point . . . is that the traditional sources of moral authority, whether scripture, papal pronouncements, or Jewish law, no longer have an exclusive or even a predominant binding power over their lives. Rather, the binding moral authority tends to reside in personal experience or scientific rationality, or either of these in conversation with particular religious or cultural traditions.

I have been talking about the contemporary cultural divide in the context of religious communities in order to highlight the historical novelty of the contemporary situation. But what about the growing number of "secularists"? These people range from the vaguely religious to the openly agnostic or atheistic. While they would probably claim no affiliation with a church or religious denomination, they nevertheless hold deep humanistic concerns about the welfare of community and nation. . . . How then do secularists relate to the matter of moral authority?

Like the representatives of religious communities, they too are divided. Yet public opinion surveys show that a decided majority of secularists are drawn toward the progressivist impulse in American culture. For these people religious tradition has no binding address, no opinion-shaping influence. Some secularists, however, (particularly many secular conservative and neo-conservative intellectuals) are drawn toward the orthodox impulse. For them, a commitment to natural law or to a high view of nature serves as the functional equivalent of the external and transcendent moral authority revered by their religiously orthodox counterparts.

In sum, the contemporary cultural conflict turns upside down (or perhaps inside out) the way cultural conflict has long been waged. Thus, we see those with apparently similar religious or cultural affiliations battling with one another. The culture war encompasses all Americans, religious and "non-religious," in very novel ways.

Political Dispositions: Cultural Conservatives versus Cultural Progressivists

The orthodox and progressivist impulses in American culture, as I have described them, contrast sources of moral truth and also the allegiances by which people, drawn toward one or the other, live and interpret the world. They also express, somewhat imperfectly, the opposing social and political dispositions to which Americans on opposing sides of the cultural divide are drawn. Here, though, a word of elaboration.

It nearly goes without saying that those who embrace the orthodox impulse are almost always cultural conservatives, while those who embrace progressivist moral assumptions tend toward a liberal or libertarian social agenda. Certainly, the associations between foundational moral commitments and social and political agendas is far from absolute; some people and organizations will cross over the lines, taking conservative positions on some issues and liberal views on others. Yet the relationship between foundational moral commitments and social and political agendas is too strong and consistent to be viewed as coincidental. This is true for most Americans (as seen in public opinion surveys), but it is especially true for the organizations engaged in the range of contemporary disputes. For the practical purposes of naming the antagonists in the culture war, then, we can label those on one side cultural conservatives or moral traditionalists, and those on the other side liberals or cultural progressives. These are, after all, the terms that the actors in the cultural war use to describe themselves. The danger of using these "political" labels, however, is that one can easily forget that they trace back to prior moral commitments and more basic moral visions: We subtly slip into thinking of the controversies debated as political rather than cultural in nature. On political matters one can compromise; on matters of ultimate moral truth, one cannot. This is why the full range of issues today seems interminable.

New and Unlikely Alliances

The real novelty of the contemporary situation emerges out of the fact that the orthodox and progressivist communities are not fighting isolated battles. Evangelical Protestants, for example, are not locked in an isolated conflict with liberal Protestants. Nor are theologically progressive Catholics struggling in isolation with their theologically conservative counterparts in the Roman hierarchy. The contemporary culture war is much larger and more complicated. *At the heart of the new cultural realignment are the pragmatic alliances being formed across faith traditions.* Because of common points of vision and concern, the orthodox wings of Protestantism, Catholicism, and Judaism are forming associations with each other, as are the progressive wings of each faith community—and each set of alliances takes form in opposition to the influence the other seeks to exert in public culture.

These institutional alliances, it should be noted, are not always influential in terms of the joint power they hold. Some of the groups, after all, are quite small and have few resources. But these institutional alliances are *culturally* significant, for the simple reason that ideological and organizational associations are being generated among groups that have historically been antagonistic toward one another. Had the disagreements in each religious tradition remained simply theological or ecclesiastical in nature, these alliances would have probably never developed. But since the divisions have extended into the broader realm of public morality, the alliances have become the expedient outcome of common concerns. In other words, although these alliances are historically "unnatural," they have become pragmatically necessary. Traditional religio-cultural divisions are superseded—replaced by the overriding differences taking form out of orthodox and progressive moral commitments.

These unlikely alliances are at the center of a fundamental realignment in American culture and, in turn, identify the key actors in an emerging cultural conflict. . . .

Points of Clarification

The first mistake we should guard against is to view the culture war as merely the accumulation of social issues debated today (such as abortion, values in schools, homosexuality, or the meaning of Columbus's discovery of America). The culture war encompasses these issues, but the source of the conflict is found in different moral visions. For this reason, it would also be a mistake to view the culture war as merely a social referendum on Ronald Reagan, George Bush, [Bill Clinton,] or other presidents and their political legacies. If this were the case, the present conflict would simply be a dispute between political "liberals" and "conservatives." The cleavages run much deeper. For the same reasons, it would be inaccurate to describe this as a collision between "religious liberals" and "religious conservatives." Nor is it a clash between what one scholar described as "New Protestants" and "Old Protestants," "New Catholics" and "Old Catholics," and by extension, "New Jews" and "Old Jews." In a similar vein, it would be wrong to confuse the contemporary culture war with the ambitions of Protestant Fundamentalism and the New Christian Right and the backlash it created among such secular activists as feminists in the National Organization for Women (NOW) or attorneys of the American Civil Liberties Union (ACLU). It is true that Evangelical and Fundamentalist Protestants are the most vocal and visible actors on the orthodox side of the new cultural divide and that the secular activists of NOW, the ACLU, or the People for the American Way are among the most visible actors on the progressive side of the divide. But to frame the contemporary culture war in this way ignores the central role played by a wide range of other cultural actors on both sides who are neither Fundamentalists on the one hand nor secular activists on the other. Besides, many of the organizations of the New Christian Right (for instance, such as the Moral Majority, Christian Voice, the Religious Roundtable) have either disappeared from public sight or gone out of business. Yet the cultural conflict continues—and it continues without any sign that it will soon abate.

THE STRUGGLE TO DEFINE AMERICA

RANDALL TERRY (spokesman for the pro-life organization Operation Rescue): The bottom line is that killing children is not what America is all about. We are not here to destroy our offspring.

FAYE WATTLETON (president of Planned Parenthood): Well, we are also not here to have the government use women's bodies as the instrument of the state, to force women into involuntary servitude—

RANDALL TERRY (*laughing*): Oh come on, Faye.

FAYE WATTLETON: —I think that as Americans celebrate the Fourth of July, our independence, and when we reflect on our personal liberties, this is a very, very somber time, in which the courts have said that the most private aspects of our lives are now . . . not protected by the Bill of Rights and the Constitution. And I believe that that is a time for Americans to reflect on the need to return to the fundamentals, and the fundamentals of personal privacy are really the cornerstones upon which our democracy is built.

RANDALL TERRY: I think that to assume or even suggest that the founding fathers of this country risked their lives and many of them died so that we can kill our offspring is pathetic.

Although Randall Terry and Faye Wattleton were debating the morality and legality of abortion, what they said goes far beyond the abortion controversy. First, the contemporary culture is not just an expression of different "opinions" or "attitudes" on this or that issue, like abortion. If this were all there was to it, the conflict I refer to would be, as someone once suggested, the "politics of distraction"—a trivial pursuit that keeps Americans from settling more important matters. No, the conflict is deeper than mere "differences of opinion" and bigger than abortion, and in fact, bigger than the culmination of all the battles being waged. As suggested earlier, the culture war emerges over fundamentally different conceptions of moral authority, over different ideas and beliefs about truth, the good, obligation to one another, the nature of community, and so on.

It is, therefore, cultural conflict at its deepest level. . . .

Though the conflict derives from differences in assumptions that are philosophical and even theological in nature, the conflict does not end as a philosophical dispute. This is a conflict over how we are to order our lives together. This means that the conflict is inevitably expressed as a clash over national life itself. Both Randall Terry and Faye Wattleton acknowledge this in their exchange. Hearing them invoke the Bill of Rights, the "founding fathers," "what America is really all about," and so on, we come to see that the contemporary culture war is ultimately a struggle over national identity—*over the meaning of America,* who we have been in the past, who we are now, and perhaps most important, who we, as a nation, will aspire to become in the new millennium. Importantly, Randall Terry and Faye Wattleton are not the only ones who see a larger relationship between a single issue in the culture war and the American character. A well-known photographer whose work has been scrutinized by the FBI claims, "We are not going down without a fight. We're not going to go down without a voice that's saying loudly and clearly, 'this is not what we think America is about.'" A young mother and activist near Sacramento, who protests the content of schoolbooks in California's public schools, said, "The battle we are fighting here is being fought all around the state and around the nation. We as parents get involved because our children are affected but in the end it is our country that is at stake." A video store owner who was prosecuted for violating pornography laws stated, "I feel like I'm fighting for America. I feel like I'm fighting for our rights as Americans. That's what I feel like." And each of the individuals . . . believes that the battle they wage has consequences for America—its institutions and its ideals. And the list goes on. Arguably, our national identity and purpose has not been more a source of contention since the Civil War.

Though intellectuals and activists of various sorts play a special role in this cultural conflict, it would be very wrong to assume that this conflict is really just the lofty and cerebral machinations of squirrelly academic types who roam the corridors of think tanks and universities. To the contrary, this culture war intersects the lives of most Americans, even those who are or would like to be totally indifferent. This is so because this conflict has an impact on virtually all of the major institutions of American society. As the "stories from the front" suggest, this conflict has a decisive impact on the *family*—not just on the critical issues of reproduction and abortion but on a wide range of other issues such as the limits (if any) of legitimate sexuality, the public and private role of women, questions of childraising, and even the definition of what constitutes a family in the first place. The cultural conflict concerns the structure and content of public *education*—of how and what American children will learn. Also affected is the content of the popular *media*—from the films that are shown to the television shows that are aired to the books that are read and to the art that is exhibited. It has a critical effect on the conduct of *law,* particularly in the ways in which Americans define rights—who should have them and who should not and with whose interests the state should be aligned. Not least, this cultural clash has tremendous consequences for electoral *politics,* the way in which Americans choose their leaders. The contemporary culture war even has a bearing on the way in which public discussion is carried out—in the way people with opposing ideals and agendas try to resolve their differences in the public forum.

Once again, what seems to be a myriad of self-contained cultural disputes actually amounts to a fairly comprehensive and momentous struggle to define the meaning of America—of how and on what terms will Americans live together, of what comprises the good society. . . .

CRITICAL-THINKING QUESTIONS

1. Why does Hunter claim that today's culture wars, although not over religion, are basically religious in character?

2. What beliefs set off "progressive" from "orthodox" people?

3. What relationship, if any, do today's political camps bear to traditional religious categories?

57

Women and Islam

Religion

CLASSIC

CONTEMPORARY

CROSS-CULTURAL

Jane I. Smith

Many Westerners have a vague notion that women in Iran, Saudi Arabia, and other Islamic societies are subject to relentless control by men. Although there is some truth to this stereotype, a more realistic account of the relationship between Islam and gender must begin with a basic understanding of this unfamiliar religion. In this article, Jane Smith provides an overview of Islamic tenets, explores some of the variations that divide the vast Islamic world, and assesses the relative social standing of the sexes—as Muslims themselves understand it.

To attempt to talk about women in Islam is of course to venture into an area fraught with the perils of overgeneralization, oversimplification, and the almost unavoidable limitations of a Western bias. The first problem is simply one of raw numbers. There are perhaps close to half a billion Muslim women inhabiting all major areas of the world today. Is it possible to say anything that holds true for all of them, let alone for their sisters over the past fourteen centuries of Islam?

Then one must consider all the various elements that comprise the picture of Islamic womanhood. Many of these elements are directly related to the religion of Islam itself, such as past and present legal realities, roles permitted and enforced as a result of Muslim images of women, and the variety of Islamic and hetero-Islamic rites and practices in which Islamic women have traditionally participated. Other elements contributing to the full picture of women in Islam—such as education, political rights, professional employment opportunities, and the like—have less to do with the religion per se but are still influenced by it.

The Holy Qur'ān (sometimes transliterated as "Koran") still forms the basis of prevailing family law in most areas of the Muslim world. It has always been and still is considered to be the last in a series of divine revelations from God given in the seventh century C.E. to humanity through the vehicle of his final prophet Muhammad. The Qur'ān is therefore the literal and unmitigated word of God, collected and ordered by the young Muslim community but untainted with the thoughts and interpretations of any persons, including Muhammad himself. It is obvious, then, why the regulations formulated by the Qur'ān in regard to women have been adhered to with strictness and why changes in Muslim family law are coming about only very slowly in the Islamic world.

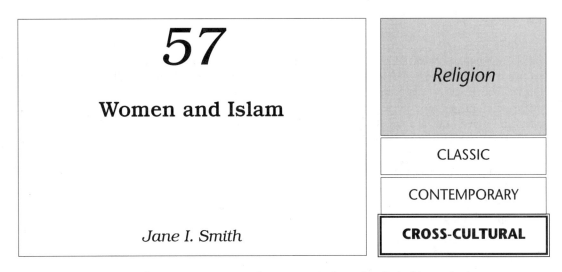

Source: Reprinted by permission of the State University of New York Press, from *Women in World Religions* by Arvind Sharma and Katherine K. Young (eds.),

The circumstances of women in pre-Islamic Arabia are subject to a variety of interpretations. On the one hand, certain women—soothsayers, priestesses, queens, and even singular individuals—did play powerful roles in society. On the other hand, whatever the earlier realities for women in terms of marriage, divorce, and inheritance of property, it is clear that the Qur'ān did introduce very significant changes that were advantageous for women. Contemporary Muslims are fond of pointing out, quite correctly, that Islam brought legal advantages for women quite unknown in corresponding areas of the Western Christian world. What, then, does the Qur'ān say about women?

The earliest messages of the Qur'ān, and the twin themes that run through all the chapters, are of the realities of the oneness of God and the inevitability of the day of judgment. All persons, men and women, are called upon to testify to those realities. . . . Religiously speaking, then, men and women are fully equal in the eyes of God according to the Qur'ān.

Before looking at the specifics of the legal injunctions for women, it is necessary to consider two verses that have caused a great deal of consternation to Westerners. One is 2:228, which says literally that men are a step above women, and the other is 4:34, clarifying that men are the protectors of women (or are in charge of women) because God has given preference to one over the other and because men provide support for women. Perhaps because these verses have been so troublesome for non-Muslims (especially feminists), they have been subject to an enormous amount of explanation and interpretation by contemporary Muslim apologists eager to present a defense of their religion. These writers, men and women, affirm that it is precisely because men are invested with the responsibility of taking care of women, financially and otherwise, that they are given authority over the females of their families. And that, affirm many Muslim women today, is exactly the way it should be. We will return to this perspective later, particularly in light of what a desire for liberation means—and does not mean—for many Muslim women. . . . .

According to the Qur'ān, a man may marry up to four wives, so long as he is able to provide for each equally. He may marry a Muslim woman or a member of the Jewish or Christian faith, or a slave woman. A Muslim woman, however, may marry only one husband, and he must be a Muslim. Contemporary Muslim apologists are quick to point out that these restrictions are for the benefit of women, ensuring that they will not be left unprotected. In Islam, marriage is not a sacrament but a legal contract, and according to the Qur'ān a woman has clearly defined legal rights in negotiating this contract. She can dictate the terms and can receive the dowry herself. This dowry (*mahr*) she is permitted to keep and maintain as a source of personal pride and comfort.

Polygamy (or more strictly polygyny, plurality of wives) is practiced by only a small percentage of the contemporary Muslim population, and a man with more than two wives is extremely rare. Many countries are now taking steps to modify the circumstances in which a husband may take more than one wife, although only in two countries, Turkey and Tunisia, are multiple marriages actually illegal. Other countries have made such moves as requiring the husband to have the permission of the court (as in Iraq and Syria) or to get the permission of the first wife (as in Egypt), or permitting the wife to write into her marriage contract that she will not allow a cowife (as in Morocco and Lebanon). It seems reasonable to expect that other countries will make changes and modifications. It is interesting to note that while for some finances have dictated monogamy—most husbands have simply not been able to afford more than one wife—changing economic realities may again dictate that a man contemplate the possibility of having several wives to work and supply income for the family.

Muslim women traditionally have been married at an extremely young age, sometimes even before puberty. This practice is related, of course, to the historical fact that fathers and other male relatives generally have chosen the grooms themselves, despite the guarantee of the Qur'ān that marriage is a contract into which male and female enter equally. While it is true that technically a girl cannot be forced into a marriage she does not want, pressures from family and the youth of the bride often have made this prerogative difficult to exercise. Today, the right of a male member of the family to contract an engagement for a girl against her wishes has been legally revoked in most places, although it is still a common practice, especially in rural areas. . . .

In the contemporary Islamic world, divorce rates vary considerably from one country to the next. Muslim apologists insist that divorce is not nearly as common in Islamic countries as it is, for example, in the United States. This statement is generally true, although in some countries, such as Morocco, the rate is high and continues to grow. Often what is really only the breaking of the engagement contract is included in divorce statistics, skewing the measure. Many countries are now considering serious changes in divorce procedures. The simultaneous triple repudiation generally has been declared illegal, and in many countries divorce initiated by either party, the man or the woman, must take place in the court of law. Other countries add special stipulations generally favorable to the woman. It remains true, however, that men can divorce for less cause than women, and often divorces hung up in courts with male judges can prove enormously difficult for women to gain.

In accordance with Islamic law, custody of the children traditionally has gone to the father at some time between the age of seven and nine for boys and between seven and puberty for girls, depending on the legal school. This practice too is slowly changing, and in most areas women who have been divorced by their husbands are allowed to keep their sons until puberty and their daughters until they are of an age to be married.

It is considered one of the great innovations of the Qur'ān over earlier practices that women are permitted to inherit and own property. Non-Muslims have generally found great difficulty with the Qur'ānic stipulation that a woman is allowed to inherit property but that the inheritance should be only half that of a male. According to the Islamic understanding, however, the rationale is precisely that which applies to the verse saying that men are in charge of women. Because women are permitted to keep and maintain their own property without responsibility for taking care of their families financially, it is only reasonable that the male, who must spend his own earning and inheritance for the maintenance of women, should receive twice as much. . . .

According to the Qur'ān, women should not expose themselves to public view with lack of modesty. It does not say that they should be covered specifically from head to toe, nor that they should wear face veils or masks or other of the paraphernalia that has adorned many Islamic women through the ages. The Qur'ān also suggests that the wives of the Prophet Muhammad, when speaking to other men, should do so from behind a partition, again for purposes of propriety. It has been open to question whether this statement is meant to apply to all women. In the early Islamic community, these verses were exaggerated and their underlying ideas elaborated and defined in ways that led fairly quickly to a seclusion of women which seems quite at odds with what the Qur'ān intended or the Prophet wanted. When the community in Medina was established, women participated fully with men in all activities of worship and prayer. Soon they became segregated, however, to the point where an often-quoted *hadīth* (no doubt spurious) attributed to Muhammad has him saying that women pray better at home than in the mosque, and best of all in their own closets. Today a number of contemporary Muslim writers are urging a return to the practices of the young Muslim community, with women no longer segregated from the mosque or relegated to certain rear or side portions as they generally have been, but participating fully in worship with men. . . .

What is popularly known as "veiling" is part of the general phenomenon of the segregation of women and yet is also distinctly apart from it. The two are increasingly seen as separate by contemporary Islamic women seeking to affirm a new identity in relation to their religion. Veils traditionally have taken a number of forms: a veil covering the face from just below the eyes down; a *chador* or *burka* covering the entire body, including the face, often with a woven screen in front through which women can see but not be seen; and a full face mask with small slits through the eyes, still worn in some areas of the Arabian Gulf. These costumes, so seemingly oppressive to Western eyes, at least have allowed women to observe without being observed, thus affording their wearers a degree of anonymity that on some occasions has proven useful.

The general movement toward unveiling had its ostensible beginning in the mid-1920s, when the Egyptian feminist Huda Sha'rawi cast off her veil after arriving in Egypt from an international meeting of women. She was followed literally and symbolically by masses of women in the succeeding years, and Egyptian women as well as those in other Middle Eastern countries made great strides in adopting Western dress. At the present time in the history of Islam, however, one finds a quite different phenomenon. Partly in reaction against Western liberation and Western ideals in general, women in many parts of the Islamic world are self-consciously adopting forms of dress by which they can identify with Islam rather than with what they now see as the imperialist West. Islamic dress, generally chosen by Muslim women themselves rather than forced upon them by males, signals for many an identification with a way of life that they are increasingly convinced represents a more viable alternative than that offered by the West. . . .

We see, then, that while legal circumstances for women have undergone some significant changes in the past half-century, the dictates of the Qur'ān continue to be enormously influential in the molding of new laws as well as in the personal choices of Muslim men and women. . . .

I have stressed here the insistence of the Qur'ān on the religious and spiritual equality of men and women. And aside from some unfortunate hadīth with very weak chains of authority suggesting that the majority of women will be in the Fire on the Day of Judgment because of their mental and physical inferiority, religious literature in general, when talking about human responsibility and concomitant judgment, makes women full partners with men under the divine command to live lives of integrity and righteousness. . . .

Of course, women do participate in many of the activities and duties considered incumbent on all good Muslims, but generally these practices have a somewhat different function for them than for men. Prayer for women, as we have said, is usually in the home rather than in the mosque, and does not necessarily follow the pattern of the regularized five times a day. Participation in the fast itself is normally the same as for the men (except when women are pregnant, nursing, or menstruating), but the particular joys of preparing the fast-breaking meals are for the women alone. While the husband determines the amount of money or goods to be distributed for almsgiving, another responsibility of all Muslims, it is often the wife who takes charge of the actual distribution.

The last duty incumbent on Muslims after the testimony to the oneness of God and prophethood of his apostle Muhammad, the prayer, the fast, and paying the almstax is the pilgrimage once in a lifetime to the holy city of Mecca. Women do participate in this journey, and as transportation becomes easier and the care provided for pilgrims in Saudi Arabia becomes more regularized with modernization, increasing numbers of females join the throngs which gather to circumambulate the Xaaba at Mecca each year. . . .

Saints in Islam are both male and female. One is normally recognized as a saint not by any process of canonization but because of some miraculous deed(s) performed or through a dream communication after death with a living person requesting that a shrine be erected over his or her tomb. Often a woman is favored with these dreams and after the construction of the shrine she becomes the carekeeper of the tomb, a position of some honor and responsibility. . . .

While women in the Islamic world have been segregated and secluded, and historically have been considered second-class citizens by the vast majority of males in the community, they have not been totally without power. They have been able to maintain a degree of control over their own lives and over the men with whom they live through many of the religious practices described above. The fact that they alone have the ability to bear children, the influence they continue to play in the lives of their sons, and the power they have over their sons' wives are subtle indications that there are certain checks and balances on the obvious authority invested by the Qur'ān in men. From sexuality to control of the network of communications in the family to manipulation of such external agencies as spirits and supernatural beings, women have had at their control a variety of means to exert their will over the men in their families and over their own circumstances. The subtle means of control available to women throughout the world have of course been exploited: withholding sexual favors (a questionable but often-quoted hadı¯ th says that if a woman refuses to sleep with her husband, the angels will curse her until the morning), doing small things to undermine a husband's honor such as embarrassing him in front of guests, indulging in various forms of gossip and social control, and the like. . . .

Until fairly recently, education for women in the Muslim world has been minimal. Girls were given the rudiments of an Islamic education, mainly a little instruction in the Qur'ān and the traditions so as to be able to recite their prayers properly. Beyond that their training was not academic but domestic. In the late nineteenth and early twentieth century, Islamic leaders awoke with a start to the reality that Muslims were significantly behind the West in a variety of ways, including technology and the education necessary to understand and develop it. Many of these leaders recognized that if Islamic nations were to compete successfully in the contemporary world, it had to be with the aid of a well-educated and responsible female sector. Thus, this century has seen a number of educational advances for women, and in some countries, such as Egypt, Iraq, and Kuwait, women constitute very significant numbers of the university population. Nonetheless, illiteracy in many Muslim nations continues to be high, and the gap between male and female literacy rates is even increasing in some areas. In Saudi Arabia, where at present the economic resources are certainly available, large numbers of Saudi girls are receiving a full education, though separated from boys, and are taught either by men through television transmission or by women.

In education as in most areas of life, the male understanding of women as encouraged by certain parts of the Islamic tradition continues to play an important role. The Qur'ān does state, along with the stipulation that women can inherit only half of what men inherit, that the witness (in the court of law) of one man is equal to that of two women. This unfortunately has been interpreted by some in the history of Islam to mean that women are intellectually inferior to men, unstable in their judgment, and too easily swayed by emotion. Such perspectives are certainly not shared by all but nonetheless have been influential (and in some places are increasingly so today) in making it difficult for a woman to have access to the same kinds of educational opportunities that are available to men. Certain subjects are deemed "appropriate" for a woman to study, particularly those geared to make her the best and most productive wife, mother, and female participant in the family structure.

The prevalent view, confirmed by the Qur'ān, is that women should be modest and should neither expose themselves to men nor be too much in public places, where they will be subject to men's observation or forced to interact with males not in their immediate families. This view obviously has contributed to the difficulties of receiving a full education and of securing employment outside the home. More employment opportunities are open to women today than in the past, however, and in many countries women hold high-level positions in business, government, civil service, education, and other sectors. Statistics differ greatly across the Islamic world and are difficult to assess because they often fail to take into account the rural woman who may work full-time in the fields or other occupation outside the house but does not earn an independent salary. . . .

Saudi Arabia presents an interesting case study of the confrontation of Islamic ideas with contemporary reality. Women are greatly inhibited in the labor arena; because of conservative religious attitudes they must be veiled and covered, are not permitted to drive or even ride in a taxi with a strange man, and in general are unable to participate on the social and professional level with males. However, in a country in which production is both necessary and economically possible and which suffers from a lack of manpower, the use of women in the work force or increased importation of foreign labor seem the only two (both undesirable) alternatives. Thus more Saudi women are working, and because of their right to inherit, are accumulating very substantial amounts of money. It is interesting to note the rapid rate of construction of new banks exclusively for women in places like Jiddah and Riyadh.

The aforementioned Qur'ān verse about the witness of two women being equal to that of one man and the supporting literature attesting to female intellectual, physical (and in fact sometimes moral) inferiority have made it difficult for Muslim women to achieve equal political rights. In most Arab countries (except Saudi Arabia and certain of the Gulf States), as well as in most other parts of the Islamic world, women have now been given the vote. Centuries of passivity in the political realm, however, have made it difficult for women to take advantage of the opportunities now available to them. In some countries, such as Egypt, women are playing major political roles, but generally women politicians find little support from men or even from other women for their aspirations. This is not to underestimate the strong current in Islamic thinking which encourages the full participation of women in politics, as well as in the educational and professional fields.

Like an intricate and complex geometric pattern on a Persian rug or a frieze decorating a mosque, the practices, roles, opportunities, prescriptions, hopes, and frustrations of Islamic women are woven together in a whole. The colors are sometimes bold and striking, at other times muted and subtle. Some contemporary Muslim women are progressive and aggressive, no longer content to fit the traditionally prescribed patterns. Others are passive and accepting, not yet able to discern what new possibilities may be open to them, let alone whether or not they might want to take advantage of such opportunities. Some are Westernized as their mothers and grandmothers were and have every intention of staying that way, while others are increasingly clear in their feelings that the West does not have the answers and that Islam, particularly the Islam of the Qur'ān and the community of the Prophet Muhammad, is God's chosen way for humankind. For the latter, their dress, their relationships with their husbands and families, and their verbal assent to Islamic priorities reflect this conviction that the time has come to cease a fruitless preoccupation with things Western and to reaffirm their identity as Muslim women.

It is difficult for Western feminists to grasp exactly what the Muslim woman may mean by "liberation." For many Islamic women, the fruits of liberation in the West are too many broken marriages, women left without the security of men who will provide for them, deteriorating relations between men and women, and sexual license that appears as rank immorality. They see the Islamic system as affirmed by the Qur'ān as one in which male authority over them ensures their care and protection and provides a structure in which the family is solid, children are inculcated with lasting values, and the balance of responsibility between man and woman is one in which absolute equality is less highly prized than cooperation and complementarity.

The new Islamic woman, then, is morally and religiously conservative and affirms the absolute value of the true Islamic system for human relationships. She is intolerant of the kind of Islam in which women are subjugated and relegated to roles insignificant to the full functioning of society, and she wants to take full advantage of educational and professional opportunities. She may agree, however, that certain fields of education are more appropriate for women than others, and that certain professions are more natural to males than to females. She participates as a contributor to and decisionmaker for the family, yet recognizes that in any complex relationship final authority must rest with one person. And she is content to delegate that authority to her husband, father, or other male relative in return for the solidarity of the family structure and the support and protection that it gives her and her children.

That not all, or even most, Muslim women subscribe to this point of view is clear. And yet, at the time of this writing, it seems equally clear that, if Western observers are to understand women in the contemporary Islamic world, they must appreciate a point of view that is more and more prevalent. The West is increasingly identified with imperialism, and solutions viable for women in the Islamic community are necessarily different from the kinds of solutions that many Western women seem to have chosen for themselves. For the Muslim the words of the Qur'ān are divine, and the prescriptions for the roles and rights of females, like the other messages of the holy book, are seen as part of God's divinely ordered plan for all humanity. Change will come slowly, and whatever kinds of liberation ultimately prevail will be cloaked in a garb that is—in one or another of its various aspects—essentially Islamic.

CRITICAL-THINKING QUESTIONS

1. In what formal ways does Islam confer on men authority over women?
2. In what formal and informal ways does Islam give power to women to affect their own lives and those of men?
3. From a Muslim perspective, what are some of the problems with Western living and, particularly, Western feminism?

Education

CLASSIC

CONTEMPORARY

CROSS-CULTURAL

58

Education and Inequality

Samuel Bowles and Herbert Gintis

Education has long been held to be a means to realizing U.S. ideals of equal opportunity. As Lester Ward notes at the beginning of this selection, the promise of education is to allow "natural" abilities to win out over the "artificial" inequalities of class, race, and sex. Samuel Bowles and Herbert Gintis claim that this has happened very little in the United States. Rather, they argue, schooling has more to do with maintaining *existing social hierarchy.*

Universal education is the power, which is destined to overthrow every species of hierarchy. It is destined to remove all artificial inequality and leave the natural inequalities to find their true level. With the artificial inequalities of caste, rank, title, blood, birth, race, color, sex, etc., will fall nearly all the oppression, abuse, prejudice, enmity, and injustice, that humanity is now subject to. (Lester Frank Ward, *Education* © 1872)

A review of educational history hardly supports the optimistic pronouncements of liberal educational theory. The politics of education are better understood in terms of the need for social control in an unequal and rapidly changing economic order. The founders of the modern U.S. school system understood that the capitalist economy produces great extremes of wealth and poverty, of social elevation and degradation. Horace Mann and other school reformers of the antebellum period knew well the seamy side of the burgeoning industrial and urban centers. "Here," wrote Henry Barnard, the first state superintendent of education in both Connecticut and Rhode Island, and later to become the first U.S. Commissioner of Education, "the wealth, enterprise and professional talent of the state are concentrated . . . but here also are poverty, ignorance, profligacy and irreligion, and a classification of society as broad and deep as ever divided the plebeian and patrician of ancient Rome."[1] They lived in a world in which, to use de Tocqueville's words, ". . . small

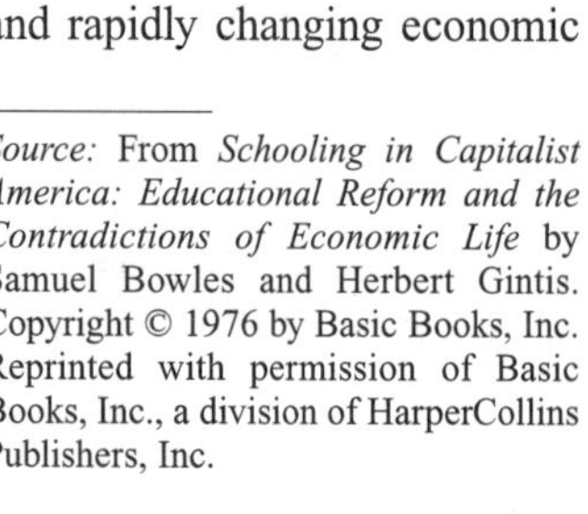

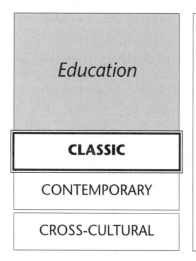

aristocratic societies . . . are formed by some manufacturers in the midst of the immense democracy of our age [in which] . . . some men are opulent and a multitude . . . are wretchedly poor."[2] The rapid rise of the factory system, particularly in New England, was celebrated by the early school reformers; yet, the alarming transition from a relatively simple rural society to a highly stratified industrial economy could not be ignored. They shared the fears that de Tocqueville had expressed following his visit to the United States in 1831:

> When a workman is unceasingly and exclusively engaged in the fabrication of one thing, he ultimately does his work with singular dexterity; but at the same time he loses the general faculty of applying his mind to the direction of the work. . . . [While] the science of manufacture lowers the class of workmen, it raises the class of masters. . . . [If] ever a permanent inequality of conditions . . . again penetrates into the world, it may be predicted that this is the gate by which they will enter.[3]

While deeply committed to the emerging industrial order, the farsighted school reformers of the mid-nineteenth century understood the explosive potential of the glaring inequalities of factory life. Deploring the widening of social divisions and fearing increasing unrest, Mann, Barnard, and others proposed educational expansion and reform. In his Fifth Report as Secretary of the Massachusetts Board of Education, Horace Mann wrote:

> Education, then beyond all other devices of human origin, is the great equalizer of the conditions of men—the balance wheel of the social machinery. . . . It does better than to disarm the poor of their hostility toward the rich; it prevents being poor.[4]

Mann and his followers appeared to be at least as interested in disarming the poor as in preventing poverty. They saw in the spread of universal and free education a means of alleviating social distress without redistributing wealth and power or altering the broad outlines of the economic system. Education, it seems, had almost magical powers:

> The main idea set forth in the creeds of some political reformers, or revolutionizers, is, that some people are poor because others are rich. This idea supposed a fixed amount of property in the community . . . and the problem presented for solution is, how to transfer a portion of this property from those who are supposed to have too much to those who feel and know that they have too little. At this point, both their theory and their expectation of reform stop. But the beneficent power of education would not be exhausted, even though it should peaceably abolish all the miseries that spring from the coexistence, side by side, of enormous wealth and squalid want. It has a higher function. Beyond the power of diffusing old wealth, it has the prerogative of creating new.[5]

The early educators viewed the poor as the foreign element that they were. Mill hands were recruited throughout New England, often disrupting the small towns in which textile and other rapidly growing industries had located. Following the Irish potato famine of the 1840s, thousands of Irish workers settled in the cities and towns of the northeastern United States. Schooling was seen as a means of integrating this "uncouth and dangerous" element into the social fabric of American life. The inferiority of the foreigner was taken for granted. The editors of the influential *Massachusetts Teacher,* a leader in the educational reform movement, writing in 1851, saw ". . . the increasing influx of foreigners . . ." as a moral and social problem:

> Will it, like the muddy Missouri, as it pours its waters into the clear Mississippi and contaminates the whole united mass, spread ignorance and vice, crime and disease, through our native population?
>
> If . . . we can by any means purify this foreign people, enlighten their ignorance and bring them up to our level, we shall perform a work of true and perfect charity, blessing the giver and receiver in equal measure. . . .
>
> With the old not much can be done; but with their children, the great remedy is *education.* The rising generation must be taught as our own children are taught. We say *must be* because in many cases this can only be accomplished by coercion.[6]

Since the mid-nineteenth century the dual objectives of educational reformers—equality of opportunity and social control—have been intermingled, the merger of these two threads sometimes so nearly complete that it becomes impossible to distinguish between the two. Schooling has been at once something done for the poor and to the poor.

The basic assumptions which underlay this commingling help explain the educational reform movement's social legacy. First, educational reformers did not question the fundamental economic institutions of capitalism: Capitalist ownership and control of the means of production and dependent wage labor were taken for granted. In fact, education was to help preserve and extend the capitalist order. The function of the school system was to accommodate workers to its most rapid possible development. Second, it was assumed that people (often classes of people or "races") are differentially equipped by nature or social origins to occupy the varied economic and social levels in the class structure. By providing equal opportunity, the school system was to elevate the masses, guiding them sensibly and fairly to the manifold political, social, and economic roles of adult life.

Jefferson's educational thought strikingly illustrates this perspective. In 1779, he proposed a two-track educational system which would prepare individuals for adulthood in one of the two classes of society: the "laboring and the learned."[7] Even children of the laboring class would qualify for leadership. Scholarships would allow ". . . those persons whom nature hath endowed with genius and virtue . . ." to ". . . be rendered by liberal education worthy to receive and able to guard the sacred deposit of the rights and liberties of their fellow citizens."[8] Such a system, Jefferson asserted, would succeed in ". . . raking a few geniuses from the rubbish."[9] Jefferson's two-tiered educational plan presents in stark relief the outlines and motivation for the stratified structure of U.S. education which has endured up to the present. At the top, there is the highly selective aristocratic tradition, the elite university training future leaders. At the base is mass education for all, dedicated to uplift and control. The two traditions have always coexisted although their meeting point has drifted upward over the years, as mass education has spread upward from elementary school through high school, and now up to the post-high-school level.

Though schooling was consciously molded to reflect the class structure, education was seen as a means of enhancing wealth and morality, which would work to the advantage of all. Horace Mann, in his 1842 report to the State Board of Education, reproduced this comment by a Massachusetts industrialist:

> The great majority always have been and probably always will be comparatively poor, while a few will possess the greatest share of this world's goods. And it is a wise provision of Providence which connects so intimately, and as I think so indissolubly, the greatest good of the many with the highest interests in the few.[10]

Much of the content of education over the past century and a half can only be construed as an unvarnished attempt to persuade the "many" to make the best of the inevitable.

The unequal contest between social control and social justice is evident in the total functioning of U.S. education. The system as it stands today provides eloquent testimony to the ability of the well-to-do to perpetuate in the name of equality of opportunity an arrangement which consistently yields to themselves disproportional advantages, while thwarting the aspirations and needs of the working people of the United States. However grating this judgment may sound to the ears of the undaunted optimist, it is by no means excessive in light of the massive statistical data on inequality in the United States. Let us look at the contemporary evidence.

We may begin with the basic issue of inequalities in the years of schooling. As can be seen in [Figure 1], the number of years of schooling attained by an individual is strongly associated with parental socioeconomic status. This figure presents the estimated distribution of years of schooling attained by individuals of varying socioeconomic backgrounds. If we define socioeconomic background by a weighted sum of income, occupation, and educational level of the parents, a child from the ninetieth percentile may expect, on the average, five more years of schooling than a child in the tenth percentile.[11]

... We have chosen a sample of white males because the most complete statistics are available for this group. Moreover, if inequality for white males can be documented, the proposition is merely strengthened when sexual and racial differences are taken into account.

Additional census data dramatize one aspect of educational inequalities: the relationship between family income and college attendance. Even among those who had graduated from high school in the early 1960s, children of families

FIGURE 1: Educational Attainments Are Strongly Dependent on Social Background Even for People of Similar Childhood IQs

Notes: For each socioeconomic group, the left-hand bar indicates the estimated average number of years of schooling attained by all men from that group. The right-hand bar indicates the estimated average number of years of schooling attained by men with IQ scores equal to the average for the entire sample. The sample refers to "non-Negro" men of "nonfarm" backgrounds, aged 35–44 years in 1962. Source: Samuel Bowles and Valerie Nelson, "The 'Inheritance of IQ' and the Intergenerational Transmission of Economic Inequality," *The Review of Economics and Statistics,* vol. LVI, no. 1 (Feb. 1974).

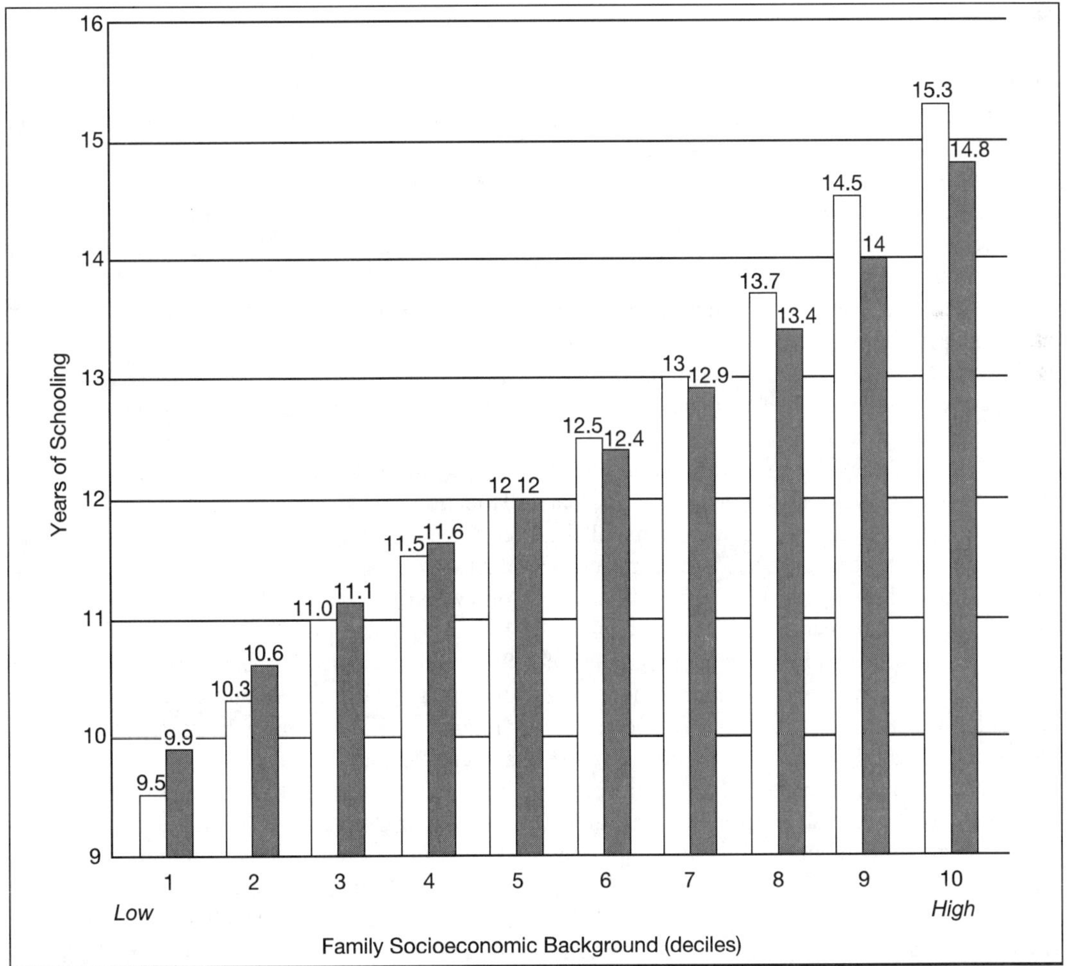

earning less than $3,000 per year were over six times as likely *not* to attend college as were the children of families earning over $15,000.[12] Moreover, children from less well-off families are *both* less likely to have graduated from high school and more likely to attend inexpensive, two-year community colleges rather than a four-year B.A. program if they do make it to college.[13]

Not surprisingly, the results of schooling differ greatly for children of different social backgrounds. Most easily measured, but of limited importance, are differences in scholastic achievement. If we measure the output of schooling by scores on nationally standardized achievement tests, children whose parents were themselves highly educated outperform the children of parents with less education by a wide margin. Data collected for the U.S. Office of Education Survey of Educational Opportunity reveal, for example, that among white high-school seniors, those whose parents were in the top education decile were, on the average, well over three grade levels in measured scholastic achievement ahead of those whose parents were in the bottom decile.[14]

Given these differences in scholastic achievement, inequalities in years of schooling among individuals of different social backgrounds are to be expected. Thus one might be tempted to argue that the close dependence of years of schooling attained on background displayed in the left-hand bars of [Figure 1] is simply a reflection of unequal intellectual abilities, or that inequalities in college attendance are the consequences of differing levels of scholastic achievement in high school and do not reflect any additional social class inequalities peculiar to the process of college admission.

This view, so comforting to the admissions personnel in our elite universities, is unsupported by the data, some of which is presented in [the figure]. The right-hand bars of [the figure] indicate that even among children with identical IQ test scores at ages six and eight, those with rich, well-educated, high-status parents could expect a much higher level of schooling than those with less-favored origins. Indeed, the closeness of the left-hand and right-hand bars in [the figure] shows that only a small portion of the observed social class differences in educational attainment is related to IQ differences across social classes.[15] The dependence of education attained on background is almost as strong for individuals with the same IQ as for all individuals. Thus, while [the figure] indicates that an individual in the ninetieth percentile in social class background is likely to receive five more years of education than an individual in the tenth percentile, it also indicated that he is likely to receive 4.25 more years schooling than an individual from the tenth percentile with the same IQ. Similar results are obtained when we look specifically at access to college education for students with the same measured IQ. Project Talent data indicates that for "high ability" students (top 25 percent as measured by a composite of tests of "general aptitude"), those of high socioeconomic background (top 25 percent as measured by a composite of family income, parents' education, and occupation) are nearly twice as likely to attend college than students of low socioeconomic background (bottom 25 percent). For "low ability" students (bottom 25 percent), those of high-social background are more than four times as likely to attend college as are their low-social background counterparts.[16]

Inequality in years of schooling is, of course, only symptomatic of broader inequalities in the educational system. Not only do less well-off children go to school for fewer years, they are treated with less attention (or more precisely, less benevolent attention) when they are there. These broader inequalities are not easily measured. Some show up in statistics on the different levels of expenditure for the education of children of different socioeconomic backgrounds. Taking account of the inequality in financial resources for each year in school and the inequality in years of schooling obtained, Jencks estimated that a child whose parents were in the top fifth of the income distribution receives roughly twice the educational resources in dollar terms as does a child whose parents are in the bottom fifth.[17]

The social class inequalities in our school system, then, are too evident to be denied. Defenders of the educational system are forced back on the assertion that things are getting better; the inequalities of the past were far worse. And, indeed, there can be no doubt that some of the inequalities of the past have been mitigated. Yet new inequalities have apparently developed to take their place, for the available historical evidence lends little support to the idea that our schools are on the road to equality of educational opportunity. For example, data from a recent U.S. Census survey reported in Spady indicate that graduation from college has become no less dependent on one's social background. This is true despite the fact that high-school graduation is becoming increasingly equal across social classes.[18] Additional data confirm this impression. The statistical association (coefficient of correlation) between parents' social status and years of education attained by individuals who completed their schooling three or four decades ago is virtually identical to the same correlation for individuals who terminated their schooling in recent years.[19] On balance, the available data suggest that the number of years of school attained by a child depends upon family background as much in the recent period as it did fifty years ago.

Thus, we have empirical reasons for doubting the egalitarian impact of schooling. . . . We conclude that U.S. education is highly unequal, the chances of attaining much or little schooling being substantially dependent on one's race and parents' economic level. Moreover, where there is a discernible trend toward a more equal educational system—as in the narrowing of the black education deficit, for example—the impact on the structure of economic opportunity is minimal at best.

CRITICAL-THINKING QUESTIONS

1. Describe how the educational system of the United States has historically had two objectives: increasing opportunity on the one hand and stabilizing an unequal society on the other. Which is emphasized in most public discussions of schooling?

2. In what respects, according to Bowles and Gintis, has schooling supported the capitalist economic system? How have such supports shaped the content of the educational system?

3. What are Bowles and Gintis's conclusions about the relationship between schooling and natural ability? Between schooling and social background?

NOTES

1. H. Barnard, *Papers for the Teacher: 2nd Series* (New York: F. C. Brownell, 1866), pp. 293–310.

2. A. de Tocqueville, as quoted in Jeremy Brecher, *Strike!* (San Francisco: Straight Arrow Books, 1972), pp. xi, xii.

3. Ibid., p. 172.

4. Horace Mann as quoted in Michael Katz, ed., *School Reform Past and Present* (Boston: Little, Brown, 1971), p. 141.

5. Ibid., p. 145.

6. *The Massachusetts Teacher* (Oct., 1851), quoted in Katz, pp. 169–70.

7. D. Tyack, *Turning Points in American Educational History* (Waltham, Mass.: Blaisdell, 1967), p. 89.

8. Ibid., p. 10.

9. Ibid., p. 89.

10. Mann, quoted in Katz, p. 147.

11. This calculation is based on data reported in full in Samuel Bowles and Valerie Nelson, "The 'Inheritance of IQ' and the Intergenerational Transmission of Economic Inequality," *The Review of Economics and Statistics,* 56, 1 (Feb., 1974). It refers to non-Negro males from nonfarm backgrounds, aged 35–44 years. The zero-order correlation coefficient between socioeconomic background and years of schooling was estimated at 0.646. The estimated standard deviation of years of schooling was 3.02. The results for other age groups are similar.

12. These figures refer to individuals who were high-school seniors in October 1965, and who subsequently graduated from high school. College attendance refers to both two- and four-year institutions. Family income is for the twelve months preceding October 1965. Data is drawn from U.S. Bureau of the Census, *Current Population Reports,* Series P-60, No. 183 (May, 1969).

13. For further evidence, see ibid.; and Jerome Karabel, "Community Colleges and Social Stratification," *Harvard Educational Review,* 424, 42 (Nov., 1972).

14. Calculation based on data in James S. Coleman et al., *Equality of Educational Opportunity* (Washington, D.C.: U.S. Government Printing Office, 1966), and the authors.

15. The data relating to IQ are from a 1966 survey of veterans by the National Opinion Research Center; and from N. Bayley and E. S. Schaefer, "Correlations of Maternal and Child Behaviors with the Development of Mental Ability: Data from the Berkeley Growth Study," *Monographs of Social Research in Child Development,* 29, 6 (1964).

16. Based on a large sample of U.S. high-school students as reported in John C. Flannagan and William W. Cooley, *Project Talent, One Year Follow-up Study,* Cooperative Research Project, No. 2333 (Pittsburgh: University of Pittsburgh, School of Education, 1966).

17. C. Jencks et al., *Inequality: A Reassessment of the Effects of Family and Schooling in America* (New York: Basic Books, 1972), p. 48.

18. W. L. Spady, "Educational Mobility and Access: Growth and Paradoxes," in *American Journal of Sociology,* 73, 3 (Nov. 1967); and Peter Blau and Otis D. Duncan, *The American Occupational Structure* (New York: John Wiley, 1967). More recent data support the evidence of no trend toward equality. See U.S. Bureau of Census, op. cit.

19. Ibid., Blau and Duncan.

59

Savage Inequalities: Children in U.S. Schools

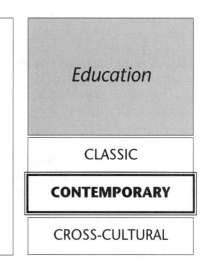

Jonathan Kozol

Education

CLASSIC

CONTEMPORARY

CROSS-CULTURAL

The job of our schools, we like to believe, is to give children a chance to develop their abilities and compete with others for their place in society. But has the game been "fixed" right from the start? Comparing two schools in New York City, Jonathan Kozol points to "savage inequalities" that perpetuate—or even increase—class differences.

"In a country where there is no distinction of class," Lord Acton wrote of the United States 130 years ago, "a child is not born to the station of its parents, but with an indefinite claim to all the prizes that can be won by thought and labor. It is in conformity with the theory of equality . . . to give as near as possible to every youth an equal state in life." Americans, he said, "are unwilling that any should be deprived in childhood of the means of competition."

It is hard to read these words today without a sense of irony and sadness. Denial of "the means of competition" is perhaps the single most consistent outcome of the education offered to poor children in the schools of our large cities; and nowhere is this pattern of denial more explicit or more absolute than in the public schools of New York City.

Average expenditures per pupil in the city of New York in 1987 were some $5,500. In the highest spending suburbs of New York (Great Neck or Manhasset, for example, on Long Island) funding levels rose above $11,000, with the highest districts in the state at $15,000. "Why . . . ," asks the city's Board of Education, "should our students receive less" than do "similar students" who live elsewhere? "The inequity is clear."

But the inequality to which these words refer goes even further than the school board may be eager to reveal. "It is perhaps the supreme irony," says the nonprofit Community Service Society of New York, that "the same Board of Education which perceives so clearly the inequities" of funding between separate towns and cities "is perpetuating similar inequities" right in New York. And, in comment on the Board of Education's final statement—"the inequity is clear" the CSS observes, "New York City's

Source: From *Savage Inequalities: Children in America's Schools* by Jonathan Kozol. Copyright © 1991 by Jonathan Kozol. Reprinted by permission of Crown Publishers, a division of Random House, Inc.

poorest. . . districts could adopt that eloquent statement with few changes."

New York City's public schools are subdivided into thirty-two school districts. District 10 encompasses a large part of the Bronx but is, effectively, two separate districts. One of these districts, Riverdale, is in the northwest section of the Bronx. Home to many of the city's most sophisticated and well-educated families, its elementary schools have relatively few low-income students. The other section, to the south and east, is poor and heavily nonwhite.

The contrast between public schools in each of these two neighborhoods is obvious to any visitor. At Public School 24 in Riverdale, the principal speaks enthusiastically of his teaching staff. At Public School 79, serving poorer children to the south, the principal says that he is forced to take the "tenth-best" teachers. "I thank God they're still breathing," he remarks of those from whom he must select his teachers.

Some years ago, District 10 received an allocation for computers. The local board decided to give each elementary school an equal number of computers, even though the schools in Riverdale had smaller classes and far fewer students. When it was pointed out that schools in Riverdale, as a result, had twice the number of computers in proportion to their student populations as the schools in the poor neighborhoods, the chairman of the local board replied, "What is fair is what is determined . . . to be fair."

The superintendent of District 10, Fred Goldberg, tells *The New York Times* that "every effort" is made "to distribute resources equitably." He speculates that some gap might exist because some of the poorer schools need to use funds earmarked for computers to buy basic supplies like pens and paper. Asked about the differences in teachers noted by the principals, he says there are no differences, then adds that next year he'll begin a program to improve the quality of teachers in the poorer schools. Questioned about differences in physical appearances between the richer and the poorer schools, he says, "I think it's demographics."

Sometimes a school principal, whatever his background or his politics, looks into the faces of the children in his school and offers a disarming statement that cuts through official ambiguity. "These are the kids most in need," says Edward Flanery, the principal of one of the low-income schools, "and they get the worst teachers." For children of diverse needs in his overcrowded rooms, he says, "you need an outstanding teacher. And what do you get? You get the worst."

In order to find Public School 261 in District 10, a visitor is told to look for a mortician's office. The funeral home, which faces Jerome Avenue in the North Bronx, is easy to identify by its green awning. The school is next door, in a former roller-skating rink. No sign identifies the building as a school. A metal awning frame without an awning supports a flagpole, but there is no flag.

In the street in front of the school there is an elevated public transit line. Heavy traffic fills the street. The existence of the school is virtually concealed within this crowded city block.

In a vestibule between the outer and inner glass doors of the school there is a sign with these words: "All children are capable of learning."

Beyond the inner doors a guard is seated. The lobby is long and narrow. The ceiling is low. There are no windows. All the teachers that I see at first are middle-aged white women. The principal, who is also a white woman, tells me that the school's "capacity" is 900 but that there are 1,300 children here. The size of classes for fifth and sixth grade children in New York, she says, is "capped" at thirty-two, but she says that class size in the school goes "up to thirty-four." (I later see classes, however, as large as thirty-seven.) Classes for younger children, she goes on, are "capped at twenty-five," but a school can go above this limit if it puts an extra adult in the room. Lack of space, she says, prevents the school from operating a prekindergarten program.

I ask the principal where her children go to school. They are enrolled in private school, she says.

"Lunchtime is a challenge for us," she explains. "Limited space obliges us to do it in three shifts, 450 children at a time."

Textbooks are scarce and children have to share their social studies books. The principal says there is one full-time pupil counselor and another who is here two days a week: a ratio of 930 children to one counselor. The carpets are patched and sometimes taped together to conceal an open space. "I could use some new rugs," she observes.

To make up for the building's lack of windows and the crowded feeling that results, the staff puts plants and fish tanks in the corridors. Some of the plants are flourishing. Two boys, released from class, are in a corridor beside a tank, their noses pressed against the glass. A school of pinkish fish inside the tank are darting back and forth. Farther down the corridor a small Hispanic girl is watering the plants.

Two first grade classes share a single room without a window, divided only by a blackboard. Four kindergartens and a sixth grade class of Spanish-speaking children have been packed into a single room in which, again, there is no window. A second grade bilingual class of thirty-seven children has its own room but again there is no window.

By eleven o'clock, the lunchroom is already packed with appetite and life. The kids line up to get their meals, then eat them in ten minutes. After that, with no place they can go to play, they sit and wait until it's time to line up and go back to class.

On the second floor I visit four classes taking place within another undivided space. The room has a low ceiling. File cabinets and movable blackboards give a small degree of isolation to each class. Again, there are no windows.

The library is a tiny, windowless and claustrophobic room. I count approximately 700 books. Seeing no reference books, I ask a teacher if encyclopedias and other reference books are kept in classrooms.

"We don't have encyclopedias in classrooms," she replies. "That is for the suburbs."

The school, I am told, has twenty-six computers for its 1,300 children. There is one small gym and children get one period, and sometimes two, each week. Recess, however, is not possible because there is no playground. "Head Start," the principal says, "scarcely exists in District 10. We have no space."

The school, I am told, is 90 percent black and Hispanic; the other 10 percent are Asian, white or Middle Eastern.

In a sixth grade social studies class the walls are bare of words or decorations. There seems to be no ventilation system, or, if one exists, it isn't working.

The class discusses the Nile River and the Fertile Crescent.

The teacher, in a droning voice: "How is it useful that these civilizations developed close to rivers?"

A child, in a good loud voice: "What kind of question is that?"

In my notes I find these words: "An uncomfortable feeling—being in a building with no windows. There are metal ducts across the room. Do they give air? I feel asphyxiated...."

On the top floor of the school, a sixth grade of thirty children shares a room with twenty-nine bilingual second graders. Because of the high class size there is an assistant with each teacher. This means that fifty-nine children and four grown-ups—sixty-three in all—must share a room that, in a suburban school, would hold no more than twenty children and one teacher. There are, at least, some outside windows in this room— it is the only room with windows in the school—and the room has a high ceiling. It is a relief to see some daylight.

I return to see the kindergarten classes on the ground floor and feel stifled once again by lack of air and the low ceiling. Nearly 120 children and adults are doing what they can to make the best of things: eighty children in four kindergarten classes, thirty children in the sixth grade class, and about eight grown-ups who are aides and teachers. The kindergarten children sitting on the worn rug, which is patched with tape, look up at me and turn their heads to follow me as I walk past them.

As I leave the school, a sixth grade teacher stops to talk. I ask her, "Is there air conditioning in warmer weather?"

Teachers, while inside the building, are reluctant to give answers to this kind of question. Outside, on the sidewalk, she is less constrained: "I had an awful room last year. In the winter it was 56 degrees. In the summer it was up to 90. It was sweltering."

I ask her, "Do the children ever comment on the building?"

"They don't say," she answers, "but they know."

I ask her if they see it as a racial message.

"All these children see TV," she says. "They know what suburban schools are like. Then they look around them at their school. This was a roller-rink, you know. . . . They don't comment on it but you see it in their eyes. They understand." . . .

Two months later, on a day in May, I visit an elementary school in Riverdale. The dogwoods and magnolias on the lawn in front of P.S. 24 are in full blossom on the day I visit. There is a well-tended park across the street, another larger park three blocks away. To the left of the school is a playground for small children, with an innovative jungle gym, a slide and several climbing toys. Behind the school there are two playing fields for older kids. The grass around the school is neatly trimmed.

The neighborhood around the school, by no means the richest part of Riverdale, is nonetheless expensive and quite beautiful. Residences in the area—some of which are large, freestanding houses, others condominiums in solid red-brick buildings—sell for prices in the region of $400,000; but some of the larger Tudor houses on the winding and tree-shaded streets close to the school can cost up to $1 million. The excellence of P.S. 24, according to the principal, adds to the value of these homes. Advertisements in *The New York Times* will frequently inform prospective buyers that a house is "in the neighborhood of P.S. 24."

The school serves 825 children in the kindergarten through sixth grade. This is . . . a great deal smaller than the 1,300 children packed into the former skating rink; but the principal of P.S. 24, a capable and energetic man named David Rothstein, still regards it as excessive for an elementary school.

The school is integrated in the strict sense that the middle- and upper-middle-class white children here do occupy a building that contains some Asian and Hispanic and black children; but there is little integration in the classrooms since the vast majority of the Hispanic and black children are assigned to "special" classes on the basis of evaluations that have classified them "EMR"—"educable mentally retarded"—or else, in the worst of cases, "TMR"—"trainable mentally retarded."

I ask the principal if any of his students qualify for free-lunch programs. "About 130 do," he says. "Perhaps another thirty-five receive their lunches at reduced price. Most of these kids are in the special classes. They do not come from this neighborhood."

The very few nonwhite children that one sees in mainstream classes tend to be Japanese or else of other Asian origins. Riverdale, I learn, has been the residence of choice for many years to members of the diplomatic corps.

The school therefore contains effectively two separate schools: one of about 130 children, most of whom are poor, Hispanic, black, assigned to one of the twelve special classes; the other of some 700 mainstream students, almost all of whom are white or Asian.

There is a third track also—this one for the students who are labeled "talented" or "gifted." This is termed a "pull out" program since the children who are so identified remain in mainstream classrooms but are taken out for certain periods each week to be provided with intensive and, in my opinion, excellent instruction in some areas of reasoning and logic often known as "higher-order skills" in the contemporary jargon of the public schools. Children identified as "gifted" are admitted to this program in first grade and, in most cases, will remain there for six years. Even here, however, there are two tracks of the gifted. The regular gifted classes are provided with only one semester of this specialized instruction yearly. Those very few children, on the other hand, who are identified as showing the most promise are assigned, beginning in the third grade, to a program that receives a full-year regimen.

In one such class, containing ten intensely verbal and impressive fourth grade children, nine are white and one is Asian. The "special" class I enter first, by way of contrast, has twelve children of whom only one is white and none is Asian. These racial breakdowns prove to be predictive of the schoolwide pattern.

In a classroom for the gifted on the first floor of the school, I ask a child what the class is doing. "Logic and syllogisms," she replies. The room is fitted with a planetarium. The principal says that all the elementary schools in District 10 were given the same planetariums ten years ago but that certain schools, because of overcrowding, have been forced to give them up. At P.S. 261, according to my notes, there was a domelike space that had been built to hold a planetarium, but the planetarium had been removed to free up space for the small library collection. P.S. 24, in contrast, has a spacious library that holds almost 8,000 books. The windows are decorated with attractive, brightly colored curtains and look out on flowering trees. The principal says that it's inadequate, but it appears spectacular to me after the cubicle that holds a meager 700 books within the former skating rink.

The district can't afford librarians, the principal says, but P.S. 24, unlike the poorer schools of District 10, can draw on educated parent volunteers who staff the room in shifts three days a week. A parent organization also raises independent funds to buy materials, including books, and will soon be running a fund-raiser to enhance the library's collection.

In a large and sunny first grade classroom that I enter next, I see twenty-three children, all of whom are white or Asian. In another first grade, there are twenty-two white children and two others who are Japanese. There is a computer in each class. Every classroom also has a modern fitted sink.

In a second grade class of twenty-two children, there are two black children and three Asian children. Again, there is a sink and a computer. A sixth grade social studies class has only one black child. The children have an in-class research area that holds some up-to-date resources. A set of encyclopedias (World Book, 1985) is in a rack beside a window. The children are doing a Spanish language lesson when I enter. Foreign languages begin in sixth grade at the school, but Spanish is offered also to the kindergarten children. As in every room at P.S. 24, the window shades are clean and new, the floor is neatly tiled in gray and green, and there is not a single light bulb missing.

Walking next into a special class, I see twelve children. One is white. Eleven are black. There are no Asian children. The room is half the size of mainstream classrooms. "Because of overcrowding," says the principal, "we have had to split these rooms in half." There is no computer and no sink.

I enter another special class. Of seven children, five are black, one is Hispanic, one is white. A little black boy with a large head sits in the far corner and is gazing at the ceiling.

"Placement of these kids," the principal explains, "can usually be traced to neurological damage."

In my notes: "How could so many of these children be brain-damaged?"

Next door to the special class is a woodworking shop. "This shop is only for the special classes," says the principal. The children learn to punch in time cards at the door, he says, in order to prepare them for employment.

The fourth grade gifted class, in which I spend the last part of the day, is humming with excitement. "I start with these children in the first grade," says the teacher. "We pull them out of mainstream classes on the basis of their test results and other factors such as the opinion of their teachers. Out of this group, beginning in third grade, I pull out the ones who show the most potential, and they enter classes such as this one."

The curriculum they follow, she explains, "emphasizes critical thinking, reasoning and logic." The planetarium, for instance, is employed not simply for the study of the universe as it exists. "Children also are designing their own galaxies," the teacher says.

A little girl sitting around a table with her classmates speaks with perfect poise: "My name is Susan. We are in the fourth grade gifted program."

I ask them what they're doing and a child says, "My name is Laurie and we're doing problem-solving."

A rather tall, good-natured boy who is half-standing at the table tells me that his name is David. "One thing that we do," he says, "is logical thinking. Some problems, we find, have more than one good answer. We need to learn not simply to be logical in our own thinking but to show respect for someone else's logic even when an answer may be technically incorrect."

When I ask him to explain this, he goes on, "A person who gives an answer that is not 'correct' may nonetheless have done some interesting thinking that we should examine. 'Wrong' answers may be more useful to examine than correct ones."

I ask the children if reasoning and logic are innate or if they're things that you can learn.

"You know some things to start with when you enter school," Susan says. "But we also learn some things that other children don't."

I ask her to explain this.

"We know certain things that other kids don't know because we're *taught* them."

CRITICAL-THINKING QUESTIONS

1. In principle, what should our schools do for all children?

2. Point to specific differences in schools that Kozol claims amount to "savage inequalities." Do you agree with his argument that schools stack the deck against poor children?

3. What about parents who claim they have earned the right to give their children whatever privileges they can afford to? Would you support a government-imposed equal-funding rule to give children in every neighborhood roughly the same quality of schooling?

60

Academic Achievement in Southeast Asian Refugee Families

Nathan Caplan, Marcella H. Choy, and John K. Whitmore

Education

CLASSIC

CONTEMPORARY

CROSS-CULTURAL

Many analysts pronounce the U.S. educational system in crisis. But are schools to blame for the modest achievement of some children? In this selection, the authors argue that socialization has a greater impact on academic performance than the quality of our schools. Even though most of the Southeast Asian boat people are poor, have had limited exposure to Western culture, know virtually no English, and live in low-income metropolitan areas, their children are excelling in the U.S. school system.

The scholastic success of Asian children is well recognized. Their stunning performance—particularly in the realm of science and mathematics—has prompted American educators to visit Japanese and Taiwanese schools in an effort to unearth the foundations of these achievements. Experts recommend that American schools adopt aspects of their Asian counterparts, such as a longer school year or more rigorous tasks, in order to raise the scholastic level of U.S. students.

Yet there is no need to go abroad to understand why these children do so well. The achievement of Asian-American students indicates that much may be learned about the origins of their triumph within the American school system itself. More specifically, during the late 1970s and early 1980s, devastating political and economic circumstances forced many Vietnamese, Lao and Chinese-Vietnamese families to seek a new life in the United States. This resettlement of boat people from Indochina offered a rare opportunity to examine the academic achievement of their children.

These young refugees had lost months, even years of formal schooling while living in relocation camps. Like their parents, they suffered disruption and trauma as they escaped from Southeast Asia. Despite their hardships and with little knowledge of English, the children quickly adapted to their new schools and began to excel.

In researching the economic and scholastic accomplishments of 1,400 refugee households in the early 1980s, our group at the University of Michigan studied the forces that shaped the performance of these children. Some of the standard explanations for educational excellence—parental encouragement and dedication to learning—applied to the young students, but other theories proved inadequate.

Source: "Indochinese Refugee Families and Academic Achievement," by Nathan Caplan, Marcella H. Choy, and John K. Whitmore, in *Scientific American,* February, 1992, pp. 36–42.

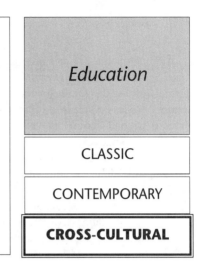

Although some of our findings are culturally specific, others point overwhelmingly to the pivotal role of the family in the children's academic success. Because this characteristic extends beyond culture, it has implications for educators, social scientists and policymakers as well as for the refugees themselves. It is clear that the U.S. educational system can work—if the requisite familial and social supports are provided for the students outside school.

Our study encompassed many features of resettlement. We gathered survey and other data on 6,750 persons in five urban areas—Orange County, Calif., Seattle, Houston, Chicago, and Boston—and obtained information about their background and home life as well as economic and demographic facts. We discovered that with regard to educational and social status, the refugees proved to be more ordinary than their predecessors who fled Vietnam in 1975 during the fall of Saigon. These newer displaced persons had had limited exposure to Western culture and knew virtually no English when they arrived. Often they came with nothing more than the clothes they wore.

From this larger group, we chose a random sample of 200 nuclear families and their 536 school-age children. Twenty-seven percent of the families had four or more children. At the time of the study, these young refugees had been in the United States for an average of three and a half years. We collected information on parents and their children during interviews conducted in their native tongues; we also gained access to school transcripts and other related documents.

All the children attended schools in low-income, metropolitan areas—environs not known for outstanding academic records. The refugees were fairly evenly distributed throughout the school levels: Grades one through eleven each contained about 8 percent of the children in the study; kindergarten and twelfth grade each contained about 5 percent. We converted the students' letter grades into a numerical grade point average (GPA): An A became a four; a D became a one. After calculations, we found that the children's mean GPA was 3.05, or a B average. Twenty-seven percent had an overall GPA in the A range, 52 percent in the B range and 17 percent in the C range. Only 4 percent had a GPA below a C grade.

Even more striking than the overall GPAs were the students' math scores. Almost half of the children earned As in math; another third earned Bs. Thus, four out of five students received either As or Bs. It is not surprising that they would do better in this subject. Their minds could most easily grasp disciplines in which English was not so crucial: math, physics, chemistry and science. As expected, their grades in the liberal arts were lower: In areas where extensive language skills were required, such as English, history or social studies, the combined GPA was 2.64.

To place our local findings in a national context, we turned to standardized achievement test scores, in particular, the California Achievement Test (CAT) results. In this arena as well, we found that the performance of the newly arrived students was exceptional. Their mean overall score on the CAT was in the 54th percentile; that is, they outperformed 54 percent of those taking the test—placing them just above the national average. Interestingly, their scores tended to cluster toward the middle ranges: They showed a more restricted scope of individual differences.

The national tests also reflected an above-average ability in math when the Indochinese children were compared with children taking the exam at equivalent levels. Half of the children studied obtained scores in the top quartile. Even more spectacularly, 27 percent of them scored in the 10th decile—better than 90 percent of the students across the country and almost three times higher than the national norm. The CAT math scores confirmed that the GPAs of these children were not products of local bias but of true mathematical competence.

Again, the lowest scores were found in the language and reading tests. In this case, the mean score was slightly below the national average. For reasons discussed earlier, this finding was expected. It remains remarkable, however, that the students' scores are so close to the national average in language skills.

The GPA and CAT scores show that the refugee children did very well, particularly in light of their background. A history marked by significant physical and emotional trauma as well as a lack of formal education would not seem to predispose them to an easy transition into U.S. schools. Yet even though they had not forgotten their difficult experiences, the children were able to focus on the present and to work toward the future. In so doing, they made striking scholastic progress. Moreover, their achievements held true for the majority, not for just a few whiz kids.

Clearly, these accomplishments are fueled by influences powerful enough to override the impact of a host of geographic and demographic factors. Using various statistical approaches, we sought to understand the forces responsible for this performance. In the process, a unique finding caught our attention, namely, a positive relation between the number of siblings and the children's GPA.

Family size has long been regarded as one of the most reliable predictors of poor achievement. Virtually all studies on the topic show an inverse relation: The greater the number of children in the family, the lower the mean GPA and other measures associated with scholastic performance. Typically, these reports document a 15 percent decline in GPA and other achievement-related scores with the addition of each child to the family. The interpretation of this finding has been subject to disagreement, but there is no conflict about its relation to achievement.

For the Indochinese students, this apparent disadvantage was somehow neutralized or turned into an advantage. We took this finding to be an important clue in elucidating the role of the family in academic performance. We assumed that distinctive family characteristics would explain how these achievements took place so early in resettlement as well as how these children and their parents managed to overcome such adversities as poor English skills, poverty and the often disruptive environment of urban schools.

Because they were newcomers in a strange land, it was reasonable to expect that at least some of the reasons for the children's success rested on their cultural background. While not ignoring the structural forces present here in the United States—among them the opportunity for education and advancement—we believed that the values and traditions permeating the lives of these children in Southeast Asia would guide their lives in this country.

Knowledge of one's culture does not occur in a vacuum; it is transmitted through the family. Children often acquire a sense of their heritage as a result of deliberate and concentrated parental effort in the context of family life. This inculcation of values from one generation to another is a universal feature of the conservation of culture.

We sought to determine which values were important to the parents, how well those values had been transmitted to the children and what role values played in promoting their educational achievement. In our interviews we included twenty-six questions about values that were derived from a search of Asian literature and from social science research. Respondents were asked to rate the perceived importance of these values.

We found that parents and children rated the perceived values in a similar fashion, providing empirical testimony that these parents had served their stewardship well. For the most part, the perspectives and values embedded in the cultural heritage of the Indochinese had been carried with them to the United States. We also determined that cultural values played an important role in the educational achievement of the children. Conserved values constituted a source of motivation and direction as the families dealt with contemporary problems set in a country vastly different from their homeland. The values formed a set of cultural givens with deep roots in the Confucian and Buddhist traditions of East and Southeast Asia.

The family is the central institution in these traditions, within which and through which achievement and knowledge are accomplished. We used factor analyses and other statistical procedures to determine value groupings and their relation to achievement. These analyses showed that parents and children honor mutual, collective obligation to one another and to their relatives. They strive to attain respect, cooperation and harmony within the family.

Nowhere is the family's commitment to accomplishment and education more evident than in time spent on homework. During high school, Indochinese students spend an average of three hours and ten minutes per day; in junior high, an average of two and a half hours; and in grade school, an average of two hours and five minutes. Research in the United States shows that American students study about one and a half hours per day at the junior and senior high school levels.

Among the refugee families, then, homework clearly dominates household activities during weeknights. Although the parents' lack of education and facility with English often prevents them from engaging in the content of the exercise, they set standards and goals for the evening and facilitate their children's studies by assuming responsibility for chores and other practical considerations.

After dinner, the table is cleared, and homework begins. The older children, both male and female, help their younger siblings. Indeed, they seem to learn as much from teaching as from being taught. It is reasonable to suppose that a great amount of learning goes on at these times—in terms of skills, habits, attitudes and expectations as well as the content of a subject. The younger children, in particular, are taught not only subject matter but how to learn. Such sibling involvement demonstrates how a large family can encourage and enhance academic success. The familial setting appears to make the children feel at home in school and, consequently, perform well there.

Parental engagement included reading regularly to young children—an activity routinely correlated to academic performance. Almost one half (45 percent) of the parents reported reading aloud. In those families, the children's mean GPA was 3.14 as opposed to 2.97 in households where the parents did not read aloud. (This difference, and all others to follow in which GPAs are compared, is statistically reliable.) It is important to note that the effects of being read to held up statistically whether the children were read to in English or in their native language.

This finding suggests that parental English literacy skills may not play a vital role in determining school performance. Rather, other aspects of the experience—emotional ties between parent and child, cultural validation and wisdom shared in stories read in the child's native language, or value placed on reading and learning—extend to schoolwork. Reading at home obscures the boundary between home and school. In this context, learning is perceived as normal, valuable and fun.

Egalitarianism and role sharing were also found to be associated with high academic performance. In fact, relative equality between the sexes was one of the strongest predictors of GPA. In those homes where the respondents disagreed that a "wife should always do as her husband wishes," the children earned average GPAs of 3.16. But children from homes whose parents agreed with the statement had an average GPA of 2.64. In households where the husband helped with the dishes and laundry, the mean GPA was 3.21; when husbands did not participate in the chores, the mean GPA was 2.79.

This sense of equality was not confined to the parents—it extended to the children, especially in terms of sex-role expectations and school performance. GPAs were higher in households where parents expected both boys and girls to help with chores. Families rejecting the idea that a college education is more important for boys than for girls had children whose average GPA was 3.14;

children from families exhibiting a pro-male bias had a mean GPA of 2.83.

Beyond the support and guidance provided by the family, culturally based attributions proved to be important to refugees in their view of scholastic motivation. The "love of learning" category was rated most often by both parents and students as the factor accounting for their academic success. There appeared to be two parts to this sentiment. First, the children experienced intrinsic gratification when they correctly worked a problem through to completion. The pleasure of intellectual growth, based on new knowledge and ideas and combined with increased competence and mastery, was considered highly satisfying. Second, refugee children felt a sense of accomplishment on seeing their younger siblings learn from their own efforts at teaching. Both learning and imparting knowledge were perceived as pleasurable experiences rather than as drudgery.

The gratification accompanying accomplishment was, in turn, founded on a sense of the importance of effort as opposed to ability. The refugees did not trust fate or luck as the determinant of educational outcome; they believed in their potential to master the factors that could influence their destiny. And their culture encompasses a practical approach to accomplishment: setting realistic goals. Without the setting of priorities and standards for work, goals would remain elusive. But anyone endorsing the values of working in a disciplined manner and taking a long-term view could establish priorities and pursue them .

Belief in one's own ability to effect change or attain goals has long been held to be a critical component of achievement and motivation—and our findings support this conclusion. Parents were asked a series of questions relating to their perceived ability to control external events influencing their lives. Those who had a clear sense of personal efficacy had children who attained higher GPAs.

We had some difficulty, however, interpreting the perception of efficacy as an idea generated solely by the individual. Despite a vast social science literature asserting the contrary, we believe that these refugees' sense of control over their lives could be traced to family identity. It seemed to us that the sense of familial efficacy proved critical, as opposed to the more Western concept of personal efficacy.

Other cultural values show us that the refugee family is firmly linked not only to its past and traditions but to the realities of the present and to future possibilities. This aptitude for integrating the past, present and future appears to have imparted a sense of continuity and direction to the lives of these people.

Education was central to this integration and to reestablishment in the United States. It was and still is the main avenue for refugees in American society to succeed and survive. In contrast, education in Indochina was a restricted privilege. The future of the refugee children, and of their families, is thus inextricably linked to schools and to their own children's performances within them. The emphasis on education as the key to social acceptance and economic success helps us understand why academic achievement is reinforced by such strong parental commitment.

Outside school, the same sense of drive and achievement can be seen in the parents. Having a job and being able to provide for the family is integral to family pride. Shame is felt by Asian families on welfare. Reflecting the same determination and energy that their children manifest in school, Indochinese parents have found employment and climbed out of economic dependency and poverty with dispatch.

Two of the twenty-six values included as a measure of cultural adaptation entailed integration and the acceptance of certain American ways of life: the importance of "seeking fun and excitement" and of "material possessions." These ideas are of particular concern because they address the future of refugee families and mark the potential power and consequence of American life on the refugees and subsequent generations. Not surprisingly, when our subjects were asked to indicate which values best characterized their nonrefugee neighbors, these two items were most frequently cited.

More interesting, however, was our finding that these same two values were correlated with a lower GPA. We found that parents who attributed greater importance to fun and excitement had children who achieved lower GPAs: 2.90 as opposed to 3.14. The results for material possessions were similar: GPAs were 2.66 versus 3.19.

It is not clear why these negative associations exist. Do they reflect less strict parents or families who have integrated so quickly that cultural stability has been lost? We believe it is the latter explanation. Refugees who held that "the past is as important as the future" had children whose GPAs averaged 3.14. Children of those who did not rate the preservation of the past as highly had an average GPA of 2.66. This item was one of the most powerful independent predictors of academic performance. Our findings run contrary to expectations. Rather than adopting American ways and assimilating into the melting pot, the most successful Indochinese families appear to retain their own traditions and values. By this statement we are in no way devaluing the American system. The openness and opportunity it offers have enabled the Indochinese to succeed in the United States even while maintaining their own cultural traditions.

Although different in origins, both traditional Indochinese and middle-class American values emphasize education, achievement, hard work, autonomy, perseverance and pride. The difference between the two value systems is one of orientation to achievement. American mores encourage independence and individual achievement, whereas Indochinese values foster interdependence and a family-based orientation to achievement. And in view of the position of these refugees in society during the early phase of resettlement in this country, this approach appears to have worked well as the best long-term investment. It appears to be the reason why these children are highly responsive to American schools.

The lack of emphasis on fun and excitement also does not indicate misery on the part of these refugee children. Despite evidence that the suicide rate is growing among some Asian-American children, we found that those in our sample were well adjusted. Our interviews revealed no damaging manipulation of their lives by their parents; moreover, their love of learning sustained their academic pursuits.

The Indochinese values that encourage academic rigor and excellence are not culturally unique: earlier studies of other groups have found similar results. The children of Jewish immigrants from Eastern Europe, for example, excelled in the U.S. school system. In 1961 Judith R. Kramer of Brooklyn College and Seymour Leventman of the University of Pennsylvania reported that nearly 90 percent of the third generation attended college, despite the fact that the first generation had little or no education when they arrived in the United States. Their emphasis on family and culture was held to be instrumental in this success.

In 1948 William Caudill and George DeVos of the University of California at Berkeley found that Japanese students overcame prejudice in U.S. schools immediately after World War II and thrived academically. Their success was attributed to cultural values and to parental involvement. More recently, a study by Reginald Clark of the Claremont Graduate School documented the outstanding achievement of low-income African-American students in Chicago whose parents supported the school and teachers and structured their children's learning environment at home.

These findings, as well as our own, have significance for the current national debate on education. It is clear that the American school system—despite widespread criticism—has retained its capacity to teach, as it has shown with these refugees. We believe that the view of our schools as failing to educate stems from the unrealistic demand that the educational system deal with urgent social service needs. Citizens and politicians expect teachers and schools to keep children off the streets and away from drugs, deal with teenage pregnancy, prevent violence in the schools, promote safe sex and perform myriad other tasks and responsibilities in addition to teaching traditional academic subjects.

As the social needs of our students have moved into the classroom, they have consumed the scarce resources allocated to education and have compromised the schools' academic function. The primary role of teachers has become that of parent by proxy; they are expected to transform the attitude and behavior of children, many of whom come to school ill prepared to learn.

If we are to deal effectively with the crisis in American education, we must start with an accurate definition of the problem. We must separate teaching and its academic purpose from in-school social services. Only then can we assess the true ability of schools to accomplish these two, sometimes opposing, functions—or we can identify and delegate these nonacademic concerns to other institutions.

Throughout this article we have examined the role of the family in the academic performance of Indochinese refugees. We firmly believe that for American schools to succeed, parents and families must become more committed to the education of their children. They must instill a respect for education and create within the home an environment conducive to learning. They must also participate in the process so that their children feel comfortable learning and go to school willing and prepared to study.

Yet we cannot expect the family to provide such support alone. Schools must reach out to families and engage them meaningfully in the education of their children. This involvement must go beyond annual teacher-parent meetings and must include, among other things, the identification of cultural elements that promote achievement.

Similarly, we cannot adopt the complete perspective of an Indochinese or any other culture. It would be ludicrous to impose cultural beliefs and practices on American children, especially on those whose progress in this country has been fraught with blocked access.

We can, however, work to ensure that families believe in the value of an education and, like the refugees, have rational expectations of future rewards for their efforts. Moreover, we can integrate components of the refugees' experience regarding the family's role in education. It is possible to identify culturally compatible values, behaviors and strategies for success that might enhance scholastic achievement. It is in this regard that the example of the Indochinese refugees—as well as the Japanese and Jewish immigrants before them—can shape our priorities and our policies.

CRITICAL-THINKING QUESTIONS

1. How do Indochinese children compare with their U.S. counterparts on such measures of academic performance as grade-point average (GPA), mathematics scores, and the California Achievement Test (CAT)?
2. How do the values of Indochinese and many lower socioeconomic families in the United States differ? How are these differences reflected in children's academic achievement?
3. What remedies do the authors propose for the crisis in U.S. education? What do these proposals demand of our families? Do you think the solutions are realistic?

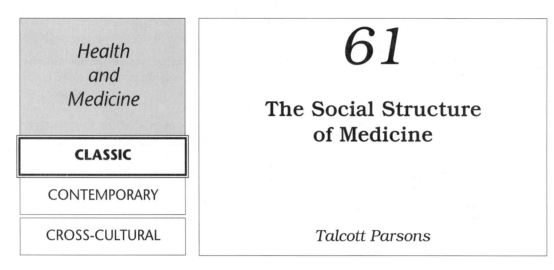

Health and Medicine

CLASSIC

CONTEMPORARY

CROSS-CULTURAL

61

The Social Structure of Medicine

Talcott Parsons

Talcott Parsons, one of the most influential U.S. sociologists during the twentieth century, contributed greatly to the development of structural-functional analysis. In this selection, he examines the significance of health and illness within a social system, with particular attention to the social roles of physicians and patients.

A little reflection will show immediately that the problem of health is intimately involved in the functional prerequisites of the social system. . . . Certainly by almost any definition health is included in the functional needs of the individual member of the society so that from the point of view of functioning of the social system, too low a general level of health, too high an incidence of illness, is dysfunctional. This is in the first instance because illness incapacitates for the effective performance of social roles. It could of course be that this incidence was completely uncontrollable by social action, an independently given condition of social life. But insofar as it is controllable, through rational action or otherwise, it is clear that there is a functional interest of the society in its control, broadly in the minimization of illness. As one special aspect of this, attention may be called to premature death. From a variety of points of view, the birth and rearing of a child constitute a "cost" to the society, through pregnancy, child care, socialization, formal training, and many other channels. Premature death, before the individual has had the opportunity to play out his full quota of social roles, means that only a partial "return" for this cost has been received.

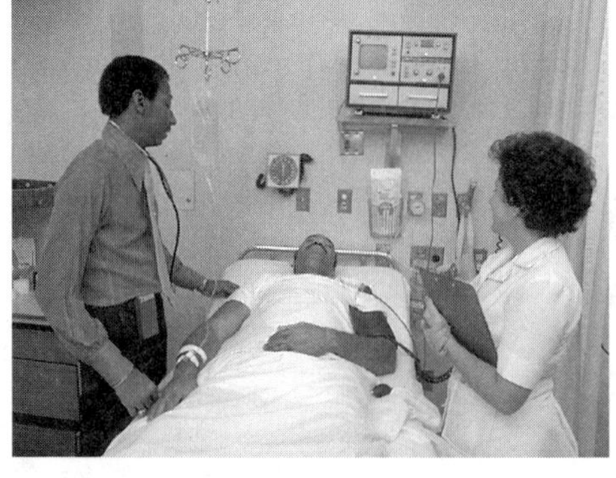

All this would be true were illness purely a "natural phenomenon" in the sense that, like the vagaries of the weather, it was not, to our knowledge, reciprocally involved in the motivated interactions of human beings. In this case illness would be something which merely "happened

Source: From *The Social System* by Talcott Parsons. Copyright © 1951, copyright renewed 1979 by Talcott Parsons. Reprinted with the permission of The Free Press, a Division of Simon & Schuster.

to" people, which involved consequences which had to be dealt with and conditions which might or might not be controllable but was in no way an expression of motivated behavior.

This is in fact the case for a very important part of illness, but it has become increasingly clear, by no means for all. In a variety of ways motivational factors accessible to analysis in action terms are involved in the etiology of many illnesses, and conversely, though without exact correspondence, many conditions are open to therapeutic influence through motivational channels. To take the simplest kind of case, differential exposure, to injuries or to infection, is certainly motivated, and the role of unconscious wishes to be injured or to fall ill in such cases has been clearly demonstrated. Then there is the whole range of "psychosomatic" illness about which knowledge has been rapidly accumulating in recent years. Finally, there is the field of "mental disease," the symptoms of which occur mainly on the behavioral level. . . .

Summing up, we may say that illness is a state of disturbance in the "normal" functioning of the total human individual, including both the state of the organism as a biological system and of his personal and social adjustments. It is thus partly biologically and partly socially defined. . . .

Medical practice . . . is a "mechanism" in the social system for coping with the illnesses of its members. It involves a set of institutionalized roles. . . . The immediately relevant social structures consist in the patterning of the role of the medical practitioner himself and, though to common sense it may seem superfluous to analyze it, that of the "sick person" himself. . . .

The role of the medical practitioner belongs to the general class of "professional" roles, a subclass of the larger group of occupational roles. Caring for the sick is thus not an incidental activity of other roles though, for example, mothers do a good deal of it—but has become functionally specialized as a full-time "job." This, of course, is by no means true of all societies. As an occupational role it is institutionalized about the technical content of the function which is given a high degree of primacy relative to other status-determinants. It is thus inevitable both that incumbency of the role should be achieved and that performance criteria by standards of technical competence should be prominent. Selection for it and the context of its performance are to a high degree segregated from other bases of social status and solidarities. . . . Unlike the role of the businessman, however, it is collectivity-oriented not self-oriented.

The importance of this patterning is, in one context, strongly emphasized by its relation to the cultural tradition. One basis for the division of labor is the specialization of technical competence. The role of physician is far along the continuum of increasingly high levels of technical competence required for performance. Because of the complexity and subtlety of the knowledge and skill required and the consequent length and intensity of training, it is difficult to see how the functions could, under modern conditions, be ascribed to people occupying a prior status as one of their activities in that status, following the pattern by which, to a degree, responsibility for the health of her children is ascribed to the mother-status. There is an intrinsic connection between achieved statuses and the requirements of high technical competence. . . .

High technical competence also implies specificity of function. Such intensive devotion to expertness in matters of health and disease precludes comparable expertness in other fields. The physician is not, by virtue of his modern role, a generalized "wise man" or sage—though there is considerable folklore to that effect—but a specialist whose superiority to his fellows is confined to the specific sphere of his technical training and experience. For example one does not expect the physician as such to have better judgment about foreign policy or tax legislation than any other comparably intelligent and well-educated citizen. There are of course elaborate subdivisions of specialization within the profession. . . . The physician is [also] expected to treat an objective problem in objective, scientifically justifiable terms. For example, whether he likes or dislikes the particular patient as a person is supposed to be irrelevant, as indeed it is to most purely objective problems of how to handle a particular disease.

. . . The "ideology" of the profession lays great emphasis on the obligation of the physician to put the "welfare of the patient" above his personal interests, and regards "commercialism" as the most serious and insidious evil with which it has to contend. The line, therefore, is drawn primarily vis-à-vis "business." The "profit motive" is supposed to be drastically excluded from the medical world. This attitude is, of course, shared with the other professions, but it is perhaps more pronounced in the medical case than in any single one except perhaps the clergy. . . .

An increasing proportion of medical practice is now taking place in the context of organization. To a large extent this is necessitated by the technological development of medicine itself, above all the need for technical facilities beyond the reach of the individual practitioner, and the fact that treating the same case often involves the complex cooperation of several different kinds of physicians as well as of auxiliary personnel. This greatly alters the relation of the physician to the rest of the instrumental complex. He tends to be relieved of much responsibility and hence necessarily of freedom, in relation to his patients other than in his technical role. Even if a hospital executive is a physician himself he is not in the usual sense engaged in the "practice of medicine" in performing his functions any more than the president of the Miners' Union is engaged in mining coal.

As was noted, for common sense there may be some question of whether "being sick" constitutes a social role at all—isn't it simply a state of fact, a "condition"? Things are not quite so simple as this. The test is the existence of a set of institutionalized expectations and the corresponding sentiments and sanctions.

There seem to be four aspects of the institutionalized expectation system relative to the sick role. First is the exemption from normal social role responsibilities, which of course is relative to the nature and severity of the illness. This exemption requires legitimation by and to the various alters involved and the physician often serves as a court of appeal as well as a direct legitimatizing agent. It is noteworthy that like all institutionalized patterns the legitimation of being sick enough to avoid obligations can not only be a right of the sick person but an obligation upon him. People are often resistant to admitting they are sick and it is not uncommon for others to tell them that they *ought* to stay in bed. The word generally has a moral connotation. It goes almost without saying that this legitimation has the social function of protection against "malingering."

The second closely related aspect is the institutionalized definition that the sick person cannot be expected by "pulling himself together" to get well by an act of decision or will. In this sense also he is exempted from responsibility—he is in a condition that must "be taken care of." His "condition" must be changed, not merely his "attitude." Of course the process of recovery may be spontaneous but while the illness lasts he can't "help it." This element in the definition of the state of illness is obviously crucial as a bridge to the acceptance of "help."

The third element is the definition of the state of being ill as itself undesirable with its obligation to want to "get well." The first two elements of legitimation of the sick role thus are conditional in a highly important sense. It is a relative legitimation so long as he is in this unfortunate state which both he and alter hope he can get out of as expeditiously as possible.

Finally, the fourth closely related element is the obligation—in proportion to the severity of the condition, of course—to seek *technically competent* help, namely, in the most usual case, that of a physician and to *cooperate* with him in the process of trying to get well. It is here, of course, that the role of the sick person as patient becomes articulated with that of the physician in a complementary role structure.

It is evident from the above that the role of motivational factors in illness immensely broadens the scope and increases the importance of the institutionalized role aspect of being sick. For then the problem of social control becomes much more than one of ascertaining facts and drawing lines. The privileges and exemptions of the sick role may become objects of a "secondary gain" which the patient is positively motivated, usually unconsciously, to secure or to retain. The problem, therefore, of the balance of motivations to recover becomes of first importance. In general motivational balances of great functional significance to the social system are institutionally controlled, and it should, therefore, not be surprising that this is no exception.

A few further points may be made about the specific patterning of the sick role and its relation to social structure. It is, in the first place, a "contingent" role into which anyone, regardless of his status in other respects, may come. It is, furthermore, in the type case temporary. One may say that it is in a certain sense a "negatively achieved" role, through failure to "keep well," though, of course, positive motivations also operate, which by that very token must be motivations to deviance. . . .

The orientation of the sick role vis-à-vis the physician is also defined as collectively-oriented. It is true that the patient has a very obvious self-interest in getting well in most cases, though this point may not always be so simple. But once he has called in a physician the attitude is clearly marked, that he has assumed the obligation to cooperate with that physician in what is regarded as a common task. The obverse of the physician's obligation to be guided by the welfare of the patient is the latter's obligation to "do his part" to the best of his ability. This point is clearly brought out, for example, in the attitudes of the profession toward what is called "shopping around." By that is meant the practice of a patient "checking" the advice of one physician against that of another without telling physician A that he intends to consult physician B, or if he comes back to A that he has done so or who B is. The medical view is that if the patient is not satisfied with the advice his physician gives him he may properly do one of two things, first he may request a consultation, even naming the physician he wishes called in, but in that case it is physician A not the patient who must call B in, the patient may not see B independently, and above all not without A's knowledge. The other proper recourse is to terminate the relation with A and become "B's patient." The notable fact here is that a pattern of behavior on the part not only of the physician but also of the patient, is expected which is in sharp contrast to perfectly legitimate behavior in a commercial relationship. If he is buying a car there is no objection to the customer going to a number of dealers before making up his mind, and there is no obligation for him to inform any one dealer what others he is consulting, to say nothing of approaching the Chevrolet dealer only through the Ford dealer.

The doctor-patient relationship is thus focused on these pattern elements. The patient has a need for technical services because he doesn't—nor do his lay associates, family members, etc.—"know" what is the matter or what to do about it, nor does he control the necessary facilities. The physician is a technical expert who by special training and experience, and by an institutionally validated status, is qualified to "help" the patient in a situation institutionally defined as legitimate in a relative sense but as needing help. . . .

CRITICAL-THINKING QUESTIONS

1. Does Parsons understand illness as a biological condition, that is, "something that happens to people"? What are the social elements in health and illness?
2. According to Parsons, what are the distinctive characteristics of the social role of the physician?
3. What are the major elements of "the sick role"? In what respects does Parsons view the social roles of physicians and patients as complementary? Can you see ways in which they may be in conflict?

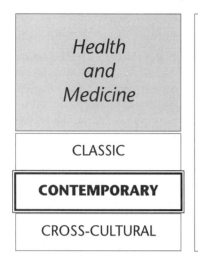

Health and Medicine

CLASSIC

CONTEMPORARY

CROSS-CULTURAL

62

The Health of Latino Families

Ruth E. Zambrana, Claudia Dorrington, and David Hayes-Bautista

Although affluent people in the United States benefit from excellent medical care, the poor have limited access to health services. Those who are hit hard by unemployment, poverty, and a lack of health insurance are especially likely to experience high rates of illness, disability, and early death. This selection examines why many Latino women, men, and children in the United States have more health problems than members of other racial and ethnic groups

HEALTH WITHIN THE FAMILY CONTEXT: AN OVERVIEW

. . . [T]he health of women, men, and children is affected by their living conditions, the community resources available to them to enhance their physical and mental functioning, and their social environment. Documentation of the multidimensional factors that influence use of health services and health outcomes has led scholars to a new theoretical discourse, which in essence examines the interrelationships among individual attributes, family and behavioral risk factors, and institutional arrangements. Population characteristics alone are not focal explanations for low use of health and human services and poor health outcome among Latinos; rather, there is a focus on institutional arrangements and sociocultural barriers that occur at the level of the provider but are influenced by features of the larger society, such as discrimination and racism, poverty, and immigration law. For example, the high cost of medical care, difficulties of accessibility, language barriers, undocumented immigrant status, long waiting lines, lack of transportation, lack of evening and weekend services, lack of child care, and lack of knowledge of available resources assume a central role in understanding access to the use of appropriate health and human services among Latino families (De La Rosa, 1989; Giachello, 1994). Evidence suggests significant barriers associated with the allocation and distribution of economic resources and related health and human services for Latino families. These correlates of social inequality include poverty, lack of health insurance, segregated residential communities, and limited access to quality health and human service support services. All these significantly contribute to the persistent health and social disparities among Latinos. . . .

Source: From "Family and Child Health: A Neglected Vision," by Ruth E. Zambrana, Claudia Dorrington, and David Hayes-Bautista, in *Understanding Latino Families: Scholarship, Policy, and Practice*, ed. Ruth E. Zambrana, pp. 157–59, 165–68, 170–76.

MATERNAL AND CHILD HEALTH

Overall, Latino women have higher fertility rates and tend to begin childbearing at younger ages than the general population. They are also less likely to use health services or to have public or private insurance. Among all racial and ethnic groups, Latinas are the least likely to use prenatal care. In 1987, the percentages of women receiving late (in the third trimester) or no prenatal care at all were 12.7 percent and 11.1 percent for Latinas and African American women, respectively, compared with 5 percent for non-Hispanic White women (U.S. Department of Health and Human Services, 1991). Among poor and racial and ethnic women, about 60 percent initiate care in the first trimester compared to 80 percent of the general population. Compared to women who receive timely prenatal care, women who do not receive prenatal care are three times more likely to deliver low-birthweight infants, and their infants are five times more likely to die in the first year of life (U.S. Department of Health and Human Services, 1991).

Patterns of use of prenatal care vary by Hispanic subgroup. Puerto Rican women are the most likely to receive late or no prenatal care (17 percent), followed by Central American (13.5 percent) and Mexican-origin (13 percent) women (U.S. Department of Health and Human Services, 1991). Several studies have demonstrated that Mexican-born women are the least likely of all groups in California to begin prenatal care during the first trimester. Among Mexican-origin women, Mexican-born women were less likely to initiate care in the first trimester than either African American or Mexican American women (Zambrana, Hernandez, Scrimshaw, & Dunkel-Schetter, 1991). Mexican immigrant women confront a number of barriers to prenatal care: low income; low education; limited financial access to prenatal care programs, including pregnancy-related social services; monolingual Spanish speaking; and the stressors of being immigrant, and undocumented. . . .

Several studies have found that the generational status (or nativity) of the mother is an important predictor of low birthweight. U.S.-born (second-generation) Mexican-origin women were more likely than Mexican-born women to give birth to infants under 2,500 grams. This occurred despite the fact that, compared to Mexican-born women, U.S.-born women had higher education levels, better incomes, and higher health care use rates (Guendelman, Gould, Hudes, & Eskenazi, 1990). Cultural practices, such as abstention from substances, have been found to serve as protective factors and contribute to more favorable pregnancy outcomes. Overall, Latinas are more likely to abstain from the use of drugs, alcohol, and cigarettes than women of other racial and ethnic groups (U.S. Department of Health and Human Services, 1991). However, second-generation Mexican-origin and Puerto Rican women are more likely than Mexican-born women to smoke or use alcohol and drugs (Guendelman et al., 1990). These differences in use of substances, combined with different family structure arrangements (that is, increases in women without partners) may explain the generational differences in low birthweight.

The overall health profile of Latino children reflects their tendency to be poorer and to live in "severely distressed" environmental conditions. Compared to other U.S. children, Latino children are less likely to have health insurance, to receive routine medical checkups, to have a source of health care, or to be immunized for infant and childhood diseases. They are also five times more likely to be involved in accidental injury and half as likely as non-Hispanic white children to have seen a dentist by age eleven (Children's Defense Fund, 1991).

Less than half of poor Latino children are covered by public health insurance. In a national study of barriers to care for children, it was found that only 27.8 percent of Latino children were covered by Medicaid, about 40 percent reported some form of private insurance, and almost one-third reported no insurance (Cornelius, 1993). An examination of data regarding older children from the 1984 National Health Interview Survey revealed that compared to non-Hispanic whites, Latino adolescents are nearly three times as likely to be uninsured. That year, 30 percent of Latino adolescents and 44 percent of Latino young adults were completely uninsured (Lieu, Newacheck, & McManus, 1993).

Due to their low immunization rates, Latino children are at higher risk than non-Hispanic white children for such preventable illnesses as pertussis, tetanus, polio, diphtheria, measles, and rubella. The U.S. childhood vaccinations programs (polio, DPT, measles) have not been made available to significant numbers of low-income racial and ethnic children in the last ten years. The national rate in 1985 for adequate immunization of two-year-olds was 44 percent compared to 25 percent for Latino two-year-olds in California (Lazarus & Gonzalez, 1989). A possible consequence has been a measles epidemic; 25,000 cases have been identified since 1988, and more than 60 deaths were recorded in 1990 alone. The children most at risk of morbidity and possible mortality from these preventable diseases are low-income African American and Hispanic children under the age of five (National Vaccine Advisory Committee, 1991). In a study of hospital admission rates in Los Angeles County, low-income areas (which are heavily populated by Latinos and African Americans) were more likely than high-income areas to have hospital admission rates for conditions that could have been treated early in a primary-care setting. Latino and African American children living in poor areas were much more likely than non-Hispanic white children living in affluent areas to be hospitalized for pneumonia, bronchitis, asthma, gastroenteritis, and ear infections (Valdez & Dallek, 1991). Finally, higher rates of obesity have been reported among Latino school-age children in comparison with non-Latinos (U.S. Department of Health and Human Services, 1991). . . .

HEALTH BEHAVIORS, CHRONIC DISEASE PATTERNS, AND MORTALITY RATES

Recent analyses of intragroup data show significant differences in morbidity and mortality rates (Desenclos & Hahn, 1992). The disproportionate share of illness and mortality burdens experienced by Puerto Rican and Mexican-origin groups reflects their low socioeconomic status in comparison to Cuban and other Hispanic groups. Health behaviors or behavioral risk factors have a significant relationship to chronic disease patterns and mortality. Latinos tend to engage in a range of moderate lifestyle behaviors, although there are differences by nativity, gender, and generational status. Overall, the data suggest that Latino immigrants, particularly Mexican immigrants, tend to exhibit more positive lifestyle behaviors than the native born. Such lifestyle behaviors may be major contributors to better infant health, longer life spans, and lower incidences of heart disease and certain forms of cancer (Hayes-Bautista, 1990; Scribner & Dwyer, 1989; Valdez et al., 1993). . . .

An accurate and comprehensive review of Latino patterns of substance use is limited by lack of data. However, substance use among Latinos represents a growing health care issue. Alcohol use represents a serious behavioral risk factor in Hispanic communities, especially among the Mexican American and Puerto Rican male population (Austin & Gilbert, 1989). Overall, Mexican American men abuse alcohol 5.5 times more frequently than other drugs, compared to non-Hispanic whites. Furthermore, liver disease is the sixth leading cause of death among Latinos, and Latino elderly are twice as likely to die from cirrhosis of the liver as non-Hispanic whites. Evidence suggests a higher prevalence of frequent and heavy drinking among U.S.-born Latino males and females than among immigrants (Valdez et al., 1993). Hispanic women generally appear to be less at risk for alcohol problems than women in general; however, the amount of drinking and incidence of heavy drinking are increasing among young and acculturated Mexican American women (Austin & Gilbert, 1989).

Smoking prevalence among Latino populations is higher than among the non-Hispanic White population, specifically among Latino adult and adolescent males, but it is lower than among the African American population. Overall it appears that Cuban men, ages 25–34, and Puerto Rican women, ages 25–54, have higher rates of smoking and higher consumption of cigarettes than other Hispanic subgroups (U.S. Department of Health and Human Services, 1991). On the other hand, many Hispanic females never smoke, and, if they do they begin smoking at a later age, they smoke fewer cigarettes and are more likely to quit. Tobacco use rates among Latinas have been far lower than those of non-Hispanic white and African American women, although with acculturation, researchers have noted an increasing number of young Hispanic female smokers. Paralleling the increase in tobacco use has been a marked increase in the rates of lung cancer and other pulmonary diseases, especially among Latino males (Maxwell & Jacobson, 1989; Valdez et al., 1993).

Regarding other drug use among Latinos, reliable data are even more limited and vary by subgroup and gender. Contrary to the stereotype, the prevalence of other drug use does not seem to vary substantially by race and ethnicity. Among Latinos, 17 percent of the men and 11.7 percent of the women reported use of illicit drugs in 1990. However, the type of drugs used and the method of use seems to vary. African Americans and Latinos are more likely to use cocaine and crack cocaine than non-Hispanic whites. For both males and females, current and lifetime use of crack is higher among African Americans and Latinos. In addition, emergency-room data indicate that Latinos are more likely to report primary presenting problems with heroin, PCP, or cocaine than non-Hispanic whites. Mexican Americans appear to have higher rates of marijuana and other drug use than other Latino groups. On the other hand, Mexican immigrants are less likely to have a diagnosis of drug abuse/dependence compared to non-Hispanic whites (U.S. Department of Health and Human Services, 1991).

Related to the use of drugs is the prevalence of HIV/AIDS among the Latino population. Latinos accounted for 16 percent of all AIDS cases between 1982 and 1992. By 1989, 40 percent of Latino AIDS cases were related to the use of intravenous drugs and 7 percent to homosexual/bisexual male contact and intravenous drug use. Nationwide, Puerto Ricans had the highest incidence of AIDS related to intravenous drug use. As of 1992, Hispanic women represented 21 percent of all women diagnosed with AIDS, and Hispanic men accounted for 16 percent of all men so diagnosed. Among children, 25 percent of all children with AIDS are Latino. As of 1991, AIDS was the fifth leading cause of death among Latinos. The risk of contracting AIDS for Latinos is 2.8 times higher than for non-Hispanic whites. The cumulative incidence of AIDS among Hispanic women is 8.1 times higher than for non-Hispanic women. The majority of cases among women and children are reportedly related to intravenous drug use by the women's partners (Office of Minority Health, 1990). Latinas as a group tend to be sexually conservative with respect to the number of past sexual partners and age at sexual initiation. Recent Latina immigrants tend to be the most sexually conservative, followed by bilingual Latinas, and then non-Hispanic white women. However, sexual practices are clearly related to the prevalence of AIDS and other sexually transmitted diseases. In one study, approximately half of the Latinas reported rarely or never using contraceptive birth control measures. The use of contraception and other protective sexual practices was highly related to educational level, age, and traditional values (Rapkin & Erickson, 1990).

Nutrition and diet are other important areas where limited information is available for Latino groups. However, the research suggests that obesity, which is related to high blood pressure, high cholesterol, and diabetes, among other health problems, is a relatively serious problem among certain Latino groups, especially among women. Data from the HHANES study found that between 30 percent and 40 percent of Puerto Rican, Cuban, and Mexican-origin women were overweight, compared to just under 25 percent of a comparable sample of non-Hispanic white women. Cuban Americans were found to have the highest percentage of overweight men, almost 30 percent, in comparison to 24 percent of non-Hispanic white men and 19 percent of Mexican Americans. . . .

Overall, the leading causes of death for Latinos in order of frequency are heart disease (25 percent), cancer (17 percent), nonintentional injuries (9 percent), stroke (6 percent), and homicide (5 percent). Liver disease, pneumonia/influenza, diabetes, HIV infection, and perinatal conditions each account for 3 percent of mortality. However, the actual prevalence of diabetes among Latinos is much higher than the mortality rates might suggest, because most diabetics die from complications of diabetes, primarily heart and kidney disease. Latino males are more likely than non-Hispanic White males to die as a result of homicide, unintentional injuries, cirrhosis, and infections. The low overall rate of mortality among Latinas, in comparison to non-Hispanic white females, is related to lower rates of suicide and unintentional injuries. However, although the incidence of breast cancer is significantly lower among Latinas, they are 2.4 times more likely to die from both cervical and breast cancer, due to limited knowledge of early symptoms of the disease and limited access to preventive and primary care. Furthermore, the burden of premature mortality varies widely by Latino subgroup. Mortality rates are highest for Puerto Ricans, followed by Mexican-origin persons and Cubans (Desenclos & Hahn, 1992).

The socioeconomic characteristics of the Latino population represent a set of shared risk attributes with other poor and racial/ethnic groups in the United States. The correlates of poverty, such as poor housing, lower educational attainment, inadequate nutrition, use of substances, and unsafe and poor quality environmental conditions, all contribute to the higher prevalence of both acute and chronic health conditions (Adler, Boyce, Chesney, Folkman, & Syme, 1993). Latinos of higher socioeconomic status, as defined by education and income, have health care patterns similar to the general population. The data suggest that the overall well-being and health status of Latinos are being adversely affected by their lack of access to quality health care services, as well as other supportive human service programs.

OBSTACLES IN PROMOTING LATINO FAMILY HEALTH

The dramatic increase and the diversity in Latino populations in the United States, coupled with their lack of access to health care and public social service resources, constitute a serious policy concern. Latino health and human service needs require serious consideration and attention from legal scholars, health and human service practitioners, and policymakers. The issues encompass both institutional changes and family-focused efforts. Although increased attention has been directed at public health policy and welfare reform in the 1990s, Latinos, as an emerging culturally distinct population, have received little or no attention. This results from the commonplace assumption that "all minorities suffer from the same problems and have the same needs" (Hayes-Bautista, 1990).

Recent scholarly developments and data on the unique health and human services needs of Latino families and children provide a relevant base from which to shape appropriate, effective, and responsive services for Latinos (Furino, 1992; U.S. Department of Health and Human Services, 1993). In effect, what is abundantly clear is that health promotion involves improving the standard of living and is the most important area of public health policy in this decade. Terris (1990) succinctly states the core of the solution:

> The concept of health promotion refers to the development of healthful living standards. These have a profound effect on positive health, which is not only a subjective state of well-being (including such elements as vitality, freedom from excess fatigue, and freedom from environmental discomforts such as excessive heat, cold, smog and noise), but also has a functional component, namely the ability of an individual to participate effectively in society; at work; at home; and in the community. (p. 285)

Improvements in the standard of living are crucial to Latino families and children, but equally important is access to primary and preventive services. All current data on use of public health and social service programs show that Latino families and children are not receiving needed services due to lack of awareness of services, lack of understanding of eligibility, and sociocultural and language barriers that impede access. Ginzberg (1991) states:

> Many Hispanics are poorly positioned to access the health care system by virtue of below average family income, above average employment in establishments that do not regularly provide health insurance and a sizeable number who live in states with low Medicaid enrollments. (p. 238)

In addition, immigration status and the effects of differential eligibility within a single family are economically and psychologically damaging to Latinos. Immigration status is an obstacle to health care access, and clearly an obstacle to maximizing contributions to society. For example, differential definitions of *resident* for purposes of eligibility for county-funded services lead to inequitable access to health and family-support resources.

Another significant barrier is the severe underrepresentation of Latinos in the health and social service professions. Within the overall context of an oversupply of medical professional personnel, the system has failed to provide support, financial or affirmative, for health professionals who are bilingual and bicultural. Recent data from the Association of American Medical Colleges note that Latino enrollment in U.S. medical schools is a meager 1.7 percent for Mexican Americans, 2 percent for Puerto Ricans, and 1.7 percent for "other Hispanics" (Ginzberg, 1991). In our view, two potential pools of health personnel must be incorporated into the existing health care delivery system if we are to be responsive to the Latino community: the native-born Latino provider and the Foreign Medical Graduate (FMG). For native-born providers, the issues of affirmative action, recruitment, admissions, and retention to medical and related health professional schools remain salient. A vital program in the effort to increase the Latino physician supply is the National Health Service Corps, a mechanism to recruit and train Latino physicians in conjunction with the Hispanic Centers of Excellence in medical schools throughout the country. If training and educational resources were allocated for Latino health-service providers, this would represent an important commitment on the part of the United States to provide primary-care services in a culturally acceptable way to Latinos in the United States. The licensure of FMGs remain a legal limbo filled with unlicensed but trained personnel. This important and vital resource has remained unused within the Latino community.

The current health care and human service systems continue a long-standing tradition of unresponsiveness and ineffectiveness in addressing the needs and concerns of vulnerable and at-risk populations. A national health insurance program linked with a family income maintenance program and a child-care program can strengthen families, rather than serve to debilitate them. Furthermore, we need a focus on preventing problems, not on repairing the damage of neglect. These programs must be designed as an integrated system to provide comprehensive, family-focused, culturally and linguistically appropriate, community-based linked networks of health and human services, guided by the principles of prevention and primary-care interventions (Darder et al., 1993; Latino Coalition for a Healthy California, 1993).

This commitment requires reflection on our values as a nation. Current health and human service legislation must seek to redress the current inequities. Latinos bear a persistent and disproportionate burden of morbidity and mortality. In effect, Latinos, who have limited economic resources, confront extraordinary financial and sociocultural barriers to obtaining minimal health and human services. Current patterns set the foundation for a new generation of Latinos, who will continue to experience the adverse social, psychological, and medical effects of living in a society that denies them adequate access to health care and child and family welfare services. With certainty, it can be argued that Latino families and children have not elected to be economically and socially disadvantaged, but rather that the society in which they live has made that choice for them.

CRITICAL-THINKING QUESTIONS

1. Describe the major health risks that Latino mothers, children, and men face. How do these risks vary within Latino groups (e.g., between Puerto Rican Americans, Mexican Americans, and Cuban Americans)?
2. Health represents a complex relationship between individual behavior, community environments, and societal resources. How do the consequences of social inequality interact with cultural factors in influencing Latino health and help-seeking behavior?
3. The authors of this selection discuss several obstacles to promoting Latino family health. Do any of these obstacles characterize other poor people in the United States as well? Or are most of these health barriers unique to Latino families?

REFERENCES

ADLER, N. E., T. BOYCE, M. CHESNEY, S. FOLKMAN, and L. SYME. 1993. Socioeconomic inequalities in health. *Journal of the American Medical Association,* 289(24):3140–45.

AUSTIN, G. A., and M. J. GILBERT. 1989. Substance abuse among Latino youth. In *Prevention Research Update* (No. 3, Spring). Portland, Ore.: Western Center for Drug-Free Schools and Communities.

CHILDREN'S DEFENSE FUND. 1991. *An opinion maker's guide to children in election year 1992.* Washington, D.C.

CORNELIUS, L. 1993. Barriers to medical care for white, black, and Hispanic children. *Journal of the National Medical Association,* 85(4):281–88.

DARDER, A., Y. R. INGLE, and B. G. COX. 1993. *The policies and the promise: The public schooling of Latino children.* Claremont, Calif.: The Tomás Rivera Center.

DE LA ROSA. 1989. Health care needs of Hispanic Americans and the responsiveness of the health care system. *Health and Social Work,* 14(2), 104–13.

DESENCLOS, J. C. A., and R. A. HAHN. 1992. Years of potential life lost before age 65, by race, Hispanic origin, and sex—United States, 1986–1988. *Morbidity and Mortality Weekly Report,* 6(42):13–23.

FURINO, A. 1992. *Health policy and the Hispanic.* Boulder, Colo.: Westview.

GIACHELLO, A. L. 1994. Hispanics' access to health care: Issues for the 1990's. In *Latino health: America's growing challenge for the 21st century,* eds. C. Molina and M. Aguirre-Molina, 83–114. Washington, D.C.: American Public Health Association.

GINZBERG, E. L. 1991. Access to health care for Hispanics. *Journal of the American Medical Association,* 265(2):238–42.

GUENDELMAN, S., J. B. GOULD, M. HUDES, and B. ESKENAZI. 1990. Generational differences in perinatal health among the Mexican American population: Findings from HHANES 1982–84. *American Journal of Public Health,* 80(Suppl.):61–65.

HAYES-BAUTISTA, D. 1990. *Latino health indicators and the underclass model: From paradox to new policy models.* Los Angeles: Chicano Studies Research Center, University of California, Los Angeles.

LATINO COALITION FOR A HEALTHY CALIFORNIA. 1993. *The American Health Security Act: A Latino perspective.* San Francisco: The Latino Coalition for a Healthy California.

LAZARUS, W., and M. GONZALEZ. 1989. *California: The state of our children 1989.* Oakland, Calif.: Children Now.

LIEU, T. A., P. W. NEWACHECK, and M. A. MCMANUS. 1993. Race, ethnicity, and access to ambulatory care among U.S. adolescents. *American Journal of Public Health,* 83:960–65.

MAXWELL, B., and M. JACOBSON. 1989. *Marketing disease to Hispanics—The selling of alcohol, tobacco, and junk foods.* Washington, D.C.: The Center for Science in the Public Interest.

NATIONAL VACCINE ADVISORY COMMITTEE. 1991. The measles epidemic: The problems, barriers, and recommendations. *Journal of the American Medical Association,* 266:1547–52.

Office of Minority Health, Public Health Service, U.S. Department of Health and Human Services. 1990. AIDS/HIV infection and minorities. In *Closing the gap* (0-860-815). Washington, D.C.: Government Printing Office.

RAPKIN, A. J., and P I. ERICKSON. 1990. Acquired Immune Deficiency Syndrome: Ethnic differences in knowledge and risk factors among women in an urban family planning clinic. *AIDS* (August).

SCRIBNER, R., and J. DWYER. 1989. Acculturation and low birthweight among Latinos in Hispanic HANES. *American Journal of Public Health,* 79(9):1263–67.

TERRIS, M. 1990. Public health policy for the 1990s. *Annual Reviews of Public Health,* 11:39–51.

U.S. Department of Health and Human Services. 1991. *Health status of minorities and low-income groups* (3d ed.). Washington, D.C.

U.S. Department of Health and Human Services, Public Health Service. 1993. *Surgeon general's report: Blueprint for improving Hispanic and Latino health: Implementation strategies.* Washington, D.C.: Government Printing Office.

VALDEZ, R. B., and G. DALLEK. 1991. *Does the health care system serve black and Latino communities in Los Angeles County? An analysis of hospital use in 1987.* Claremont, Calif.: The Tomás Rivera Center.

VALDEZ, R. B., D. J. DELGADO, R. C. CERVANTES, and S. BOWLER. 1993. *Cancer in U.S. Latino communities: An exploratory review.* Santa Monica, Calif.: RAND.

ZAMBRANA, R. E., M. HERNANDEZ, C. DUNKEL-SCHETTER, and S. SCRIMSHAW. 1991. Ethnic differences in the substance use patterns of low income pregnant women. *Journal of Family and Community Health,* 13(4):1–11.

Health and Medicine

CLASSIC

CONTEMPORARY

CROSS-CULTURAL

63

Female Genital Mutilation

Efua Dorkenoo and Scilla Elworthy

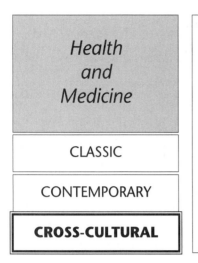

During the last decade, numerous women's organizations around the world have focused on a variety of health-related issues and problems including domestic violence, rape, sexual harassment, and poverty. In this selection, Efua Dorkenoo and Scilla Elworthy examine the complex cultural issues surrounding female genital mutilation, a practice that has received international attention since the early 1990s.

THE FACTS

. . . [F]emale genital mutilation covers four types of operation:

1. *Circumcision,* or cutting of the prepuce or hood of the clitoris, known in Muslim countries as Sunna (tradition). This, the mildest type, affects only a small proportion of the millions of women concerned. It is the only type of mutilation that can correctly be called circumcision, though there has been a tendency to group all kinds of mutilations under the misleading term 'female circumcision.'
2. *Excision,* meaning the cutting of the clitoris and of all or part of the labia minora.
3. *Infibulation,* the cutting of the clitoris, labia minora and at least part of the labia majora. The two sides of the vulva are then pinned together by silk or catgut sutures, or with thorns, thus obliterating the vaginal introitus except for a very small opening, preserved by the insertion of a tiny piece of wood or a reed for the passage of urine or menstrual blood. These operations are done with special knives, with razor blades or pieces of glass. The girl's legs are then bound together from hip to ankle and she is kept immobile for up to forty days to permit the formation of scar tissue.
4. *Intermediate,* meaning the removal of the clitoris and some parts of the labia minora or the whole of it. Various degrees are done according to the demands of the girl's relatives. . . .

Most frequently these operations are performed by an old woman of the village or by a traditional birth attendant and only rarely by qualified nurses or doctors. The age at which the mutilations are carried out varies from area to area, and according to whether legislation against the practice is foreseen or not. It varies from a few days old (for example, the Jewish Falashas in Ethiopia, and the nomads of the Sudan) to about seven years (as in Egypt and many countries of Central Africa) or—more rarely—adolescence, as among the Ibo of Nigeria. Most experts are agreed that the age of mutilation is becoming younger, and has less and less to do with initiation into adulthood.[1]

Source: From "Female Genital Mutilation," by Efua Dorkenoo and Scilla Elworthy, in *Female Genital Mutilation: Proposals for Change,* an MRG Report, 92/3. Reprinted with permission.

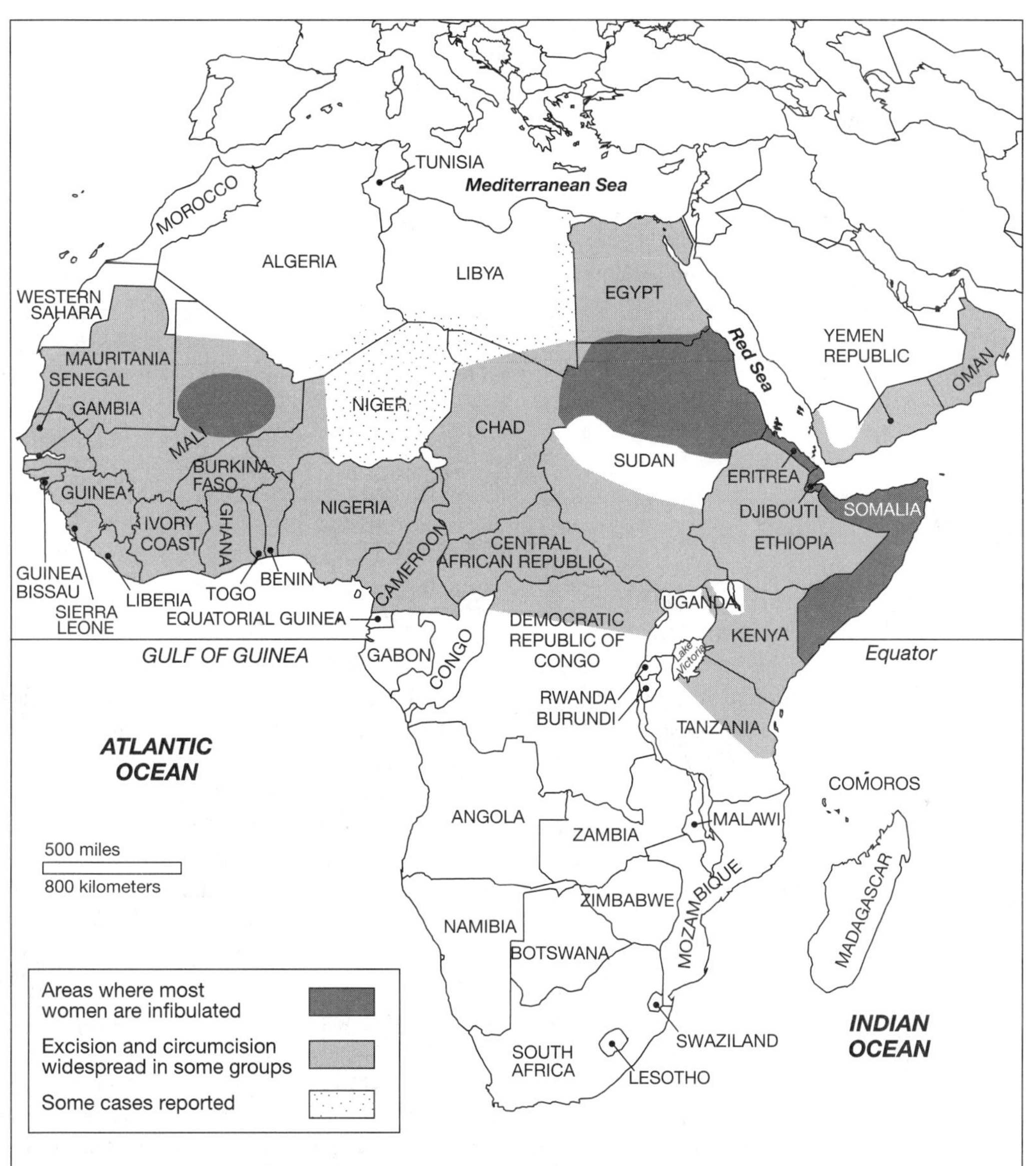

Female Genital Mutilation in Africa

Physical Consequences

Health risks and complications depend on the gravity of the mutilation, hygienic conditions, the skill and eyesight of the operator, and the struggles of the child. Whether immediate or long term, they are grave.[2] Death from bleeding is not uncommon, while long-term complications include chronic infections of the uterus and vagina, painful menstruation, severe pain during intercourse, sterility and complications during childbirth. Though evidence has yet to be collected, it is also likely that bleeding or open wounds increase the likelihood of HIV transmission and AIDS.

There is great difficulty in obtaining accurate research on the sexual experiences of mutilated women, because the majority are reluctant to speak on the subject and are generally ambivalent on questions of sexual enjoyment.[3] However, in all types of mutilation, even the "mildest" clitoridectomy, a part of a woman's body containing nerves of vital importance to sexual pleasure is amputated.

Psychological Consequences

Even less research has been done to date on the psychological consequences of these traditions. However, many personal accounts and research findings contain repeated references to anxiety prior to the operation, terror at the moment of being seized by an aunt or village matron, unbearable pain, and the subsequent sense of humiliation and of being betrayed by parents, especially the mother. On the other hand, there are references to special clothes and good food associated with the event, to the pride felt in being like everyone else, in being "made clean," in having suffered without screaming.

To be different clearly produces anxiety and mental conflict. An unexcised, non-infibulated girl is despised and made the target of ridicule, and no one in her community will marry her. Thus what is clearly understood to be her life's work, namely marriage and child-bearing, is denied her. So, in tight-knit village societies where mutilation is the rule, it will be the exceptional girl who will suffer psychologically, unless she has another very strong identity which she has lost.[4]

There is no doubt that genital mutilation would have overwhelming psychological effects on an unmotivated girl, unsupported by her family, village, peers and community. To those from other cultures unfamiliar with the force of this particular community identity, the very concept of amputation of the genitals carries a shock value which does not exist for most women in the areas concerned. For them, not to amputate would be shocking.

These observations concern social-psychological factors rather than the central question, namely, what effects do these traumatic operations have on little girls at the moment of operation and as they grow up? The fact is that we simply don't know. We do not know what it means to a girl or woman when her central organ of sensory pleasure is cut off, when her life-giving canal is stitched up amid blood and fear and secrecy, while she is forcibly held down and told that if she screams she will cause the death of her mother or bring shame on the family.

THE PRACTICE

The Area Covered

The countries where one or more forms of female genital mutilation are practised number more than twenty in Africa, from the Atlantic to the Red Sea, the Indian Ocean and the eastern Mediterranean. Outside Africa, excision is also practised in Oman, South Yemen and in the United Arab Emirates (UAE). Circumcision is practised by the Muslim populations of Indonesia and Malaysia and by Bohra Muslims in India, Pakistan and East Africa.[5]

On the map of Africa, an uninterrupted belt is formed across the centre of the continent, which then expands up the length of the Nile. This belt, with the exception of the Egyptian buckle, corresponds strikingly with the pattern of countries that have the highest child mortality rates (more than 30 percent for children from one to four years of age).[6] These levels reflect deficiencies of medical care, of clean drinking water, of sanitary infrastructure and of adequate nutrition in most of the countries.

The gravity of the mutilations varies from country to country. Infibulation is reported to affect nearly all the female population of Somalia, Djibouti and the Sudan (except the non-

Muslim population of southern Sudan), southern Egypt, the Red Sea coast of Ethiopia, northern Kenya, northern Nigeria and some parts of Mali. The most recent estimate of women mutilated is 74 million.[7]

Ethnic groups closely situated geographically are by no means affected in the same way: For example, in Kenya, the Kikuyu practise excision and the Luo do not; in Nigeria, the Yoruba, the Ibo and the Hausa do, but not the Nupes or the Fulanis; in Senegal, the Woloff have no practice of mutilation. There are many other examples.

As the subject of female genital mutilation began to be eligible at least for discussion, reports of genital operations on non-consenting females have appeared from many unexpected parts of the world. During the 1980s, women in Sweden were shocked by accounts of mutilations performed in Swedish hospitals on daughters of immigrants. In France, women from Mali and Senegal have been reported to bring an *exciseuse* to France once a year to operate on their daughters in their apartments.[8] In July 1982 a Malian infant died of an excision performed by a professional circumciser, who then fled to Mali. In the same year, reports appeared in the British press that excision for non-medical reasons had been performed in a London private clinic.

Legislation

In Africa. Formal legislation forbidding genital mutilation, or more precisely infibulation, exists in the Sudan. A law first enacted in 1946 allows for a term of imprisonment up to five years and/or a fine. However, it is not an offence (under Article 284 of the Sudan Penal Code for 1974) "merely to remove the free and projecting part of the clitoris."

Many references have been made to legislation in Egypt, but after researching the available materials, all that has been traced is a resolution signed by the Minister of Health in 1959, recommending only partial clitoridectomy for those who want an operation, to be performed only by doctors.[9]

In late 1978, largely due to the efforts of the Somali Women's Democratic Organization (SWDO), Somalia set up a commission to abolish infibulation. In 1988 at a seminar held in Mogadishu, it was recommended that SWDO should propose a bill to the competent authorities to eradicate all forms of female genital mutilation.

In September 1982, President Arap Moi took steps to ban the practices in Kenya, following reports of the deaths of fourteen children after excision. A traditional practitioner found to be carrying out this operation can be arrested under the Chiefs Act and brought before the law.

Official declarations against female genital mutilation were made by the late Captain Thomas Sankara and Abdou Diouf, the heads of state in Burkina Faso and Senegal respectively.

In Western Countries. A law prohibiting female excision, whether consent has been given or not, came into force in Sweden in July 1982, carrying a two-year sentence. In Norway, in 1985, all hospitals were alerted to the practice. Belgium has incorporated a ban on the practice. Several states in the U.S.A. have incorporated female genital mutilation into their criminal code.

In the U.K., specific legislation prohibiting female circumcision came into force at the end of 1985. A person found guilty of an offence is liable to up to five years' imprisonment or to a fine. Female genital mutilation has been incorporated into child protection procedures at local authority levels. As yet no person has been committed in the English courts for female circumcision but since 1989 there have been at least seven local authority legal interventions which prevented parents from sexually mutilating their daughters or wards.

France does not have specific legislation on female sexual mutilation but under Article 312–3 of the French Penal Code, female genital mutilation can be considered as a criminal offence. Under this code, anybody who exercises violence or seriously assaults a child less than fifteen years old can be punished with imprisonment from ten to twenty years, if the act of violence results in a mutilation, amputation of a limb, the loss of an eye or other parts of the body or has unintentionally caused the death of the child.

In 1989, a mother who had paid a traditional woman exciser to excise her week-old daughter, in 1984, was convicted and given a three-year suspended jail sentence. In 1991 a traditional exciser was jailed for five years in France.

Contemporary Practices

Opinions are very divided as to whether the practice is disappearing because of legislation or social and economic changes. Esther Ogunmodede, for instance, believes that in Nigeria, Africa's most populous country, the tradition is disappearing but extremely slowly, with millions of excisions still taking place. She reports that in areas where the operations are done on girls of marriageable age, they are "running away from home to avoid the razor." This confirms Fran Hosken's assertion that operations are being done at earlier and earlier ages, in order that the children should be "too young to resist." Fran Hosken does not think that the custom is dying out, and she indisputably has the best published range of information concerning all the countries where the practice is known.

An interesting development took place in Ethiopia during the years of civil warfare which only ended in 1991. When the Eritrean People's Liberation Front (EPLF) occupied large areas from January 1977 to December 1978, among many other reforms they categorically and successfully forbade genital mutilation and forced marriage. In fact, the reason given for the large numbers of young women in the EPLF army was that they were running away from home in other parts of Ethiopia to avoid forced marriage and the knife.[10] Although it appears the practice continues in remote areas, because the consciousness of Eritrean women has changed dramatically during the war years, it is easier to persuade men and women to let go of this practice.

Since 1983, the number of educational programmes initiated to raise public awareness of the health risk associated with female genital mutilation at local, national and international levels have increased. The media have played a major role in bringing this issue from the domestic to the public domain. As a result of these efforts it can be said that the taboo surrounding even public mention of the practice has at last been broken. There is an increase in public awareness of the harmful effects of female genital mutilation.

It has been noted that female genital mutilation is becoming unpopular amongst the urban elite in some African countries. In Sierra Leone, for example, Koso-Thomas claims that urban men are willing to marry uncircumcised women, in particular when the marriage is not pre-arranged.[11]

In general, among urban educated women, reasons often cited against female genital mutilation include the pointlessness of mutilation, health risks and reduction of sexual sensitivity. The last reason points to a changing attitude towards women's fundamental human rights amongst urban Africans.

In the main, the practice continues to be widespread among large sectors and groups within Africa. Those in favour of the practice are noted in the 1986 UN study to be a passive majority who refer back to traditional society, without necessarily sharing that society's values.[12] In some cases, the practice appears to be spreading to population groups who traditionally never practised female genital mutilation, as observed with city women in Wau, Sudan, who regard it as fashionable, and among converted Muslim women in southern Sudan who marry northern Sudanese men.[13] Furthermore, even in areas where some groups are turning against the practice, the absolute numbers affected may be increasing. Rapid population growth in Africa means greater numbers of female children are born, who in turn are exposed to the risk of mutilation.

THE ISSUES

Female genital mutilation is a complex issue, for it involves deep-seated cultural practices which affect millions of people. However, it can be divided into (at least) four distinct issues.

Rights of Women

Female genital mutilation is an extreme example of the general subjugation of women, sufficiently extreme and horrifying to make women and men question the basis of what is done to women, what women have accepted and why, in the name of society and tradition.

The burning of Indian widows and the binding of the feet of Chinese girl children are other striking examples, sharp enough and strange enough to throw a spotlight on other less obvious ways in which women the world over submit to oppression. It is important to remember that all these practices are, or were, preserved under centuries of tradition, and that foot-binding was only definitively stopped by a massive social and political revolution (replacing the many traditions which it swept away by offering an entirely new social system, revolutionary in many aspects: land ownership, class system, education, sex equality, etc.) which had been preceded by years of patient work by reformers.

Thus, to be successful, campaigns on female genital mutilation should consider carefully not only eliminating but also replacing the custom. (The example of Eritrea, previously quoted, is illuminating here.) Furthermore, such success may be predicated on long-term changes in attitudes and ideologies by both men and women.

A major international expression of the goal of equal rights for women was taken in December 1979, when the U.N. General Assembly adopted the Convention on the Elimination of All Forms of Discrimination Against Women. This came into force in September 1981. The comprehensive convention calls for equal rights for women, regardless of their marital status, in all fields: political, economic, social, cultural and civil. Article 5(a) obliges states' parties to take:

> All appropriate measures to modify the social and cultural patterns of conduct of men and women, with a view to achieving the elimination of prejudices and customary and all other practices which are based on the idea of the inferiority or superiority of either of the sexes or on stereotyped roles for men and women.

To succeed in abolishing such practices will demand fundamental attitudinal shifts in the way that society perceives the human rights of women. The starting point for change should be educational programmes that assist women to recognize their fundamental human rights. This is where UNESCO, the U.N. Centre for Human Rights and international agencies could help by supporting awareness-building programmes.

Rights of Children

An adult is free to submit her or himself to a ritual or tradition, but a child, having no formed judgement, does not consent but simply undergoes the operation (which in this case is irrevocable) while she is totally vulnerable. The descriptions available of the reactions of children—panic and shock from extreme pain, biting through the tongue, convulsions, necessity for six adults to hold down an eight-year-old, and death—indicate a practice comparable to torture.

Many countries signatory to Article 5 of the Universal Declaration of Human Rights (which provides that no one shall be subjected to torture, or to cruel, inhuman or degrading treatment) violate that clause. Those violations are discussed and sometimes condemned by various U.N. commissions. Female genital mutilation, however, is a question of torture inflicted not on adults but on girl children, and the reasons given are not concerned with either political conviction or military necessity but are solely in the name of tradition.

The Declaration of the Rights of Children, adopted in 1959 by the General Assembly, asserts that children should have the possibility to develop physically in a healthy and normal way in conditions of liberty and dignity. They should have adequate medical attention, and be protected from all forms of cruelty.

It is the opinion of Renée Bridel, of the Fédération Internationale des Femmes de Carrières Juridiques, that "One cannot but consider Member States which tolerate these practices as infringing their obligations as assumed under the terms of the Charter [of the U.N.].[14]

In September 1990, the United Nations Convention on the Rights of the Child went into force. It became part of international human rights law. Under Article 24(3) it states that: "States Parties shall take all effective and appropriate measures with a view to abolishing traditional practices prejudicial to the health of children." This crucial article should not merely remain a paper provision, to be given lip service by those entrusted to implement it. Members of the U.N. should work at translating its provisions into specific implementation programmes at grassroots level. Much could be learned (by African states in particular) from countries with established child protection systems.

The Right to Good Health

No reputable medical practitioner insists that mutilation is good for the physical or mental health of girls and women, and a growing number offer research indicating its grave permanent damage to health and underlining the risks of death. Medical facts, carefully explained, may be the way to discourage the practice, since these facts are almost always the contrary of what is believed, and can be shown and demonstrated.

Those U.N. agencies and government departments specifically entrusted with the health needs of women and children must realize that it is their responsibility to support positive and specific preventative programmes against female genital mutilation, for while the practice continues the quality of life and health will inevitably suffer. However, this approach, if presented out of context, ignores the force of societal pressures which drive women to perform these operations, regardless of risk, in order to guarantee marriage for their daughters, and to conform to severe codes of female behaviour laid down by male-dominated societies.

The Right to Development

The practice of female genital mutilation must be seen in the context of underdevelopment,[15] and the realities of life for the most vulnerable and exploited sectors—women and children. International political and economic forces have frequently prevented development programmes from meeting the basic needs of rural populations. With no access to education or resources, and with no effective power base, the rural and urban poor cling to traditions as a survival mechanism in time of socio-economic change.

In societies where marriage for a woman is her only means of survival, and where some form of excision is a prerequisite for marriage, persuading her to relinquish the practice for herself or for her children is an extraordinarily difficult task. Female (and some male) African analysts of development strategies are today constantly urging that the overall deteriorating conditions in which poor women live be made a major focus for change, for unless development affects their lives for the better, traditional practices are unlikely to change.

DIRECTIONS FOR THE FUTURE

The mutilation of female genitals has been practised in many areas for centuries. The greatest determination, combined with sensitivity and understanding of local conditions, will be needed if it is to be abolished. In every country and region where operations are carried out, the situation is different, as is the political will, whether at local or national levels. In Western countries the way forward is relatively clear. In Africa the problem is more profound and the economic and political conditions vastly more difficult, while international agencies have hardly begun to explore their potential role.

What all three have in common is that, to date, nearly all programmes have been individual or *ad hoc* efforts, with little integration into other structures, with minimal evaluation or monitoring, and lacking in long-term goals and strategies. To achieve real change will require more resources, more detailed planning, and more real, sustained commitment from governments and international organizations.

CRITICAL-THINKING QUESTIONS

1. What are the four types of female genital mutilation? How widespread are these practices?
2. What do Dorkenoo and Elworthy mean when they describe female genital mutilation as a "complex" issue? Do they feel that this practice can be abolished or not?
3. Many Western countries have denounced female genital mutilation as barbaric. But what about comparable practices in the United States and other Western nations? Even though they are voluntary, are silicone breast transplants, face-lifts, or liposuction more "civilized" in making women's bodies more acceptable to men?

NOTES

1. Fran Hosken, *The Hosken Report—Genital and Sexual Mutilation of Females* (third enlarged/revised edition, Autumn, 1982, published by Women's International Network News, 187 Grant St, Lexington, Mass. 02173, USA). This is the most detailed and comprehensive collection of information available.

2. The consequences of sexual mutilations on the health of women have been studied by Dr. Ahmed Abu-el-Futuh Shandall, Lecturer in the Department of Obstetrics and Gynaecology at the University of Khartoum, in a paper entitled, "Circumcision and Infibulation of Females" (*Sudanese Medical Journal,* Vol. 5, No. 4, 1967); and by Dr. J.A. Verzin, in an article entitled "The Sequelae of Female Circumcision," (*Tropical Doctor,* October, 1975). A bibliography on the subject has been prepared by Dr. R. Cook for the World Health Organization.

3. Readers interested to read more about research on the sexual experience of circumcised women may want to read Hanny Lightfoot-Klein, *Prisoners of Ritual: An Odyssey into Female Genital Mutilation in Africa* (New York, The Haworth Press, 1989).

4. These feelings of rejection are clearly articulated by Kenyan girls in "The Silence over Female Circumcision in Kenya," in *Viva,* August, 1978.

5. Q.R. Ghadially, "Ali for 'Izzat': The Practice of Female Circumcision among Bohra Muslims," *Manushi,* No. 66, New Delhi, India, 1991.

6. See map of Childhood Mortality in the World, 1977 (Health Sector Policy Paper, World Bank, Washington, D.C., 1980).

7. See Hosken for details and estimates of ethnic groups involved.

8. *F Magazine,* No. 4, March, 1979 and No. 31, October, 1980.

9. Marie Assaad, *Female Circumcision in Egypt—Current Research and Social Implications* (American University in Cairo, 1979), p. 12.

10. "Social Transformation of Eritrean Society," paper presented to the People's Tribunal, Milan, 24–26 May 1980, by Mary Dines of Rights and Justice.

11. Koso-Thomas, *The Circumcision of Women: A Strategy for Elimination* (London, Zed Books, 1987).

12. UN Commission on Human Rights, Report of the Working Group on Traditional Practices Affecting Women and Children, 1986.

13. Ellen Ismail et al., *Women of the Sudan* (Bendestorf, Germany, EIS, 1990).

14. *L'enfant mutilé* by Renée Bridel, delegate of the FIFCJ to the UN, Geneva, 1978. See also Raqiya Haji Dualeh Abdalla, *Sisters in Affliction* (London, Zed Press, 1982) and Asma El Dareer, *Woman Why Do You Weep?* (London, Zed Press, 1982).

15. Belkis Woldes Giorgis, *Female Circumcision in Africa,* ST/ECA/ATRCW 81/02.

Population and Urbanization

CLASSIC

CONTEMPORARY

CROSS-CULTURAL

64

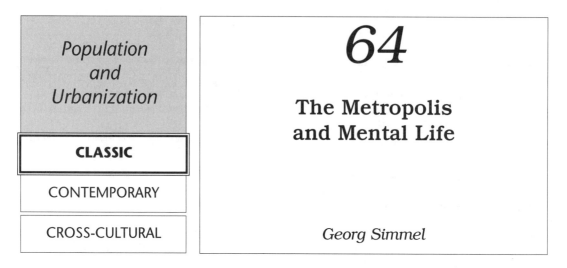

The Metropolis and Mental Life

Georg Simmel

In this, one of his best-known essays, Simmel examines what might be called the "spiritual condition" of the modern world. His focus is the city, in which forces of modernity—including anonymity, a detached sophistication, and a preoccupation with commercial matters—are most clearly evident. Note that Simmel finds reason both to praise this new world and to warn of its ability to destroy our humanity.

The deepest problems of modern life derive from the claim of the individual to preserve the autonomy and individuality of his existence in the face of overwhelming social forces, of historical heritage, of external culture, and of the technique of life. The fight with nature which primitive man has to wage for his *bodily* existence attains in this modern form its latest transformation. The eighteenth century called upon man to free himself of all the historical bonds in the state and in religion, in morals and in economics. Man's nature, originally good and common to all, should develop unhampered. In addition to more liberty, the nineteenth century demanded the functional specialization of man and his work; this specialization makes one individual incomparable to another, and each of them indispensable to the highest possible extent. However, this specialization makes each man the more directly dependent upon the supplementary activities of all others. Nietzsche sees the full development of the individual conditioned by the most ruthless struggle of individuals; socialism believes in the suppression of all competition for the same reason. Be that as it may, in all these positions the same basic motive is at work: The person resists to being leveled down and worn out by a social-technological mechanism. An inquiry into the inner meaning of specifically modern life and its products, into the soul of the cultural body, so to speak, must seek to solve the equa-

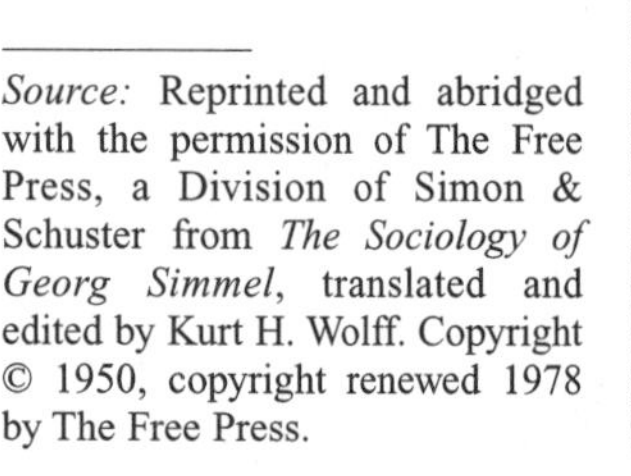
Source: Reprinted and abridged with the permission of The Free Press, a Division of Simon & Schuster from *The Sociology of Georg Simmel*, translated and edited by Kurt H. Wolff.

tion which structures like the metropolis set up between the individual and the superindividual contents of life. Such an inquiry must answer the question of how the personality accommodates itself in the adjustments to external forces. This will be my task today.

The psychological basis of the metropolitan type of individuality consists in the *intensification of nervous stimulation* which results from the swift and uninterrupted change of outer and inner stimuli. Man is a differentiating creature. His mind is stimulated by the difference between a momentary impression and the one which preceded it. Lasting impressions, impressions which differ only slightly from one another, impressions which take a regular and habitual course and show regular and habitual contrasts—all these use up, so to speak, less consciousness than does the rapid crowding of changing images, the sharp discontinuity in the grasp of a single glance, and the unexpectedness of onrushing impressions. These are the psychological conditions which the metropolis creates. With each crossing of the street, with the tempo and multiplicity of economic, occupational and social life, the city sets up a deep contrast with small town and rural life with reference to the sensory foundations of psychic life. The metropolis exacts from man as a discriminating creature a different amount of consciousness than does rural life. Here the rhythm of life and sensory mental imagery flows more slowly, more habitually, and more evenly. Precisely in this connection the sophisticated character of metropolitan psychic life becomes understandable—as over against small town life, which rests more upon deeply felt and emotional relationships. These latter are rooted in the more unconscious layers of the psyche and grow most readily in the steady rhythm of uninterrupted habituations. The intellect, however, has its locus in the transparent, conscious, higher layers of the psyche; it is the most adaptable of our inner forces. In order to accommodate to change and to the contrast of phenomena, the intellect does not require any shocks and inner upheavals; it is only through such upheavals that the more conservative mind could accommodate to the metropolitan rhythm of events. Thus the metropolitan type of man—which, of course, exists in a thousand individual variants—develops an organ protecting him against the threatening currents and discrepancies of his external environment which would uproot him. He reacts with his head instead of his heart. In this an increased awareness assumes the psychic prerogative. Metropolitan life, thus, underlies a heightened awareness and a predominance of intelligence in metropolitan man. The reaction to metropolitan phenomena is shifted to that organ which is least sensitive and quite remote from the depth of the personality. Intellectuality is thus seen to preserve subjective life against the overwhelming power of metropolitan life, and intellectuality branches out in many directions and is integrated with numerous discrete phenomena.

The metropolis has always been the seat of the money economy. Here the multiplicity and concentration of economic exchange gives an importance to the means of exchange which the scantiness of rural commerce would not have allowed. Money economy and the dominance of the intellect are intrinsically connected. They share a matter-of-fact attitude in dealing with men and with things; and, in this attitude, a formal justice is often coupled with an inconsiderate hardness. The intellectually sophisticated person is indifferent to all genuine individuality, because relationships and reactions result from it which cannot be exhausted with logical operations. In the same manner, the individuality of phenomena is not commensurate with the pecuniary principle. Money is concerned only with what is common to all: It asks for the exchange value, it reduces all quality and individuality to the question: How much? All intimate emotional relations between persons are founded in their individuality, whereas in rational relations man is reckoned with like a number, like an element which is in itself indifferent. Only the objective measurable achievement is of interest. Thus metropolitan man reckons with his merchants and customers, his domestic servants and often even with persons with whom he is obliged to have social intercourse. These features of intellectuality contrast with the nature of the small circle in which the inevitable knowledge of individuality as inevitably produces a warmer tone of behavior, a behavior which is beyond a mere objective balancing of service and return. In the sphere of the economic psychology of the small group it is of importance that under primitive conditions production serves the customer who orders the goods, so that the producer and the consumer are acquainted. The modern metropolis, however, is supplied almost entirely by production for the market, that is, for entirely unknown purchasers who never personally enter the producer's actual field of vision. Through this anonymity the interests of each party acquire an unmerciful matter-of-factness; and the intellectually calculating economic egoisms of both parties need not fear any deflection because of the imponderables of personal relationships. The money economy dominates the metropolis; it has displaced the last survivals of domestic production and the direct barter of goods; it minimizes, from day to day, the amount of work ordered by customers. The matter-of-fact attitude is obviously so intimately interrelated with the money economy, which is dominant in the metropolis, that nobody can say whether the intellectualistic mentality first promoted the money economy or whether the latter determined the former. The metropolitan way of life is certainly the most fertile soil for this reciprocity, a point which I shall document merely by citing the dictum of the most eminent English constitutional historian: Throughout the whole course of English history, London has never acted as England's heart but often as England's intellect and always as her moneybag!

In certain seemingly insignificant traits, which lie upon the surface of life, the same psychic currents characteristically unite. Modern mind has become more and more calculating. The calculative exactness of practical life which the money economy has brought about corresponds to the ideal of natural science: to transform the world into an arithmetic problem, to fix every part of the world by mathematical formulas. Only money economy has filled the days of so many people with weighing, calculating, with numerical determinations, with a reduction of qualitative values to quantitative ones. Through the calculative nature of money a new precision, a certainty in the definition of identities and differences, an unambiguousness in agreements and arrangements has been brought about in the relations of life-elements—just as externally this precision has been effected by the universal diffusion of pocket watches. However, the conditions of metropolitan life are at once cause and effect of this trait. The relationships and affairs of the typical metropolitan usually are so varied and complex that without the strictest punctuality in promises and services the whole structure would break down into an inextricable chaos. Above all, this necessity is brought about by the aggregation of so many people with such differentiated interests, who must integrate their relations and activities into a highly complex organism. If all clocks and watches in Berlin would suddenly go wrong in different ways, even if only by one hour, all economic life and communication of the city would be disrupted for a long time. In addition an apparently mere external factor, long distances, would make all waiting and broken appointments result in an ill-afforded waste of time. Thus, the technique of metropolitan life is unimaginable without the most punctual integration of all activities and mutual relations into a stable and impersonal time schedule. Here again the general conclusions of this entire task of reflection become obvious, namely, that from each point on the surface of existence—however closely attached to the surface alone—one may drop a sounding into the depth of the psyche so that all the most banal externalities of life finally are connected with the ultimate decisions concerning the meaning and style of life. Punctuality, calculability, exactness are forced upon life by the complexity and extension of metropolitan existence and are not only most intimately connected with its money economy and intellectualistic character. These traits must also color the contents of life and favor the exclusion of those irrational, instinctive, sovereign traits and impulses which aim at determining the mode of life from within, instead of receiving the general and precisely schematized form of life from without. . . .

The same factors which have thus coalesced into the exactness and minute precision of the form of life have coalesced into a structure of the highest impersonality; on the other hand, they have promoted a highly personal subjectivity. There is perhaps no psychic phenomenon which has been so unconditionally reserved to the metropolis as has the blasé attitude. The blasé attitude results first from the rapidly changing and closely compressed contrasting stimulations of the nerves. From this, the enhancement of metropolitan intellectuality, also, seems originally to stem. Therefore, stupid people who are not intellectually alive in the first place usually are not exactly blasé. A life in boundless pursuit of pleasure makes one blasé because it agitates the nerves to their strongest reactivity for such a long time that they finally cease to react at all. In the same way, through the rapidity and contradictoriness of their changes, more harmless impressions force such violent responses, tearing the nerves so brutally hither and thither that their last reserves of strength are spent; and if one remains in the same milieu they have no time to gather new strength. An incapacity thus emerges to react to new sensations with the appropriate energy. This constitutes that blasé attitude which, in fact, every metropolitan child shows when compared with children of quieter and less changeable milieus.

This physiological source of the metropolitan blasé attitude is joined by another source which flows from the money economy. The essence of the blasé attitude consists in the blunting of discrimination. This does not mean that the objects are not perceived, as is the case with the half-wit, but rather that the meaning and differing values of things, and thereby the things themselves, are experienced as insubstantial. They appear to the blasé person in an evenly flat and gray tone; no one object deserves preference over any other. This mood is the faithful subjective reflection of the completely internalized money economy. By being the equivalent to all the manifold things in one and the same way, money becomes the most frightful leveler. For money expresses all qualitative differences of things in terms of "how much?" Money, with all its colorlessness and indifference, becomes the common denominator of all values; irreparably it hollows out the core of things, their individuality, their specific value, and their incomparability. All things float with equal specific gravity in the constantly moving stream of money. All things lie on the same level and differ from one another only in the size of the area which they cover. In the individual case this coloration, or rather discoloration, of things through their money equivalence may be unnoticeably minute. However, through the relations of the rich to the objects to be had for money, perhaps even through the total character which the mentality of the contemporary public everywhere imparts to these objects, the exclusively pecuniary evaluation of objects has become quite considerable. The large cities, the main seats of the money exchange, bring the purchasability of things to the fore much more impressively than do smaller localities. That is why cities are also the genuine locale of the blasé attitude. In the blasé attitude the concentration of men and things stimulate the nervous system of the individual to its highest achievement so that it attains its peak. Through the mere quantitative intensification of the same conditioning factors this achievement is transformed into its opposite and appears in the peculiar adjustment of the blasé attitude. In this phenomenon the nerves find in the refusal to react to their stimulation the last possibility of accommodating to the contents and forms of metropolitan life. The self-preservation of certain personalities is brought at the price of devaluating the whole objective world, a devaluation which in the end unavoidably drags one's own personality down into a feeling of the same worthlessness.

Whereas the subject of this form of existence has to come to terms with it entirely for himself, his self-preservation in the face of the large city demands from him a no less negative behavior of a social nature. This mental attitude of metropolitans toward one another we may designate, from a formal point of view, as reserve. If so many inner reactions were responses to the continuous external contacts with innumerable people as are those in the small town, where one knows almost everybody one meets and where one has a positive relation to almost everyone, one would be completely atomized internally and come to an unimaginable psychic state. Partly this psychological fact, partly the right to distrust which men have in the face of the touch-and-go elements of metropolitan life, necessitates our reserve. As a result of this reserve we frequently do not even know by sight those who have been our neighbors for years. And it is this reserve which in the eyes of the small-town people makes us appear to be cold and heartless. Indeed, if I do not deceive myself, the inner aspect of this outer reserve is not only indifference but, more often than we are aware, it is a slight aversion, a mutual strangeness and repulsion, which will break into hatred and fight at the moment of a closer contact, however caused. The whole inner organization of such an extensive communicative life rests upon an extremely varied hierarchy of sympathies, indifferences, and aversions of the briefest as well as of the most permanent nature. The sphere of indifference in this hierarchy is not as large as might appear on the surface. Our psychic activity still responds to almost every impression of somebody else with a somewhat distinct feeling. The unconscious, fluid, and changing character of this impression seems to result in a state of indifference. Actually this indifference would be just as unnatural as the diffusion of indiscriminate mutual suggestion would be unbearable. From both these typical dangers of the metropolis, indifference and indiscriminate suggestibility, antipathy protects us. A latent antipathy and the preparatory stage of practical antagonism affect the distances and aversions without which this mode of life could not at all be led. The extent and the mixture of this style of life, the rhythm of its emergence and disappearance, the forms in which it is satisfied—all these, with the unifying motives in the narrower sense, form the inseparable whole of the metropolitan style of life. What appears in the metropolitan style of life directly as dissociation is in reality only one of its elemental forms of socialization.

This reserve with its overtone of hidden aversion appears in turn as the form or the cloak of a more general mental phenomenon of the metropolis: It grants to the individual a kind and an amount of personal freedom which has no analogy whatsoever under other conditions. The metropolis goes back to one of the large developmental tendencies of social life as such, to one of the few tendencies for which an approximately universal formula can be discovered. The earliest phase of social formations found in historical as well as in contemporary social structures is this: a relatively small circle firmly closed against neighboring, strange, or in some way antagonistic circles. However, this circle is closely coherent and allows its individual members only a narrow field for the development of unique qualities and free, self-responsible movements. Political and kinship groups, parties and religious associations begin in this way. The self-preservation of very young associations requires the establishment of strict boundaries and a centripetal unity. Therefore they cannot allow the individual freedom and unique inner and outer development. From this stage social development proceeds at once in two different, yet corresponding, directions. To the extent to which the group grows—numerically, spatially, in significance and in content of life—to the same degree the group's direct, inner unity loosens, and the rigidity of the original demarcation against others is softened through mutual relations and connections. At the same time, the individual gains freedom of movement, far beyond the first jealous delimitation. The individual also gains a specific individuality to which the division of labor in the enlarged group gives both occasion and necessity. . . .

It is not only the immediate size of the area and the number of persons which, because of the universal historical correlation between the enlargement of the circle and the personal inner and outer freedom, has made the metropolis the locale of freedom. It is rather in transcending this visible expanse that any given city becomes the seat of cosmopolitanism. The horizon of the city expands in a manner comparable to the way in which wealth develops; a certain amount of property increases in a quasi-automatical way in ever more rapid progression. As soon as a certain limit has been passed, the economic, personal, and intellectual relations of the citizenry, the sphere of intellectual predominance of the city over its hinterland, grow as in geometrical progression. Every gain in dynamic extension becomes a step, not for an equal, but for a new and larger extension. From every thread spinning out of the city, ever new threads grow as if by themselves, just as within the city the unearned increment of ground rent, through the mere increase in communication, brings the owner automatically increasing profits. At this point, the quantitative aspect of life is transformed directly into qualitative traits of character. The sphere of life of the small town is, in the main, self-contained and autarchic. For it is the decisive nature of the metropolis that its inner life overflows by waves into a far-flung national or international area. . . .

The most profound reason, however, why the metropolis conduces to the urge for the most individual personal existence—no matter whether justified and successful—appears to me to be the following: The development of modern culture is characterized by the preponderance of what one may call the "objective spirit" over the "subjective spirit." This is to say, in language as well as in law, in the technique of production as well as in art, in science as well as in the objects of the domestic environment, there is embodied a sum of spirit. The individual in his intellectual development follows the growth of this spirit very imperfectly and at an ever increasing distance. If, for instance, we view the immense culture which for the last hundred years has been embodied in things and in knowledge, in institutions and in comforts, and if we compare all this with the cultural progress of the individual during the same period—at least in high status groups—a frightful disproportion in growth between the two becomes evident. Indeed, at some points we notice a retrogression in the culture of the individual with reference to spirituality, delicacy, and idealism. This discrepancy results essentially from the growing division of labor. For the division of labor demands from the individual an ever more one-sided accomplishment, and the greatest advance in a one-sided pursuit only too frequently means dearth to the personality of the individual. In any case, he can cope less and less with the overgrowth of objective culture. The individual is reduced to a negligible quantity, perhaps less in his consciousness than in his practice and in the totality of his obscure emotional states that are derived from this practice. The individual has become a mere cog in an enormous organization of things and powers which tear from his hands all progress, spirituality, and value in order to transform them from their subjective form into the form of a purely objective life. It needs merely to be pointed out that the metropolis is the genuine arena of this culture which outgrows all personal life. Here in buildings and educational institutions, in the wonders and comforts of space-conquering technology, in the formations of community life, and in the visible institutions of the state, is offered such an overwhelming fullness of crystallized and impersonalized spirit that the personality, so to speak, cannot maintain itself under its impact. On the one hand, life is made infinitely easy for the personality in that stimulations, interests, uses of time, and consciousness are offered to it from all sides. They carry the person as if in a stream, and one needs hardly to swim for oneself. On the other hand, however, life is composed more and more of these impersonal contents and offerings which tend to displace the genuine personal colorations and incomparabilities. This results in the individual's summoning the utmost in uniqueness and particularization, in order to preserve his most personal core. He has to exaggerate this personal element in order to remain audible even to himself. . . .

CRITICAL-THINKING QUESTIONS

1. In what respects does the metropolis symbolize modern society?

2. What does Simmel mean by suggesting that in modern cities, people experience an "intensification of nervous stimulation"? How do we react "with our heads instead of with our hearts"?

3. What does Simmel see as the achievements of modern urban life? What does he think has been lost in the process?

65

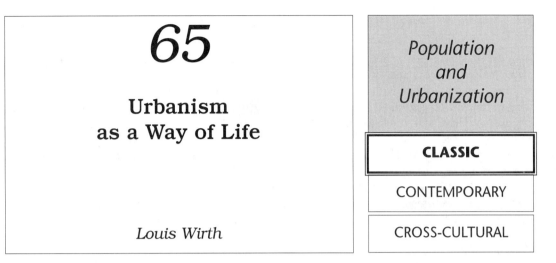

Urbanism as a Way of Life

Louis Wirth

Population and Urbanization

CLASSIC

CONTEMPORARY

CROSS-CULTURAL

For many decades, sociologists in Europe and the United States have commented on the distinctive qualities of urban social life. In 1938, U.S. sociologist Louis Wirth integrated these various insights into a comprehensive theory of urbanism. Although it has been challenged and reformulated over the years, Wirth's theory remains probably the best-known sociological statement on urbanism.

A SOCIOLOGICAL DEFINITION OF THE CITY

Despite the preponderant significance of the city in our civilization, our knowledge of the nature of urbanism and the process of urbanization is meager, notwithstanding many attempts to isolate the distinguishing characteristics of urban life. Geographers, historians, economists, and political scientists have incorporated the points of view of their respective disciplines into diverse definitions of the city. While in no sense intended to supersede these, the formulation of a sociological approach to the city may incidentally serve to call attention to the interrelations between them by emphasizing the peculiar characteristics of the city as a particular form of human association. A sociologically significant definition of the city seeks to select those elements of urbanism which mark it as a distinctive mode of human group life. . . .

For sociological purposes a city may be defined as a relatively large, dense, and permanent settlement of socially heterogeneous individuals. On the basis of the postulates which this minimal definition suggests, a theory of urbanism may be formulated in the light of existing knowledge concerning social groups.

A THEORY OF URBANISM

Given a limited number of identifying characteristics of the city, I can better assay the consequences or further characteristics of them in the light of general sociological theory and empirical research. I hope in this manner to arrive at the essential propositions comprising a theory of urbanism. Some of these propositions can be supported by a considerable body of already available research materials; others may be accepted as hypotheses for which a certain amount of pre-

Source: From *American Journal of Sociology,* Vol. 44, No. 1, July 1938, pp. 1–24, copyright © 1938 by The University of Chicago Press. Reprinted by permission of the University of Chicago Press.

sumptive evidence exists, but for which more ample and exact verification would be required. At least such a procedure will, it is hoped, show what in the way of systematic knowledge of the city we now have and what are the crucial and fruitful hypotheses for future research.

The central problem of the sociologist of the city is to discover the forms of social action and organization that typically emerge in relatively permanent, compact settlements of large numbers of heterogeneous individuals. We must also infer that urbanism will assume its most characteristic and extreme form in the measure in which the conditions with which it is congruent are present. Thus the larger, the more densely populated, and the more heterogeneous a community, the more accentuated the characteristics associated with urbanism will be. . . .

Some justification may be in order for the choice of the principal terms comprising our definition of the city, a definition which ought to be as inclusive and at the same time as denotative as possible without unnecessary assumptions. To say that large numbers are necessary to constitute a city means, of course, large numbers in relation to a restricted area or high density of settlement. There are, nevertheless, good reasons for treating large numbers and density as separate factors, because each may be connected with significantly different social consequences. Similarly the need for adding heterogeneity to numbers of population as a necessary and distinct criterion of urbanism might be questioned, since we should expect the range of differences to increase with numbers. In defense, it may be said that the city shows a kind and degree of heterogeneity of population which cannot be wholly accounted for by the law of large numbers or adequately represented by means of a normal distribution curve. Because the population of the city does not reproduce itself, it must recruit its migrants from other cities, the countryside, and—in the United States . . .—from other countries. The city has thus historically been the melting-pot of races, peoples, and cultures, and a most favorable breeding-ground of new biological and cultural hybrids. It has not only tolerated but rewarded individual differences. It has brought together people from the ends of the earth *because* they are different and thus useful to one another, rather than because they are homogeneous and like-minded.

A number of sociological propositions concerning the relationship between (a) numbers of population, (b) density of settlement, (c) heterogeneity of inhabitants and group life can be formulated on the basis of observation and research.

Size of the Population Aggregate

Ever since Aristotle's *Politics,* it has been recognized that increasing the number of inhabitants in a settlement beyond a certain limit will affect the relationships between them and the character of the city. Large numbers involve, as has been pointed out, a greater range of individual variation. Furthermore, the greater the number of individuals participating in a process of interaction, the greater is the *potential* differentiation between them. The personal traits, the occupations, the cultural life, and the ideas of the members of an urban community may, therefore, be expected to range between more widely separated poles than those of rural inhabitants.

That such variations should give rise to the spatial segregation of individuals according to color, ethnic heritage, economic and social status, tastes and preferences, may readily be inferred. The bonds of kinship, of neighborliness, and the sentiments arising out of living together for generations under a common folk tradition are likely to be absent or, at best, relatively weak in an aggregate the members of which have such diverse origins and backgrounds. Under such circumstances competition and formal control mechanisms furnish the substitutes for the bonds of solidarity that are relied upon to hold a folk society together.

Increase in the number of inhabitants of a community beyond a few hundred is bound to limit the possibility of each member of the community knowing all the others personally. Max Weber, in recognizing the social significance of this fact, explained that from a sociological point of view large numbers of inhabitants and density of settlement mean a lack of that mutual acquaintanceship which ordinarily inheres between the inhabitants in a neighborhood.[1] The increase in numbers thus involves a changed character of the social relationships. As Georg Simmel points out: "[If] the unceasing external contact of numbers of persons in the city should be met by the same number of inner reactions as in the small town, in which one knows almost every person he meets and to each of whom he has a positive relationship, one would be completely atomized internally and would fall into an unthinkable mental condition."[2] The multiplication of persons in a state of interaction under conditions which make their contact as full personalities impossible produces that segmentalization of human relationships which has sometimes been seized upon by students of the mental life of the cities as an explanation for the "schizoid" character of urban personality. This is not to say that the urban inhabitants have fewer acquaintances than rural inhabitants, for the reverse may actually be true; it means rather that in relation to the number of people whom they see and with whom they rub elbows in the course of daily life, they know a smaller proportion, and of these they have less intensive knowledge.

Characteristically, urbanites meet one another in highly segmental roles. They are, to be sure, dependent upon more people for the satisfactions of their life-needs than are rural people and thus are associated with a greater number of organized groups, but they are less dependent upon particular persons, and their dependence upon others is confined to a highly fractionalized aspect of the other's round of activity. This is essentially what is meant by saying that the city is characterized by secondary rather than primary contacts. The contacts of the city may indeed be face to face, but they are nevertheless impersonal, superficial, transitory, and segmental. The reserve, the indifference, and the blasé outlook which urbanites manifest in their relationships may thus be regarded as devices for immunizing themselves against the personal claims and expectations of others.

The superficiality, the anonymity, and the transitory character of urban social relations make intelligible, also, the sophistication and the rationality generally ascribed to city-dwellers. Our acquaintances tend to stand in a relationship of utility to us in the sense that the role which each one plays in our life is overwhelmingly regarded as a means for the achievement of our own ends. Whereas the individual gains, on the one hand, a certain degree of emancipation or freedom from the personal and emotional controls of intimate groups, he loses, on the other hand, the spontaneous self-expression, the morale, and the sense of participation that comes with living in an integrated society. This constitutes essentially the state of *anomie,* or the social void, to which Durkheim alludes in attempting to account for the various forms of social disorganization in technological society.

The segmental character and utilitarian accent of interpersonal relations in the city find their institutional expression in the proliferation of specialized tasks which we see in their most developed form in the professions. The operations of the pecuniary nexus lead to predatory relationships, which tend to obstruct the efficient functioning of the social order unless checked by professional codes and occupational etiquette. The premium put upon utility and efficiency suggests the adaptability of the corporate device for the organization of enterprises in which individuals can engage only in groups. The advantage that the corporation has over the individual entrepreneur and the partnership in the urban-industrial world derives not only from the possibility it affords of centralizing the resources of thousands of individuals or from the legal privilege of limited liability and perpetual succession, but from the fact that the corporation has no soul.

The specialization of individuals, particularly in their occupations, can proceed only, as Adam

Smith pointed out, upon the basis of an enlarged market, which in turn accentuates the division of labor. This enlarged market is only in part supplied by the city's hinterland; in large measure it is found among the large numbers that the city itself contains. The dominance of the city over the surrounding hinterland becomes explicable in terms of the division of labor which urban life occasions and promotes. The extreme degree of interdependence and the unstable equilibrium of urban life are closely associated with the division of labor and the specialization of occupations. This interdependence and this instability are increased by the tendency of each city to specialize in those functions in which it has the greatest advantage.

In a community composed of a larger number of individuals than can know one another intimately and can be assembled in one spot, it becomes necessary to communicate through indirect media and to articulate individual interests by a process of delegation. Typically in the city, interests are made effective through representation. The individual counts for little, but the voice of the representative is heard with a deference roughly proportional to the numbers for whom he speaks.

While this characterization of urbanism, in so far as it derives from large numbers, does not by any means exhaust the sociological inferences that might be drawn from our knowledge of the relationship of the size of a group to the characteristic behavior of the members, for the sake of brevity the assertions made may serve to exemplify the sort of propositions that might be developed.

Density

As in the case of numbers, so in the case of concentration in limited space certain consequences of relevance in sociological analysis of the city emerge. Of these only a few can be indicated.

As Darwin pointed out for flora and fauna and as Durkheim noted in the case of human societies,[3] an increase in numbers when area is held constant (i.e., an increase in density) tends to produce differentiation and specialization, since only in this way can the area support increased numbers. Density thus reinforces the effect of numbers in diversifying men and their activities and in increasing the complexity of the social structure.

On the subjective side, as Simmel has suggested, the close physical contact of numerous individuals necessarily produces a shift in the media through which we orient ourselves to the urban milieu, especially to our fellow-men. Typically, our physical contacts are close but our social contacts are distant. The urban world puts a premium on visual recognition. We see the uniform which denotes the role of the functionaries, and are oblivious to the personal eccentricities hidden behind the uniform. We tend to acquire and develop a sensitivity to a world of artifacts, and become progressively farther removed from the world of nature.

We are exposed to glaring contrasts between splendor and squalor, between riches and poverty, intelligence and ignorance, order and chaos. The competition for space is great, so that each area generally tends to be put to the use which yields the greatest economic return. Place of work tends to become dissociated from place of residence, for the proximity of industrial and commercial establishments makes an area both economically and socially undesirable for residential purposes.

Density, land values, rentals, accessibility, healthfulness, prestige, aesthetic consideration, absence of nuisances such as noise, smoke, and dirt determine the desirability of various areas of the city as places of settlement for different sections of the population. Place and nature of work income, racial and ethnic characteristics, social status, custom, habit, taste, preference, and prejudice are among the significant factors in accordance with which the urban population is selected and distributed into more or less distinct settlements. Diverse population elements inhabiting a compact settlement thus become segregated from one another in the degree in which their requirements and modes of life are incompatible and in the measure in which they are antagonistic. Similarly, persons of homogeneous status and needs unwittingly drift into, consciously select, or are forced by circumstances into the same area. The different parts of the city acquire specialized functions, and the city consequently comes to resemble a mosaic of social worlds in which the transition from one to the other is abrupt. The juxtaposition of divergent personalities and modes of life tends to produce a relativistic perspective and a sense of toleration of differences which may be regarded as prerequisites for rationality and which lead toward the secularization of life.[4]

The close living together and working together of individuals who have no sentimental and emotional ties foster a spirit of competition, aggrandizement, and mutual exploitation. Formal controls are instituted to counteract irresponsibility and potential disorder. Without rigid adherence to predictable routines a large compact society would scarcely be able to maintain itself. The clock and the traffic signal are symbolic of the basis of our social order in the urban world. Frequent close physical contact, coupled with great social distance, accentuates the reserve of unattached individuals toward one another and, unless compensated by other opportunities for response, gives rise to loneliness. The necessary frequent movement of great numbers of individuals in a congested habitat causes friction and irritation. Nervous tensions which derive from such personal frustrations are increased by the rapid tempo and the complicated technology under which life in dense areas must be lived.

Heterogeneity

The social interaction among such a variety of personality types in the urban milieu tends to break down the rigidity of caste lines and to complicate the class structure; it thus induces a more ramified and differentiated framework of social stratification than is found in more integrated societies. The heightened mobility of the individual, which brings him within the range of stimulation by a great number of diverse individuals and subjects him to fluctuating status in the differentiated social groups that compose the social structure of the city, brings him toward the acceptance of instability and insecurity in the world at large as a norm. This fact helps to account, too, for the sophistication and cosmopolitanism of the urbanite. No single group has the undivided allegiance of the individual. The groups with which he is affiliated do not lend themselves readily to a simple hierarchical arrangement. By virtue of his different interests arising out of different aspects of social life, the individual acquires membership in widely divergent groups, each of which functions only with reference to a single segment of his personality. Nor do these groups easily permit a concentric arrangement so that the narrower ones fall within the circumference of the more inclusive ones, as is more likely to be the case in the rural community or in primitive societies. Rather the groups with which the person typically is affiliated are tangential to each other or intersect in highly variable fashion.

Partly as a result of the physical footlooseness of the population and partly as a result of their social mobility, the turnover in group membership generally is rapid. Place of residence, place and character of employment, income, and interests fluctuate, and the task of holding organizations together and maintaining and promoting intimate and lasting acquaintanceship between the members is difficult. This applies strikingly to the local areas within the city into which persons become segregated more by virtue of differences in race, language, income, and social status than through choice or positive attraction to people like themselves. Overwhelmingly the city-dweller is not a home-owner, and since a transitory habitat does not generate binding traditions and sentiments, only rarely is he a true neighbor. There is little opportunity for the individual to obtain a conception of the city as a whole or to survey his place in the total scheme. Consequently he finds it difficult to determine what is to his own "best interests" and to decide between the issues and leaders presented to him by the agencies of mass suggestion. Individuals who are thus detached from the organized bodies which integrate society comprise the fluid masses that make collective behavior in the urban community so unpredictable and hence so problematical.

Although the city, through the recruitment of variant types to perform its diverse tasks and the accentuation of their uniqueness through competition and the premium upon eccentricity, novelty, efficient performance, and inventiveness, produces a highly differentiated population, it also exercises a leveling influence. Wherever large numbers of differently constituted individuals congregate, the process of depersonalization also enters. This leveling tendency inheres in part in the economic basis of the city. The development of large cities, at least in the modern age, was largely dependent upon the concentrative force of steam. The rise of the factory made possible mass production for an impersonal market. The fullest exploitation of the possibilities of the division of labor and mass production, however, is possible only with standardization of processes and products. A money economy goes hand in hand with such a system of production. Progressively as cities have developed upon a background of this system of production, the pecuniary nexus which implies the purchasability of services and things has displaced personal relations as the basis of association. Individuality under these circumstances must be replaced by categories. When large numbers have to make common use of facilities and institutions, those facilities and institutions must serve the needs of the average person rather than those of particular individuals. The services of the public utilities, of the recreational, educational, and cultural institutions, must be adjusted to mass requirements. Similarly, the cultural institutions, such as the schools, the movies, the radio, and the newspapers, by virtue of their mass clientele, must necessarily operate as leveling influences. The political process as it appears in urban life could not be understood unless one examined the mass appeals made through modern propaganda techniques. If the individual would participate at all in the social, political, and economic life of the city, he must subordinate some of his individuality to the demands of the larger community and in that measure immerse himself in mass movements. . . .

On the basis of the three variables, number, density of settlement, and degree of heterogeneity, of the urban population, it appears possible to explain the characteristics of urban life and to account for the differences between cities of various sizes and types. . . .

CRITICAL-THINKING QUESTIONS

1. What basic issue should a sociological theory of urbanism address? Why is Wirth's approach to studying urbanism also termed "ecological"?
2. How does Wirth define a city? How do the three defining factors give rise to an urban way of life?
3. According to Wirth, what are the qualities of social relationships in cities? What moral consequences seem to follow?

NOTES

1. *Wirtschaft und Gesellschaft* (Tübingen, 1925), part I, chap. 8, p. 514.

2. "Die Grossstädte und das Geistesleben," *Die Grossstadt,* ed. Theodor Petermann (Dresden, 1903), pp. 187–206.

3. E. Durkheim, *De la division du travail social* (Paris, 1932), p. 248.

4. The extent to which the segregation of the population into distinct ecological and cultural areas and the resulting social attitude of tolerance, rationality, and secular mentality are functions of density as distinguished from heterogeneity is difficult to determine. Most likely we are dealing here with phenomena which are consequences of the simultaneous operation of both factors.

66

The Urban Real Estate Game: Traditional and Critical Perspectives

Joe R. Feagin and Robert Parker

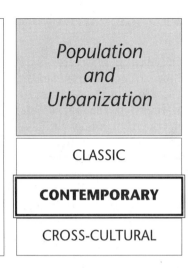

Population and Urbanization

CLASSIC

CONTEMPORARY

CROSS-CULTURAL

Feagin and Parker argue that traditional urban sociology has emphasized demographic and technological dimensions of city growth, while accepting the validity of classical economics' market model. Traditionalists explain the growth and change of cities in terms of various demands made by countless urban consumers. A newer, critical perspective sees the process of urban development as dominated by powerful economic interests—industrial executives, developers, and politicians sympathetic to their aims. The authors condemn the traditional model and argue the virtues of the critical approach.

INTRODUCTION

Locating new factories. Relocating offices. Buying hotels. Building office towers. Mortgaging whole streets of houses. Buying and selling utility companies. Bulldozing apartment buildings for office construction. Purchasing large blocks of urban land to secure a land monopoly. Going bankrupt because of overextension in real estate. These actions are part of the real estate game played in every American city. The only place most Americans are able to play anything analogous to this is on the *Monopoly* game board in living-room encounters with their friends. The board game mimics the real world of real estate buying, selling, and development, but the parallels between playing *Monopoly* on the board and playing the real estate game in cities are limited, for in the everyday world of urban development and decline there are real winners and real losers.

In U.S. cities the powerful elites controlling much development—the industrial executives, developers, bankers, and their political allies—have built major development projects, not just the hotels and houses of the *Monopoly* game, but also shopping malls, office towers, and the like. They typically build with little input from local community residents. Executives heading industrial firms and real estate developers have frequently been able to win a string of favorable concessions from city officials: cheap land, industrial parks, tax decreases, and utility services subsidized by rank-and-file taxpayers. In many cities these industrial executives and developers threaten to go elsewhere if these governmental subsidies are not provided. Yet in the 1970s and 1980s some citizen groups . . . tried to change this way of doing city business.

Source: From "Building American Cities: Traditional and Critical Perspectives," by Joe R. Feagin and Robert Parker, in *Building American Cities: The Urban Real Estate Game,* 2d ed., pp. 1–13, 16–17, 22, 23, 30–31.

Periodically, the voters in cities, from Santa Monica and Berkeley on the West Coast, to Cleveland in the Midwest, to Burlington and Hartford on the East Coast, voted out pro-development political officials in favor of candidates more tuned to slow growth and enhancing the local quality of life. For instance, in the 1980s the residents of Santa Monica, California, voted out a city council allied with landlords, developers, and bankers. They elected in their place a progressive council determined to break with the developer-oriented dominance of city politics. The new council has rejected policies favoring developers and has used a policy called "linked development" to force those developers building new office complexes and shopping centers to take action to meet important local needs. One Santa Monica city council agreement with a developer building a million-square-foot hotel-office complex specified that he must include landscaped park areas, a day-care center, energy conservation measures, and a positive plan for hiring minority workers.[1]

Who Decides on Development?

Some powerful developers, bankers, and other development decision makers are becoming known to the public. There is, for example, Gerald D. Hines, a Houston mechanical engineer whose $200 million estimated net worth was just under the amount necessary to be listed among the nation's 400 richest people by *Forbes* in 1987.[2] Still, Gerald D. Hines Interests of Houston, one of the largest U.S. development firms, controlled buildings worth more than $4.5 billion. In the early 1980s Hines celebrated the laying of the foundation of a Republic Bank office complex in Houston with a lavish $35,000 reception for top business and government leaders; it included a brass ensemble playing fanfares, fine wine and cheeses, and other culinary delights. The massive building itself, red granite in a neo-Gothic style, is just one of more than 360 such office buildings, shopping malls, and other urban projects that have been built by Hines' company in cities from New York to San Francisco.

Residential developers have also shaped U.S. cities in fundamental ways. The famous firm Levitt and Sons is among the 2 percent of developer-builders that have constructed the lion's share of U.S. residential housing since World War II. Using nonunion labor, Levitt and Sons pulled together in one corporation the various aspects of the house manufacturing and marketing process, from controlling the source of nails and lumber to marketing the finished houses. After World War II, Levittowns—names now synonymous with suburbs—were built in cities on the East Coast. One subdivision, Levittown, New Jersey, was carefully planned so that the acreage was within one political jurisdiction. According to Herbert Gans, the company executives had the boundaries of a nearby township changed so that it was not part of the area in which this Levittown would be built, thus giving Levitt and Sons more political control. William Levitt was the key figure in this development firm for decades, and he reportedly built his suburbs with little concern for the expressed tastes of his potential customers; Levitt was not especially "concerned about how to satisfy buyers and meet their aspirations. As the most successful builder in the East . . . he felt he knew what they wanted."[3] Profitability was the basic standard; community-oriented features were accepted when they enhanced profit. No surveys of potential buyers were made to determine consumer preferences, but a great deal of attention was given to advertising, marketing, and selling the houses to consumers. Friendly salespeople were selected and trained by a professional speech teacher. Buyers who were viewed as "disreputable" were excluded; and blacks were excluded until the state government began to enforce a desegregation law.[4]

Developers such as Hines and Levitt and Sons have been a major force in making and remaking the face of American cities. They are key figures in shaping city diversity and decentralization. Since World War II, U.S. cities have exploded horizontally and vertically with thousands of large-scale developments—shopping centers, office towers, business parks, multiple-use projects, convention centers, and residential subdivisions. The "built environments" of our cities have expanded to the point that their growing, and dying, pains have become serious national problems. Trillions of dollars have been invested in tearing down, constructing, and servicing the many and diverse physical structures scattered across hundreds of urban landscapes. For large development projects to be completed in downtown or outlying areas of cities, older buildings are often leveled, even when local citizens oppose such development. The major U.S. developers often see their projects as the "cutting-edge of western civilization." Yet these massive expenditures of capital for large-scale urban development, for lavish towers and the parties celebrating them, are made in cities with severe urban problems—extreme poverty, housing shortages, severe pollution—for whose solution little money allegedly can be found.[5]

Cities are not chance creations; rather, they are human developments. They reflect human choices and decisions. But exactly who decides that our cities should be developed the way they are? Who chooses corporate locations? Who calculates that sprawling suburbs are the best way to house urbanites? Who decides to put workers in glassed-in office towers? Who determines that shopping is best done in centralized shopping centers? Who creates the complex mazes of buildings, highways, and open spaces? There is an old saying that "God made the country, but man made the town." Cities are indeed human-engineered environments. But which men and women made the cities? And what determines how they shape our cities?

GROWTH AND DECLINE OF CITIES: TRADITIONAL SOCIAL SCIENCE PERSPECTIVES

The Traditional Approach: The Market Knows Best

Examination of urban development and decline has been dominated by a conflict between the market-centered approaches of traditional social scientists and the newer critical analyses developed in recent decades. Traditional social scientists have dominated research and writing about American cities. Beginning in the 1920s and 1930s, there was a major spurt of activity in urban sociology and ecology at the University of Chicago, where researchers such as Robert Park and Ernest W. Burgess drew on the nineteenth-century social philosopher Herbert Spencer to develop their concept of city life, organization, and development; they viewed the individual and group competition in markets in metropolitan areas as resulting in "natural" regularities in land-use patterns and population distributions—and thus in an urban ecological or geographical map of concentric zones of land use, moving out from a central business district zone, with its office buildings, to an outlying commuter zone, with residential subdivisions.[6]

Much urban research between the 1940s and the 1970s established the dominance of the traditional market-centered paradigm in urban sociology, geography, economics, political science, and other social science disciplines. Largely abandoning the concern of the earlier social scientists with urban space and land-use zones, sociological, economic, and geographical researchers have for the most part accented demographic analysis and have typically focused on population trends such as migration flows, suburbanization, and other deconcentration, and on statistical distributions of urban and rural populations in examining modern urban development. Writing in the *Handbook of Sociology,* the urban analysts Kasarda and Frisbie review mainstream research and a small portion of the newer critical research, but they explicitly regard the ecological approach in sociology, geography, and economics as the "dominant (and arguably, the only) general theory of urban form" that has been tested by empirical verification.[7] Books such as Berry and Kasarda's *Contemporary Urban Ecology,* Micklin and Choldin's *Sociological Human Ecology,* and textbooks like Choldin's *Cities and Suburbs* have been influential in establishing a conventional perspective accenting the role of a competitive market in urban development and emphasizing market-centered city growth as beneficial to all urban interest groups. The political scientists in this tradition have also given attention to capitalism-generated growth and the role of the market in city development; they alone have given much attention to the importance of government in urban development. However, their view of government typically accents a pluralism of competing interest groups and an array of government officials acting for the general welfare, a perspective that, as we will discuss, is rather limited.[8]

Consumers and Workers as Dominant

Conventional social scientists have accepted uncritically the workings of the dominant market and the processes of capital accumulation. This perspective on competitive urban markets is grounded in neoclassical economic theory; it sees urban society as the "algebraic sum of the individuals . . . the sum of the interests of individuals."[9] In this view, given a "freemarket" system, urban consumers and business firms will freely buy and sell. "If consumers want certain goods they will demand them. Businessmen will sense this demand through the marketplace and seek to satisfy the consumers' wishes. Everyone is happy."[10] Urban sociologist John Kasarda has written of profit-seeking entrepreneurs operating in self-regulating markets as a wise guiding force in city development.[11] Similarly, economists Bradbury, Downs, and Small, reviewing problems of city decline, argue that "market forces are extremely powerful; so it would be folly to try [governmental] policies that ignored their constructive roles in guiding the form and structure of economic change."[12] From this perspective capitalists follow the profit logic of capital investments that seeks out "good business climates" (low taxes and pro-business governments) in certain cities, such as those in the South. This conventional view implies that whatever exists as the economics and geography of the urban landscape today is fundamentally good for all concerned, if it has resulted from competitive market activity. The rather utopian competitive market idea, Lewis Mumford has suggested, was taken over from earlier theologians: "the belief that a divine providence ruled over economic activity and ensured, so long as man did not presumptuously interfere, the maximum public good through the dispersed and unregulated efforts of every private, self-seeking individual."[13]

Imbedded in this common market assumption is the idea that individual workers and consumers are often more important than corporate decision makers in shaping urban patterns, because the capitalists mostly react to the demands of consumers. A study of the U.S. business creed accented this point: "One way of shedding awkward responsibility is to believe that the consumer is the real boss."[14] Such analysts accept the business view of individual consumers and workers as "voting" in the marketplace with their consumer choices: Cities are viewed as having been created by average Americans whose demands for such things as autos and single-family houses have forced developers, builders, and industrial executives to respond. Consumers are often termed "kings" and "queens" when it comes to urban development. For decades not only urban scholars but also business leaders have argued that through their consumption choices "the masses of Americans have elected Henry Ford. They have elected General Motors. They have elected the General Electric Company, and Woolworth's and all the other great industrial and business leaders of the day."[15]

One assumption in much traditional urban research is that no one individual or small group of individuals has a determinate influence on patterns of urban land uses, building, and development. Mainstream sociologists and land economists such as William Alonso and Richard Muth have argued that urban commercial and residential land markets are determined by free competitive bidding. According to these theories, thousands of consumers, and thousands of firms, are pictured as autonomous atoms competing in a market system, largely without noneconomic (for example, political) relations and conventions, atoms that have a "taste" for commodities such as more space and housing. As their incomes grow, they will seek more space. Conventional analysts offer this as an explanation of why cities grow, expand, or die. Actors in this competitive bidding are recognized as having different interests, even different incomes, which affect the bidding process. However, the fact that a small group of the most powerful decision makers (such as major developers) can do far more to shape the land and building markets than simply outbid their competitors is not seriously analyzed. And the negative consequences of market-generated growth (for example, water pollution from sewer crises) in these same cities are seldom discussed.[16]

David L. Birch, Director of the Massachusetts Institute of Technology's Program on Neighborhood and Regional Change, has offered a worker-driven theory in explaining why many cities have had too much office space. Birch argues that the story of the current high vacancy rates in office buildings in many U.S. cities began decades ago when the "war babies" began to enter the labor force. This movement into the labor force caused a huge increase in employment. Birch argues that both sexes decided they did not want to work in factories. Rather, they "wanted to work in offices. They wanted to join the service economy, wear white shirts, and become managers or clerks."[17] According to this line of reasoning, there was only one thing for developers and builders to do; in order to satisfy this new generation of workers and consumers, "we built them offices." Yet the power of workers and consumers in shaping the urban office landscape has never been as profound as Birch and others describe. Indeed, it is the industrialists, investors, developers, bankers, and their associates who have the capital to invest in job creation and to build office buildings and other workplaces—in places they decide upon and in terms of their corporate restructuring and profit needs.

Accenting Technology and Downplaying Inequality

Traditional social scientists often view the complexity of cities as largely determined by historical changes in transportation and communication technologies, whose economic contexts, histories, and alternatives are not reviewed. Changes in urban form are explained in terms of technological transformation, including shifts in water, rail, and automotive transport systems, without reference to the decisions of powerful decision makers such as investors and top government officials. Water-borne commerce favors port and river cities, while auto, train, and truck technologies facilitate the location of cities apart from water systems. In an opening essay for a 1985 book *The New Urban Reality,* Paul Peterson views technological innovations as independent forces giving "urban development its rate and direction."[18] And in the influential book *Urban Society,* mainstream ecological researcher Amos Hawley looked at the relocation of industry from the industrial heartland to outlying areas and explained this decentralization substantially in terms of technological changes in transport and in communication.[19] Transport and communication technologies are certainly important in urban centralization and decentralization. But the corporate history and capitalistic decision-making *context* that led to the dominance of, for example, automobiles—and not mass transit—in the U.S. transport system should be more carefully examined. . . .

Some Major Omissions

Missing from most traditional research on cities is a major discussion of such major factors in urban development as capital investment decisions, power and resource inequality, class and class conflict, and government subsidy programs. The aforementioned collection, *The New Urban Reality,* has important essays by prominent geographers, economists, political scientists, and sociologists on urban racial demography and the black underclass, but there is no significant discussion of capital investment decisions made by investors and developers and the consequences of these decisions for urban development. Moreover, in the recent summary volume, *Sociological Human Ecology,* prominent ecologists and demographers have reviewed the question of how humans survive in changing social environments, including cities, but without discussing inequality, power, conflict, or the role of governments.[20] Traditional urban scholars such as the geographer Berry and the sociologist Kasarda briefly note that in market-directed societies the role of government has been primarily "limited to combating crises that threaten the societal mainstream," that government involvement tends to be incremental, and that state government dealing with the "social consequences of laissez-faire urbanization" are "ineffective in most cases."[21] In his influential urban textbook, *Urban Society,* sociologist Amos Hawley has devoted little space to the government role in city growth and decline. This neglect of the role of government has been most common among mainstream urban sociologists, geographers, and economists. As we will see, the mainstream political scientists among contemporary urban researchers have given more attention to government, but generally with a pluralistic emphasis.[22]

An Important Government Report

However, the federal government has used this traditional urban research for policy purposes. In the 1980s a major federal government report, *Urban America in the Eighties,* publicly articulated the traditional urban perspective for the general public. Prepared by the President's Commission for a National Agenda for the Eighties, this report called on the federal government to refrain from assisting the troubled northern cities. Free-enterprise markets are viewed as driving the basically healthy changes in urban development. And these markets know best. The *Urban America* report's strong conclusions were publicly debated—particularly those suggesting that the federal government should neglect dying northern cities and should, at most, assist workers in leaving Frostbelt cities for the then-booming cities of the Sunbelt. Some northern mayors protested the report's conclusions, but many Sunbelt mayors were enthusiastic. While northern officials were concerned about the report's conclusions, few publicly disputed the report's basic assumptions about how cities grow or die.[23]

This market-knows-best view of the Frostbelt-Sunbelt shift in capital investment and of urban growth more generally drew on the work of traditional urban researchers. Prepared under the direction of prominent business leaders, this report conveys the view of cities found in mainstream urban research: that cities are "less conscious creations" than "accumulations—the products of ongoing change." Again, choices by hundreds of thousands of individual consumers and workers are emphasized as the fundamental determinants of urban landscapes. Changes in cities, such as the then-increasing prosperity of many Sunbelt cities, reflect "nothing more than an aggregate of countless choices by and actions of individuals, families, and firms."[24] The urban land and building market is again viewed as self-regulating; according to this theory the market efficiently allocates land uses and maximizes the benefits for everyone living in the cities. The hidden hand of the market receives heavy emphasis in this conventional accounting. In the policy-oriented conclusions, the authors of *Urban America* pursued this market logic to its obvious conclusion: Those impersonal individuals and firms actively working in cities and shaping urban space know best, and government officials should thus not intervene when impersonal decisions lead to the decline of cities in the North. Growth in, and migration to, booming cities such as those in the Sunbelt should simply be recognized, and, at most, governments should encourage workers to move from dying cities to booming cities.

GROWTH AND DECLINE OF CITIES: THE CRITICAL URBAN PERSPECTIVE

Basic Themes in the New Approach

Since the 1970s the dominance of the mainstream urban research in the United States has been challenged by a critical urban perspective, called by some the "new urban sociology." Both European and American researchers have developed a critical urban paradigm grounded in concepts of capital investment flows, class and inequality, activist governments, and powerful business elites. European researchers such as Henri Lefebvre, Manuel Castells, and David Harvey had developed critiques of the traditional urban approaches by the late 1960s and early 1970s.[25] This European influence was soon felt in U.S. urban studies. By the late 1970s critical urban studies were pursued and published by Michael Peter Smith, Mark Gottdiener, Allen Scott, John Mollenkopf, Norman and Susan Fainstein, Richard Child Hill, Ed Soja, Michael Dear, Richard Walker, Allen Whitt, Todd Swanstrom, and Harvey Molotch, to mention just a few of the growing number of critical social scientists in the United States.[26] The critical urban approach accents issues neglected in most traditional sociological, economic, and political science analysis. While there is still much ferment and debate among contributors to the critical urban perspective, there is some consensus on three fundamental themes.

The first major theme is that city growth and decline, internal city patterns, and city centralization and decentralization are shaped by both economic factors and political factors. Although some critical scholars accent the economic over the political, and others the political over the economic, in this book we will focus on both the economic and political factors. In [Figure 1] we show the economic and political influences on cities, as well as the interaction between these economic and political influences. Most Western cities are shaped by capitalistic investments in production, workers, workplaces, land, and buildings. These urban societies are organized along class (also race and gender) lines; and their social institutions are substantially shaped by the commodity production and capital investment processes. Capital investment is centered in corporations calculating profit at the firm level; this can result in major urban social costs associated with the rapid inflow of capital investment and accompanying growth and also with capital outflow (disinvestment) and accompanying urban decline. But [Figure 1] indicates that there are governmental (state) factors in urban growth, structuring, and decline as well. Governments protect the right to own and dispose of privately held property as owners see fit. Moreover, governments in capitalistic societies are often linked to business elites and the investment process; various levels of government play a part in fostering corporate profit making. But government officials also react to citizen protests, to class, race, and community-based struggles; as a result, they often try to cope with the costs of capitalist-generated growth and decline. In addition, in cities with relatively inde-

FIGURE 1

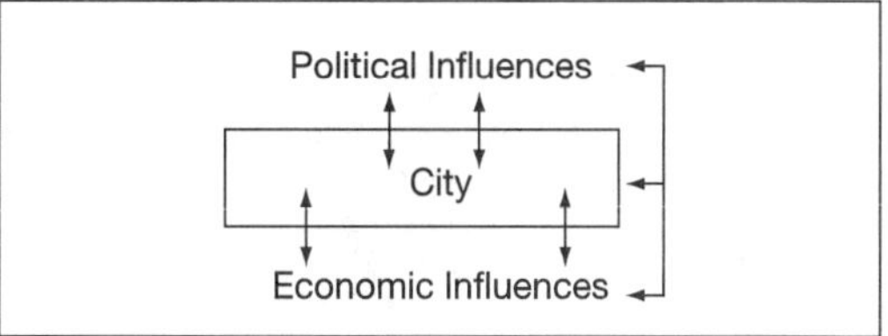

pendent political organizations (for example, "machines"), politicians may develop interests of their own and work *independently* of individual capitalists and citizen groups to shape and alter cities. In the urban worlds there is much interaction between the political and economic structures and political and economic decision makers.

A second important theme to be found in many critical urban arguments has to do with the central role of *space.* Some critical scholars only implicitly touch on spatial issues, while others feature the spatial dimension at the center of their city analysis. As [Figure 2] is designed to illustrate, we human beings live not only economic and political lives as workers affected by investments in markets and voters affected by political advertising, but also lives as occupiers of space, in households and families living in the home and neighborhood spaces of our cities. On the one side, we have the group of profit-oriented industrialists, developers, bankers, and landowners who buy, sell, and develop land and buildings just as they do with other for-profit commodities. Exchange value, the value (price) of commodities exchanged in markets, is usually the dominant concern in their decisions about buying and selling land and buildings. The investment actions of developers and others seeking to profit off the sale of, and construction on, land are centered in exchange-value considerations. On the other side, we have the group of American tenants and homeowners, low-income and middle-income, black and white, who are usually much more concerned with the *use value* of space, of home and neighborhood, than with the exchange value.

FIGURE 2 Capital's Global Investment Space

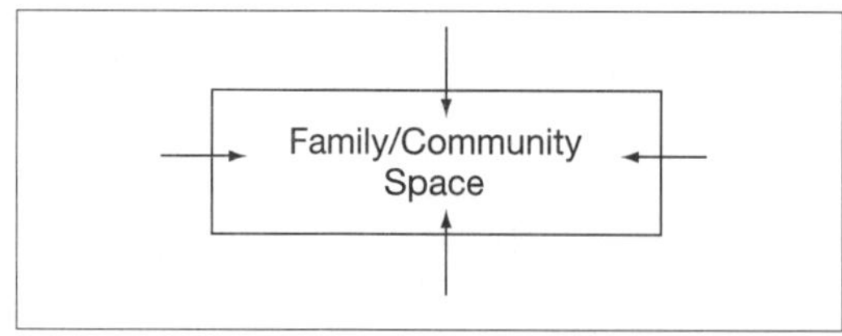

Corporate exchange-value decisions frequently come into conflict with the use-value concerns of many Americans. A concern with use value can mean that the utility of space, land, and building for everyday life, for family life, and for neighborhood life is much more important than land or building profitability. Such use-value concerns are behind the actions of neighborhood residents who have fought against numerous office buildings, malls, and redevelopment projects in order to keep them from intruding on their home and neighborhood spaces. Some zoning and other government land-use controls have thrown up barriers to the unrestrained expansion of capitalistic investment. Historically, much pressure for land-use regulation has come from worker-homeowners concerned with protecting family spaces and neighborhoods against industrial and commercial encroachment.[27]

Capitalist investors operate today in a worldwide investment space, so they may move factory and office jobs (or real estate capital) quickly from one city or country to another. However, workers and consumers generally spend their lives in more constricted family and home spaces. They often invest their lives in particular communities and cities and cannot move so easily to a city in another region or country, so they suffer when investors relocate quickly to other areas on the globe. Capital accumulation, capital investment, and the capitalistic class structure interact with space to generate urban and rural spatial patterns of production, distribution, and consumption. The aforementioned competition of local urban politicians for capital investments by corporate actors had not only job and construction effects, but also effects on the livability of local urban space. Uneven economic development also means uneven spatial development. Some places, homes and neighborhoods, stay viable and livable, while other urban communities become difficult to live in because of capital flight to other places across the nation or the globe.

A third basic theme in the new critical perspective is that of *structure* and *agency,* which is suggested in [Figure 3]. While most critical scholars tend to accent either structure (for example, institutions) or agency (for example, decision makers) in research on urban development, a number of scholars such as Lefebvre, Gottdiener, and Giddens, have called for research giving more attention to *both* dimensions. Some focus on the concrete actors involved in making cities, such as developers and business elites or citizens protesting development, while others prefer to emphasize the complex web of institutions and structures, such as state bureaucracies and capital investment circuits. . . . Economic systems and governments do not develop out of an inevitable and unalterable structural necessity, but rather in a contingent manner; they result from the conscious actions taken by individual decision makers in various class, race, gender, and community-based groups, acting under particular historical circumstances. The most powerful actors have the most influence on how our economic and political institutions develop. Yet they, in turn, are shaped by those institutions.[28]

A Structural Dimension: Private Property

The U.S. legal system, a critical part of our governmental structure, institutionalizes and protects the right to private property. Yet this legal system is critical to the perpetuation of great inequalities in real estate ownership and control. Most Americans own or control little property, other than their homes. Essential to the maintenance of inequality in land decision making is the legal protection of individualized property ownership. The rights of private property give owners, especially the large property owners, a great deal of control over land and buildings. Within broad limits land can be developed, and buildings constructed, as owners desire. This unbridled use of private property has not always been the case in the United States. The early Puritans, for example, had highly planned towns from Maine to Long Island. For two generations Puritan towns were designed by pioneers whose strong religious values influenced the layout of urban areas. The private ownership and control of property were not central; more important communal and collective goals often overrode private property interests. But the Puritan group-centered town planning soon gave way to intensified private landholding, even in New England. Fee-simple (unrestricted transfer) ownership of land became central to the expanding capitalistic system of eighteenth-century America. Early immigrants from Europe were generally hostile to landlords and vigorously sought to own their own land. Ownership of even a small piece of property was a sign of independence from landlords; many immigrants had come to the colonies to escape oppressive European landlords. Land was seen as a civil right by the many small farmers.[29]

FIGURE 3 Institutional Structures (Economy/State)

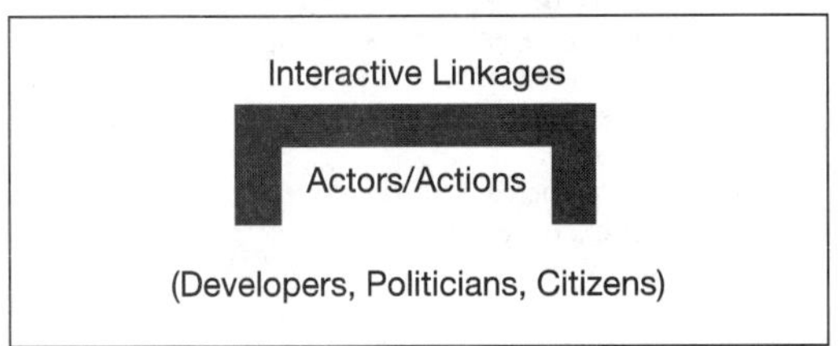

Yet this early and heavy commitment to the sacredness of privately held property had a major negative effect on development once the United States was no longer primarily a country of small farmers. By the early decades of the nineteenth century, there were fewer landholders and ever more tenants without land. In many cases, the growing number of Americans with little or no real estate property were seen as unworthy. Yet the strong commitment to private property, on the part of both propertied and landless Americans, has continued to legitimate the private disposal of property by the powerful landowning and development decision makers. As a result, over the last two centuries control over urban land development has become more concentrated in the hands of executives of banks, insurance firms, development corporations, and industrial companies.[30] In addition, there are major social costs for a private property system that gives owners of large amounts of land the right to use the land more or less as they wish. Those who build and develop large projects on central-city land have shown that they can transfer certain social costs onto other people nearby. A good example is the modern skyscraper with its mirrored glass walls, which often generate heat problems for nearby buildings, and with its thousands of workers whose exit in the evenings can create massive traffic jams. Such social costs of skyscraper development are generally not paid for by the developers and owners of the buildings. . . .

POWERFUL AGENTS OF URBAN CHANGE: PRIVATE PRODUCERS

Neglecting Powerful Agents

. . . Mainstream scholars often portray . . . land and building markets as "natural" markets guided by an invisible hand. But they are not natural. In reality, these markets are the creation of the most powerful players on the urban scene—the array of visible real estate decision makers in industry, finance, development, and construction. Over decades of urban development these powerful decision makers have both shaped, and been shaped by, the structures and institutions of urban real estate capitalism. Not only some of the critical analyses, such as the research of Harvey, but also traditional urban analyses, such as Berry and Kasarda's *Contemporary Urban Ecology* and Micklin and Choldin's *Sociological Human Ecology,* have largely ignored the central role of specific capitalistic and political actors in basic decisions about shaping urban land and built environments, the complex array of residential subdivisions, shopping malls, factories, warehouses, and office buildings.[31]

Among the primary decision makers in the urban real estate game are the capitalistic producers. Today real estate capitalism is organized around a complicated network of entrepreneurs and executives heading corporations of varying size. The size and complexity of the urban development industry can be seen in [Table 1], which lists major real estate and development decision makers. The categories refer to sets of major decisions that are critical to urban development.[32]

Looking at the private sector, we see that category 1 encompasses those corporate executives whose location decisions (for example, the choice of locating a factory in a northern city or a Sunbelt city) often set the other decision makers into motion. Category 2 covers the developers, land speculators, and landowners who buy, package, and develop land for use by industrial corporations and others.[33] Category 3 encompasses, among others, those bankers and financial corporations that make the loans for land purchase, construction, and related development. Category 4 includes the various design and construction actors who actually construct urban projects. And category 5 covers a variety of supporting actors, including real estate brokers and chamber of commerce executives.

TABLE 1 Urban Development: Decision Categories and Selected Decision Makers

1. Industrial and commercial location decisions
   Executives of industrial companies
   Executives of commercial companies
2. Development decisions
   Executives of development companies (developers)
   Land speculators and landowners
   Apartment owners and landlords
3. Financial decisions
   Commercial bankers
   Executives of savings and loan associations ("thrifts")
   Executives of insurance companies
   Executives of mortgage companies
   Executives of real estate investment trusts
4. Construction decisions
   Builders and developer-builders
   Executives of architectural and engineering firms
   Construction subcontractors
5. Support decisions
   Chamber of commerce executives
   Real estate brokers
   Executives of leasing companies
   Apartment management firms

Today a single corporation may include subsidiaries and other organizational units involved in a variety of decisions across several categories. Within one firm there may be a development subdivision, which not only develops projects but also engages in land speculation; a real estate brokerage subsidiary; and an architectural subsidiary. A major insurance company may have a lending department, as well as its own urban land development subsidiary. Large integrated real estate development companies are often involved in major decisions in more than one category. Frequently, local developers, realtors, and bankers are the major decision makers in local development projects; studies of community decision makers show clearly the role and power of local business people in all types of cities in the North and South.[34] However, major real estate decisions are made not only by local individuals and real estate companies but also by powerful regional and national firms, such as the Hines and Levitt firms cited earlier. There are complex interconnections between influential interests external to cities and those that are part of the internal power structure of a particular city. An example would be a major insurance company, such as the Prudential Life Insurance Company, which, in connection with other local and national companies, finances and owns real estate and development projects in cities across the United States. . . .

GOVERNMENT AND URBAN DEVELOPMENT

Pluralist and Market Politics Analyses

In addition to economic structures and decision makers, we must give substantial attention to political structures and decision makers in understanding city building. Most social scientists have either neglected the role of government in city development or have assumed a pluralist or "market politics" perspective. The pluralist outlook has dominated much political science analysis of U.S. cities: Political decision makers, on the whole, promote the general welfare because their decisions result from responding to and coordinating pressures from a multiplicity of contending pressure groups. Advocates of urban pluralism see a competitive market in the urban political sphere that is analogous to the economic market; there is a political market in which individual voters and an array of diverse interest groups, in ever changing coalitions, compete for influence on local governments within a general value consensus.[35] Yet traditional pluralists have tended to neglect private economic decision making. . . .

Critical Perspectives on Government

In contrast to this market-knows-best perspective on urban economics and politics, critical urban analysts note the overwhelming evidence that certain groups have *far* more power than others to shape both economic and political decisions. Just as markets generally favor powerful capitalist investors over ordinary consumers, the urban political process favors the interests of powerful business and other groups over ordinary voters. Neither U.S. markets nor U.S. political arrangements are neutral. And both economic and political arrangements are dominated by the few. Some critical social scientists emphasize the economic and political decision makers, while others accent economic and governmental structures. But all critical analysts reject the pluralist and market-knows-best perspectives. Certain critical researchers such as Ralph Miliband and G. William Domhoff have accented the importance of specific business decision makers, particularly the capitalists, in state decisions. They view powerful economic decision makers as generally dominant over governmental decision makers and their decisions. Miliband and Domhoff have emphasized the specific ties between the capitalist class and various governments, including the movement of business leaders into and out of key political positions. In the United States, at the federal and local government levels, there is the everyday reality of interpersonal connections between business leaders and governmental officials. Domhoff has demonstrated that in the United States individual capitalists and their close subordinates do in fact rule by serving in critical governmental positions at both the national and the local levels. These governmental actors generally work hard to maintain favorable conditions for capitalists' enterprises and profits.[36]

CONCLUSION: THE NEED FOR PUBLIC BALANCE SHEETS

In this [excerpt] we have examined the traditional social science and governmental perspectives on urban growth and development and have seen them to be substantially grounded in neoclassical economics. These traditional perspectives put heavy emphasis on a "free" land and property market, on allegedly equal individuals competing freely, on private property, on efficient land use, and on the benefits that markets in land are supposed to bring to all urbanites. But the realities are not what these perspectives suggest. As we have seen from examples, there are no free competitive markets in cities, because corporate location, urban land purchase, and urban development are disproportionately controlled, often monopolized, by powerful capitalistic decision makers. The newer critical perspective, also described in this [selection], focuses on these power and inequality realities of city growth and decline.

For the most part, the actions of urban industrialists, developers, bankers, and their political allies are visible and quantifiable. Using the language of the accountant and the economist and calculating profit and loss on their private balance sheets, they are prepared to spell out what they see as the need for and benefits of constant urban growth. Down to the last square foot, they can tell us how much new office space is needed and how much has been created. They inform us of the number of jobs produced by their construction projects, and, once completed, they speculate with great precision about the number of additional employees the employers in their urban monuments will require. They calculate, and often exaggerate, the expected amount of additional tax revenues their large projects will generate, and, using the concept of the multiplier effect, speculate upon the economic benefits of their actions for the city as a whole.

On the other hand, the negative fallout from urban development is noticeably absent from the industrialists' and developers' lexicon. Just as critical, and usually just as obvious, the *social costs* generated by urban growth are less studied and are sometimes more difficult to specify and quantify. For example, why do we not attempt to measure the long-term physical and psychological impact of increasing pedestrian and auto congestion on consumers and workers? How can we eliminate unsafe pollution levels and prevent health damage? How should we measure the psychological impact on urbanites of routinely being deprived of sunlight as high-rise skyscrapers obstruct the sun? And what is the total community cost of the growing numbers of the homeless and those displaced by the processes of condominium conversion and gentrification in our cities? Finally, how can we calculate the fading sense of community that is produced in many neighborhoods as constant development and redevelopment converge to constitute the modern city?

In the last few years a start on studying social costs has been made. The idea that what is efficient and rational for developers is not necessarily so for workers, consumers, and society as a whole has even been documented in a study of Phoenix, Arizona, by the Center for Business Research at Arizona State University. According to this study the benefits of Phoenix's growth to businesses included more customers, improved market potential, greater availability of labor, and higher profits; the study's research manager stated that "most businesses enjoy a substantial net benefit from urban growth." His evaluation of the net effect of urban growth for ordinary citizens was less favorable. The benefits of expanded job opportunities, a greater selection of goods, and higher incomes for some workers are offset by higher taxes, an increased cost of living, urban sprawl and traffic congestion, water and air pollution, destruction of the natural environment and depletion of resources, waste disposal, a higher crime rate, greater demand for social services, and problems such as homelessness.[37]

Industrial and real estate capitalism does indeed shape the major development projects in cities—the factories, shopping centers, suburbs, business parks, office towers, and apartment complexes. Once the decisions of the powerful are made, smaller scale builders must work around the larger-scale projects, and average workers and their families have to choose within the limits provided. Workers and consumers, especially those with inadequate economic resources, endure the brunt of many social costs of our capitalistic development system. And these costs . . . have been enormous. However, we must not forget that group struggle is at the heart of capitalist cities. Citizens' movements are pressing for the community costs of urban development and decline to be addressed and eliminated.

CRITICAL-THINKING QUESTIONS

1. According to Feagin and Parker, what role do residents have in a city's development? In their view, what role *should* residents have?

2. What are some of the specific criticisms made of the traditional "market-knows-best" approach?

3. What are the basic assertions of the critical urban perspective? What political values appear to underlie this view? What sort of city would be consistent with these values?

NOTES

1. D. Lindorff, "About-Face in Santa Monica," *Village Voice* (December 2–8, 1981), 20.

2. "Who's Gone This Year," *Forbes,* 140 (October 26, 1987), 308. See also H. Banks, "Real Men Don't Need Tax Breaks," *Forbes,* 135 (June 3, 1985), 78, 80.

3. H. Gans, *The Levittowners* (New York: Random House, 1967), p. 6.

4. Ibid., pp. 5–13.

5. "The Master Builder," *Newsweek* (August 31, 1981), 45; J. R. Feagin, "Sunbelt Metropolis and Development Capital," in *Sunbelt/Snowbelt: Urban Development and Regional Restructuring,* ed. L. Sawers and W. K. Tabb (New York: Oxford University Press, 1984), pp. 110–11.

6. R. E. Park and E. W. Burgess, *Introduction to the Science of Society* (Chicago: University of Chicago Press, 1924), p. 507.

7. W. P. Frisbie and J. D. Kasarda, "Spatial Processes," in *The Handbook of Sociology,* ed. N. Smelser (Newbury Park, Calif.: Sage, 1988), pp. 629–66.

8. B. J. L. Berry and J. Kasarda, *Contemporary Urban Ecology* (New York: Macmillan, 1977); M. Micklin and H. M. Choldin, eds., *Sociological Human Ecology* (Boulder: Westview, 1984); Harvey M. Choldin, *Cities and Suburbs: An Introduction to Urban Sociology* (New York: McGraw-Hill, 1985). This paragraph draws on J. R. Feagin, *Free Enterprise City: Houston in Political-Economic Perspective* (New Brunswick, N.J.: Rutgers, 1988), pp. 15–21.

9. S. E. Harris, *The Death of Capital* (New York: Pantheon, 1977), p. 64.

10. Ibid., p. 65.

11. J. Kasarda, "The Implications of Contemporary Redistribution Trends for National Urban Policy," *Social Science Quarterly,* 61 (Dec., 1980), 373–400.

12. K. Bradbury, A. Downs, and K. Small, *Urban Decline and the Future of American Cities* (Washington, D.C.: The Brookings Institution, 1982), p. 296.

13. L. Mumford, *The City in History* (New York: Harcourt, Brace and World, 1961), p. 452.

14. F. X. Sutton et al., *The American Business Creed* (Cambridge: Harvard University Press, 1956), pp. 361–62.

15. E. A. Filene, *Successful Living in the Machine Age* (New York: Simon & Schuster, 1932), p. 98.

16. W. Alonso, *Location and Land Use* (Cambridge: Harvard University Press, 1964); Richard Muth, *Cities and Housing* (Chicago: University of Chicago Press, 1969).

17. D. L. Birch, "Wide Open Spaces," *Inc.,* 9 (Aug., 1987), 28.

18. P. E. Peterson, "Introduction: Technology, Race, and Urban Policy," in *The New Urban Reality* (Washington, D.C.: Brookings Institution, 1985), pp. 2–12.

19. A. Hawley, *Urban Society,* 2d ed. (New York: Wiley, 1981).

20. Micklin and Choldin, eds., *Sociological Human Ecology.*

21. Berry and Kasarda, *Contemporary Urban Ecology,* pp. 353, 402.

22. Hawley, *Urban Society,* pp. 228–29, 262–63; see also Frisbie and Kasarda, "Spatial Processes."

23. President's Commission for a National Agenda for the Eighties, Panel on Policies and Prospects, *Urban America in the Eighties: Perspectives and Prospects* (Washington, D.C.: U.S. Government Printing Office, 1980).

24. Ibid., pp. 12, 104.

25. M. Castells, "Is There an Urban Sociology?" in *Urban Sociology,* ed. C. G. Pickvance (London: Tavistock, 1976), pp. 33–57; M. Castells, *The Urban Question* (London: Edward Arnold, 1977); D. Harvey, *The Urbanization of Capital* (Baltimore: Johns Hopkins University Press, 1985); H. Lefebvre, *La revolution urbaine* (Paris: Gallimard, 1970).

26. M. P. Smith, *The City and Social Theory* (New York: St. Martin's, 1979); S. Fainstein, N. Fainstein, M. P. Smith, D. Judd, and R. C. Hill, *Restructuring the City* (New York: Longman, 1983); R. C. Hill, "Urban Political Economy," in *Cities in Transformation,* ed. M. P. Smith (Beverly Hills: Sage, 1984), pp. 123–38; J. Allen Whitt, *Urban Elites and Mass Transportation* (Princeton, N.J.: Princeton University Press, 1982); M. Gottdiener, *The Social Production of Urban Space* (Austin: University of Texas Press, 1985); G. L. Clark and Michael Dear, *State Apparatus: Structures and Language of Legitimacy* (Boston: Allen and Unwin, 1984), pp. 131–45; J. R. Logan and H. M. Molotch, *Urban Fortunes: The Political Economy of Place* (Berkeley and Los Angeles: University of California Press, 1987).

27. Other pressures for land-use controls have stemmed from local merchants concerned with protecting their business places for profitable marketing uses. In such cases the commitment by local merchants to land is primarily to its use value as a place to make a profit. Thus we actually have three basic interests in land: (1) in the exchange value of the land itself, (2) in the use value of the land for living, family, and neighborhood; (3) in the use value of the land for local commercial or industrial profit making.

28. See M. Gottdiener and J. R. Feagin, "The Paradigm Shift in Urban Sociology," *Urban Affairs Quarterly,* 24 (Dec., 1988), 163–87.

29. Sam Bass Warner, *The Urban Wilderness* (New York: Harper and Row, 1972), pp. 16–17. See also pp. 8–15.

30. Ibid., p. 18.

31. Berry and Kasarda, *Contemporary Urban Ecology;* Micklin and Choldin, eds., *Sociological Human Ecology;* Choldin, *Cities and Suburbs: An Introduction to Urban Sociology.*

32. D. C. McAdams and J. R. Feagin, "A Power Conflict Approach to Urban Land Use," Austin, Texas, University of Texas, unpublished monograph 1980; and D. Claire McAdams, "Powerful Actors in Public Land Use Decision Making Processes" (Ph.D. diss., University of Texas, 1979), chaps. 1–3.

33. The term "corporation" is used in this [reading] for the various organizational arrangements, including partnerships, that capitalists utilize in profit making, whether or not legally incorporated.

34. J. Walton "A Systematic Survey of Community Power Research," in *The Structure of Community Power,* eds., M. Aiken and P. Mott (New York: Random House, 1970), pp. 443–64.

35. See R. Dahl, *Who Governs?* (New Haven: Yale University Press, 1961); T. M. Guterbock, "The Political Economy of Urban Revitalization," *Urban Affairs Quarterly,* 15 (March, 1980): 429–38.

36. R. Miliband, "State Power and Class Interests," *New Left Review,* 138 (1983), 57–68; R. Miliband, *The State in Capitalist Society* (London: Weidenfeld and Nicolson, 1969); G. W. Domhoff, *Who Rules America?* (Englewood Cliffs, N.J.: Prentice-Hall, 1967); this and the next few paragraphs draw on Feagin, *Free Enterprise City: Houston in Political-Economic Perspective,* pp. 34–40.

37. T. R. Rex, "Businesses Enjoy Benefits; Individuals, Society Pay Costs," *Arizona Business,* 34 (Aug., 1987), 3.

67

Let's *Reduce* Global Population!

J. Kenneth Smail

Population and Urbanization

CLASSIC

CONTEMPORARY

CROSS-CULTURAL

A familiar concern is holding the line on world population increase. But, some people are asking, has population growth already gone too far? In this selection, Ken Smail argues that the long-term "carrying capacity" of the planet may only be half the number of people we have now. And the time left to begin reducing population is running out fast.

The main point of this essay is simply stated. Within the next half-century, it is essential for the human species to have in place a flexible voluntary, equitable, and internationally coordinated plan to dramatically reduce world population by at least two-thirds. This process of voluntary consensus building—local, national, and global—must begin now.

The mathematical inevitability that human numbers will continue their dramatic increase over the next two generations (to perhaps 9 billion or more by the year 2050), the high probability that this numerical increase will worsen the problems that already plague humanity (economic, political, environmental, social, moral, etc.), and the growing realization that the Earth may only be able to support a global human population in the 2 to 3 billion range at an "adequate to comfortable" standard of living, only reinforce this sense of urgency.

There are, however, hopeful signs. In recent years, we have finally begun to come to terms with the fact that the consequences of the twentieth century's rapid and seemingly uncontrolled population growth will soon place us—if it has not done so already—in the greatest crisis our species has yet encountered.

TEN INESCAPABLE REALITIES

In order better to appreciate the scope and ramifications of this still partly hidden crisis, I shall briefly call attention to ten essential and inescapable realities that must be fully understood and soon confronted.

First, during the present century world population will have grown from somewhere around 1.6 billion in 1900 to slightly more than 6 billion by

Source: This is a revised version of an essay published as a pamphlet by Negative Population Growth (Smail, 1995) and then—after revision and expansion—as a journal article in *Population and Environment* (Smail, 1997) and *Politics and the Life Sciences* (Smail, 1997). Reprinted with permission of the author (e-mail address: Smail@kenyon.edu).

the year 2000, an almost fourfold increase in but 100 years. This is an unprecedented numerical expansion. Throughout human history, world population growth measured over similar 100-year intervals has been virtually nonexistent or, at most, modestly incremental; it has only become markedly exponential within the last few hundred years. To illustrate this on a more easily comprehensible scale, based on the recent rate of increase of nearly 90 million per year, human population growth during the 1990s alone amounted to nearly 1 billion, an astonishing 20 increase in but little more than a single decade. Just by itself, this increase is equivalent to the total global population in the year 1800 and is approximately triple the estimated world population (ca. 300 million) at the height of the Roman Empire. It is a chastening thought that even moderate demographic projections suggest that this billion-per-decade rate of increase will continue well into the century, and that the current global total of 6 billion (late 1999 estimate) could easily reach 9 to 10 billion by mid-twenty-first century.

Second, even if a fully effective program of zero population growth (ZPG) were implemented immediately, by limiting human fertility to what demographers term the *replacement rate* (roughly 2.1 children per female), global population would nevertheless continue its rapid rate of expansion. In fact, demographers estimate that it would take at least two to three generations (fifty to seventy-five years) at ZPG fertility levels just to reach a point of population stability, unfortunately at numbers considerably higher than at present. This powerful *population momentum* results from the fact that an unusually high proportion (nearly one-third) of the current world population is under the age of fifteen and has not yet reproduced. Even more broad-based population profiles may be found throughout the developing world, where the under-fifteen age cohort often exceeds 40 percent and where birth rates have remained high even as mortality rates have fallen. While there are some recent indications that fertility rates are beginning to decline, the current composite for the less-developed world—excluding China—is still nearly double (ca. 3.8) that needed for ZPG.

Third, in addition to fertility levels, it is essential to understand that population growth is also significantly affected by changes in mortality rates. In fact, demographic transition theory suggests that the earlier stages of rapid population expansion are typically fueled more by significant reductions in death rates (i.e., decreased childhood mortality and/or enhanced adult longevity) than by changes in birth rates. Nor does recent empirical data suggest that average human life expectancy has reached anywhere near its theoretical upper limit, in either the developing or developed worlds. Consequently, unless there appears a deadly pandemic, a devastating world war or a massive breakdown in public health (or a combination of all three), it is obvious that ongoing global gains in human longevity will continue to make a major contribution to world population expansion over the next half-century, regardless of whatever progress might be made in reducing fertility.

Fourth, all previous examples of significant human population expansion—and subsequent (occasionally rapid) decline—have been primarily local or, at most, regional phenomena. At the present time, given the current global rate of increase of some 220,000 people per day (more than 9,000 per hour), it is ludicrous to speak of significant empty spaces left on Earth to colonize, certainly when compared with but a century ago. And it is ridiculous to suggest that "off Earth" (extraterrestrial) migration will somehow be sufficient to siphon away excess human population, in either the near or more distant future.

Fifth, given the data and observations presented thus far, it becomes increasingly apparent that the time span available for implementing an effective program of population "control" may be quite limited, with a window of opportunity—even in the more optimistic scenarios—that may not extend much beyond the middle of the next century. As mentioned previously, most middle-of-the-road demographic projections for the year 2050 two generations from now—are in the 8 to 9 billion range. Several observations might help to bring these demographic estimates and the above-mentioned "limited" time span into somewhat better perspective:

- the year 2050 is closer to the present than the year 1950
- an infant born in 2000 will be only 50 years old in the year 2050
- a young person entering the job market in the early twenty-first century will have reached retirement age in the year 2050

These observations also make it quite clear that *those already* born—ourselves, our children, and our grandchildren—will have to confront the overwhelming impact of an additional 3–4 billion people.

Sixth, the Earth's long-term carrying capacity, in terms of resources, is indeed finite, despite the continuing use of economic models predicated on seemingly unlimited growth, and notwithstanding the high probability of continued scientific/technological progress. Some further terminological clarification may be useful. "Long-term" is most reasonably defined on the order of several hundred years, at least; it emphatically does not mean the five to fifteen year horizon typical of much economic forecasting or political prognostication. Over this much longer time span, it thus becomes much more appropriate—perhaps even essential to civilizational survival—to define a sustainable human population size in terms of optimums rather than maximums. Further, *what "could" be supported in the short term is not necessary what "should" be humanity's goal over the longer term.*

As far as resources are concerned, whether these be characterized as renewable or nonrenewable, it is becoming increasingly apparent that the era of inexpensive energy (derived from fossil fuels), adequate food supplies (whether plant or animal), readily available or easily extractable raw materials (from wood to minerals), plentiful fresh water, and readily accessible "open space" is rapidly coming to a close, almost certainly within the next half-century. And finally, the consequences of future scientific/technological advances—whether in terms of energy production, technological efficiency, agricultural productivity, or creation of alternative materials—are much more likely to be incremental than revolutionary, notwithstanding frequent and grandiose claims for the latter.

Seventh, rhetoric about "sustainable growth" is at best a continuing exercise in economic self-deception and at worst a politically pernicious oxymoron. Almost certainly, working toward some sort of *steady-state sustainability* is much more realistic scientifically, (probably) more attainable economically, and (perhaps) more prudent politically. Assertions that the Earth might be able to support a population of 10, 15, or even 20 billion people for an indefinite period of time at a standard of living superior to the present are not only cruelly misleading but almost certainly false. Rather, extrapolations from the work of a growing number of ecologists, demographers, and numerous others suggest the distinct possibility that *the Earth's true carrying capacity—defined simply as humans in long-term adaptive balance with their ecological setting, resource base, and each other—may already have been exceeded by a factor of two or more.*

To the best of my knowledge, no evidence contradicts this sobering—perhaps even frightening—assessment. Consequently, since at some point in the not-too-distant future the negative consequences and ecological damage stemming from the mutually reinforcing effects of excessive human reproduction and overconsumption of resources could well become irreversible, and because there is only one Earth with which to experiment, it is undoubtedly better for our species to err on the side of prudence, exercising wherever possible a cautious and careful stewardship.

Eighth, only about 20 percent of the current world population (ca. 1.2 billion people) could be said to have a *generally adequate* standard of living, defined here as a level of affluence roughly approximating that of the so-called "developed" world (Western Europe, Japan, and North America). The other 80 percent (ca. 4.8 billion), incorporating most of the inhabitants of what have been termed the "developing nations," live in conditions ranging from mild deprivation to severe deficiency. Despite well-intentioned efforts to the contrary, there is little evidence that this imbalance is going to decrease in any significant way, and a strong likelihood that it may get worse, particularly in view of the fact that more than 90 percent of all future population expansion is projected to occur in these less-developed regions of the world. In fact, there is growing concern that when this burgeoning population growth in the developing world is combined with excessive or wasteful per capita energy and resource consumption in much of the developed world, widespread environmental deterioration (systemic breakdown?) in a number of the Earth's more heavily stressed ecosystems will become increasingly likely. This is especially worrisome in regions already beset by shortsighted or counterproductive economic policies, chronic political instability, and growing social unrest, particularly when one considers that nearly all nations in the less-developed world currently have an understandable desire—not surprisingly expressed as a fundamental right—to increase their standard of living (per capita energy and resource consumption) to something approximating "first world" levels.

Ninth, to follow up on the point just made, the total impact of human numbers on the global environment is often described as the product of three basic multipliers: (1) population size; (2) per capita energy and resource consumption (affluence); and (3) technological efficiency in the production, utilization, and conservation of such energy and resources. This relationship is usually expressed by some variant of the now well-known I = PAT equation: Impact = Population × Affluence × Technology. This simple formula enables one to demonstrate much more clearly the quantitative scope of humanity's dilemma over the next fifty to seventy-five years, particularly if the following projections are anywhere near accurate:

- human population could well *double* by the end of the twenty-first century, from our current 6 billion to perhaps 12 billion or more
- global energy and resource consumption could easily *quadruple* or more during the same period, particularly if (as just indicated in item 8) the less-developed nations are successful in their current efforts to significantly improve their citizens' standard of living to something approaching developed-world norms
- new technologies applied to current energy and resource inefficiencies might be successful in reducing per capita waste or effluence *by half*, or even *two-thirds*, in both the developed and developing worlds

Given these reasonable estimates, the conclusion seems inescapable that the human species' total impact on the Earth's already stressed ecosystem could easily *triple to quadruple* by the middle of the twenty-first century. This impact could be even greater if current (and future) efforts at energy and resource conservation turn out to be less successful than hoped for, or if (as seems likely) the mathematical relationship between these several multipliers is something more than simply linear. It is therefore very important to keep a close watch—for harbingers of future trends and/or problems—on current events in the growing group of nations now experiencing rapid economic development and modernization, with particular attention being given to ongoing changes in India and China, two states whose combined size represents nearly half the population of the less-developed world.

Tenth, and finally, there are two additional considerations—matters not usually factored into the I = PAT equation—that must also be taken into account in any attempt to coordinate appropriate responses to the rapidly increasing global environmental impact described in points 6 through 9. First, given current and likely ongoing scientific uncertainties about environmental limits and ecosystem resilience, not to mention the potential dangers of irreversible damage if such limits are stretched too far (i.e., a permanently reduced carrying capacity), it is extremely important to design into any future planning an adequate safety factor (or sufficient margin for error). In other words, any attempt at "guided social engineering" on the massive scale that will clearly be necessary over the next century will require at least as much attention to safety margins, internal coordination, and systems redundancy as may be found in other major engineering accomplishments—from designing airplanes to building the Channel Tunnel to landing astronauts on the moon.

In addition, such planning must consider yet another seemingly intractable problem. Because the human species not only shares the Earth—but has also co-evolved—with literally millions of other life forms, the closely related issues of wilderness conservation and biodiversity preservation must also be taken fully into account, on several different levels (pragmatic, aesthetic, and moral). In simplest terms, it has now become a matter of critical importance to ask some very basic questions about what proportion of the Earth's surface the human species has the right to exploit or transform—or, conversely, how much of the Earth's surface should be reserved for the protection and preservation of all other life forms. As many have argued, often in eloquent terms, our species will likely be more successful in confronting and resolving these questions—not to mention the other complex problems that are now crowding in upon us—*if we can collectively come to regard ourselves more as the Earth's long-term stewards than its absolute masters.*

To sum up, if the above "inescapable realities" are indeed valid, it is obvious that rational, equitable, and attainable population goals will have to be established in the very near future. It is also obvious that these goals will have to address—and in some fashion resolve—a powerful internal conflict: how to create and sustain an adequate standard of living for *all* the world's peoples, minimizing as much as possible the growing inequities between rich and poor, while simultaneously neither overstressing nor exceeding the Earth's longer-term carrying capacity. *I submit that these goals cannot be reached, or this conflict resolved, unless and until world population is dramatically reduced—to somewhere around 2 to 3 billion people—within the next two centuries.*

CRITICAL-THINKING QUESTIONS

1. Why, according to this reading, is simply holding the line on population increase not enough?
2. What about the fact that humans share the earth with millions of other life forms? In facing up to the problem of population increase, what responsibility do we have for other species?
3. All in all, do you agree with Smail that we must find a way to reduce global population? Why or why not?

REFERENCES

Smail, J. Kenneth. 1995. Confronting the 21st century's hidden crisis: Reducing human numbers by 80%. *NPG Forum*. Teaneck, N.J.: Negative Population Growth.

———. 1997. Averting the 21st century's demographic crisis: Can human numbers be reduced by 75%? *Population and Environment*, 18 (6): 565–80.

———. Beyond population stabilization: The case for dramatically reducing global human numbers. Roundtable: World Population Policy commentary and responses. *Politics and the Life Sciences*, 16, 2 (September, 1997): 183–236.

Environment and Society

CLASSIC

CONTEMPORARY

CROSS-CULTURAL

68

Why Humanity Faces Ultimate Catastrophe

Thomas Robert Malthus

In this selection, from "An Essay on the Principle of Population," Thomas Robert Malthus foretells human calamity. His dire prediction is based on a single assertion: Human beings will overwhelm the earth's capacity to provide for us. Many of today's environmentalists (sometimes termed "neo-Malthusians") accept this principle and echo his early warning.

STATEMENT OF THE SUBJECT: RATIOS OF THE INCREASE OF POPULATION AND FOOD

In an inquiry concerning the improvement of society, the mode of conducting the subject which naturally presents itself is

1. To investigate the causes that have hitherto impeded the progress of mankind towards happiness
2. To examine the probability of the total or partial removal of the causes in [the] future

To enter fully into this question, and to enumerate all the causes that have hitherto influenced human improvement, would be much beyond the power of an individual. The principal object of the present essay is to examine the effects of one great cause intimately united with the very nature of man; which, though it has been constantly and powerfully operating since the commencement of society, has been little noticed by the writers who have treated this subject. The facts which establish the existence of this cause have, indeed, been repeatedly stated and acknowledged; but its natural and necessary effects have been almost totally overlooked; though probably among these effects may be reckoned a very considerable portion of that vice and misery, and of that unequal distribution of the bounties of nature, which it has been the unceasing object of the enlightened philanthropist in all ages to correct.

The cause to which I allude is the constant tendency in all

Source: From *On the Principle of Population,* Vol. I, by T. R. Malthus (New York: E. P. Dutton & Co., Inc., 1914; orig. 1798).

animated life to increase beyond the nourishment prepared for it.

It is observed by Dr. Franklin that there is no bound to the prolific nature of plants or animals but what is made by their crowding and interfering with each other's means of subsistence. Were the face of the earth, he says, vacant of other plants, it might be gradually sowed and overspread with one kind only, as for instance with fennel: and were it empty of other inhabitants, it might in a few ages be replenished from one nation only, as for instance with Englishmen.[1]

This is incontrovertibly true. Through the animal and vegetable kingdoms Nature has scattered the seeds of life abroad with the most profuse and liberal hand; but has been comparatively sparing in the room and the nourishment necessary to rear them. The germs of existence contained in this earth, if they could freely develop themselves, would fill millions of worlds in the course of a few thousand years. Necessity, that imperious, all pervading law of nature, restrains them within the prescribed bounds. The race of plants and the race of animals shrink under this great restrictive law; and man cannot by any efforts of reason escape from it.

In plants and irrational animals, the view of the subject is simple. They are all impelled by a powerful instinct to the increase of their species; and this instinct is interrupted by no doubts about providing for their offspring. Wherever therefore there is liberty, the power of increase is exerted; and the super-abundant effects are repressed afterwards by want of room and nourishment.

The effects of this check on man are more complicated. Impelled to the increase of his species by an equally powerful instinct, reason interrupts his career, and asks him whether he may not bring beings into the world for whom he cannot provide the means of support. If he attends to this natural suggestion, the restriction too frequently produces vice. If he hear it not, the human race will be constantly endeavouring to increase beyond the mean of subsistence. But as, by the law of our nature which makes food necessary to the life of man, population can never actually increase beyond the lowest nourishment capable of supporting it, a strong check on population, from the difficulty of acquiring food, must be constantly in operation. This difficulty must fall somewhere, and must necessarily be severely felt in some or other of the various forms of misery, or the fear of misery, by a large portion of mankind.

That population has this constant tendency to increase beyond the means of subsistence, and that it is kept to its necessary level by these causes, will sufficiently appear from a review of the different states of society in which man has existed. But, before we proceed to this review, the subject will, perhaps, be seen in a clearer light if we endeavour to ascertain what would be the natural increase of population if left to exert itself with perfect freedom; and what might be expected to be the rate of increase in the production of the earth under the most favourable circumstances of human industry.

It will be allowed that no country has hitherto been known where the manners were so pure and simple, and the means of subsistence so abundant, that no check whatever has existed to early marriages from the difficulty of providing for a family, and that no waste of the human species has been occasioned by vicious customs, by towns, by unhealthy occupations, or too severe labour. Consequently in no state that we have yet known has the power of population been left to exert itself with perfect freedom.

Whether the law of marriage be instituted, or not, the dictate of nature and virtue seems to be an early attachment to one woman; and where there were no impediments of any kind in the way of a union to which such an attachment would lead, and no causes of depopulation afterwards, the increase of the human species would be evidently much greater than any increase which has been hitherto known. . . .

It may safely be pronounced, . . . that population, when unchecked, goes on doubling itself every twenty-five years, or increases in a geometrical ratio.

The rate according to which the productions of the earth may be supposed to increase, it will not be so easy to determine. Of this, however, we may be perfectly certain, that the ratio of their increase in a limited territory must be of a totally different nature from the ratio of the increase of population. A thousand millions are just as easily doubled every twenty-five years by the power of population as a thousand. But the food to support the increase from the greater number will by no means be obtained with the same facility. Man is necessarily confined in room. When acre has been added to acre till all the fertile land is occupied, the yearly increase of food must depend upon the melioration of the land already in possession. This is a fund, which, from the nature of all soils, instead of increasing, must be gradually diminishing. But population, could it be supplied with food, would go on with unexhausted vigour; and the increase of one period would furnish the power of a greater increase the next, and this without any limit. . . .

Europe is by no means so fully peopled as it might be. In Europe there is the fairest chance that human industry may receive its best direction. The science of agriculture has been much studied in England and Scotland; and there is still a great portion of uncultivated land in these countries. Let us consider at what rate the produce of this island might be supposed to increase under circumstances the most favourable to improvement.

If it be allowed that by the best possible policy, and great encouragements to agriculture, the average produce of the island could be doubled in the first twenty-five years, it will be allowing, probably, a greater increase than could with reason be expected.

In the next twenty-five years, it is impossible to suppose that the produce could be quadrupled. It would be contrary to all our knowledge of the properties of land. The improvement of the barren parts would be a work of time and labour; and it must be evident to those who have the slightest acquaintance with agricultural subjects that, in proportion as cultivation extended, the additions that could yearly be made to the former average produce must be gradually and regularly diminishing. That we may be the better able to compare the increase of population and food, let us make a supposition, which, without pretending to accuracy, is clearly more favourable to the power of production in the earth than any experience we have had of its qualities will warrant.

Let us suppose that the yearly additions which might be made to the former average produce, instead of decreasing, which they certainly would do, were to remain the same; and that the produce of this island might be increased every twenty-five years by a quantity equal to what it at present produces. The most enthusiastic speculator cannot suppose a greater increase than this. In a few centuries it would make every acre of land in the island like a garden.

If this supposition be applied to the whole earth, and if it be allowed that the subsistence for man which the earth affords might be increased every twenty-five years by a quantity equal to what it at present produces, this will be supposing a rate of increase much greater than we can imagine that any possible exertions of mankind could make it.

It may be fairly pronounced, therefore, that, considering the present average state of the earth, the means of subsistence, under circumstances the most favourable to human industry, could not possibly be made to increase faster than in an arithmetical ratio.

The necessary effects of these two different rates of increase, when brought together, will be very striking. Let us call the population of this island eleven millions; and suppose the present produce equal to the easy support of such a number. In the first twenty-five years the population would be twenty-two millions, and the food being also doubled, the means of subsistence would be equal to this increase. In the next twenty-five years, the population would be forty-four millions, and the means of subsistence only equal to the support of thirty-three millions. In the next period the population would be eighty-eight millions, and the means of subsistence just equal to the support of half that number. And, at the conclusion of the first century, the population would be a hundred and seventy-six millions, and the means of subsistence only equal to the support of fifty-five millions, leaving a population of a hundred and twenty-one millions totally unprovided for.

Taking the whole earth, instead of this island, emigration would of course be excluded; and, supposing the present population equal to a thousand millions, the human species would increase as the numbers, 1, 2, 4, 8, 16, 32, 64, 128, 256, and subsistence as 1, 2, 3, 4, 5, 6, 7, 8, 9. In two centuries the population would be to the means of subsistence as 256 to 9; in three centuries as 4096 to 13, and in two thousand years the difference would be almost incalculable. . . .

CRITICAL-THINKING QUESTIONS

1. According to Malthus, at what rate does human population increase? At what rate can the earth's food supplies be increased?

2. Malthus published his essay in 1798; in the two centuries since then, has his dire prediction come to pass? Why or why not?

3. Following Malthus's thinking, what should be the cornerstone of the world's program to protect the environment? Do you agree with his position or not?

NOTE

1. Franklin's Miscell, p. 9.

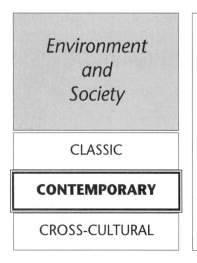

Environment and Society

CLASSIC

CONTEMPORARY

CROSS-CULTURAL

69

The State of the World's Natural Environment

Lester R. Brown

For a decade, the Worldwatch Institute has issued annual reports on the state of the world's natural environment. Their data point to a steady deterioration of the world's natural environment. This troubling trend, they explain, is not simply a technical problem; rather, it results from the ways in which we organize our lives and how we view the planet that supports our existence.

In early 1992, the U.S. National Academy of Sciences and the Royal Society of London issued a report that began: "If current predictions of population growth prove accurate and patterns of human activity on the planet remain unchanged, science and technology may not be able to prevent either irreversible degradation of the environment or continued poverty for much of the world."

It was a remarkable statement, an admission that science and technology can no longer ensure a better future unless population growth slows quickly and the economy is restructured. This abandonment of the technological optimism that has permeated so much of the twentieth century by two of the world's leading scientific bodies represents a major shift, but perhaps not a surprising one given the deteriorating state of the planet. That they chose to issue a joint statement, their first ever, reflects the deepening concern about the future among scientists.

This concern is not limited to the scientific community. People everywhere are worried about the planet's continuing deterioration. Attendance at the U.N. Conference on Environment and Development and the parallel nongovernmental events in June in Rio de Janeiro totalled 35,000 people, dwarfing the turnout at the predecessor meetings in Stockholm in 1972. Some 106 heads of state and government participated in the Earth Summit, the largest gathering of national political leaders in history. The 9,000 journalists in Rio for the meetings exceeded the number of total participants in Stockholm.

Despite the intensifying global interest in the planet's future, the U.N. conference fell short of both hopes and expectations. Many of the difficulties centered on the U.S. insistence that goals and timetables for restricting carbon emissions be removed from the climate treaty, leaving it little more than a statement of good intentions. The

---

Source: "A New Era Unfolds" by Lester R. Brown, in *State of the World 1993: A Worldwatch Institute Report on Progress toward a Sustainable Society,* edited by Lester R. Brown et al.

convention designed to protect biological diversity had some flaws, but perhaps the most serious one was the missing U.S. signature.

The Earth Summit was not a total loss by any means. The climate treaty, which was signed by 154 participating countries, including the United States, recognizes that global warming is a serious issue. And it does provide for setting up an international system for governments to report each year on changes in carbon emissions. This information flow itself will focus attention on the threat of climate change. . . .

[T]he broad indicators showed a continuing wholesale deterioration in the earth's physical condition. During the twenty years since Stockholm, farmers have lost nearly 500 billion tons of topsoil through erosion at a time when they were called on to feed 1.6 billion additional people. Atmospheric concentrations of carbon dioxide (CO_2), the principal greenhouse gas, climbed 9 percent. In Rio, the risks to life on earth posed by the loss of stratospheric ozone and the associated increase of ultraviolet radiation were on everyone's mind; a threat not even imagined in 1972.

The environmental concerns that brought delegates to Rio exist in part because of an economic accounting system that misleads and a biological accounting system that is largely nonexistent. The internationally accepted system of national economic accounting used to calculate gross national product (GNP) rightly subtracts the depreciation of plant and equipment from the overall output of goods and services. But it takes no account of the depreciation of natural capital, such as the loss of topsoil from erosion, the destruction of forests by acid rain, or the depletion of the protective stratospheric ozone layer. As a result, the economic accounting system now used by governments greatly overstates progress. Failing to reflect reality, it generates environmentally destructive economic policies.

The biological accounting system is fragmentary at best. No one knows how many species of plants and animals are lost each year; indeed, lacking a global inventory of the earth's biological resources, no one even knows how many species there are. Visual evidence, occasional national surveys, and satellite data tell us that forests are disappearing in many countries. Similarly, incomplete data indicate that grasslands are deteriorating. Closely associated with the reduced grass and tree cover is the loss of topsoil. Despite the essential economic role of soil, no global data gathering system measures its gains or losses.

Nor does the biological accounting system warn when carrying capacity thresholds are crossed. We learn that cattle numbers are excessive only when the rangeland begins to deteriorate. We discover that demands on forests are excessive only when they begin to disappear. We find that we have been overfishing only when the catch drops precipitously. Lacking information on sustainable yields, governments have permitted demands on these natural systems to become excessive, leading to their gradual destruction.

The result of this flawed economic accounting system and largely nonexistent biological accounting system is widespread degradation and destruction of the economy's environmental support systems. Industrial firms are allowed to internalize profits while externalizing costs, passing on to society such expenses as those for health care associated with polluted air or those arising from global warming.

An expanding economy based on such an incomplete accounting system would be expected to slowly undermine itself, eventually collapsing as support systems are destroyed. And that is just what is happening. The environmentally destructive activities of recent decades are now showing up in reduced productivity of croplands, forests, grasslands, and fisheries; in the mounting cleanup costs of toxic waste sites; in rising health care costs for cancer, birth defects, allergies, emphysema, asthma, and other respiratory diseases; and in the spread of hunger.

Rapid population growth, environmental degradation, and deepening poverty are reinforcing each other in a downward spiral in many countries. In its *World Development Report 1992,* the World Bank reported that per capita GNP had fallen in forty-nine countries during the eighties. Almost all these nations, containing 846 million people, are low-income, largely agrarian economies experiencing rapid population growth and extensive degradation of their forests, grasslands, and croplands.

As the Royal Society/National Academy statement implies, it may not be possible to reverse this fall in living standards of nearly one sixth of humanity if rapid population growth continues and existing patterns of economic activity are not changed. Just how difficult it will be is only now becoming clear. There is also a real risk that the demographic pressures and environmental deterioration that are replacing progress with decline will spread, enveloping even more of humanity during the nineties.

ENVIRONMENTAL DEGRADATION: THE ECONOMIC COSTS

Many people have long understood, at least intuitively, that continuing environmental degradation would eventually exact a heavy economic toll. Unfortunately, no global economic models incorporate the depletion and destruction of the earth's natural support systems. Only now can we begin to piece together information from several recent independent studies to get a sense of the worldwide economic effects of environmental degradation. Among the most revealing of these are studies on the effects of air pollution and acid rain on forests in Europe, of land degradation on livestock and crop production in the world's dryland regions, of global warming on the U.S. economy, and of pollution on health in Russia.

These reports and other data show that the fivefold growth in the world economy since 1950 and the increase in population from 2.6 billion to 5.5 billion have begun to outstrip the carrying capacity of biological support systems and the ability of natural systems to absorb waste without being damaged. In country after country, demands for crops and for the products of grasslands, forests, and fisheries are exceeding the sustainable yield of these systems. Once this happens, the resource itself begins to shrink as natural capital is consumed. Overstocking grasslands, overcutting forests, overplowing, and overfishing are now commonplace. Every country is practicing the environmental equivalent of deficit financing in one form or another.

Perhaps the most visible environmental deficit is deforestation, the result of tree cutting and forest clearing that exceeds natural regrowth and tree planting. Each year this imbalance now costs the world some 17 million hectares of tropical forests alone. Over a decade, the destruction of tropical forests clears an area the size of Malaysia, the Philippines, Ghana, the Congo, Ecuador, El Salvador, and Nicaragua. Once tropical forests are burned off or clear-cut, the land rapidly loses its fertility, since most of the nutrients in these ecosystems are stored in the vegetation. Although these soils can be farmed for three to five years before fertility drops and can be grazed for five to ten years before becoming wasteland, they typically will not sustain productivity over the long term. Clearing tropical forests is, in effect, the conversion of a highly productive ecosystem into wasteland in exchange for a short-term economic gain.

As timber resources are depleted in the Third World, transforming countries that traditionally exported forest products into importers, logging companies are turning to remote temperate-zone forests. Canada, for example, is now losing 200,000 hectares a year as cutting exceeds regeneration by a wide margin. Similarly, as Japanese and Korean logging firms move into Siberia, the forests there are also beginning to shrink.

It is not only the axe and the chainsaw that threaten forests, but also emissions from power plant smokestacks and automobile exhaust pipes. In Europe, air pollution and acid rain are damaging and destroying the region's traditionally well managed forests. Scientists at the

International Institute for Applied Systems Analysis (IIASA) in Austria have estimated the effect on forest productivity of sulfur dioxide emissions from fossil-fuel-burning power plants, factories, and automobiles. They concluded that 75 percent of Europe's forests are now experiencing damaging levels of sulfur deposition. Forests in every country on the continent are affected—from Norway and Portugal in the west to the European part of the former Soviet Union in the east.

The IIASA study estimated that losses associated with the deterioration of Europe's forests total $30.4 billion each year, roughly equal to the annual output of the German steel industry. . . .

Land degradation is also taking a heavy economic toll, particularly in the drylands that account for 41 percent of the earth's land area. In the early stages the costs show up as lower land productivity. But if the process continues unarrested, it eventually creates wasteland, destroying the soil as well as the vegetation. Using data for 1990, a U.N. assessment of the earth's dryland regions estimated that the degradation of irrigated cropland, rainfed cropland, and rangeland now costs the world more than $42 billion a year in lost crop and livestock output, a sum that approximates the value of the U.S. grain harvest. . . .

Excessive demand directly threatens the productivity of oceanic fisheries as well. The U.N. Food and Agriculture Organization (FAO), which monitors oceanic fisheries, indicates that four out of seventeen of the world's fishing zones are now overfished. It also reports that most traditional marine fish stocks have reached full exploitation. Atlantic stocks of the heavily fished bluefin tuna have been cut by a staggering 94 percent. It will take years for such species to recover, even if fishing were to stop altogether.

Dwindling fish stocks are affecting many national economies. In Canada, for example—where the fishing industry traditionally landed roughly 1.5 million tons of fish a year, worth $3.1 billion—depletion of the cod and haddock fisheries off the coast of Nova Scotia has led to shrinking catches and heavy layoffs in the fishing and fish processing industries. In July 1992, in an unprecedented step, Canada banned all cod fishing off the coast of Newfoundland and Labrador for two years in a bid to save the fishery. To cushion the massive layoffs in the industry, the mainstay of Newfoundland's economy, Ottawa authorized a $400-million aid package for unemployment compensation and retraining.

As overfishing of the North Atlantic by U.S., Canadian, and European fleets decimated stocks there during the seventies, the ships turned to the South Atlantic, particularly to the fisheries off the African coast. Unable to control fishing in the 200-mile Exclusive Economic Zones granted by the 1979 Law of the Sea Treaty, some African countries saw their fisheries decimated. Namibia, for instance, watched the catch in its zone fall from nearly 2 million tons in 1980 to less than 100,000 tons a decade later. After banning European ships from its waters in 1990, stocks started to recover.

Inland fisheries are also suffering from environmental mismanagement—water diversion, acidification, and pollution. The Aral Sea, located between Kazakstan and Uzbekistan, as recently as 1960 yielded 40 million kilograms of fish per year. Shrinking steadily over the last three decades as the river water feeding it was diverted for irrigation, the sea has become increasingly salty, eventually destroying the fish stock. Today it is effectively dead. A similar situation exists in Pakistan, where Deg Nullah, a small but once highly productive freshwater lake that yielded 400,000 kilograms of fish annually, is now barren—destroyed by pollution. Acidification is also taking a toll. Canada alone now counts 14,000 dead lakes.

In the United States, pollution has severely affected the Chesapeake Bay, one of the world's richest estuaries. Its fabulously productive oyster beds, which yielded 8 million bushels per year a century ago, now produce scarcely a million bushels. Elsewhere, fish have survived, such as in the U.S. Great Lakes and New York's Hudson River, but many species are unsafe for human consumption because of pollution with PCBs and other toxic chemicals. Half the shellfish-growing areas off Nova Scotia in eastern Canada have been closed because of contamination.

The rising atmospheric concentration of greenhouse gases is potentially the most economically disruptive and costly change that has been set in motion by our modern industrial society. William Cline, an economist with the Washington-based Institute for International Economics, has looked at the long-term economic effects of global warming. As part of this study he analyzed the effect of a doubling of greenhouse gases on the U.S. economy, which could come as early as 2025. He estimates that heat, stress and drought would cost U.S. farmers $18 billion in output, that increased electricity for air conditioning would require an additional $11 billion, and that dealing with sea level rise would cost an estimated $7 billion per year. In total, Cline estimates the cost at nearly $60 billion, roughly 1 percent of the 1990 U.S. GNP. . . .

Not all countries would be affected equally. Some island countries, such as the Republic of the Maldives in the Indian Ocean, would become uninhabitable. Low-lying deltas, such as in Egypt and Bangladesh, would be inundated, displacing millions of people. In the end, rising seas in a warming world would be not only economically costly, but politically disruptive as well.

Every society is paying a price for environmental pollution. Contamination of air, water, and soil by toxic chemicals and radioactivity, along with increased ultraviolet radiation, is damaging human health, running up health care costs. An assessment of urban air quality jointly undertaken by the World Health Organization and the United Nations Environment Programme reports that 625 million people are exposed to unhealthy levels of sulfur dioxide from fossil fuel burning. More than a billion people, a fifth of the planet's population, are exposed to potentially health-damaging levels of air pollutants of all kinds. One study for the United States estimates that air pollution may cost the nation as much as $40 billion annually in health care and lost productivity.

In Bulgaria, research that was declassified following democratization showed that those living near heavy industrial complexes had asthma rates nine times higher than people living elsewhere. Skin diseases occurred seven times as often. Liver disease was four times as frequent, and nervous system diseases three times as high.

New data from Russia, Europe's largest country, show all too well the devastating effect of pollution by chemical and organic toxins on human health. At an October 1992 news conference, Vladimir Pokrovsky, head of the Russian Academy of Medical Sciences, shocked the world with his frankness, "We have already doomed ourselves for the next twenty-five years." He added: "The new generation is entering adult life unhealthy. The Soviet economy was developed at the expense of the population's health." Data released by the Academy show 11 percent of Russian infants suffering from birth defects. With half the drinking water and a tenth of the food supply contaminated, 55 percent of school-age children suffer health problems. The Academy reported that the increase in illness and early death among those aged twenty-five to forty was particularly distressing. The bottom line is that Russian life expectancy is now falling.

Another source of higher future health care costs is stratospheric ozone depletion. Epidemiologists at the U.S. Environmental Protection Agency (EPA) estimate that the upward revision in early 1991 of the rate of ozone loss could mean an additional 200,000 skin cancer fatalities in the United States over the next five decades. Worldwide, this translates into millions of deaths. The number of people with cataracts would also increase dramatically in a world where people are exposed to greater doses of ultraviolet radiation than ever recorded. Other associated health care costs include a projected higher incidence of infectious diseases associated with the suppression of immune systems, the economic costs of which are difficult to even estimate.

In addition to the environmental deficits the world is now experiencing, huge environmental cleanup bills are accumulating. For example, the estimated costs for cleaning up hazardous waste sites in the United States center on $750 billion, roughly three fourths the 1990 U.S. federal budget. And a national survey in Norway has discovered some 7,000 hazardous waste sites, the product of decades of irresponsible dumping. Cleanup is estimated to cost tiny Norway $3–6 billion.

There is no reason to believe that these bills for the United States and Norway are very different from those of other industrial countries. In a world generating more than a million tons of hazardous waste a day, much of it carelessly disposed of, the costs of cleanup are enormous. The alternative to cleaning up these sites is to ignore them and let toxic wastes eventually leak into underground aquifers. One way or another, society will pay—either in cleanup bills or in rising health care costs.

In addition to toxic chemical wastes, damaging nuclear waste is also a threat to human health. National governments in countries with nuclear power plants have failed to design a system for safely disposing of their wastes. At present, radiated fuel at most plants is stored in pools of cooling water at the site itself. No one has yet put a price tag on safely disposing of nuclear waste and decommissioning the nuclear power plants that generate it. Coping with the health problems associated with nuclear waste is, being left to future generations, a part of the nuclear legacy.

Several military powers face the related threat of radiation wastes generated at nuclear weapons manufacturing facilities, which are released into the surrounding areas. In the United States, the cleanup bill for all these sites, including some of the more publicized ones such as Rocky Flats in Colorado and the Savannah River site in South Carolina, is estimated at $200 billion. For the former Soviet Union, where the management of radioactive waste has been even more irresponsible, the costs are likely to be far greater. Again, the question is not whether society will pay the bill for nuclear wastes, but whether it will be in the form of cleanup or in rising health care costs in exposed communities.

The environmental deficits and debts that the world has incurred in recent decades are enormous, often dwarfing the economic debts of nations. Perhaps more important is the often overlooked difference between economic deficits and environmental ones. Economic debts are something we owe each other. For every borrower there is a lender; resources simply change hands. But environmental debts, especially those that lead to irreversible damage or losses of natural capital, can often be repaid only in the deprivation and ill health of future generations.

CRITICAL-THINKING QUESTIONS

1. In what ways are the world's environmental problems social issues?
2. Do you think global gatherings—like the United Nations Conference on Environment and Development held in Rio de Janeiro in 1992—can turn the tide of environmental deterioration?
3. Why do you think the author of this selection stresses the economic costs of environmental problems?

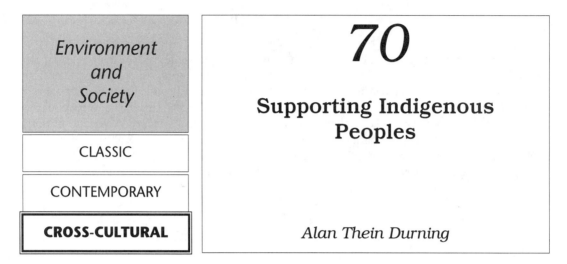

Environment and Society

CLASSIC

CONTEMPORARY

CROSS-CULTURAL

70

Supporting Indigenous Peoples

Alan Thein Durning

A particular concern of many environmentalists (and social scientists) is the steady loss of this planet's cultural diversity as thousands of small societies are pushed aside by the relentless march of economic development. This selection describes the problem and points out that protecting indigenous peoples is not just a matter of justice—the well-being of everyone in the world depends on it.

In July of 1992, an aged chief of the Lumad people in the Philippines—a man with a price on his head for his opposition to local energy development—sat at the base of the cloud-covered volcano Mount Apo and made a simple plea.

"Our Christian brothers are enjoying their life here in the plains," said eighty-six-year-old Chief Tulalang Maway, sweeping his arm toward the provincial town of Kidapawan and the agricultural lands beyond, lands his tribe long ago ceded to immigrants from afar. Turning toward the mountain—a Lumad sacred site that he has vowed to defend "to the last drop of blood"—Maway slowly finished his thought, "We only ask them to leave us our last sanctuary."

Chief Maway's words could have been spoken by almost any tribal Filipino, or, for that matter, any Native American, Australian aborigine, African pygmy, or member of one of the world's thousands of other distinct indigenous cultures. All have ancient ties to the land, water, and wildlife of their ancestral domains, and all are endangered by onrushing forces of the outside world. They have been decimated by violence and plagues. Their cultures have been eroded by missionaries and exploited by wily entrepreneurs. Their subsistence economies have been dismantled in the pursuit of national development. And their homelands have been invaded by commercial resource extractors and overrun by landless peasants.

Chief Maway's entreaty, in its essence, is the call of indigenous peoples everywhere: the plea that their lands be spared further abuse, that their birthright be returned to them. It is a petition that the world's dominant cultures have long ignored, believing the passing of native peoples and their antiquated ways was an inevitable, if lamentable, cost of progress. That view, never morally defensible, is now demonstrably untenable.

Source: "Supporting Indigenous Peoples," by Alan Thein Durning, in *State of the World 1993: A Worldwatch Institute Report on Progress Toward a Sustainable Society,* edited by Lester R. Brown et al.

Indigenous peoples are the sole guardians of vast, little-disturbed habitats in remote parts of every continent. These territories, which together encompass an area larger than Australia, provide important ecological services: They regulate hydrological cycles, maintain local and global climatic stability, and harbor a wealth of biological and genetic diversity. Indeed, indigenous homelands may provide safe haven for more endangered plant and animal species than all the world's nature reserves. Native peoples, moreover, often hold the key to these vaults of biological diversity. They possess a body of ecological knowledge—encoded in their languages, customs, and subsistence practices—that rivals the libraries of modern science.

The human rights enshrined in international law have long demanded that states shield indigenous cultures, but instead these cultures have been dismembered. A more self-interested appeal appears to be in order: Supporting indigenous survival is an objective necessity, even for those callous to the justice of the cause. As a practical matter, the world's dominant cultures cannot sustain the earth's ecological health—a requisite of human advancement—without the aid of the world's endangered cultures. Biological diversity is inextricably linked to cultural diversity.

Around the globe, indigenous peoples are fighting for their ancestral territories. They are struggling in courts and national parliaments, gaining power through new mass movements and international campaigns, and—as on the slopes of Mount Apo—defending their inheritance with their lives. The question is, Who will stand with them?

STATE OF THE NATIONS

Indigenous peoples (or "native" or "tribal" peoples) are found on every continent and in most countries. [See Table 1] The extreme variations in their ways of life and current circumstances defy ready definition. Indeed, many anthropologists insist that indigenous peoples are defined only by the way they define themselves: They think of themselves as members of a distinct people. Still, many indigenous cultures share a number of characteristics that help describe, if not define, them.

They are typically descendants of the original inhabitants of an area taken over by more powerful outsiders. They are distinct from their country's dominant group in language, culture, or religion. Most have a custodial concept of land and other resources, in part defining themselves in relation to the habitat from which they draw their livelihood. They commonly live in or maintain strong ties to a subsistence economy; many are, or are descendants of, hunter-gatherers, fishers, nomadic or seasonal herders, shifting forest farmers, or subsistence peasant cultivators. And their social relations are often tribal, involving collective management of natural resources, thick networks of bonds between individuals, and group decision making, often by consensus among elders.

Measured by spoken languages, the single best indicator of a distinct culture, all the world's people belong to 6,000 cultures; 4,000–5,000 of these are indigenous ones. Of the 5.5 billion humans on the planet, some 190 million to 625 million are indigenous people. (These ranges are wide because of varying definitions of "indigenous." The higher figures include ethnic nations that lack political autonomy, such as Tibetans, Kurds, and Zulus, while the lower figures count only smaller, subnational societies.) In some countries, especially those settled by Europeans in the past five centuries, indigenous populations are fairly easy to count. [See Table 2] By contrast, lines between indigenous peoples and ethnic minorities are difficult to draw in Asia and Africa, where cultural diversity remains greatest.

Regardless of where lines are drawn, however, human cultures are disappearing at unprecedented rates. Worldwide, the loss of cultural diversity is keeping pace with the global loss of

TABLE 1 Indigenous Peoples of the World, 1992

Region	*Indigenous Peoples*
Africa and Middle East	Great cultural diversity throughout continent; "indigenous" share hotly contested lands. Some 25–30 million nomadic herders or pastoralists in East Africa, Sahel, and Arabian peninsula include Bedouin, Dinka, Masai, Turkana. San (Bushmen) of Namibia and Botswana and pygmies of central African rain forest, both traditionally hunter-gatherers, have occupied present home lands for at least 20,000 years. (25–350 million indigenous people overall, depending on definitions; 2,000 languages)
Americas	Native Americans concentrated near centers of ancient civilizations: Aztec in Mexico, Mayan in Central America, and Incan in Andes of Bolivia, Ecuador, and Peru. In Latin America, most Indians farm small plots; in North America, 2 million Indians live in cities and on reservations.(42 million; 900 languages)
Arctic	Inuit (Eskimo) and other Arctic peoples of North America, Greenland, and Siberia traditionally fishers, whalers, and hunters. Sami (Lapp) of northern Scandinavia are traditionally reindeer herders. (2 million; 50 languages)
East Asia	Chinese indigenous peoples, numbering up to 82 million, mostly subsistence farmers such as Bulang of south China or former pastoralists such as ethnic Mongolians of north and west China. Ainu of Japan and aboriginal Taiwanese now largely industrial laborers. (12–84 million; 150 languages)
Oceania	Aborigines of Australia and Maoris of New Zealand, traditionally farmers, fishers, hunters, and gatherers. Many now raise livestock. Islanders of South Pacific continue to fish and harvest marine resources. (3 million; 500 languages)
South Asia	Gond, Bhil, and other adivasis, or tribal peoples, inhabit forest belt of central India. In Bangladesh, adivasis concentrated in Chittagong hills on Burmese border, several million tribal farmers and pastoralists in Afghanistan, Pakistan, Nepal, Iran, and central Asian republics of former Soviet Union. (74–91 million; 700 languages)
Southeast Asia	Tribal Hmong, Karen, and other forest-farming peoples form Asia ethnic mosaic covering up lands. Indigenous population follows distribution of forest: Laos has more forest and tribal peoples, Myanmar and Vietnam have less forest and fewer people, and Thailand and mainland Malaysia have the least. Tribal peoples are concentrated at the extreme ends of the Philippine and Indonesian archipelagos. Island of New Guinea—split politically between Indonesia and Papua New Guinea—populated by indigenous tribes. (32–55 million; 1,950 languages)

Source: Worldwatch Institute.

biological diversity. Anthropologist Jason Clay of Cultural Survival in Cambridge, Massachusetts, writes, "there have been more . . . extinctions of tribal peoples in this century than in any other in history." Brazil alone lost eighty-seven tribes in the first half of the century. One-third of North American languages and two-thirds of Australian languages have disappeared since 1800—the overwhelming share of them since 1900.

Cultures are dying out even faster than the peoples who belong to them. University of Alaska linguist Michael Krauss projects that half the world's languages—the storehouses of peoples' intellectual heritages—will disappear within a century. These languages, and arguably the cultures they embody, are no longer passed on to sufficient numbers of children to ensure their survival. Krauss likens such cultures to animal species doomed to extinction because their populations are below the threshold needed for adequate reproduction. Only 5 percent of all languages, moreover, enjoy the relative safety of having at least a half-million speakers.

To trace the history of indigenous peoples' subjugation is simply to recast the story of the rise of the world's dominant cultures: the spread of Han Chinese into Central and Southeast Asia, the ascent of Aryan empires on the Indian subcontinent, the southward advance of Bantu cultures across Africa, and the creation of a world economy first through European colonialism and then through industrial development. Surviving indigenous cultures are often but tattered remnants of their predecessors' societies.

TABLE 2 Estimated Populations of Indigenous Peoples, Selected Countries, 1992

Country	*Population*[a]	*Share of National Population*
	(million)	(percent)
Papua New Guinea	3.0	77
Bolivia	5.6	70
Guatemala	4.6	47
Peru	9.0	40
Ecuador	3.8	38
Myanmar	14.0	33
Laos	1.3	30
Mexico	10.9	12
New Zealand	0.4	12
Chile	1.2	9
Philippines	6.0	9
India	63.0	7
Malaysia	0.8	4
Canada	0.9	4
Australia	0.4	2
Brazil	1.5	1
Bangladesh	1.2	1
Thailand	0.5	1
United States	2.0	1
Former Soviet Union	1.4	>1

[a] Generally excludes those of mixed ancestry.
Source: Worldwatch Institute

When Christopher Columbus reached the New World in 1492, there were perhaps 54 million people in the Americas, almost as many as in Europe at the time; their numbers plummeted, however, as plagues radiated from the landfalls of the conquistadors. Five centuries later, the indigenous peoples of the Americas, numbering some 42 million, have yet to match their earlier population. Similar contractions followed the arrival of Europeans in Australia, New Zealand, and Siberia.

Worldwide, virtually no indigenous peoples remain entirely isolated from national societies. By indoctrination or brute force, nations have assimilated native groups into the cultural mainstream. As a consequence, few follow the ways of their ancestors unchanged. Just one tenth of the Penan hunter-gatherers continue to hunt in the rain forests of Malaysian Borneo. A similar share of the Sami (Lapp) reindeer-herders of northern Scandinavia accompany their herds on the Arctic ranges. Half of North American Indians and many New Zealand Maori dwell in cities.

Tragically, indigenous peoples whose cultures are besieged frequently end up on the bottom of the national economy. They are often the first sent to war for the state, as in Namibia and the Philippines, and the last to go to work: Unemployment in Canadian Indian communities averages 50 percent. They are overrepresented among migrant laborers in India, beggars in Mexico, and uranium miners in the United States. They are often drawn into the shadow economy: They grow drug crops in northern Thailand, run gambling casinos in the United States, and sell their daughters into prostitution in Taiwan. Everywhere, racism against them is rampant. India's adivasis, or tribal people, endure hardships comparable to the "untouchables," the most downtrodden caste.

Native peoples' inferior social status is sometimes codified in national law and perpetuated by institutionalized abuse. Many members of the hill tribes in Thailand are denied citizenship, and until 1988 the Brazilian constitution legally classified Indians as minors and wards of the state. In the extreme, nation-states are simply genocidal: Burmese soldiers systemically raped, murdered, and enslaved thousands of Arakanese villagers in early 1992. Guatemala has exterminated perhaps 100,000 Mayans in its three-decade counterinsurgency. Similar numbers of indigenous people have died in East Timor and Irian Jaya since 1970 at the hands of Indonesian forces intent on solidifying their power.

In much of the world, the oppression that indigenous peoples suffer has indelibly marked their own psyches, manifesting itself in depression and social disintegration. Says Tamara Gliminova of the Khant people of Siberia, "When they spit into your soul for this long, there is little left."

HOMELANDS

Indigenous peoples not yet engulfed in modern societies live mostly in what Mexican anthropologist Gonzalo Aguirre Beltran called "regions of refuge," places so rugged, desolate, or remote that they have been little disturbed by the industrial economy. They remain in these areas for tragic reasons. Peoples in more fertile lands were eradicated outright to make way for settlers and plantations, or they retreated—sometimes at gun point—into these natural havens. Whereas indigenous peoples exercised de facto control over most of the earth's ecosystems as recently as two centuries ago, the territory they now occupy is reduced to an estimated 12–19 percent of the earth's land area—depending, again, on where the line between indigenous peoples and ethnic nations is drawn. And governments recognize their ownership of but a fraction of that area.

Gaining legal protection for the remainder of their subsistence base is most indigenous peoples' highest political priority. If they lose this struggle, their cultures stand little chance of surviving. As the World Council of Indigenous Peoples, a global federation based in Canada, wrote in 1985, "Next to shooting Indigenous Peoples, the surest way to kill us is to separate us from our part of the Earth." Most native peoples are bound to their land through relationships both practical and spiritual, routine and historical. Tribal Filipino Edtami Mansayagan, attempting to communicate the pain he feels at the destruction of the rivers, valleys, meadows, and hillsides of his people's mountain domain, exclaims, "these are the living pages of our unwritten history." The question of who shall control resources in the regions of refuge is the crux of indigenous survival.

Indigenous homelands are important not only to endangered cultures; they are also of exceptional ecological value. Intact indigenous communities and little-disturbed ecosystems overlap with singular regularity, from the coastal swamps of South America to the shifting sands of the Sahara, from the ice floes of the circumpolar north to the coral reefs of the South Pacific. When, for example, a National Geographic Society team in Washington, D.C., compiled a map of Indian lands and remaining forest cover in Central America in 1992, they confirmed the personal observation of Geodisio Castillo, a Kuna Indian from Panama: "Where there are forests there are indigenous people, and where there are indigenous people there are forests."

Because populations of both indigenous peoples and unique plant and animal species are numerically concentrated in remnant habitats in the tropics—precisely the regions of refuge that Beltran was referring to—the biosphere's most diverse habitats are usually homes to endangered cultures. The persistence of biological diversity in these regions is no accident. In the Philippines and Thailand, both representative cases, little more than a third of the land officially zoned as forest remains forest-covered; the tracts that do still stand are largely those protected by tribal people.

The relationship between cultural diversity and biological diversity stands out even in global statistics. Just nine countries together account for 60 percent of human languages. Of these nine centers of cultural diversity, six are also on the roster of biological "megadiversity" countries—nations with exceptional numbers of unique plant and animal species. . . . By the same token, two-thirds of all megadiversity countries also rank at the top of the cultural diversity league, with more than 100 languages spoken in each.

Everywhere, the world economy now intrudes on what is left of native lands, as it has for centuries. Writes World Bank anthropologist Shelton Davis: "The creation of a . . . global economy . . . has meant the pillage of native peoples' lands, labor and resources and their enforced acculturation and spiritual conquest. Each cycle of global economic expansion—the search for gold and spices in the sixteenth century, the fur trade and sugar estate economics of the seventeenth and eighteenth centuries, the rise of the great coffee, copra and . . . tropical fruit plantations in the late nineteenth and early twentieth centuries, the modern search for petroleum, strategic minerals, and tropical hardwoods—was based upon the exploitation of natural resources or primary commodities and led to the displacement of indigenous peoples and the undermining of traditional cultures."

The juggernaut of the money economy has not slowed in the late twentieth century; if anything, it has accelerated. Soaring consumer demand among the world's fortunate and burgeoning populations among the unfortunate fuel the economy's drive into native peoples' territories. Loggers, miners, commercial fishers, small farmers, plantation growers, dam builders, oil drillers—all come to seek their fortunes. Governments that equate progress with export earnings aid them, and military establishments bent on controlling far-flung territories back them.

Logging, in particular, is a menace because so many indigenous peoples dwell in woodlands. Japanese builders, for example, are devouring the ancient hardwood forests of tropical Borneo, home of the Penan and other Dayak peoples for disposable concrete molds. Most mahogany exported from Latin America is now logged illegally on Indian reserves and most nonplantation teak cut in Asia currently comes from tribal lands in the war-torn hills of Myanmar.

The consequences of mining on native lands are also ruinous. In the late eighties, for instance, tens of thousands of gold prospectors infiltrated the remote northern Brazilian haven of the Yanomami, the last large, isolated group of indigenous peoples in the Americas. The miners turned streams into sewers, contaminated the environment with the 1,000 tons of toxic mercury they used to purify gold, and precipitated an epidemic of malaria that killed more than a thousand children and elders. Just in time, the Brazilian government recognized and began defending the Yanomami homeland in early 1992, a rare and hopeful precedent in the annals of indigenous history. Still, in Brazil overall, mining concessions overlap 34 percent of Indian lands. . . .

Other energy projects, especially large dams, also take their toll on native habitats. In the north of Canada, the provincial electric utility Hydro Quebec completed a massive project called James Bay I in 1985, inundating vast areas of Cree Indian hunting grounds and unexpectedly contaminating fisheries with naturally occurring heavy metals that had previously been locked away in the soil. The Cree and neighboring Inuit tribes have organized against the project's next gigantic phase, James Bay II. The $60-billion project would tame eleven wild rivers, altering a France-sized area to generate 27,000 megawatts of exportable power. As Matthew Coon-Come, Grand Chief of the Cree, says, "The only people who have the right to build dams on our territory are the beavers.". . .

Commercial producers have also taken over indigenous lands for large-scale agriculture. The Barabaig herders of Tanzania have lost more than 400 square kilometers of dry-season range to a mechanized wheat farm. Private ranchers in Botswana have enclosed grazing lands for their own use, and Australian ranchers have usurped aboriginal lands. In peninsular Malaysia, palm and rubber plantations have left the Orang Asli (Original People) with tiny fractions of their ancient tropical forests.

Less dramatic but more pervasive is the ubiquitous invasion of small farmers onto indigenous lands. Sometimes sponsored by the state but ultimately driven by population growth and maldistribution of farmland, poor settlers encroach on native lands everywhere. In Indonesia during the eighties, for example, the government shifted 2 million people from densely populated islands such as Java to 800,000 hectares of newly cleared plots in sparsely populated indigenous provinces such as Irian Jaya, Kalimantan, and Sumatra. Half the area settled was virgin forest—much of it indigenous territory. . . .

Few states recognize indigenous peoples' rights over homelands, and where they do, those rights are often partial, qualified, or of ambiguous legal force. Countries may recognize customary rights in theory, but enforce common or statutory law against those rights whenever there is a conflict; or they may sanction indigenous rights but refuse to enforce them. Through this cloud of legal contradictions a few countries stand out as exceptional. Papua New Guinea and Ecuador acknowledge indigenous title to large shares of national territory, and Canada and Australia recognize rights over extensive areas. . . . Still, across all the earth's climatic and ecological zones—from the Arctic tundra to the temperate and nontropical forests to the savannahs and deserts—native peoples control slim shares of their ancestral domains. . . .

STEWARDS

Sustainable use of local resources is simple self-preservation for people whose way of life is tied to the fertility and natural abundance of the land. Any community that knows its children and grandchildren will live exactly where it does is more apt to take a longer view than a community without attachments to local places.

Moreover, native peoples frequently aim to preserve not just a standard of living but a way of life rooted in the uniqueness of a local place. Colombian anthropologist Martin von Hildebrand notes, "The Indians often tell me that the difference between a colonist [a non-Indian settler] and an Indian is that the colonist wants to leave money for his children and that the Indians want to leave forests for their children."

Indigenous peoples' unmediated dependence on natural abundance has its parallel in their peerless ecological knowledge. Most forest-dwelling tribes display an utter mastery of botany. One typical group, the Shuar people of Ecuador's Amazonian lowlands, uses 800 species of plants for medicine, food, animal fodder, fuel, construction, fishing, and hunting supplies.

Native peoples commonly know as much about ecological processes that affect the availability of natural resources as they do about those resources' diverse uses. South Pacific islanders can predict to the day and hour the beginning of the annual spawning runs of many fish. Whaling peoples of northern Canada have proved to skeptical western marine biologists that bowhead whales migrate under pack ice. Coastal aborigines in Australia distinguish between eighty different tidal conditions.

Specialists trained in western science often fail to recognize indigenous ecological knowledge because of the cultural and religious ways in which indigenous peoples record and transmit that learning. Ways of life that developed over scores of generations could only thrive by encoding ecological sustainability into the body of practice, myth, and taboo that passes from parent to child. . . .

What are the conditions in which traditional systems of ecological management can persist in the modern world? First, indigenous peoples must have secure rights to their subsistence base—rights that are not only recognized but enforced by the state and, ideally, backed by international law. Latin American tribes such as the Shuar of Ecuador, when threatened with losing their land, have cleared their own forests and taken up cattle ranching, because these actions prove ownership in Latin America. Had Ecuador backed up the Shuar's land rights, the ranching would have been unnecessary.

Second, for indigenous ecological stewardship to survive the onslaught of the outside world, indigenous peoples must be organized politically and the state in which they reside must allow democratic initiatives. The Khant and Mansi peoples of Siberia, just as most indigenous people in the former Soviet Union, were nominally autonomous in their customary territories under Soviet law, but political repression precluded the organized defense of that terrain until the end of the eighties. Since then, the peoples of Siberia have begun organizing themselves to turn paper rights into real local control. In neighboring China, in contrast, indigenous homelands remain pure legal fictions because the state crushes all representative organizations.

Third, indigenous communities must have access to information, support, and advice from friendly sources if they are to surmount the obstacles of the outside world. The tribal people of Papua New Guinea know much about their local environments, for example, but they know little about the impacts of large-scale logging and mining. Foreign and domestic investors have often played on this ignorance, assuring remote groups that no lasting harm would result from leasing parts of their land to resource extractors. If the forest peoples of Papua New Guinea could learn from the experience of indigenous peoples elsewhere—through supportive organizations and indigenous peoples' federations—they might be more careful.

A handful of peoples around the world have succeeded in satisfying all three of these conditions. . . .

RISING FROM THE FRONTIER

From the smallest tribal settlements to the U.N. General Assembly, indigenous peoples' organizations are making themselves felt. Their grassroots movements have spread rapidly since 1970, gaining strength in numbers and through improvement of their political skills. They have pooled their talents in regional, national, and global federations to broaden their influence. This uprising, which like any movement has its share of internal rivalries, may eventually bring fundamental advances in the status of all endangered cultures. . . .

In a world where almost all nations have publicly committed themselves to the goal of sustainable development and most have signed a global treaty for the protection of biological diversity, the questions of cultural survival and indigenous homelands cannot be avoided much longer. As guardians and stewards of remote and fragile ecosystems, indigenous cultures could play a crucial role in safeguarding humanity's planetary home. But they cannot do it alone. They need the support of international law and national policy, and they need the understanding and aid of the world's more numerous peoples.

Giving native peoples power over their own lives raises issues for the world's dominant culture as well—a consumerist and individualist culture born in Europe and bred in the United States. Indeed, indigenous peoples may offer more than a best-bet alternative for preserving the outlying areas where they live. They may offer living examples of cultural patterns that can help revive ancient values within everyone: devotion to future generations, ethical regard for nature, and commitment to community among people. The question may be, then, Are indigenous peoples the past, or are they the future?

CRITICAL-THINKING QUESTIONS

1. How many indigenous cultures are there on this planet? What general traits do they have in common?
2. Why are the world's tribal peoples disappearing?
3. The author asserts that sustaining the world's natural environment depends on assuring the future of indigenous peoples. Why is this so?

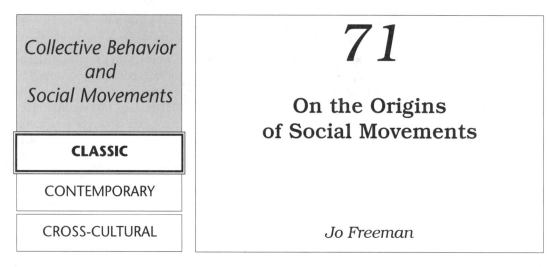

Collective Behavior and Social Movements

CLASSIC

CONTEMPORARY

CROSS-CULTURAL

71

On the Origins of Social Movements

Jo Freeman

According to Jo Freeman, a "spark of life" sometimes transforms a group of like-minded people into a social movement. In this excerpt from her work, Freeman analyzes this process, illustrating her ideas with an account of the civil rights movement and the women's movement in the United States.

Most movements have inconspicuous beginnings. The significant elements of their origins are usually forgotten or distorted by the time a trained observer seeks to trace them out. Perhaps this is why the theoretical literature on social movements usually concentrates on causes (Gurr, 1970; Davies, 1962; Oberschall, 1973) and motivations (Toch, 1965; Cantril, 1941; Hoffer, 1951; Adorno et al., 1950), while the "spark of life" by which the "mass is to cross the threshold of organizational life" (Lowi, 1971:41) has received scant attention. . . .

From where do the people come who make up the initial, organizing cadre of a movement? How do they come together, and how do they come to share a similar view of the world in circumstances that compel them to political action? In what ways does the nature of the original center affect the future development of the movement?

Before answering these questions, let us first look at data on the origins of [two] social movements prominent in the sixties and seventies: civil rights . . . and women's liberation. These data identify recurrent elements involved in movement formation. The ways in which these elements interact, given a sufficient level of strain, would support the following propositions:

***Proposition** 1.* The need for a *preexisting communications network* or infrastructure within the social base of a movement is a primary prerequisite for "spontaneous"

Source: From *Social Movements of the Sixties and Seventies,* ed. Jo Freeman, pp. 8–13, 17–30, copyright © 1983 by Jo Freeman. Reprinted by permission.

activity. Masses alone do not form movements, however discontented they may be. Groups of previously unorganized individuals may spontaneously form into small local associations—usually along the lines of informal social networks—in response to a specific strain or crisis. If they are not linked in some manner, however, the protest does not become generalized but remains a local irritant or dissolves completely. If a movement is to spread rapidly, the communications network must already exist. If only the rudiments of a network exist, movement formation requires a high input of "organizing" activity.

Proposition 2. Not just any communications network will do. It must be a network that is *cooptable* to the new ideas of the incipient movement.[1] To be cooptable, it must be composed of like-minded people whose backgrounds, experiences, or location in the social structure make them receptive to the ideas of a specific new movement.

Proposition 3. Given the existence of a cooptable communications network, or at least the rudimentary development of a potential one, and a situation of strain, one or more precipitants are required. Here, two distinct patterns emerge that often overlap. In one, a *crisis* galvanizes the network into spontaneous action in a new direction. In the other, one or more persons begin *organizing* a new organization or disseminating a new idea. For spontaneous action to occur, the communications network must be well formed or the initial protest will not survive the incipient stage. If it is not well formed, organizing efforts must occur; that is, one or more persons must specifically attempt to construct a movement. To be successful, organizers must be skilled and must have a fertile field in which to work. If no communications network already exists, there must at least be emerging spontaneous groups that are acutely attuned to the issue, albeit uncoordinated. To sum up, if a cooptable communications network is already established, a crisis is all that is necessary to galvanize it. If it is rudimentary, an organizing cadre of one or more persons is necessary. Such a cadre is superfluous if the former conditions fully exist, but it is essential if they do not.

THE CIVIL RIGHTS MOVEMENT

The civil rights movement has two origins, although one contributed significantly to the other. The first can be dated from December 7, 1955, when the arrest of Rosa Parks for occupying a "white" seat on a bus stimulated both the Montgomery Bus Boycott and the formation of the Montgomery Improvement Association. The second can be dated either from February 1, 1960, when four freshmen at A & T College in Greensboro, North Carolina, sat in at a white lunch counter, or from April 15–17, when a conference at Shaw University in Raleigh, North Carolina, resulted in the formation of the Student Non-Violent Co-ordinating Committee. To understand why there were two origins one has to understand the social structure of the southern black community, as an incipient generation gap alone is inadequate to explain it.

Within this community the two most important institutions, often the only institutions, were the church and the black college. They provided the primary networks through which most southern blacks interacted and communicated with one another on a regular basis. In turn, the colleges and churches were linked in a regional communications network. These institutions were also the source of black leadership, for being a "preacher or a teacher" were the main status positions in black society. Of the two, the church was by far the more important; it touched on more people's lives and was the largest and oldest institution in the black community. Even during slavery there had been an "invisible church." After emancipation, "organized religious life became the chief means by which a structured or organized social life came into existence among the Negro masses" (Frazier, 1963:17). Furthermore, preachers were more economically independent of white society than were teachers.

Neither of these institutions represented all the segments of black society, but the segments they did represent eventually formed the main social base for supplying civil rights activists. The church was composed of a male leadership and a largely middle-aged, lower-class female followership. The black colleges were the homes of black intellectuals and middle-class youth, male and female.

Both origins of the civil rights movement resulted in the formation of new organizations, despite the fact that at least three seemingly potential social movement organizations already existed. The wealthiest of these was the Urban League, founded in 1910. It, however, was not only largely restricted to a small portion of the black and white bourgeoisie but, until 1961, felt itself to be "essentially a social service agency" (Clark, 1966:245).

Founded in 1909, the National Association for the Advancement of Colored People (NAACP) pursued channels of legal change until it finally persuaded the Supreme Court to abolish educational segregation in *Brown* v. *Board of Education.* More than any other single event, this decision created the atmosphere of rising expectations that helped precipitate the movement. The NAACP suffered from its own success, however. Having organized itself primarily to support court cases and utilize other "respectable" means, it "either was not able or did not desire to modify its program in response to new demands. It believed it should continue its important work by using those techniques it had already perfected" (Blumer, 1951:199).

The Congress of Racial Equality, like the other two organizations, was founded in the North. It began "in 1942 as the Chicago Committee of Racial Equality, which was composed primarily of students at the University of Chicago. An offshoot of the pacifist Fellowship of Reconciliation, its leaders were middle-class intellectual reformers, less prominent and more alienated from the mainstream of American society than the founders of the NAACP. They regarded the NAACP's legalism as too gradualist and ineffective, and aimed to apply Gandhian techniques of non-violent direct action to the problem of race relations in the United States. A year later, the Chicago Committee joined with a half dozen other groups that had emerged across the country, mostly under the encouragement of the F. O. R. to form a federation known as the Congress of Racial Equality" (Rudwick & Meier, 1970:10).

CORE's activities anticipated many of the main forms of protest of the civil rights movement, and its attitudes certainly seemed to fit CORE for the role of a major civil rights organization. But though it became quite influential, at the time the movement actually began, CORE had declined almost to the point of extinction. Its failure reflects the historical reality that organizations are less likely to create social movements than be created by them. More important, CORE was poorly situated to lead a movement of southern blacks. Northern-based and composed primarily of pacifist intellectuals, it had no roots in any of the existing structures of the black community, and in the North these structures were themselves weak. CORE could be a source of ideas, but not of coordination.

The coordination of a new movement required the creation of a new organization. But that was not apparent until after the Montgomery bus boycott began. That boycott was organized through institutions already existing in the black community of Montgomery.

Rosa Parks's refusal to give up her seat on the bus to a white man was not the first time such defiance of segregation laws had occurred. There had been talk of a boycott the previous time, but after local black leaders had a congenial meeting with the city commissioners, nothing happened—on either side (King, 1958:37–41). When Parks, a former secretary of the local NAACP, was arrested, she immediately called E. D. Nixon, at that time the president of the local chapter. He not only bailed her out but informed a few influential women in the city, most of whom were members of the Women's Political Council. After numerous phone calls between their members, it was the WPC that actually suggested the boycott, and E. D. Nixon who initially organized it (ibid.:44–45).

The Montgomery Improvement Association (MIA) was formed at a meeting of eighteen ministers and civic leaders the Monday after Parks's conviction and a day of successful boycotting, to provide ongoing coordination. No one then suspected that coordination would be necessary for over a year, with car pools organized to provide alternative transportation for seventeen thousand riders a day. During this time the MIA grew slowly to a staff of ten in order to handle the voluminous correspondence, as well as to provide rides and keep the movement's momentum going. The organization, and the car pools, were financed by $250,000 in donations that poured in from all over the world in response to heavy press publicity about the boycott. But the organizational framework for the boycott and the MIA was the church. Most, although not all, of the officers were ministers, and Sunday meetings with congregations continued to be the main means of communicating with members of the black community and encouraging them to continue the protest.

The boycott did not end until the federal courts ruled Alabama's bus segregation laws unconstitutional late in 1956—at the same time that state courts ruled the boycott illegal. In the meantime, black leaders throughout the South had visited Montgomery, and out of the discussions came agreement to continue antisegregation protests regularly and systematically under the aegis of a new organization, the Southern Christian Leadership Conference. The NAACP could not lead the protests because, according to an SCLC pamphlet, "during the late fifties, the NAACP had been driven out of some Southern states. Its branches were outlawed as foreign corporations and its lawyers were charged with barratry, that is, persistently inciting litigation."

On January 10, 1957, over one hundred people gathered in Atlanta at a meeting called by four ministers, including Martin Luther King. Bayard Rustin drew up the "working papers." Initially called the Southern Leadership Conference on Transportation and Nonviolent Integration, the SCLC never developed a mass base even when it changed its name. It established numerous "affiliates" but did most of its work through the churches in the communities to which it sent its fieldworkers.

The church was not just the only institution available for a movement to work through; in many ways it was ideal. It performed "the central organizing function in the Negro community" (Holloway, 1969:22), providing both access to large masses of people on a regular basis and a natural leadership. As Wyatt Tee Walker, former executive director of SCLC, commented, "The Church today is central to the movement. If a Negro's going to have a meeting, where's he going to have it? Mostly he doesn't have a Masonic lodge, and he's not going to get the public schools. And the church is the primary means of communication" (Brink & Harris, 1964:103). Thus the church eventually came to be the center of the voter registration drives as well as many of the other activities of the civil rights movement.

Even the young men and women of SNCC had to use the church, though they had trouble doing so because, unlike most of the officers of SCLC, they were not themselves ministers and thus did not have a "fraternal" connection. Instead they tended to draw many of their resources and people from outside the particular town in which they were working by utilizing their natural organizational base, the college.

SNCC did not begin the sit-ins, but came out of them. Once begun, the idea of the sit-in spread initially by means of the mass media. But such sit-ins almost always took place in towns where there were Negro colleges, and groups on these campuses essentially organized the sit-in activities of their communities. Nonetheless, "CORE, with its long emphasis of nonviolent direct action, played an important part, once the sit-ins began, as an educational and organizing agent" (Zinn, 1964:23). CORE had very few staff in the South, but there were enough to at least hold classes and practice sessions in nonviolence.

It was SCLC, however, that was actually responsible for the formation of SNCC; though it might well have organized itself eventually. Ella Baker, then executive secretary of SCLC, thought something should be done to coordinate the rapidly spreading sit-ins in 1960, and many members of SCLC thought it might be appropriate to organize a youth group. With SCLC money, Baker persuaded her alma mater, Shaw University, to provide facilities to contact the groups at centers of sit-in activity. Some two hundred people showed up for the meeting, decided to have no official connection with SCLC beyond a "friendly relationship," and formed the Student Non-Violent Co-ordinating Committee (Zinn, 1964:32–34). It had no members, and its fieldworkers numbered two hundred at their highest point, but it was from the campuses, especially the southern black colleges, that it drew its sustenance and upon which its organizational base rested. . . .

THE WOMEN'S LIBERATION MOVEMENT[2]

Women are not well organized. Historically tied to the family and isolated from their own kind, only in the nineteenth century did women in this country have the opportunity to develop independent associations of their own. These associations took years and years of careful organizational work to build. Eventually they formed the basis for the suffrage movement of the early twentieth century. The associations took less time to die. Today the Women's Trade Union League, the General Federation of Women's Clubs, the Women's Christian Temperance Union, not to mention the powerful National Women's Suffrage Association, are all either dead or a pale shadow of their former selves.

As of 1960, not one organization of women had the potential to become a social movement organization, nor was there any form of "neutral" structure of interaction to provide the base for such an organization. The closest exception to the former was the National Women's Party, which has remained dedicated to feminist concerns since its inception in 1916. However, the NWP has been essentially a lobbying group for the Equal Rights Amendment since 1923. From the beginning, the NWP believed that a small group of women concentrating their efforts in the right places was more effective than a mass appeal, and so was not appalled by the fact that as late as 1969 even the majority of avowed feminists in this country had never heard of the ERA or the NWP.

The one large women's organization that might have provided a base for a social movement was the 180,000-member Federation of Business and Professional Women's Clubs. Yet, while it has steadily lobbied for legislation of importance to women, as late as "1966 BPW rejected a number of suggestions that it redefine . . . goals and tactics and become a kind of 'NAACP for women' . . . out of fear of being labeled 'feminist' " (Hole & Levine, 1971:89).

Before any social movement could develop among women, there had to be created a structure to bring potential feminist sympathizers together. To be sure, groups such as the BPW, and institutions such as the women's colleges, might be a good source of adherents for such a movement. But they were determined not to be the source of leadership.

What happened in the 1960s was the development of two new communications networks in which women played prominent roles that allowed, even forced, an awakened interest in the old feminist ideas. As a result, the movement actually has two origins, from two different strata of society, with two different styles, orientations, values, and forms of organization. The first of these will be referred to as the "older branch" of the movement, partially because it began first and partially because it was on the older side of the "generation gap" that pervaded the sixties. Its most prominent organization is the National Organization for Women (NOW), which was also the first to be formed. The style of its movement organizations tends to be traditional with elected officers, boards of directors, bylaws, and the other trappings of democratic procedure. Conversely, the "younger branch" consisted of innumerable small groups engaged in a variety of activities whose contact with one another was always tenuous (Freeman, 1975:50).

The forces that led to NOW's formation were set in motion in 1961 when President Kennedy established the President's Commission on the Status of Women at the behest of Esther Petersen, then director of the Women's Bureau. Its 1963 report, *American Women,* and subsequent committee publications documented just how thoroughly women were denied many rights and opportunities. The most significant response to the activity of the President's commission was the establishment of some fifty state commissions to do similar research on a state level. The Presidential and State Commission activity laid the groundwork for the future movement in two significant ways: (1) It unearthed ample evidence of women's unequal status and in the process convinced many previously uninterested women that something should be done; (2) It created a climate of expectations that something would be done. The women of the Presidential and State Commissions who were exposed to these influences exchanged visits, correspondence, and staff, and met with one another at an annual commission convention. They were in a position to share and mutually reinforce their growing awareness and concern over women's issues. These commissions thus provided an embryonic communications network.

During this time, two other events of significance occurred. The first was the publication of Betty Friedan's *The Feminine Mystique* in 1963. A quick best seller, the book stimulated many women to question the *status quo* and some women to suggest to Friedan that an organization be formed to do something about it. The second event was the addition of "sex" to the 1964 Civil Rights Act.

Many thought the "sex" provision was a joke, and the Equal Employment Opportunity Commission treated it as one, refusing to enforce it seriously. But a rapidly growing feminist coterie within the EEOC argued that "sex" would be taken more seriously if there were "some sort of NAACP for women" to put pressure on the government.

On June 30, 1966, these three strands of incipient feminism came together, and NOW was tied from the knot. At that time, government officials running the Third National Conference of Commissions on the Status of Women, ironically titled "Targets for Action," forbade the presentation of a suggested resolution calling for the EEOC to treat sex discrimination with the same consideration as race discrimination. The officials said one government agency could not be allowed to pressure another, despite the fact that the state commissions were not federal agencies. The small group of women who desired such a resolution had met the night before in Friedan's hotel room to discuss the possibility of a civil rights organization for women. Not convinced of its need, they chose instead to propose the resolution. When conference officials vetoed it, they held a whispered conversation over lunch and agreed to form an action organization "to bring women into full participation in the mainstream of American society now, assuming all the privileges and responsibilities thereof in truly equal partnership with men." The name NOW was coined by Friedan who was at the conference doing research on a book. When word leaked out, twenty-eight women paid five dollars each to join before the day was over (Friedan, 1967:4).

By the time the organizing conference was held the following October 29 through 30, over three hundred men and women had become charter members. It is impossible to do a breakdown on the composition of the charter membership, but one of the officers and board is possible. Such a breakdown accurately reflected NOW's origins. Friedan was president, two former EEOC commissioners were vice presidents, a representative of the United Auto Workers Women's Committee was secretary-treasurer, and there were seven past and present members of the State Commissions on the Status of Women on the twenty member board. One hundred twenty-six of the charter members were Wisconsin residents—and Wisconsin had the most active state Commission. Occupationally, the board and officers were primarily from the professions, labor, government, and communications fields. Of these, only those from labor had any experience in organizing, and they resigned a year later in a dispute over support of the Equal Rights Amendment. Instead of organizational experience, what the early NOW members had was experience in working with and in the media, and it was here that their early efforts were aimed.

As a result, NOW often gave the impression of being larger than it was. It was highly successful in getting in the press; much less successful in either bringing about concrete changes or forming an organization. Thus it was not until 1970, when the national press simultaneously did major stories on the women's liberation movement, that NOW's membership increased significantly.

In the meantime, unaware of and unknown to NOW, the EEOC, or the State Commissions, younger women began forming their own movement. Here, too, the groundwork had been laid some years before. The different social action projects of the sixties had attracted many women, who were quickly shunted into traditional roles and faced with the self-evident contradiction of working in a "freedom movement" but not being very free. No single "youth movement" activity or organization is responsible for forming the younger branch of the women's liberation movement, but together they created a "radical community" in which like-minded people continually interacted or were made aware of one another. This community provided the necessary network of communication and its radical ideas the framework of analysis that "explained" the dismal situation in which radical women found themselves.

Papers had been circulated on women and individual temporary women's caucuses had been held as early as 1964 (see Hayden & King, 1966). But it was not until 1967 and 1968 that the groups developed a determined, if cautious, continuity and began to consciously expand themselves. At least five groups in five different cities (Chicago, Toronto, Detroit, Seattle, and Gainesville, Florida) formed spontaneously, independently of one another. They came at an auspicious moment, for 1967 was the year in which the blacks kicked the whites out of the civil rights movement, student power was discredited by SDS, and the New Left was on the wane. Only draft resistance activities were on the increase, and this movement more than any other exemplified the social inequities of the sexes. Men could resist the draft. Women could only counsel resistance.

At this point, there were few opportunities available for political work. Some women fit well into the secondary role of draft counseling. Many didn't. For years their complaints of unfair treatment had been forestalled by movement men with the dictum that those things could wait until after the Revolution. Now these political women found time on their hands, but still the men would not listen.

A typical example was the event that precipitated the formation of the Chicago group, the first independent group in this country. At the August 1967 National Conference for New Politics convention a women's caucus met for days, but was told its resolution wasn't significant enough to merit a floor discussion. By threatening to tie up the convention with procedural motions the women succeeded in having their statement tacked to the end of the agenda. It was never discussed. The chair refused to recognize any of the many women standing by the microphone, their hands straining upwards. When he instead called on someone to speak on "the forgotten American, the American Indian," five women rushed the podium to demand an explanation. But the chairman just patted one of them on the head (literally) and told her, "Cool down, little girl. We have more important things to talk about than women's problems."

The "little girl" was Shulamith Firestone, future author of *The Dialectic of Sex,* and she didn't cool down. Instead she joined with another Chicago woman she met there who had unsuccessfully tried to organize a women's group that summer, to call a meeting of the women who had halfheartedly attended those summer meetings. Telling their stories to those women, they stimulated sufficient rage to carry the group for three months, and by that time it was a permanent institution.

Another somewhat similar event occurred in Seattle the following winter. At the University of Washington an SDS organizer was explaining to a large meeting how white college youth established rapport with the poor whites with whom they were working. "He noted that sometimes after analyzing societal ills, the men shared leisure time by 'balling a chick together.' He pointed out that such activities did much to enhance the political consciousness of the poor white youth. A woman in the audience asked, 'And what did it do for the consciousness of the chick?' " (Hole & Levine, 1971:120). After the meeting, a handful of enraged women formed Seattle's first group.

Subsequent groups to the initial five were largely organized rather than formed spontaneously out of recent events. In particular, the Chicago group was responsible for the formation of many new groups in Chicago and in other cities. Unlike NOW, the women in the first groups had had years of experience as trained organizers. They knew how to utilize the infrastructure of the radical community, the underground press, and the free universities to disseminate women's liberation ideas. Chicago, as a center of New Left activity, had the largest number of politically conscious organizers. Many traveled widely to leftist conferences and demonstrations, and most used the opportunity to talk with other women about the new movement. In spite of public derision by radical men, or perhaps because of it, young women steadily formed new groups around the country.

ANALYSIS

From these data there appear to be four essential elements involved in movement formation: (1) the growth of a preexisting communications network that is (2) cooptable to the ideas of the new movement; (3) a series of crises that galvanize into action people involved in a cooptable network, and/or (4) subsequent organizing effort to weld the spontaneous groups together into a movement. Each of these elements needs to be examined in detail.

COMMUNICATIONS NETWORK

. . . The women's liberation movement . . . illustrates the importance of a network precisely because the conditions for a movement existed *before* a network came into being, but the movement didn't exist until afterward. Analysts of socioeconomic causes have concluded that the movement could have started anytime within a twenty-year period. Strain for women was as great in 1955 as in 1965 (Ferriss, 1971). What changed was the organizational situation. It was not until new networks emerged among women aware of inequities beyond local boundaries that a movement could grow past the point of occasional, spontaneous uprisings. The fact that two distinct movements, with two separate origins, developed from two networks unaware of each other is further evidence of the key role of preexisting communications networks as the fertile soil in which new movements can sprout.

References to the importance of a preexisting communications network appear frequently in case studies of social movements, though the theoretical writers were much slower to recognize their salience. According to Buck (1920: 43–44), the Grange established a degree of organization among American farmers in the nineteenth century that greatly facilitated the spread of future farmers' protests. Lipset has reported that in Saskatchewan, "the rapid acceptance of new ideas and movements . . . can be attributed mainly to the high degree of organization. . . . The role of the social structure of the western wheat belt in facilitating the rise of new movements has never been sufficiently appreciated by historians and sociologists. Repeated challenges and crises forced the western farmers to create many more community institutions (especially cooperatives and economic pressure groups) than are necessary in a more stable area. These groups in turn provided a structural basis for immediate action in critical situations. [Therefore] though it was a new radical party, the C. C. F. did not have to build up an organization from scratch" (1959:206).

Similarly, Heberle (1951:232) reports several findings that Nazism was most successful in small, well-integrated communities. As Lipset put it, these findings "sharply challenge the various interpretations of Nazism as the product of the growth of anomie and the general rootlessness of modern urban industrial society" (1959:146).

Indirect evidence attesting to the essential role of formal and informal communications networks is found in diffusion theory, which emphasizes the importance of personal interaction rather than impersonal media communication in the spread of ideas (Rogers, 1962; Lionberger, 1960). This personal influence occurs through the organizational patterns of a community (Lionberger, 1960:73). It does not occur through the mass media. The mass media may be a source of information, but they are not a key source of influence.

Their lesser importance in relation to preexisting communications networks was examined in one study on "The Failure of an Incipient Social Movement" (Jackson, Peterson, Bull, Monsen, & Richmond, 1960). In 1957 a potential tax protest movement in Los Angeles generated considerable interest and publicity for a little over a month but was dead within a year. According to the authors, this did not reflect a lack of public notice. They concluded that "mass communication alone is probably insufficient without a network of communication specifically linking those interested in the matter. . . . If a movement is to grow rapidly, it cannot rely upon its own network of communication, but must capitalize on networks already in existence" (p. 37).

A major reason it took social scientists so long to acknowledge the importance of communications networks was because the prevailing theories of the post–World War II era emphasized increasing social dislocation and anomie. Mass society theorists, as they were called, hypothesized that significant community institutions that linked individuals to governing elites were breaking down, that society was becoming a mass of isolated individuals. These individuals were seen as increasingly irresponsible and ungovernable, prone to irrational protests because they had no mediating institutions through which to pursue grievances (Kornhauser, 1959).

In emphasizing disintegrating vertical connections, mass society theorists passed lightly over the role of horizontal ones, only occasionally acknowledging that "the combination of internal contact and external isolation facilitates the work of the mass agitator" (Kornhauser, 1959:218). This focus changed in the early seventies. Pinard's study of the Social Credit Party of Quebec (1971) severely criticized mass society theory, arguing instead that "when strains are severe and widespread a new movement is more likely to meet its early success among the more strongly integrated citizens" (Pinard, 1971:192).

This insight was expanded by Oberschall (1973), who created a six-cell table to predict both the occurrence and type of protest. As did the mass society theorists, Oberschall said that even when there are grievances, protest will not occur outside institutional channels by those who are connected, through their own leadership or patron/client relationships, with governing elites. Among those who are segmented from such elites, the type of protest will be determined by whether there is communal, associational, or little organization. In the latter case, discontent is expressed through riots or other short-lived violent uprisings. "It is under conditions of strong . . . ties and segmentation that the possibility of the rapid spread of opposition movements on a continuous basis exists" (p. 123).

The movements we have studied would confirm Oberschall's conclusions, but not as strongly as he makes them. In all these cases a preexisting communications network was a necessary but insufficient condition for movement formation. Yet the newly formed networks among student radicals, welfare recipients, and women can hardly compare with the longstanding ties provided by the southern black churches and colleges. Their ties were tenuous and may not have survived the demise of their movements.

The importance of segmentation, or lack of connection with relevant elites, is less obvious in the sixties' movements. The higher socioeconomic status of incipient feminists and Movement leaders would imply greater access to elites than is true for blacks or welfare recipients. If Oberschall were correct, these closer connections should either have permitted easier and more rapid grievance solutions or more effective social control. They did neither. Indeed, it was the group most closely connected to decision-making elites—women of the Presidential and State Commission—who were among the earliest to see the need of a protest organization. Women of the younger branch of the movement did have their grievances against the men of the New Left effectively suppressed for several years, but even they eventually rejected this kind of elite control, even when it meant rejecting the men.

Conversely, Piven and Cloward show that the establishment of closer ties between leaders of local welfare rights groups and welfare workers through advisory councils and community coordinators led to a curtailment of militance and the institutionalization of grievances (1977:326–31). They also argue that the development of government-funded community programs effectively coopted many local black movement leaders in the North and that federal channeling of black protest in the South into voter registration projects focused the movement there into traditional electoral politics (ibid.:253). In short, the evidence about the role of segmentation in movement formation is ambiguous. The effect may be varied considerably by the nature of the political system.

CO-OPTABILITY

A recurrent theme in our studies is that not just any communications network will do. It must be one that is co-optable to the ideas of the new movement. The Business and Professional Women's (BPW) clubs were a network among women, but having rejected feminism, they could not overcome the ideological barrier to new political action until after feminism became established. . . .

On the other hand, the women on the Presidential and State Commissions and the feminist coterie of the EEOC were co-optable largely because their immersion in the facts of female status and the details of sex discrimination cases made them very conscious of the need for change. Likewise, the young women of the "radical community" lived in an atmosphere of questioning, confrontation, and change. They absorbed an ideology of "freedom" and "liberation" far more potent than any latent "antifeminism" might have been. . . .

Exactly what makes a network co-optable is harder to elucidate. Pinard (1971:186) noted the necessity for groups to *"possess* or *develop* an ideology or simply subjective interests congruent with that of a new movement" for them to "act as mobilizing rather than restraining agents toward that movement," but did not further explore what affected the "primary group climate." More illumination is provided by the diffusion of innovation studies that point out the necessity for new ideas to fit in with already established norms for changes to happen easily. Furthermore, a social system that has as a value "innovativeness" (as the radical community did) will more rapidly adopt ideas than one that looks upon the habitual performance of traditional practices as the ideal (as most organized women's groups did in the fifties). Usually, as Lionberger (1960: 91) points out, "people act in terms of past experience and knowledge." People who have had similar experiences are likely to share similar perceptions of a situation and to mutually reinforce those perceptions as well as their subsequent interpretation. A co-optable network, then, is one whose members have had common experiences that predispose them to be receptive to the particular new ideas of the incipient movement and who are not faced with structural or ideological barriers to action. If the new movement as an "innovation" can interpret these experiences and perceptions in ways that point out channels for social action, then participation in a social movement becomes the logical thing to do.

THE ROLE OF CRISES

As our examples have illustrated, similar perceptions must be translated into action. This is often done by a crisis. For blacks in Montgomery, this was generated by Rosa Parks's refusal to give up her seat on a bus to a white man. For women who formed the older branch of the women's movement, the impetus to organize was the refusal of the EEOC to enforce the sex provision of Title VII, precipitated by the concomitant refusal of federal officials at the conference to allow a supportive resolution. For younger women there were a series of minor crises.

While not all movements are formed by such precipitating events, they are quite common as they serve to crystallize and focus discontent. From their own experiences, directly and concretely, people feel the need for change in a situation that allows for an exchange of feelings with others, mutual validation, and a subsequent reinforcement of innovative interpretation. Perception of an immediate need for change is a major factor in predisposing people to accept new ideas (Rogers, 1962: 280). Nothing makes desire for change more acute than a crisis. Such a crisis need not be a major one; it need only embody collective discontent.

ORGANIZING EFFORTS

A crisis will only catalyze a well-formed communications network. If such networks are embryonically developed or only partially co-optable, the potentially active individuals in them must be linked together by someone. . . . As Jackson et al. (1960:37) stated, "Some protest may persist where the source of trouble is constantly present. But interest ordinarily cannot be maintained unless there is a welding of spontaneous groups into some stable organization." In other words, people must be organized. Social movements do not simply occur.

The role of the organizer in movement formation is another neglected aspect of the theoretical literature. There has been great concern with leadership, but the two roles are distinct and not always performed by the same individual. In the early stages of a movement, it is the organizer much more than any leader who is important, and such an individual or cadre must often operate behind the scenes. The nature and function of these two roles was most clearly evident in the Townsend old-age movement of the thirties. Townsend was the "charismatic" leader, but the movement was organized by his partner, real estate promoter Robert Clements. Townsend himself acknowledges that without Clements's help, the movement would never have gone beyond the idea stage (Holzman, 1963).

The importance of organizers is pervasive in the sixties' movements. Dr. King may have been the public spokesperson of the Montgomery Bus Boycott who caught the eye of the media, but it was E. D. Nixon who organized it. Certainly the "organizing cadre" that young women in the radical community came to be was key to the growth of that branch of the women's liberation movement, despite the fact that no "leaders" were produced (and were actively discouraged). The existence of many leaders but no organizers in the older branch of the women's liberation movement readily explains its subsequent slow development. . . .

The function of the organizer has been explored indirectly by other analysts. Rogers (1962) devotes many pages to the "change agent" who, while he does not necessarily weld a group together or "construct" a movement, does many of the same things for agricultural innovation that an organizer does for political change. Mass society theory makes frequent reference to the "agitator," though not in a truly informative way. Interest groups are often organized by single individuals and some of them evolve into social movements. Salisbury's study of farmers' organizations finds this a recurrent theme. He also discovered that "a considerable number of farm groups were subsidized by other, older, groups. . . . The Farm Bureau was organized and long sustained by subsidies, some from federal and state governments, and some by local businessmen" (Salisbury, 1959:13).

These patterns are similar to ones we have found in the formation of social movements. Other organizations, even the government, often serve as training centers for organizers and sources of material support to aid the formation of groups and/or movements. The civil rights movement was the training ground for many an organizer of other movements. . . . The role of the government in the formation of the National Welfare Rights Organization was so significant that it would lead one to wonder if this association should be considered more of an interest group in the traditional sense than a movement "core" organization.

From all this it would appear that training as an organizer or at least as a proselytizer or entrepreneur of some kind is a necessary background for those individuals who act as movement innovators. Even in something as seemingly spontaneous as a social movement, the professional is more valuable than the amateur.

CRITICAL-THINKING QUESTIONS

1. Why has the role of communications networks in the formation of social movements only recently received the attention of researchers?
2. How do leadership roles emerge in social movements? Are "leaders" the same as "organizers"?
3. Cite some similarities and differences in the development of the civil rights movement and the women's movement.

NOTES

1. The only use of this significant word appears rather incidentally in Turner (1964): 123.

2. Data for this section are based on my observations while a founder and participant in the younger branch of the Chicago women's liberation movement from 1967 through 1969 and editor of the first (at that time, only) national newsletter. I was able, through extensive correspondence and interviews, to keep a record of how each group around the country started, where the organizers got the idea from, who they had talked to, what conferences were held and who attended, the political affiliations (or lack of them) of the first members, and so forth. Although I was a member of Chicago NOW, information on the origins of it and the other older branch organizations comes entirely through ex post facto interviews of the principals and examination of early papers in preparation for my dissertation on the women's liberation movement. Most of my informants requested that their contribution remain confidential.

REFERENCES

ADORNO, L. W., et al. 1950. *The authoritarian personality.* New York: Harper & Row.

BLUMER, H. 1951. Social movements. In *New outline of the principles of sociology,* ed. A. M. Lee. New York: Barnes and Noble.

BRINK, W., and L. HARRIS. 1964. *The Negro revolution in America.* New York: Simon & Schuster.

BUCK, S. J. 1920. *The agrarian crusade.* New Haven, Conn.: Yale University Press.

CANTRIL, H. 1941. *The psychology of social movements.* New York: Wiley.

CLARK, K. B. 1966. The civil rights movement: Momentum and organization. *Daedalus,* Winter.

DAVIES, J. C. 1962. Toward a theory of revolution. *American Sociological Review,* 27(1):5–19.

FERRISS, A. L. 1971. *Indicators of trends in the status of American women.* New York: Russell Sage Foundation.

FIRESTONE, S. 1971. *Dialectics of sex.* New York: Morrow.

FRAZIER, E. F. 1963. *The Negro church in America.* New York: Schocken.

FREEMAN, J. 1975. *The politics of women's liberation.* New York: Longman.

FRIEDAN, B. 1963. *The feminine mystique.* New York: Dell.

———. 1967. NOW: How it began. *Women Speaking,* April.

GURR, T. 1970. *Why men rebel.* Princeton, N.J.: Princeton University Press.

HAYDEN, C., and M. KING. 1966. A kind of memo. *Liberation,* April.

HEBERLE, R. 1951. *Social movements.* New York: Appleton-Century-Crofts.

HOFFER, E. 1951. *The true believer.* New York: Harper & Row.

HOLE, J., and E. LEVINE. 1971. *Rebirth of feminism.* New York: Quadrangle.

HOLLOWAY, H. 1969. *The politics of the Southern Negro.* New York: Random House.

HOLZMAN, A. 1963. *The Townsend movement: A political study.* New York: Bookman.

JACKSON, M., et al. 1960. The failure of an incipient social movement. *Pacific Sociological Review,* 3(1):40.

KING, M. L., JR. 1958. *Stride toward freedom.* New York: Harper & Row.

KORNHAUSER, W. 1959. *The politics of mass society.* Glencoe, Ill.: Free Press.

LIONBERGER, H. F. 1960. *Adoption of new ideas and practices.* Ames: Iowa State University Press.

LIPSET, S. M. 1959. *Agrarian socialism.* Berkeley: University of California Press.

LOWI, T. J. 1971. *The politics of discord.* New York: Basic Books.

OBERSCHALL, A. 1973. *Social conflict and social movements.* Englewood Cliffs, N.J.: Prentice-Hall.

PINARD, M. 1971. *The rise of a third party: A study in crisis politics.* Englewood Cliffs, N.J.: Prentice-Hall.

PIVEN, F. F., and R. CLOWARD. 1977. *Poor people's movements: Why they succeed, how they fail.* New York: Pantheon.

ROGERS, E. M. 1962. *Diffusion of innovations.* New York: Free Press.

RUDWICK, E., and A. MEIER. 1970. Organizational structure and goal succession: A comparative analysis of the NAACP and CORE, 1964–1968. *Social Science Quarterly,* 51 (June).

SALISBURY, R. H. 1969. An exchange theory of interest groups. *Midwest Journal of Political Science,* 13(1), (February).

TOCH, H. 1965. *The social psychology of social movements.* Indianapolis, Ind.: Bobbs-Merrill.

ZINN, H. 1964. *SNCC: The new abolitionists.* Boston: Beacon Press.

72

The Animal Rights Movement as a Moral Crusade

James M. Jasper and Dorothy Nelkin

Collective Behavior and Social Movements

CLASSIC

CONTEMPORARY

CROSS-CULTURAL

Although the number of animal rights organizations in the United States is small compared to the membership of other social movements, animal rights activists have enjoyed numerous victories since the 1980s. Why has this small group been so successful? James M. Jasper and Dorothy Nelkin provide some of the answers. They describe the animal rights movement as a "moral crusade" that relies, for example, on sympathetic media coverage, sentimental views about pets, and coalitions with other recent protest movements to achieve their objectives.

On a warm spring day in May, 1980, Henry Spira was on Manhattan's posh Fifth Avenue with a flatbed truck filled with white rabbits. With him were 300 more demonstrators, many of them dressed in bunny suits. On the sidewalk in front of the headquarters of the cosmetics giant Revlon, they were protesting that company's extensive use of white rabbits to test the safety of new products. The demonstrators were angry about procedures in which substances were placed in rabbits' eyes to test if these ingredients caused redness, swelling, or cloudiness. Many demonstrators had been drawn to the protest by full-page advertisements in the *New York Times* and other papers that asked, "How many rabbits does Revlon blind for beauty's sake?"

After a friend left him a cat in 1973, Spira, a burly man in his early fifties, had become increasingly outraged over humans' treatment of animals, wondering about "the appropriateness of cuddling one animal while sticking a knife and fork into others." He grew more and more critical of such common practices as wearing furs and leather and eating meat. For more than a year he had talked to Revlon officials, hoping to persuade them to contribute several hundred thousand dollars to help develop alternative tests that did not use live animals. When Revlon officials listened politely but then ignored him, he put together a coalition of 400 animal groups, mostly humane societies operating spay clinics and offering cats and dogs for adoption. And he gathered funds for the newspaper ads. He felt public opinion would be on his side: "I think there are very few people on the street who'll say, 'Yeah, go around and blind rabbits to produce another mascara.' "[1]

Following the May rally, public protests continued alongside Spira's private negotiations, and

---

Source: Reprinted with the permission of The Free Press, a Division of Simon & Schuster, from *The Animal Rights Crusade: The Growth of a Moral Protest* by James M. Jasper and Dorothy Nelkin.

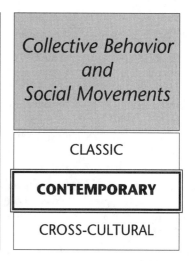

in December of 1980 Revlon capitulated, announcing that it would provide Rockefeller University $750,000 for research on alternative tests. Soon other companies followed Revlon's lead; by 1987 many had ended live animal testing; and the cosmetics industry claimed to have contributed about $5 million to alternatives research.

Four years after the Revlon demonstration, another effort to liberate animals unfolded in the laboratories of the University of Pennsylvania Medical School. On Memorial Day weekend in 1984, five members of the Animal Liberation Front (ALF) surreptitiously entered the deserted research lab of Thomas Gennarelli, who headed a team of researchers studying the effects of severe head injuries. Underway for fourteen years, these experiments currently involved severe shocks and injuries—similar to whiplash in car accidents—to the heads of baboons. The intruders destroyed equipment worth $20,000 and removed sixty hours of videotapes made to document the experiments.

The members of the ALF shared Henry Spira's goal of eliminating any use of animals for human needs, but they felt a stronger sense of urgency that compelled them to break the law. In most of their break-ins—Pennsylvania was one of more than 100 entries—the ALF has liberated animals rather than videotapes. Its members value animal lives so highly that they feel a moral obligation to act to save them, even to damage property in doing so. Violence against property, they claim, is justified to stop violence against living beings (the animals they liberate). As one activist put it, "Property laws are artificial constructs. We feel we answer to a higher law."[2]

Perhaps the most important result of the Memorial Day break-in is what then happened to the videotapes. The ALF, an illegal group designated as a "terrorist" organization by the FBI, passed the tapes to another animal rights group, People for the Ethical Treatment of Animals (PETA). PETA edited the tapes into a twenty-minute film called *Unnecessary Fuss,* which portrayed bantering among researchers and joking about the injured animals—"mocking them," as animal activists put it. It also appeared that the animals were not fully anesthetized. Scientists were painted as callous, even sadistic, and so brutal that discussion with them about their methods would be useless: Direct action against such research was the only appropriate response. The film proved a powerful instrument for PETA in its efforts to recruit new and committed members to an emerging protest movement.

The Revlon and University of Pennsylvania incidents are just two among thousands of recent animal rights protests, lawsuits, break-ins, and other actions that have targeted scientific laboratories, cosmetic and pharmaceutical firms, slaughterhouses and butchers, fur ranchers and retailers, rodeos and circuses, hunters and trappers, carriage drivers, and even zoos. Since the late 1970s, new animal "rights" organizations have rejuvenated the older and larger animal welfare movement, and together they are reshaping public awareness of animals. As many as 10 to 15 million Americans send money to animal protection groups, which have proliferated: By 1990, there were several thousand animal welfare and several hundred animal rights organizations in the United States. Some focus on particular animals (The Beaver Defenders, Bat Conservation International); others have a religious bent (Life for God's Stray Animals, Jews for Animal Rights); some are organized around tactics (the Animal Legal Defense Fund); others protest particular uses or abuses of animals (Students United Protesting Research Experiments on Sentient Subjects); still others represent links with related causes (Feminists for Animal Rights). The pull of these groups was evident in June 1990, when 30,000 people participated in a march on Washington for animal rights, with slogans such as "Fur Is Dead," "No Tax Dollars for Torture," and "Blinding Bunnies Is Not Beautiful."

Renewed concerns about animals have generated a powerful social movement driven by a simple moral position: Animals are similar enough to humans to deserve serious moral consideration. They are sentient beings entitled to dignified lives, and they should be treated as ends, not as means. Protectors ask how we can love our pets, yet experiment on identical animals in laboratories; how we can cuddle one animal, yet eat another. They have themselves mostly given up meat, dairy products, and eggs; they refuse to wear leather shoes or belts; they do not patronize the products of certain corporations; and many will not wear wool—let alone fur—garments. While some would allow occasional animal research if subjects are fully sedated and the benefits outweigh the harm, others say this concession violates the inherent right of animals to a full life independent of human goals. Movement leaders often use the morally charged language of good and evil, and their political actions and rhetorical style often display an absolutism that discourages discussion or negotiation with those who disagree.

The new movement has exploded into Americans' awareness. Animal rights has been the cover story of magazines as diverse as *Newsweek, U.S. News and World Report*, *New York Magazine,* the *Atlantic Monthly,* the *New Republic,* the *Village Voice*, the *Progressive* , and the lawyers' weekly *National Law Journal*; its issues have been featured in network television series like *L.A. Law, MacGyver,* and *Designing Women*; it has been examined in major news programs such as *48 Hours*. Despite a tendency to focus on secretive and sensationalist ALF commandos, most media coverage has been sympathetic to the ideas of the movement. Typically, the activists are portrayed as eccentric, but their positions are treated with respect. Comic strips such as *Doonesbury* and *Bloom County* have favorably portrayed animal activists and their issues. *Saturday Night Live* at least recognized the controversy over fur coats in a skit titled "They're Better Off Dead." Celebrities such as Bob Barker, Doris Day, Casey Kasem, River Phoenix, and several of *The Golden Girls* have given their support to the cause.

Consumer goods have followed suit. One Barbie Doll is an "animal loving" Barbie, marketed as an animal rights volunteer—even as real-life activists attack the mink stole sold by the Spiegel Company for other Barbie Dolls. Vegetarian food is sold for the dogs of those with strict animal rights sensibilities. Public opinion polls show a slippage of support for scientific research using animals, even when it generates information about human health. Activists have delivered a crippling blow to the American fur industry—from which it may never recover. Animal protection is not only one of today's fastest-growing protest movements, it is one of the most effective.

The social roots of this movement lie in the changed relationship between humans and their fellow creatures that resulted from urbanization and industrialization in Western societies, as city dwellers began to encounter animals only as family pets, and less and less as instruments of labor and production. Animals have accompanied men and women throughout their history, some as members of the family to be cherished, others as tools to be used. But in modern times the balance between these attitudes—one sentimental, the other instrumental—has been questioned, as more and more people insist that all animals be treated as though they were partners—"companion animals"—rather than objects.

In the United States, the first societies to prevent cruelty to animals were founded in the 1860s as part of the more general humanitarian impulse of the time. While these societies persisted, further expansion of this animal welfare movement took place in the 1950s, with the founding of such organizations as the Humane Society of the United States. Most of these groups concentrated on problems associated with the growing number of pets: overpopulation and frequent abandonment, the issue of shelters, and the frequency of brutality and cruelty. These humane societies and welfare organizations saw animal cruelty coming from poorly educated or abusive individuals, not from the systematic activities of institutions.

A new ideological agenda for animal protection emerged dramatically in the late 1970s, combining ideas from several sources. It retained the animal welfare tradition's concern for animals as sentient beings that should be protected from unnecessary cruelty. But animal activists added a new language of "rights" as the basis for demanding animal liberation. In the individualist culture of America, "rights talk" is often the only way to express moral values and demands. Rights—whether of patients, women, fetuses, or animals—are accepted as a moral trump card that cannot be disputed. Justified in terms of tradition, nature, or fundamental moral principles, rights are considered non-negotiable. Protectors compare animal rights to human rights, and the charge of "speciesism" takes its place alongside racism and sexism. Wildlife traffickers are engaged in a "monkey slave trade," laboratories become "torture chambers," and animal testing is a "holocaust."

The moral vision of animal rightists is partly drawn from other movements, especially feminism and environmentalism. At the core of these ideologies is a critique of "instrumentalism," the confusion of ends and means said to prevail in contemporary society. According to this critique, instrumental attitudes reduce nature and women, as well as other humans—all with inherent value as ends in themselves—to the status of things and tools. At the same time, instrumentalism promotes technologies, markets, and bureaucracies—all intended to be the means for attaining the good life—to the status of ends. Uneasiness with instrumental attitudes is widespread: Many people feel that there is something wrong with basing all decisions on economic values; that science lacks a human face; that consumer society creates artificial needs rather than satisfying real ones; that humans are treated like cogs in a machine.

Recent protest movements—ranging from Christian fundamentalists to radical feminists—insist that policies and decisions be guided by moral values and social needs, not by profits, technological feasibility, or bureaucratic inertia. Just as environmentalists question the exploitation of nature for commercial purposes, so animal rights advocates demand the end of animal exploitation for human gain. Animals, like human beings or nature, should be treated as ends rather than as means. This view grounded the mistreatment of animals in institutions rather than blaming misguided individuals. Rather than searching for individual scientists who inflicted unusual pain on their animal subjects, activists condemned all research using live animals, thereby attacking the heart of biomedical science. Instead of criticizing the occasional circus for its cruelty in training animals, they rejected any use of animals to entertain people as exploitation and humiliation. Here was a new view of the relationship between animals and human institutions, one that often condemned the very essence of those institutions. The appeal of this critique helps explain the transformation of animal protection into a radical animal rights movement.

But a fuller explanation lies in common cultural beliefs and implicit understandings about animals in our society, since the treatment of other species often reflects a culture's moral concerns. Animals were the first subject of painting—on the walls of caves—and the first metaphors in human thought—for example, as symbols of tribes and families. They may have been the first objects to be worshiped, perceived as embodiments of spirits. Animals exhibit enough diversity of behavior and attributes to provide an extensive vocabulary for our own thinking. Throughout recorded history, men and women have found that animals were "good to think with," a rich source of symbols that humans could use to impose order on the world. They are blank slates onto which people have projected their beliefs about the state of nature, about "natural" forms of hierarchy and social organization, about language and rationality, and about moral behavior. Lessons are drawn from the supposed behavior of tortoises and hares, from the social organization of ants and grasshoppers, from the territoriality of lions and wolves.

We also project onto animals the characteristics of humans—sensitivity to pain, emotional bonds such as love and loyalty, the ability to plan and communicate. People have long endowed animals with human characteristics—crafty foxes, greedy pigs, lazy cats. Conversely, they use animals to characterize humans—people chatter like magpies, work like mules, and squirrel things away. We speak of male chauvinist pigs; we complain that Uncle Pete hogs the sports section. We use expressions like rat's nest, rat race, dirty rat, and smelling a rat. The sloth was even unlucky enough to be named after one of the seven deadly sins. But we can also romanticize animals, projecting onto them traits that make them better than people: a goodness, innocence, and purity rarely found in human company. Animals often come to represent the best in human nature, those qualities we cherish and try to protect.

If animals share so many human characteristics, what are the essential differences? The distinction between humans and other animals is the key issue in the growing number of disputes over animal protection. "A life is a life," whether human or nonhuman, is a common refrain in animal rights rhetoric. Ironically, science itself has helped to blur the boundaries between humans and other animals. Evolutionary biology, after all, is controversial among Christian fundamentalists precisely because it violates the long assumed distinction between man and the animal world. While religious movements like creationists struggle to maintain boundaries, believing Man was created in God's image, animal rightists have taken biologists literally, denying moral distinctions between species as the "effluvium of a discredited metaphysics."[3]

For most people, the boundaries between animals and humans are intuitively clear. A human life is simply worth more than a non-human life, and while animals deserve some moral consideration, they are not to be exempt from human use. Such distinctions, however, remain matters of belief, not of evidence; they are affected by cultural preferences, personal values, and moral sentiments—traits not entirely open to rational persuasion. Rhetoric that compares animal suffering with the holocaust, that equates speciesism with racism, has emotive power for those who blur the boundaries between humans and other species. For others, these metaphors appear outlandish, threatening, dangerously defying accepted categories. The conflict between animal advocates and animal users is far more than a matter of contrasting tastes or interests. Opposing world views, concepts of identity, ideas of community, are all at stake. The animal rights controversy is about the treatment of animals, but it is also about our definition of ourselves and of a moral society. For this reason, it cannot be easily resolved.

Animal rights is a moral crusade. Its adherents act upon explicit moral beliefs and values to pursue a social order consistent with their principles. Their fervent moral vision crowds out other concerns. Most moral crusades focus on single issues: Some focus on abortion; others on drunken driving; still others on the evils of pornography. Their members—moral missionaries—often insist they have no broader partisan agenda. They are less interested in material benefits for themselves than in correcting perceived injustices. Animals are a perfect cause for such a crusade; seen as innocent victims whose mistreatment demands immediate redress, they are an appealing lightning rod for moral concerns.

The symbolic importance of animals in this crusade underscores the importance of ideas in inspiring social movements, shaping their tactics, and enhancing or limiting their effects. To organize a crusade, movement leaders appeal to the moral sentiments of like-minded citizens, inciting their anger with emotive rhetoric and strategies ranging from colorful public rallies to clandestine break-ins that free animals from laboratories. The language of moral crusades is sometimes shrill, self-righteous, and uncompromising, for bedrock principles are non-negotiable. In the strident style of Old Testament prophets, scolding and condemning their society, organizers point to evils that surround them and to catastrophes that will befall society in the absence of reform. Extreme and even illegal strategies and tactics are seen as justified in order to stop widespread immoral practices. Their sense of moral urgency encourages believers to ignore laws and conventional political processes, and they organize themselves into groups structured for quick action, not participatory debate. Proselytizing and interventionist in their style, such crusades frequently appear dangerous to those who do not share their judgmental and uncompromising views.

Yet animal protection groups vary widely in their aims and thus in their shrillness. Contrasting goals, tactics, and philosophical positions bring forth different organizations that form a continuum from reformist to radical. However, they tend to cluster into three kinds of groups that we label welfarist, pragmatist, and fundamentalist. In the humane tradition of the ASPCA, animal *welfarists* accept most current uses of animals, but seek to minimize their suffering and pain. They view animals as distinct from humans, but as objects entitled to compassion. Their reformist position, advocated through public education and lobbying for protective legislation, has long enjoyed wide public support and continues to do so. Welfarist groups like the SPCAs and the Humane Society of the United States existed before the animal rights movement appeared, and remain the largest, most powerful organizations.

In the late 1970s, however, more radical groups formed on the fringes of the animal welfare movement, redefining the issue of animal welfare as one of animal rights. Some of these new advocates organized around the well-articulated and widely disseminated utilitarian perspective of philosopher Peter Singer. Because animals could feel pain and pleasure, Singer argued that they deserved moral consideration, and he demanded drastic reduction in their use. The *pragmatist* groups feel that certain species deserve greater consideration than others, and would allow humans to use animals when the benefits deriving from their use outweigh their suffering. They seek to reduce animal use through legal actions, political protest, and negotiation. Henry Spira is a prominent example of a pragmatist.

Some of these new advocates, however, demanded the immediate abolition of all exploitation of animals, on the grounds that animals have inherent, inviolable rights. These more extreme animal rights *fundamentalists* believe that people should never use animals for their own pleasures or interests, regardless of the benefits. Some see even the ownership of pets as a distortion of the animals' natural lives. Insisting that increased understanding of head injuries does not justify harming baboons, the Animal Liberation Front expresses the fundamentalists' position, as well as their compelling sense of urgency. Although far less numerous than pragmatist or welfarist organizations, these groups set the tone of the new animal rights movement. And they are growing in size and wealth.

These distinctions are not absolute or rigid. Some activists, for example, believe in full animal rights, but pursue their goals with pragmatic strategies. Many shift their language and tactics depending on the issue or political arena. And all are tempted to indulge in fundamentalist rhetoric that simplifies the moral issues and demonizes opponents. But these three labels are useful to highlight important differences and tensions within a movement often described in monolithic terms. For the movement itself is divided over many issues: whether the same attention should be given to helping wild animals and domestic ones, whether insects or reptiles should be championed as fervently as furry mammals, and, especially, whether destructive tactics are acceptable.

Nevertheless, welfarists, pragmatists, and fundamentalists cooperate on specific issues, and their interests as well as rhetoric often merge. Together, they form a remarkably powerful animal protection movement, in which the pragmatists and fundamentalists represent the radical wing—the animal rights crusade. These crusaders would like to challenge Americans to rethink their fundamental beliefs about themselves and their connection to the world around them. They wonder if the boundaries we have drawn between ourselves and other animals are as rigid as we suppose. They would force us to extend the rights we promote for humans to other species. They want nothing short of a moral revolution that would change our food and clothing, our science and health care, our entire relationship to the natural world.

CRITICAL-THINKING QUESTIONS

1. In the previous reading, Jo Freeman maintains that social movements develop when 1) there is an effective communications network, 2) the communications network is co-optable, 3) a crisis propels like-minded people into action, and 4) people are organized to act. Are these characteristics useful or not in explaining the emergence and success of the animal rights movement?

2. Why do Jasper and Nelkin describe the animal rights movement as a "moral crusade" rather than, for example, a "lunatic fringe" or a terrorist group that vandalizes and destroys scientific research laboratories?

3. Jasper and Nelkin propose a continuum of animal rights organizations that includes welfarists, pragmatists, and fundamentalists. Prepare a short typology of these three groups in terms of their a) beliefs, b) major goals, and c) primary strategies to accomplish their goals. Using your typology, describe what you think are the strengths and weaknesses of each group in developing acceptable public policies that protect animals.

NOTES

1. Quoted in "Animals in Testing. How the CPI Is Handling a Hot Issue," *Chemical Week* 135, 23 (December 5, 1984), 38.

2. Quoted in Richard J. Brenneman, "Animal 'liberator' promises more raids on labs," *Sacramento Bee* (July 2, 1984), B1.

3. James Rachels, *Created from Animals* (New York: Oxford University Press, 1990).

Collective Behavior and Social Movements

CLASSIC

CONTEMPORARY

CROSS-CULTURAL

73

Abortion Movements in Poland, Great Britain, and the United States

Janet Hadley

Perhaps one of the best-known feminist slogans during the early 1970s was that "A woman has a right to choose" whether or not to terminate a pregnancy. About 38 percent of the world's population lives in countries where abortion has been available on request. Although abortion has been legal in the United States and most of Europe for at least twenty-five years, it remains an explosive issue in many countries and has spawned "for" and "against" social movements and collective behavior. In this reading, Janet Hadley examines some of the controversies and campaigns of abortion rights movements in Poland, the United States, and Great Britain.

In recent years in the United States, in Poland, and in Ireland, too, national politics has at times been convulsed by the issue of abortion. In Germany the historic reunification of East and West almost foundered amid wrangling about conflicting abortion laws. How can abortion, hardly an issue comparable to the great affairs of state, such as the economy or national security, have an impact such as this?

This is an account, first, of how post-Communist Poland found itself in the grip of the abortion debate and secondly how the issue came to be such a seemingly permanent shadow on the political landscape in the United States, in the wake of the Supreme Court's 1973 landmark decision on abortion in the case of *Roe* v. *Wade*. It offers some ideas about why.

The account focuses on abortion, primarily as a method of birth control, which women have always sought out, legally when they can, illegally when they must. The controversies and campaigns recorded and the ideas offered here concentrate on women's access to affordable, safe and legal abortion—an essential part of women's reproductive freedom in a world where five hundred women die every day from the complications of unsafe abortion (World Health Organization, 1993).

The way abortion has at times dominated public debate in both Poland and the United States can hardly be exaggerated, but the contexts are very different. At times, during the 1992 American presidential election campaign, it seemed as if the fate of the United States for the next four years hung solely on the thread of the abortion issue. Economic issues, national security, even political scandals were all pushed into the background. But no one was too surprised to encounter this wild card in the United States' electoral politics. It had been thus, on and off, for around twenty years, since the 1973

Source: Janet Hadley, "God's Bullies: Attacks on Abortion," *Feminist Review*, Vol. 48 (Fall 1994), pp. 94–113. Reprinted with permission of Taylor & Francis Ltd., Oxford, U.K.

Supreme Court judgement which had sanctioned abortion as a woman's constitutional right.

It was, however, probably a lot harder for anyone to have predicted events in Poland where, for more than four years, well before the forty-year-old Communist regime was finally sloughed off, abortion took centre stage. The renascent right in Poland selected abortion as the first block of the social welfare system for demolition. The battle over it highlights the new relationship between the Roman Catholic Church—once the main element of opposition alongside Solidarity—and the state. As the democratization of Eastern Europe got under way, abortion was one of the first laws to come under fire (Einhorn, 1993).

In some ways the abortion debate in Poland, which of all the former Soviet bloc countries has undergone by far the most draconian reversal of its abortion law, is quite straightforward: The opponents of abortion are solidly Roman Catholic and perceive their efforts as part of the task of rescuing Poland from its years of godlessness. The debate in Poland harks back to the relatively straightforward arguments which took place in Britain at the time of the passing of the Abortion Act in 1967.

In the United States, on the other hand, the issue has been linked to a much more extensive catalogue of perceived "social degeneracy." Opposition to abortion in the United States involves a curious alliance of religious and secular New Right groupings and much of the driving force has been provided, not by the Roman Catholic Church, but by evangelical Christians. . . .

POLAND: NO PLACE TO BE A WOMAN

. . . What we have been witnessing in Poland since 1989, according to one observer, is the "Church's colossal efforts to replace a totalitarian state with a theocracy" (Kissling, 1992). Weekly Masses from Rome are broadcast on Polish TV these days. Scientific conferences open with High Mass, blessings and so on, and military personnel are sent on pilgrimages. Classes in religion (i.e., Roman Catholicism) are mandatory for children in state schools. There is little doubt that the bishops of Poland, who behave more like leaders of a political party than as simple guardians of moral values, have their sights set not only on banning abortion but also divorce, provision of contraception, and other hallmarks of a secular society. One commentator wrote in 1991:

> From the very beginning until its unexpected culmination in June [1991—when a draft anti-abortion bill was rejected by parliament in the face of huge pro-choice demonstrations] the Polish controversy on abortion was a classic example of political conflict. Nobody cared any more about subtle moral or political arguments. It was clear that who wins the abortion debate will control the political situation in Poland. (Szawarski, 1991)

The irony is that not only was June 1991 far from being the "culmination," but also that nobody today could be said to have won. (Women, of course, lost.)

The final law, signed by President Lech Walesa in February 1993, was seen by opponents of abortion as a compromise. It is much weaker than they would have liked. The original anti-abortion bill, first published in 1989, promised three years' imprisonment for a woman who induced her own abortion, as well for any doctor caught performing an illegal operation. Under the new law, two years' imprisonment awaits an abortionist, but a woman inducing her own abortion will not face gaol [jail].

The new law allows abortion when a woman's life or health is in danger, after rape or incest, or if there is suspected fetal abnormality. But prenatal testing is only permissible if there is a family history of genetic disorder. There are token provisions urging local authorities to provide contraceptive services.

The Church's Power and Influence

The religious context of the abortion row in Poland goes a long way to explaining how it came to be such a passionate, extreme and dominating issue. Around 95 percent of its 39 million people consider themselves Catholic and there is a very strong family tradition of Catholicism, which during the Communist era greatly strengthened the Church as a focus of national identity and a shelter for opposition. Having a Polish Pope helps too; when John Paul II visited in 1991, he urged his fellow Poles to free themselves from a law permitting abortion, which he called a tragic inheritance of Communism.

Even when the Communist grip seemed at its most unyielding, the Church consistently harried the authorities on issues of sexual control. In a recent survey, conducted since the fall of the Communists, and reported in the *Guardian* (9/14/93), 95 percent of Polish women said they rely on personal experience for their sex education and 73 percent said they had had an unplanned pregnancy.

The only sex-education manual ever produced in Poland had to be withdrawn because of Church protest. Roman Catholic opposition to contraception has been effective—76 percent of the urban population and 87 percent of the rural population use only Church-approved 'natural' methods of fertility control (Mrugala, 1991). (Priests often determine what is sold in local pharmacies.) Poland's 1956 abortion law contained no conscience clause, but the Church's success in pressuring doctors can be judged from the fact that in some state hospitals, staff refusal made it impossible to get an abortion. As early as 1973, Church protests over the rising abortion rate and the behaviour of "callous young women" forced the government to set up a commission to consider whether the law needed amending (Okolski, 1988).

But the pressures on women to have abortions were very strong. Even for those who wanted it, contraception has never been easily available, and was of notoriously poor quality. Abortion—which was free in state hospitals after 1959, and easy to obtain—was therefore the main method of birth control. Women only had to report that they were "in a difficult life situation." "Poland's hard life finds more and more women choosing abortions," reported *The New York Times* in 1983, citing families in some cities waiting eighteen years to obtain a small apartment. Despite the Church's denunciations, there were an estimated 600,000 abortions a year, compared to just 700,000 live births.

Times may have been hard in 1983, but the economic "shock therapy" of post-Communist Poland has brought unimaginable hardship in its wake. Unemployment is now 2.8 million and will be one-fifth of the workforce in three years' time. The bishops have deplored this, by urging *women* to leave the labour market, to ease unemployment and ensure that men's wages increase. They have made no adverse comment on the virtual shutdown of state-financed child care.

The Bishops, the State, and the Medical Profession

The episcopate first floated the idea of outlawing abortion in 1988, deeming it to be a mortal threat to the "biological substance of the nation." In the spring of 1989 an Unborn Child Protection Bill was published and the Pope hurried to send his congratulations.

In 1990, however, long before the legislative battle had got into its stride, the Ministry of Health took its own initiative, saying that women wanting abortion would now need the permission of three physicians and of a psychologist, whose appointment had been approved by the local bishop, and that an abortion for social reasons must be requested in writing (*The New York Times*, 4/21/92). The psychologist's job is to dissuade women, mainly by putting the frighteners on them. Sterilization and the in-vitro fertilization programme were suspended.

As Poland created its first parliament, abortion became the bellwether for fitness to serve. Anyone supporting abortion rights was traduced as a surreptitious advocate for Communism. Throughout 1990 and 1991 the battle raged, overshadowing the upheavals of the new market economy. Huge demonstrations in favour of abortion took place in Warsaw and women's groups began to get organized to defend abortion rights. Solidarity was split on the issue. Bills were proposed and defeated in dizzying succession. Parish priests threatened to withhold sacraments from anyone who did not sign the petitions against "killing innocent children."

The anti-abortion movement targeted not only abortion but family planning provision, too, blocking the launch of an information campaign in the textile city of Lodz, where there has been an unusually high rate of congenital abnormalities among babies born to women working in the textile factories (Rich, 1991). Their activity was partly financed by pro-life organizations from the United States, such as Human Life International. This evangelical group, fired by a vision of "re-Christianized united Europe stretching from the Atlantic to the Urals," vowed to "flood Eastern Europe" with films, videos (such as *The Silent Scream* which has been shown in Polish schools), fetal models and other propaganda. In 1992, Operation Rescue blockaded a clinic in the Baltic port of Gdynia, with protesters from the United States, Canada and the U.K.

Although one smear in circulation was that "only communists and Jews favor abortion," there is little direct evidence that the anti-abortion campaign was fuelled by a nationalist pro-natalism—a desire to demographically overwhelm Poland's minorities. There was, however, a definite bid to appeal to a repressive notion of proper and traditional Polish "womanhood." The term "emancipation for women" is laden with Communist overtones and has often in reality meant the notorious "double burden" or overloading of women, in Poland and Eastern Europe in general, in which they have been expected to shoulder full-time jobs as well as forty hours a week shopping, cooking, cleaning, laundry, with only the aid of very poor-quality pre-school child care and medical care (Jankowska, 1993). Against such a reality, a misty vision of womanhood may have a definite allure.

May 1992 brought another turn of the screw. A new code of medical ethics made it professionally unethical for doctors to perform abortions except in cases of rape or incest or when the woman's life was in danger. Violations would lead to suspension of the doctor's license. The code effectively ended hospital abortions and prenatal testing: Some institutions put up signs, "No Abortions."

The issue continued to rock the government, which twice postponed a final vote on abortion. By the end of 1992, the conflict was extreme enough to threaten the fragile coalition government, an improbable seven-party affair. A million people signed a petition for a referendum. Meanwhile, 61 percent of Poles said they favoured the provisions of the 1956 law.

Turning the Clock Back

Nevertheless, when the government could postpone a vote no longer, a law was finally passed early in 1993. Under the new law, only 3 percent of the abortions previously performed in Poland are now deemed legal. Two years in gaol awaits an illegal abortionist, but there is no punishment for a woman who obtains an illegal operation. Although it is the most restrictive abortion law in Europe, apart from Ireland's, pro-choice campaigners comforted themselves with the rueful thought that things could easily have been much worse.

The legislation satisfies no one. Both sides have vowed to fight on. Even before President Lech Walesa signed the new law, the 1992 doctors' code—a *de facto* ban on abortions in Poland—was having its effect. The Warsaw police morgue has begun receiving bodies of women bearing witness to botched abortions. For the last three years, cases of infanticide have steadily increased.

Deaths will be outnumbered by injuries. Romania, where abortion was illegal until the fall of Ceauşescu in 1989, shows the way. Staff at a clinic for women in Bucharest, set up by Marie Stopes International, found that 80 percent of patients were suffering from past incompetent abortions.

A helpline set up in Warsaw by pro-abortion campaigners is receiving calls from men seeking advice because their wives are refusing to have sex any more. Women are phoning for help, reporting that even in circumstances which comply with the new law, they are being refused operations. In Poland's deep Catholic south, a pregnant Cracow woman, furnished with a police report confirming that she had been raped, was refused help at the hospital (Hoell, 1993).

All the desolately familiar symptoms of outlawed abortion are there: police raids on clinics, small ads appearing in the newspapers: "Gynaecologist: Interventions." The price is $350–1,000: The average monthly wage is $200. For professional women "medical tours" can be arranged—to the Ukraine, to Kaliningrad, even to Holland. (But not to the Czech Republic, which in the wake of Poland's new law, moved swiftly to outlaw abortions for foreign visitors.)

Paradoxically, the last few years have seen a burgeoning of women's organizations, formed to defend abortion and women's rights. It is an irony, comments Hanna Jankowska, "when the word 'feminist' sounds in this country like an insult" (1993). But sustaining the momentum of such organizations is uphill work. People are consumed by the effort to cope with the effects of 38 percent inflation.

There are signs that the Church may have overplayed its hand in its attempt to introduce a legislative version of "absolute morality" as part of a plan to create a theocratic Poland. There was strong public support for a referendum on abortion, which the Church opposed, and its popularity has dropped by half since Communism collapsed, according to opinion polls *(Catholic Herald*, 9/9/93). The Irish Church found itself in similar trouble after the referendum on abortion in Ireland in 1992, an event which was much reported in the Polish media.

But it is hard to draw sound parallels with Ireland: The Republic is certainly behind the times, but there are signs that slowly things are creeping forward for women in Ireland. Nothing compares with the crudeness with which the clock hands have been wrenched *back* in Poland.

In September 1993, the political coalition which fostered the anti-abortion legislation suffered a crushing defeat in national elections. The pace of reform was thought to be the main culprit, but the unpopularity of the anti-abortion law was also held to blame. Proabortion campaigners are preparing a new bill to reverse the law, scarcely before the ink is dry. In January 1994, Polish doctors amended their medical code, somewhat relaxing the abortion guidelines and increasing scope for prenatal diagnosis of fetal abnormalities.

The bishops and their allies intend to press on towards a theocratic state. They have stated: "We must reject the false and harmful belief—which unfortunately is grounded in social consciousness—that a secular state is perceived as the only and fundamental guarantee of freedom and equality of citizens" (Szawarski, 1991). If they succeed in creating a model Roman Catholic state, it will be women who suffer most directly. That is why no one in Poland, on whichever side of the abortion divide, underestimates the importance of the struggle around abortion as a stalking horse for what may yet come.

It is not possible to yoke together the national experience of abortion politics in Poland with that of the United States, only to offer them as two distinct examples of how abortion seemed at times to be the tail that wagged the dog of national politics. It has been quite remarkable to find abortion ricocheting around the political arena in Poland and other Eastern European countries. But the issue has played a crucial part in the politics of the United States for almost twenty years: in itself an astonishing phenomenon.

USA, 1973—THE SUPREME COURT LIGHTS THE FUSE

Until the historic U.S. Supreme Court judgment of 1973, in the case of *Roe* v. *Wade* (which I shall call plain *Roe*), abortion was not a major issue in the United States. In the late 1960s, when campaigners for abortion reform in California asked people to sign petitions, it took so long for people to think and talk before deciding where they stood that no more than four or five signatures could be gathered in an afternoon's work (Luker, 1984).

But the spark of *Roe* caught dry tinder at once and is still burning. Today, everyone has an opinion on abortion: After thousands of opinion polls, hours of TV debating, radio phone-ins and miles of newsprint, people know with certainty whether they are "pro-choice" or "pro-life."

In the late nineteenth century it was doctors who pressed for anti-abortion legislation in the United States, partly to strengthen the delineation of medicine as a regulated, elite profession. Making abortion illegal, unless performed by a doctor, was an effective way of cutting the ground from under the "quacks." The laws granted doctors alone the discretion to decide when a woman's life was sufficiently endangered to justify the loss of fetal life.

For almost seventy years legal abortion was a matter for medical judgement. Its prevalence and the criteria used varied enormously. Women who could not get legal abortions resorted to illegal practitioners and practices. But in the 1950s and 1960s exclusive medical control over abortion began to crumble.

Briefly, women's lives were changing as they entered the labour market in increasing numbers—for a married woman an unintended pregnancy became much more of a disaster than in the past; secondly, the improvements of medicine and obstetrics made pregnancy and childbirth much safer and made it harder for doctors to cloak a decision to perform an abortion for a wealthy patient behind the excuse that continuing the pregnancy would gravely endanger her health. Doctors' work became much more hospital-based and could be more easily scrutinized and regulated than when they worked in private consulting rooms.

Thirdly, women began to question the right of doctors and lawyers, or anyone, to decide whether or not they should have to continue an unintended pregnancy. Finally, the effects of the Thalidomide cases and the advent of effective contraception all played a part in dragging decisions and policies on abortion into the harsh public light of politics.

Some states began to permit abortion. Between 1967 and 1973, seventeen states rescinded their restrictions on abortion. Thousands of women crossed state boundaries to obtain abortions (Gold, 1990). Abortion was happening, despite its continuing prohibition under federal law.

Several decades of Supreme Court decisions—for instance, acknowledging it was no business of the state (or states) to seek to outlaw the use and purchase of contraceptives—had smoothed the path towards the *Roe* judgment, but nonetheless, when it eventually came, it was quite dramatic. The court said that a woman's right to obtain an abortion, like her right to use contraception without government interference is constitutionally protected, as part of her fundamental right to privacy. And that because the right to privacy is fundamental (rights under the American constitution are ranked, and *fundamental* trumps every other kind of right) states must show a "compelling interest" before they can intervene.

The court stressed that, of course, the decision to abort must be made together with a doctor. But it devised a sliding scale of maternal/fetal rights, practically sanctioning "abortion on demand" in the first trimester and gradually increasing the amount of protection afforded to the fetus as the weeks of pregnancy progressed.

No Room for Compromise

The significance of the Supreme Court ruling in 1973 was that it turned abortion into a constitutional issue, declaring it a fundamental right of the female citizen, and sweeping away all the various state restrictions. In doing so it called into question the deeply held beliefs of people accustomed to thinking that *theirs* was the majority opinion and set the state on a collision course with an indefatigable group of its citizens. As long as abortion had been purely a medical issue, as it is in Britain (see below) it had been much more difficult to challenge, and far less in the public domain.

The absolute divide between right-to-life/pro-life/anti-choice/anti-abortion people, and the rest is thc cmbryo or fetus. If you believe that the embryo or later the fetus is a person, a human being in the fullest sense, the moral equivalent of a woman, everything else falls into place. The Supreme Court questioned this notion and opened the door to the years of court challenge, endless legislative pressure and single-issue pressure-group politics. For those who believe that abortion is the equivalent of homicide there can hardly be a compromise.

The impact of the *Roe* judgement was enormous. Overnight literally, the opposition mobilized.[1] Its attack has had two aims: to upset and overturn the judicial applecart and at the same time to erect as many obstacles as possible between a woman and a legal abortion. It's been a busy twenty years: *Roe* has been harried almost to extinction by state regulations, such as imposed waiting periods, demands for "informed consent," such as making the woman look at images of fetal development—at all stages, no matter how early her own pregnancy. As pro-choice campaigner Lawrence Lader said, after *Roe,* "We thought we had won. We were wrong" (*Family Planning World*, Jan/Feb, 1992).

At first, state attempts to regulate abortion after *Roe* received a cool response in the Supreme Court, but as the new right has gained power and judges appointed to the court became more conservative, so the judgements have hardened against abortion rights.

Wide-ranging Success for Abortion's Opponents

The cultural and political climate today is of course very different from that surrounding *Roe* in 1973. On the day of the Supreme Court's ruling on *Roe*, newspapers reported an agreement which might bring an end to the war in Vietnam and carried obituaries of former President Lyndon B. Johnson, whose presidency was marked domestically by the civil rights movement, Black Power and the movement against the war in Vietnam. This is not the place to rehearse the cultural "backlash" of the years since then except to highlight how wide-ranging it has been.

Susan Faludi, for instance, recounts the fate of a script for the TV show *Cagney and Lacey.* In "Choices," as the early 1980s' episode was to be called, Cagney—the single woman in the feisty female cop duo—became pregnant. CBS programming executives went beserk at the mere idea of abortion (even as an option to be rejected). They demanded numerous rewrites until in the final version, Cagney only mistakenly thinks she is pregnant. "Lacey . . . tells her that if she had been pregnant she should have got married. Abortion is never offered as a choice" (Faludi, 1992:186).

The anti-abortion lobby drew comfort not only from *Cagney and Lacey* but also from the White House. As the violence against clinics increased in 1984 after Ronald Reagan's election to a second term as president, he refused to condemn the actions and their perpetrators (Blanchard & Prewitt, 1993).[2]

Opinion polls show that Americans' attitude to abortion was and generally remains "permit but discourage." It was not very hard to convert such ambivalence into support for restrictions on government funding and so on. The most significant curtailment of rights for low-income women was the Hyde Amendment of 1979 which denied Medicaid funding for abortion, except where a woman's life is in danger. There have also been severe and wide-ranging restrictions on the use of public facilities for abortion: It is illegal, for instance, to perform a private abortion in a private building standing on publicly owned land. By 1979 no federal funds could be used to provide abortion or abortion-related services (Petchesky, 1984).

Today, only half the United States' medical schools even offer the option of training in abortion procedures, and fewer and fewer young doctors are willing to perform abortions. Many gynaecologists still performing abortions are reaching retirement, and in a 1985 study, two-thirds of the gynaecologists in the United States stated that they would not terminate pregnancy. Who would choose to conduct their professional working life in a bullet-proof vest, with an armed guard at the clinic door? In 1988, 83 percent of all United States counties lacked any facilities for abortion, and those counties contain 31 percent of U.S. women aged between fifteen and forty-four (Alan Guttmacher Institute, 1993).

A shadowy world of unlicensed, unregulated abortion facilities in private doctors' offices is beginning to emerge. There are estimated to be several dozen in New York City alone, and a doctor there was recently prosecuted for a botched abortion on a twenty-one-year-old immigrant woman, who subsequently gave birth to a severely mutilated infant (*Family Planning World*, May/June, 1993).

And yet, despite all the legislative obstacles and the physical harassment, the anti-abortion movement has made no dent in the number of abortions taking place in the United States. The overall figure has hovered steadily around 1.6 million a year.

Who Opposes Abortion Rights?

The intimidation of anti-abortion activists, such as Operation Rescue, or the Lambs of Christ, and the violence and terrorism against abortion clinics is what immediately comes to mind when thinking about abortion's opponents, but it is not the only face of the opposition.

After the *Roe* judgment, the Catholic Church was the first into action, with plangent denunciation and millions of dollars poured into new anti-abortion organizations. But as the New Right in the Republican party set out deliberately to woo the anti-abortion voters, as part of its efforts to shift the party itself to the right, the anti-abortion alliance became a curious blend—from Catholics to born-again Christian evangelicals, to more secular "New Right" types. It was ultimately to prove a volatile coalition.

Abortion has been and still is the kernel of a protracted campaign against the social trends of the second half of the twentieth century, and for a reinstatement of "traditional family values." The Reagan presidency boosted the legitimacy, power and influence of "God's bullies" as they have been aptly called. Although the specific goal of the antiabortionists is to outlaw abortions, it is important to see this in a wider context of conservatism, attacks on welfare and so on.

The movement has two faces—first, the lobbyists and court challengers, as well as the image-makers, whose ideological offensive has sought to control the public perception of abortion and the women who seek it (Petchesky, 1984). In 1990 alone there were 465 abortion-related bills presented to state legislatures (McKeegan, 1992). The anti-abortion lobby has used its muscle in the ballot box with considerable effect. Single-issue voting can tip the scales when results are close and election turnouts are low. Packing state legislatures and other elected bodies has been a systematic strategy and for twenty years abortion has wracked the United States, from school boards to Congress.

Secondly, there is the face of direct action, some of it peaceful, but nevertheless extremely intimidating, some of it violent and explicitly women-hating. In 1991 in Wichita, south Kansas, there were more than 2,600 arrests as 30,000 anti-abortion protesters blockaded an abortion clinic. In the last fifteen years around a hundred clinics have been bombed or set on fire. Others have had medical equipment wrecked. Clinic staff and their families have been harassed; doctors have been shot at; in March 1993, one was even killed.

Pregnant women arriving at abortion clinics have had to run a gauntlet of screaming demonstrators, some hurling plastic fetal models, some videotaping their faces and noting the numbers on their car license plates for subsequent tracing and personal harassment.

A study of men convicted of anti-abortion violence concluded that they are "clearly acting out of a desire to maintain the dependent status of women." Many also favour policies such as capital and corporal punishment (Blanchard & Prewitt, 1993). Somewhat in a grey area of legality lie the fake abortion clinics which have been set up and are listed in the Yellow Pages, which harangue women who turn up hoping to arrange an abortion, and force them to look at often gruesome pictures of fetuses. . . .

WHY HAS BRITAIN'S ABORTION DEBATE BEEN DIFFERENT?

It seems worth briefly comparing the struggle in the United States with that in Britain, whose political process has never been gripped by the throat as it has in the United States. Pro-choice Republican Senator Robert Packwood explained what the attentions of a single-minded group such as the U.S. anti-abortion lobby mean to his daily political life:

> [The pro-lifers] are a frightening force. They are people who are with you 99 percent of the time, but if you vote against them on this issue it doesn't matter what else you stand for. (Tribe, 1992)

That's hard to imagine in Britain. Of course, there have been times when abortion has been a hot issue in the U.K., swelling MPs' mailbags and prompting heated exchanges on *Question Time,* but it has at no time been such dynamite, compelling British MPs to refer their every political step to its impact on those of their supporters who oppose abortion. Part of the reason is that Britain is relatively indifferent to religion and has no comparably powerful, organized fundamentalist or Roman Catholic population. Also, laws made in the United States Supreme Court positively invite legal challenge and counter-challenge. Laws made by Parliament are more resilient in general.

What's more, part of the reason is in the abortion law itself. It is for doctors, says Britain's 1967 Abortion Act—two doctors—to decide whether a woman needs an abortion, under the terms specified by the law. The rights of women do not remotely enter into it. Many campaigners who have defended the provisions of the 1967 Act, from no less than sixteen parliamentary attempts to curtail its scope, believe that it is the Act's reliance on doctors that has allowed it to escape relatively unscathed after twenty-five years.

When opponents of abortion in Britain have attacked the Act, its defenders have quite legitimately and cogently been able to point out that it is not *women* who make the final decision, but (respectable) professionals. (Funding cuts in the National Health Service and excessive Department of Health regulations have more stealthily debilitated abortion provision in Britain—that is another story.) Although the inherent paternalism in the framing of the Act is not only demeaning but has also led to unfair geographical differences in women's access to a sympathetic, prompt abortion service, the pragmatic, defensive value of investing the responsibility in the medical profession is worth noting.

CRITICAL-THINKING QUESTIONS

1. The United States has witnessed numerous murders of physicians who provide abortion services and bombings of Planned Parenthood clinics. Why, in contrast, has Poland not experienced such violent attacks on the medical profession and on women who seek abortions?

2. Why, in contrast to the United States and Poland, has there been little debate about abortion in Great Britain?

3. Opponents of abortion in Europe and the United States often describe abortion as a break-

down of "social values" and the "traditional family." In contrast, proponents of abortion emphasize a woman's reproductive rights. According to Hadley, how do politics, religion, and economics ultimately shape policy and many women's destiny in abortion debates?

NOTES

1. Kristin Luker (Luker, 1984) describes how would-be activists phoned around frantically in the days after the court decision, trying to find an organization to join. Many of them—women, married, housewives with small children, had never joined anything before—not even the school parent-teacher association.

2. Ronald Reagan not only refused to condemn the violence, in 1984 he wrote a bizarre call-to-arms against abortion, with help from Malcolm Muggeridge *(Abortion and the Conscience of the Nation*. Thomas Nelson, Nashville, 1984).

REFERENCES

ALAN GUTTMACHER INSTITUTE. 1993. *Abortion in the United States: Facts in brief.* New York.

BLANCHARD, D., and T. J. PREWITT. 1993. *Religious violence and abortion*. University Press of Florida.

EINHORN, B. 1993. Polish backlash. *Everywoman*, April, 1993.

FALUDI, S. 1992. *Backlash*. London: Vintage.

GOLD, RACHEL BENSON. 1990. *Abortion and women's health: The turning point for America*. New York: Alan Guttmacher Institute.

HOELL, S. 1993. Strict new law drives abortion underground in Poland. *Reuters*, 14 December.

JANKOWSKA, H. 1993. The reproductive rights campaign in Poland. *Women's Studies International Forum*, 16, 3:291–96.

KISSLING, F. 1992. The Church's heavy hand in Poland. *Planned Parenthood in Europe* 21, 2 (May):18–19.

LUKER, K. 1984. *Abortion and the politics of motherhood*. Berkeley: University of California Press.

MCKEEGAN, M. 1992. *Mutiny in the ranks of the right*. New York: The Free Press, Maxwell Macmillan International.

MRUGALA, G. 1991. Polish family planning in crisis: The Roman Catholic influence. *Planned Parenthood in Europe* 20, 2, (September):4–5.

OKOLSKI, M. 1988. 'Poland' in Sachdev, P., *International handbook on abortion*. New York: Greenwood Press.

PETCHESKY, R. 1984. *Abortion and woman's choice*. New York, Longman.

RICH, VERA. 1991. Poland: Abortion and contraception. *Lancet*, 338, 875, (13 July):108–9.

SZAWARSKI, Z. 1991. Abortion in Poland. *British Journal of Obstetrics and Gynaecology*, 98 (December):1202–4.

TRIBE, L. 1992. *Abortion: The clash of absolutes*. New York, Norton.

WORLD HEALTH ORGANIZATION. 1993. *Progress in human reproductive research*, No. 25. Geneva.

Social Change and Modernity

CLASSIC

CONTEMPORARY

CROSS-CULTURAL

74

Anomy and Modern Life

Emile Durkheim

In this excerpt from his classic study of suicide, Emile Durkheim asserts that human aspiration, which is not bounded by nature as in other creatures, must be framed by limits imposed by society. Modern societies, however, have lost some of their moral power over the individual. The consequence is a societal condition of anomy (or anomie), which people experience as a lack of moral regulation. In the extreme, anomy prompts people to suicide; more generally, an anomic society contains people with weak and vacillating moral values who have difficulty reining in their own ambitions and desires.

No living being can be happy or even exist unless his needs are sufficiently proportioned to his means. In other words, if his needs require more than can be granted, or even merely something of a different sort, they will be under continual friction and can only function painfully. . . .

In the animal, at least in a normal condition, this equilibrium is established with automatic spontaneity because the animal depends on purely material conditions. All the organism needs is that the supplies of substance and energy constantly employed in the vital process should be periodically renewed by equivalent quantities; that replacement be equivalent to use. When the void created by existence in its own resources is filled, the animal, satisfied, asks nothing further. Its power of reflection is not sufficiently developed to imagine other ends than those implicit in its physical nature. . . .

Edvard Munch, *The Scream*, Oslo, National Gallery, Scala/Art Resource, NY. © 1998 Artists Rights Society (ARS), New York/ADAGP, Paris.

This is not the case with man, because most of his needs are not dependent on his body or not to the same degree. . . . But how determine the quantity of well-being, comfort or luxury legitimately to be craved by a human being? Nothing appears in man's organic nor in his psychological constitution which sets a limit to such tendencies. The functioning of individual life does not require them to cease at one point rather than at another; the proof being that they have constantly increased since the be-

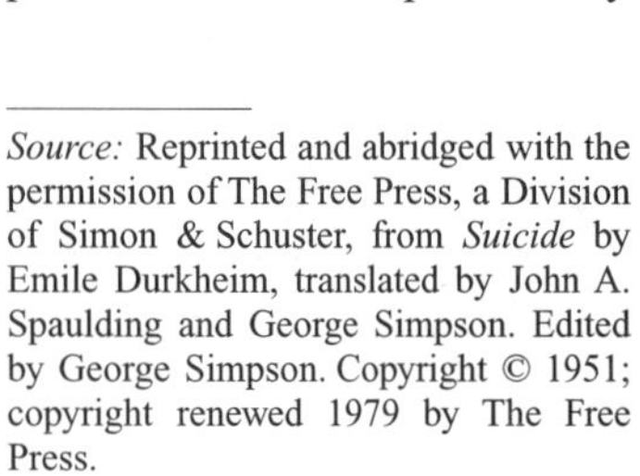

Source: Reprinted and abridged with the permission of The Free Press, a Division of Simon & Schuster, from *Suicide* by Emile Durkheim, translated by John A. Spaulding and George Simpson. Edited by George Simpson. Copyright © 1951; copyright renewed 1979 by The Free Press.

ginnings of history, receiving more and more complete satisfaction, yet with no weakening of average health. . . . It is not human nature which can assign the variable limits necessary to our needs. They are thus unlimited so far as they depend on the individual alone. Irrespective of any external regulatory force, our capacity for feeling is in itself an insatiable and bottomless abyss.

But if nothing external can restrain this capacity, it can only be a source of torment to itself. Unlimited desires are insatiable by definition and insatiability is rightly considered a sign of morbidity. Being unlimited, they constantly and infinitely surpass the means at their command; they cannot be quenched. Inextinguishable thirst is constantly renewed torture. It has been claimed, indeed, that human activity naturally aspires beyond assignable limits and sets itself unattainable goals. But how can such an undetermined state be any more reconciled with the conditions of mental life than with the demands of physical life? All man's pleasure in acting, moving and exerting himself implies the sense that his efforts are not in vain and that by walking he has advanced. However, one does not advance when one walks toward no goal, or—which is the same thing—when his goal is infinity. Since the distance between us and it is always the same, whatever road we take, we might as well have made the motions without progress from the spot. Even our glances behind and our feeling of pride at the distance covered can cause only deceptive satisfaction, since the remaining distance is not proportionately reduced. To pursue a goal which is by definition unattainable is to condemn oneself to a state of perpetual unhappiness. Of course, man may hope contrary to all reason, and hope has its pleasures even when unreasonable. It may sustain him for a time; but it cannot survive the repeated disappointments of experience indefinitely. What more can the future offer him than the past, since he can never reach a tenable condition nor even approach the glimpsed ideal? Thus, the more one has, the more one wants, since satisfactions received only stimulate instead of filling needs. . . .

To achieve any other result, the passions first must be limited. Only then can they be harmonized with the faculties and satisfied. But since the individual has no way of limiting them, this must be done by some force exterior to him. A regulative force must play the same role for moral needs which the organism plays for physical needs. This means that the force can only be moral. The awakening of conscience interrupted the state of equilibrium of the animal's dormant existence; only conscience, therefore, can furnish the means to re-establish it. Physical restraint would be ineffective; hearts cannot be touched by physio-chemical forces. So far as the appetites are not automatically restrained by physiological mechanisms, they can be halted only by a limit that they recognize as just. Men would never consent to restrict their desires if they felt justified in passing the assigned limit. But, for reasons given above, they cannot assign themselves this law of justice. So they must receive it from an authority which they respect, to which they yield spontaneously. Either directly and as a whole, or through the agency of one of its organs, society alone can play this moderating role; for it is the only moral power superior to the individual, the authority of which he accepts. It alone has the power necessary to stipulate law and to set the point beyond which the passions must not go. . . .

. . . Man's characteristic privilege is that the bond he accepts is not physical but moral; that is, social. He is governed not by a material environment brutally imposed on him, but by a conscience superior to his own, the superiority of which he feels. Because the greater, better part of his existence transcends the body, he escapes the body's yoke, but is subject to that of society.

But when society is disturbed by some painful crisis or by beneficent but abrupt transitions, it is momentarily incapable of exercising this influence; thence come the sudden rises in the curve of suicides which we have pointed out above.

In the case of economic disasters, indeed, something like a declassification occurs which suddenly casts certain individuals into a lower state than their previous one. Then they must reduce their requirements, restrain their needs, learn greater self-control. All the advantages of social influence are lost so far as they are concerned; their moral education has to be recommenced. But society cannot adjust them instantaneously to this new life and teach them to practice the increased self-repression to which they are unaccustomed. So they are not adjusted to the condition forced on them, and its very prospect is intolerable; hence the suffering which detaches them from a reduced existence even before they have made trial of it.

It is the same if the source of the crisis is an abrupt growth of power and wealth. Then, truly, as the conditions of life are changed, the standard according to which needs were regulated can no longer remain the same; for it varies with social resources, since it largely determines the share of each class of producers. The scale is upset; but a new scale cannot be immediately improvised. Time is required for the public conscience to reclassify men and things. So long as the social forces thus freed have not regained equilibrium, their respective values are unknown and so all regulation is lacking for a time. The limits are unknown between the possible and the impossible, what is just and what is unjust, legitimate claims and hopes and those which are immoderate. Consequently, there is no restraint upon aspiration. . . . Appetites, not being controlled by a public opinion become disoriented, no longer recognize the limits proper to them. . . . With increased prosperity desires increase. At the very moment when traditional rules have lost their authority, the richer prize offered these appetites stimulates them and makes them more exigent and impatient of control. The state of de-regulation or anomy is thus further heightened by passions being less disciplined, precisely when they need more disciplining. . . .

This explanation is confirmed by the remarkable immunity of poor countries. Poverty protects against suicide because it is a restraint in itself. No matter how one acts, desires have to depend upon resources to some extent; actual possessions are partly the criterion of those aspired to. So the less one has the less he is tempted to extend the range of his needs indefinitely. Lack of power, compelling moderation, accustoms men to it, while nothing excites envy if no one has superfluity. Wealth, on the other hand, by the power it bestows, deceives us into believing that we depend on ourselves only. Reducing the resistance we encounter from objects, it suggests the possibility of unlimited success against them. The less limited one feels, the more intolerable all limitation appears. Not without reason, therefore, have so many religions dwelt on the advantages and moral value of poverty. It is actually the best school for teaching self-restraint. Forcing us to constant self-discipline, it prepares us to accept collective discipline with equanimity, while wealth, exalting the individual, may always arouse the spirit of rebellion which is the very source of immorality. This, of course, is no reason why humanity should not improve its material condition. But though the moral danger involved in every growth of prosperity is not irremediable, it should not be forgotten.

If anomy never appeared except, as in the above instances, in intermittent spurts and acute crisis, it might cause the social suicide-rate to vary from time to time, but it would not be a regular, constant factor. In one sphere of social life, however—the sphere of trade and industry—it is actually in a chronic state.

For a whole century, economic progress has mainly consisted in freeing industrial relations from all regulation. Until very recently, it was the function of a whole system of moral forces to exert this discipline. First, the influence of religion was felt alike by workers and masters, the poor and the rich. It consoled the former and taught them contentment with their lot by informing them of the providential nature of the social order, that the share of each class was assigned by God himself, and by holding out the hope for just compensation in a world to come in return for the inequalities of this world. It governed the latter, recalling that worldly interests are not man's entire lot, that they must be subordinate to other and higher interests, and that they should therefore not be pursued without rule or measure. Temporal power, in turn, restrained the scope of economic functions by its supremacy over them and by the relatively subordinate role it assigned them. Finally, within the business world proper, the occupational groups by regulating salaries, the price of products and production itself, indirectly fixed the average level of income on which needs are partially based by the very force of circumstances. However, we do not mean to propose this organization as a model. Clearly it would be inadequate to existing societies without great changes. What we stress is its existence, the fact of its useful influence, and that nothing today has come to take its place.

Actually, religion has lost most of its power. And government, instead of regulating economic life, has become its tool and servant. The most opposite schools, orthodox economists and extreme socialists, unite to reduce government to the role of a more or less passive intermediary among the various social functions. The former wish to make it simply the guardian of individual contracts; the latter leave it the task of doing the collective bookkeeping, that is, of recording the demands of consumers, transmitting them to producers, inventorying the total revenue and distributing it according to a fixed formula. But both refuse it any power to subordinate other social organs to itself and to make them converge toward one dominant aim. On both sides nations are declared to have the single or chief purpose of achieving industrial prosperity; such is the implication of the dogma of economic materialism, the basis of both apparently opposed systems. And as these theories merely express the state of opinion, industry, instead of being still regarded as a means to an end transcending itself, has become the supreme end of individuals and societies alike. Thereupon the appetites thus excited have become freed of any limiting authority. By sanctifying them, so to speak, this apotheosis of well-being has placed them above all human law. Their restraint seems like a sort of sacrilege. For this reason, even the purely utilitarian regulation of them exercised by the industrial world itself through the medium of occupational groups has been unable to persist. Ultimately, this liberation of desires has been made worse by the very development of industry and the almost infinite extension of the market. So long as the producer could gain his profits only in his immediate neighborhood, the restricted amount of possible gain could not much overexcite ambition. Now that he may assume to have almost the entire world as his customer, how could passions accept their former confinement in the face of such limitless prospects?

Such is the source of the excitement predominating in this part of society, and which has thence extended to the other parts. There the state of crisis and anomy is constant and, so to speak, normal. From top to bottom of the ladder, greed is aroused without knowing where to find ultimate foothold. Nothing can calm it, since its goal is far beyond all it can attain. Reality seems valueless by comparison with the dreams of fevered imaginations; reality is therefore abandoned, but so too is possibility abandoned when it in turn becomes reality. A thirst arises for novelties, unfamiliar pleasures, nameless sensations, all of which lose their savor once known. Henceforth one has no strength to endure the least reverse. The whole fever subsides and the sterility of all the tumult is apparent, and it is seen that all these new sensations in their infinite quantity cannot form a solid foundation of happiness to support one during days of trial. The wise man, knowing how to enjoy achieved results without having constantly to replace them with others, finds in them an attachment to life in the hour of difficulty. But the man who has always pinned all his hopes on the future and lived with his eyes fixed upon it, has nothing in the past as a comfort against the present's afflictions, for the past was nothing to him but a series of hastily experienced stages. What blinded him to himself was his expectation always to find further on the happiness he had so far missed. Now he is stopped in his tracks; from now on nothing remains behind or ahead of him to fix his gaze upon. Weariness alone, moreover, is enough to bring disillusionment, for he cannot in the end escape the futility of an endless pursuit.

We may even wonder if this moral state is not principally what makes economic catastrophes of our day so fertile in suicides. In societies where a man is subjected to a healthy discipline, he submits more readily to the blows of chance. The necessary effort for sustaining a little more discomfort costs him relatively little, since he is used to discomfort and constraint. But when every constraint is hateful in itself, how can closer constraint not seem intolerable? There is no tendency to resignation in the feverish impatience of men's lives. When there is no other aim but to outstrip constantly the point arrived at, how painful to be thrown back! Now this very lack of organization characterizing our economic condition throws the door wide to every sort of adventure. Since imagination is hungry for novelty, and ungoverned, it gropes at random. Setbacks necessarily increase with risks and thus crises multiply, just when they are becoming more destructive.

Yet these dispositions are so inbred that society has grown to accept them and is accustomed to think them normal. It is everlastingly repeated that it is man's nature to be eternally dissatisfied, constantly to advance, without relief or rest, toward an indefinite goal. The longing for infinity is daily represented as a mark of moral distinction, whereas it can only appear within unregulated consciences which elevate to a rule the lack of rule from which they suffer. The doctrine of the most ruthless and swift progress has become an article of faith. But other theories appear parallel with those praising the advantages of instability, which, generalizing the situation that gives them birth, declare life evil, claim that it is richer in grief than in pleasure and that it attracts men only by false claims. Since this disorder is greatest in the economic world, it has most victims there.

Industrial and commercial functions are really among the occupations which furnish the greatest number of suicides. . . . Almost on a level with the liberal professions, they sometimes surpass them; they are especially more afflicted than agriculture, where the old regulative forces still make their appearance felt most and where the fever of business has least penetrated. Here is best recalled what was once the general constitution of the economic order. And the divergence would be yet greater if, among the suicides of industry, employers were distinguished from workmen, for the former are probably most stricken by the state of anomy. The enormous rate of those with independent means (720 per million) sufficiently shows that the possessors of most comfort suffer most. Everything that enforces subordination attenuates the effects of this state. At least the horizon of the lower classes is limited by those above them, and for this same reason their desires are more modest. Those who have only empty space above them are almost inevitably lost in it, if no force restrains them.

CRITICAL-THINKING QUESTIONS

1. How do most creatures restrain their desires? How are human beings distinctive in this way?
2. Why does modern society afford to individuals less moral regulation? Why is this especially true of people (such as rock stars) who experience sudden fame and fortune?
3. How would Durkheim explain the relatively high suicide rate among rock stars and other celebrities?

75

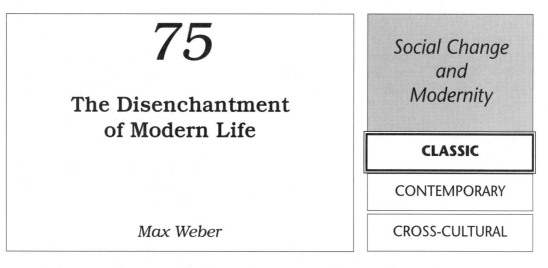

The Disenchantment of Modern Life

Max Weber

Social Change and Modernity

CLASSIC

CONTEMPORARY

CROSS-CULTURAL

In this excerpt from a speech, "Science as a Vocation," delivered at Munich University in 1918, Weber claims that the rise of science has changed our way of thinking about the world. Where, in the past, humans confronted a world of mystical forces beyond our comprehension, now we assume that all things yield to human comprehension. Thus, Weber concludes, the world has become "disenchanted." Notice, however, that something is lost in the process for, unlike the churches of the past, science can provide no answer to questions of ultimate meaning in life.

Scientific progress is a fraction, the most important fraction, of the process of intellectualization which we have been undergoing for thousands of years and which nowadays is usually judged in such an extremely negative way. Let us first clarify what this intellectualist rationalization, created by science and by scientifically oriented technology, means practically.

Does it mean that we, today, for instance, everyone sitting in this hall, have a greater knowledge of the conditions of life under which we exist than has an American Indian or a Hottentot? Hardly. Unless he is a physicist, one who rides on the streetcar has no idea how the car happened to get into motion. And he does not need to know. He is satisfied that he may "count" on the behavior of the streetcar, and he orients his conduct according to this expectation; but he knows nothing about what it takes to produce such a car so that it can move. The savage knows incomparably more about his tools. When we spend money today I bet that even if there are colleagues of political economy here in the hall, almost every one of them will hold a different answer in readiness to the question: How does it happen that one can buy something for money—sometimes more and sometimes less? The savage knows what he does in order to get his daily food and which institutions serve him in this pursuit. The increasing intellectualization and rationalization do *not,* therefore, indicate an increased and general knowledge of the conditions under which one lives.

It means something else, namely, the knowledge or belief that if one but wished one *could* learn it at any time. Hence, it means that principally there are no mysterious incalculable forces that come into play, but rather that one can, in principle, master all things by calculation. This means that the world is disenchanted. One need no longer have recourse to magical means in order to master or implore the spirits, as did the

Source: Excerpts from *From Max Weber: Essays in Sociology* by Max Weber, edited by H. H. Gerth & C. Wright Mills, translated by H. H. Gerth & C. Wright Mills.

savage, for whom such mysterious powers existed. Technical means and calculations perform the service. This above all is what intellectualization means. . . .

Science today is a "vocation" organized in special disciplines in the service of self-clarification and knowledge of interrelated facts. It is not the gift of grace of seers and prophets dispensing sacred values and revelations, nor does it partake of the contemplation of sages and philosophers about the meaning of the universe. This, to be sure, is the inescapable condition of our historical situation. We cannot evade it so long as we remain true to ourselves. And if Tolstoi's question recurs to you: As science does not, who is to answer the question: "What shall we do, and, how shall we arrange our lives?" or, in the words used here tonight: "Which of the warring gods should we serve? Or should we serve perhaps an entirely different god, and who is he?" then one can say that only a prophet or a savior can give the answers. . . .

To the person who cannot bear the fate of the times like a man, one must say: May he rather return silently, without the usual publicity build-up of renegades, but simply and plainly. The arms of the old churches are opened widely and compassionately for him. After all, they do not make it hard for him. One way or another he has to bring his "intellectual sacrifice"—that is inevitable. If he can really do it, we shall not rebuke him. For such an intellectual sacrifice in favor of an unconditional religious devotion is ethically quite a different matter than the evasion of the plain duty of intellectual integrity, which sets in if one lacks the courage to clarify one's own ultimate standpoint and rather facilitates this duty by feeble relative judgments. In my eyes, such religious return stands higher than the academic prophecy, which does not clearly realize that in the lecture-rooms of the university no other virtue holds but plain intellectual integrity: Integrity, however, compels us to state that for the many who today tarry for new prophets and saviors, the situation is the same as resounds in the beautiful Edomite watchman's song of the period of exile that has been included among Isaiah's oracles:

> He calleth to me out of Seir, Watchman, what of the night? The watchman said, The morning cometh, and also the night: if ye will enquire, enquire ye: return, come.

The people to whom this was said has enquired and tarried for more than two millennia, and we are shaken when we realize its fate. From this we want to draw the lesson that nothing is gained by yearning and tarrying alone, and we shall act differently. We shall set to work and meet the "demands of the day," in human relations as well as in our vocation. This, however, is plain and simple, if each finds and obeys the demon who holds the fibers of his very life.

CRITICAL-THINKING QUESTIONS

1. In what sense do members of a traditional society know more about their world than we do? In what sense do we know more?
2. What is "Tolstoi's question"? Why can science not answer it?
3. What does Weber see as the great burden of living in a modern society? In other words, what comforts of the past are less available to modern people?

76

The Search for Meaning in Modern America

Robert N. Bellah, Richard Madsen, William M. Sullivan, Ann Swidler, and Steven M. Tipton

Social Change and Modernity

CLASSIC

CONTEMPORARY

CROSS-CULTURAL

In the pursuit of their individual dreams, people in the United States seem to have lost the ability to connect with others to form a meaningful human community. In other words, although freed from the grasp of tradition, modern Americans too often seem to be rootless and lonely, unsure of what to believe, and uncommitted to goals beyond their immediate pleasures. This selection from a widely read study of U.S. culture explores the promise—and also the pitfalls—of modern society.

. . . Much of the thinking about our society and where it should be going is rather narrowly [focused] on our political economy. This focus makes sense in that government and the corporations are the most powerful structures in our society and affect everything else, including our culture and our character. But as an exclusive concern, such a focus is severely limited. Structures are not unchanging. They are frequently altered by social movements, which grow out of, and also influence, changes in consciousness, climates of opinion, and culture. We have followed Tocqueville and other classical social theorists in [focusing] on the mores—the "habits of the heart"—that include consciousness, culture, and the daily practices of life. It makes sense to study the mores not because they are powerful—in the short run, at least, power belongs to the political and economic structures—but for two other reasons. A study of the mores gives us insight into the state of society, its coherence, and its long-term viability. Secondly, it is in the sphere of the mores, and the climates of opinion they express, that we are apt to discern incipient changes of vision—those new flights of the social imagination that may indicate where society is heading.

A CHANGE OF ERAS?

. . . John Donne, in 1611, at the very beginning of the modern era, with the prescience that is sometimes given to great poets, vividly described that process:

'Tis all in peeces, all cohaerence gone;
All just supply, and all Relation:
Prince, Subject, Father, Sonne, are things forgot,
For every man alone thinkes he hath got
To be a Phoenix, and that then can bee
None of that kinde, of which he is, but hee.[1]

Source: From *Habits of the Heart: Individualism and Commitment in American Life* by Robert N. Bellah, Richard Madsen, William M. Sullivan, Ann Swidler, and Steven M. Tipton (Berkeley, Calif.: University of California Press, 1985), pp. 275–93, 294–96.

Donne lived in a world where the ties of kinship and village and feudal obligation were already loosening, though only a few perceived how radical the consequences would be.

America was colonized by those who had come loose from the older European structures, and so from the beginning we had a head start in the process of modernization. Yet the colonists brought with them ideas of social obligation and group formation that disposed them to recreate in America structures of family, church, and polity that would continue, if in modified form, the texture of older European society. Only gradually did it become clear that every social obligation was vulnerable, every tie between individuals fragile. Only gradually did what we have called ontological individualism, the idea that the individual is the only firm reality, become widespread. Even in our day, when separation and individuation have reached a kind of culmination, their triumph is far from complete. The battles of modernity are still being fought.

But today the battles have become half-hearted. There was a time when, under the battle cry of "freedom," separation and individuation were embraced as the key to a marvelous future of unlimited possibility. It is true that there were always those, like Donne, who viewed the past with nostalgia and the present with apprehension and who warned that we were entering unknown and dangerous waters. It is also true that there are still those who maintain their enthusiasm for modernity, who speak of the third wave or the Aquarian Age or the new paradigm in which a dissociated individuation will reach a final fulfillment. Perhaps most common today, however, is a note of uncertainty, not a desire to turn back to the past but an anxiety about where we seem to be headed. In this view, modernity seems to be a period of enormously rapid change, a transition from something relatively fixed toward something not yet clear. Many might find still applicable Matthew Arnold's assertion that we are

> Wandering between two worlds, one dead,
> The other powerless to be born.[2]

There is a widespread feeling that the promise of the modern era is slipping away from us. A movement of enlightenment and liberation that was to have freed us from superstition and tyranny has led in the twentieth century to a world in which ideological fanaticism and political oppression have reached extremes unknown in previous history. Science, which was to have unlocked the bounties of nature, has given us the power to destroy all life on earth. Progress, modernity's master idea, seems less compelling when it appears that it may be progress into the abyss. And the globe today is divided between a liberal world so incoherent that it seems to be losing the significance of its own ideals, an oppressive and archaic communist statism, and a poor, and often tyrannical, Third World reaching for the very first rungs of modernity. In the liberal world, the state, which was supposed to be a neutral nightwatchman that would maintain order while individuals pursued their various interests, has become so overgrown and militarized that it threatens to become a universal policeman.

Yet in spite of those daunting considerations, many of those we talked to are still hopeful. They realize that though the processes of separation and individuation were necessary to free us from the tyrannical structures of the past, they must be balanced by a renewal of commitment and community if they are not to end in self-destruction or turn into their opposites. Such a renewal is indeed a world waiting to be born if we only had the courage to see it.

THE CULTURE OF SEPARATION

One of the reasons it is hard to envision a way out of the impasse of modernity is the degree to which modernity conditions our consciousness. If modernity is "the culture of separation," Donne characterized it well when he said "'Tis all in peeces, all cohaerence gone." When the world comes to us in pieces, in fragments, lacking any overall pattern, it is hard to see how it might be transformed.

A sense of fragmentariness is as characteristic of high intellectual culture as of popular culture. Starting with science, the most respected and influential part of our high culture, we can see at once that it is not a whole, offering a general interpretation of reality, as theology and philosophy once did, but a collection of disciplines each having little to do with the others. . . .

These developments in the realm of high culture have had devastating consequences for education. Here, particularly in higher education, students were traditionally supposed to acquire some general sense of the world and their place in it. In the contemporary multiversity, it is easier to think of education as a cafeteria in which one acquires discrete bodies of information or useful skills. Feeble efforts to reverse these trends periodically convulse the universities, but the latest such convulsion, the effort to establish a "core curriculum," often turns into a battle between disciplines in which the idea of a substantive core is lost. The effort is thus more symptomatic of our cultural fracture than of its cure.

When we turn from intellectual culture to popular culture, particularly the mass media, the situation is, if anything, even more discouraging. Within the disciplinary and subdisciplinary "compartments" of intellectual culture, though there is little integration between them, there is still meaning and intensity in the search for truth. In popular culture, it is hard to say even that much. To take an extreme example, television, it would be difficult to argue that there is any coherent ideology or overall message that it communicates. There is a sense in which the broadcasters' defense of their role—that they are merely mirroring the culture—has a certain plausibility. They do not support any clear set of beliefs or policies, yet they cast doubt on everything. Certainly, they do not glorify "the power structure." Big business is not admirable: Its leaders are frequently power-hungry bullies without any moral restraints (J. R. Ewing, for example). Government is under a cloud of suspicion: Politicians are crooks. Labor is badly tarnished: Labor leaders are mobsters. The debunking that is characteristic of our intellectual culture is also characteristic of the mass media. While television does not preach, it nevertheless presents a picture of reality that influences us more than an overt message could. As Todd Gitlin has described it,

> . . . [T]elevision's world is relentlessly upbeat, clean and materialistic. Even more sweepingly, with few exceptions prime time gives us people preoccupied with personal ambition. If not utterly consumed by ambition and the fear of ending up as losers, these characters take both the ambition and the fear for granted. If not surrounded by middle-class arrays of consumer goods, they themselves are glamorous incarnations of desire. The happiness they long for is private, not public; they make few demands on society as a whole, and even when troubled they seem content with the existing institutional order. Personal ambition and consumerism are the driving forces of their lives. The sumptuous and brightly lit settings of most series amount to advertisements for a consumption-centered version of the good life, and this doesn't even take into consideration the incessant commercials, which convey the idea that human aspirations for liberty, pleasure, accomplishment and status can be fulfilled in the realm of consumption. The relentless background hum of prime time is the packaged good life.[3]

Gitlin's description applies best to daytime and prime-time soaps. It does not apply nearly so well to situation comedies, where human relations are generally more benign. Indeed, the situation comedy often portrays people tempted to dishonesty or personal disloyalty by the prospect of some private gain, who finally decide to put family or friends ahead of material aggrandizement. Yet, finally, both soaps and situation comedies are based on the same contrast: human decency versus brutal competitiveness for economic success. Although the soaps show us that the ruthlessly powerful rich are often unhappy and the situation comedies show us that decent "little people" are often happy, they both portray a world dominated by economic competition, where the only haven is a very small circle of warm personal relationships. Thus the "reality" that looms over a narrowed-down version of "traditional morality" is the overwhelming dominance of material ambition.

Of course, in television none of these things is ever really argued. Since images and feelings are better communicated in this medium than ideas, television seeks to hold us, to hook us, by the sheer succession of sensations. One sensation being as good as another, there is the implication that nothing makes any difference. We switch from a quiz show to a situation comedy, to a bloody police drama, to a miniseries about celebrities, and with each click of the dial, nothing remains.

But television operates not only with a complete disconnectedness between successive programs. Even within a single hour or half-hour program, there is extraordinary discontinuity. Commercials regularly break whatever mood has built up with their own, often very different, emotional message. Even aside from commercials, television style is singularly abrupt and jumpy, with many quick cuts to other scenes and other characters. Dialogue is reduced to clipped sentences. No one talks long enough to express anything complex. Depth of feeling, if it exists at all, has to be expressed in a word or a glance.

The form of television is intimately related to the content. Except for the formula situation comedies (and even there, divorce is increasingly common), relationships are as brittle and shifting as the action of the camera. Most people turn out to be unreliable and double-dealing. Where strong commitments are portrayed, as in police dramas, they are only between buddies, and the environing atmosphere, even within the police force, is one of mistrust and suspicion.

If popular culture, particularly television and the other mass media, makes a virtue of lacking all qualitative distinctions, and if the intellectual culture, divided as it is, hesitates to say anything about the larger issues of existence, how does our culture hold together at all? The culture of separation offers two forms of integration—or should we say pseudo-integration?—that turn out, not surprisingly, to be derived from utilitarian and expressive individualism. One is the dream of personal success. As Gitlin has observed, television shows us people who are, above all, consumed by ambition and the fear of ending up losers. That is a drama we can all identify with, at least all of us who have been (and who has not?) exposed to middle-class values. Isolated in our efforts though we are, we can at least recognize our fellows as followers of the same private dream. The second is the portrayal of vivid personal feeling. Television is much more interested in how people feel than in what they think. What they think might separate us, but how they feel draws us together. Successful television personalities and celebrities are thus people able freely to communicate their emotional states. We feel that we "really know them." And the very consumption goods that television so insistently puts before us integrate us by providing symbols of our version of the good life. But a strange sort of integration it is, for the world into which we are integrated is defined only by the spasmodic transition between striving and relaxing and is without qualitative distinctions of time and space, good and evil, meaning and meaninglessness. And however much we may for a moment see something of ourselves in another, we are really, as Matthew Arnold said in 1852, "in the sea of life enisled . . . We mortal millions live *alone.*"[4]

THE CULTURE OF COHERENCE

But that is not the whole story. It could not be the whole story, for the culture of separation, if it ever became completely dominant, would collapse of its own incoherence. Or, even more likely, well before that happened, an authoritarian state would emerge to provide the coherence the culture no longer could. If we are not entirely a mass of interchangeable fragments within an aggregate, if we are in part qualitatively distinct members of a whole, it is because they are still operating among us, with whatever difficulties, traditions that tell us about the nature of the world, about the nature of society, and about who we are as people. Primarily biblical and republican, these traditions are, as we have seen, important for many Americans and significant to some degree for almost all. Somehow families, churches, a variety of cultural associations, and; even if only in the interstices, schools and universities, do manage to communicate a form of life, a *paideia,* in the sense of growing up in a morally and intellectually intelligible world.

. . . [C]ommunities of memory . . . are concerned in a variety of ways to give a qualitative meaning to the living of life, to time and space, to persons and groups. Religious communities, for example, do not experience time in the way the mass media present it—as a continuous flow of qualitatively meaningless sensations. The day, the week, the season, the year are punctuated by an alternation of the sacred and the profane. Prayer breaks into our daily life at the beginning of a meal, at the end of the day, at common worship, reminding us that our utilitarian pursuits are not the whole of life, that a fulfilled life is one in which God and neighbor are remembered first. Many of our religious traditions recognize the significance of silence as a way of breaking the incessant flow of sensations and opening our hearts to the wholeness of being. And our republican tradition, too, has ways of giving form to time, reminding us on particular dates of the great events of our past or of the heroes who helped to teach us what we are as a free people. Even our private family life takes on a shared rhythm with a Thanksgiving dinner or a Fourth of July picnic.

In short, we have never been, and still are not, a collection of private individuals who, except for a conscious contract to create a minimal government, have nothing in common. Our lives make sense in a thousand ways, most of which we are unaware of, because of traditions that are centuries, if not millennia, old. It is these traditions that help us to know that it does make a difference who we are and how we treat one another. Even the mass media, with their tendency to homogenize feelings and sensations, cannot entirely avoid transmitting such qualitative distinctions, in however muted a form.

But if we owe the meaning of our lives to biblical and republican traditions of which we seldom consciously think, is there not the danger that the erosion of these traditions may eventually deprive us of that meaning altogether? Are we not caught between the upper millstone of a fragmented intellectual culture and the nether millstone of a fragmented popular culture? The erosion of meaning and coherence in our lives is not something Americans desire. Indeed, the profound yearning for the idealized small town that we found among most of the people we talked to is a yearning for just such meaning and coherence. But although the yearning for the small town is nostalgia for the irretrievably lost, it is worth considering whether the biblical and republican traditions that small town once embodied can be reappropriated in ways that respond to our present need. Indeed, we would argue that if we are ever to enter that new world that so far has been powerless to be born, it will be through reversing modernity's tendency to obliterate all previous culture. We need to learn again from the cultural riches of the human species and to reappropriate and revitalize those riches so that they can speak to our condition today. . . .

SOCIAL ECOLOGY

. . . Without derogating our modern technological achievements, we now see that they have had devastatingly destructive consequences for the natural ecology. We are engaged in an effort to mitigate and reverse the damage and regain an ecological balance whose complete loss could prove fatal. Modernity has had comparable destructive consequences for social ecology. Human beings have treated one another badly for as long as we have any historical evidence, but modernity has given us a capacity for destructiveness on a scale incomparably greater than in previous centuries. And social ecology is damaged not only by war, genocide, and political repression. It is also damaged by the destruction of the subtle ties that bind human beings to one another, leaving them frightened and alone. It has been evident for some time that unless we begin to repair the damage to our social ecology, we will destroy ourselves long before natural ecological disaster has time to be realized.

For several centuries, we have been embarked on a great effort to increase our freedom, wealth, and power. For over a hundred years, a large part of the American people, the middle class, has imagined that the virtual meaning of life lies in the acquisition of ever-increasing status, income, and authority, from which genuine freedom is supposed to come. Our achievements have been enormous. They permit us the aspiration to become a genuinely human society in a genuinely decent world, and provide many of the means to attain that aspiration. Yet we seem to be hovering on the very brink of disaster, not only from international conflict but from the internal incoherence of our own society. What has gone wrong? How can we reverse the slide toward the abyss?

In thinking about what has gone wrong, we need to see what we can learn from our traditions, as well as from the best currently available knowledge. What has failed at every level—from the society of nations to the national society to the local community to the family—is integration: We have failed to remember "our community as members of the same body," as John Winthrop put it. We have committed what to the republican founders of our nation was the cardinal sin: We have put our own good, as individuals, as groups, as a nation, ahead of the common good.

The litmus test that both the biblical and republican traditions give us for assaying the health of a society is how it deals with the problem of wealth and poverty. The Hebrew prophets took their stand by the *'anawim,* the poor and oppressed, and condemned the rich and powerful who exploited them. The New Testament shows us a Jesus who lived among the *'anawim* of his day and who recognized the difficulty the rich would have in responding to his call. Both testaments make it clear that societies sharply divided between rich and poor are not in accord with the will of God. Classic republican theory from Aristotle to the American founders rested on the assumption that free institutions could survive in a society only if there were a rough equality of condition, that extremes of wealth and poverty are incompatible with a republic. Jefferson was appalled at the enormous wealth and miserable poverty that he found in France and was sanguine about our future as a free people only because we lacked such extremes. Contemporary social science has documented the consequences of poverty and discrimination, so that most educated Americans know that much of what makes our world and our neighborhoods unsafe arises from economic and racial inequality.[5] Certainly most of the people to whom we talked would rather live in a safe, neighborly world instead of the one we have.

But the solution to our problems remains opaque because of our profound ambivalence. When times are prosperous, we do not mind a modest increase in "welfare." When times are not so prosperous, we think that at least our own successful careers will save us and our families from failure and despair. We are attracted, against our skepticism, to the idea that poverty will be alleviated by the crumbs that fall from the rich man's table, as the neocapitalist ideology tells us. Some of us often feel, and most of us sometimes feel, that we are only someone if we have "made it" and can look down on those who have not. The American dream is often a very private dream of being the star, the uniquely successful and admirable one, the one who stands out from the crowd of ordinary folk who don't know how. And since we have believed in that dream for a long time and worked very hard to make it come true, it is hard for us to give it up, even though it contradicts another dream that we have—that of living in a society that would really be worth living in.

What we fear above all, and what keeps the new world powerless to be born, is that if we give up our dream of private success for a more genuinely integrated societal community, we will be abandoning our separation and individuation, collapsing into dependence and tyranny. What we find hard to see is that it is the extreme fragmentation of the modern world that really threatens our individuation; that what is best in our separation and individuation, our sense of dignity and autonomy as persons, requires a new integration if it is to be sustained.

The notion of a transition to a new level of social integration, a newly vital social ecology, may also be resisted as absurdly utopian, as a project to create a perfect society. But the transformation of which we speak is both necessary and modest. Without it, indeed, there may be very little future to think about at all.

RECONSTITUTING THE SOCIAL WORLD

The transformation of our culture and our society would have to happen at a number of levels. If it occurred only in the minds of individuals (as to some degree it already has), it would be powerless. If it came only from the initiative of the state, it would be tyrannical. Personal transformation among large numbers is essential, and it must not only be a transformation of consciousness but must also involve individual action. But individuals need the nurture of groups that carry a moral tradition reinforcing their own aspirations. Implicitly or explicitly, a number of the communities of memory . . . hold ethical commitments that require a new social ecology in our present situation. But out of existing groups and organizations, there would also have to develop a social movement dedicated to the idea of such a transformation. We have several times spoken of the civil rights movement as an example. It permanently changed consciousness, in the sense of individual attitudes toward race, and it altered our social life so as to eliminate overt expressions of discrimination. If the civil rights movement failed fundamentally to transform the position of black people in our society, it was because to do that would have required just the change in our social ecology that we are now discussing. So a movement to transform our social ecology would, among other things, be the successor and fulfillment of the civil rights movement. Finally, such a social movement would lead to changes in the relationship between our government and our economy. This would not necessarily mean more direct control of the economy, certainly not nationalization. It would mean changing the climate in which business operates so as to encourage new initiatives in economic democracy and social responsibility, whether from "private" enterprise or autonomous small- and middle-scale public enterprises. In the context of a moral concern to revive our social ecology, the proposals of the proponents of the Administered Society and Economic Democracy . . . could be considered and appropriate ones adopted.[6]

To be truly transformative, such a social movement would not simply subside after achieving some of its goals, leaving the political process much as it found it. One of its most important contributions would be to restore the dignity and legitimacy of democratic politics. We have seen . . . how suspicious Americans are of politics as an area in which arbitrary differences of opinion and interest can be resolved only by power and manipulation. The recovery of our social ecology would allow us to link interests with a conception of the common good. With a more explicit understanding of what we have in common and the goals we seek to attain together, the differences between us that remain would be less threatening. We could move to ameliorate the differences that are patently unfair while respecting differences based on morally intelligible commitments. Of course, a political discourse that could discuss substantive justice and not only procedural rules would have to be embodied in effective political institutions, probably including a revitalized party system.

It is evident that a thin political consensus, limited largely to procedural matters, cannot support a coherent and effective political system.

For decades that has become ever clearer. We have been afraid to try for a more substantial consensus for fear that the effort may produce unacceptable levels of conflict. But if we had the courage to face our deepening political and economic difficulties, we might find that there is more basic agreement than we had imagined. Certainly, the only way to find out is to raise the level of public political discourse so that the fundamental problems are addressed rather than obscured.[7]

If we are right in our stress on a revitalized social ecology, then one critically important action that government could take in a new political atmosphere would be, in Christopher Jencks's words, to reduce the "punishments of failure and the rewards of success."[8] Reducing the inordinate rewards of ambition and our inordinate fears of ending up as losers would offer the possibility of a great change in the meaning of work in our society and all that would go with such a change. To make a real difference, such a shift in rewards would have to be a part of reappropriation of the idea of vocation or calling, a return in a new way to the idea of work as a contribution to the good of all and not merely as a means to one's own advancement.

If the extrinsic rewards and punishments associated with work were reduced, it would be possible to make vocational choices more in terms of intrinsic satisfactions. Work that is intrinsically interesting and valuable is one of the central requirements for a revitalized social ecology. For professionals, this would mean a clearer sense that the large institutions most of them work for really contribute to the public good. A bright young lawyer (or a bright old lawyer, for that matter) whose work consists in helping one corporation outwit another is intelligent enough to doubt the social utility of what he or she is doing. The work may be interesting—even challenging and exciting—yet its intrinsic meaninglessness in any larger moral or social context necessarily produces an alienation that is only partly assuaged by the relatively large income of corporate lawyers. Those whose work is not only poorly rewarded but boring, repetitive, and unchallenging are in an even worse situation. Automation that turns millions of our citizens into mere servants of robots is already a form of despotism, for which the pleasures of private life—modest enough for those of minimum skill and minimum wage—cannot compensate. The social wealth that automation brings, if it is not siphoned into the hands of a few, can be used to pay for work that is intrinsically valuable, in the form of a revival of crafts (that already flourish in supplying goods for the wealthy) and in the improvement of human services. Where routine work is essential, its monotony can be mitigated by including workers in fuller participation in their enterprises so that they understand how their work contributes to the ultimate product and have an effective voice in how those enterprises are run.

Undoubtedly, the satisfaction of work well done, indeed "the pursuit of excellence," is a permanent and positive human motive. Where its reward is the approbation of one's fellows more than the accumulation of great private wealth, it can contribute to what the founders of our republic called civic virtue. Indeed, in a revived social ecology, it would be a primary form of civic virtue. And from it would flow a number of positive consequences. For one thing, the split between private and public, work and family, that has grown for over a century, might begin to be mended. If the ethos of work were less brutally competitive and more ecologically harmonious, it would be more consonant with the ethos of private life and, particularly, of family life. A less frantic concern for advancement and a reduction of working hours for both men and women would make it easier for women to be full participants in the workplace without abandoning family life. By the same token, men would be freed to take an equal role at home and in child care. In this way, what seemed at first to be a change only in the nature of work would turn out to have major consequences for family life as well.

Another consequence of the change in the meaning of work from private aggrandizement to public contribution would be to weaken the motive to keep the complexity of our society invisible. It would become part of the ethos of work to be aware of our intricate connectedness and interdependence. There would be no fear of social catastrophe or hope of inordinate reward motivating us to exaggerate our own independence. And with such a change, we might begin to be better able to understand why, though we are all, as human beings, morally deserving of equal respect, some of us begin with familial or cultural advantages or disadvantages that others do not have. Or perhaps, since we would not conceive of life so much in terms of a race in which all the prizes go to the swiftest, we might begin to make moral sense of the fact that there are real cultural differences among us, that we do not all want the same thing, and that it is not a moral defect to find other things in life of interest besides consuming ambition. In short, a restored social ecology might allow us to mitigate the harm that has been done to disadvantaged groups without blaming the victims or trying to turn them into carbon copies of middle-class high achievers.

It should be clear that we are not arguing . . . that a few new twists in the organization of the economy would solve all our problems. It is true that a change in the meaning of work and the relation of work and reward is at the heart of any recovery of our social ecology. But such a change involves a deep cultural, social, and even psychological transformation that is not to be brought about by expert fine-tuning of economic institutions alone. On the contrary, at every point, institutional changes, educational changes, and motivational changes would go hand in hand. For example, part of our task might well involve a recovery of older notions of the corporation. As Alan Trachtenberg has written:

> The word [corporation] refers to any association of individuals bound together into a *corpus,* a body sharing a common purpose in a common name. In the past, that purpose had usually been communal or religious; boroughs, guilds, monasteries, and bishoprics were the earliest European manifestations of the corporate form. . . . It was assumed, as it is still in nonprofit corporations, that the incorporated body earned its charter by serving the public good. . . . Until after the Civil War, indeed, the assumption was widespread that a corporate charter was a privilege to be granted only by a special act of a state legislature, and then for purposes clearly in the public interest. Incorporation was not yet thought of as a right available on application by a private enterprise.[9]

As late as 1911 . . . a leading Boston businessman, Henry Lee Higginson, could say, following earlier Protestant notions of stewardship, that corporate property "belongs to the community."

Reasserting the idea that incorporation is a concession of public authority to a private group *in return for* service to the public good, with effective public accountability, would change what is now called the "social responsibility of the corporation" from its present status, where it is often a kind of public relations whipped cream decorating the corporate pudding, to a constitutive structural element in the corporation itself. This, in turn, would involve a fundamental alteration in the role and training of the manager. Management would become a profession in the older sense of the word, involving not merely standards of technical competence but standards of public obligation that could at moments of conflict override obligations to the corporate employer. Such a conception of the professional manager would require a deep change in the ethos of schools of business administration, where "business ethics" would have to become central in the process of professional formation. If the rewards of success in business management were not so inordinate, then choice of this profession could arise from more public-spirited motives. In short, personal, cultural, and structural change all entail one another.

SIGNS OF THE TIMES

Few of those with whom we talked would have described the problems facing our society in exactly the terms we have just used. But few have found a life devoted to "personal ambition and consumerism" satisfactory, and most are seeking in one way or another to transcend the limitations of a self-centered life. If there are vast numbers of a selfish, narcissistic "me generation" in America, we did not find them, but we certainly did find that the language of individualism, the primary American language of self-understanding, limits the ways in which people think.

Many Americans are devoted to serious, even ascetic, cultivation of the self in the form of a number of disciplines, practices, and "trainings," often of great rigor. There is a question as to whether these practices lead to the self-realization or self-fulfillment at which they aim or only to an obsessive self-manipulation that defeats the proclaimed purpose. But it is not uncommon for those who are attempting to find themselves to find in that very process something that transcends them. For example, a Zen student reported: "I started Zen to get something for myself, to stop suffering, to get enlightened. Whatever it was, I was doing it for myself. I had hold of myself and I was reaching for something. Then to do it, I found out I had to give up that hold on myself. Now it has hold of me, whatever 'it' is."[10] What this student found is that the meaning of life is not be discovered in manipulative control in the service of the self. Rather, through the disciplined practices of a religious way of life, the student found his self more grasped than grasping. It is not surprising that "self-realization" in this case has occurred in the context of a second language, the allusive language of Zen Buddhism, and a community that attempts to put that language into practice.

Many Americans are concerned to find meaning in life not primarily through self-cultivation but through intense relations with others. Romantic love is still idealized in our society. It can, of course, be remarkably self-indulgent, even an excuse to use another for one's own gratification. But it can also be a revelation of the poverty of the self and lead to a genuine humility in the presence of the beloved. We have noted in the early chapters of this book that the therapeutically inclined, jealous though they are of their personal autonomy, nonetheless seek enduring attachments and a community within which those attachments can be nurtured. As in the case of self-cultivation, there is in the desire for intense relationships with others an attempt to move beyond the isolated self, even though the language of individualism makes that sometimes hard to articulate.

Much of what is called "consumerism," and often condemned as such, must be understood in this same ambiguous, ambivalent context. Attempts to create a beautiful place in which to live, to eat well and in a convivial atmosphere, to visit beautiful places where one may enjoy works of art, or simply lie in the sun and swim in the sea, often involve an element of giving to another and find their meaning in a committed relationship.[11] Where the creation of a consumption-oriented lifestyle, which may resemble that of "the beautiful people" or may simply involve a comfortable home and a camper, becomes a form of defense against a dangerous and meaningless world, it probably takes on a greater burden than it can bear. In that case, the effort to move beyond the self has ended too quickly in the "little circle of family and friends" of which de Tocqueville spoke, but even so the initial impulse was not simply selfish.

With the weakening of the traditional forms of life that gave aesthetic and moral meaning to everyday living, Americans have been improvising alternatives more or less successfully. They engage, sometimes with intense involvement, in a wide variety of arts, sports, and nature appreciation, sometimes as spectators but often as active participants. Some of these activities involve conscious traditions and demanding practices, such as ballet. Others, such as walking in the country or jogging, may be purely improvisational, though not devoid of some structure of shared meaning. Not infrequently, moments of intense awareness, what are sometimes called "peak experiences," occur in the midst of such activities. At such moments, a profound sense of well-being eclipses the usual utilitarian preoccupations of everyday life. But the capacity of such experiences to provide more than a momentary counterweight to pressures of everyday life is minimal. Where these activities find social expression at all, it is apt to be in the form of what we have called the lifestyle enclave. The groups that form around them are too evanescent, too inherently restricted in membership, and too slight in their hold on their members' loyalty to carry much public weight. Only at rare moments do such largely expressive solidarities create anything like a civic consciousness, as when a local professional sports team wins a national championship and briefly gives rise to a euphoric sense of metropolitan belongingness. . . .

THE POVERTY OF AFFLUENCE

At the very beginning of the modern era, Thomas Hobbes . . . summed up his teaching about human life by arguing that the first "general inclination of mankind" is "a perpetual and restless desire of power after power, that ceaseth only in death."[12] But we are beginning to see now that the race of which he speaks has no winner, and if our power is our only end, the death in question may not be merely personal, but civilizational.

Yet we still have the capacity to reconsider the course upon which we are embarked. The morally concerned social movement, informed by republican and biblical sentiments, has stood us in good stead in the past and may still do so again. But we have never before faced a situation that called our deepest assumptions so radically into question. Our problems today are not just political. They are moral and have to do with the meaning of life. We have assumed that as long as economic growth continued, we could leave all else to the private sphere. Now that economic growth is faltering and the moral ecology on which we have tacitly depended is in disarray, we are beginning to understand that our common life requires more than an exclusive concern for material accumulation.

Perhaps life is not a race whose only goal is being foremost. Perhaps true felicity does not lie in continually outgoing the next before. Perhaps the truth lies in what most of the world outside the modern West has always believed, namely that there are practices of life, good in themselves, that are inherently fulfilling. Perhaps work that is intrinsically rewarding is better for human beings than work that is only extrinsically rewarded. Perhaps enduring commitment to those we love and civic friendship toward our fellow citizens are preferable to restless competition and anxious self-defense. Perhaps common worship, in which we express our gratitude and wonder in the face of the mystery of being itself, is the most important thing of all. If so, we will have to change our lives and begin to remember what we have been happier to forget.

We will need to remember that we did not create ourselves, that we owe what we are to the communities that formed us, and to what Paul Tillich called "the structure of grace in history" that made such communities possible. We will need to see the story of our life on this earth not as an unbroken success but as a history of suffering as well as joy. We will need to remember the millions of suffering people in the world today and the millions whose suffering in the past made our present affluence possible.

Above all, we will need to remember our poverty. We have been called a people of plenty, and though our per capita GNP has been surpassed by several other nations, we are still enormously affluent. Yet the truth of our condition is our poverty. We are finally defenseless on this earth. Our material belongings have not brought us happiness. Our military defenses will not avert nuclear destruction. Nor is there any increase in productivity or any new weapons system that will change the truth of our condition.

We have imagined ourselves a special creation, set apart from other humans. In the late twentieth century, we see that our poverty is as absolute as that of the poorest of nations. We have attempted to deny the human condition in our quest for power after power. It would be well for us to rejoin the human race, to accept our essential poverty as a gift, and to share our material wealth with those in need.

Such a vision is neither conservative nor liberal in terms of the truncated spectrum of present American political discourse. It does not seek to return to the harmony of a "traditional" society, though it is open to learning from the wisdom of such societies. It does not reject the modern criticism of all traditions, but it insists in turn on the criticism of criticism, that human life is lived in the balance between faith and doubt. Such a vision arises not only from the theories of intellectuals, but from the practices of life that Americans are already engaged in. Such a vision seeks to combine social concern with ultimate concern in a way that slights the claims of neither. Above all, such a vision seeks the confirmation or correction of discussion and experiment with our friends, our fellow citizens.

CRITICAL-THINKING QUESTIONS

1. In what ways is U.S. culture "individualistic"? What are some of the consequences of living within a "culture of separation"?
2. According to the authors, how is the cultural "fragmentation" of modern life evident in academic life? In the mass media?
3. Explain the authors' notion of the "impasse of modernity." That is, what do the members of modern, industrial societies need to enhance the meaning of life? What suggestions do the authors make toward reconstructing human community?

NOTES

1. John Donne, "An Anatomie of the World: The First Anniversary."

2. Matthew Arnold, "Stanzas from the Grand Chartreuse" (1855).

3. T. Gitlin, *Inside Prime Time* (New York: Pantheon, 1983), pp. 268–69. Conversations with Todd Gitlin and Lisa Heilbronn were helpful in clarifying our views of television.

4. Matthew Arnold, "To Marguerite." Emphasis in original.

5. L. Rainwater, *What Money Buys: Inequality and the Social Meanings of Income* (New York: Basic Books, 1974).

6. On many of these issues, an approach refreshingly free of ideological narrowness is provided by recent Catholic social teaching. See the collection of documents from Vatican II and after: *Renewing the Earth: Catholic Documents on Peace, Justice and Liberation*, eds., D. J. O'Brien and T. A. Shannon (Garden City, N.Y.: Image Books, 1977). See also Pope John Paul II's 1981 encyclical letter *Laborem Exercens,* contained in G. Baum, *The Priority of Labor* (New York: Paulist Press, 1982), which provides a useful commentary. C. K. Wilber and K. P. Jameson use these teachings to reflect about the American economy in their *An Inquiry into the Poverty of Economics* (Notre Dame, Ind.: University of Notre Dame Press, 1983).

7. On the modern fear of politics and the need to connect politics and vision see S. Wolin, *Politics and Vision: Continuity and Innovation in Western Political Thought* (Boston: Little, Brown, 1960), especially chapter 10. For a helpful consideration of some of these issues see M. Walzer, *Spheres of Justice: A Defense of Pluralism and Equality* (New York: Basic Books, 1983). For a critique of the dangers of too thin a moral consensus see D. Callahan, "Minimalist Ethics," *Hastings Center Report* II (October 1981), 19–25.

8. C. Jencks et al., *Inequality: A Reassessment of the Effect of Family and Schooling in America* (New York: Basic Books, 1972), p. 8. On pp. 230–32 Jencks discusses the various ways, preferably indirect, in which this could be done. Daniel Yankelovich criticizes Jencks for being wildly out of touch with popular American consciousness in making his suggestion about limiting income (*New Rules: Searching for Self-Fulfillment in a World Turned Upside Down* [New York: Random House, 1981], pp. 137–39). But he in no way answers Jencks's argument.

9. A. Trachtenberg, *The Incorporation of America: Culture and Society in the Gilded Age* (New York: Hill and Wang, 1982), pp. 5–6.

10. S. M. Tipton, *Getting Saved from the Sixties* (Berkeley and Los Angeles: University of California Press, 1982), p. 115.

11. The differences between private vacations and public holidays, or holy days, illustrate the moral limits of expressive alternatives to traditional civic and religious forms of enacting our social solidarity. The vacation began its short, century-long history as a stylish middle-class imitation of the aristocrat's seasonal retreat from court and city to country estate. Its character is essentially individualistic and familial: "Everyone plans his own vacation, goes where he want to go, does what he wants to do," writes Michael Walzer. Vacations are individually chosen, designed, and paid for, regardless of how class-patterned vacation behavior may be or how many

vacation spots depend on public funds for their existence. The experience vacations celebrate is freedom—the freedom to break away from the ordinary places and routines of the workaday world and "escape to another world" where every day is "vacant" and all time is "free time." There we have "our own sweet time" to do with as we will and empty days to fill at our own pace with activities of our own choosing. Public holidays, by contrast, were traditionally provided for everyone in the same form and place, at the same time, to celebrate together by taking part in the fixed communal rites, meals, and celebrations that already filled them. In ancient Rome, the *dies vacantes,* in a telling reversal of meaning, were those ordinary working days devoid of religious festivals or public games. Public holy days such as the Sabbath are the common property of all. "Sabbath rest is more egalitarian than the vacation because it can't be purchased: It is one more thing that money can't buy. It is enjoined for everyone, enjoyed by everyone," Walzer observes. The Sabbath requires a shared sense of obligation and solemnity, backed not only by a shared impulse to celebrate but by a common mechanism of enforcement. God created the Sabbath for everyone and *commanded* all of the faithful to rest although in our society today individuals are free to choose to respect it or not. Nonetheless, the Sabbath signifies a freedom interwoven with civic equality and unity under an ultimate authority that is not merely a man-made social idea (Walzer, *Spheres of Justice,* pp. 190–96).

12. Thomas Hobbes, *Leviathan* (1651), ed. C. B. MacPherson (Harmondsworth, England: Penguin Books, 1968), p. 161.

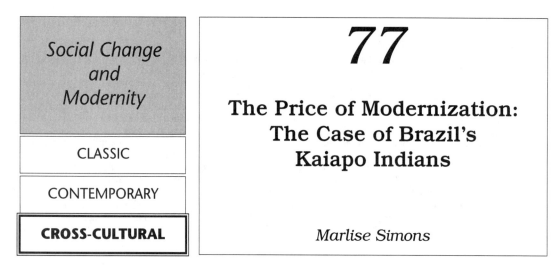

Social Change and Modernity

CLASSIC

CONTEMPORARY

CROSS-CULTURAL

77

The Price of Modernization: The Case of Brazil's Kaiapo Indians

Marlise Simons

Among the billions of poor people throughout the Third World, few will have a chance for a better life. But this is exactly what has happened to the Kaiapo, people who live deep in Brazil's rain forest. Has affluence been the blessing that the Kaiapo imagined it would be? To at least some of their number, the modernization of the Kaiapo amounts to little more than the systematic destruction of their traditional way of life.

It is getting dark when Chief Kanhonk sits down in the yard outside his home, ready for a long evening of conversation. Night birds are calling from the bush that sparkles with fireflies. Whooping frogs make a racket by the river. No one seems worried by the squadron of bats sweeping low overhead.

It is that important moment of the day when Indians of the Amazon, who use no written language, meet to talk, pass on information, and tell stories. The night is when they recall ancestral customs, interpret dreams, and comment on changes in nature and other events of the day. But from a nearby home come the sounds of a powerful rival: A television set is screeching cartoons at a group of children. I understand now why, that morning, by way of saying hello, these naked children of the rain forest had shouted things like "He-Man" and "Flintstones."

Three years ago, when money from the sale of gold nuggets and mahogany trees was pouring into Gorotire, Chief Kanhonk agreed to bring in television, or the "big ghost," as it is called here. A shiny satellite dish now stands on the earthen plaza like an alien sculpture, signaling that Gorotire—a small settlement of some 800 people on the Fresco River, a tributary of the Amazon—has become one of the wealthiest Indian villages in Brazil.

Yet Chief Kanhonk appears to regret his decision. "I have been saying that people must buy useful things like knives or fishing hooks," he says darkly. "Television does not fill the stomach. It only shows our children and grandchildren white people's things."

The "big ghost" is just one of the changes that have been sweeping over Gorotire, but it seems to be worrying the elders the most. Some believe it is powerful enough to rob them of their culture. Bebtopup, the oldest medicine man in the village,

Source: "The Amazon's Savvy Indians," by Marlise Simons, *The New York Times Magazine,* February 26, 1989, pp. 36–37, 48–52.

explains his misgivings: "The night is the time the old people teach the young people. Television has stolen the night."

When I discuss this with Eduardo Viveiros, a Brazilian anthropologist who works with a more isolated Amazonian tribe, he seems less worried. "At least they quickly understood the consequences of watching television," he says. "Many people never discover. Now Gorotire can make a choice."

It was the issue of choice that first drew me to the Kaiapo Indians of the lower Amazon Basin. They seemed to be challenging the widely held notion that forest Indians are defenseless in face of the pressures of the competitive and predatory Western world around them. Unlike most of Brazil's 230,000 Indians, they go out into the white world to defend their interests, and it is no longer unusual to see Kaiapo men—in their stunning body paint and feathered headdresses—showing up in Congress in Brasilia, the nation's capital, or lobbying by doing a war dance outside a government office. They have even bought Western gadgets to record and film their festivals.

Once the masters of immense stretches of forest and savannas, the Kaiapo were for hundreds of years among the most skillful farmers and hunters and fiercest warriors of central Brazil. They terrified other tribes with their raids. From the seventeenth to the nineteenth centuries, they not only resisted the slaving raids of the Portuguese invaders but they also attacked white traders and gold prospectors with such a vengeance that royal orders came from Portugal to destroy the Kaiapo. The white man's wrath and his diseases killed many, yet there are still close to 3,600 Kaiapo in more than a dozen different villages near the Xingu River. They have quarreled and regrouped, but their lands, several vast reservations, are more secure than those of many other tribes.

After many years of isolation in the forest, the Kaiapo now have to deal with the growing encroachments of white society. "They are going through a great transition," says Darrell Posey, an American anthropologist who has worked in Gorotire for more than a decade. "Their survival is a miracle in itself. But I worry whether they can go on making the changes on their own terms."

Colombia, Ecuador, Peru, and Venezuela—four of nine nations in the Amazon Basin, which harbors some 800,000 Indians—each have large numbers of tropical-forest Indians. But nowhere are pressures on Indian land as great as they are in Brazil. As the Amazon is opened up, developers bring in highways, settlers, cattle ranchers, mines, and hydroelectric dams. In Brazil alone, more than ninety tribes have disappeared since the beginning of this century.

The clearing of large areas of the rain forest and the fate of the Indians are also rapidly becoming an issue of international concern. Interest in the region has risen as ecological concerns, such as ozone depletion, the greenhouse effect, and other changes in the global environment become political issues. More attention is paid to scientists who are alarmed at the destruction of the rain forest—a vital flywheel in the world's climate and the nursery of at least half of the world's plant and animal species.

This has also prompted an increasing interest in the highly structured world of the forest Indians and their ancient and intricate knowledge of nature that permits them to survive in the tropical jungle without destroying it. (The Hall of South American Peoples, which includes a life-size model of a Kaiapo warrior, recently opened at the Museum of Natural History in New York City.)

As Indians find greater support among environmentalists, they also get more organized in their fight to protect their habitat. The Kaiapo held their first international congress last week in Altamira, in central Brazil, protesting government plans to build several massive dams that would flood Indian land.

In Brazil, Indian tribes occupy 10 percent of the nation's territory, although much of their land has not been demarcated. Brazil's past military regimes elevated Indian affairs to a national-security issue, because many tribes live in large areas of border land. It is official policy to integrate Indians into the larger society, and the National Indian Foundation, with its 4900 employees, is in charge of implementing this.

In my eighteen years in Latin America, I have heard many politicians and anthropologists discuss what is usually called "the Indian problem," what to "do" about cultures that have changed little in thousands of years. One school of thought holds that the remote tribes should be kept isolated and protected until they can slowly make their own choices. Another school accepts that the Indian world is on the wane, and talks about "guiding" the Indians toward inevitable change—a process that should take several generations.

But some anthropologists and politicians, including the Brazilian government, believe in still more rapid integration. When Romeo Jucá was head of the Indian Foundation, he said that it was only right for Indians to exploit their wealth, even if it meant acculturation. "We have to be careful how fast we go," he said, "but being Indian does not mean you have to be poor."

Gerardo Reichel-Dolmatoff is one of Latin America's most respected anthropologists. He insists that the Indians are their own best guides into Western society. An Austrian-born Colombian, Reichel-Dolmatoff has worked in Colombia's forests, at the Amazon's headwaters, for almost fifty years. "We cannot choose for them," he insists. "And we cannot put them into reserves, ghettos, ashokas. They are not museum exhibits. . . . If Indians choose the negative aspects of our civilization, we cannot control that. If there is one basic truth in anthropology, it is that cultures change. Static cultures do not exist."

The Indians themselves are pleading for more protection and respect for their cultures. Conrad Gorinsky, son of a Guyana Indian mother and himself a chemist in London, recently said: "We don't want the Indians to change because we have them comfortably in the back of our mind like a kind of Shangri-La, something we can turn to even if we work ourselves to death in New York. But we are hounding and maligning them instead of recognizing them as the guardians of the forests, of the world's genetic banks, of our germ plasm and lifelines."

The aboriginal peoples we call Indians are as different from one another as, say, Europeans are. Even the most isolated groups remain separate fiefdoms with widely varying experiences, beliefs, and histories. The degree of contact they have with the outside world is just as varied.

I first met Kaiapo tribesmen three years ago in Belém, a large city at the mouth of the Amazon. I saw them again in Brasilia, the capital. In both places, they demonstrated their political skills and capacity to mobilize, showing up in large numbers to protest measures by the government. They seemed particularly adept at commanding the attention of the press. Their body paint, feathers, and other paraphernalia made them appear warlike, exotic, and photogenic.

Back in Gorotire, as it turns out, they are more "ordinary." Wearing feathers and beads, explains Kubei, a chief's son, is for special occasions. "It's our suit and tie." Besides the satellite dish, the Kaiapo also have their own small airplane. Their new wealth has also given them the luxury of hiring non-Indians to help plant new fields. But they remain ready to attack white intruders; some of the adult men have markings on their chests that record the number of outsiders they have killed.

Two roads fan out from the center of Gorotire. A new sand track leads east on a five-hour drive to the town of Redenção. The other road goes south and, in a sense, it leads into the past. Dipping into the forest, it becomes a path that meanders through open patches where the Kaiapo women grow corn, sweet potatoes, bananas, manioc. On the plain ahead, it joins an ancient trail system that once reached for hundreds of miles into northern and western Brazil.

One morning, Beptopup (medicine man, shaman, connoisseur of nature), the anthropologist Darrell Posey (who speaks the Kaiapo language), and I wander into the bush. Beptopup walks past the plants the way you go down a street where you know everyone. Stopping, nodding, his face lighting up with happy recognition, he sometimes goes into a song—a soft, high-pitch chant for a particular plant.

He picks leaves, each one familiar, each one useful. One serves to remove body hair. Another, he says, can prevent pregnancy. The underside of one leaf is so rough it is used to sandpaper wood and file fingernails. Beptopup collects his plants in the morning, he says, because "that is when they have the most strength."

Stopping at a shrub, we look at the large circle around its stem, where nothing grows. "This and other plants have been sent to a laboratory for analysis," says Posey. "We think this one has a natural weedkiller."

Beptopup holds up a branch of what he calls the "eye of the jaguar." "This was our flashlight," he says, showing how to set it afire and swing it gently so its strong glow will light one's path.

One afternoon, when the heat has crept into everything, the women and children come back from the fields to their village. They stop and sit in a creek to escape the swirling gnats and buzzing bees. Others sit outside their homes, going about their age-old business. One woman plucks the radiant feathers of a dead macaw. Another removes her eyebrows and eyelashes, because the Kaiapo women think they are ugly. (A nurse once told me that this custom might have a hygienic origin—to ward off parasites, for instance.) Kaiapo women also deepen their foreheads by shaving the top of their head in a triangle that reaches the crown—a fearsome sight to the unaccustomed eye.

I envy a mother who is clearly enjoying herself fingerpainting her three children. She draws black designs with genipap juice. On the face and the feet she puts red dye from the "urucu," or annatto, plant; Indians say it keeps away chiggers and ticks.

Change has come to Gorotire along the other road, the one leading east to Redenção. Recent Kaiapo history is full of "firsts," but a notable turning point came when prospectors struck gold on Gorotire land in 1980. The Kaiapo raided the camp, twenty miles from the village, but failed to drive away the trespassers. Then they made a deal.

Last fall, when I was visiting Gorotire, about 2,000 gold diggers were stripping the land to the bone farther upstream, and the River Fresco passed the village the color of mud, its water contaminated with oil and mercury. I heard no one complain about that. Gorotire gets 7 percent of the mine's profits—several pounds of gold a week.

In 1984, a lumber company completed the first road. It signed a contract with the Indian Foundation for Gorotire's mahogany (the Indians are wards of the Brazilian government). Most of the mahogany is gone now, and the government agency split the profits with the Kaiapo. Gorotire chose to spend its gold and timber profits on new water and electricity lines and rows of brick houses. Only about half of the inhabitants now live in traditional palm-frond huts.

The young Kaiapo who earn a salary as supervisors at the gold camp have bought their own gas stoves, radios, sofas, and mattresses. For the community, the four tribal chiefs ordered several boats, trucks, and a small plane that ferries people and goods among nearby Kaiapo villages.

One evening, a truck arriving from Redenção—bringing rice, sugar, bottled gas, oil for the generator—is another reminder of how fast Gorotire is adapting to a Western economy. From being a largely self-sufficient community of hunters and farmers, it is now increasingly dependent on outside goods. In Gorotire, it is clearly money, no longer disease or violence, that has become the greatest catalyst for change. Money has given the Kaiapo the means and the confidence to travel and lobby for their rights. At the same time, it is making them more vulnerable.

I have seen other villages where Indians have received large sums of money—for the passage of a railroad or a powerline, or from a mining company. Such money is usually released in installments, through banks, but its arrival has put new strains on the role of the chiefs. Money and goods have introduced a new, materialistic expression of power in societies that have been egalitarian. Among most Indians, a man's prestige has always depended not on what he acquires but on what he gives away.

In Gorotire, some of the young men complain that the chiefs are not distributing community money and goods equally, that the chiefs' relatives and favorites are getting a bigger share and more privileges.

Darrell Posey, the anthropologist, believes the greatest political change came with the road. With it, he says, "the Kaiapo chiefs lost control of which people and what goods would come in." Previously, the chiefs had been the sole distributors. They had also played the vital roles of keeping the peace and leading the ceremonies. Now, the chiefs hardly know the liturgy of the ceremonies; their main task seems to be to deal with the outside world.

The transition is also changing the role of the medicine man. Bebtopup, for example, has an arsenal of remedies for the common ailments—fevers, diarrheas, snake bites, wounds. But he and his colleagues have lost prestige because they do not know how to deal with the diseases brought to Gorotire by white men, such as the pneumonia that strikes the children and the malaria spreading from the gold miners' camp.

Anthropologists sometimes say that when outsiders visit the Indian world, they often focus on themes central not to Indians but to themselves. This might explain why I was so bothered by the garbage, the flotsam of Western civilization.

Gorotire's setting is Arcadian. It lies on a bluff overlooking the River Fresco, with views of the forests across and the mountains behind. Spring rains bring waterfalls and blossoms. But these days the village is awash with rusting cans, plastic wrappers, tapes sprung from their cassettes, discarded mattresses, and clothes. New domestic animals such as dogs, pigs, and ducks have left a carpet of droppings. And giant rats, which suddenly appeared some years ago, seem to be everywhere; some have bitten small children.

"Indians have never had garbage that was not biodegradable," says Sandra Machado, a Brazilian researching Kaiapo farming techniques here. "No one wants to take care of it."

It is a mild moonlit evening, and in the men's house many Kaiapo are watching soccer on television. The bank of the river is a quieter place to talk.

"If you look beyond the garbage and the stone houses, this is still a strong and coherent indigenous culture," says Darrell Posey, speaking of the mixed feelings he has about a decade of developments in Gorotire. "Despite everything, the language is alive, the festivals and initiation rights are observed."

Posey says that the Kaiapo in Gorotire and in other villages continue with their age-old natural farming techniques, using plants to fix nitrogen in the soil, chunks of termite nests instead of chemical fertilizers, plant infusions to kill pests, the nests of ferocious ants to protect fruit trees from other ant predators.

Biologists often complain that there have been many studies of exotic rituals, paraphernalia, and kinships of Indians, but that Western science has paid scant attention to the Indians' use of animals and plants.

Like others working in the Amazon region, Posey worries about the gap between the old and the young. "The old chiefs are turning over decisions to the young because they can drive a truck or operate a video machine or go to the bank," he says. "But the young people don't see the relevance of learning the tribal knowledge and it's being lost."

"You can afford to lose one generation," he adds, "because grandparents do the teaching of their grandchildren. But you cannot afford to lose two generations."

Gorotire has a small Government school, designed to help Indians integrate into the national society. The teacher, who speaks only Portuguese, has started organizing annual Independence Day parades. On the blackboard is a list of patriotic holidays, including Independence

Day and the Day of the Soldier. I ask the children later what a soldier is. "Something of white people," one of them says.

Chief Poropot agrees that everyone must learn Portuguese. "The language of the Kaiapo is very ancient and it will never end," he says. "But the women and the children need to learn Portuguese to defend themselves."

Defend themselves?

"If they go to shop in Redenção, they have to talk," he says. "If they get sick, they cannot tell the doctor what they have."

Thirty miles from Gorotire, in the village of Aukre, another Kaiapo tribe is choosing a different strategy for change. Its best-known member is Paiakan, thirty-seven years old, the son of Chief Tikiri.

Calm and articulate, Paiakan has been named to "keep an eye on the whites" in the state capital of Belém. He acts as a kind of roving ambassador for the Kaiapo, even though each village is autonomous. When Kaiapo interests are threatened, he sends out warnings to the communities.

Paiakan's contacts with the outside world and the many pitfalls it holds for Indians have made him more conservative, he says, more so than in the early days, in the 1970s, when he first left home to work on the Trans-Amazonian Highway. As his father's main adviser, he has insisted that Aukre remain a traditional village.

It is built in the age-old circle of mud-and-thatch huts. There is no television, running water, pigs, or piles of garbage. Paiakan and his father have also banned logging and gold digging. This appears to have saved Aukre from the consumerism—and widespread influenza and malaria—of Gorotire.

"The lumber men have come to us with their bags of money," he says. "And we know we have a lot of gold. But we do not want to bring a lot of money in. The Indian still does not know the value of white man's objects or how to treat them." Paiakan cites clothing as an example. "The Indian wears something until it is stiff with dirt, then he throws it out."

But people now want things from the "world of the whites," he continues. "Pressure from the white society is so strong, there is no wall that can stop it." It is the task of the chief to measure the change, provide explanations, he says. "If someone wants to get a radio or a tape recorder, the chiefs cannot stop it."

In Aukre, where two aging chiefs are still in charge of buying goods for the community, they say that they will not buy gadgets. "We explain we cannot buy this thing for you because we do not have the batteries you need and we cannot repair it," Paiakan says.

Of late, Paiakan has been invited abroad to campaign for the protection of the rain forest. He knows the problem only too well. Ranchers have moved almost to the reservation's doorstep, felled trees, and set massive forest fires. Because of deforestation, there have been unusual changes in the water level of the Fresco River.

"Our people are getting very disoriented," says Paiakan. "It would be as if people from another planet came to your cities and started to tear down your houses. The forest is our home." With all the destruction going on, he continues, "the breath of life is drifting up and away from us."

At the age of seventy-eight and retired from teaching at the University of California at Los Angeles, the anthropologist Gerardo Reichel-Dolmatoff lives in Bogotá, Colombia, and is still writing. After studying changes in the Amazon for five decades, he is not optimistic about the prospects for the Indians.

"In Colombia, I don't know of a single case where an aboriginal culture has found a strong adaptive mechanism," he says. "Physical survival is possible. But I have not seen the ancient values replaced by a workable value system. I wish I could be more positive. But in fifty years I have seen too many traditions being lost, too many tribes disappear.

"For 500 years we have witnessed the destruction of the Indians. Now we are witnessing the destruction of the habitat. I suggest more field work, and immediate field work, because soon it will be too late."

At a conference on ethnobiology last fall, Reichel-Dolmatoff urged scientists to insist on spreading the message that Western science has much to learn from Indians, from their well-adapted lives and deeply felt beliefs, their view that whatever man subtracts he must restore by other means.

What suggestions has he made to Indians?

"Indians have to stay in touch with their language—that is absolutely essential," he says. "It embodies their thought patterns, their values, their philosophy." Moreover, he says, talented young Indians should be given a modern academic education, but also the chance to keep in touch with their people. "They come from cultures based on extraordinary realism and imagery. They should not be forced to enter at the lowest level of our society."

One night, I ask the chiefs in Gorotire: What happens if the gold runs out? After all, most of the mahogany is already gone. Young tribesmen have wanted to invest some of the income, and the chiefs have accepted the idea. Gorotire has bought a home in Belém for Kaiapo who travel there, as well as three houses in Redenção. There is talk of buying a farm, a curious thought, perhaps, for a community that lives on 8 million acres of land. But the Kaiapo, so they say, want it so that white farmers can grow rice for them.

And there is talk of planting new mahogany trees. Soon the conversation turns to a bird that a tribesman explains is very important. It is the bird, he says, that spreads the mahogany seeds.

CRITICAL-THINKING QUESTIONS

1. What have been the short-term consequences of the Kaiapo's new wealth? What are their long-term prospects?
2. What arguments can be made in support of continued effort by the Kaiapo to economically develop their resources? What arguments can be made against doing so?
3. In what ways are other countries involved in the changes taking place in the Amazon Basin?

Photo Credits

Alex Colville (1920–), *To Prince Edward Island*, 1965, acrylic emulsion on masonite, 61.9 × 92.5 cm. National Gallery of Canada, Ottawa, © NGC/MBAC, ***1***; Doranne Jacobson/International Images, ***18***; Pearson Education/PH College, ***31***; Corbis, ***51***; Andy Sacks/Stone, ***71***, Ken Karp/Pearson Education/PH College, ***93***; Jim West/Impact Visuals Photo & Graphics, Inc., ***113***; Campbell/Corbis-Sygma, ***138***; Scott Cunningham/Merrill Education, ***186***; Bettmann/Corbis, ***206***; Corbis, ***226***; Laimute E. Druskis/Pearson Education/PH College, ***247***; U.S. Department of Agriculture, ***266***; Kenneth Meyer, ***287***; Edward Hopper (1882–1967), *Room in New York*, 1932, oil on canvas, 29 × 36 in. UNL-Sheldon Memorial Art Gallery and Sculpture Garden, F. M. Hall Collection, 1932.H-166, ***315***; J. Gerard-Smith/PhotoEdit, ***336***; John Giordano/SABA Press Photos, Inc., ***356***; Pearson Education/PH College, ***376***; New York Convention & Visitors' Bureau, ***396***; Bobbie Kingsley/Photo Researchers, Inc., ***428***; Corbis, ***446***; Edvard Munch, *The Scream*, Oslo, National Gallery, Scala/Art Resource, N.Y. © 1998 Artists Rights Society (ARS), New York/ADAGP, Paris, ***476***.